R A S I A

INDIAN

OCEAN

PACIFIC

OCEAN

Peking

Yellow R.

Indus R.

▲ Mohenjo-Daro

SIAN GULF

▲ Java

Volume II: Since 1650   HISTORY OF

WESTERN CIVILIZATION

The Coronation of Elizabeth II in Westminster Abbey, June 2, 1953.

Volume II: Since 1650

ESTERN

THE MACMILLAN COMPANY, New York
Macmillan New York, London
A DIVISION OF THE CROWELL-COLLIER PUBLISHING COMPANY

CARLTON J. H. HAYES
Seth Low Professor Emeritus of History in Columbia University

MARSHALL WHITHED BALDWIN
Professor of History in New York University

CHARLES WOOLSEY COLE
Rockefeller Foundation and Former President of Amherst College

HISTORY OF
CIVILIZATION

Prefatory Note

This book is a thorough revision of the second volume of a work which was published originally in 1949, under the title of *History of Europe,* and in a second edition in 1956. The new version, like its predecessor, tells the modern story since 1650, but it has been reorganized and very largely rewritten. It embodies numerous amendments of both statement and interpretation necessitated by advancing historical scholarship and broadening knowledge. As befits its title, *History of Western Civilization,* it treats of cultural as well as political and economic developments. And it brings the story down to date through current stormy years of "cold" war between communist and free words, liquidation of colonial empires, and novel impacts of Asia and Africa on Europe and America.

Moreover, the publishers have given the work an attractive and useful new format, with double-columned pages, with a profusion of pertinent maps and illustrations, with select lists of supplementary readings for each of the six parts into which this volume is divided, and with an exhaustive index. Of the half-hundred maps about half are adapted from excellent ones provided originally by Mr. Francis Barkoczy, to whom the authors gratefully acknowledge their indebtedness.

C.J.H.H.
M.W.B.
C.W.C.

CONTENTS

Maps

Volume II: Since 1650

HISTORY OF
WESTERN CIVILIZATION

The Palace of Versailles as seen from the park.
Courtesy Bettmann Archive

Cardinal Richelieu. After a contemporary engraving.

Courtesy Bettmann Archive

PART VII

POWER POLITICS,

AND THE

Molière (Jean-Baptiste Poquelin, 1622–1673).

Courtesy Bettmann Archive

From Richelieu to Voltaire

COLONIAL RIVALRY

"ENLIGHTENMENT"

DEFINITELY "modern times" are inaugurated by the age covering the second half of the seventeenth century and most of the eighteenth. In this age, Western Civilization is firmly established on the American continents, not only by Spaniards and Portuguese, but by Dutch, French, and English, while on the European continent there is an unsteady "balancing" among a set of great powers, each of which pursues its own interests under absolutist divine-right monarchs. During the greater part of the age, France under the Bourbons is chief of the great powers. It humbles the Habsburgs of Austria and makes Spain a satellite. Presently, however, two new great powers emerge: Prussia and Russia, the former at the expense of Austria, and the latter at the expense of Sweden, Poland, and the Turks.

England, unlike the Continent, experiences in the seventeenth century a protracted struggle between king and parliament, involving civil war and temporary Puritan dictatorship, and issuing eventually in rejection of absolutism and establishment of constitutional parliamentary government. Detailed treatment of this revolutionary development we nevertheless defer, in order to associate it with the great American and French liberating revolutions of an ensuing age which it presaged. Here it suffices to point out that, under its peculiar regime, England absorbs Scotland and, as the "United Kingdom" of Great Britain, wages a long and eventually triumphant duel with France for commercial, naval, and colonial supremacy. A vast British Empire is in the making. Incidentally, Britain now opposes French hegemony within Europe, as previously it had opposed that of Spain. The defeat of France by Prussia and the latter's growing prestige in the second half of the eighteenth century are attributable to British support as well as to the generalship of Frederick the Great.

The age is not exclusively one of power politics, English political revolution, or colonial conflict. Above and beyond all these, it is an age of remarkable scientific and intellectual achievement and of attendant concern with "natural law" and "natural rights." In a word, it is an "enlightened" age, when, perhaps a bit naively, there is widespread faith in "reason" and "progress," and when "reform" is in the air. Even the despotic dynastic sovereigns of the age tend to be "enlightened." Yet long after such sovereigns disappear, and indeed until our own day, ideals of "enlightenment" will have recurrent vogue and abiding effects.

The decrease in religious fanaticism and even in religious zeal, which had been noticeable in the last stages of the Thirty Years' War, and in the peace of Westphalia, became even more marked in the ensuing years, though France in the late seventeenth century was something of an exception. At first the trend was toward "tolerance," then toward "rational" or "pietist" religion, and finally, in the eighteenth century, even toward irreligion and godlessness. French Huguenots were still to suffer for their Protestantism and Irishmen for their Catholicism, but the age of predominantly religious war and combat was drawing to a close.

CHAPTER 34

The Age of Louis XIV

A. Background: Henry IV, Richelieu, and Mazarin

From about 1659 to about 1763 France was the foremost nation of Europe, and its preëminence was not clearly lost until 1815. French strength arose in part from a favorable geographic position, a relatively large population, and fertile lands. But in addition to these factors, a centralized government, an excellent army, and a considerable degree of national unity helped to make France strong. The foundations of this governmental structure were laid, or rather re-laid, by two men—Henry IV and Richelieu. The edifice was completed by Louis XIV.

For a century after the conclusion of the Hundred Years' War in 1453, a succession of French kings had been consolidating the state. But then had ensued a half-century of demoralizing civil-religious wars and foreign interventions. When these were finally ended by Henry IV in 1598, through the edict of Nantes and the treaty of Vervins with Spain, France was in a sorry state. The national treasury was empty, commerce disrupted, and agriculture impaired. With the aid of his chief minister, the Huguenot Duke of Sully, and the natural recuperative powers of France, Henry IV, by avoiding further wars, restored the prosperity of the nation.

Henry IV brought to his task certain advantages. He was personally attractive, affable and gracious to high and low. If he was self-centered and showed but little loyalty to his friends and supporters, still he was intelligent, brave, quick to decide, and firm in enforcement. Most important of all, Henry understood France and the French. In the wars, he had traveled the length and breadth of the country. Often without funds, he had known poverty and learned to understand peasants and townsmen as well as nobles. It was not without reason that his subjects called him Henry "the Great," or "Good" King Henry. Of all the long line of French monarchs Henry IV is one of two that are remembered with warmth and affection in France, the other being Louis IX (Saint Louis).

In rebuilding the prosperity of France, Sully was Henry's chief agent. Sully reformed the tax system so thoroughly and so improved collections that after 1600 there was usually a surplus of a million *livres* each year. He repaired and improved the roads and planted shade trees along them. He built bridges, encouraged fairs, and improved water ways. He zealously sought to aid French agriculture, which seemed to him the source of the country's wealth. At the same time, Henry IV had another Huguenot aide, Barthélemy de Laffemas, who as Controller-General of Commerce was equally vigorous in seeking to develop industry and trade. Under his guidance, Henry established factories for tapestries, silks, and linens, and supported them with loans, privileges, and tax exemptions. Under Henry, too, interest in colonies grew, and Quebec was founded in 1608.

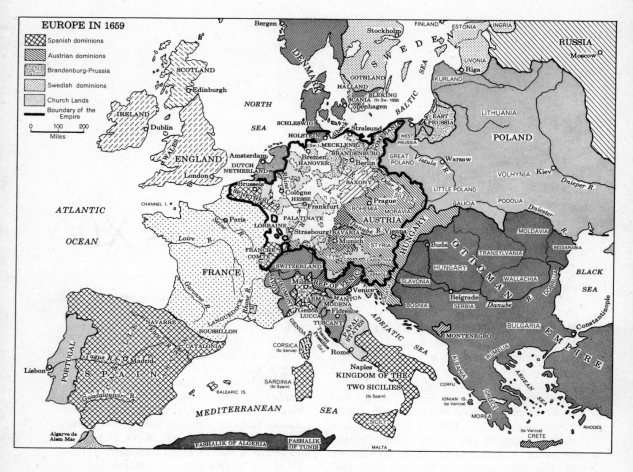

EUROPE IN 1659

Spanish dominions
Austrian dominions
Brandenburg-Prussia
Swedish dominions
Church Lands
Boundary of the Empire

0   100   200
Miles

In the long run, Henry IV's work in the political sphere was even more significant than his success in the rehabilitation of French economic life. During the religious wars, all the political elements of France had gotten out of hand. The nobles had levied taxes, raised armies, and waged wars. The Estates General (the old medieval legislature) had made laws and negotiated with foreign countries. France had come close to the old confused anarchy of early feudal times.

Again aided by Sully, Henry IV reduced France to order in a very few years and made the authority of the king and the central government paramount throughout the land. The nobles he brought to heel by pensions and favors, by a ruthless suppression of plots and fighting, and by giving much of the real power in the government to middle-class officials. As for the Estates General, he ignored it, and when he needed help and advice he summoned an

Assembly of Notables whose members were hand-picked by him and were mainly bourgeois officials. The towns were made to feel the increasing weight of royal power. Henry changed their charters and reduced their financial independence.

In thus vindicating and strengthening royal authority in France, Henry IV was helped both by his personal popularity with the French people and by the fact that they were so sick of internal disorder, strife, and religious disputation that they welcomed a strong hand at the helm. Yet it seemed for a while as if all that Henry had done might go for nought, since in 1610 he was assassinated in Paris by a religious maniac. To the throne succeeded Henry's son, Louis XIII, a child of eight; while to actual power, as regent, succeeded Henry's widow, Marie de' Medici, an ambitious and scheming woman, but quite incompetent.

Surrounding herself with favorites,

Marie dismissed the able Sully and other capable ministers. She tried to restrain the nobles by honors and bribes instead of firmness. In foreign policy, she sought to appease Spain at any cost. The savings of Henry IV were soon exhausted, and as a financial crisis loomed, Marie summoned the Estates General (1614). But the three estates (clergy, nobles, and commoners) spent their time in bickering with each other. They neither aided the government by voting taxes, nor took steps to increase their own power and lead France toward a constitutional monarchy. After a few weeks Marie locked the Estates General out of their meeting places and contemptuously sent them home. They were not to meet again for a hundred and seventy-five years.

After this fiasco with the legislature, matters went from bad to worse. There were revolts of nobles and of Huguenots. And Marie's pro-Spanish policy was generally unpopular with a people who looked upon Spain as their national enemy. Nonetheless the Regent arranged for the marriage of the young King to Anne of Austria, who was the daughter of Philip III and sister of Philip IV of Spain. As Louis XIII grew older he chafed under his mother's rule and at length pushed her aside. The King, however, was more interested in hunting and music than in affairs of state, and it is doubtful whether matters would have improved, if a great statesman had not risen to be chief minister in 1624. It is the principal claim to fame of Louis XIII that for eighteen years (1624–1642), in the face of all opposition, he kept Cardinal Richelieu in power.

Born of a noble family, Armand de Richelieu (1585–1642), despite early preference for an army career, had been trained for the church, and had become at twenty-one a bishop of the small diocese of Luçon. Some years later, as a delegate to the Estates General, he had attracted the notice of Marie de' Medici, who gave him a post in the government and later secured his nomination as a cardinal of the Roman Church. But Marie's favor seemed a handicap rather than a help when she was deposed by her son in 1617. Nevertheless, Richelieu handled the negotiations between the King and Marie so adroitly that he won the respect, though not the affection, of Louis XIII. He was given a place in the ministry in 1624, and soon made himself the King's chief minister. Thereafter, though his enemies conspired against him repeatedly and sought to get rid of him, Richelieu retained the confidence of the King and remained in office till his death.

In giving Richelieu power, Louis XIII displayed excellent judgment, for the Cardinal was a great statesman, possibly the greatest that France has ever produced. A master of diplomacy, a far-sighted administrator, a skilled courtier, Richelieu had a penetrating insight into military and economic as well as political affairs. If the needs of war prevented him from reorganizing French finances as he would have liked, still he did a good deal to carry on the work of Henry IV in encouraging industry and commerce. Under him, for example, a West Indian company was formed and colonies developed in those islands, a Canadian company was organized and strengthened, and an East India company founded.

Toward the end of his life Richelieu explained his policy in a simple fashion. His aim, he said, had always been to make France strong by destroying the power of the Huguenots, abasing the pretentions of the nobles, and humbling the proud house of Habsburg. By the first two objectives, he sought to increase the power of the crown and the central government in France. By the third, he desired to win for France a preëminent position in Europe.

In destroying the power of the Huguenots, Richelieu, Cardinal though he was, was not moved by religious motives. In his devotion to France and the French crown, he seemed ever ready to sacrifice religious to political considerations. But the Edict of Nantes (1598) had given the Protestants not only religious toleration but a privileged political position. With their fortified cities, their assemblies, and their special rights, they formed a state within the state. As such they were a threat to the national unity which Richelieu desired, and their privileges were an impediment to that uniformity of administration which the Cardinal sought.

Richelieu's opportunity came when the Huguenots, egged on by England, started a revolt which centered in the seaport of La Rochelle. Richelieu went thither with the royal armies and was the real commander of the long siege (1627–1628). Eventually he forced the town's surrender by building a breakwater across the mouth of the harbor. Then, after putting down the remnants of the Protestant revolt in the south of France, he concluded with the Huguenots the peace of Alais (1629). It left them religious liberty and freedom of conscience and equal political rights— everything, said Richelieu, which a good Huguenot would think it worth dying for. But it took from them their fortified cities and their special political privileges, everything through which they could make trouble. Thereafter the Huguenots made no further difficulties in France and Richelieu's compromise lasted for more than half a century.

The repression of the great nobles was an even more serious task and one which Richelieu undertook in the face of redoubtable opposition. It had long been customary to name noblemen as governors of the various provinces and as high administrative officers of the crown. Many nobles had at their command armed troops and fortified castles. Thereby they could thwart the will of the king, and even defy him in open revolt. Moreover, the nobles at court, jealous of Richelieu's advancement and spurred on by the intrigues of Marie de' Medici and the King's weak and foolish brother, the Duke of Orleans, hampered the Cardinal at every turn and plotted against him whenever opportunity offered.

Into the ranks of the noble courtiers, Richelieu struck terror. By means of a matchless system of spies and by consummate guile, he ferreted out conspiracies and put the leaders to death. As early as 1626 he had the King decree the demolition of all fortified castles not needed for the defense of the realm, and to this day the ruins of many an ancient château bear eloquent witness to the Cardinal's activity.

The noble governorships were not abolished by the Cardinal, but their importance was reduced in two ways. First, Richelieu appointed nobles as governors in parts of the country where they had few friends or supporters. Second, he made greatly increased use of a special kind of officials called "intendants." These were usually lawyers of bourgeois origin utterly dependent on the King. Richelieu sent them out in the country with authority to try cases, to arrange for military supplies, and to put down rebellion. Gradually real power shifted into the hands of these intendants, and when, in the next reign, they were assigned for long periods to a definite locality, the noble governors became merely ornamental.

What Richelieu was really doing by developing the office of intendant was inaugurating a bureaucratic administration. The intendants were servants of the crown and had no power save as such. They became the eyes and ears of the king. Through them, the central government could enforce its will; from them, it could secure reports on conditions; by them, it could carry on the task of administering an extensive country. Dimly the country realized what Richelieu was doing, and the nobles hated him both for his aims and his accomplishments. The rest of the country, and especially the middle classes, tended to welcome a centralized all-powerful monarchy as the surest guarantee of internal peace and order.

How Richelieu set about accomplishing his third purpose—the humbling of the Habsburgs—we have already noted. By subsidizing the Swedes and then throwing the weight of France into the Thirty Years' War, he prevented the triumph of the Catholic and Habsburg causes. But he did not live to see the complete success of his policies, for he died in 1642 shortly before the death of Louis XIII, the master whom he had served so well.

It was under Louis XIII, and with some encouragement from Richelieu, that there developed a definite intellectual and cultural movement that was to quicken and flower in the next reign. The Cardinal himself created the French Academy (*Académie Française*), a group of learned and distinguished men who began purifying literary style and standardizing the French language. One of the most famous of literary hostesses, Madame de Rambouillet

(1588–1665), gathered at her town house (or *Hôtel*) a group of writers that at one time or another included the first important French dramatist, Pierre Corneille (1606–1684), the poet and critic François de Malherbe (1555–1628), the letter-writer and poet Vincent de Voiture (1597–1648), and Madame de Sévigné (1626–1696) who penned incomparable letters to her daughter and others. This self-conscious literary group, though it was somewhat affected, won for writers and their works both recognition and appreciation.

There was at the same time, in other circles, a re-awakening of Catholic religious ardor in France. Much of it went into charity, better organized than ever before by St. Vincent de Paul (1576–1660), who founded the Lazarist (Vincentian) order and the Sisters of Charity, established foundling hospitals, and even enlisted the services of society ladies of Paris. St. Francis de Sales (1567–1622), though he was bishop of Geneva, preached often and with great effect in the chief cities of France, and his books like *Treatise on the Love of God* were notable for the purity and the clarity of their French. Of quite another sort was Blaise Pascal (1623–1662). A genius in mathematics, he turned to religion in his later years and became a prominent figure in the Jansenist movement which centered in the convent of Port Royal des Champs and which was a sort of Puritan wing of French Catholicism. His writings, of which the ironic *Provincial Letters* are the best known, constitute in their style one of the high water marks of French prose.

Louis XIII was succeeded by his son Louis XIV, who at his accession in 1643 was only five years old. In spite of arrangements to the contrary made by the dead King, power passed to his widow, Anne of Austria, as Regent. Since she was a Habsburg, she might well have undone the work of Richelieu by a pro-Spanish policy (as Marie de' Medici had started to undo the work of Henry IV), save for one man. That man was Jules Mazarin (Giulio Mazarini), an Italian who had become a naturalized Frenchman and an aide of Richelieu. An astute diplomat with a real love of intrigue, Mazarin had made himself so useful to Richelieu that he had been rewarded with a cardinal's hat and posts of high responsibility. By his charm and tact, Mazarin won the respect, the trust, and even the love of Anne, the Regent, and until his death in 1661, he was her chief minister.

How Mazarin brought to fulfillment the policies of Richelieu in the Peace of Westphalia and the treaty of the Pyrenees has been described elsewhere.[1] But his brilliant successes in foreign affairs were not duplicated within France. Disliked as a foreigner, envied because he was so powerful, criticized because he made himself enormously rich, the Cardinal was soon the

[1] See above, p. 405.

Peasant Family. Mathieu Le Nain (d. 1677).

Courtesy Detroit Institute of Arts

most hated man in France. The opposition to Mazarin developed into a confused sort of rebellion, called the Fronde, which lasted from 1648 to 1653.

The Fronde had a comic-opera aspect. Noble ladies dashed around France on horseback, even leading troops on occasion. Satirical songs, called *Mazarinades*, were sung in the streets. But it had a serious side as well. Both the great French generals, Condé and Turenne, sided with the *Frondeurs*, though the latter gave them only temporary support. On several occasions the rebels were in control of Paris and the Regent had to flee with the King, while Mazarin had to retire from the scene. But the rebels had no clear-cut objectives, and when they won victories they usually did not know what to do.

Eventually the rebellion petered out, but it had some permanent importance. It was the last occasion on which the nobles in old, feudal fashion took arms against the crown. It made the French people more willing to accept strong royal rule as a guarantee against civil disorder. Finally, it made such an impression on Louis XIV that when he came to power he sternly saw to it that there were no more Frondes.

B. Louis XIV, Exemplar of Absolute Monarchy

On the death of Cardinal Mazarin in 1661, everyone wondered who would be the Richelieu or the Mazarin of the ensuing period. They were not left long in doubt, for Louis XIV, who was now of age, announced that he would be his own chief minister. The remainder of his extremely long reign (1643–1715) is known as the period of his personal rule—the Age of Louis XIV. Louis XIV had a good mind, though he was by no means brilliant, and his education had been somewhat neglected. He was short, well built, and handsome in a rather heavy-featured way. His courtesy was impeccable; his bearing most dignified; his nature imperious. He was a man of strong passions but considerable self control. Avid for glory, he wished especially to distinguish his reign by great military victories. Very seriously did Louis XIV

take his task of being king. Day after day, he went over documents, listened to reports, and sat through long council meetings. His confidence in his own judgment was unshakable. While he would give ear to various opinions at great length, once he had made up his mind he would brook no discussion or dissent.

As King of the strongest monarchy in Europe, Louis XIV had a very special position and one which he filled with great dignity. In theory his power was absolute and he was accountable for his acts only to God. His will was law. In practice, however, his authority was conditioned by difficulty of communication and enforcement, and by a vast mass of surviving traditional rights and privileges, personal, municipal, provincial, and ecclesiastical, which even the King did not consider it proper to put aside lightly. Yet the King was thought of as sacred, a monarch by divine right. It was truly sacrilege to oppose him. He was regarded, too, as the father of his people. Paris and Lyons and Bordeaux were "his good cities." Frenchmen were not citizens, but "subjects of the King." Courtiers fawned on him. Officials abased themselves before him. He was surrounded by a rigid and ceremonious etiquette from the time he got up until he went to bed.

Such was the man who, heir to the labors of Henry IV and Richelieu, built up for France a highly centralized government, which was in its day the most efficient in Europe. Louis XIV was served by a group of able ministers. Colbert handled financial and economic matters and the navy; Le Tellier and his son Louvois directed the army; Lionne, Pomponne, and Colbert de Croissy successively administered foreign affairs. With the aid of these and other ministers, Louis XIV reorganized the royal councils such as the Council of Finance, and established new ones like the Council of Commerce. These councils, which had legislative and judicial as well as executive powers, he manned with able lawyers and bourgeois officials, though for tradition's sake a duke or two was usually included on each.

The office of intendant, as developed by

Louis XIV. Hyacinthe Rigaud (d. 1743).

Courtesy Bettmann Archive

Richelieu, became the cornerstone of the administration outside of Paris. The intendants were carefully selected, and assigned for long periods to a "generality" (France was divided into some thirty generalities for financial and other purposes). An intendant who did well in an unimportant area was often promoted to a more important one and might hope to reach the highest posts in the government. While the chief duty of the intendants was to administer the collection of taxes, they became the King's general handy men. They intervened in lawsuits, raised troops, reported on crops, issued local regulations, and saw to the enforcement of the royal laws. Gradually their duties became so heavy that they had to be given assistants, called sub-delegates.

As the power and efficiency of the royal government grew, its older organs tended to become less important. The King interfered in town elections, and the local intendant saw to it that properly submissive mayors were chosen. More and more, the estates (legislatures) of the provinces which still retained them, met mainly to vote sums of money to the King. The chief business of the church assembly, which met every five years, came to be the voting of a "gratuitous gift" to the crown. The noble provincial governors, though they retained some theoretical military powers, were active mainly in public ceremonies and had no thought but to please the King. The great courts, or *parlements*, of which there were about a dozen, were kept in line by the intendants and ministers who let them know clearly what the King desired.

For the upper classes, the center of life in France came to be the royal court, first at Paris and then at Versailles. Thither flocked great churchmen, wealthy bishops and abbots, who owed their places to the King's choice and hoped for further favors from him. Thither came all nobles who could afford it, for the principal way to riches and power was through pensions and offices which the King bestowed. Henry IV and Richelieu had broken the political power of the nobility. Louis XIV completed the task by making the nobles into courtiers. To be sure, poorer nobles still lived on their estates, and all nobles were exempt from many taxes like the *taille*, or land tax, and enjoyed social precedence over commoners. But where once they had been the real rulers of the outlying districts, nobles now had but two careers open to them, that of courtier near the King's person, or that of officer in the King's army. In either case, their success depended on royal favor.

The lot of the peasant was not greatly changed. He still tilled the soil and hoped to produce enough at the harvest to carry him over the winter. But of the taxes and dues he paid, an increasing proportion went to the King, and if a peasant found himself in a law court it was more often a royal one than that of the local landlord.

Persons of the middle class could hope to attain power and even the status of a noble by becoming royal officials or members of a *parlement*. As business men they felt the weight of royal authority in two ways. First, the crown was increasingly active in regulating industry and commerce. Second, it vigorously sought to encourage production and trade in order to promote the prosperity of France.

Until his death in 1683, Colbert was the minister who had active charge of all economic matters. He was a convinced mercantilist and sought by use of the royal authority to regulate and encourage industry and commerce, so that French production would be greatly increased, so that the French would have a large merchant marine and rich colonies, and so that the masses of Frenchmen would be usefully employed. To these ends, Colbert reformed the French tariffs. By tariff act of 1664 he simplified the import and export duties. With the tariff of 1667 he declared economic war on Holland, England, and Italy by raising drastically the import duties on the goods these countries sent to France.

At the same time, Colbert reduced export duties on French goods, negotiated commercial treaties, subsidized increases in the merchant marine, and protected it from foreigners and pirates by building up a large and powerful navy. Moreover, he launched France on a period of real colonial development. Gathering up the remnants of the ventures of previous decades, he refounded in 1664 an East India Company and a West India Company and supported them lavishly with royal funds. The former, in the face of great difficulties and losses, slowly won for France a foothold in the trade to India, despite the opposition of the Dutch and English. The West India Company sent colonists to Canada as well as to the West Indies (Martinique, Guadeloupe, Santo Domingo), strengthened these colonies, increased their trade with France, and gained for the French a share of the slave trade with West Africa. Colbert also founded a Levant Company and a Company of the North which, while failures from a financial point of view, laid the foundations of future French trade in the Near East and the Baltic.

Internally, Colbert sought to increase agricultural production, and he developed French horsebreeding so that France would not have to import horses. But his main interest was in industry. By organizing companies, by granting loans, privileges, and tax exemptions, and by importing skilled foreign workers, Colbert stimulated domestic manufacture of many commodities, and made France largely independent of other countries.

At the same time that he encouraged industry, Colbert endeavored to regulate it, for he believed that quality must be maintained in order to give the domestic consumer good value and to win and retain foreign markets. Elaborate regulations were issued for the textile industry, specifying the length and width of the fabrics and sometimes the number of threads in the warp. Detailed instructions on the best dyeing methods were prepared. Royal inspectors were appointed, and arrangements were made to mark with a seal each properly woven piece of cloth.

Nor did Colbert's efforts stop here. He sought to increase the population by subsidizing large families. The poor and idle were put to productive labor. The administration of forests was reorganized. Roads were reconstructed, and canals built, the most famous of the latter being the Languedoc Canal, 175 miles long, from the Atlantic to the Mediterranean.

Moreover, Colbert drastically reorganized French finances. He chastised corrupt financiers, forced the tax farmers to bid competitively for the right to collect the royal taxes, lowered taxes like the *taille* from which the nobles were exempt, and raised those like *aides* (on beverages) which almost everyone had to pay. It was Colbert's work in rebuilding France economically which made possible many of the great cultural achievements of the reign of Louis XIV and also the long wars which that monarch waged.

C. French Cultural Leadership

With an increasing royal income, Louis XIV found himself in a position to support and encourage all sorts of cultural activities. He did so partly that he might dazzle the rest of Europe with the magnificence of his reign, partly that he might have about him a setting suitable for so great a King, and partly that he might be known to history as a patron of the arts and of learning. Nor were his efforts unavailing. His reign is known in French history as "The Great Century." The artistic style of the epoch the French call "The Great Style." Louis was known to contemporaries, French and foreign alike, as "Louis the Great" and the "Sun King."

It can be argued that French art, literature, and learning were already making rapid progress before Louis XIV came to power, and that all the King did was to subsidize and take the credit for it. Indeed, it is hard to see how a king could create men of talent and genius. Nonetheless, it is clear that he did recognize their worth and gave them an opportunity to come to the fore. In addition, he brought to France many distinguished foreigners whose presence added lustre to his court.

With the King's sanction, Colbert undertook to organize and support the arts and sciences in much the same way that he brought order and prosperity to the economic life of the country. The French Academy, composed of leading writers and literary figures, had been founded, as we have said, by Richelieu and was still a semi-private organization. Colbert took it in hand, gave it the King for a patron, lodged it in the Louvre, and told it to hurry on with the great French dictionary it was preparing. Similarly he revivified the Academy of Painting and Sculpture, enforcing its monopoly of the right to teach art.

Important, too, was the Academy of Sciences founded by Colbert in 1666 and numbering at first fifteen members. It met frequently and performed experiments of which some were perhaps more novel than significant, as for example the first dissection of an elephant's trunk. The results of its work were published in an important scientific periodical, the *Journal des Savants*. With Colbert's aid, a Royal Observatory was built and equipped at Paris. At Paris, likewise, a notable botanical garden, called the *Jardin du Roi*, was developed, and a large royal library established.

But Colbert did more than organize and regulate. With royal funds he subsidized and pensioned men distinguished in any cultural field. Thus, Jean Racine received a pension for his incomparable classical tragedies, which, despite their cold dignity, are considered by the French as the greatest dramas ever written. Pierre Corneille, known as the "father of French tragedy," had long since written his greatest works like the *Cid*, but he too received a pension. Molière was subsidized and called on to write and act in plays for court festivals. With an unsurpassed sense of the comic and a remarkable ability for biting if good-humored satire, Molière wrote comedies such as *Le Misanthrope, Tartuffe, Les Précieuses Ridicules,* and *Le Bourgeois Gentilhomme,* which have delighted later generations.

This was indeed the great age, the golden age, of French literature. For in addition to the writers already mentioned, a number of others achieved special distinction. Madame de Sévigné continued her letters, which have charmed millions of readers with their pictures of court and country life. La Fontaine, in rhymed fables about animals, satirized human foibles. Boileau won fame by his precise but witty poems. La Rochefoucauld polished his incisive epigrams and maxims. Bishop Bossuet brought the eloquence of church preaching to a rotound climax. Such was the prestige of French letters under Louis XIV, that French became the language of the polite and the learned all over Europe, at the same time that French power was making it the language of diplomacy.

As outward evidence of his glory, Louis XIV reared magnificent edifices in a new style which, though based on the principles and elements of the classical Italian renaissance (dome, pillar, pilaster, round arch), was made into something distinctively French by the genius of architects like Le Vau, Perrault, and the Mansarts. The Observatory and the Hôtel des Invalides were constructed at Paris, together with triumphal arches and new city gates. Domestic architecture for both town and country houses gained a new dignity.

But the great palace of Versailles, which cost something like 40,000,000 *livres,* outshone all else. Immense in size, set in the middle of formal gardens with walks and fountains designed by the landscape architect Le Nôtre, Versailles, with all its dignity, was more than a building. It was the symbol of the reign. With its mirrored halls, its great mural paintings, its impressive façade, its gilt and its marble, it became the seat of the court of Louis XIV. It was the setting in which the "Sun King" shone in all his splendor. That the court was now removed some eleven miles from Paris was perhaps indicative of the growing gap between the King and his people. But the people were not to make themselves felt for a century yet. And in the meantime, most European princes sought to pattern themselves after Louis XIV and to build palaces in imitation of Versailles.

To decorate Versailles and his other châteaux, Louis XIV had a whole corps of artists and other craftsmen, headed by the painter Le Brun, who turned out vast canvases depicting with classic formality the triumphs of the King in peace and war, and also thousands of designs and sketches for tapestries, rugs, and articles of furniture. The *Gobelins,* founded by Henry IV, became a state establishment where tapestries were woven, while the similar *Savonnerie* made rugs. For the furniture and interior decoration, there were numerous skilled cabinetmakers, goldsmiths, glassworkers, embroiderers, and sculptors, who made Versailles a veritable museum of all that was finest and most costly in contemporary production.

French painting of the era will be discussed in a later chapter, but it may be noted here that in all the art of the period, from the tragedies to the doorknobs, and from Versailles to the chairs inside it, there was a common spirit. It has been called the spirit of classicism because it drew its inspiration from ancient Greece and Rome via the Italian Renaissance, and because it sought magnificence, dignity, symmetry, and balance rather than charm, delicacy, or daintiness. To the modern eye, the "grand style" is a little heavy, a little stiff, a little too formal. But it was a synthesis that arose from the spirit of the time and from the organizing efforts of men like Colbert and Le Brun. It went with the manners and the clothes. It seemed definitely to fit the age, the country, and Louis XIV.

All Europe was impressed and dazzled by the achievements of the French. The upper classes all over the Continent, from England to Russia, imitated French poetry and drama, French clothes and furniture, French architecture and tapestries. France set the style, and since then it has been from France that people have sought women's dresses and perfumes, laces and fine cooking, and all those articles that make for luxury and the most civilized living.

D. Wars of Louis XIV against Spain, Holland, and the Holy Roman Empire

Had Louis XIV devoted the strength of his government and the wealth of his country to promoting the prosperity of the people and encouraging the arts of peace, the future history of Europe would doubtless have been different. Instead, he was determined to win military glory and to add to the prestige and possessions of the house of Bourbon. He wanted France, he said, to expand her territories till they reached the "natural boundaries" which God had presumably established for the country in the form of the Rhine, the Pyrenees, the Alps, and the sea. He therefore plunged France into a series of long wars which dissipated French financial resources, wasted French man-power, and impaired French prosperity. Moreover, by his aggressive tactics Louis XIV made himself hated and feared by most other nations, so that they banded together to fight off the French as they had formerly joined to strike down Spain. Such a heritage did Louis XIV leave behind him, that for a century after his death France was generally regarded as an aggressor nation, a threat to her neighbors and to the peace of Europe.

To wage his wars, Louis XIV built up a big military machine. On the sea, Colbert created, out of the decayed fleet that Mazarin had left behind, a large navy, which was powerful enough to defeat the combined English and Dutch fleets in the Battle of Beachy Head (1690). Two years later it suffered a defeat at La Hogue, and thereafter, by what was probably a crucial mistake in policy, the French devoted their main efforts to land warfare and sent to sea chiefly privateers and commerce raiders which harried enemy shipping but left in English hands the real control of the seaways and all the dominance that such control brought with it.

On land, the story was different. There, the war minister, Louvois, who encouraged his master's ardor for military glory, made the French army supreme. He regularized the enlisting and levying of men and increased the size of the forces. It was Louvois who introduced into Europe the true "standing army," a force kept continuously in being and ready for service. No longer did the French army consist of feudal levies or semi-private regiments "owned" by their colonels and called up or brought up to full strength only when war threatened. Now the royal authority was complete and apparent at all levels. Discipline was tightened. The different branches (infantry, cavalry, artillery, engineers) were more clearly distinguished and more carefully organized. Where formerly troops had struggled along the roads in nondescript costumes, Louvois made them wear uniforms and march in step. He also created an elaborate and effective system of supply. Food for the troops and fodder for the horses were collected and deposited at convenient depots. The output of cannon, muskets, swords, pikes, gunpowder, and other munitions was vastly increased in quantity and improved in quality. Under

Louvois the formation and equipping of armies became business-like and scientific.

Louvois had helpful aides. Marshal Vauban, the greatest military engineer of the time, and perhaps of all time, fortified the frontier cities, ringed France about with well-nigh impregnable fortresses, and planned elaborate siege operations against enemy fortifications. Able officers enforced the new order on the army. There was, for example, Colonel Martinet, whose very name has become a synonym for a rigid disciplinarian. In addition, there were skilled generals to command the armies in actual battle. Condé and Turenne had already distinguished themselves in the later phases of the Thirty Years' War. The Duke of Luxembourg, whose father had been executed by Richelieu, was the most brilliant general of the later period of the reign of Louis XIV.

With the strongest and best trained army in Europe, Louis XIV was not long in finding occasion to use it. In 1667–1668 he waged against Spain the "War of Devolution." The excuse for it was a quite unjustified claim he advanced, on his wife's behalf, to the Spanish Netherlands. By diplomacy, he persuaded or threatened other countries into neutrality, then threw the weight of his armies against the fortress cities of the Belgian Netherlands. His triumph was checked, however, when Holland, England, and Sweden formed a triple alliance to put a stop to the war and to preserve the "balance of power" in Europe. This caused Louis XIV to accept a compromise in the treaty of Aix-la-Chapelle, by which Spain, while retaining the greater part of the Belgian Netherlands, surrendered to France an important section, including the fortified cities of Charleroi, Tournai, and Lille. The taste for conquest of the "Sun King" was whetted, but his appetite was hardly appeased.

Louis blamed the Dutch for the check he had met. Moreover, the Dutch were the chief rivals of the growing French commerce and industry. Even Colbert, who hated wars because they were so expensive, believed it would be a good idea to destroy Dutch trade by military means. With these thoughts in mind, Louis proceeded to break up the triple alliance by negotiating the secret treaty of Dover with King Charles II of England,[1] and buying off Sweden with favors and pensions. Holland alone did not seem formidable, for it was a small country and was torn by civil strife. On the one side, the head of the Orange family, with the title of *Stadholder*, supported by the country districts, the nobles, and the Calvinist clergy, aspired to centralize the state and transform it into an hereditary monarchy. On the other side, the aristocrats, big business men, religious liberals, and townsfolk found an able leader in John De Witt, the "Grand Pensionary," who wished to preserve the republic and the rights of the several provinces. For over twenty years, the latter party had been in power, but as the young Prince of Orange, William III, grew to maturity, signs were not lacking of a reaction in favor of his party.

Under these circumstances, Louis XIV declared war against Holland in 1672, anticipating an easy victory. French troops occupied Lorraine, marched down the Rhine, invaded Holland, and threatened the great commercial city of Amsterdam. John De Witt, whom the Dutch unjustly blamed for their reverses, was murdered; and at the order of William III, who assumed supreme command, they cut the dikes and flooded a large part of northern Holland to check the French advance.

By refusing to accept the generous peace terms which the Dutch now offered, Louis XIV again aroused general apprehension throughout Europe. The Emperor Leopold, the Great Elector of Brandenburg, and other German rulers joined with Spain to help Holland. The French in a series of victories defeated their German opponents and invaded Spanish territory in the Netherlands and Franche Comté. But King Charles II of England was obliged by his Parliament to join the anti-French alliance, and Louis XIV decided at length that it was time to make peace. By the treaties of Nimwegen (1678, 1679), it was Spain which had to pay the penalties of Louis' second war. The Dutch lost nothing. But Spain ceded to France the long-coveted province of Franche Comté with its capital city of

[1] See below, p. 509.

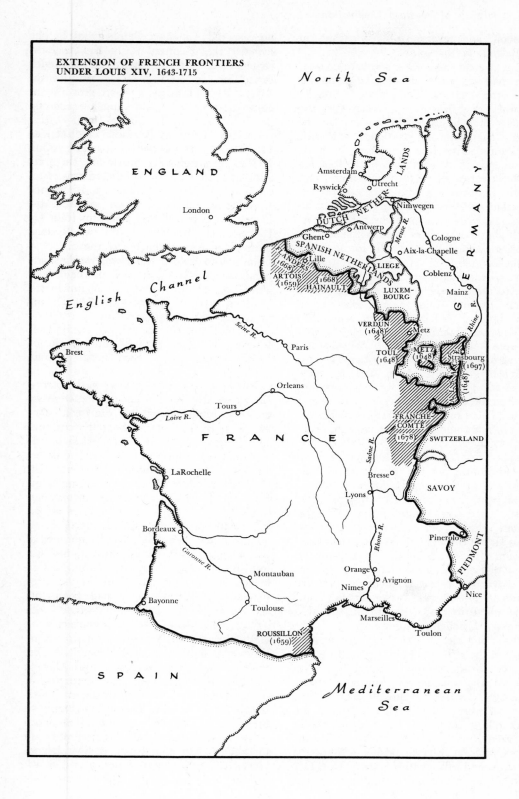

EXTENSION OF FRENCH FRONTIERS
UNDER LOUIS XIV, 1643-1715

North Sea

ENGLAND

NETHER-LANDS

Amsterdam

Ryswick

Utrecht

London

Nimwegen

DUTCH NETHER

Antwerp

Cologne

Ghent

SPANISH NETHERLANDS

Aix-la-Chapelle

Channel

FLANDERS (1668)

Lille

LIEGE

Coblenz

English

ARTOIS (1659)

HAINAULT (1668)

LUXEM-BOURG

Mainz

GERMANY

Meuse R.

VERDUN (1648)

Metz

Rhine R.

Seine R.

Brest

Paris

TOUL (1648)

METZ (1648)

Strasbourg (1697)

(1648)

Orleans

Loire R.

Tours

FRANCE

FRANCHE-COMTÉ (1678)

SWITZERLAND

LaRochelle

Saône R.

Bresse

SAVOY

Lyons

Bordeaux

Garonne R.

Rhone R.

Pinerolo

Montauban

Orange

Avignon

PIEDMONT

Bayonne

Nimes

Nice

Toulouse

Marseilles

SPAIN

ROUSSILLON (1659)

Toulon

Mediterranean
Sea

Besançon, and several strong fortresses in the Belgian Netherlands.

Thus at great financial and economic cost, Louis had extended the French frontiers nearer the "natural boundaries." But he was not yet satisfied. No sooner was the war over than he established special courts, called "chambers of reunion," and had them adjudge to him numerous areas as "dependencies" of territories he had gained by the treaties of Westphalia and Nimwegen. In this way, he took over such important cities as Strasbourg and Luxembourg, as well as many lesser towns. At length alarmed by these encroachments, the Emperor Leopold in 1686 formed the League of Augsburg, composed of Austria, Spain, Sweden, and several lesser states, in order to preserve the territories of the Holy Roman Empire from further seizures. In 1688, Louis XIV sent a large army into the Rhenish Palatinate to enforce a preposterous claim to that valuable district. The war which resulted was Louis's third major struggle and has been variously styled the War of the League of Augsburg, or the War of the Palatinate. In America it was paralleled by a conflict between French and English colonists, known as King William's War.

In his first two wars, Louis had been able to count on the neutrality of the English King Charles II, whom he subsidized. But now a decisive change came about, since the English, for domestic reasons, drove out Charles's successor, James II, and brought in, as their new king, William III of Orange, the implacable enemy of Louis XIV. William, whose main desire was to defeat France, adroitly ingratiated himself with the English and threw all Britain's strength on the side of the anti-French alliance.

Neglecting the colonial and commercial phases of the struggle, Louis devoted French energies to the conflict in Europe. The War of the League of Augsburg lasted from 1689 to 1697. Though Condé and Turenne were now dead, the Duke of Luxembourg brilliantly led the splendidly organized French armies and won resounding victories at Fleurus (1690), Steinkirk (1692), and Neerwinden (1693). The allied armies were held at bay and France

was spared invasion, while the French ravaged the Palatinate. On the sea, the struggle went against France, and a French expedition to Ireland ended disastrously. After years of strife, ruinous to all the combatants, Louis XIV finally sued for peace.

By the treaty of Ryswick which ended the War of the League of Augsburg, Louis XIV: (1) surrendered nearly all the places adjudged to him by the "chambers of reunion," except Strasbourg, and returned Lorraine to its duke; (2) allowed the Dutch to garrison the chief fortresses of the Spanish (Belgian) Netherlands as a barrier against French aggression; (3) promised to reduce the French tariffs and commercial restrictions which had been aimed against the Dutch; (4) acknowledged William III as King of England and promised not to support any attempt to oust him from his throne. France lost no territory and even secured full recognition of its ownership of the whole province of Alsace.

But the wars of Louis were costing France dearly. Taxes and debts were increasing. Financial officials were compelled to use peculiar money-raising devices such as forcing payments from the guilds or selling new and useless offices. Industries, started so optimistically by Colbert, were languishing. The costs of winning glory for the "Sun King" seemed increasingly high.

In addition, Louis had in 1685 taken an ill-advised step. Urged by a number of his advisers, including Louvois, his war minister, he revoked the Edict of Nantes, by which the Huguenots had been granted religious toleration. Louis had been told that most French Protestants would, with a little persuasion, become converted to Catholicism, and he was eager to secure thoroughgoing unity of the country. The results of his action were disastrous. Despite ruthless pressure, such as the quartering of rough soldiery on peaceful Protestant households, most of the Huguenots clung to their religious beliefs. A hundred thousand or more left the country they loved and migrated to Holland, England, Switzerland, Germany, and even to America and South Africa. Since many of them were able merchants, manufacturers, and craftsmen, France suffered a serious economic blow. What France lost, her neighbors gained. The Huguenots took with them secrets and skills of French industry and built up commercial competition with France.

E. War of the Spanish Succession and Close of the Reign of Louis XIV

One of the reasons which led Louis XIV to negotiate the treaty of Ryswick in 1697, was the development of a situation in Spain which bade fair to give the French monarch golden opportunities for new territorial gains. Spain was still accounted a great power and held not only a vast overseas dominion but the southern (Belgian) Netherlands and much of Italy. The King of Spain at the time was a prematurely senile Habsburg, Charles II, who had reigned ingloriously since 1665 and had no direct heirs. Louis XIV might hope, therefore, to claim the Spanish inheritance for his children, on the ground that their Spanish mother's dowry had never been paid. On the other hand, the Emperor Leopold I (1658–1705) was a Habsburg and the nearest male relative of Charles II, and he was naturally eager to take over, for his line, the Spanish inheritance.

As the question of the Spanish succession loomed larger, attempts were made to solve it peacefully. Louis XIV, Leopold I, and William III of England negotiated a number of "partition treaties," which would have divided the Spanish inheritance and preserved a balance of power in Europe by preventing either France or the Empire from gaining too much. Charles II was not consulted about the matter, though as absolute ruler of Spain he was supposed to have the right to dispose of his own territories.

One of the greatest triumphs of the diplomatic art of Louis XIV was the way in which he ingratiated himself with the Spanish King whom he had so long and so often fought. French agents likewise won the favor of the Spanish people. Charles II, the last of the Spanish Habsburgs, a month before his pitiful death (1700), dictated a will that awarded his whole inheritance to Philip of Anjou, grandson of Louis XIV, with the resolute provision that in no circumstances should the Spanish possessions be divided.

When the news reached Versailles, the Sun King hesitated. The advantage of accepting the will of Charles II would be mainly dynastic; it would put the Bourbon family in a position more exalted than that of the Habsburgs under the Emperor Charles V. But the cost would be heavy, and France, already worn by a lengthening series of wars, would have to shoulder it. For other European powers would certainly strive to maintain some sort of balance between themselves and France. William III would surely not allow the French to take over the Spanish (Belgian) Netherlands without a struggle; and neither Holland nor England would willingly permit the Spanish colonies, so long closed to their ships, to be opened to French commerce. And, of course, the Habsburgs of Austria and the Holy Roman Empire were practically certain, for family reasons, as well as in German interests, to join Holland and England against any combination of France and Spain. On the other hand, if Louis XIV adhered to the previous partition treaties, he could gain considerably for France, ensure peace to Europe, and appear as an honorable and temperate ruler.

Hesitation was but an interlude. Ambition triumphed over fear, and the glory of the Bourbon family over the welfare of France. In the great hall of mirrors at Versailles, the Grand Monarch heralded his grandson as Philip V, the first Bourbon King of Spain. And when Philip left for Madrid, his aged grandfather proudly kissed him, and the Spanish ambassador exultantly declared, "The Pyrenees no longer exist."

Louis knew that war was inevitable, and he hastily prepared for it by seizing the "barrier fortresses" held by the Dutch, by recognizing the son of James II as the rightful King of England in place of William III, by negotiating alliances with Savoy and Bavaria, and by summoning up the armies of France and Spain. Meanwhile, William III and the Emperor Leopold formed against France a "Grand Alliance" of England, Holland, and Austria, to which the German states of Brandenburg-Prussia,

Hanover, and the Palatinate adhered. Later, by means of a favorable commercial agreement called the Methuen treaty (1703), England persuaded Portugal to join the Grand Alliance; and the Duke of Savoy was prevailed upon, by the promise of being recognized as king instead of duke, to change sides and enter the Alliance. It was the aim of the Allies to place the Emperor Leopold's second son, the Habsburg Archduke Charles, on the Spanish throne, to open up the Spanish colonies to foreign trade, and to set limits to the power of Louis XIV.

The War of the Spanish Succession, the fourth major war of Louis XIV, lasted from 1702 to 1713. Although William III died at its very outset, it was vigorously pushed by the English government of his sister-in-law, Queen Anne (1702–1714). On the high seas and in the colonies of America a bitter struggle known as "Queen Anne's War" ensued. And in Europe, the military campaigns were on a hitherto unprecedented scale. Fighting was carried on in the Netherlands, in southern Germany, in Italy, and in Spain. Many of the battles were in the open field, but the war was also punctuated by protracted sieges of fortress cities.

The tide of war turned steadily for several years against the Bourbons. The great French generals were all dead, and the Allies possessed the ablest military leaders of the time in the self-possessed English Duke of Marlborough and the daring Prince Eugene of Savoy. The battle of Blenheim (1704) drove the French out of Germany, and the capture of Gibraltar in the same year gave England a foothold in Spain and a naval base for the Mediterranean. Prince Eugene crowded the French out of Italy (1706); and by the victories of Ramillies (1706), Oudenarde (1708), and Malplaquet (1709), Marlborough cleared the Netherlands. On land and sea one Franco-Spanish reverse followed another. The Allies were preparing to invade France and dictate peace at Paris.

Then it was that Louis XIV displayed an energy and devotion worthy of a better cause. He appealed to the patriotism of the French people. He set an example of

untiring application to toil. He melted down rich ornaments at Versailles to make coins. Nor was he disappointed in his expectations. New recruits hurried to the front. Rich and poor poured in their contributions. A supreme effort was made to stay the advancing enemy.

The fact that Louis XIV came out of the war as well as he did was owing to this remarkable uprising of the French (and of the Spaniards), and also to dissension among the Allies. The Tory party came to power in England, dismissed Marlborough, and showed some eagerness to make peace on moderate terms. Then, too, the unexpected accession of the Archduke Charles to the imperial and Austrian thrones (1711) made his claim to the Spanish crown as menacing to the European balance of power as that of Philip, for his possession of it would have made him another Charles V.

These circumstances rendered possible the conclusion of the peace of Utrecht (1713) with the following major provisions: (1) Philip V, the Bourbon grandson of Louis XIV, was acknowledged King of Spain and of Spain's overseas dominion on the condition that the crowns of France and Spain should never be united. (2) The Austrian Habsburgs were indemnified by securing Naples, Milan, Sardinia (which they exchanged for Sicily seven years later), and the Spanish Belgian Netherlands (which were known from 1713 until 1797 as the Austrian Netherlands). (3) England received the lion's share of the commercial and colonial spoils. From France she obtained Newfoundland, Nova Scotia, and Hudson Bay, and from Spain, Minorca and Gibraltar. She also secured a favorable tariff on the goods she sent into Spain through the port of Cadiz and a monopoly of slave trade to Spanish America (the Asiento), together with the privilege of sending one ship of merchandise each year to the Spanish colonies. France promised not to recognize or assist the Stuart pretenders (descendants of James II) to the English throne. (4) The Dutch recovered their barrier fortresses, whose garrisons were to be paid for in part by Austria; and the Scheldt River was to be open only to Dutch ships. (5) The Elector of Brandenburg was acknowledged as King of Prussia, an important step forward in the fortunes of the house of Hohenzollern. (6) The duchy of Savoy was likewise recognized as a kingdom, and was awarded Sicily which it had to exchange for Sardinia in 1720.

Thus France gained no territory and actually lost important colonies. In return for all her losses, for the crushing debts, the decline of trade, the mounting taxes, France had only the satisfaction of seeing a Bourbon on the throne of Spain. France might now hope for Spanish collaboration in diplomacy and war, and the Bourbons seemed clearly the foremost royal house in Europe. Louis XIV had gained dynastic ends at the cost of heavy national sacrifices.

In the wake of the War of the Spanish Succession, came to the masses of the French nation pestilence and famine, excessive taxes and debasement of the coinage, and the threat of national bankruptcy —a dangerous array of disorders. Louis XIV survived the treaty of Utrecht but two years. His long reign had seen France built up into a strong, centralized power, with its arts flourishing as never before and its people making strides forward in industry and commerce. But it had seen all the gains compromised by costly wars inspired by dynastic ambition and by desire for conquest.

La Danse dans un Pavillon de Jardin (The Minuet in a Pavilion). By Jean Antoine Watteau (d. 1721).

Courtesy The Cleveland Museum of Art. Gift of Commodore Louis D. Beaumont

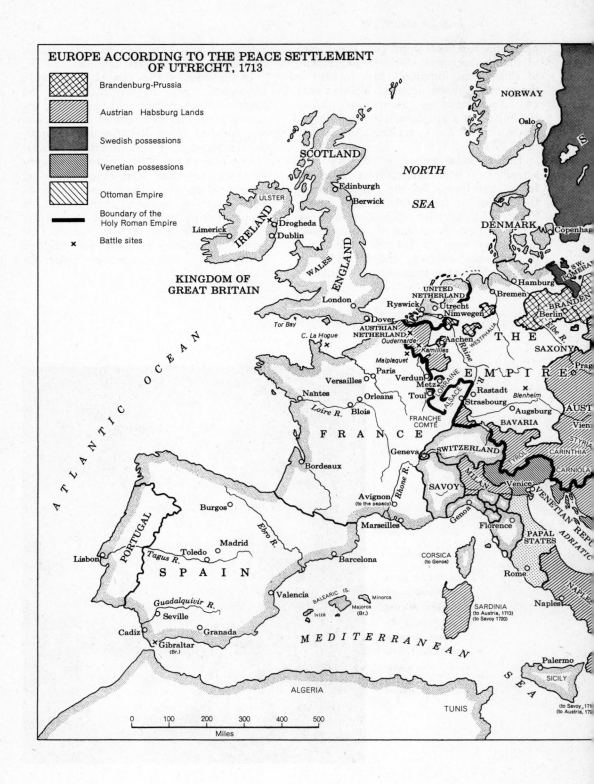

EUROPE ACCORDING TO THE PEACE SETTLEMENT OF UTRECHT, 1713

Brandenburg-Prussia

Austrian Habsburg Lands

Swedish possessions

Venetian possessions

Ottoman Empire

Boundary of the Holy Roman Empire

× Battle sites

NORWAY

Oslo

SCOTLAND

Edinburgh
Berwick

NORTH SEA

DENMARK

Copenhagen

ULSTER

IRELAND

Limerick
Drogheda
Dublin

S.W. POMERANIA

Hamburg
Bremen

BRANDEN
Berlin

WALES

ENGLAND

London

UNITED NETHERLAND
Ryswick Utrecht
Nimwegen

Elbe R.

THE

SAXONY

Prag

Tor Bay

Dover

AUSTRIAN NETHERLAND
Oudenarde
Kamillies

Aachen
WESTPHALIA

Rhine

C. La Hogue

Malplaquet

Paris

Versailles
Verdun
Metz
Toul

LORRAINE
ALSACE

EMPIRE

Rastadt
Strasbourg

Blenheim

AUST

Vien

Nantes

Orleans

Augsburg

STYRIA

Loire R.

Blois

FRANCHE COMTÉ

BAVARIA

CARINTHIA

KINGDOM OF GREAT BRITAIN

ATLANTIC OCEAN

FRANCE

Bordeaux

Geneva

SWITZERLAND

TYROL

CARNIOLA

MILAN

Venice

SAVOY

VENETIAN REP.

ADRIATIC

Rhone R.

Avignon
(to the papacy)

Marseilles

Genoa

Florence

PAPAL STATES

PORTUGAL

Burgos

Ebro R.

Madrid

Toledo

Tagus R.

Lisbon

SPAIN

Barcelona

CORSICA
(to Genoa)

Rome

NAPLES

Valencia

BALEARIC IS.
Minorca

Guadalquivir R.

Iviza

Majorca
(Br.)

SARDINIA
(to Austria, 1713)
(to Savoy 1720)

Naples

Seville

Granada

Cadiz

Gibraltar
(Br.)

MEDITERRANEAN

SEA

Palermo

SICILY

ALGERIA

TUNIS

(to Savoy, 1715
(to Austria, 172

0   100   200   300   400   500
Miles

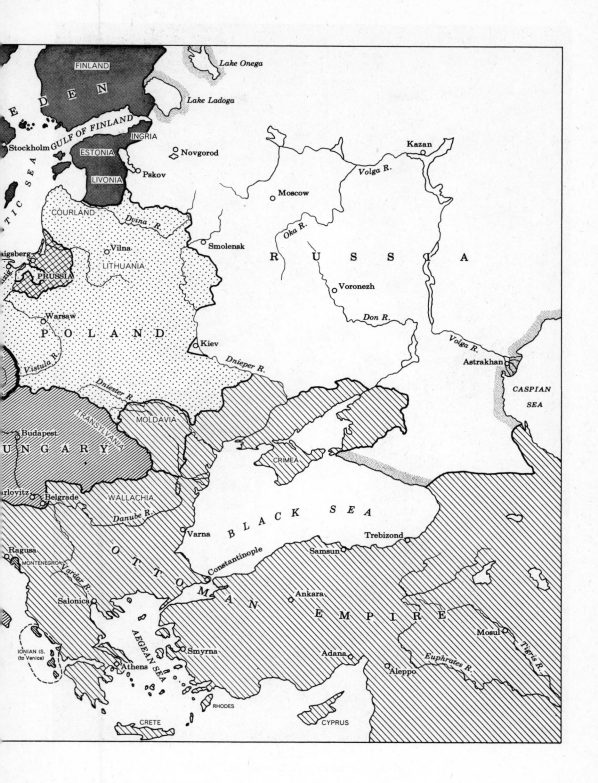

Catherine the Great. By G. B. Lampl (d. 1838).

CHAPTER 35

Rise of Russia and Prussia

A. The Great Northern War: Decline of Sweden and Poland

During the latter part of the seventeenth century and the early part of the eighteenth, drastic changes occurred in the relative strength of countries of eastern and north-central Europe. Two states—Russia and Prussia—consolidated and extended their territories and became notably more important. Two states—Sweden and Poland—declined rather rapidly in strength and significance. One state—Austria—lost weight in Germany but gained by expansion to the east and southeast, while still another state—the previously expanding Ottoman Empire—began to recede.

At the close of the Thirty Years' War in 1648, Sweden dominated the Baltic, and was recognized as the leading Protestant power on the European continent. Much Russian and Polish trade passed through the Swedish port of Riga, and much German commerce went in and out on Swedish ships via the ports of Stettin and Stralsund. Gustavus Adolphus' successor was his brilliant but erratic daughter, Maria Christina, on whose conversion to Catholicism and retirement to Rome the Swedish crown passed to the warlike Charles X (1654–1660). He engaged in simultaneous wars with Russia, Poland, Brandenburg, and Denmark, and by a series of peace treaties with them in 1660–1661 Sweden was confirmed in its extensive Baltic possessions.

The basis of Swedish power was threefold: commerce, army, and alliance with France. But these were not sufficient to enable Sweden to maintain its predominance in the north. Its own population was small, its resources scanty, and its administration inefficient. Its peasantry was poor and backward, its nobility self-seeking, its politics disorderly. Moreover, though its territories were extensive, they were scattered around the edge of the Baltic Sea, and control of them depended on communication by ships and thus on naval supremacy. Nor could it command any deep loyalty on the part of its subjects across the Baltic—Germans, Russians, Finns, Estonians, Latvians, Danes, or Poles. And despite subsidies and diplomatic support from France, the military strength of Sweden proved insufficent to cope with the waxing power of Russia and Prussia.

Had Sweden kept the peace, clung tenaciously to its possessions, and concentrated its attention upon internal development, its power might have endured longer. But King Charles XI (1660–1697), at the behest of Louis XIV, took Sweden into the Franco-Dutch War, with resulting defeat of Swedish forces on land and sea by those of Prussia and Denmark. Only French support secured the restoration of Sweden's territories at the peace table. In his remaining years Charles XI increased the power of the crown, bettered its finances, and strengthened the army and navy. But all his achievements were to go for nought in the catastrophe which marked the astounding reign of his successor.

Charles XII (1697–1718) came to the throne at the age of fifteen a precocious and sensitive boy filled with martial ardor and fanatical courage. When Saxony, Denmark, and Russia formed an alliance in 1699 to seize some of the Swedish territories, they expected an easy victory, for Sweden's ally France was occupied with the question of the Spanish succession. Instead, they precipitated the Great Northern War which lasted until 1721. In it, Charles XII, by the fury with which he defended his dominion, earned the title of the "madman of the North" and went down to final defeat only amid spectacular exploits and after an incredible struggle against overwhelming odds.

Seizing the initiative, Charles XII invaded Denmark and forced its terrified king to make peace (1700) and pay a huge indemnity. Then Charles hastened into Estonia and annihilated a Russian army at Narva (1700). Turning into Poland, he captured Warsaw and Cracow, forced the Polish parliament to oust King Augustus II, who was also Elector of Saxony, and place a friendly noble, Stanislaus Lesczynski, on the Polish throne (1704). Charles, youth though he was, had defeated all his enemies. Callous to the horrors of war, and arrogant with pride, he sent out orders "to slay, burn, and destroy" in the territories he had conquered. But his enemies were now aroused and stubborn. The Russian Tsar Peter reorganized his armies and occupied Karelia and Ingria. Augustus II rallied his forces and regained his Polish throne. Though Charles could still have made a satisfactory peace, he persisted, with increasing stubbornness, in the war that was bleeding Sweden.

Invading Russia, Charles XII met the armies of Peter and suffered an overwhelming defeat at Poltava (1709). Fleeing with the pitiful remnant of his forces, Charles escaped southward into the Ottoman Empire, where he stirred up the Sultan to attack Russia. While he lingered in Turkey, Charles' enemies overran all the Swedish territory except Sweden itself, Finland, and the Baltic port of Stralsund. At this port, Charles suddenly appeared (1714) with a single attendant. Though Prussia and Great Britain had now joined the coalition against him, still Charles would not sue for peace. It was while directing an invasion of Nor-

way in 1718 that Charles XII, at the age of thirty-six, met his death.

The peace which Charles would not seek was made shortly after his death, and none too soon for exhausted and enfeebled Sweden. By the treaties of Stockholm (1719–1720), Sweden gave up all her German territories except a small district in western Pomerania which included Stralsund. Denmark received Holstein; Hanover, the mouths of the Elbe and Weser rivers; Prussia, the mouth of the Oder, with Stettin. Augustus of Saxony recovered the Polish crown, while Great Britain, Denmark, and Prussia became the chief commercial heirs of declining Sweden. By the treaty of Nystad (1721), Russia secured from Sweden the territories of Karelia, Ingria, Estonia, Livonia, and a narrow strip of southern Finland which included the fortress of Viborg. By this treaty Peter the Great gained his long-sought "window to the west," and Russia's power was increased as much as Sweden's was reduced.

In the remainder of the eighteenth century, Sweden rapidly fell to the position of a second-rate power. When an ambitious and assertive party of nobles, called the "Hats," gained control and unwisely took Sweden into another war with Russia (1741) and then into the Seven Years' War (1756), the disastrous results quickly showed that even the continued support of France could not bolster Sweden or maintain it as an important factor in European politics. The economic difficulties that arose from the Swedish defeats and loss of territory led the country into some interesting experiments. A bank of Stockholm had been founded in 1656 and had issued paper notes which were much easier to handle than the clumsy Swedish copper coins, some of which weighed as much as forty-three pounds. Brought under parliamentary control and renamed the Bank of Sweden, this institution became important in the eighteenth century. By 1762, its notes in circulation had risen in amount to 45,000,000 Swedish dollars, and over-issue had led to some depreciation in their value.

The decline of Poland was more prolonged and less dramatic than that of Sweden, but it was no less painful and even more calamitous. By the end of the seventeenth century, Swedish commercial domination of the Baltic had impaired Polish prosperity. Poland's cities were not growing, nor was she developing a strong middle class of merchants and traders. Her peasantry was depressed, and the only strong class was the nobility, which owned most of the land, maintained their own political and social privileges, quarreled fiercely among themselves, and intrigued with foreign powers.

A strong national government might have remedied Poland's internal conditions and protected her against neighboring countries that were ever ready to take advantage of Poland's lack of natural frontiers to seize some of her territory. But at the very time when strong, absolute monarchies were being established in all other countries on the Continent, the Polish government was becoming almost anarchical. Since the sixteenth century the Polish monarchy had been elective, and the noble electors disfigured every reign by their squabbles about the succession. They used their power to

wrest concession after concession from their monarchs until the kings became hardly more than figureheads.

Weakened by wars with Sweden and Russia, Poland was also enfeebled by the lawlessness of the nobles. To make matters worse, the nobles insisted more and more on their political rights, such as the so-called *liberum veto*, by which any of them in the diet, or parliament, could rise in his place and, by saying "I disapprove," prevent the passage of a measure or even secure the dissolution of the session. John III Sobieski, who was king from 1674 to 1696, had led a revolt against his predecessor and had intrigued with France. Though he won immortal fame by a brilliant victory over the Turks (1673) and by defeating them again before beleaguered Vienna (1683), internal conditions in Poland, under his rule, went from bad to worse. At Sobieski's death (1697), there were eighteen candidates for the Polish throne. The election was won by Frederick Augustus, Elector of Saxony, who, to improve his chances, had hastily

SWEDEN BEFORE AND AFTER THE
GREAT NORTHERN WAR, 1699-1721

Lazienski Palace, Warsaw (XVIII Century).

become a Catholic and who arrived late on the scene with ample bribe-money when the finances of his rivals were already exhausted.

For the next sixty-six years, save when Stanislaus Lesczynski, the puppet of the Swedish King Charles XII, was precariously balanced on the throne, the electors of Saxony were kings of Poland. Such resources as Poland could muster after the long and painful war with Sweden, the Saxon rulers cheerfully used for their German projects. The nobles, as unruly as ever, increasingly sought wealth and advantages by negotiating with foreign powers, even when a betrayal of Polish interests was involved. Thus was the way prepared for the tragic partitions of Poland in the latter half of the eighteenth century, when three times (1772, 1793, 1795) her powerful and ruthless neighbors divided up her territories, and at last erased the Polish state from the political map of Europe.

Poland's fate was the result not only of foreign rule, a weak kingship, and a turbulent nobility that sought ever to increase its power, but also of other factors. Though it seemed like a geographic unit, its boundaries were mainly in open plains hard to defend. Nor was it a national unit like France or England, for it contained a large minority of Lithuanians who spoke a different language and smaller numbers of Latvians who spoke another, not to mention Ruthenians (Ukrainians) and Russian Cossacks over against the Russian border. Nor was Poland unified in religion. While the Poles and most of the Lithuanians were Roman Catholics, many of its people in the east adhered to the Orthodox Church; there were large numbers of Jews in the cities; and in the west were sizeable groups of Protestant Germans. Appeals from the Protestants to German rulers, and from the Orthodox to the Russian tsars, formed a convenient basis for foreign interference in Polish affairs.

B. Russia from Peter the Great to Catherine the Great

To the Parisian or Londoner of 1600, Russia seemed a distant half-wild land that lay so far out on the fringes of Europe as to be scarcely a factor in its life or part of its civilization. Yet developments were taking place that were to bring Russia into main currents of Western European life. The time would come when Russia would be the most populous and powerful of European states.

In the century and a half that followed the capture (1453) of Constantinople by the Turks, Russia stood out as the heir of Byzantine culture. From the old Eastern Roman Empire she had derived her religion (Orthodox Christianity), her alphabet, her art and architecture. Moreover her vigorous, ruthless rulers, Ivan III the "Great" (1462–1505) and Ivan IV the "Terrible" (1533–1584), thought of themselves as successors of the Eastern Emperors. They adopted the title of Tsar (or Czar, a form of the word Caesar), the ancient imperial symbol of the double-headed eagle, and much of the old Byzantine court etiquette. Moreover, as they enlarged the grand-duchy of Moscow into the state of Russia and shook off the Tatar yoke, they assumed something of the role of the old Eastern Empire as a barrier between the rest of Europe and the great spaces and wild tribes of Asia.

There was in Russian life a definite eastern tinge derived partly from Constantinople and partly from contact and intermixture with the Tatars and other Asiatic peoples. The Russian men wore long beards; the upper-class women were kept in seclusion; the manner of dress was more oriental than western. During the sixteenth and seventeenth centuries, Russians were spreading rapidly eastward, so that Russia thenceforward was an Asiatic as well as a European power. Russia's contacts with the nations to the west were long limited by several factors. Not only did her emigrants tend to go eastward, but the very nature of the country made agriculture more important than industry or trade, so that her commercial relations with outside lands were comparatively slight. Her Orthodox Christianity kept her aloof from both Catholics and Protestants to the west. Furthermore, as long as her immediate neighbors—Sweden, Poland, and the Ottoman Empire—were strong, Russia was shut off from the west by hostile territories. After Gustavus Adolphus secured Karelia in 1617, Russia was cut off from all contact with the Baltic and could trade directly with western Europe only by the long and difficult Arctic Ocean route.

At the close of the sixteenth century, the direct line of Ivan the Great died out and there ensued what were known as the "Troublous Times" (1605–1613). Harassed by the struggles of contestants for the throne, invaded by Swedes, Poles, and Turks, Russia seemed to be sinking into anarchy. To remedy the situation a meeting of nobles at Moscow in 1613 chose one of their own number, Michael Romanov, to be the new Tsar. Aided by his father, who was Orthodox Patriarch of Moscow, Michael slowly reduced the country to order. His successor, Alexius (1645–1676), was able, by joining with groups of frontiersmen, to wrest part of the Ukraine from Polish rule.

At the death of Alexius, there were new troubles as to the succession, but by 1694 Peter, a grandson of Michael, had become the sole ruler. Brought up amid scenes of blood and violence, gigantic in stature, subject to terrible fits of rage, ruthless and unprincipled, Peter was a remarkable leader, administrator, and statesman. His achievements won him the title of "the Great." Interested in ships from childhood, Peter, thwarted in an attempt to take Azov on the Black Sea from the Turks (1695), built a fleet which enabled him to capture that city the next year. Already eager to gain for Russia "windows" on the Black and Baltic Seas, Peter in 1697 sent a special embassy to seek the aid of the Western powers against the Turks. Those powers were too busy with the question of the Spanish succession to heed Russian pleas. But Peter, who accompanied the embassy in the guise of a sea captain, avidly absorbed useful knowledge about armies, navies, forts, shipbuilding, industry, and trade in Prussia, Holland, England, and the other countries he visited. Everywhere he went he enlisted sailors, craftsmen, engineers, and technicians, and sent them back to Russia to work on his projects.

While traveling from Vienna to Venice, Peter heard news of a mutiny among the royal bodyguard, or *streltsi*, at Moscow. Though the rising had been quickly put down, Peter hurried home to wreak a bloody vengeance and show the elements who opposed him that his authority was not to be questioned. Some seven thousand of the mutineers were executed, a number of them by Peter in person, for it amused him to demonstrate that he could behead a man with a single stroke. But Peter came back for more than vengeance.

Peter the Great. After a picture by Sir Godfrey Kneller (d. 1723).

Impressed by the superior culture and technology of western Europe, the Tsar was determined to "westernize" Russia. In part, he sought to alter external ways. Beards and mustaches were taxed heavily and Peter with his own hand cut off the hirsute adornments of some of the chief nobles. French and German clothes were made compulsory. Women were brought into the social gatherings of the court. The use of tobacco was encouraged. January 1 was substituted for September 1 as New Year's day.

Peter sought likewise to effect deeper reforms. He tried to build up trade and industry. State factories were started and manned by serfs. Shipping was subsidized, and the middle class of traders and business men, which was very small in Russia, was favored and helped. Much of the westernization was superficial. When Peter tried to establish the German guild system in Russia he met with little success. But his efforts mark a turning point in Russian history, for henceforward Russia came more and more into the main currents of Western civilization.

Determined to make Russia an absolute monarchy like that of Louis XIV, Peter acted with such skill and energy that Russian rule became more autocratic than any in the west. He created a strong army, trained and disciplined by expert foreign officers. Any remaining traces of local self-government were wiped out or enfeebled, and the old local divisions were replaced by "govern-

ments" (gubernii), each headed by an army officer who extorted taxes to pay for Peter's reforms. The old Duma of the nobles was changed into an advisory Senate, and each town was endowed, in western style, with a town hall and aldermen to go in it, but even here all real power rested with agents of the Tsar. The church, too, was brought under complete royal control, for though Peter, professing devotion to the Orthodox faith, harried all heretics, he also abolished the patriarchate of Moscow and transferred its authority to a "Holy Synod" whose members were chosen by the Tsar and were subservient to him. Thenceforth the Tsars exalted the Russian Orthodox Church as the source of order, while the Church rapidly became the right-hand support of Tsardom.

Effective, too, were Peter's alterations of the social structure of the country. He swamped the old nobility (the boyars) by creating tens of thousands of new nobles. To these he gave lands and privileges, and, in return, demanded that they serve him in the army and the government administration. The lands of the new nobles were worked by serfs. Until about 1600, the Russian peasants had been relatively free and had worked their lands in communal groups. During the course of the seventeenth century they had lost much of their freedom and had been bound more and more closely to the soil, at a time when most of the serfs of western Europe were gaining freedom. This trend came to completion through the work of Peter the Great. The peasants were registered by a rural census and forbidden to leave the land. They were put entirely under the control of the landowners, who regarded them more and more as a sort of livestock that went with the estates. If the nobles were to serve the Tsar, the serfs were to be forced to serve the nobles.

Peter's forceful achievements within his country were matched by success in war and foreign policy. To be sure, he made little progress against the Turks. In fact, in 1711, he had to restore Azov to them to avoid a military disaster. But against Sweden, despite his initial defeat at Narva, he was successful at Poltava and thereafter. The treaty of Nystad (1721) marked Russia's triumph. To symbolize the country's new orientation westward, Peter built on the waste marshes near the mouth of the Neva river a great new modern city and called it St. Petersburg (now Leningrad). Thither he transferred from Moscow his government. The capital of Russia was no longer to be in the old "holy city" steeped in the Russian past, with churches that bespoke Byzantium and with its memories of the Tatars. Henceforth for almost two centuries, Russia was to be ruled from a city built by Peter's orders, on land won by Peter's armies; a city linked to the rest of Europe by its position and its "western" architecture.

One of Russia's three strong neighbors— Sweden—was disposed of by Peter the Great in the early part of the eighteenth century. It remained for the Tsarina Catherine II the "Great," in the latter part of the century, to take care of the other two— Poland and the Ottoman Empire. In the interval (1725–1762) between Peter I and Catherine II, there were several disputes over the succession in Russia, and the country was ruled mainly by women more or less directly connected with the Romanov family. These female rulers were for the most part notable for their loose morals and ugly manners. Of them, Anne (1730–1740) was reared in Germany and surrounded herself with German favorites and advisers, while Elizabeth (1741–1762), a daughter of Peter the Great, hated Germans, employed native Russian advisers, and warred on Prussia.

But Catherine II, who ruled Russia from 1762 to 1796, was of a different stamp. She came of a minor German princely family and had been brought as a girl to Russia to marry a weak and half-mad heir to the throne. At once she set herself to win the favor of the Russians. She learned their language, she adopted their religion; she slighted Germans and surrounded herself with Russians. In 1762, her husband came to the throne as Peter III, and his brief rule was not without significance, for in his crazy admiration of the Prussian King Frederick II, he took Russia out of the war then raging against Prussia and aided Frederick. But within a few months Peter was removed from power by a revolt of the guards regiment abetted by Catherine. Shortly afterwards Peter died in captivity,

officially of "apoplexy," but actually by assassination.

Despite the fact that Catherine was a German with no Romanov or even Russian blood, she was proclaimed Tsarina by those who had got rid of her husband, and during the thirty-four years of her reign, her authority was never successfully challenged. Completely immoral, utterly without scruples, surrounded by favorites who were frequently her lovers, Catherine II was a strong ruler at home and notably successful in foreign affairs. Though she had no real love of learning, she was eager to be thought "progressive" and "enlightened." She founded some secondary schools and an Academy at St. Petersburg. She corresponded with learned men and philosophers in France. She discussed forward-looking reforms of all sorts and popularized French language, manners, architecture, and cookery in the court circles, with such success that French became the first and Russian the second language of the next generation of Russian nobles.

Actually, for all this show, Catherine accomplished few real reforms in Russia and these were more designed to strengthen her authority than to benefit the people. Administratively she reorganized the "governments" and "districts." The courts of justice were improved and set in order. But at the same time Catherine further subjugated the Church by taking over its lands and the million serfs that lived on them. To reward the nobles who were the class from which she derived her support, she gave to distinguished generals and administrators large estates and great numbers of serfs, and she distributed in a similar fashion much of the foreign land she acquired by conquest or diplomacy.

It was really in foreign affairs that Catherine won the right to be called "Great," for here she proved herself a worthy successor of Peter I and displayed an equal ruthlessness and an even greater cynicism. In 1764, aided by Frederick the Great of Prussia, Catherine secured the election of one of her favorites, Stanislaus Poniatowski, as King of Poland, ending the rule there of the Saxon Electors. Determined to keep Poland weak and ill-governed, Catherine not only intrigued constantly among the quarreling groups of nobles but in 1768

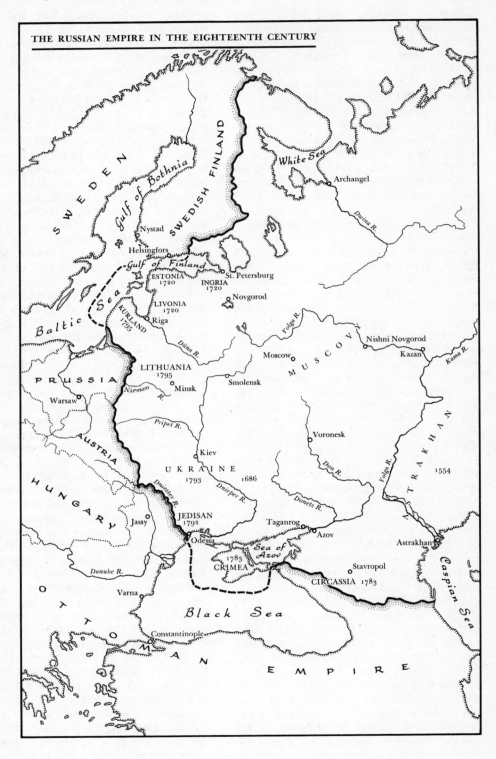

THE RUSSIAN EMPIRE IN THE EIGHTEENTH CENTURY

S W E D E N

Gulf of Bothnia

White Sea

Archangel

Nystad

SWEDISH FINLAND

Helsingfors

Dwina R.

Gulf of Finland

Baltic Sea

ESTONIA
1720

INGRIA
1720

St. Petersburg

Novgorod

LIVONIA
1720

KURLAND
1795

Riga

Volga R.

Nishni Novgorod

Diina R.

Moscow

M U S C O V Y

Kazan

Kama R.

LITHUANIA
1795

P R U S S I A

Minsk

Smolensk

Warsaw

Niemen R.

Pripet R.

Voronesk

A S T R A K H A N

Kiev

Don R.

Volga R.

1554

U K R A I N E
1793   1686

Dnieper R.

H U N G A R Y

Dniester R.

Donetz R.

Jassy

JEDISAN
1792

Odessa
1783

CRIMEA

Taganrog

Azov

Sea of
Azov

Astrakhan

Caspian Sea

Danube R.

Stavropol

CIRCASSIA 1783

Varna

Black Sea

O T T O M A N

Constantinople

E M P I R E

negotiated a treaty by which the Poles promised not to reform or change their anarchical form of government without her consent.

Then by a series of negotiations with Poland's other neighbors, Austria and Prussia, Catherine prepared the way for the first partition of Poland. In 1772 all was ready. By prearrangement, and despite the frantic protests of the Poles, Prussia took from Poland West Prussia except the town of Danzig. Austria took Galicia except Cracow. Catherine seized all of Poland east of the Duna and Dnieper rivers. Thus Poland was deprived of about a fourth of its territory, a third of its population, and almost half of its wealth.

Sobered by this catastrophe, many of the Polish nobles sought to reform the government and to strengthen what remained of their nation. But Catherine always worked to prevent the fruition of their projects and stirred up dissident groups to maintain the old anarchy. In 1791 the Poles were able, by means of a new constitution, to put through a series of important improvements in their government. The *liberum veto* was abolished, and the monarchy made hereditary. But again Catherine intervened, pointing out that such changes violated the treaty of 1768. Joining with Prussia, she partitioned Poland again in 1793, defeating the Poles who were led by the heroic Kosciusko and who sought to defend their country and their new constitution. Prussia took Posen and western Poland almost up to Warsaw, while Russia occupied another large slice of eastern and southeastern Poland.

In vain did Kosciusko assume a military dictatorship and lead a desperate national revolt. He was defeated, wounded, and captured. In 1795 Prussia and Russia, again joined by Austria, completed the task of wiping Poland off the map. Though the boundaries they drew did not long endure, Poland was not to reappear as an independent national state for one hundred and twenty-three years, and, from 1815 onwards, the majority of Poles and the greater part of their country lay under Russian rule.

If acquisition of territory is the gauge of success, Catherine the Great was almost equally successful in her dealings with the Ottoman Empire. From 1768 to 1774, she waged war on the Turks and with such good fortune that the resulting treaty of Kuchuk Kainarji (1774) was a decisive turning point in the decline of Turkey and the rise of Russia in southeastern Europe.

When Catherine died in 1796 she left a record of very considerable accomplishments. If it can be said that Peter the Great made Russia a European power, it can be maintained with equal justice that Catherine the Great made Russia a great power. The eighteenth century witnessed a marvelous growth of the Russian Empire in Europe, as the seventeenth had seen it spread out over northern Asia. Russia had acquired wide lands and a capital on the Baltic. It had secured valuable ports on the Black Sea. It had pushed its boundaries westward to the middle of the continent. It now counted among its subjects, not only Russians, but Ukrainians, Byelorussians, Lithuanians, Estonians, Letts, and Poles, as well as a whole medley of Asiatic tribes and peoples.

C. Austria and the Holy Roman Empire in the Eighteenth Century

In the late middle age and early modern times, the Habsburgs of Austria, as Holy Roman Emperors, had had considerable influence and some control throughout Germany. But after 1648, a change gradually occurred. The peace of Westphalia so increased the independence of the several German states, both large and small, that Austria had to win their alliance or support almost as if she were dealing with foreign powers. Yet Austria did not sink to the position of a second-rate power, for, while it lost influence in Germany and the west, it made compensating gains in Italy, and also in the east at the expense of the Ottoman Empire and Poland. But these gains bore with them seeds of future trouble, since more and more they made of Habsburg Austria a conglomerate state of alien peoples with only a relatively small German nucleus in the old hereditary lands around Vienna.

In Germany, to be sure, the Habsburg Emperor, even after 1648, had a certain prestige. In a vague way, people still looked to him as the most important leader in German affairs. But the German states were taking advantage of their increased inde-

FINLAND

St. Petersburg

S W E D E N

P R U S S I A

Baltic Sea

Riga

LATVIA

Libau

Mitau

Duna R.

To Russia in 1772

Smolensk

Tilsit

Danzig

Königsberg

Niemen R.

LITHUANIA in 1795

BYELORUSSIA

POMERANIA

Marienburg

E PRUSSIA

To Prussia in 1772

Thorn

To Prussia in 1795

Grodno

Bug R.

To Russia in 1793

Posen

Gnesen

To Prussia in 1793

Warsaw

Pripet R.

SILESIA

Breslau

Oder R.

To Austria in 1795

Lublin

Vladimir

UKRAINE

Kiev

Vistula R.

AUSTRIA

Cracow

Lemberg

To Austria in 1772

Dnieper R.

Vienna

Carpathian Mts.

GALICIA

Dniester R.

Budapest

H U N G A R Y

Odessa

O T T O M A N   E M P I R E

Black Sea

PARTITIONS OF POLAND, 1772-1795

pendence to pursue their own interests. In the north, Brandenburg emerged as a powerful state. In the south, Bavaria, to strengthen itself against Austria, maintained an almost constant alliance with France. The Elector of Saxony in 1697 obtained the crown of Poland, and in 1715 the Elector of Hanover became King of Great Britain. None of these states could be counted on to follow Austrian leadership, and the others did so only when it seemed to their advantage.

In the long reign of Leopold I (1658–1705), Austria secured compensation in Hungary for her weakening hold on Germany. Strengthening his administration and suppressing dissent, Leopold heightened Habsburg authority in Hungary at the expense of old local liberties. Prompted by the pope and in alliance with Poland, Leopold engaged in a long war (1683–1699) with the Moslem Turks. At the start, the Turkish armies, with something of their former vigor, surged up to the very gates of Vienna and threatened to capture the city. But the Polish King John III (Sobieski) came south with his army and drove off the Turks. Though Leopold hesitated to continue the war, Pope Innocent XI formed a Holy League which included Venice, Poland, and Russia to drive the Moslems out of Europe. Even Louis XIV for a time lent aid to the Christian cause. Success followed success. Budapest was recovered (1686); Belgrade was taken (1688); Bosnia was liberated

(1689). But then the outbreak of the War of the League of Augsburg [1] afforded a respite to the Turks; they rallied and recaptured Belgrade. In 1697, however, Prince Eugene of Savoy defeated the Turks at Zenta and a peace conference met in the next year.

The resulting peace of Karlowitz (1699) assured to the Austrian Habsburgs the whole of Hungary, instead of only the northern portion which they had formerly held. Meanwhile, Leopold had summoned a Hungarian diet and forced it to acknowledge him as hereditary rather than elective King of Hungary. Hungarian patriots rose against the Habsburgs, and though they won few battles in their long struggle (1704–1711), they at least secured a promise that some of the traditional Hungarian privileges would be respected.

Austria had been distracted from her eastern problems by wars in the west: the War of the League of Augsburg and the War of the Spanish Succession. Though in the latter she failed to recreate the empire of Charles V, she at least made significant territorial gains. As a result of the peace of Utrecht (1713), Austria obtained the Belgian Netherlands, and in Italy both the duchy of Milan and the kingdom of the Two Sicilies. The Austrian Netherlands proved difficult to defend and not particularly profitable, and the kingdom of the Two Sicilies was lost to the Bourbons of

[1] See above, p. 428.

AUSTRIAN HABSBURG POSSESSIONS AND
THE HOLY ROMAN EMPIRE ABOUT 1740

Spain in 1738. But Milan was held by Austria, with one brief interruption, till the middle of the nineteenth century.

The Emperor who had won these lands at the peace of Utrecht was Charles VI (1711–1740). It became clear to him early in his reign that he was going to leave no male heirs. He therefore used most of his energies and diplomacy to insure the succession of his daughter, Maria Theresa. By a document called the Pragmatic Sanction, Charles declared the Habsburg dominions indivisible and capable of being inherited by a female; and by making concessions to major foreign powers, he obtained paper promises from them that they would respect the Sanction. But, as the cynical Prussian King of the time remarked, 200,000 soldiers would have been a more useful legacy.

Austria of the eighteenth century was a collection of territories brought together by conquest, marriage, and diplomacy. It was not an Empire, for the Austrian ruler was called Emperor only if he was elected head of the Holy Roman (German) Empire. It was not a national state like England or France, for it did not comprise a single predominant nationality, nor did it have a unified administration. The common monarch of the varied lands that composed the Habsburg dominions ruled as archduke in Austria, king in Bohemia, king in Hungary, duke in Milan, and prince in the Belgian Netherlands; and the administration of each of these major areas was independent of the others and affected by local traditions and privileges. Under this complicated rule were Germans, Czechs, Slovaks, Hungarians (Magyars), Rumanians, Croatians, Slovenes, Italians, Flemings, and French-speaking Walloons.

But for all the confused and varied nature of the Habsburg domains, the Austrian rulers of the eighteenth century still had great prestige in Europe. The sheer extent of their territories and the number of their subjects made them important. They were related to most of the other ruling families of Europe. They could muster large armies. They still were thought of as the chief defenders of Christendom against the Moslem Turks. All save Maria Theresa bore the proud if empty title of Holy Roman Emperor.

D. Brandenburg-Prussia from the Great Elector to Frederick the Great

Much of the power and prestige lost by the Habsburgs in Germany was gradually gained by another house, that of Hohenzollern. In the seventeenth century, the Hohenzollerns were merely one of a number of major princely families. In the eighteenth century, they possessed the most effective military power in central Europe. In the nineteenth century, they brought all Germany except Austria under their rule. Though some of the Hohenzollerns were skilled in diplomacy and not a few encouraged the arts of peace, basically their rise rested on their armies. It was a military phenomenon.

In the tenth century, the Hohenzollerns had ruled as counts over a castle on the hill of Zollern, just north of modern Switzerland. In the twelfth century, by a lucky marriage, one of them had become Burgrave of the rich city of Nuremberg. But their real start dated from 1415 when the Holy Roman Emperor made a Hohenzollern the Elector of Brandenburg, a mark, or frontier province, in the northeast of Germany. The Protestant Revolt strengthened the Hohenzollerns, for they became Lutherans and seized broad church lands. In 1614, they acquired by inheritance the duchy of Cleves on the lower Rhine, and four years later they similarly acquired the duchy of East Prussia, then a fief of the Polish crown. In the Thirty Years' War the Hohenzollerns played a sufficiently adroit game to emerge with the wealthy bishoprics of Halberstadt and Minden and the right to succeed to that of Magdeburg, much ravaged by war, but still important.

The Elector of Brandenburg and Duke of East Prussia at the end of the Thirty Years' War (1648) was Frederick William (1640–1688), usually styled the "Great Elector." At his succession, he found himself, through the gains of his ancestors, one of the leading princes of northern Germany and likewise a leader among the German Protestant rulers. His first task was rebuilding his country, devastated by war, and reorganizing and enlarging its army. This he did so successfully that he was able to act as a strong third party in a war between Sweden and Poland (1655–1660). He made himself invaluable first to one side and then to the other, and by the end of the war he had secured recognition as the outright ruler of East Prussia, for he induced the Polish king to renounce all sovereignty over that province.

But if the Great Elector raised the prestige of his state abroad, his work of internal construction was even more important. He increased his absolute powers by crushing opposition in the estates (or legislatures) of East Prussia and Cleves. He reformed the administration of Brandenburg, improved the methods of tax collection, increased the revenues, and drew into his own hands ever more despotic power. With equal skill, he centralized the separate administrations of Prussia, Cleves, and Brandenburg, merged the local armies into one military force, and made all officials subservient to him and his ministers at Berlin. Thus Frederick William welded the scattered holdings of the Hohenzollerns into a unified monarchical state.

Utterly unscrupulous though he was, the Great Elector paid much attention to the economic welfare of his people. He strove to promote agriculture, commerce, and industry, and to make his relatively poor domains as prosperous as their resources permitted. Marshes were drained to win new agricultural lands. Commercial companies were founded. Skilled Flemish workers and traders were invited to settle in Brandenburg. When Louis XIV revoked the edict of Nantes and drove thousands of French Huguenots into exile, the Great Elector seized the opportunity. He invited the refugees to come to his dominions and granted them lands and other help. To Brandenburg they brought a vital accession of industrial and commercial knowledge in weaving, glass making, and a dozen other trades. Many of the Huguenots settled around Berlin, and that capital, which had been scarcely more than a village of 8,000 inhabitants at Frederick William's accession, was a thriving little city of 20,000 people at his death.

In the rise of the Hohenzollerns, the Great Elector played a stellar role, not so much for any accessions of territory, as for his work of organization. He made a state out of what had been a collection of family holdings, a national army out of what had been feudal levies, a centralized administration out of those who had been local officials, and a progressive country out of what had been one of the more backward areas of Europe.

Much of what the Great Elector had accomplished was solidified by his son, Frederick, whose chief ambition was to win for himself the title of King, which seemed to him much more resplendent than the titles he already bore, such as Elector (of Brandenburg) or Duke (of Prussia and of Cleves). In the War of the League of Augsburg, though Frederick helped the Emperor Leopold, the latter brushed aside his pleas to be recognized as king. But on the eve of the War of the Spanish Succession, the Emperor, anxious to secure all possible support against Louis XIV, decided that a title was a cheap price for an ally and agreed in 1700 that Frederick might become a king. The title Frederick took was King of Prussia, since his duchy of Prussia, unlike Brandenburg, was completely outside the Holy Roman Empire and there could be no question of his full sovereignty in it.[1] Early in 1701, Frederick hurried to Königsberg and there assumed the royal crown. Fulfilling his promises, Frederick aided the Emperor against France in the ensuing war, and by the treaty of Utrecht in 1713 the other European powers acknowledged the new royal title of the Hohenzollerns.

Frederick I died before the peace was signed, and, if he left kingly prestige to his son Frederick William I (1713–1740), he also bequeathed an empty treasury and a country burdened by taxes and exhausted by war. The new King, thrifty and puritanical, was quite unlike his father. As soon as he came to the throne, he busied himself with dismissing useless officials and selling off the costly French-style furniture his father had collected.

The early years of the reign of Frederick William I were marked by considerable gains of territory. By the peace of Utrecht, he acquired a large part of Gelderland. In alliance with Russia, he warred on Charles XII of Sweden and acquired a portion of Pomerania, including the valuable port of

---

[1] Technically, his title was King *in* Prussia, because his duchy consisted only of *East Prussia*. *West Prussia* (including Danzig) belonged to Poland.

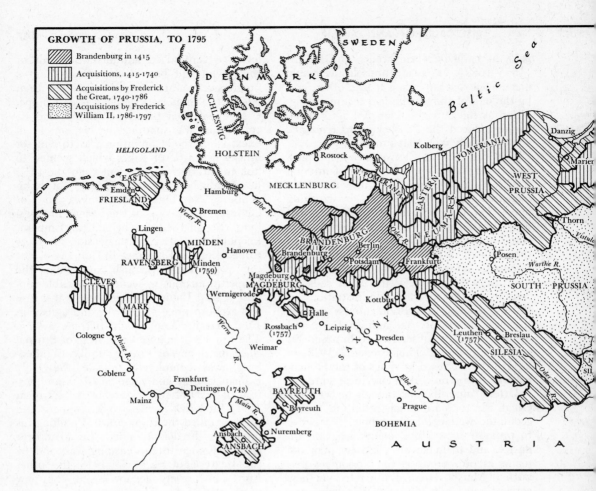

Stettin, which provided a useful commercial outlet for Berlin. But the major contributions of Frederick William to the rise of Prussia were, like those of his grandfather, in the internal sphere.

By a thrift that bordered on miserliness, Frederick William I increased his standing army from 38,000 to more than 80,000 men. At his death the Prussian army was comparable in size with the military forces of the much larger and wealthier states of France and Austria. In discipline, training, and efficiency, it was probably the best in Europe. Its officers, though drawn from noble landowning families (*Junkers*), were promoted on the basis of merit and not of wealth and influence as in other lands. The equipment of the soldiers was up to date and their training was thorough.

In internal administration, the King pushed ahead the work of centralization. He organized a "general directory" to ensure the businesslike handling of war, finance, and the royal lands. The royal estates were transformed from family holdings into crown domains and administered by public officials. The serfs on these domains were freed and encouraged to increase their productivity. For all his dislike of the French, Frederick William copied them in two respects—the creation of a bureaucracy, and the issuance of mercantilist legislation.

Though it was modeled on the French, the Prussian civil service soon surpassed it in efficiency and honesty. Junkers and bourgeois devoted their lives to the public service. The salaries and rewards were not great and the punishments for failure or laxity were severe. But a tradition was soon created of devotion to the king and to the public good. If bureaucracy brought with it formalism and red tape, it also gave Prussia a solid and honest administration.

In the field of economic legislation, Fred-

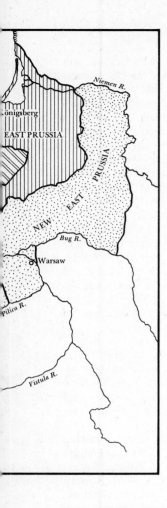

erick William followed the lines laid down by the French statesman Colbert. In the best mercantilist manner he forbade or restricted the importation of foreign manufactures and the exportation of raw materials. Industrial processes and the quality of goods were carefully regulated, and the regulations were enforced by the growing bureaucracy. In East Prussia and elsewhere, the King made every effort to improve agricultural production. He also fostered new industries, and granted rewards and protection to capable manufacturers. Yet such work of economic development was severely limited by Frederick William's thrift. He increased the state income to seven million thalers, paid off the debts left by his father, and heaped up a surplus in the treasury. But of the annual income in a normal year, five million went for military expenses, one million for a reserve fund, and only a million was left

for the court, the civil service, and economic projects.

With all his abilities, Frederick William I had many personal peculiarities which highly amused Europe. Like an angry schoolmaster, he flogged his subjects with his own royal cane. Wealthy merchants were ordered to put up fine houses to improve the appearance of Berlin. Education was more or less ignored, and the King had little sympathy for philosophy, art, or literature. One craze he did have, a passion for tall soldiers. He created the Potsdam Guard of Giants and for once spent money freely. Tall foreigners he lured into his service by promises of high pay, and sometimes, it is said, hulking peasants were kidnapped that their great stature might please the King in the military reviews which were his chief delight.

During many years this crabbed and eccentric King feared that all his savings and all his labors might go for nought, since he was mightily disappointed in his son and heir. The Crown Prince Frederick showed an interest in literature, art, and music, which struck his father as nothing short of effeminate. The King abused Frederick and disciplined him. When the Prince at length ran away, the King had him arrested and then put him through an almost slave-like training in the civil and military administration, from the lowest grades upward. It was this despised and misunderstood prince who, as Frederick II, came to the throne of Prussia in 1740, just as Maria Theresa ascended the throne of Austria. Within a few months Frederick plunged Prussia and Europe into a long conflict. His achievements in war and diplomacy were so far to outshine those of his father that history has awarded him the title of Frederick the Great as a tribute to his success, though certainly not to his methods. It was Frederick II who was to complete the work of his Hohenzollern ancestors and to make Prussia a great European power.

E. Decline of the Ottoman Empire

In the sixteenth century the strength of the Ottoman Empire had been awesome indeed, though Suleiman the Magnificent had been checked at the gates of Vienna (1529), and the Habsburg Emperor Rudolph II (1576–1612), in the "Long War" (1593–1606), had held the Turks at bay and had even made some gains against them. In the seventeenth century, Ottoman power still seemed a major threat to Christian Europe. But in actuality it was already on the wane. The three Sultans from Mohammed III (1595–1603) to Ibrahim (1640–1648) were weak and ineffective. Under them, the government became more corrupt, palace intrigues flourished, and military strength was reduced as the Turks failed to keep up with the improvements in weapons and tactics that were being developed in the west. Indeed they missed what was a golden opportunity to make territorial gains against Austria, for troubles at home prevented them from taking advantage of the Thirty Years' War which racked Europe. Similarly at sea, the once dreaded Turkish navy fell behind as the ships, cannon, and sailing techniques of the west were steadily improved and tested by long voyages and forays on the great oceans.

When, under Mohammed IV (1648–1687), the Ottoman Empire once again took the offensive, it met a vigorous defense.[1] In the ensuing peace treaty of Karlowitz (1699), the Turks gave up all their earlier conquests north of the Danube and lost much of their power to threaten Vienna and harass the Habsburg empire.

During the eighteenth century, though the decay was not obvious to the outer world, the Ottoman Empire was subject to a kind of dry rot that slowly but surely sapped its strength and vigor. The sultans were not effective leaders and they preferred the ease of palace life to the rigors of military campaigns. Actual administrative authority became lodged more and more in a "divan" or group of ministers, and these officials were more often successful court intriguers than capable public servants. Offices and privileges came to be sold corruptly, and the officeholders recouped the cost by themselves seeking bribes. The army, which had been the primary source of Ottoman strength, declined steadily in effec-

tiveness as its weapons and tactics became more and more antiquated in comparison with those developed in the wars of western Europe. Even the "janissaries"—a professional military guard made up in large part of Christian boys, recruited forcibly, converted to the Moslem faith, and subjected to thorough training—were increasingly affected by corruption. But because they were better organized than other troops they tended to become the masters of the sultan and his government.

Then too, it must be remembered that the Turks in Europe had never been more than a small minority of landholding nobles and officials, who exploited the conquered Christian peasantry of half a dozen nationalities (Rumanian, Magyar, Serb, Croatian, Bulgarian, Greek). The continuation of Moslem rule depended on military force and effective government. Had the subject peoples been better organized and better educated they might have made more trouble for their Turkish masters, but they were held together mainly by their religion and by the church organizations which the Moslems tolerated and used.

One ruler who understood the growing internal weakness of the Ottoman Empire was Catherine the Great of Russia. When some Poles who had risen against Russian intervention fled into Turkish territory, Catherine's troops pursued them and brought on a Russo-Turkish war which lasted from 1768 to 1774. The decline of the Turkish army was now revealed, and the Russian forces won a series of victories. They captured Azov, took Bucharest, and conquered a large part of Rumania. At length, the Turks made peace lest worse should befall, for Catherine was even stirring up trouble among the Greeks under Ottoman rule. By the treaty of Kuchuk Kainarji in 1774, not only did Russia gain Azov which Peter the Great had briefly held, but also the Turks were compelled to renounce all rule over the petty Tatar states on the north shore of the Black Sea and to promise to give better government to the Christians under Ottoman rule in Rumania and Greece. Russia likewise obtained the right to send ships freely through the Bosporus and the Dardanelles and to act as

---

[1] See above, pp. 346–348, 445.

Russian Capture of Azov from the Turks, 1696. From an engraving
by Adriaen Schoonebeck (d. 1714).

protector of some churches in Constantinople. Catherine had not only opened a
"window" to the south as Peter the Great
had sought to do, but she had provided
Russia with excuses to intervene almost at
will in Ottoman affairs. Within a few years
Catherine had absorbed the Tatar territory
north of the Black Sea, and another treaty
in 1792 made the Dniester River the
boundary between the Russian and Ottoman
empires.

Thus by the end of the eighteenth century Ottoman power in Europe was clearly
lessening. The sultan still ruled millions of
Christian subjects and held sway over broad
lands in Europe, Asia, and Africa. But his
armies and navies were no longer able to
cope with modern forces of the west. His
administration was increasingly ineffective.
And his subject peoples were beginning to
stir as if awakening from a long sleep.

A Dutch Banker. By Rembrandt van Rijn (d. 1669).

CHAPTER 36

Colonial and Power Rivalries in the Seventeenth and Early Eighteenth Centuries

A. The Portuguese and Spanish Oversea Dominions

During the first decades of the seventeenth century, when Portugal was still under Spanish kings and embroiled in their wars, the earlier Portuguese monopoly of the lucrative spice trade with the East Indies was broken. The Dutch won bases in Java, while the English entered actively into the trade of mainland India. But it was during the years from 1640 to 1668, when Portugal was occupied in regaining its independence from Spain, that it lost most of its farflung Eastern dominion to the Dutch. By 1700 the Portuguese held, outside of Brazil, only some stretches of seacoast in Africa, and a few posts in the Far East—Macao, Goa, Diu, and Timor.

As their trade with the Far East declined, the Portuguese paid more attention to their extensive but hitherto neglected South American colony of Brazil. Perhaps they might compensate for the losses in Asia by gains in America. In a thirteen-year war (1641–1654), waged largely by Portuguese Brazilian colonists, Dutch intruders were ousted from the coasts of Brazil, and in 1661 Holland formally renounced its attempt to win a hold in that country. From 1645 on, the heir to the Portuguese throne bore the title "Prince of Brazil," and by 1700 Portugal's trade with Brazil was equal to its commerce with all of Europe.

Then fate took a hand to enhance still more the value of Brazil. Toward the end of the seventeenth century gold was discov-

ered in the Minas Geraes district. A "gold rush" developed, and production increased rapidly. By 1780 Brazil had produced more than three-quarters of a billion dollars' worth of gold. Early in the eighteenth century diamond fields were likewise discovered, and soon Brazil was the chief diamond-producing area of the world. The government profited from the gold and diamonds by levying a head tax on the slaves brought in to work the mines. Brazil proved no mean substitute for the fabled Far East.

The Spanish overseas dominion suffered no such losses as the Portuguese in the seventeenth century. Despite the weakening of their power in Europe, the Spaniards clung to what they had won in America and the Philippines, and not only successfully defended their transatlantic colonies, but actually expanded them. Only in areas which they had not effectively occupied, did they give ground. In the West Indies, the English, the Dutch, and the French seized upon a number of islands never firmly held by the Spaniards, and in 1655 the English under Cromwell captured Jamaica. On the northeast shoulder of South America (Guiana), the Dutch and the French gained footholds; while in Central America, English logwood cutters and contraband traders were able to establish themselves in what was later to become British Honduras. At the very end of the seventeenth century, the French founded a colony near the mouth of the Mississippi and linked it up by that great waterway with their holdings in Canada.

But to compensate for these losses, the Spaniards gradually extended their sway over northern Mexico and what is now southwestern United States. In Chile, the Spanish colonists continued to war against the Araucanian Indians and to expand their settlements southward. In the fertile Plata region, despite some conflicts with the Portuguese, Spain strengthened its hold, founded new towns, and opened up new territories.

Though Spain in America was capable of making advances, it was forced into a defensive position. In the protracted wars of the seventeenth century, Dutch, English, and French vessels constantly harried Spanish shipping, and in the intervals of peace pirates of all nations continued the attack, not only in the Caribbean, but against the Peruvian coast as well. The last decades of the seventeenth century were the heyday of these "freebooters" or "buccaneers." Frequently they were protected by the governors of the Dutch, French, or English islands in the West Indies. From hidden bays they would swoop out to seize Spanish galleons and on occasion to attack, capture, and sack Spanish coastal cities in Central America.

Piratical attacks made it harder to get bullion from America to Spain. But in any case the exports of American silver were falling off rapidly. In the decade from 1651 to 1660 they amounted to less than a sixth of what they had been in the ten years from 1591 to 1600. Spain strove valiantly to guard what its American colonies produced and jealously to exclude all foreigners from its colonial trade. But even here there was a breach in the system. The importation of Negro slaves from Africa into the Spanish colonies in America had long been a monopoly of the Portuguese through an agreement known as the Asiento. By the treaty of Utrecht (1713), this Asiento was transferred to England and for some forty years afterwards it was exploited by the British.

B. Rise of Dutch Dominions

In the seventeenth century, the preëminent masters of the seaways were Dutch. In good part, they had won their independence from Spain by developing and exploiting their sea power. In the same fashion, though their country was small, their resources scanty, and their population limited, the Dutch made themselves the chief commercial nation on earth. They dominated the trade of the Baltic, taking thither cloth, French wines, and manufactured goods, and bringing back lumber, grain, furs, and naval stores. They gained a major position in the commerce with the Near East, whither they carried textiles, hardware, and silver, and whence they brought drugs, carpets, and rich fabrics. The Dutch won an important position in the trade with America; illegally they did business with Spanish, Portuguese, English, and French colonists ill-supplied by neglectful homelands; legally they developed commerce with their own American colonies, New Amsterdam and Curaçao. It was the Dutch who captured from the Portuguese the richest share of the Far Eastern trade. It was the Dutch who became the chief fishermen of Europe. By 1620, they already had some 2,000 fishing boats. They caught whales off Spitzbergen and supplied oil for the lamps and the soap of Europe. They caught herring in the North Sea and sold the dried and salted fish to the Catholic countries of Europe.

By 1660, the Dutch had won a predominant place as the carriers of Europe. Though their own products were not many or important (fine cloth, cheese, etc.), they had made their country the entrepôt of the world. Thither came goods from every clime. There Russian furs could be exchanged for East Indian cinnamon, French wine for Swedish tar, Turkish rugs for Brazilian sugar, or Caribbean tobacco for African ostrich plumes. In 1669, the French statesman, Colbert, estimated that the Dutch had some fifteen or sixteen thousand ships, as against three or four thousand for the English and five or six hundred for the French.

To a very large degree the Dutch won out in the seventeenth century because of the magnificent business organizations developed in their great city of Amsterdam, which had now far outstripped Antwerp. Dutch governments, whether of Amsterdam or of the United Provinces as a whole, were business-minded. Composed largely of

New Amsterdam (later New York) as it appeared about the time of its capture by the British (1664).

merchants, they made laws designed to aid business. For example, they, almost alone in Europe, permitted fairly free import and export of silver, and kept all tariff duties low to help the carrying trade. In making a treaty, Dutch diplomats always kept an eye on economic advantages and let lesser matters go. The Dutch fleet was ever ready to protect Dutch shipping and to fight for the right of Dutch vessels to sail anywhere. It was the Dutch who first insisted on the "freedom of the seas" as a matter of right under the slowly developing international law of the seventeenth century.

Closely associated with the government, and often run by the same men, were a number of institutions that helped Dutch trade. Insurance companies, underwriters, and brokers supplied coverage for ventures, safe or risky, at the lowest rates in Europe. The Amsterdam money market was so highly organized and so well supplied with capital that a Dutch merchant could often borrow funds at three or four per cent when his English or French competitor had to pay six or eight or ten. The Bank

of Amsterdam, founded in 1609, provided a safe place to keep deposits; and bills of exchange on it were accepted all over Europe and regarded as safer and more convenient than cash.

The Stock Exchange, or Bourse, was no less important than the Bank. Though it had first been intended as an exchange center for goods, like cloth or metals or wine, it was soon a center for deals in shares of stock, for trade in coin and bullion, and for loans. In the second half of the seventeenth century the Amsterdam Bourse was the principal money market of Europe, whither needy princes, ambitious merchants, and enterprising manufacturers came to negotiate loans. Around the Bourse grew up a whole mechanism of trade and speculation that was in some respects very modern. Goods could be bought and sold subject to future delivery. Stock could be bought on a margin or sold short. "Bulls" sought to push up prices and "bears" to depress them. Fortunes could be made or lost by speculation. From 1633 to 1637 the gambling spirit ran wild in an odd fashion. Everybody tried to get rich by buying and selling tulip bulbs, whose prices went up and up and finally collapsed.

More striking even than the Bourse as an evidence of Dutch commercial genius was the East India Company. It was founded in 1602 by the union of several smaller companies which had sprung up after Philip II stopped the Dutch from getting spice at Lisbon. With a charter that gave it the right to make peace and war and to administer colonies as well as to carry on trade, with directors from the leading Dutch cities (eight of the seventeen came from Amsterdam), and with the firm support of the government, the East India Company became the instrument through which the Dutch drove out the Portuguese from the Far Eastern trade and developed it for themselves. So rich and powerful did the company become that at times it dominated the government. It paid dividends which in some years rose to seventy-five per cent and which averaged eighteen per cent a year for almost two centuries. Its stock was for long the chief object of speculation and investment on the Amsterdam Bourse.

The West India Company, founded in 1621 to develop American trade and colonies, was less commercially successful. But it proved a remarkable instrument of warfare against the Spaniards. Between 1623 and 1636 it sent out more than eight hundred ships with crews totaling 67,000 men. By it some 600 Spanish ships were captured, including nearly a hundred "famous galleons." It was said that its activities cost Spain seventy-five million guilders. After the peace with Spain in 1648, the West India Company declined in importance.

In colonial policy the Dutch in some ways resembled the Portuguese more than the Spanish or the English. By the Dutch, colonies were regarded as bases for commerce rather than as areas for settlement and development. In America, the colonial holdings of the Dutch were not insignificant. In 1640 they possessed the Caribbean island of Curaçao, the Hudson River from its mouth to above Fort Orange (Albany), a large part of Guiana, and some of the best ports on the Brazilian coast. Subse-

quently, they were ousted from Brazil in the 1650's, from New York by the English in 1664, and from part of their Guiana colony by the British in 1803.

But it was in the Far East that the Dutch built up a really important dominion. By the 1680's they had replaced the Portuguese in the spice islands (except Timor) and had driven off their English competitors. The Dutch controlled the large East Indian islands of Java and Sumatra, and the smaller ones as well, by means of fortified trading ports, of which the greatest came to be Batavia (present-day Jakarta). By the early eighteenth century they were slowly beginning to expand their territorial holdings inland. It was their policy to keep up spice prices in Europe by ruthlessly restricting production, even if this meant pulling up the plants, cutting down the trees, and killing natives who objected. Though the Dutch were unable to capture Chinese Macao from the Portuguese, they did win a considerable share of the trade with China, and for a while in the seventeenth century they had forts and trading posts on Formosa. After the Japanese had driven out the Portuguese and their missionaries, they permitted the Dutch, who confined themselves strictly to trade, to maintain a small commercial depot in Japan. From 1638 to 1854 the Dutch were established on the small island of Deshima near Nagasaki and were the only Europeans permitted to trade with the Japanese.

So great was the Dutch commercial and colonial success in the seventeenth century that it created a host of enemies. Their chief rivals were the economically progressive national states of England and France. Three times in that century the English warred with the Dutch, largely for commercial reasons. Three times before 1700 the French fought the Dutch, who had previously been their allies in the long struggle with Spain. Against the Dutch the French raised their tariffs. An acute observer in 1713, at the Peace of Utrecht, would have realized that the days of Dutch commercial supremacy were drawing to a close. The future lay with the larger and stronger states of France and England. Yet throughout the eighteenth century Amsterdam remained an important trading city and the foremost financial center of Europe, and Dutch burghers still waxed prosperous on profits from commerce and from interest on the loans they made to all Europe.

C. Foundations of a British Empire

Though in population, as in area, England of the seventeenth century was definitely inferior to France or Spain, it had by 1713 secured an overseas dominion of considerable extent. The first British colony at Jamestown in Virginia (1607) was followed rapidly by a number of other foundations on the Atlantic seaboard of North America: Plymouth (1620), Boston (1630), Maryland (1634), Providence (1636), Hartford (1636), New Haven (1638), Carolina (1665). The northern and southern settlements were linked in a continuous strip of British holdings by the capture of New York (1664) with the adjacent area of New Jersey, and by the settlement of Pennsylvania, under William Penn, in the years following 1681.

Meanwhile the English had made numerous settlements in the West Indies, including part of St. Christopher (St. Kitts), Bermuda, Barbados, the Bahamas, Antigua, Nevis, Montserrat, some of the Virgin Islands, and Jamaica. On the Mosquito Coast of Honduras, the British obtained an increasingly firm hold. On the west coast of Africa, in competition with the Dutch and the French, they developed trading and slaving posts. In the East Indies, though forced out of the Spice Islands and even out of their post at Bantam (1683) by the Dutch, they developed important trading centers further to the west. At Surat in India, in the years after 1609, they built up a commercial depot. By the capture of Ormuz (1622) they gained control of the Persian Gulf. In 1639 they founded Madras and fortified it. A decade later they opened up trade with Bengal at the port of Hugli. From Portugal, England secured Bombay in 1661, and before long it became the center of their Indian trade. By 1690, despite the opposition of the native ruler, the British had established themselves at Calcutta.

Thus by the end of the century, with posts on both coasts, they were in an excellent position to expand their Indian trade.

If their aims and their holdings in the Far East were not unlike those of the earlier Portuguese and the Dutch, and if their West Indian plantations on the whole resembled those of the Spanish and the French, their North American colonies were somewhat different from overseas colonies of other European nations anywhere. In the first place, they were true colonies of settlement. To them, the English came in relatively large numbers—and not merely as individuals seeking to win fortunes, but as families, with women and children, in search of new homes overseas. In the second place, though some persons in the American colonies were active in commerce, fisheries, and the fur trade, the bulk of the population found its livelihood in agriculture and slowly moved in from the coast in search of tillable land. If some of the tobacco plantations of Virginia or the Carolinas, worked by indentured white servants or Negro slaves, were not unlike those of the West Indies, more typical in English North America was the family holding, or farm worked by the owner.

William Penn. After a painting by Sir Godfrey Kneller (d. 1723).

Courtesy Bettmann Archive

In the third place, the English rather freely permitted the emigration to their colonies of religious dissenters and people who did not like the religious restrictions at home. The French and Spanish strove to make their colonies conform in religion with the mother country. But the English colonies, in contrast, soon represented an almost bewildering mixture of creeds. English Catholics came to Maryland; English Congregationalists settled New England; English Quakers peopled Pennsylvania; while Anglicans went in numbers to Virginia and to mingle with Dutch Reformed colonists in New York and New Jersey. Presently other religious sects were added to the American scene. French Huguenots fled from France to South Carolina, various German religious radicals found refuge in Pennsylvania, and Presbyterians from North Ireland flocked to the middle colonies.

Partly as a result of this comparative religious tolerance, the English North American colonies became the most populous, for their size, of any European overseas holdings, and a high birthrate added to the effects of immigration. By 1698 the Atlantic seaboard colonies had a population estimated at three hundred thousand, and in the eighteenth century it tended to double every twenty-five years, so that by 1775 it was something like 2,500,000. Already in 1698 England's trade with these settlements amounted to about £1,600,000 a year, some fifteen per cent of its total commerce. Seventy-seven years later it had multiplied five times and represented almost a third of British imports and exports.

From the start England sought, with varying success, to regulate its colonial trade. But in the main it followed a policy that has been termed one of "salutary neglect," and, despite sporadic interference, it allowed the colonies a good deal of local self-government. The colonists had town governments of their own and provincial legislatures which advised the proprietors or royal governors, floated local loans, and often voted local taxes. As in other countries, the ignorance of colonial conditions in the motherland was immense. There were English statesmen who thought that Massachusetts was an island and Virginia was one of the West Indies.

But the English Parliament did take a lively interest in trade laws, and the country gentlemen who were so powerful in it joined with their merchant allies to try to better England's commerce by seeing that all the trade of the colonies flowed to the mother-country. The Navigation Act of 1651 provided, with a few exceptions, that overseas goods must be brought to England in English ships or in those of the country of origin. The Navigation Act of 1660 added the provision that certain "enumerated articles" (sugar, tobacco, indigo, ginger, dye-woods) should be exported from a colony only to England or to another English colony. The list of such goods was from time to time extended. The Staple Act of 1663 forbade the importation into the colonies of any goods not put on board ship in England. To keep trade between the English colonies from growing at the expense of that with England, another act of 1673 laid duties on the enumerated articles shipped from colony to colony. In 1696 an act for "preventing frauds" sought to plug existing loopholes in the trade laws.

Designed to profit England by making it the only source for goods sent to the colonies and the only destination for colonial exports, the English "colonial system" would, if rigidly enforced, have cramped colonial commercial development. But from the early days the American colonists found numerous ways to engage in profitable contraband and smuggling trade with French or Spanish colonies and with other areas. Often they paid their debts to England with foreign coin secured illegally in the Caribbean.

We have seen that the Dutch gradually succeeded in excluding the English from any major share in the trade with the East Indian spice islands. But it was as if some special providence were looking out for interests of the English and their East India Company. Slowly in the late seventeenth century, and more rapidly thereafter, the spice trade declined in importance, while the European market for other Eastern goods expanded, especially for cotton fabrics like calico. The British, pushed out of the East Indies and back to mainland India, found themselves trading at the main source of such fabrics. The English East India Company had its ups and downs, but by 1680 its imports of textiles outweighed its trade in spices and thereafter grew rapidly and proved most profitable. From Surat alone, in 1682, the English ordered 1,407,-800 pieces of textiles.

D. Struggle for a French Oversea Empire

The first successful French settlement overseas was at Quebec in 1608, only a year after the English foundation of Jamestown. But French colonial development was slower than English. In 1660 they had a few West Indian Islands—Martinique, Guadeloupe, Grenada, the Grenadines, St. Croix, St. Bartholomew, and parts of St. Martin and St. Christopher. On the last, oddly enough, the French held the two ends and the English the middle. They had also a foothold in Guiana (Cayenne), a string of small settlements along the St. Lawrence River and in Nova Scotia (Acadia), and some posts on the west coast of Africa and on Madagascar and Reunion. In Canada, there were fewer than 3,000 French settlers, and in the West Indies something like 27,000, about half of whom were slaves. The French population in the other holdings was infinitesimal.

But in 1661, Colbert came to office, determined to endow France with a colonial empire and to build for her a great Far Eastern commerce. So far as he could win the support of Louis XIV, he threw the weight of the government's influence and resources behind the effort to expand French overseas ventures. Far more than with England, French colonial development was dependent on governmental initiative, support, and supervision. Under his West India Company (1664) Colbert placed the West Indies, Cayenne, Canada, and the west African ports. By regulations and the use of naval power, he excluded the Dutch from trade with the French West Indies. By paying a bounty on every slave, he expanded the French slave trade between Senegal and Guinea in West Africa and the islands in the Caribbean. In every way, he sought to increase the population of the colonies. He sent soldiers to Canada,

François Xavier de Laval-Montmorency (1623?–1708), first bishop of Quebec.

Courtesy Bettmann Archive

then mustered them out and gave them land if they would stay. He sent over boatloads of girls to marry the male colonists. He encouraged the marriage of Frenchmen to Indians. He even tried to restrict the fur trade, on which the prosperity of Canada depended, so that the men would settle down in villages and raise families. But all his means proved far less successful than the device half negligently adopted by the British of letting religious dissenters emigrate to the colonies. At Colbert's death (1683), the population of Canada was only about 10,000, and of the West Indies only about 50,000.

More successful were Colbert's endeavors in other directions. Under an able governor, Frontenac, hostile Canadian Indians were subdued. Daring woodsmen and heroic missionaries (like Marquette) opened up the country around the Great Lakes and the upper Mississippi. The French competed vigorously with the English for the fur trade of Hudson Bay and toward the end of the century seemed to be gaining the upper hand. When Iberville planted a French colony in Louisiana (1699), it looked as if all North America, except a narrow strip south of the St. Lawrence and east of the Alleghenies, might become French.

French colonial trade likewise prospered. When Colbert came to power, commerce with the French West Indies was largely in foreign hands. At his death, some two hundred French ships were plying back and forth between France and the Caribbean. Sugar was rapidly coming to be the chief object of this trade, and its production rose until in the eighteenth century Martinique and Guadeloupe, together with Santo Domingo (or Haiti, where the French had settled the west half of the island neglected by the Spanish), became the sugar bowls of Europe.

In his efforts to promote French trade with the Far East, Colbert encountered various obstacles. Though the King poured millions of *livres* into the French East India Company and forced numerous officials to buy its stock, it proved impossible to get much financial support from the investing public. The English joined with the Dutch to attack French ships and to paralyze French trade in the ports of India. By 1675 the French had organized six trading posts there, but in the last years of the Dutch war they lost all save Surat and Pondichéry. When Colbert died, his East India Company, harassed by these misfortunes, was in serious financial straits. But in the next year (1684) it was reorganized, and slowly it began to gain strength and even occasionally to make some money. Despite heavy losses during the War of the League of Augsburg, the French under a vigorous soldier merchant, François Martin, greatly strengthened their position in India. By 1700 they had added to Surat and Pondichéry two posts on the Coromandel Coast and four in Bengal.

Both the French and the English had built up their overseas dominion at the expense of the Portuguese and the Spanish, and during the last half of the seventeenth century they both met and overcame considerable Dutch opposition. But by 1689, with William of Orange, implacable enemy of France, on the English throne and a major war just starting, it became clear that henceforth the most bitter rivalry was to be between the French and the English. During the ensuing hundred and twenty-six years, these two nations were repeatedly at war with each other. In the long run,

England, through her greater devotion to commerce and sea power, was to triumph. But the early rounds of the struggle were indecisive, and the keenest contemporary observer would have had some difficulty in predicting the outcome.

In the West Indies, the conflict began as early as 1625 with disputes about the joint occupation of St. Christopher. It consisted of naval engagements, commerce raiding, and attacks on the various islands, some of which passed back and forth between the contending powers. In North America, the Anglo-French conflict dated from 1613, when the English seized the French settlements in Acadia (Nova Scotia). They were returned to France by treaty in 1632, captured again by the English under Cromwell in 1654, restored to France by treaty in 1667, won again by England in 1710, and finally confirmed in the possession of the British by the treaty of Utrecht in 1713. By the same treaty France likewise abandoned all claims to the Hudson Bay area.

The French settlements along the St. Lawrence had similarly been seized by the English in 1629, but were held by them for only three years. Thereafter, Canada, as it grew in strength, seemed like an ever present threat to the English colonies to the southward. In the War of the League of Augsburg (1689–1697), called King William's War in the colonies, and the War of the Spanish Succession (1701–1713), termed there Queen Anne's War, bloody affrays occurred between French and English colonists in the frontier areas. Using Indian allies, the French raided to the south again and again. The massacres at Dover (1689), Schenectady (1690), Deerfield (1704), and Haverhill (1708), were only the most notable and successful of dozens of similar attacks.

But at the peace of Utrecht (1713) it was still hard to see how the American struggle would end. The English colonists were more numerous but were very loosely organized and ill-supported from England. The French had control of the St. Lawrence and Mississippi waterways, were firmly managed by the home government, and had the support of many Indian tribes. In India, too, the outcome was obscure, for the French strength there was growing. The native Mongol, or "Mogul," Empire of India was decaying and collapsing, and its heir would probably be the European nation best able to manipulate and intimidate the local rulers who were gaining more and more independent power. These issues of overseas supremacy were to be decided by wars of the later eighteenth century.

E. Russian Colonization Eastward, and Novel Commodities of Europe's Oversea Commerce

While the western European nations were engaged in embittered conflicts for possession of overseas areas and trade, the growing Russian nation was expanding eastward in quite a different fashion. To the east of Russia, with its chief cities of Novgorod and Moscow, lay the enormous unexplored Asiatic land mass. Into this area, the Russians spread by land in a movement not unlike that by which the English-speaking Americans were later to push westward toward the Pacific. The conquest of the Tatar states of Kazan and Astrakhan in the mid-sixteenth century had brought the Russians to the Urals and the Caspian Sea. As Russian rule moved eastward, the spearhead of its advance was a special type of frontiersmen, half-wild adventurers and doughty fighters drawn from a variety of sources and called Cossacks. Named after the area in which they lived, they were known as the Don, Astrakhan, Terek, Orenburg, Kuban, or Ural Cossacks. To them was granted a good deal of autonomy under their own chiefs, and in return for their privileges, they safeguarded the frontiers and extended the area of Russian dominion.

Another type of frontiersman was (as in later America) the fur trader. In the last half of the sixteenth century a wealthy merchant named Stroganov organized the fur trade in the Kama River region, built forts, and used Cossacks to defend the area. His nephews, aided by a band of brigands, defeated the Tatars and captured their chief city of Sibir, which was to give its name to the whole vast territory of Siberia. Pushing ever eastward in search of furs, the Russians founded fortified towns or posts like Tobolsk, Yeniseisk, and Yakutsk. By the mid-seventeenth century, the Russians had reached Lake Baikal, defeated the native Buriats, and founded Irkutsk. At about the same time, other fur traders, moving northward, reached the Kolyma River and the Arctic Ocean. In 1647 a little band of fifty-four Cossacks got all the way to the Pacific and, after defeating the wild fighters of the Tungus tribe, established a fort at Okhotsk. The next year, another group of Cossacks sailed from Kolyma Bay on the Arctic Ocean through the straits later to be explored by Bering and set up a fort at Anadyrsk on the Pacific. Within a century, the Russian frontiersmen had spread so far and so fast that this farthest post was 7,000 miles from Moscow.

Afterwards, the Russians pushed their explorations into the Kamchatka peninsula, the Amur region, the Manchurian borderlands, and across the straits to Alaska. This work was carried on by rough frontiersmen, fighters, and fur-traders, who overawed the natives they met or defeated them by their firearms and their courage. As bases they used fortified posts called *Ostrogs*, similar to the blockhouse forts of the American frontier. In the wake of the explorers who opened up the country, came settlers and traders. If there were only 70,000 Russians in all Siberia in 1662, the number increased rapidly and reached a quarter of a million by 1710. As early as 1637 a government for Siberia had been set up with its center at Tobolsk and secondary centers at Yakutsk and Irkutsk. Fur was still the basic wealth of the new land, and tribute in fur was exacted from the native tribes. To Siberia, the home government sent criminals, who were often given the opportunity to redeem themselves by opening up new areas.

When they reached the Amur river in 1644, the Russians came in contact with the Chinese, who claimed overlordship of the area. Driven out by the natives, the Russians came back, rebuilt their forts on the Amur, and began penetrating into Manchuria. In 1689, with the aid of Jesuit missionaries who accompanied the Chinese delegates as interpreters, the Russians and the Chinese signed a treaty, the first ever made by China with a European power. The Russians accepted a boundary north of the Amur, but the Chinese agreed to receive Russian traders freely. For more than two centuries peace endured between the two countries. In 1727 a new treaty permitted two hundred Russian merchants to come to Peking each year. There were not many bulky commodities sufficiently valuable to pay for transportation across thousands of miles of land to Moscow. But in exchange for their furs the Russians took costly silks and considerable quantities of tea. As a result of this early trade with China, the Russian upper classes gradually became confirmed tea drinkers.

At about the same time, the English were becoming tea drinkers too, for in the late seventeenth century their East India Company began importing this commodity, and it quickly won favor, first with the higher and then with the lower levels of society. Nor was tea the only new beverage introduced into Europe by expansion overseas. Both chocolate and coffee came into use in the latter half of the seventeenth century. Coffee houses and chocolate houses sprang up. If some claimed the new beverages to be dangerous drugs, others held them to be health-giving elixirs. In any case, people liked them. The use of these drinks increased the demand for sugar, and decade by decade the output grew, first in Madeira, then in Brazil, and later in the West Indies, while one refinery after another was built in Europe to improve the palatability of the dark sticky substance that came in the casks from America. The by-products of the growing sugar trade were also important. Rum so competed with French brandy that it was banned from France. But the English and their colonists made it in large quantities, and the English thus won an advantage in the fur trade with the Indians since rum was cheaper than the brandy of the French.

Hundreds of other new products came increasingly into the European market. Porcelain ware from China, lacquered furniture, perfumes, wall paper, drugs, silks, screens, ebony, brocades, calicos, chintz, muslins, dimities, fans, umbrellas, and even goldfish were brought in from the East. From the West, in addition to the ever growing streams of tobacco and sugar, came cabinet woods like mahogany and rosewood, codfish, naval stores, dye-woods, furs (especially beaver fur for hat making), drugs like quinine, and new vegetables and flowers. If

the exotic perfumes like civet and musk were sometimes used as a substitute for bathing, the new Indian cotton fabrics led eventually to an increasing use of underwear and thus to an improvement in personal cleanliness. The wealth of new products permitted first a tremendous expansion in the luxury of the upper classes, but by the eighteenth century articles like sugar, tobacco, tea, and cotton goods were getting cheap enough to be within the reach of large numbers of people.

The trade in these new articles represented a tremendous increase in ocean-borne commerce, which had its effects on many another phase of European life. Shipbuilding boomed and the arts of navigation and map-making were steadily improved. Old European industries grew to meet the demands of overseas markets for textiles, hardware, nails, glass, arms, gunpowder, and the like. New European industries sprang up to process the imported goods, so that by the eighteenth century sugar refiners, rum-makers, hat-makers, snuff-makers, calico-printers, and many others were dependent for their raw materials on products from overseas. Each new product tended to create subsidiary industries. Thus the manufacture of snuff-boxes had become a significant if minor trade in both England and France by the eighteenth century, while at the same time efforts to imitate Indian cottons and Chinese porcelain were gradually meeting with increased success. The governments likewise profited, for they taxed the new articles such as tea and coffee, and in France and elsewhere the sale of tobacco was made a state monopoly. If Columbus and Vasco da Gama could have returned to Europe in 1715, they would have found much that was new and different, and for those differences, they and their fellow explorers had been in no small degree responsible.

F. Protracted Rivalry of Britain and France

In the major wars that raged in Europe during the late seventeenth and the eighteenth centuries there was one constant element—a duel between France and Great Britain. From the point of view of the

French, the major stakes were the maintenance of the power and leadership which Louis XIV had won for France, and the defense and extension of the country's frontiers. Secondarily, France was interested in the development of her colonial dominion and of her foreign commerce. Great Britain was much more interested than France in colonies, commerce, and naval supremacy. But it was also concerned with preserving a balance of power in Europe. To the British, France seemed too strong, and particularly too threatening to the Low Countries directly across the Channel from England. From 1689 to 1815 France and Britain were at war half the time.

At the peace of Utrecht (1713) these major opponents seemed ill matched. England, with Scotland, had a population of something like six million, while inhabitants of France numbered about twenty-four million. The foreign trade of the French was more valuable than that of the British, and their internal trade much larger. French industry was so superior to English in most lines that during the negotiations preceding the treaty of Utrecht, English business-men fearfully repulsed the suggestion that the two countries should lower the high import tariffs they levied against each other. The French army was the largest, the best equipped, and the best organized in Europe. French financial resources, if less well managed than those of England, were considerably greater. French prestige was high, French diplomacy remarkably skilled, and France had just succeeded, despite the well-nigh united opposition of Europe, in putting a Bourbon on the throne of Spain. Only in the colonies where the British population was larger and growing faster than the French, and in the naval sphere where the British, in the War of the Spanish Succession, had finally achieved supremacy, did Great Britain seem a worthy opponent of France. Yet in the long duel from 1689 to 1815 Britain gained the upper hand. In part, this was because it was better governed than France.

In part, too, the success of Britain was due to its fortunate island position. It was never, after 1066, subject to a real invasion nor could it be, so long as its navy was strong. France, on the other hand, had long land frontiers to defend and its own territory could actually be and was invaded. It seems likely that because of the recent wars French population and wealth had actually declined from 1689 to 1715, while England was growing in both respects. Then too, though both nations were adept in persuading allies to fight their battles, the British more often succeeded in using money instead of men and their financial resources were well mobilized by the Bank of England, the National Debt, and an increasingly effective system of insurance for ships and property and of mercantile credit.

In many ways, Britain was a more modern and less feudal country than France. Neither was fully unified in language, for Gaelic was spoken in Scotland and Ireland, and Welsh in Wales just as Breton was predominant in Brittany and Basque in the southwest of France. But after 1707, when Scotland was joined with England, Britain had no interior customs duties, while France still had a tariff line dividing the north from the south and a number of minor tax systems. The old French craft and merchant guilds were still powerful, while their British counterparts were of rapidly decreasing importance. Feudal dues continued to be a weighty burden on the French peasants and had to be paid in labor, in kind, and in money. Some still existed in England, but they were no longer of real significance. Though there were notable differences between the law and the courts in England and in Scotland, France was in a much more complicated situation with some judicial power remaining in the hands of the noble landowners and dozens of different local laws, courts, and customs.

In the eighteenth century France continued the system of government developed under Louis XIV. It was an absolutist government, centralized in royal councils and in ministers chosen by the king on his own initiative. In the provinces, the intendents carried on the administration and saw to it that the wishes of the king and his councils were executed. The provincial estates, the cities, the church, and the nobles made even less trouble than they had in the days of the "Sun King." The only challenge to royal absolutism came occasionally from the higher law courts (the *parlements*), and they were privileged hereditary bodies more apt to represent the desires of the wealthy than the interests of the nation.

Likewise in the economic sphere, the traditions of Louis XIV were followed. The mercantilist regulation of industry and commerce worked out by Colbert was elaborated until it became hard and rigid. The royal finances were handled by a "controller general," who had come to be the chief minister of state. For each war, France plunged further into debt, and every effort to overcome the deficit was checkmated by the privileged classes and corporations, which paid less than their share of the tax burdens. The French monarchy was running more and more on credit, and this was lessened by every war.

Louis XIV was succeeded by his great-grandson, Louis XV (1715–1774), a boy of five years. During his childhood and young manhood the destinies of the country were guided, first for eight years by the King's cousin, the Duke of Orléans, as Regent (1715–1723), and then for many years by an elderly churchman, Cardinal Fleury, as chief minister (1726–1743). The Duke of Orléans was intellectually gifted but notoriously dissolute. His foreign policy was weak, his attempts at internal reform half hearted. His rule is most vividly remembered for the financial experiments into which he was lured by a Scottish adventurer named John Law. These led to a wild orgy of stock market speculation known as the Mississippi Bubble, which ended in a ruinous "panic" in 1721.

Cardinal Fleury was of quite different calibre. Modest, frugal, cautious, his best gift to France was seventeen years of comparative peace interrupted by only a minor war. France showed remarkable strength and recuperative powers. Commerce grew rapidly, industry flourished, and the colonies (especially the sugar islands of the West Indies) throve. But internally, Fleury was content to leave well-enough alone. He achieved no major reforms, and if he brought royal expenditures almost into line with income he made no basic improvement in the financial system. When he attempted to aid commerce by building roads with forced labor (called *corvées*), he aroused angry discontent among the peasants. Moreover, when he died at the advanced age of ninety (1743), France had already for three years been engaged in another major war which was to undo much of the good which the years of peace had wrought.

The period of Fleury seemed one of sound rule and good government compared to the next thirty-one years when Louis XV spasmodically exercised personal power. In his youth, he had displayed some amiable qualities and for a time he was called "Louis the Well-Beloved." But as he grew to manhood, he showed himself fickle, lazy, and sensuous. Easily wearied of statecraft, he was much influenced by his mistresses, of whom Mesdames de Châteauroux, de Pompadour, and du Barry were only the most famous. Madame de Pompadour was for almost twenty years a veritable prime minister in petticoats and used her power to reward and enrich her friends and wreak her vengeance on her enemies. Under Louis XV, the maladies afflicting France grew apace. The financial disorder increased; popular discontent and criticism rose; the central government at Versailles became ever more isolated from the people.

Yet the ills of France were veiled by the wealth of the country, the success of the armies, the brilliance of the court, the distinction of the artists, writers, and thinkers. Louis XV knew that troubles were brewing, but he was confident that the old system would last for a while. With cynicism he remarked, "Après moi le déluge," "After me, the deluge." The deluge was to come in the reign of his successor, Louis XVI, a well meaning but weak monarch, whose troubles we shall have occasion to examine in another connection.

Great Britain of the eighteenth century was governed by the system of limited monarchy developed after the Revolution of 1689.[1] Real power rested in Parliament, where the House of Lords was made up predominantly of landed nobles, and the House of Commons, elected on an undemocratic basis, represented mainly the country gentlemen and the rich mercantile classes of the cities. Many seats in the lower house were controlled and sometimes sold by landed nobles or gentry. There were two parties. The Whigs controlled Parliament for more than half a century after 1713. The

[1] See below, p. 512.

Tories were influential in the countryside, and the Tory squire, who was usually the local justice of the peace, exercised in his bailiwick considerable judicial and administrative authority.

The differences between the parties were not very great. The Tories were more devoutly Anglican, supported the interests of that church, and held the Stuarts in sentimental remembrance. But when the Young Pretender (grandson of James II) landed in Scotland in 1745 and sought to rouse the country, the Tories did not respond, and the Hanoverians reigned on. The Whigs, though many of them were great landowners, had considerable association with business interests and tended to show some favor to the non-Anglican Protestant sects. But they were mainly interested in maintaining their own political power.

The administration of Great Britain and its empire was in the hands of the cabinet selected from among the members of parliament by the king (actually by the prime minister) and responsible to the majority party in parliament. For twenty-one years (1721–1742), which roughly corresponded with the ministry of Fleury in France, the British prime minister was the Whig politician Sir Robert Walpole. Like Fleury, he pursued a peaceful policy in foreign affairs. His chief object was to promote prosperity and keep the taxes low. But at the end of his ministry, he was, like Fleury, propelled into a major war.

Walpole was succeeded by a series of Whigs from great landed or titled families. They were skilled in party manipulations and more or less able in diplomacy and administration. But the mid-eighteenth century produced one Whig leader of real eminence, William Pitt, later Earl of Chatham. A member of a family which had gained wealth in the East Indies and political influence by its wealth, Pitt showed himself a brilliant politician, a great orator, and an able statesman of sturdy patriotism and imperial vision.

Kings George I (1714–1727) and George II (1727–1760), more German than English, were content to leave the governing of the country to the prime ministers and cabinets, though occasionally they exercised some influence on foreign and even on domestic affairs. George III (1760–1820) was different in character and in objectives. Unlike his predecessors, he had been born and reared in England and was a solid family man of unimpeachable morals. Like an English country gentleman, he was interested in farming and he enjoyed considerable popularity with the British people. George III was determined to rule as well as to reign. He saw no reason why he, like some of the prime ministers, should not dominate Parliament through a judicious use of influence and favors. Gradually by such methods, George III was able to get rid of the Whig ministers, to constitute Tory cabinets, and to participate in government himself. From 1770 to 1782, the prime minister was Lord North, a Tory, loyal to the King and willing to see the royal power increase. Had George III been able to continue such a regime indefinitely, there might have been a rebirth of royal, at the expense of parliamentary, government.

G. Wars of the Polish Election and the Austrian Succession

The one war in which peace-loving Cardinal Fleury found himself entangled in the middle of his ministry arose from French interest in Poland, alliance with Sweden, and support of the Spanish Bourbons. In 1725, Louis XV had married the daughter of Stanislaus Leszczynski, the nobleman whom Charles XII of Sweden had briefly installed upon the throne of Poland [1] and who had been trying vainly since 1709 to regain his kingship. When Augustus II, the Elector of Saxony and King of Poland, died in 1733, Stanislaus hurried to Poland and secured election to the vacant throne. But Russia at once interfered and persuaded the Poles to depose Stanislaus and elect the son of Augustus II. Thereupon Louis XV sent an army to help his father-in-law, and the War of the Polish Election (1733–1738) began.

The war was quickly complicated by the ambitions of the masterful Elizabeth Farnese, wife of Philip V, first Bourbon King of Spain. Elizabeth had long been eager to regain some of the old Spanish holdings in Italy from the Austrian Habsburgs for the

[1] See above, p. 438.

BOURBON, HABSBURG, AND BRITISH
DOMINIONS IN EUROPE ABOUT 1740

Bourbon (French, Spanish)   Habsburg   British   0   100   200
Miles

benefit of her sons. As the Polish war broke out and Austria was preparing to help Russia against France, Philip V, appealing to Bourbon family solidarity, persuaded Fleury to bring France into an alliance with Spain against Austria. Thus the War of the Polish Election found Russia and Austria opposed by France and Spain.

The war was not so bloody or so costly as the wars of Louis XIV; and the ensuing treaty of Vienna considerably added to the prestige of the Bourbons. Though Russia and Austria kept Augustus III on the Polish throne, Austria had to grant the duchy of Lorraine to Stanislaus Leszczynski with the understanding that after his death (which occurred in 1766) it should go to France. Austria likewise had to agree to the transfer of Sicily, Naples, and Parma from Habsburg to Spanish Bourbon control. Philip V and Elizabeth had the satisfaction of putting one son on the throne of Parma and another (Charles) on the throne of the kingdom of the Two Sicilies (Naples and Sicily).

Hardly was the War of the Polish Election over, when the more significant War of the Austrian Succession occurred (1740–

1748). This was occasioned by the death of the Emperor Charles VI and the repudiation of the promises which certain other European rulers had given him that they would respect the succession of his daughter, Maria Theresa, to all the Austrian Habsburg territories. The leader in this repudiation was the ambitious and cynical Freredick II "the Great," who came to the throne of Prussia in 1740 and lost no time in trumping up a claim to the valuable Austrian province of Silesia. He enlisted against Maria Theresa the support of Louis XV of France, who planned to appropriate part or all of the Austrian (Belgian) Netherlands, and of the Elector of Bavaria, who aspired to become Holy Roman Emperor as Charles VII.

Complicating the situation was a trade war which had broken out in 1739 between Great Britain and Spain, and which was commonly called the War of Jenkins' Ear, because an otherwise obscure Captain Jenkins had aroused English feeling against Spain by relating with dramatic detail how Spaniards in America had attacked his ship, plundered it, and in the fray cut off his ear. This war was soon merged with the War of the Austrian Succession. The Spanish King Philip V, who sympathized with his fellow Bourbon, Louis XV of France, and who hoped to gain still more lands in Italy, joined the coalition against Maria Theresa. On the other hand, Great Britain, fearful of French expansion into the Austrian Netherlands and of possible Prussian designs on the German state of Hanover (which belonged to the British King), gave aid, financial and military, to Austria, and prevailed upon Holland to do likewise. Whereupon, the Franco-Prussian coalition obtained the adherence of Saxony and Savoy (Sardinia). Thus the line-up in the struggle during most of its duration (1740–1748) was Prussia, France, Spain, Bavaria, Saxony, and Savoy against Austria, Great Britain, and the Dutch Netherlands (Holland).

The War of the Austrian Succession, like others of the eighteenth century, was not so terrible or so bloody as the number of contestants might seem to indicate. The fighting was mostly in summer, and there was often, in both campaigns and battles, more maneuvering for position than actual fighting. Saxony was bribed by Austria into making peace. Spain would fight only in Italy. Savoy, as usual, changed sides. The Dutch limited themselves to activities at sea and the defense of their own lands.

Despite heroic efforts, Maria Theresa was unable to expel Frederick II from Silesia. Her generals suffered repeated reverses at his hands, and three times she was forced to recognize his possession of Silesia so as to employ her forces against Bavaria and France. By the third treaty, made at Dresden in 1745, Austria definitely ceded Silesia to Prussia. Having gained his ends, Frederick II deserted his allies and withdrew from the war. Elsewhere, Austrian arms, supported

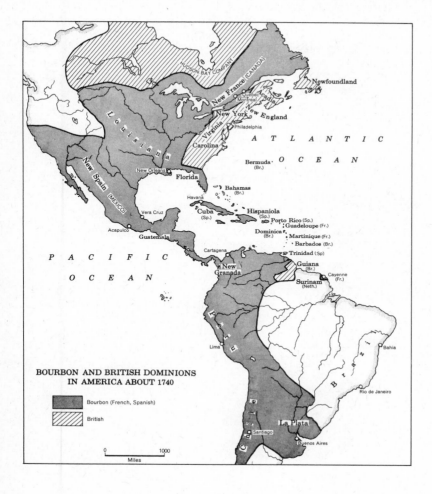

BOURBON AND BRITISH DOMINIONS IN AMERICA ABOUT 1740

Bourbon (French, Spanish)

British

0   1000
Miles

by British gold, were more successful. At the very time when Charles of Bavaria was, according to plan, being crowned Holy Roman Emperor at Frankfurt, and was thus breaking the long line of Habsburgs who had held that office. Austrian troops were marching into his capital of Munich. Soon Austria held all Bavaria, and the French were forced back across the Rhine, while at the same time the Austrians, with Sardinian aid, made some headway against the French and Spanish in Italy. But in the last years of the war, the French held off an Austrian invasion of Alsace-Lorraine and under a brilliant general, Marshal Saxe, conquered most of the Austrian Netherlands and threatened Holland.

The treaties which ended the War of the Austrian Succession were signed at Aix-la-Chapelle in 1748. They confirmed Prussia's conquest of Silesia. The Wittelsbach family of Bavaria recovered all its territories. Maria Theresa's husband, Francis of Lorraine, was recognized as Holy Roman Emperor. France for all her efforts and expenditures gained nothing.

The War of the Austrian Succession proved the initial encounter in a long struggle between Prussia and Austria for German leadership. It also proved an indecisive round in the long duel between France and Great Britain for colonial and commercial mastery. While fighting was going on in Europe, France and Britain had been harrying each other's commerce, the French mainly by privateering, the British by organized fleets. At the same time, the French and English colonists in North America engaged in a struggle which was called King George's War. In 1745, the English under Colonel William Pepperell of New Hampshire captured the French fortress of Louisburg on Cape Breton Island. In India, under an able politician and soldier, Dupleix, the French captured the English post at Madras and strengthened their position in the peninsula.

The treaty of Aix-la-Chapelle returned everything in the colonial sphere, including Louisburg and Madras, to the pre-war situation. Spain got a minor satisfaction, since in return for a money payment Great Britain renounced the slave trade contract, the Asiento, which it had obtained at the peace of Utrecht [1] and which it had since used illegally to force goods through the Spanish trade barriers in America.

---

[1] See above, p. 430.

CHAPTER 37

The Seven Years' War, and Age of the Baroque

A. The Seven Years' War in Europe, 1756–1763

Following the War of the Austrian Succession, there was a great deal of diplomatic maneuvering which so altered the alignment of European powers that it has been termed the "Diplomatic Revolution." Austria, the chief loser in that war, devoted every effort to securing allies for an attempt to recover Silesia. Saxony was readily attached to the Austrian cause, and without much difficulty Maria Theresa won as an ally the Tsarina Elizabeth of Russia, who had been much offended by the biting wit of the Prussian King Frederick II. Austria already had friendly agreements with Great Britain and Holland.

There remained the difficult task of winning the support of France. The French monarchy had been fighting the Habsburgs more or less continuously for two centuries and a half and had come to regard them as natural enemies. To Paris, Maria Theresa despatched the ablest diplomat of the age, Count Kaunitz, who sought to persuade Louis XV to abandon Prussia and join Austria, by pointing to the Prussian holdings on the lower Rhine as a possible reward in the event of a successful war. Louis XV hesitated. But Kaunitz secured the support of the King's influential mistress, Madame de Pompadour, who, like Elizabeth of Russia, had taken offense at the witty verses and sarcastic remarks of the Prussian King. Partly through Madame de Pompadour's persuasion, Louis XV finally decided to change France's traditional foreign policy and to join the Habsburg cause. A deeper reason for this action lay in the feeling that Prussia was becoming so strong as to be something of a threat to French influence in Germany.

Meanwhile, Great Britain had entered into a special agreement with Frederick II, with the object of guaranteeing the territory of Hanover and the general peace of Germany. Then, when war broke out in 1754 between French and English colonists in America, it was natural enough for Great Britain to join in a definite alliance with Prussia. Thus it befell that whereas in the War of the Austrian Succession Prussia and France had been pitted against Austria and Great Britain, in the succeeding Seven Years' War, Austria and France were in arms against Prussia and Great Britain. It will be noted that despite this change in partners the two main rivalries or duels for power were maintained. Prussia fought Austria in both wars for predominance in Germany. Britain fought France in both for commercial and colonial advantage.

The Seven Years' War lasted in Europe from 1756 to 1763. As regards the number of countries engaged, the brilliance of the generalship displayed, and the dramatic ups and downs of its course, it deserves to rank with the War of the Spanish Succession as one of the two greatest wars that Europe had so far witnessed. The coalition that was formed to check Frederick II and to make him disgorge conquered Silesia was one of the most powerful in the whole eighteenth century, for, in addition to Austria, Russia, France, and Saxony, Sweden followed her old ally France into the conflict.

Learning of the coalition that was being formed against him, Frederick II did not wait to be attacked. Without any formal declaration of war he invaded Saxony (1756), exacted large money payments, drafted Saxon recruits into his armies, and moved on across the mountains into the Habsburg territory of Bohemia. Superior Austrian armies forced him to raise the siege of Prague and to fall back into his own lands. Thereupon, from all sides, the allied armies of his enemies converged on him. Russians moved into East Prussia, Swedes from Pomerania into northern Brandenburg, and Austrians into Silesia, while the French advanced in heavy force from the west.

Frederick now displayed those qualities of military genius which justify his title of "the Great." Inferior in numbers to any one of his opponents and aided only by the fact that he was fighting on "inside lines," he moved rapidly into central Germany and at Rossbach (1757) inflicted an overwhelming defeat on the French. "I cannot tell you," wrote the French commander to Louis XV, "how many of our officers have been killed, captured, or lost." No sooner had he checked the menace from the west, than Frederick was back in Silesia. He flung his army upon the Austrians at Leuthen, captured a third of their forces, and put the rest to flight.

Frederick's victories decimated his army. He still had money, thanks to subsidies which poured in from England, but he found it more and more difficult to procure men. He gathered recruits from hostile countries, he granted pardons to deserters, he enrolled prisoners of war in the Prussian ranks. No longer was he sufficiently sure of his soldiers to take the offensive and for five years he was reduced to defensive campaigns, especially in Silesia. Meanwhile the Russians rolled on. They occupied East Prussia, penetrated into Brandenburg, and in 1759 captured Berlin itself.

After the defeat at Rossbach, the French turned their efforts against Hanover. But here they encountered unexpected resistance at the hands of an army commanded by Frederick's nephew, the Duke of Brunswick. By Brunswick the French were checked, defeated, and gradually pushed back out of Germany. These reverses, coupled with disasters to the French arms in America and India, led Louis XV to call upon his Bourbon cousins for assistance. As a result, a defensive alliance called the "Family Compact" was formed among the states of France, Spain, and the Two Sicilies (1761). But the entrance of Spain into the war (1762) was too late materially to affect its outcome.

What really saved Frederick the Great was a series of unexpected events in Russia. The Tsarina Elizabeth, who hated the Prussian King, died in 1762 and was succeeded on the Russian throne by Peter III, a dangerous madman and an ardent admirer of Frederick II. With autocratic abruptness, Peter transferred his armies from the side of Austria to the side of Prussia, and gave back to Frederick all the territories conquered by the Russian armies. Peter's reign was brief, and he was quickly succeeded by his wife Catherine II. But his acts were decisive, for without Russian support, Austria was unable to wrest Silesia from Frederick.

The treaty of Hubertusburg (1763) put an end to the Seven Years' War in Europe. Maria Theresa finally, though reluctantly, surrendered all claims to Silesia. Prussia gained a rich province, clearly humiliated Austria, and became a first-rank military power. The Hohenzollerns were henceforth the acknowledged peers of the Habsburgs.

B. The Seven Years' War as a World Conflict

The inconclusive War of the Austrian Succession had left undecided a number of important issues between France and Great Britain. Could the latter attain preëminence in commerce and in naval strength at the expense of France? Could France make good its hold on the Mississippi valley from the Great Lakes to New Orleans and thus restrict the British North American colonies to a narrow coastal strip east of the Alleghenies? Would France or would Britain fall heir to the crumbling Mogul Empire in India? All these questions were definitely settled by the Anglo-French phase of

The Marquise de Pompadour (1721–1764) after an engraving by Francois Boucher (d. 1770).

the Seven Years' War, which saw fierce battles and long campaigns fought out thousands of miles from Europe.

In America, the conflict, called the French and Indian War, actually broke out before hostilities started in Europe. The French had been pushing into the Ohio Valley. To forestall them the British built a fort at the junction of the Monongahela and Allegheny rivers. The French captured it, enlarged it, and renamed it Fort Duquesne. Shortly afterwards a young Virginian named George Washington arrived with help for the British, but was defeated and driven off on July 4, 1754. During that same year the British American colonies sought in vain, in the face of the French menace, to form an effective union at the Albany Congress. In 1755, British regular army units under General Braddock were sent to America. In an advance on Fort Duquesne, Braddock and his men were badly defeated. British attacks on Fort Niagara and on Crown Point on Lake Champlain were likewise repulsed by the French. The British then constructed Fort Edward and Fort William Henry on Lake George, while the French replied by erecting Fort Ticonderoga.

If 1755 had been unfortunate for the British, 1756 was still worse. A British squadron was defeated in the Mediterranean and the French captured the island of Minorca, which the British had held since the peace of Utrecht. In America a British attack on the French fortress of Louisburg failed, while the French under a new and brilliant leader, the Marquis de Montcalm, captured Fort William Henry and also the British fort at Oswego on Lake Ontario. By the end of 1756, it seemed as if the French were destined to dominate North America.

At this dark juncture for the British, and especially for their American colonists, an invigorating statesman entered the ministry at London in the person of William Pitt (subsequently Earl of Chatham). He stimulated new enthusiasm at home and in the colonies, recruited soldiers, organized fleets, and raised funds. American colonial volunteers now joined with British regular soldiers to provide a force of 50,000 men for simultaneous attacks on the four chief French posts of Louisburg, Ticonderoga,

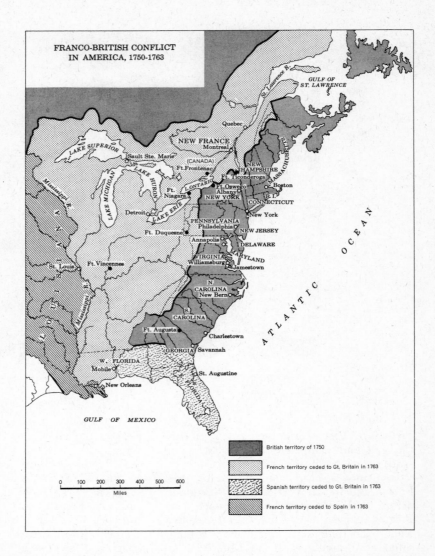

FRANCO-BRITISH CONFLICT
IN AMERICA, 1750-1763

British territory of 1750

French territory ceded to Gt. Britain in 1763

Spanish territory ceded to Gt. Britain in 1763

French territory ceded to Spain in 1763

Niagara, and Duquesne. The success of the attack on Louisburg (1758) was ensured by the support of a strong British naval squadron. Fort Duquesne was taken (1758) and rechristened Fort Pitt (now Pittsburgh). Though Ticonderoga repulsed one expedition (1758), it fell in July 1759, one day after the capture of Fort Niagara by the British.

Determined to exploit their victories, the British then launched an attack up the Hudson River valley against Montreal, and another under General Wolfe was borne on a strong fleet up the St. Lawrence against Quebec, which was defended by the redoubtable Montcalm. To capture Quebec would be well nigh decisive but very difficult. After weeks of ill success, Wolfe hit upon a daring plan. Thirty-six hundred of his men were ferried in the dead of night to a point above the city where his soldiers scrambled up a precipitous path to a high plateau, the Plains of Abraham, commanding the city. Wolfe's presence on the heights was revealed at daybreak on September 13, 1759, and Montcalm hastened to repel the attack. For a time the issue was in doubt, but a well-directed volley and an impetuous charge threw the French lines into disorder. In the moment of victory, General Wolfe, already twice wounded, received a musket ball in the breast. His death was made happy by the news of success. But no such comfort came to the mortally wounded Montcalm.

Quebec surrendered a few days later. It

was the beginning of the end of the French empire in America. In vain the French prepared a powerful fleet against the British; it was destroyed at Quiberon Bay, in October 1759, by the English Admiral Hawke. Thus deprived of assistance from the mother country, the French city of Montreal was compelled to surrender to the British in 1760, and soon all of New France (Canada) was lost. As a last despairing gesture, France drew Spain into the war in 1762, but the two powers together were utterly unable to turn the tide in America. And already the French power was crumbling in India.

After the end of the War of Austrian Succession in 1748, the French leader in India, Dupleix, had gained control of the southern part of the peninsula by using native puppet rulers. He placed princes of his choice on the thrones of Hyderabad and of Arcot, which was capital of the Carnatic, a realm that contained both the English post of Madras and the French city of Pondichéry. To thwart the French, the English backed rival candidates. They, too, had a leader of exceptional genius in Robert Clive (1725–1774), who, beginning as a clerk in the service of the East India Company, was to end his days as a wealthy lord. Both sides used sepoys, or native troops. But Clive employed them more skillfully. In 1751, by a spectacular stroke, Clive seized the citadel of Arcot with a force of only five hundred men and held it against

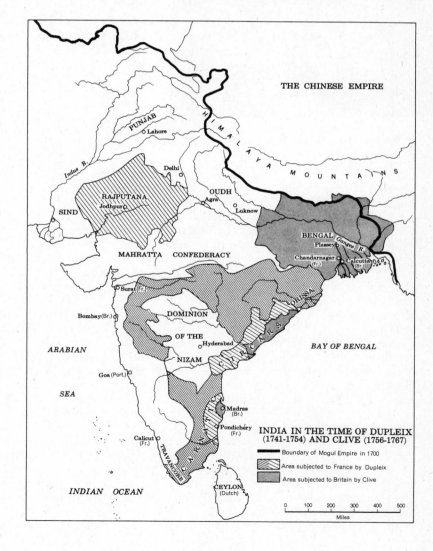

INDIA IN THE TIME OF DUPLEIX (1741-1754) AND CLIVE (1756-1767)

— Boundary of Mogul Empire in 1700

Area subjected to France by Dupleix

Area subjected to Britain by Clive

0   100   200   300   400   500
Miles

Robert, Baron Clive. After a portrait by Nathaniel Dance (d. 1811).

seized the opportunity to capture Chandernagor. When Suraj-ud-Dowlah took the French side, Clive responded by setting up a pretender to the throne of Bengal; and the contest was decided at the battle of Plassey in 1757, where Clive won a victory as brilliant as it was unexpected. There was more fighting, and finally, in 1761, Pondichéry, the center of French power in India, was captured by the British.

Though the capture of Quebec and of Pondichéry left the outcome of the colonial struggle in America and India in no doubt, the war dragged on till 1763, when France, Spain and Great Britain signed the Peace of Paris. Of all her American empire, France retained only her main West Indian islands and the tiny fishing islands of St. Pierre and Miquelon near Newfoundland. From France, Britain secured all of Canada, all the area east of the Mississippi, and the island of Grenada in the West Indies. From Spain, Britain got Florida. To Spain, Britain restored the Philippines and Cuba which had been captured by naval expeditions, and to recompense Spain for the loss of Florida, France ceded to her Louisiana, that is, the western half of the Mississippi valley. To the French were returned their posts in India, including Pondichéry and Chandernagor, but they agreed not to use them as military bases and not to build forts or maintain troops in Bengal.

Thus in the eighteenth century, as a result of the Seven Years' War, France suffered a more humiliating defeat at the hands of the British than the Netherlands had suffered in the seventeenth century, or Spain in the sixteenth. One by one Britain had downed those powers that stood in the way of her maritime and colonial expansion. For the next century and a half, she was truly to rule the waves, to be mistress of an extensive overseas empire, and to grow wealthy from a flourishing and expanding commerce.

Despite the length and the costs and the important political results of the wars that involved so many nations for fifteen of the twenty-three years between 1740 and 1763, it would be easy to exaggerate the effect of these conflicts on the life of Europe. They were by no means "total" wars. They did not pit entire nations against one another, nor require everybody to break off all deal-

repeated attacks by masses of sepoys. The English were thus enabled to place their man, Mohammed Ali, on the throne of the Carnatic, and he rewarded them richly with money and concessions. The French, instead of rushing support to Dupleix so as to recoup their losses, recalled him in disgrace.

Clive next turned his attention to Bengal, where both the French and the English had several trading centers, the British headquarters being at Calcutta and that of the French at Chandernagor. In 1756, a new, young, and violent ruler named Suraj-ud-Dowlah had come to the throne of Bengal. He quickly turned against the English, seized Calcutta, and placed 146 English prisoners in the famous "Black Hole of Calcutta," which was a tiny and stifling jail. The heat and the crowding were so severe that in one night all but twenty-three of the prisoners died. Upon receipt of the news of this atrocity, Clive organized an expedition and recovered Calcutta. Since Great Britain and France were now openly at war, Clive

ings with the "enemy" and to engage in some kind of "war work." Actual conflict was confined mainly to professional soldiers and sailors, and it interfered relatively little with the normal activities of the civilian population. Business men of warring nations often continued to trade with each other more or less openly. And even while hostilities were occurring, for example, between France and England, English gentlemen would sometimes sojourn in Paris, and French gentlemen might be entertained in London.

Life within a warring country was in most cases disturbed by no mass drafts of men, even though taxes might increase and rumors of victory or defeat might fly about. When a country was invaded the peasants in the path of any army suffered as they had suffered for a thousand years. But except in the case of invasion, life tended to go on in more or less normal fashion. During the wars there were long periods with little or no fighting. No continuous "front" was maintained. Rather, the relatively small and highly trained armies moved into each other's territories, advanced, retreated, maneuvered for position, laid siege to cities, and occasionally met in pitched battle.

Even the battles were somewhat stylized. With parade-ground discipline, columns were deployed into lines and efforts were made to outflank the opponent. In the colonial wars, the fate of continents was decided by the efforts of a few thousand men on each side. Nor were the numbers of men engaged in the crucial battles in Europe large by our standards. At Hohenfriedburg (1745) the Prussians had 65,000 men against 70,000 for Austria. The French won their great victory of Fontenoy (1745) with some 52,000 men against 46,000 for the allied army of British, Austrians, Dutch, and Hanoverians. Frederick the Great with 33,000 soldiers beat 82,000 Saxons and Austrians at Leuthen (1757) and with about 22,000 defeated the French and allied army of 42,000 men at Rossbach (1757).

The days of mass armies, of the "people in arms," still lay some decades ahead, and "total war" a century and a half beyond. It was not until the nature of government itself began to change that the character of war was drastically altered.

C. European Powers and Society in the Eighteenth Century

Despite recurrent wars, Europe seemed in the eighteenth century to have achieved a high degree of political, social, and economic stability. Politically, the national state was clearly the most significant form of organization. The foremost countries of the immediately preceding centuries—Portugal, Spain, Holland, Sweden, France, and England—had all been national states. On the other hand, the Holy Roman Empire was now little more than a name, and the Ottoman Empire was declining, while city states like Venice or Lübeck were playing very minor roles. To be sure, the Austrian Habsburgs had brought together an impressive aggregation of territories, which contained so many diverse peoples that they could scarcely be welded into a national state. But Prussia was very largely German and its expanding dominions were giving it an increasingly important position in north-central Europe. Russia, too, in the eighteenth century, was coming to resemble politically the national states of the west.

Most European countries were ruled by hereditary and absolute monarchs. France was perhaps the archetype of monarchial rule and the other countries resembled it rather closely. The Habsburgs were absolute rulers in their varied realms. The Romanovs in Russia, the Hohenzollerns in Prussia, the Wittelsbachs in Bavaria, the Bourbons in Spain and Italy were all autocratic rulers with but few theoretical limitations on their authority. Even in Holland with its republican tradition, the stadholders of the House of Orange succeeded in making their rule hereditary in the mid-eighteenth century. Poland, where the crown was both elective and weak, was shortly to disappear as a political entity. The only major exception to the general reign of absolutism was Great Britain.

Socially, the class structure of Europe, with some variation, seemed to display a considerable similarity and a marked stability. Everywhere the basis of society was the peasantry that worked the land and formed a large majority of the population. In the west, they were mostly freemen, and though many were tenants, a goodly number owned their land. Farther east, more of the peasants were serfs, and in Prussia, the Austrian lands, Poland, and Russia, serfdom was the normal condition of the agricultural workers. In the growing cities, there were still a considerable number of artisans and craftsmen who belonged to guilds and worked in shops much as they had in the middle ages. But there was also a steadily increasing number of workers who labored for wages in shops and shipyards and iron furnaces and factories. They became an urban proletariat.

From central Europe westward, there was an important middle class. It was composed of professional men like doctors and lawyers, of merchants and bankers who used their capital to make more money, of industrialists who employed from ten to hundreds of workers in shops and factories or who "put out" work to be done in the laborers' homes. The middle class was well-to-do and in general well educated. But while it had economic power, it enjoyed little social prestige. Social preëminence was reserved for the upper classes—great churchmen like bishops and archbishops, proprietors of large landed estates, titled nobles who formed the courts of the absolute monarchs. The nobles were relatively few in number, but they enjoyed a large share of the good things that life had to offer. They were no longer a warrior class, though many served as officers in the armies. It was not entirely clear what contribution they were making to the well-being of the various countries in return for the benefits they enjoyed.

Economically, Europe had behind it some three centuries of change which had considerably altered the old medieval conditions. In 1765 Europe was exploiting, largely by means of a commerce regulated by mercantilist principles, vast overseas areas in the Americas, in the Far East, and to a lesser degree in Africa. Everywhere in Europe, money had become important; even serfs and peasants, especially in the west, tended to pay dues in money rather than in labor and goods. Capitalism was well developed in commerce and finance. But it was largely confined to the urban areas and was perhaps most flourishing in seaport cities like London and Bristol, or Marseilles and Bordeaux, or Amsterdam and Cadiz. Industry was still mostly small-scale, though there were some

large factories and mines. It was closely regulated by the state and the guilds. The hand of government lay heavily on the quality of goods produced and the techniques used in producing them. The guilds were disappearing in England. Elsewhere they had grown so rigid than an outsider had little chance of getting in. People were protesting against them and finding ways of avoiding their restrictions.

In shops, whether under guild control or outside it, there was a good deal of machinery in use. Much of it was simple, made of wood and operated by hand. But some of the machinery, such as that used in spinning silk or making stockings, was fairly complicated. There was an increasing tendency to use metals and there was a growing employment of wind and water power. Transportation had been enormously improved since the middle ages. Great sailing vessels now plied all the seas. Canals had been built in many lands, and, in some countries such as France, systems of well-made highroads had replaced the oldtime cart tracks.

In England, the eighteenth century witnessed certain peculiar agricultural developments which have sometimes been termed an "agricultural revolution." At the beginning of the century, most English agricultural land, like that on the Continent consisted of open fields worked by peasant villages. Then occurred an "enclosure movement"—a fencing in of open fields and their transfer from village community to landlord —which in the space of a hundred years destroyed the English peasantry and made England a country of large estates worked by tenant farmers and hired agricultural laborers.[1] The enclosures were authorized by acts of Parliament. There were two hundred such acts between 1700 and 1760, and nearly four thousand between 1760 and 1844 when the process was complete. More than six million acres were enclosed. Theoretically the enclosure acts protected the interests of the peasant. He was supposed to receive a consolidated block equivalent to his old holdings of strips in the open field. But the acts were instituted by landowners

[1] There had been an "enclosure movement" in England in the sixteenth century, but on no such scale as this one of the eighteenth century.

and maneuvered through a parliament composed of country gentlemen. Small holders were squeezed out, and many peasant holders were unable to meet the expenses of surveying and enclosing the land and had to sell all or part of the shares they received. All lost their invaluable rights of keeping cattle, sheep, and horses in the old common pastures of the village.

The people who profited from the enclosures were the big landowners who quickly became bigger landowners. The motive behind the enclosure movement was to create large unified estates on which new and improved agricultural methods could be used. The resulting crops could be sold for cash to feed growing cities like London. Among the new techniques that could be employed, were a number that had been gradually introduced from Holland in the seventeenth century. Crops were rotated so that the land was not worn out and did not need to lie fallow. Fields were drained and limed and marled. Artificial grasses like clover improved the soil, and, as hay, made it possible to keep livestock over the winter. Turnips were useful as a rotation crop and as food for animals. So enthusiastic about this vegetable did one nobleman become that he was known as "Turnip" Townshend. At the same time, experimenters like Robert Bakewell improved stock-breeding, while other innovators like Jethro Tull devised and popularized horsedrawn agricultural implements.

With the newly enclosed fields and new techniques, many English gentlemen made handsome profits from their lands. On the other hand, the dispossessed peasants were faced with the alternative of becoming agricultural wage laborers or leaving the land to go to the cities or to America. This development of the eighteenth century was peculiar to England. Though some attempts at "scientific" farming were made in France and more so, under Charles III, in Spain, most peasants on the Continent continued to work on small holdings of land in the more traditional manner.

D. Baroque Art

In the arts, the eighteenth century, like the seventeenth, was persistently classical. The ideas of Greece and Rome, filtered through the sculptors, architects, and painters of the Renaissance, continued to constitute in men's minds standards of beauty and excellence. A Georgian country house in England or a Louis XV château in France looked rather different. But both used classical columns, pilasters, cornices, and decorations.

For all the persistence of conscious classicism there was development and change in the arts. In architecture the "classical" of the sixteenth century evolved into the baroque of the seventeenth and eighteenth by an emphasis on tendencies that had been evident even in Michelangelo and Palladio. Bernini (1598–1680) designed the impressive piazza with its curving double colonnades in front of St. Peter's basilica in Rome. His canopy over the high altar of that church, with its twisted and floriated columns, its crown of consoles, and its elaborate bronze work illustrates what came to be called "baroque." In baroque buildings a great use of colored marbles, gilt, rich ornamentation, broken lines, and fantastic effects was far different from the simpler tendency of the earlier period. In a number of churches founded by the Jesuits, especially in Italy, in the seventeenth century and the first half of the eighteenth, the baroque was carried to an extreme that came to be known as the "Jesuit style." Nor was the new trend confined to churches. Palaces, colleges, tombs, gardens, squares all showed its influence.

In Spain the architect Churriguera (1650–1725) evolved his own version of the baroque (called "Churrigueresque"), using light and airy decoration that was somewhat like the late Gothic in effect, but in its dramatic contrasts of line and surface, as in the façade of the Cathedral of Murcia, it becomes almost too exuberant in its richness. This Spanish style was to influence hundreds of churches and missions in the American colonies of Spain.

In France baroque architecture was more restrained. Its monuments, like the palace of the Luxembourg, the Invalides, and the great palace of Versailles with its enormous formal gardens filled with statues and fountains, have great dignity and make their impact rather by the grandeur of design than by the elaborateness of their decoration. During the eighteenth century the baroque in France became more delicate, freer, more intimate. Much use was made of stucco, of pastel shades of rose and blue, of light and fanciful ornamentation of shells, flowers, or cupids. This style, which came to be called "rococo," was widely and successfully imitated and developed in Germany and Austria in the palaces of dozens of princes and princelings.

The western architecture that Peter the Great brought to Russia was predominantly the baroque and his new city of St. Petersburg had more than its share of domes, columns, and ornate decorations. The leading architect in England was Sir Christopher Wren (1668–1710) and his masterpiece was the new St. Paul's Cathedral built to replace the Gothic edifice destroyed in the great London fire. But he designed many other churches in a style that was free in its use of classical elements but less ornate than much of the baroque of the continent. Toward the middle of the eighteenth century some architects moved toward a stricter classicism inspired by actual Greek or Roman buildings. The Pantheon in Paris, designed by Soufflot (1709–1780) and beginning in 1757, was definitely Roman, while the church of the Madeleine in the same city, begun by Constant d'Ivry in 1764, started out to be a domed building and ended up looking like a Greek temple.

During the seventeenth century, painting had been under the classical influence as transmitted by the Italian artists of the Renaissance. The paintings of Rubens (1577–1640), a native of the Spanish Netherlands who did much of his work in France, by their large size, rich color, and frequent use of mythology and of classical costumes and settings were quite like baroque architecture in effect. The leading Spanish artist Velasquez (1599–1660) in his court paintings was more restrained in manner. His unforgettable portraits of royal personages and their children are infused with a soft light. In France the painters Nicolas Poussin (1594–1665) and Claude Lorrain (1600–1682) were more strictly classical. In most of their works, the settings, the costumes, and even the subjects are derived from Graeco-Roman history or mythology and

are filled with temples, nymphs, and shepherds.

The classical tradition in art was continued in the eighteenth century by the great English portrait painters like Thomas Gainsborough (1727–1788) and Joshua Reynolds (1723–1792) and in France by a series of artists whose pictures represented in graceful and charming elegance scenes from the life of the court, usually in a pastoral or garden setting. Among these, Watteau (1683–1721) was notable for his skillful use of color, while Boucher (1703–1770) and Fragonard (1732–1806) were more delicate in their treatment and even more likely to depict cupids and goddesses. But as the eighteenth century wore on there was a movement toward greater realism, less dignity, and a choice of subjects from middle-class or even lower-class life. William Hogarth (1697–1764) painted London life in a satirical and almost exaggerated effort to show it as it actually was. Greuze (1725–1805) did softly sentimental pictures of French rustic scenes, Francisco Goya (1746–1828) almost caricatured the decadent court of Spain by painting its royal and noble personages exactly as they were.

In literature, too, there was tension between classicism and change in the eighteenth century. At first it was almost purely classical. Authors still composed epics in imitation of Homer, eclogues in the fashion of Vergil, and pastorals like those of Theocritus. For the sake of dignity, words like "dog" or "handkerchief" were barred from poetry. For the sake of form, dramas observed the "classical unities" of time, place, and action and were thus confined to a single main plot, in one spot, on one day. The English poets were also more or less limited to the rhymed couplet as were the French to the Alexandrine line. John Dryden (1631–1700) in his tragedies and poetry, Alexander Pope (1688–1744) even in his mock epic *The Rape of the Lock*, William Congreve (1670–1729) in his comedies, Joseph Addison (1672–1719) and Richard Steele (1622–1729) in their essays may all be thought of as classical in England, just as the plays and epics of Voltaire (1694–1778) or the comedies of Le Sage (1668–1747) represented classicism in France.

The Forge. By Francisco Goya (d. 1828).

New forms, however, were developing and new tendencies were appearing. The satires, savage in Jonathan Swift (1667–1745) or Voltaire's *Candide,* lighthearted in the *Marriage of Figaro* (1784) by Beaumarchais, were penetrating criticisms of contemporary society. The early English novels like the *Moll Flanders* of Daniel Defoe (1661?–1731), the *Tom Jones* of Henry Fielding (1707–1754), the *Roderick Random* of George Smollett (1721–1771) are new in both their form as long prose works of narrative fiction and in their realistic depiction of contemporary life. Other novels emphasized sentiment that often became sentimentality, as in Samuel Richardson (1689–1761) whose priggish story of the trials of the virtuous *Pamela* won a wide audience, or in *Paul et Virginie,* a tale of love among pastoral surroundings by Bernardin de Saint-Pierre (1737-1814). The novel of sentiment which would wring sighs and tears from its readers was becoming popular.

In English poetry, too, there was a foreshadowing of the romanticism which was to characterize the greater part of the nineteenth century. Romantic love of natural beauty was expressed by James Thomson in his *Seasons* (1726). Romantic liking for lowly scenes and simple emotions was voiced in the poems of Thomas Gray and especially in his *Elegy* (1750). Romantic fondness for legends and more primitive times was exemplified by Gray's *Bard,* by the *Reliques of Ancient English Poetry,* a collection of ballads and folk verse collected by the Anglican Bishop Thomas Percy and published in 1765, and by the poems of "Ossian" which the school teacher James Macpherson wrote and published in the 1760's pretending that they were translations from the Gaelic of a third-century Scottish poet. Most clearly of all the trend away from classicism and toward romanticism was marked at the very end of the century when William Wordsworth (1770–1850) and Samuel Taylor Coleridge (1772–1834) put out their *Lyrical Ballads* (1798) which dealt with nature and simple country folk, avoided the standard poetic words and verse forms of classical poetry, and appealed directly to the readers' emotions.

The same tendencies were also evident in Germany. Klopstock (1724–1803) wrote odes like those of "Ossian." Lessing (1729–1781) inaugurated a national and romantic German drama. Herder (1744–1803), an untiring advocate of folk lore, folk literature, and folk customs, published German folk poetry of earlier ages and was a decisive influence on younger literary men, notably Goethe (1749–1832) and Schiller (1759–1805). Schiller's first important play, *The Robbers* (1781), was essentially romantic as were Goethe's drama *Götz von Berlichingen* (1771) and his novel, *The Sorrows of Werther* (1774).

Like the literature of the eighteenth century, its music was predominantly classical but with new trends appearing toward the end of the period. The "classical" Italian opera developed in the seventeenth century was brought to the court of Louis XIV by Lully (1632–1687). Purcell (1658?–1695) composed operas like *Timon of Athens* and *Dido and Aeneas* for the court of Charles II and James II. An even greater master was George Frederick Handel (1685–1759) who followed George I from Hanover to England. He composed concertos, sonatas, and some forty operas, but is best remembered for the religious music of his later years, of which the *Messiah* is perhaps the greatest. His music was brilliantly appropriate to the baroque age.

One of the greatest composers of organ music, Johann Sebastian Bach (1685–1750) lived and worked at Weimar and Leipzig. Pious, humble, a good family man, and the father of twenty children, he knew little of the world. But his chorales, fugues, sonatas, concertos, and his four masses done for the elector of Saxony show his complete mastery of form and reach heights of mystical and majestic sublimity. His contemporary in France, Jean Philippe Rameau (1683–1764), continued the classical tradition of Lully but diverted it to a more pastoral mood that paralleled the rococo in art. One of his competitors was Christian Gluck, who, after leaving his native Germany for Austria, Italy, and England, settled in Paris and produced operas as classical in theme and setting as the architecture of Soufflot but with a notable lyric quality.

A greater master was Wolfgang Amadeus Mozart (1756–1791) of Salzburg and Vienna. Such a youthful prodigy that he

Sir Isaac Newton. From the painting by John Vanderbank, an English-Flemish painter who flourished at the beginning of the eighteenth century.

Courtesy National Portrait Gallery, London

began composing at the age of four, he had before his untimely death at the age of thirty-five created more than six hundred compositions including symphonies, sonatas, quartets, and world famous operas—the *Marriage of Figaro, Don Giovanni,* and the *Magic Flute.* His work has grace, charm and imagination fused by his genius into incomparable form. It was in Austria, too, that Franz Josef Haydn (1732–1809) brought the symphony to perfection. Within the rather rigid classical form of four movements, he still found scope for his talents in the more than one hundred symphonies that he composed. An even more important figure was in the making as the eighteenth century drew to a close. Ludwig van Beethoven (1770–1827), who had studied with both Mozart and Haydn, in his earlier work adhered rather closely to the predominant classicism. But in his later compositions he was to reach new heights of inspiration and new depths of emotion which led toward the romanticism of the nineteenth century.

E. Scientific Advance

Building on the earlier work of men like Copernicus, Kepler, and Galileo, scientists made rapid advances in their understanding of nature in the latter half of the seventeenth century and throughout the eighteenth. The greatest of them all, undoubtedly, was Sir Isaac Newton (1642–1727). Born of a humble family, he showed such skill in mathematics at the University of Cambridge that he was made a professor there when he was only twenty-seven years old. Almost every field of physical science felt the impact of Newton's inquiring mind, his remarkable powers of synthesis, and his mathematical insight. He developed improved tables of future astronomical movements. He created the science of hydrodynamics (the study of movements in liquids). In optics, he showed that the rainbow is caused by the breaking up of white light and proposed a corpuscular theory of light to which present-day physicists have turned back. In mathematics, he invented the crucial tool of calculus which he called the method of "fluxions." In kinetics, he pushed ahead Galileo's work and established three basic and simple "laws of motion."

But Newton's greatest and most influential contribution was the "law of gravitation." While still a young man he conceived the notion that the force which keeps the moon revolving around the earth, and the planets around the sun, is the same as that which makes an object fall when dropped. Though he long delayed publishing this idea while he checked over astronomical and other calculations, he gave it to the world in 1687 in his book, the *Principia* (Mathematical Principles of Natural Philosophy). It at once attracted wide attention in scientific circles, for the "law of gravitation" was significant in several respects. (1) It was universal. It applied to the stars in their courses and to a sparrow falling from a bush. (2) It was simple and could be stated simply: "Every particle of matter in the universe attracts every other particle with a force varying inversely with the square of the distance between them and directly with the product of their masses." (3) It brought together and unified a vast amount of work already done in astronomy and physics. (4) It seemed to indicate that man had finally penetrated God's design for the universe and had formulated one of the basic principles on which it was built.

Though there was some opposition to Newton's "law," it was soon confirmed by observation and experiment, and exerted enormous influence on every branch of thought. In sciences other than physics men sought to find similarly simple and basic mathematical laws. Soon in history, psychology, economics, political science, and religion, people were searching for Newtonian "laws." Indeed the whole intellectual spirit of the eighteenth century was to a very great degree molded by Newton's achievement.

It is notable that at first Newton's ideas on gravitation had seemed very difficult. There were essays and books to make them understandable and easy for earnest readers. But a half century after the publication of his *Principia*, they had become sufficiently commonplace to be discussed by schoolboys and society ladies.

Science depends for its progress to a considerable degree on accurate measurements, and in this period a number of new instruments were developed that made such measurements possible or permitted new kinds of experiments. The telescope and the microscope were repeatedly improved. The principle of the barometer was discovered by Torricelli in 1643. The air pump was invented by Otto von Guericke in 1650. The mercury thermometer was perfected by Fahrenheit (1686–1736). Two professors at the University of Leyden created the Leyden jar, an early form of the condenser which permitted the accumulation and sudden discharge of electricity. It was through working with such jars that Benjamin Franklin was led to experiments (published in 1751) which showed that lightning was an electrical phenomenon.

Using the Newtonian theories and the improved instruments, astronomers were able to make notable discoveries. Edmund Halley (1656–1742) catalogued the chief stars of the southern hemisphere and calculated the orbit of the great comet of 1682. When "Halley's Comet" returned (1759) as he had predicted and only a little late, the new astronomy scored another triumph. Like most of the scientists of the day, Halley had wide-ranging interests. His investigations (1693) improved the statistics of life-expectancy so that life insurance became much more practicable. Another versatile astronomer was William Herschel (1738–1822), a German by birth and a musician by profession, who was made royal astronomer by King George III of England in 1782. With improved telescopes he detected spots on the sun, mountains on the moon, and polar "snow" on Mars, and in 1781 discovered the planet Uranus, a major scientific event, since all the planets previously known were visible to the naked eye.

If Newton was the founder of modern physics, Robert Boyle (1627–1691) was the father of modern chemistry. He enunciated (1660) what came to be known as Boyle's law—that, temperature being constant, the volume of a confined gas varies inversely with the pressure. His book, *The Sceptical Chymist* (1661), helped to separate chemistry from alchemy with its magical and medieval traditions. In addition, he was one of the founders of the Royal Society, organized in 1662, which became a major factor in the exchange of scientific information and the forwarding of scientific discovery.

In the eighteenth century there was much progress in the understanding of gases. Joseph Black about 1755 prepared what he called "fixed air" (carbon dioxide). And a decade later Henry Cavendish, the son of an English nobleman, discovered "inflammable air" (hydrogen). Before long, Joseph Priestley isolated still another gas (1774) and showed that it was necessary for combustion and for the breathing of animals. Later the French chemist Lavoisier (1743–1794) gave it the name of oxygen. Cavendish went on to show that air was predominantly a mixture of oxygen and nitrogen and that water was a compound of oxygen and hydrogen. Lavoisier was able to dispose of the long-standing phlogiston theory that there was an impalpable substance which escaped from burning materials, and he laid the foundations for quantitative analysis and for the tremendous advances of chemistry in the next century.

Other sciences were moving forward too. A Scot, James Hutton, in an important paper in 1785 established the idea that the earth's crust as we have it today is the product of processes like erosion, glaciation, and vulcanism that can still be seen at work.

Malpighi (1628–1694) confirmed Harvey's theory of the circulation of the blood and was one of the first to describe the sexuality of plants. Anthony van Leeuwenhoek (1632–1723), using improved microscopes, saw protozoa, bacteria, and spermatozoa.

Information about plants, animals, and birds rapidly accumulated as specimens were brought back from overseas and placed in collections like that of Sir Hans Sloane, which at his death in 1753 became a nucleus of the British Museum. Carl von Linné (1707–1778), a Swedish botanist who is usually referred to as Linnaeus (the Latin form of his name), was able to develop a vastly improved system of classification for plants and animals which, with modifications, is still in use. His contemporary, the French zoölogist Buffon (1707–1788), brought together most of the existing information about animals in his encyclopedic *Natural History of Animals*. Buffon could not close his eyes to the resemblances among animals and remarked that were it not for the statements in the Bible one might be tempted to seek a common origin for the horse and the ass, the monkey and man. Thus he foreshadowed the evolutionary theories of the next century, just as his fellow scientists were gathering data and evolving theories on which the rapid advance of science in the future was to be based.

Voltaire. Bust by Jean François Houdon (d. 1828).

Courtesy Bettmann Archive

Beer Street. William Hogarth (d. 1764).

CHAPTER 38

Religion and the Enlightenment

A. Vogue of Rationalism and Deism

Much influenced by Newtonianism, there gradually developed a new philosophy which was essentially materialistic, that is, which tried to explain everything in the universe in terms of matter and motion, and of forces which could be detected by the human senses. Even before Newton, the French philosopher and mathematician René Descartes had worked out a philosophic system which put God and the human soul to one side as not being susceptible of human observation and which otherwise was quite materialistic. The English thinker Thomas Hobbes went further and insisted that everything, including the human soul, must be understood in terms of matter and motion. Baruch Spinoza, a gentle Jewish philosopher of Amsterdam, who made his living by grinding lenses, set forth a philosophy called pantheism. To him, what man called spirit was merely an aspect of matter; and, on the other hand, God was the natural universe. There was also a concern about materialism in the philosophy of William Leibnitz (1646–1716) who is distinguished in the history of mathematics for having discovered the calculus at about the same time as Newton. Leibnitz strove to compose the differences between Catholics and Protestants and to reconcile Christianity with the new developments in science. He put great stress on pure reason, and thought that by it man could transcend the material universe. He revived an ancient atomic theory and held that everything was made up of what he called "monads," but to him these were spiritual rather than material entities. Thus he sought to deal with matter by spiritualizing it, in contrast to Hobbes who had dealt with the spirit by insisting that it was material.

The trend toward rationalism and materialism culminated in the eighteenth century in the work of David Hume, a Scottish student of history and economics as well as of psychology and philosophy. To Hume all thought seemed based on the impressions which came through the human senses. Thought was therefore "merely a practical instrument for the convenient interpretation of our human experience." By thought, man could arrive at no truth about God, or the soul, or the after-life, or anything that lay outside of human experience, and since the truth could not be known about such matters they might best be ignored. Hume was completely skeptical about all the religious beliefs that had been accepted for generations.

Nor was Hume the only religious skeptic. True, some scientists, including Newton, accepted the Christian revelation as useful and necessary to supplement what man could find out about the universe for himself. But other scientists and most philosophers of the time were skeptical of "revelation." Hobbes and Spinoza questioned the divine inspiration and historical accuracy of the Bible.

Gradually there developed a body of religious thought which is called "Deism." Deists denied the divinity of Christ and all peculiarly Christian tenets of faith. They tried to elaborate a "natural religion" based on reason and on those beliefs that seemed common to all the different religions of mankind. By the eighteenth century, many thinkers were in general agreement as to the essential points of a "natural" and "rational" Deist religion. They could be summed up under three heads. (1) There is a God. (2) He demands righteous living of men. (3) He rewards and punishes men in a life after death. Many of the Deists agreed, likewise, that virtue could be summed up as adherence to the Christian Golden Rule.

Most of the "advanced" thinkers of the eighteenth century were Deists. Many churchmen in England and France, while performing their duties as ministers or priests and giving lip service to their respective Protestant or Catholic creeds, were really Deists at heart. But Deism was confined mainly to intellectuals. The masses and many of the upper and governing classes, and some intellectuals also, clung to Christian beliefs and fought Deism not only with word and pen but by censorship and the penalties of the law. In this controversy, the foremost of the *Philosophes*, as the advanced or "enlightened" thinkers were called in France, was a Frenchman, François Arouet (1694–1778), better known by his pen name of Voltaire. Sprung from a middle class family, Voltaire devoted his life to writing. He wrote poems and plays, histories and essays, pamphlets and books; and his personal correspondence was prodigious. Voltaire's religious views were disapproved by the royal government of France, and he spent much of his life in Lorraine, in Prussia, or finally on the Swiss border.

Wherever he was, Voltaire kept his pen busy. His writings were witty, graceful, and persuasive. Contemporaries thought them readable. In every field—social, political, or economic—Voltaire pleaded for rationalism, for the rule of "nature." As a Deist, he regarded much of Christianity as misleading mythology. As a reformer, he considered the Catholic Church, especially in France, an irrational institution handed down from the "dark ages" and designed to exploit men

by preying upon their superstitions. Seizing upon cases of religious persecution in his native country, Voltaire publicized them widely, denounced the church and its hierarchy bitterly, and pleaded for a "rational" approach to religious matters.

But Voltaire's militant Deism was not the end product of the rise of religious doubt in the eighteenth century. Soon the more skeptical were questioning the "natural and rational" religion of the Deists, including Voltaire himself. If there were no "rational" grounds for believing in the divinity of Christ, in the Christian miracles, and in the Biblical revelations, could not the same thing also be said of God and of the afterlife? A German *philosophe* named Holbach, who lived in Paris where he maintained a salon much frequented by fellow intellectuals, published two works, *Christianity Unveiled* (1767) and *The System of Nature* (1770), in which he attacked all religion and denied the existence of God. In the ensuing years Holbach's views won a number of converts, and by the end of the century there was a current of Atheism, as well as of Deism, among the intellectuals. Thus had rationalism progressed from a questioning of religious beliefs, to Deism, and finally to atheism. Yet, on the whole, Deism remained the typical religion of the *philosophes* of the eighteenth-century Age of Enlightenment. It was preached in their books and spread in their gatherings. It was furthered by secret societies like the Freemasons, which sprang up in eighteenth-century England and soon had lodges all over Europe. It profoundly shocked and disturbed the large majority of persons, who were still sincerely Christian.

The organized churches fought back at rationalism with more or less vigor. On the continent, the Jesuits were especially active in replying to the *philosophes* and striving to uphold the Catholic Christian faith. Because they had been so successful and so influential, they were singled out for the most virulent attacks by the rationalists, and these found allies among absolutist sovereigns of the age who felt themselves more "enlightened" than the Jesuits and who at the same time perceived in the Jesuits a potential menace to their own absolutism. It was "enlightened" despots who drove the

Jesuits out of Portugal in 1759 and out of France and Spain eight years later, and who in 1773 prevailed upon Pope Clement XIV to decree the formal suppression of the Society.

B. Pietism

In rural areas and small towns, and among the masses generally, Deism and other forms of rationalism made little headway. But especially in Protestant countries, there were other religious movements that did win many followers among the lower and middle classes. These movements were varied but they had certain tendencies in common. They reacted against the long theological debates of Protestant sects with one another. They minimized dogmas and emphasized the effort to lead Christlike lives. They turned away from argument and cultivated faith and religious emotions. They ignored rationalism and, frankly mystical, stressed a direct relationship of man to God.

In Germany the movement came to be called "Pietism" and can be traced to a book published by Philip Spener in 1675. Spener pleaded with his fellow Lutherans for less formal religion and more personal piety and holiness. Many welcomed the freshness and human warmth of the Pietist approach to religion, and, while Pietism never developed a separate church, it was a strong influence among eighteenth-century Protestants in Germany. Leibnitz himself was influenced by the Pietists, particularly in his interest in reducing acrimonious debate among Christians. Of a rather different sort was Emanuel Swedenborg (1688–1772), an able scientist and engineer who in 1745 had what he regarded as divine revelations and thereafter turned to writing mystical works on "divine love and wisdom" and on the "new Jerusalem." Another mystic of great power was William Blake (1757–1827) whose poems, and particularly his copper plate illustrations for them, are filled with a surging sense of divinity and eternity.

Contemporary with Spener was an Englishman, George Fox, who founded a sect, the "Friends," or "Quakers" as they were popularly known. Self-taught and by no means an intellectual, Fox was very earnest. He called churches "steeple houses," thought external observances like hat-tipping silly, and denounced war, violence, and bloodshed. He preached in England, Scotland, and America his doctrine that Christianity is no matter of clergy or churches, but a strictly personal experience. Man should be guided by the "inner light" given him by God. The Friends were soon famous for their plain-living and plain-speaking, for their refusal to take oaths, and for their staunch pacifism. While most of the Friends were humble folk, they could count among their numbers such an aristocrat as William Penn, founder of Pennsylvania.

At first the Anglican Church was little influenced by the tendencies exemplified by the Pietists or the Quakers. Yet it seemed to many in need of some sort of rejuvenation. Its services were often perfunctory and many of its clergymen worldly and even rationalist. It brought little religious emotion into the lives of the masses. The opportunity that these conditions offered was seized by John Wesley (1703–1791). At Oxford, he became the leader of a group of students who called themselves the Holy Club, but

John Wesley. After a painting by George Romney (d. 1802).

Courtesy Bettmann Archive

were nicknamed "Methodists" by reason of their methodical abstinence from frivolity and their methodical cultivation of personal piety and charity. Wesley became for a while a missionary in America and in 1738 underwent a profound religious experience, or "conversion." Then for fifty years he traveled an average of 5,000 miles a year. He preached some 40,000 sermons and with his brother Charles wrote hundreds of hymns. To Wesley anyone was a Christian who "accepted" Christ and lived methodically according to "Christian principles."

Wesley and his early associates were all Anglicans. But their emphasis on emotion, their neglect of ritual, their puritanical way of life, and their appeal to the lower classes made a breach between them and the established Church of England. Gradually the followers of Wesley came to form an independent body known as Wesleyans or Methodists, and governed by conferences of their own preachers and bishops. Before the end of the eighteenth century there were many Methodist churches in England. In North America too, Methodism rapidly became important; in fact it was as a young Anglican missionary to the Indians in Georgia that Wesley had first come into contact with Pietism through some German Protestant missionaries. George Whitefield, who was closely associated with the Wesley brothers, made several trips to America and in 1771 Francis Asbury crossed the Atlantic and gave great impetus to Methodism in the colonies. With their itinerant preachers, evangelical hymns, and their revival meetings, the Methodists made such rapid progress, especially in the frontier areas, that they became the largest of the Protestant sects in the next century.

Even within the Catholic Church there were seventeenth-century movements that somewhat resembled Pietism and persisted into the eighteenth century. One was Jansenism already mentioned in connection with Pascal. Jansen (1585–1638) was a Catholic bishop in the Spanish Netherlands who taught that above and beyond the ministrations of the church every Christian in order to be saved must experience a "conversion" and must lead a life of holiness. Louis XIV took steps against Jansenism and Pope Clement XI declared it heretical in 1713.[1] But it continued on to merge after 1870 with the sect of "Old Catholics" in the Netherlands.

The other movement, Quietism, was inaugurated by a Spanish priest named Miguel de Molinos (1640–1697); he taught that while the Catholic Church could start a man on the road to salvation, true holiness depended upon a direct indwelling of God in the individual conscience and a passive acceptance by each believer of whatever befell him. For a while Quietism won distinguished supporters in France including the famous Bishop Fénelon. But eventually it was opposed by the Jesuits and by Louis XIV and the views of Molinos were also held to be heretical.

Though the religious development of Russia was very different from that of western Europe, there were movements within its Orthodox Church that were not wholly dissimilar from Pietism. In 1654 the patriarch of Moscow had sought to revise and modernize the liturgy of the Russian Church. A number of priests and their followers clung tenaciously to the older forms, seceded from the church, and came to be known as "Old Believers." Among them arose several dissenting sects which, beside opposing the established church, tended to regard individual conscience as the final authority in religion and the sole guide to spiritual life. One of these sects, whose followers were known as Dukhobors, was composed mainly of peasants. Their beliefs were rather like those of the English Quakers, for they stressed the "inner light" and refused to do military service. The Dukhobors and similar sects were persecuted by both the government of the tsars and the Orthodox Church.[2]

The effects of Pietism were not wholly restricted to the field of religion. Pietist influence came into philosophy through the person of Immanuel Kant (1724–1804), a quiet and retiring professor of Königsberg in East Prussia. Reared in Pietist surroundings, Kant wrote on many topics but left his impress mainly by answering the ration-

---

[1] After 1713 the Pope specifically condemned Jansenist teachings concerning free will, grace, and predestination.

[2] A considerable number of Dukhobors later found refuge in Canada.

alism and skepticism of men like Holbach and Hume. He insisted that God, the freedom of the human will, and the immortality of the soul are subjects which cannot be understood by ordinary human reason. But man has, innately, other inner faculties by which he instinctively can know about, understand, and respond to such subjects. This philosophic point of view, known as "idealism," avoided most of the problems raised by eighteenth-century rationalism, by insisting that the basic matters of religion were not subject to reason alone. It was the basis of much of the religious and philosophic thought of the succeeding century.

C. The "Enlightenment," and Political and Economic Speculation

"Enlightened" thought of the eighteenth century expressed itself not only directly in religious skepticism and Deism, and indirectly in Pietism, but in a variety of other ways. Of course "enlightened" philosophers were not all of one mind; they differed in interests and emphases. Among most of them, however, certain general trends of thought can be discerned. (1) With the substitution of the natural for the supernatural, of science for theology, of this-worldly secularism for ecclesiastical other-worldliness, there was a stressing of *natural law*. The whole universe could now be regarded as a great Newtonian machine, perhaps originally created by God, but left by Him to function according to the rules He had established. (2) *Nature*, as man saw it, was the outer aspect of this world machine. What was natural was good. Everything worked out for the best if left alone. Man must not interfere. He must not try to go against nature. His laws should be merely explanations and declarations of what was natural. (3) Man could find out about natural law, and the workings of nature could be discovered and understood by *human reason*, as Newton had found out about gravitation. Man should trust his reason. What was *rational* was good. What was irrational or merely traditional was bad. (4) If man by reason learned about nature and natural law and sought to conform to them, if he did away with irrational laws and insti-

tutions, if he educated youth along natural and rational lines, then *human progress* would be rapid indeed. In fact man and society could by proper education approach perfection. (5) Individual human beings, endowed with reason to understand the universe, were important. They were born equal and made unequal only by education and experience. They were possessed of natural rights which should be respected. Man should treat man in a *humanitarian* fashion.

Such views slowly penetrated the field of political science and produced by the eighteenth century certain distinctive views on questions of government. Back in 1651, in the midst of civil war and troublous times in England, Thomas Hobbes had published a book called *Leviathan*. In it, he pointed to good order as the purpose of government, and strong government as the means to order. It was his notion that man in "the state of nature," before governments were established, was little better than a beast. His life was violent, nasty, brutish, and short. To escape such ills men set up a ruler and gave over to him all their rights. Thereafter they had to obey him, and even if he was unjust, they had no recourse against him.

Similar in some ways, but very different in conclusion, were the political ideas of John Locke, who lived at the time of the "Glorious Revolution," [1] approved of it, and tried in his writings to justify it. Locke believed, like Hobbes, that men in a state of nature chose a sovereign to improve their lot. But they did so mainly that he might defend the natural rights of the individual. Part of their rights men gave up to their new ruler by a "social contract." They retained under this contract, however, the rights to life, liberty, and property. If the sovereign unjustly or tyranically interfered with his subjects' remaining rights, or if he failed to protect them, then the people were entitled to drive him out and to select a new ruler who would maintain and defend their rights.

Locke's ideas were extremely popular in the eighteenth century. They led Voltaire and many of the other *philosophes* to believe that the ideal kind of government was

---

[1] In 1689. See below, pp. 511–512.

John Locke. After Sir Godfrey Kneller (d. 1723).

Courtesy Bettmann Archive

rule by a just, wise king, who was rational in his behavior, who understood nature and natural law, and who protected the natural rights of his subjects. He might be an absolute ruler, a despot, but if he were "enlightened" and ruled in an "enlightened" fashion, all was well. In fact, so great were the difficulties and dangers of rule by groups or by all the people that many held "enlightened despotism" to be the best possible form of government.

Most political thinkers spun their ideas by rational arguments from suppositions about the nature of man. But one French writer, Montesquieu, in a famous work entitled *The Spirit of the Laws* (1748), adopted another method. He studied and compared existing governments and political institutions. In England, he thought he discerned the ideal system. Because he did not fully realize how powerful the Parliament had become, he thought that in the British government the powers were divided evenly among the executive (the king), the legislature (parliament), and the judiciary (the judges). Each branch checked and balanced

the others, and, by this division of power, justice was secured and the natural rights of men preserved. Montesquieu's interpretation of British government had great influence on the formulation of the American constitution and also upon the development of the idea of *limited* monarchy as the proper form of government.

Some eighteenth-century thinkers moved beyond the notion of enlightened despotism or limited monarchy and developed democratic theories which held that the people should rule themselves. Of such thinkers, the most famous was a French Swiss named Jean-Jacques Rousseau (1712–1778). Rousseau was a pioneer in the movement which in the next century was called romanticism. Though he put his own children in an orphan asylum, his book on education, *Émile* (1762), persuaded many people that children were naturally good, and that man was evil because he was perverted by faulty teaching and by bad laws and institutions. He believed likewise that men in a "state of nature" were good, and he popularized the idea of the "noble savage." Like Locke he maintained that men set up governments by means of a "social contract," and his major political work is called the *Social Contract* (1761). But Rousseau went further than Locke, for he maintained that men are born free and they can best maintain their freedom and their rights if they are ruled by a government of their own choosing which by its acts expresses the popular will. Rousseau believed that such democracy could only work well in small states like his native Geneva. Others, however, using his vigorous phrases and his highly charged catchwords, extended the idea of democracy and of republicanism to larger countries. Within fifteen years of Rousseau's death, France itself would be experimenting with a democratic republic.

The ideas of the enlightenment gradually influenced economic thought. During previous centuries, economics had been thoroughly ensnarled with the politics of state action. It was indeed quite properly called "political economy." Almost everybody had accepted the basic mercantilist notion that individuals seeking their selfish ends must be checked and controlled by the government for the sake of the wealth, strength, and unity of the whole nation. In practice, such beliefs had led to policies of high tariffs, subsidies, industrial regulations, navigation acts, and colonial exclusiveness. In England, it is true, the destruction of a strong and effective royal government had brought about a gradual relaxation of internal controls on industry. But the parliament of landlords and merchants had maintained thoroughly mercantilist policies on imports, shipping, and colonies. In other countries, there had long been much government control of internal economic life as well as of foreign trade. Many states modeled their policies on those applied in France by Colbert.

Toward the end of the seventeenth century, complaints began to be raised in England and France about specific mercantilist regulations. Some businessmen protested against high tariffs; others denounced monopolistic companies; still others argued against the prohibition of the export of coin. There was a growing belief that nations had set too much store by gold and silver and that ships and shops and raw materials were just as important forms of wealth.

The philosopher David Hume in a series of essays insisted that the government would do well to leave foreign commerce alone, that there was no need to worry about a balance of trade, and that prosperous neighbors helped a country instead of hurting it. In France there developed a whole school of thinkers called the "Physiocrats," whose slogan was *laissez-faire* (leave alone). Led by a court physician named Quesnay, the physiocrats were mainly interested in agriculture. They held that agriculture alone really produced a national profit, a "net product." Industry and commerce were sterile, since they merely transformed goods or moved them from place to place. There was no reason, therefore, to regulate manufacturing or trade; and agriculture would be most helped by leaving commerce in farm products and especially in grain completely free. Wealth circulated best if it circulated naturally. It should be left alone. A French minister named Turgot tried to introduce physiocratic reforms in France in 1774–1776. But the opposition was too strong and he was forced out of office.

The culmination of *laissez-faire* think-

ing, and of eighteenth century economic thought, was reached in *An Inquiry into the Nature and Causes of the Wealth of Nations* (1776) by a Scottish professor named Adam Smith. This work was a literary masterpiece of brilliant and persuasive eloquence; it was also a notable synthesis which drew together the best of the thought of Hume and the Physiocrats and a host of earlier writers. Smith destroyed the foundations of mercantilist thought by showing that goods, not money, are true wealth, and by demonstrating that restrictions and regulations on industry and trade tended to lessen the production of goods. Wine, he pointed out, could be produced in Scotland in hothouses, if the import duty on wine were high enough. But it would cost thirty times as much as French wine. It would be better for the Scots to use their land, labor, and capital where they could employ them most effectively, and then exchange their products with France for wine.

Not only did Smith attack the reasoning which had buttressed the mercantilist regulations, but he also advanced positive arguments for *laissez-faire*. He reasoned that if men are left alone to seek their own ends they will be guided as if by "an invisible hand" to work and to use their land, labor, and capital in the way most beneficial to the whole country. Economic forces should be left alone under the sway of natural economic laws, without human interference. It is noteworthy that Smith's work which showed the folly of colonial regulations and restrictions appeared in the very year in which the American Declaration of Independence broke up the English colonial system. The lesson was not lost on some people. But though most thinkers became disciples of Adam Smith and adherents of *laissez-faire*, it was a generation or more before the British government began to adopt a *laissez-faire* policy. Other nations were still slower.

The enlightened *philosophes* of the eighteenth century were not on the whole greatly interested in history. To them the record of the past was mainly one of ignorance and superstition. They preferred, therefore, to look forward to an era of progress guided by reason, rather than looking backward. Nonetheless, there was in the period considerable development of historical method and knowledge, and some of the major figures wrote histories that reached a wide audience. Thus Voltaire's *Age of Louis XIV* and his *Life of Charles XII* (of Sweden), and Hume's *History of England* were received with enthusiasm.

Already in the seventeenth century a French Benedictine monk named Mabillon (1632–1707) had formulated the rules and scientific principles for the study and interpretation of historical documents. The monks of the Congregation of St. Maur, to which he belonged, carried his work forward, and in 1733 began to publish a monumental collection of the sources of French history. At about the same time, a learned Italian priest, Muratori, was engaged in a similar enterprise for his country. Moreover, the growth of well-ordered libraries meant that historical materials were collected and cared for more effectively than in the past. The library of the Vatican, the Laurentian library at Florence, the Royal Library at Paris, and the royal Prussian library were all greatly expanded in the eighteenth century, while the library of the British Museum grew rapidly from the nucleus of a private gift.

One of the fertile historical minds of the period was that of Vico (1668–1744), a Neapolitan professor who not only worked out theories as to the successive periods of history but also subjected the sources of Greek and Roman history to searching criticism. Vico thought of art, literature, and political institutions as all being the products of a changing historical environment. To a degree, his attitude was exemplified by Winckelmann, who has been called the founder of scientific archaeology and who published the first treatise on the treasures of the buried cities of Pompeii and Herculaneum.

The continuing interest in ancient history is illustrated by the greatest and most typical historical work of the eighteenth century, the *Decline and Fall of the Roman Empire* by Edward Gibbon (1737–1794), a well-to-do English gentleman. Gibbon was an agnostic, though he had been both a Catholic and a Protestant. With rationalism and wit he contrasted pagan "civilization" with Christian "barbarism" and attributed the decay of the Roman Empire, with all that it had meant for the well-being of mankind, to the triumph of Christianity.

More prophetic of the future was the work of Herder (1744–1803), a German Lutheran pastor. He wrote no important histories himself nor did he collect documents, but he did plead for a scientific study of history. In his *Ideas on the Philosophy of History* he urged that history should show how human actions are modified by time and place; it should explain how the human race has developed; it should be national; and it should above all be humanitarian and promote a real understanding of human nature.

D. Humanitarianism

The Enlightenment involved, with many of its devotees, a humanitarianism. For example, an Italian nobleman and professor, Beccaria, in a treatise *On Crimes and Punishments* (1761), pleaded for more humane treatment of criminals. He condemned torture and capital punishment and held that justice should seek to prevent rather than to punish crime. The Quakers denounced the slave trade, and the Pennsylvania Quakers in 1761 forbade their members to engage in it. Before long Englishmen like Thomas Clarkson and William Wilberforce were engaged in an active campaign against slavery and the slave trade, and in 1787 anti-slavery committees were organized both in England and in France.

Humanitarianism, aided by scepticism and rationalism, also affected other areas of public policy. The belief in witches which had been normal in the seventeenth century came to seem a superstition, and gradually witches ceased to be tried and executed. The last witch trial in Scotland was in 1722, the last in Germany in 1793. The same forces, combined with the insistence of dissenting sects like the Quakers, led toward a gradual rise of religious toleration. The laws against Protestants were eased in France and those against Catholics in England. Even for the Jews, who had long been clannish and subjected in most countries to repressive laws designed to keep them segregated, a new day began to dawn. Their own "enlightened" philosopher, Moses Mendelssohn (1729–1786), urged them to be more understanding of other religions, to be less clannish, and to seek to be good citizens in the countries where they resided. Despite the fact that Frederick the Great disliked and harried Jews, he began the process of giving them more rights. Joseph II of Austria in 1781–1782 repealed most of the anti-Jewish laws and even permitted them to attend universities. In England and the Netherlands, where the Jews had been tolerated for some time, they were treated progressively in the eighteenth century much like other citizens.[1]

E. The Enlightened Despots

Just after the middle of the eighteenth century, between 1751 and 1765, there appeared in France an encyclopedia composed of seventeen large volumes of text and four of illustrations. So famous that it is known as "The Encyclopedia," it forms a monument of eighteenth-century learning, rationalism, and "enlightenment." It was edited by Denis Diderot, who wrote many of the articles and who was imprisoned and constantly harried by the authorities because of the skeptical tone of the work. While some of the articles were written by hacks, others were contributed by major *philosophes*. Voltaire wrote on history, Rousseau on music, Quesnay on economics, d'Alembert on mathematics. To a degree, the Encyclopedia hid its skepticism on religious matters behind a superficial acknowledgment of orthodox views. But tucked way in unexpected minor articles were scathing, if indirect, attacks on the church, the priesthood, and traditional faith. In other fields, all the diversity, all the faith in nature and reason, all the insistence on natural rights, all the belief in man, education, and progress, which were exemplified by eighteenth-century thinkers, were spread upon the pages. So important and effective was the work that "encyclopedist" became a synonym for *philosophe* or "liberal thinker." When a churchman or a conservative wished to attack the rationalist trend of eighteenth-century thought, he denounced the Encyclopedia.

But there were some in high places who gave heed to the encyclopedists. There were rulers who hypocritically or sincerely sought to play the role of "enlightened despots" about whom the thinkers were writing. In Austria, though Maria Theresa had striven earnestly to strengthen her realm and increase its prosperity, she was by no means "enlightened," for she was fearful of the new ideas, averse to radical changes, and quite devoted to the Catholic religion. But her son, Joseph II, who was associated with her after 1765 and was sole ruler from 1780 to 1790, was of a more "enlightened" type. He had read the *philosophes* and could quote them. While it can be argued whether he drew more of his inspiration from them or from the older Austrian mercantilist writers, there can be little doubt about his devotion to reason and reform.

With little regard to opposition or to tradition, Joseph II plunged ahead on a path of reform and tried by the despotic enforcement of his ideas to bring the Austrian domains "up-to-date." Though the masses of his subjects were Catholics, Joseph was eager not only to purge Catholicism of "superstition" but also to subject the church completely to the state. He forbade the publication of papal bulls in his territories without his permission. He nominated bishops who shared his views. He confiscated church lands. He abolished many monasteries, ordered the clergy to be trained in state schools, and gave to heretics and Jews equal rights with Catholics.

Joseph, in traditional more than philosophic manner, attempted to extend his lands by going to war with the Turks (1786). But he was also bent on centralizing his despotic government. He divided his dominions into thirteen provinces, each under a military commander. Local assemblies and legislatures were abolished and age-old customs and privileges ignored. Everything was henceforth to be managed from Vienna. The army was reorganized after the Prussian model and reluctant peasants were forced to serve in it. German was made the official language in all the diverse Habsburg lands, where so many tongues were spoken. In his effort to reconstruct society, Joseph went

---

[1] Not until the nineteenth century, however, were either Jews or Catholics admitted to the British Parliament.

still further. He ordered that all serfs were to become free men, able to marry without consent of their lord, permitted to sell their holdings, and privileged to pay a fixed rent in money rather than in labor. Nobles were to bear their share of the taxes.

Many of Joseph's social and economic reforms met with bitter opposition. The peasants disliked military service and did not understand about "freedom." The nobles resented loss of feudal rights. The provinces hated to see their assemblies and privileges destroyed. The Austrian Netherlands rose in revolt rather than surrender their local laws; the Tyrol did likewise; and angry protests came from Hungary. When Joseph II was dying (1790), he confessed that "after all my trouble I have made few happy and many ungrateful." He directed that most of his reforms be cancelled and proposed as his epitaph the gloomy sentence, "Here lies a man who, with the best intentions, never succeeded in anything."

There were other "enlightened" rulers in the eighteenth century. The English Georges and Louis XV of France were least affected by rationalist or liberal thought. Catherine the Great of Russia made at least a pretense of interest in the *philosophes*. She corresponded with Diderot, bought his library when he was in financial difficulties, and was as eager to be thought modern as she was to increase her own autocratic power. Charles IV of Naples (1738–1759) and III of Spain (1759–1788) was more genuine in his "enlightenment." He centralized and reformed the administration, reduced the public debt, built roads and canals, encouraged "scientific farming," fostered commerce and industry, reorganized the army, rejuvenated the navy, improved the government of the Spanish colonies, and sent thither emigrants from Spain. In addition, he suppressed the Jesuits and checked the activities of the Inquisition. During the reign of Charles III the revenues of Spain tripled, the population grew, and Spain's prestige increased abroad. In Portugal, Charles's neighbor, King Joseph I (1750–1777), shone in the reflected glory of a minister, Pombal, who was both an "enlightened" philosopher and an astute statesman. Under Pombal, royal authority was strengthened, at the expense of the nobles and clergy, and was exercised to promote education and the material well-being of the middle classes.

Sweden had an "enlightened" despot in Gustavus III (1771–1792); Sardinia, in Charles Emmanuel III (1730–1773); and Tuscany, in Leopold I (1765–1790), a brother of Joseph II of Austria and his successor as Holy Roman Emperor. But of them all the most famous was Frederick the Great of Prussia, whose exploits in war and diplomacy we have already noticed. Frederick was much more than a military genius and a ruthless diplomat. He was thoroughly imbued with the rationalist philosophy of the French thinkers whose language he spoke by choice, whose works he read, and whose company he sought. Voltaire himself came as a guest to the Prussian court, and there were long conversations and witty interchanges until the "prince of philosophers" went too far in correcting the amateur poems of the Prussian King.

Frederick took his duties as an "enlightened" despot most seriously. In a work written in French on the theory of government, Frederick declared, "The monarch is not the absolute master but only the first servant of the state." Like a faithful servant, Frederick labored many hours a day on documents and despatches, with only occasional interruptions for military parades, conversations over a coffee table, or, as relaxation, some literary work and a little flute playing. Even in the midst of his long and desperate wars, Frederick never lost his zeal for internal administration and reform.

Frederick accomplished much for the economic development of Prussia. He encouraged landowners to try out the new agricultural methods that were being introduced in England, to drain marshes, to plow waste lands, to plant fruit trees, to breed better farm animals, and to grow root crops adapted to the sandy soils of north Germany. Frederick brought in immigrants, built roads and canals, and tried to improve industry and trade. Though he kept the peasants in a state of serfdom, he was eager to reduce their financial burdens. Taxes were not light, but Frederick spent the public funds with care. He was not the man to

Frederick the Great. After a drawing by
H. Hamberg.

pices, moreover, the laws of the land were published in clear and compact form for the information of the public and the guidance of the courts. Torture in criminal investigations was abolished and other humane reforms decreed.

In religious matters, Frederick was devoid of Protestant zeal, and in fact of any zeal at all. It was part of his "enlightenment" to be skeptical about Christian faith and morals, to doubt the Bible, and to sneer at clergymen. "All religions must be tolerated," he affirmed, "and every person allowed to go to heaven in his own fashion." To the scandal of many of his Lutheran subjects, he welcomed Catholics in Prussia and told them they might build their churches as high as they pleased. To the amazement of all Christians, he declared, "If Turks should come to populate the land, I myself shall build them mosques." Only against Jews did he discriminate, and in their case not because of their religion but because of qualities which he fancied were inherent in their race. He obliged Jews to adopt surnames and to obtain special licenses to live in Prussia. He arbitrarily expelled them from this or that locality, favored them when they seemed serviceable, and at other times harassed them with restrictions.

There was another matter in which Frederick was not "enlightened." Cosmopolitan and humanitarian he might be in some respects, but he was no pacifist. Like his father he lavished time, money, and attention on the army and rebuilt it with care when it was shattered by war. Tireless drill, strict discipline, up-to-date arms, and, most of all, Frederick's enthusiasm and ability rendered the Prussian army the envy and the model of Europe in the second half of the eighteenth century. For all his "enlightenment," Frederick is best remembered for his extraordinary feats on the bloody fields of war. And in some ways he thus symbolizes the eighteenth century, which, under a veneer of rationalism among the intellectuals and polish among the courtiers, was a period in which society rested upon the exploited peasants and in which the lot of the lower classes was little bettered by all the "progress."

lavish fortunes on courtiers or mistresses like Louis XV of France. His officials dared not be extravagant for fear of corporal punishment, or, what was worse, being held up to ridicule by Frederick's sarcastic tongue.

Into the intellectual life of his time, Frederick entered heart and soul. He invigorated the Berlin Academy of Sciences and showed his faith in education by establishing numerous elementary schools. Though he disliked German literature and thought the works of Lessing and Goethe vulgar, he was fond of French writers and eagerly read the latest works from Paris.

To Frederick, the law seemed often formal and unreasonable. On one occasion, when he thought an injustice had been done to a poor man, he dismissed the judges, condemned them to a year's imprisonment, and compelled them to make good out of their own pockets the loss sustained by their victim. Under Frederick's "enlightened" aus-

SELECT SUPPLEMENTARY READINGS FOR PART VII

General. David Ogg, *Europe in the Seventeenth Century* (1925); *New Cambridge Modern History*, vol. v (1961), vol. vii (1957); C. J. H. Hayes, *Political and Cultural History of Modern Europe*, vol. i (1936); S. B. Clough and C. W. Cole, *Economic History of Europe* (1952); C. J. Friedrich, *The Age of the Baroque* (1952); F. L. Nussbaum, *The Triumph of Science and Reason, 1660–1685* (1953); J. B. Wolf, *The Emergence of the Great Powers, 1685–1715* (1951); Paul Hazard, *The European Mind: the Critical Years, 1680–1715* (1935); Preserved Smith, *A History of Modern Culture*, 2 vols. (1930–1934).

Chapter 34. A. J. Grant, *French Monarchy, 1483–1789*, 4th ed., 2 vols. (1920); Quentin Hurst, *Henry of Navarre* (1938); J. B. Perkins, *Richelieu and the Growth of the French Power* (1900), *France under Mazarin*, 2 vols. (1886), *France under Louis XIV*, 2 vols. (1897), *France under the Regency* (1892); Anthony Blunt, *Art and Architecture in France, 1500–1700* (1953); L. B. Packard, *Age of Louis XIV* (1929); James Farmer, *Versailles and the Court under Louis XIV* (1905); A. J. Grant, *The Huguenots* (1934); C. W. Cole, *Colbert and a Century of French Mercantilism*, 2 vols. (1939), and *French Mercantilism, 1683–1700* (1943); H. W. Van Loon, *Fall of the Dutch Republic*, 2nd ed. (1924); G. M. Trevelyan, *England under Queen Anne*, 3 vols (1930–1934), (for the War of the Spanish Succession).

Chapter 35. Frank Nowak, *Medieval Slavdom and the Rise of Russia* (1930); Stephen Graham, *Ivan the Terrible* (1933); Eugene Schuyler, *Peter the Great*, 2 vols. (1884); B. H. Sumner, *Peter the Great and the Emergence of Russia* (1951), and *Peter the Great and the Ottoman Empire* (1949); I. Andersson, *A History of Sweden* (1956); F. G. Bengtsson, *Charles XII* (1960); E. F. Heckscher, *An Economic History of Sweden* (1954); John A. Gade, *Charles XII of Sweden* (1916); R. N. Bain, *Slavonic Europe, a Political History of Poland and Russia from 1447 to 1796* (1908); R. H. Lord, *Second Partition of Poland* (1915); K. Waliszewski, *Catherine II of Russia* (1894); W. F. Reddaway, *et al.* (eds.), *The Cambridge History of Poland*, 2 vols. 1941–50); D. Halecki, *A History of Poland* (1956); G. P. Gooch, *Maria Theresa and other Studies* (1951); Mehmed Pasha, *Ottoman Statecraft* (1935); H. Gibb and H. Bowen, *Islamic Society and the West*, vol. 1, *Islamic Society in the Eighteenth Century*, 2 pts. (1950–1957); Lord Eversley, *Turkish Empire*, 3rd ed. (1924); Ferdinand Schevill, *History of the Balkan Peninsula*, rev. ed. (1933); S. B. Fay, *The Rise of Brandenburg-Prussia to 1786* (1937); C. E. Maurice, *Life of Frederick William, the Great Elector* (1926); R. R. Ergang, *The Potsdam Führer, King Frederick William I* (1941); G. P. Gooch, *Frederick the Great* (1947); W. H. Bruford, *Germany in Eighteenth Century* (1935).

Chapter 36. W. C. Abbott, *Expansion of Europe*, rev. ed. (1924); L. B. Packard, *The Commercial Revolution, 1400–1776* (1927); P. A. Means, *The Spanish Main* (1935); H. W. Van Loon, *Golden Book of the Dutch Navigators* (1916); V. Barbour, *Capitalism in Amsterdam in the Seventeenth Century* (1950); J. J. van Klaveren, *The Dutch Colonial System* (1953); C. H. Haring, *The Spanish Empire in America* (1947); J. B. Brebner, *The Explorers of North America* (1933); J. A. Williamson, *Short History of British Expansion*, 2 vols. (1930); G. M. Wrong, *Rise and Fall of New France*, 2 vols. (1928); H. I. Priestley, *France Overseas through the Old Regime* (1939).

Chapter 37. J. O. Lindsay, *The Old Regime, 1713–1763* (1957); Penfield Roberts, *The Quest for Security, 1715–1740* (1947); W. L. Dorn, *Competition for Empire, 1740–1763* (1940); W. F. Reddaway, *Frederick the Great and the Rise of Prussia* (1904); Norwood Young, *Life of Frederick the Great* (1919); J. F. Bright, *Maria Theresa* (1897); A. H. Buffington, *The Second Hundred Years' War, 1689–1815* (1929); Howard Robinson, *Development of the British Empire*, rev. ed. (1936); J. D. Perkins, *France under Louis XV*, 2 vols. (1897); Basil Williams, *Life of William Pitt, Earl of Chatham*, 2 vols. (1913); J. S. Corbett, *England in the Seven Years' War*, 2 vols. (1907); H. Dodwell, *Dupleix and Clive, the Beginning of Empire* (1930); W. H. Moreland and A. C. Chatterjee, *A Short History of India* (1936); G. M. Wrong, *Rise and Fall of New France*, 2 vols. (1928); W. T. Waugh, *James Wolfe, Man and Soldier* (1928); Sir George Forrest, *Life of Lord Clive*, 2 vols. (1918).

Chapter 38. L. Gershoy, *From Despotism to Revolution* (1944); Geoffrey Brunn, *The Enlightened Despots, 1763–1789* (1941); Dorothy Stimson, *The Gradual Acceptance of the Copernican Theory* (1917); L. T. More, *Isaac Newton* (1937); J. W. N. Sullivan, *Isaac Newton* (1937); Charles Singer, *Discovery of the Circulation of the Blood* (1923); F. Masson, *Robert Boyle* (1914); A. Wolfe, *History of Science, Philosophy and Technology in the Eighteenth Century* (1939); H. Higgs, *Physiocrats* (1897); Carl Becker, *The Heavenly City of the Eighteenth-Century Philosophers* (1932); Kingsley Martin, *French Liberal Thought in the Eighteenth Century* (1929); R. R. Palmer, *Catholics and Unbelievers in Eighteenth-Century France* (1939); E. de and J. de Goncourt, *French XVIII Century Painters* (1948); Emil Kaufmann, *Architecture in the Age of Reason* (1955); B. Willey, *The Eighteenth Century Background* (1940).

For Voltaire, see the studies by R. Aldington (1925), G. Brandes (1934), H. N. Brailsford (1935), and N. L. Torrey (1938). For Rousseau, see the studies by A. Cobban (1934), H. Fairchild (*The Noble Savage*, 1928), F. C. Green (1955), M. Josephson (1931), R. B. Mowat (1938), and E. H. Wright (1929).

James I of England (VI of Scotland) by Pieter de Jode (d. 1634).

From Cromwell to Napoleon

PART VIII

REVOLUTIONARY

Spanish Uprising of May Second and French Mass Shooting at Madrid. Francisco Goya (d. 1828).

Courtesy Bettmann Archive

TRANSITION

WHILE EUROPE was engaged in colonial rivalries and dynastic wars, while scientific knowledge was being greatly refined and extended, while religious attitudes were changing and thought was becoming "enlightened," there was in process, within the area of Western civilization, a special historical development which was to be of outstanding importance in laying solid foundations for the free world of the nineteenth and twentieth centuries. This development was predominantly political, though it was thoroughly ensnarled with social, religious, economic, and intellectual factors. It is a series of revolutions, beginning with those in England of the seventeenth century and including the American and French Revolutions of the late eighteenth century.

The English revolutions had definite religious origins, though the political and economic aspirations of the middle class and the country gentry gave them much of their driving force. Thereafter the revolutions sometimes had religious implications, but other factors were more significant. The American Revolution must be thought of as part of European history, for its causes were part of British imperial development and it had major repercussions not only in Britain but on the Continent. The French Revolution was the most shattering that was to occur before the twentieth century. Its effects were profound and far-reaching. Europe and the world were never, after it, to be the same again. It was to be the focus not only of political ideas of enduring influence like liberty, equality, and democracy, but also it was to create a division between "Right" (conservative) and "Left" (liberal or radical) that was permanent, and to give rise to an intense nationalism in France that was eventually to be communicated by a kind of contagion to every country on every continent.

Attempts have been made to draw parallels among the various revolutions and there are certain similarities among their courses and their events. But each arose from peculiar circumstances and each developed in a manner different from the others. It is, nevertheless, a fact that there grew up a kind of revolutionary tradition. The leaders of each successive revolt were aware of the ideas and the techniques of the previous ones and sometimes quite consciously sought to follow the examples or avoid the mistakes of their predecessors.

CHAPTER 39

The English Revolutions

A. Opposition to the Stuart Kings James I and Charles I

In almost every country of Continental Europe, the seventeenth century was marked by a tendency toward absolute monarchy.[1] At the beginning of the century, while the Tudor Queen Elizabeth was still alive, it might reasonably have been predicted that the political development of England would follow that on the Continent. Yet a peculiar combination of social, economic, and religious conditions, of political traditions, and of the personalities of Elizabeth's successors made the century's development in England unique.

When James VI of Scotland succeeded his cousin Elizabeth in 1603 and became James I of England, the first of its Stuart kings, he was already a thorough believer in strong monarchy and determined to continue the firm rule of his Tudor predecessors. Unlike these, however, he was not content to be absolute in practice. He must expound in writing the theory of divine-right monarchy, that the king derived his authority from God and was responsible only to God. The king's will was law, and the people should obey him without question, as children obey their father.

James in England faced certain disadvantages. He was regarded as a foreigner, a point emphasized by his Scottish accent. He understood the Scottish people, but the

---

[1] The one exception was Poland. See above, p. 437.

English and their ways were something of a mystery to him. He made the mistake of giving special honors and rewards to Scottish favorites who came with him to England. Brought up in bleak, stony Scotland, James thought of England as a land blessed with milk and honey, and endowed with unlimited wealth and resources. Though he was not really extravagant, he liked display and appeared wasteful to many of his subjects, especially the Puritans.

In England James I also found certain traditional restrictions on royal power. There was a two-house parliament of lords and commons, which dated back to the thirteenth century and which in the course of time had acquired very considerable powers over taxation and legislation. The Tudors had handled it by cajolery, bribery, pressure, and popular appeal, and had called it together infrequently. Besides, there was a series of medieval charters, of which Magna Carta of 1215 was the most important. Though this dealt with medieval feudal problems, some of its wording seemed to guarantee the liberties of Englishmen against royal tyranny. There was also the common law, a collection of customs and precedents built up over centuries by English judges and governing the law courts of the land. Much of the common law was designed to protect the individual and his rights, and there were lawyers who were ready to insist that even the king was bound by it.

BRITISH KINGDOMS IN THE
SEVENTEENTH CENTURY

ORKNEY IS.

ATLANTIC OCEAN

HEBRIDES

KINGDOM OF SCOTLAND

Culloden
Aberdeen

NORTH SEA

Glencoe

Stirling Dunbar
Glasgow Edinburgh
Selkirk

NORTH CHANNEL

Newcastle
Durham

Londonderry
Donegal Belfast
Armagh
Sligo

ISLE OF MAN

York
Marston Hull
Moor

KINGDOM OF IRELAND

Kells
Drogheda
Galway Athlone
Boyne R. Dublin
Wicklow

IRISH SEA

Liverpool

Lincoln

Chester

Limerick

Nottingham
Naseby
Coventry

Waterford

WALES

KINGDOM OF ENGLAND Cambridge

Cork

Oxford
London
Windsor Thames R. Canterbury Dover
Bristol Calais
Portsmouth

Exeter

Plymouth

ENGLISH CHANNEL

FRANCE

CHANNEL IS.

In addition, James I faced, though neither he nor his contemporaries understood it clearly, an almost insoluble financial problem. The flow of silver from America was forcing up prices all over Europe with startling rapidity.[1] James came to the throne in the middle of this price rise. On the one hand, his revenues were more or less fixed by custom. The King was supposed to live "of his own," that is, on the regular income of the royal estates and dues together with the customs duties. Land and other taxes were voted only reluctantly and as emergency measures. Yet every year the price of the goods and services needed by the King and his government was going up. Either James had to turn to Parliament for added grants

of money, which that body would give only in return for increased control over policy, or he had to try to squeeze out added funds without recourse to Parliament, a procedure which seemed tyrannical to many people.

Finally, and perhaps most crucially of all, James was confronted by a very difficult religious problem. He approved most heartily of the Anglican Church, with its bishops, its ritual, and its tradition of royal supremacy. But within that church, there was growing up a strong body of opinion, Calvinist in tone, which wished to simplify or eliminate the ceremonies, to reduce the powers of the bishops, and to give more weight to meetings of ministers. Those who held these views were called Puritans because they wished to "purify" the Anglican Church,

[1] See above, pp. 406–407.

and they were especially numerous in certain cities, especially London, in the increasingly powerful business classes, and in Parliament. Even more radical were the thoroughgoing Calvinists, who wanted to do away with bishops altogether and to make either Presbyterianism or Congregationalism the state religion in England, and if these radicals were few in 1603, their numbers grew rapidly in the ensuing years. Both the Puritans and the more extreme "Independents" were characterized by a fanatical fear and hatred of Catholicism, by a great faith in the Bible with a strong tendency to emphasize the spirit and teachings of the Old Testament just as much as, if not more than, the precepts of the New, 'and by a simplicity of manner, speech, dress, and Sabbath observance that seemed like stark austerity to their more easygoing fellow-citizens.

With all these problems, it was clear that James's task as ruler was not going to be an easy one. From the start financial difficulties crowded in upon him. When Parliament refused him added revenues, the King resorted to the imposition of additional customs duties, the grant of monopolies (which interfered with free business), the sale of titles, and the solicitation of "benevolences" (forced loans). Parliament promptly protested against such practices. But Parliament's objections only increased the wrath of the King. The noisiest parliamentarians were imprisoned or sent home with royal scoldings. In 1621, the Commoners entered in their journal a "great protestation" against the King's interference. This so angered James that with his own royal hand he tore the protestation out of the journal and presently dissolved the unruly Parliament. But the quarrel continued and James's last Parliament had the audacity to impeach his lord treasurer.

The dispute with Parliament was embittered by religious conflict. The Puritans, with increasing vigor, were raising objections to Anglican ceremonies, reminiscent of "popery," such as the use of the ring in marriages. They were denouncing Maypole dances, Christmas games, and all festivities not in keeping with an austerely Calvinist view of life. In 1604, a large number of Puritan ministers presented to the King a petition on the reform of the Anglican Church and their proposals were discussed at a conference at the royal palace of Hampton Court. Taking offence at what he believed were disparagements of the Anglican bishops, James I declared that as for those Puritans who would do away with bishops he would make them conform or "harry them out of the land." James did accede to one of the Puritan requests and appointed a board of scholars to make a new English translation of the Bible. It appeared in 1611 and is called the King James version. It is a masterpiece of English prose, despite its many authors. Fresh and colorful with the vigor of the vernacular, it greatly influenced the style and manner of many later works of English literature.

The religious bitterness was intensified by a rising tide of anti-Catholic feeling. James was suspected of harboring friendly feelings toward the Catholics and wishing to grant them toleration. But when a plot by some fanatical Catholics to blow up the King and the House of Lords was discovered (1605), public opinion forced the application of fierce penalties upon Catholic priests and their adherents. James increased his unpopularity by his foreign policy, for he showed himself determined to make friends with Catholic Spain, the hated enemy of England. To this policy he sacrificed Sir Walter Raleigh, who was executed in 1618 for attacks on Spain which would have been rewarded by Elizabeth. James's failure to take any real part in the Thirty Years' War was motivated partly by his desire to save money and partly by his eagerness to appease Spain. But the fact that he did not help his Calvinist son-in-law, Frederick of the Palatinate, added to the Puritan feeling against him.

Despite the difficulties and troubles of the reign, considerable commercial and colonial progress was made by the English under James I. The East India Company founded by Elizabeth, after some initial setbacks, and in the face of Dutch jealousy and opposition, sponsored a number of successful ventures in Asia. In America, colonies were founded at Jamestown in Virginia (1607) and at Plymouth in New England (1620). The latter was the work of Congregationalists or Separatists, who were opposed to the religious situation in England

and to the laws which punished dissent from Anglicanism. The Bermuda islands were settled in 1612, and were soon, like Virginia, growing tobacco. But the greater the growth of English commerce and colonies, the more the difficulties of the crown increased, for it was the trading classes and the London merchants who were most strongly Puritan, and whose representatives in Parliament were most eager to limit the royal power.

At the death of James in 1625, he was succeeded by his son, Charles, who had been reared in England and should have understood the English better than his father. He was handsome, dignified, and well-mannered. But he proved himself stubborn and unyielding. No less than James, he was eager to maintain all the royal prerogatives. In religion, he was a good Anglican, but he leaned toward that wing called "high church" which believed in forms and ceremonies and which, to rigid Puritans, seemed almost Catholic. From the start, Charles I was in trouble. He married a French Catholic princess who brought hated French priests in her train. He clashed with, and dissolved, his first Parliament, which had attacked his showy but worthless favorite, the Duke of Buckingham. When he made popular moves like sending a fleet against the Spanish port of Cadiz or seeking to aid the French Protestants at La Rochelle, the expeditions failed miserably. A second Parliament which tried to impeach Buckingham was dissolved, and a third was summoned only when the financial situation seemed desperate.

The third Parliament in 1628 granted subsidies to the King, but only in return for his signature to its *Petition of Right*, by which Charles promised not to levy taxes without its authorization, not to establish martial law in peace time, not to quarter soldiers on private houses, and not to order arbitrary arrests or imprisonments. But even these concessions were not enough. Only the assassination of Buckingham prevented Parliament from impeaching that unpopular minister. And soon the House of Commons was attempting to check the unauthorized collection of customs duties by the King (the customs were a major and growing item in the revenues), and to prevent the introduction of "popish" ceremonies into the Anglican Church.

Charles was now so thoroughly disgusted with Parliament that he determined to rule without it. For eleven years (1629–1640), in spite of financial and religious difficulties, he carried on a "personal," as distinct from a parliamentary, government. Had this attempt been in the long run successful, England might well have been transformed into an absolute monarchy like France, and the growth of political liberty and democracy might have been long postponed.

Without the consent of Parliament, Charles was bound not to collect direct taxes. He was therefore driven to the most peculiar expedients. He revived old feudal laws and collected fines for their infraction. He sold monopolies on wine, salt, soap, and coal for large sums, thereby enraging the trading classes, who lost business, and the people, who paid higher prices. Even more obnoxious was a device called "ship money." The king had long had the right to exact money or ships from seaboard towns for the support of the navy. But Charles now sought to regularize these contributions and to collect them from inland towns as well. To test the legality of this procedure, a certain John Hampden, egged on by his Puritan friends, refused to pay the twenty shillings required of him. The majority of the judges, subservient to the King, held that ship money was legal. But Hampden was hailed as a hero by the opponents of the crown.

Opposition to financial exactions continued to go hand in hand with bitter religious disputes. Charles had entrusted the conduct of religious affairs to William Laud, a high-church Anglican whom he named archbishop of Canterbury. Restrictions on Puritans were increased, and certain practices and vestments of the Catholic Church were reinstated in the Anglican Church. Puritan clergy were forced to read from the pulpits a royal declaration encouraging sinful Sunday sports like archery and dancing on the green.

Meanwhile Charles was creating the mechanism of arbitrary rule. Aided by Laud and the able Thomas Wentworth, Earl of Strafford, he developed a strong Privy Council which issued orders to the local justices of the peace. The prerogative courts (like the Star Chamber)[1] were strengthened, and they firmly enforced the King's will. The common-law courts were manned with judges who would support the King. Much that Charles did was worthy. Strafford gave Ireland the best English rule it had ever had. The royal government showed a real concern for the poorer classes and sought to improve their condition. Regulations against economic abuses were elaborated. But all such economic legislation only irked the Puritan business classes, and all Charles' good intentions were vitiated by his arbitrary methods.

In his Scottish policy Charles overreached himself. With the zealous aid of Archbishop Laud, he sought to reform the Scottish Presbyterian Church in an Anglican direction. The angry Scottish Presbyterians signed a covenant, swearing to defend their religion (1638); and, deposing the bishops set over them by the King, they rose in revolt. Failing to crush the rebellion and in desperate need of money for his army, Charles summoned at last another English parliament (1640). After three weeks of bootless wrangling, this so-called Short Parliament was dissolved. Still unable to check the advance of the rebellious Scots into northern England, Charles convoked (1640) a new Parliament, which, because it lasted for twenty years, has been called the Long Parliament. In both England and Scotland, absolute monarchy now faced a crisis —and indeed a rebellion.

B. The Great Rebellion and Cromwell's Puritan Dictatorship

Under the leadership of Puritans like John Pym, John Hampden, and Oliver Cromwell, the Long Parliament, confident of its own strength and the King's weakness, began to assert its authority. With blow after blow it hewed away at the royal authority. The prerogative courts were abolished. The King's financial expedients, like ship money, were forbidden. The King's power to dissolve parliament was annulled, and a "triennial act" required the legislature to meet every three years whether summoned by the King or not. Parliament went

[1] See above, p. 288.

further and after long proceedings forced the execution of the King's most loyal servants, Strafford and Laud.

Despite these many victories for Parliament, the King's position was temporarily improved. His armed forces turned back the Scottish invaders, and the outbreak of a rebellion in Ireland seemed to require, for its suppression, a larger royal army which might eventually be utilized to overcome the Parliament. Besides, Parliament itself was becoming divided between extremists and moderates. Charles chose this juncture to make an attempt to strengthen his position. In person he appeared in Parliament (1642) and sought to arrest five members who were his leading opponents. This act produced a definite break between the King and the legislature. Parliament proceeded to pass ordinances without the royal seal and to issue a call to arms. The levy of troops contrary to the King's will was sheer rebellion. Charles in turn raised the royal standard at Nottingham and called his loyal subjects to suppress the rebellion. The issue was squarely joined between absolute monarchy and the revolutionary forces of parliament and Puritanism.

The division of the country between King and Parliament cut across every class and section of the country. Even families were split. But in a general way the King had the support of the titled nobles, the country gentlemen or squires, the "high church" Anglicans, and the remaining Catholics. The royal cause was likewise strong in the north and west of England. In support of Parliament, on the other hand, rallied a minority of the nobility and gentry, and a large majority of the middle-class townsfolk, especially in London, together with the Puritans, Presbyterians, Congregationalists, and religious radicals. Parliament found its strongest support in the south and east of England. The lower classes were less concerned about the issues but tended to go with the leaders of their respective districts. Thus the artisans of London fought for Parliament, and the peasants of the north of England for the King. In common speech, the close cropped heads of the "God-fearing" supporters of Parliament won them the nickname of "Roundheads," while the royalist upper classes, not thinking it a sinful

Trial of Archbishop Laud, in the House of Lords. Wenceslaus Hollar (d. 1677)

vanity to wear their hair in long curls, were called "Cavaliers."

In the Long Parliament, the predominance in religious matters lay with the Presbyterians, who were more radical than those Puritans who merely wished to reform the Anglican Church, and less extreme than the Independents (mainly Congregationalists). The parliamentary majority, therefore, made a "solemn league and covenant" with the Scottish Presbyterians, to establish Presbyterianism throughout the British Isles. Though the royal army won some engagements in 1642 and 1643, it was crushed by the parliamentary forces at Marston Moor (1644). At once the Presbyterian majority in parliament abolished the office of bishop, decreed the removal of altars, and tolerated the smashing of crucifixes, images, and stained glass windows. At this point, the Presbyterians seemed ready to make peace with the King and to restore him to power, if he would accept the new religious settlement.

But the parliamentary army was growing restive. Oliver Cromwell, a stern Independent, had organized a cavalry regiment of "honest sober Christians," who charged into battle singing psalms and acquired by their steel-like invincibility the name of "Ironsides." So successful were Cromwell's troops that a large part of the parliamentary forces were reorganized on his plan into the "New Model" army. This army was strongly Independent in sympathy, hostile to Presbyterian and Anglican alike, and in favor of no compromise with the King.

The New Model army defeated Charles again at Naseby (1645) and compelled his surrender the next year. Then, after some hesitation, its leaders turned against the irresolute Presbyterian majority in parliament. A certain Colonel Pride, backed by his soldiers, "purged" the House of Commons of 143 Presbyterian members (1648), leaving only some sixty Independents to deliberate on the nation's affairs. This "Rump," or sitting part of Parliament, acting on its own authority, appointed a "high court of justice" by whose sentence Charles I was beheaded on January 30, 1649. The Rump then decreed England to be a Commonwealth with neither king nor House of Lords. In the next year, the parliamentary

Oliver Cromwell. After a mezzotint by Peter Lily (d. 1680).

Courtesy Bettmann Archive

army was placed under the supreme command of Oliver Cromwell.

During the ensuing eight years Oliver Cromwell was practical dictator in England. A country gentleman by birth, he had pleaded the Puritan cause in Parliament in 1628, and emerged as a leader of the Independents in the Long Parliament and as the ablest soldier in the civil war. In private life, Cromwell liked music, art, and a cup of wine. But everywhere he carried with him an austere Calvinist conviction that he was doing God's work, and his fiercely eloquent speeches were interlarded with Biblical phrases. His force of character was great, his temper occasionally violent, his statesmanship of a high order. Though he was the leader of the Independents (or Congregationalists) who formed only a minority of the country, the fact that he had the backing of a victorious army made him the real power in the land.

Leaving the Rump to legislate, Cromwell in 1650 put down with fire and rivers of blood the rebellion of the Irish. Then he turned against the Scots, who, dismayed at the ousting of the Presbyterians from Parliament, had rallied to the cause of Prince Charles, son of the executed King. At Worcester (1651) the Scots were defeated, and all the British Isles were at the mercy of

Cromwell and his army. The Rump meanwhile had passed the first great English Navigation Act, which aimed to restrict commerce with England to English ships and was designed to prevent Dutch vessels from trading with England. This law led to a brief Anglo-Dutch naval war, in which the English fared well, but of which Cromwell did not thoroughly approve. In fact, he was becoming disgusted with the Rump and in 1653 he turned it out saying, "Your hour is come, the Lord hath done with you."

For the next five years, Cromwell attempted to provide some legal foundation for his Puritan dictatorship, though without success. First, he assembled a legislature named by himself on the recommendation of Independent ministers. It was given the name of Barebones' Parliament after one of its members with the peculiarly Puritan name of Praisegod Barebones. But it ventured to quarrel with Cromwell, and he dismissed it. Then Cromwell had an Instrument of Government (the first important written constitution in Europe) drawn up. It conferred upon him the title of "Lord Protector" of England for life, and provided for a one-house parliament for England, Scotland, and Ireland, elected by persons not identified with the royalist party. Despite this exclusion of royalists from the polls, the Independents could not win a majority in the new parliament. Before long it was at odds with the Protector, and in 1655 Cromwell abruptly sent it home. Thereafter he made no pretense of consulting popular wishes. The British Isles were divided into areas and each was placed under the rule of a general. Cromwell's power was more absolute than that of Charles I had ever been. With a firm hand he put down Presbyterian, Catholic, and Anglican alike, and repressed the activities of extreme radicals, whether political (the "Levelers"), or economic (the "Diggers"), or religious (the "Fifth Monarchy men").

Despite the dictatorial and tyrannical form of his rule, Cromwell's authority was unshakable and he enjoyed some popularity. He was the beloved leader of an army respected for its rigid discipline and feared for its mercilessness. Under his strict enforcement of order, industry flourished and commerce throve. His conduct of foreign affairs was so skillful that it satisfied English patriotism by increasing England's prestige, and brought profit to many English purses. With the Dutch and the French, Cromwell made advantageous commercial treaties. For the first time in centuries Jews were allowed to come into England, and they brought with them capital and commercial knowledge. By an alliance with France against Spain, the English army won Dunkirk, while the English navy seized Jamaica, sank a Spanish fleet, and brought home shiploads of Spanish silver.

But with all its success Cromwell's rule struck no deep roots in England. His death in 1658 left the army without a master and the country without a government. Oliver's son Richard abdicated after a brief attempt to succeed his father. The army restored the Rump, forced it to recall the ousted Presbyterian members, and then finally obliged the reconstituted Long Parliament to summon a new and freely elected "Convention Parliament." Meanwhile, one of the generals, Monck by name, negotiated for a restoration of the Stuart family to the kingship. In 1660, King Charles II returned from exile and disembarked at Dover. His entry into London was a veritable triumph, "the wayes strew'd with flowers, the bells ringing, the streets hung with tapistry, fountaines running with wine."

England might relax from the long tension of civil war and dictatorship at this royal Restoration, but it could never be the same again. Twenty years of Calvinist rule, with sports and plays and frivolous music banned, had put an end to "Merrie England." The literature had taken on a dreary cast and the greatest poet of the time, John Milton, had latterly been busy with government work and controversial pamphlets. It was only after Cromwell's death that he turned to the composition of his great religious epic, *Paradise Lost*. The grievances and ideals that had inspired the Great Rebellion were being forgotten, and a new generation welcomed with relief the replacement of a stern dictatorship by a restored monarchy which, it was hoped, would operate within the known limits of law and custom.

C. Temporary Stuart Restoration

The narrow basis of Cromwell's popular support explains to some degree the ease with which Charles II won back the crown. The Scots and Irish had hated Cromwell as a bloody conqueror. The Anglicans and the Presbyterians in England had disapproved of his rule. The experiment with Congregationalist republicanism had convinced the majority of people that the old monarchy was a better system. All they now asked were assurances against royal despotism and, where the coin was promises, Charles II was a ready buyer. He swore to observe Magna Carta and the "Petition of Right," to respect Parliament, and to refrain from interfering with religious policy and from levying illegal taxes.

At the return of Charles II, the Anglican bishops and Cavalier nobles resumed their offices. Things seemed to slip back into the old grooves. But the strong monarchy of the Tudors or of the first two Stuarts—James I and Charles I—was not restored. The prerogative courts were not reëstablished, nor was the Privy Council given back its wide powers. Most of the King's old feudal privileges and revenues were abandoned, and there was less talk of the "divine right" of kings. Parliament emerged stronger than before, with a much firmer control of religious and financial matters. Though many a Cavalier noble or squire could not win back the estates he had sold or mortgaged under Cromwell's heavy taxation, it was the landed classes who were dominant during the restoration period (1660–1689). Charles II retained his throne and no small measure of power by coöperating with them, humoring the Parliaments in which they sat, and retreating skillfully whenever the opposition to his policies became too strong.

At the beginning of the reign, the position of the country landholder was strengthened in a way that seemed unimportant but had significant long-run implications. Parliament abolished the surviving feudal fees, dues, and services, so that it was no longer necessary to make payments to the king or another for inheriting an estate, for the wardship of a minor, the marriage of an heiress, and so on. Thus England abandoned the feudal theory that land was held in return for military service to the crown or the overlord, and confirmed the newer principle that land is private property.

In religious policy the Cavalier nobles and squires, staunchly Anglican, had their way. Two thousand Calvinist clergymen were deprived of their offices by an Act of Uniformity (1662), which required clergymen to accept the Anglican prayer-book, while a "Five Mile Act" (1665) kept them at least that distance from their old churches. A Corporation Act (1661) excluded from town offices "dissenters" from Anglicanism, and a Conventicle Act (1664) sought to prevent their religious meetings. Yet in the midst of this triumph of Anglicanism the King had his reservations.

At heart Charles II, and also his brother James, were Catholics, for their mother was a Catholic and they had grown up in exile in the strongly Catholic atmosphere of the French court. Charles, in the secret treaty of Dover (1670), promised Louis XIV, in return for a large pension, to reintroduce Catholicism into England, but, sensing the fierce hatred of "popery" even among the Anglicans, he kept his views to himself, and his formal conversion to the faith of Rome was postponed until the time of his death. James, Duke of York, and heir to the throne, was less tactful or more forthright. His conversion was announced in 1672. At the same time, Charles II, by a royal "declaration of indulgence," suspended the laws against both dissenters and Catholics. This stirred a big wave of anti-Catholic sentiment. Charles II was compelled to withdraw his declaration, and James to give up the public offices he held.

Anti-Catholic feeling reached another high point in 1678 when wild tales of a "popish plot" gained currency. There was no such "plot," but crowds rioted and several noted Catholics were executed as a sacrifice to popular feeling. In the next year, a bill was introduced into Parliament which would have excluded James and any other Catholic from the throne. The Exclusion Bill failed to pass. But from the discussions which it occasioned there gradually emerged in Parliament and in the country two parties. The one which came to be called "Whig" favored the bill and attracted the support of dissenters, of the business classes, and of those landowners who were liberal in their Anglicanism and who wished to strengthen Parliament against the King. The other party, called "Tory," was more rigidly Anglican. Since it upheld the idea of a strong hereditary monarchy and wished both to maintain the *status quo* and at all costs to avoid a renewal of civil war, it opposed the Bill. In the last years of Charles' reign the Whigs were somewhat discredited, and some of them were involved in an abortive rising which sought at Charles' death to put his illegitimate but Protestant son, the Duke of Monmouth, on the throne instead of James.

In economic matters, the Restoration witnessed a relaxation of the internal economic controls used by the Tudors and the first two Stuarts. The guilds had decayed and were unable to reëstablish their monopolies. The old regulations on industry and the grain trade were enforced with less effectiveness. The relief of the poor fell more and more into the hands of the local parish authorities. But with this decrease in the government's control of economic affairs in England, went a strengthening of the regulations on colonial and foreign trade. A Navigation Act of 1660 reënforced the one passed in 1651, and the system was further developed by acts of 1663 and 1673. These laws, taken together, were the bases of English colonial policy and an expression of English mercantilism. Their object was to build up English shipping and to make sure that the trade of the English colonies profited England alone.

This economic legislation was aimed as a direct blow at Dutch dominance in commerce and it led to two more Anglo-Dutch wars. In the first of these (1664–1667) the British seized the Dutch colony of New Amsterdam and rechristened it New York in honor of James, Duke of York. But the Dutch fleet swept the Channel clear of English shipping and the Dutch Admiral De Ruyter even sailed up the Thames and terrorized London. The second of the Anglo-Dutch wars (1672–1674) was merged in the attack of the French on Holland. During its course, the English public and parliamentary pressure forced Charles II to withdraw from the attack on Holland and then to join the anti-French alliance. The English were coming to see that their chief rival, the real threat to their commercial and colonial progress, was not Holland but France. They were coming to realize, too, that the union of Catholicism and absolutism which Louis XIV represented in Europe was what they feared both abroad and at home. Henceforth, for nearly a century and a half, England's wars were with France.

The mid-1660's were memorable years in the history of London, which had been rapidly growing into an important center of trade and industry, and now ranked in Europe with Amsterdam or Paris or Lisbon. In 1665, London was swept by the plague. Though two thirds of the population (estimated at 460,000) fled to avoid the contagion, more than 75,000 died amid scenes of terror. The next spring the Dutch Admiral De Ruyter sailed up the Thames, burning English shipping and bringing dismay to the almost defenseless metropolis. The following autumn a great fire swept over London and reduced most of the older sections of the city to ashes. From these tribulations London rose larger and more important than ever. Its commerce kept the Thames busy with ships plying to every part of Europe, to the Near East, to the American colonies, and to India. Its merchant class was growing rapidly in wealth. The goldsmiths had become private bankers and were accepting deposits and lending out large sums.

Though parliament had voted Charles II a royal revenue that totaled about £1,200,000, the sum was insufficient for the expenses of his government. Despite his pension from Louis XIV, Charles was forced to borrow continually. In 1672, he announced that instead of paying back a million and a quarter pounds he had borrowed from a group of goldsmiths, he would consider the sum as a permanent loan. This hardly added to the popularity of the crown.

A puritanically minded business man had other reasons for disapproving of Charles, for the royal court represented a complete reaction from the austerity of Cromwell's time. Surrounded by a bevy of mistresses, Charles set an example of blatant immorality which was imitated by many of the upper

James II. After a portrait by Sir Godfrey Kneller (d. 1723).

Courtesy Bettmann Archive

classes. Manners, copied from the French, were polished, but language was coarse. Gambling was all the rage. The theatres had been opened again, and the witty dramatists of the time imitated French models with bawdy gusto. The courtiers and their imitators, with gaudy clothes and indolent manners, flocked to see such plays as William Wycherley's *The Gentleman Dancing Master*, or Sir George Etherege's *The Man of Mode or Sir Fopling Flutter*. It was all a far cry from the psalms and sermons of Cromwell's day.

It was his good-natured tact which carried Charles II sucessfully through a difficult reign of twenty-five years. Without principles, he sought only to maintain his position and to increase his authority. He was always ready to compromise or to retreat. So skillfully did he use the feeling against the Whigs, which arose from their excesses, that during the last four years of his reign he was able to rule without Parliament. When he died in 1685, the position of the crown seemed firm and even strong. But the ensuing years were to witness dramatic changes.

Uprisings in Scotland and in England (led by the Duke of Monmouth) greeted the accession of James II, but were easily put down. The country wanted no more civil war. Indeed, James might have ruled successfully had he been a Protestant, or had he been willing to play a secondary role and give real power to Parliament. It was the combination of his Catholicism with his attempts to rule more and more despotically that roused the fear and opposition of the English leaders and of the masses of the people.

In the three years following 1685, James gave ample evidence that he was eager to increase his own power and to favor Catholicism. Even the Tories, who believed in strong royal rule, were shocked by his attempt to create a standing professional army and to officer it with Catholics. In addition, he relaxed the laws against Catholics and dissenters by a new "declaration of indulgence" (1687) and sought to place Catholics in high posts in the universities of Oxford and Cambridge, and in the town and royal governments. When he ordered a second "declaration of indulgence" read from the church pulpits (1688), seven Anglican bishops objected, and, since no jury would convict them, they were acquitted of the charges brought against them.

D. The "Glorious" Revolution of 1688–1689

Though James had alienated both Whigs and Tories, he might have kept his throne but for a change in the prospective royal succession. He was now fifty-five years old and his heirs were his two daughters by a first marriage: Mary, wife of her cousin William III, Stadholder of Holland; and Anne, married to a Danish prince. Both of these daughters and both their husbands were Protestants. So long as his heirs were Protestants, the country might have been willing to put up with James II. But in the late spring of 1688, a son was born to James by his second and Catholic wife, Mary of Modena. The boy would not only take precedence over his sisters in the succession, but obviously he would be reared in the Catholic faith. Almost at once, the English leaders, Whig and Tory alike, began conspiring to oust James and to bring in William and Mary as rulers. William listened with interest to the proposals, since he was eager to swing England into line against France for the war that was then in the making.[1]

In November 1688, William landed in

[1] See above, p. 428.

England with a small Dutch army. Welcomed enthusiastically by the Protestant masses, the Dutch Stadholder entered London without opposition. James, deserted by his army, fled to France. The revolution was quite bloodless in England. In Ireland, however, there was a popular Catholic rising in favor of James, which William was able to crush in the decisive battle of the Boyne (1690). An irregular parliament presented William and Mary with the crown as joint sovereigns, declaring that James had tried to overthrow the constitution of the kingdom, and, by his flight, had left the throne vacant.

The inner meaning of this revolution was that henceforth Parliament, not the king, was to be supreme in the British Isles. If Parliament could put aside the rightful king and his son (James, called the "Old Pretender"), and give the crown to others, then its authority was final. To be sure, the king still seemed to have considerable power, but the "Glorious" Revolution was a decisive turning point in the growth of parliamentary supremacy. It must be remembered that the Parliament of the time was by no means democratic. The system of election was such that in the country it was the big landowners who had the real influence, and in the towns and cities it was the wealthy members of the middle class. For nearly a century and a half after the Revolution, England was to be ruled by an aristocratic Parliament which represented not the people as a whole, but rather the landlords and wealthy merchants.

In establishing its own power, however, the aristocratic Parliament enacted legislation which, by limiting royal authority, did protect all citizens from royal tyranny. The Declaration of Rights (1689), which became law as the Bill of Rights, provided that the sovereign must be an Anglican, that the King could not suspend laws by declaration or otherwise, and that he could not maintain any army or levy taxes without the consent of Parliament. It provided that the King should not interfere with free speech, free elections, or free discussion in Parliament, and that the people should be allowed to make petitions to the King. It likewise demanded impartial juries and frequent parliaments. In addition, Parliament adopted a new device for strengthening its

position. From 1689 on, it granted taxes and made appropriations for the army for one year only, and it similarly passed the Mutiny Act (requiring soldiers to obey orders under penalty of court martial) only for a year at a time. A compromise on religion was also part of the "settlement" of 1689. While the "Toleration Act" (1689) imposed exceptionally severe restrictions and penalties on Catholics and debarred non-Anglicans from public affairs, it accorded to the dissenting Protestant sects full freedom of conscience and of public worship.

Here were the first fruits of the Revolution of 1689. Absolute monarchy was finally overthrown in Britain. Parliament was entrenched in power. The Protestant character of the state was confirmed. The influence and predominance of the British aristocracy were strengthened.

William III accepted the changes in the system of government because his main interest was in bringing England into the War of the League of Augsburg (1689–1697) against France, and this he was able to do successfully, with the support of Parliament and the English people. But there were other results of the new position of Parliament. Now that taxes and expenditures were increasingly under its control, people were more ready to lend money to the government and in 1693 it became possible to organize a regular national debt. At the start people who subscribed to loans received ten per cent interest, but the rate fell rapidly to four and even three per cent. In the eighteenth century the English Government could raise large sums of money at a very low cost. In 1694, moreover, the Bank of England was founded, and though it was a private institution, it proved itself invaluable to the government in holding deposits, sending funds abroad, advancing short term credits, and managing the national debt. During the same period, England reformed and regularized its coinage, and the techniques of buying and selling stock in the various companies and of writing insurance were rapidly improved. By 1700 England not only had a more business-like government, and one friendly to the commercial interests, but it also had a financial system that was able to meet the growing demands of the ensuing decades.

E. Triumph of Parliamentary Government

Since William III was more interested in foreign war and diplomacy than in domestic affairs, he tended to leave the management of English matters to his ministers. He found that the wheels of government turned more smoothly if, when the Whigs held a majority of seats in the House of Commons, all the ministers were Whigs. On the other hand, if the Tories gained the upper hand, it seemed better to have the king's ministers, or the "cabinet" as they began to be called, Tories instead of Whigs. Thus the tenure of a cabinet came slowly to be dependent on its ability to command a majority in parliament. In fact, as the ministers were members of one of the houses of the legislature, they came gradually to be a sort of committee whose duty it was to see that the will of Parliament was carried out. Since the cabinet enforced the laws and carried on the administration, it was clear that Parliament was getting control of the executive as well as the legislative functions of the British Government.

In 1701, Parliament again asserted its authority by determining who should succeed William III. By an Act of Settlement, it excluded the Catholic heirs of James II, together with all other Catholics, and directed that the crown should pass to Anne and her heirs. If she had no children, it was to go at her death to Sophia of Hanover and her heirs. This Sophia was a granddaughter of James I and the daughter of the Calvinist Count Palatine of the Rhine whose election as King of Bohemia had inflamed the Thirty Years' War.[1] The Act likewise provided that England should not be required to wage war on behalf of the foreign possessions of its ruler without the consent of Parliament, and it placed a number of other restrictions on the crown. Of these the most important was that royal judges should hold office "during good behavior" and not "at the king's pleasure." Unsuitable judges were to be removed only at the request of Lords and Commons. Parliament was gaining control of the judiciary as well as the executive.

Anne, who succeeded William III in 1702, was more English than he and more active

[1] See above, p. 395.

in English affairs. She was the last English sovereign who vetoed acts of Parliament, and toward the close of her reign she chose a Tory cabinet in the face of a Whig majority in the House of Commons. It was this cabinet that negotiated the Peace of Utrecht on terms reasonably favorable to Louis XIV. Though Anne might act as if she were sovereign by right instead of the will of Parliament, she was uneasily conscious that her half-brother, the son of James II, had a better claim to the throne than she and that this "Old Pretender," as he came to be called, had many supporters in England, and especially in Scotland, who would have liked to see him on the throne of England as James III.

It was partly to ensure the succession of the Protestant descendants of Sophia of Hanover that the parliaments of England and of Scotland in 1707 passed the Act of Union which finally fused the two kingdoms into one—Great Britain. The English Parliament at Westminster was transformed into a British Parliament by the inclusion of Scottish lords and commoners. Though the Union had been opposed in Scotland and was put through there only by bribery and pressure, it gave new prosperity to the northern kingdom by bringing it into the English commercial and colonial system and removing trade barriers between the two parts of the island. It gave to able Scots a chance to win wider political power in the new united government.

At Anne's death (1714) there were, indeed, plots to put the Old Pretender on the throne. The next year "James III" actually landed in Scotland, rallied some support, and advanced toward England. But his army of clansmen was defeated at Preston, and he soon had to return to the continent. Meanwhile, the son of Sophia of Hanover had come to London and as George I had firmly seated his ponderous form on the British throne.

George I (1714–1727) was dazzled by the fortune that thus dropped a rich kingdom in his lap. But he was slow of wit; he spoke no English; and he was far more interested in German affairs than in British. After some half-hearted attempts to carry on cabinet meetings in broken Latin, George simply stopped attending them and left his

English ministers to handle the complicated parliamentary politics which he did not understand.

George II (1727–1760) spoke broken English, but his heart, too, was in German Hanover where he was an absolutist prince. In so far as the first two Georges understood British politics at all, they favored the Whigs, who had consistently supported the Hanoverian succession, whereas many Tories had been "Jacobites," or partisans of the Stuart pretender. In general, these Kings left the Whig cabinet to rule the country, and the Whigs, profiting from the discredit of the Tories and consolidating their position by bribery and parliamentary manipulation, were able to maintain themselves in power during the whole of the two reigns. The Kings accepted every act of Parliament and never ventured to exercise the royal right of veto, which fell into disuse. The first two Georges reigned, but they did not rule. And the British were content to have it so, for to them the Kings were foreigners who were endured because they were symbols representing the Protestant royal succession.

It was during this period of Whig ascendancy that cabinet government emerged and that the office of prime minister came into existence. For twenty-one years (1721–1742) Sir Robert Walpole managed to retain the royal favor and the control of a majority in the House of Commons. Though he disclaimed any such title, he was generally recognized as "prime" minister, prime in importance, prime in executive authority, with the selection of the rest of the cabinet virtually in his hands. Thenceforth it became a tradition that the crown should appoint from the majority party in Parliament the prime minister, or head of the cabinet, and that all other cabinet ministers should be appointed by the crown upon the nomination of the prime minister.

The king was still the head of the state and in law still the ruler of his kingdom. In his name were all laws passed and treaties made. Under him both church and state were administered. But in practice, by the traditions and precedents that made up the unwritten British constitution, most of the king's functions were delegated to his "government"—to a prime minister and cabinet who were not his agents but representatives of Parliament. It was the cabinet that carried on the real business of government. Thus, by the mid-eighteenth century the king could not levy taxes, make laws, maintain an army, control the judiciary, or even appoint ministers, save with parliamentary sanction. The British system of government had evolved through two revolutions and much religious and political turmoil, from a more or less "absolute" monarchy under the Tudors, to the "limited" monarchy of the Hanoverians. The limitations on British monarchy in the eighteenth century consisted in the well-nigh complete power of Parliament, and this Parliament was dominated by a wealthy oligarchy of landowners aided by powerful commercial interests. But even under the Whig oligarchy of the eighteenth century, Britain was an object of admiration to thoughtful men on the continent of Europe, for in limiting royal powers Parliament had built up a respect for courts and for law which went far toward protecting individual rights, and Parliament itself was a forum where citizens could plead the public interests.

CHAPTER 40

The American Revolution

A. Conflict Between Britain and Its Colonies

The American Revolution was not merely a matter of British concern. It had important effects on France and indeed on the whole later history of Europe and the world. In part, it arose because the English had transported overseas, to their thirteen colonies along the North American seaboard, their own system of law and courts which protected and maintained the rights of individuals, and because they had permitted a considerable degree of self-government by provincial legislature, while at the same time they subjected the colonials to irksome mercantilist regulations. The American colonials were conscious of their rights as Britishers and had sufficient political experience to know how to organize for their defense.

Until the end of the Seven Years' War, two factors kept American discontent in check. In the first place, the British policy tended to be one of "salutary neglect." Trade laws, though strict, were enforced sporadically. Evasion was easy, and sober New England merchants smuggled their goods blithely through the loopholes they so readily found. In the second place, the existence of French Canada to the north and French Louisiana to the west kept the English colonists vividly aware of the value of the British army and navy as agencies of defense.

Both these factors were changed at the close of the Seven Years' War. Canada became British, and at the same time the British government decided to tighten up the enforcement of its trade regulations and to make the colonies pay a share of the costs of imperial defense. This program was sponsored by King George III and the ministers through whom he was trying to gain more influence in the government of Great Britain. Indeed, during the whole of the struggle between Britain and the colonies, there was a parallel political conflict within Britain. The center of the strife was King George III himself, for he was trying to build a party of his own among the ruling Whigs, so that he might regain some of the power that his predecessors had lost. By patronage, influence, corruption, and favors, the king sought to rule and to see to it that the government was in the hands of followers like Lord Bute or Lord North. In opposition to the King, the "old Whigs," like the Marquess of Rockingham, Edmund Burke, and later Charles James Fox, sought to thwart the King's efforts and to maintain the parliamentary supremacy that had been gradually built up since 1689. With this group were usually aligned the elder William Pitt (Earl of Chatham) and his large following.

In pursuance of the new policies with regard to the colonies, the British prime minister, George Grenville, in 1764 put through Parliament the Sugar Act. It actually reduced the duties on sugar and molasses brought from the British West Indies to New England, much of which was made into rum for exchange for furs and slaves.

But while the duties were cut, a determined effort to collect them and to check smuggling was made. "Writs of assistance" were issued to the customs collectors to enable them to search private houses. In the next year (1765) the Stamp Act was passed. This sought to raise £100,000 from the colonies by a stamp tax on legal documents, pamphlets, and newspapers. The opposition to these acts in the colonies was immediate and became effective when the colonists began to refuse to purchase British goods. Trade with Britain fell off precipitously. Respectable citizens formed groups called "Sons of Liberty." More important, even, nine colonies, led by Virginia and Massachusetts, sent delegates to a congress which met in New York and adopted resolutions opposing the Stamp Act as contrary to the traditional rights of the colonists.

In fact, in the debates over the Stamp Act the constitutional issue between Britain and the colonies was sharply drawn. The British government held that the colonists were "virtually represented" in Parliament just as were the new cities of Liverpool or Sheffield which elected no members to it. But the Americans, who had developed a system by which the member of a legislature actually represented the district in which he lived, insisted that they were not represented in Parliament and could not, therefore, properly be taxed by it. So violent was the colonial opposition to the Stamp Act that Grenville was forced out of office and Rockingham, the new prime minister, sympathetic to the Americans, secured the repeal of the hated law.

But in 1767 occurred a new attempt to make the colonies provide revenues. Charles Townshend, chancellor of the exchequer, put through a series of acts which levied duties on the importation into the colonies of certain goods, such as glass, lead, paper, and tea, and provided for rigorous collection. Again the colonies protested, and by agreements stopped their importation of British goods. The colonists had previously argued that external duties on trade could be imposed by Parliament and that only internal taxes were improper. Now they opposed the new levies, and their antagonism was only heightened when the legislature in Massachusetts was dissolved for expressing its disapproval of the Townshend Acts. The sale of British goods in the colonies fell off rapidly. People wore homespun cloth and drank sassafras tea.

Resistance led to violence in Boston. Customs officials were beaten up and troops were brought in from Halifax to keep order. Finally in March 1770 blood was shed. The "Boston Massacre" started mildly enough when some snowballs were thrown at the red-coated soldiers. But before it was over shots were fired and four Bostonians were killed. It was by chance that it was on the same day that the new ministry of Lord North got Parliament to repeal all the Townshend duties save only the tax on tea.

Feeling had run too high, however, to be easily soothed. The more radical of the American leaders like Samuel Adams of Massachusetts and Patrick Henry of Virginia kept up their agitation. "Committees of Correspondence" were organized and chapters of Freemasons communicated anti-British sentiments to each other. The duty on tea had been retained to maintain in principle the British right to levy taxes on the colonies, and it was to this principle that the colonists now objected. On December 16, 1773, men dressed up like Indians seized three ships in Boston Harbor and dumped 342 chests of tea into the water.

The "Tea Party" brought a quick reaction intended to cow the rebellious colonists. The British Parliament, led by Lord North, passed the famous five "intolerable acts" (1774). Massachusetts was practically deprived of self-government. Boston Harbor was closed. Troops were quartered on the colonists. In the same year, though for different reasons, Parliament passed a law that seemed to many of the colonials equally threatening. The Quebec Act was intended to settle some of the questions regarding western lands, Canada, and the Indians. But by granting complete religious freedom to the Catholics in Canada it stirred the ire of the New England Calvinists, and by assigning to Quebec all the land north of the Ohio River, it seemed to ignore the claims of four colonies to westward expansion and to eliminate possibilities of settlement, speculation, and trade with the Indians.

Thus it was that when the first Continen-

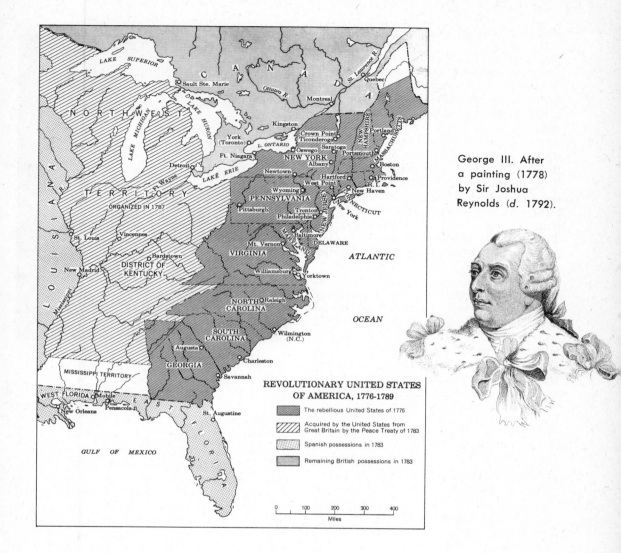

LAKE SUPERIOR

C A N A D A

Sault Ste. Marie

Ottawa R.

St. Lawrence R.

Quebec

Montreal

N O R T H W E S T

LAKE MICHIGAN

LAKE HURON

Kingston

York (Toronto)

L. ONTARIO

Oswego

Crown Point

Ticonderoga

Saratoga

NEW HAMPSHIRE

Portland

Portsmouth

MASSACHUSETTS

Ft. Niagara

NEW YORK

Albany

Boston

Detroit

LAKE ERIE

R. Wayne

Newtown

Hartford

West Point

Providence

R. I.

New Haven

T E R R I T O R Y

ORGANIZED IN 1787

Wyoming

PENNSYLVANIA

CONNECTICUT

New York

Pittsburgh

Trenton

Philadelphia

St. Louis

Vincennes

Baltimore

MARYLAND

DELAWARE

Mt. Vernon

ATLANTIC

DISTRICT OF KENTUCKY

VIRGINIA

New Madrid

Bardstown

Williamsburg

Yorktown

LOUISIANA

Mississippi R.

NORTH CAROLINA

Raleigh

OCEAN

SOUTH CAROLINA

Wilmington (N.C.)

Augusta

GEORGIA

Charleston

MISSISSIPPI TERRITORY

Savannah

WEST FLORIDA

Mobile

New Orleans

Pensacola

EAST FLORIDA

St. Augustine

GULF OF MEXICO

REVOLUTIONARY UNITED STATES OF AMERICA, 1776-1789

The rebellious United States of 1776

Acquired by the United States from Great Britain by the Peace Treaty of 1783

Spanish possessions in 1783

Remaining British possessions in 1783

0   100   200   300   400
Miles

George III. After a painting (1778) by Sir Joshua Reynolds (d. 1792).

tal Congress met at Philadelphia in September 1774, though it had been summoned to secure the redress of grievances and concert measures of opposition that would force the British to recognize the rights of the colonists, there was much that the more radical members could point to as reason for going further. The Congress passed a Declaration of Rights and Grievances, and Lord North, under some pressure from friends of America like the Earl of Chatham and Edmund Burke, put through a Conciliatory Resolve. But this last step came too late, for in April 1775 hostilities broke out at Lexington and Concord. The American Revolution was beginning.

B. The War of American Independence

Matters would hardly have issued in armed conflict if the political and economic events just outlined had not been reënforced by other factors. Americans had long felt that they were being exploited by England and its manufacturers and merchants. Even rich Virginia planters were deeply in debt to British mercantile houses and the debts were passed on from father to son. The industries of the colonists had been throttled, their commerce restricted, and their finances restrained. The privilege of being part of the British commercial empire and collecting bounties on the production of goods like indigo and naval stores no longer seemed an adequate compensation. In addition, the British were woefully ignorant about the colonies and treated the colonials as social inferiors. They ignored even the religious needs of the colonists. There was, for instance, no Anglican bishop in America, so that an Anglican from Virginia or New York, in order to be confirmed, had to journey to England. Moreover, it must be remembered that by 1775 many of the inhabitants of the colonies were not English. There were many Scotch, Scotch-Irish, Germans, or French who had no particular ties of affection to the mother country.

Leading colonists were also much affected by the currents of eighteenth century thought. They had read Locke on natural rights and on the social contract between sovereign and subject. Some of them had read Montesquieu on the limitation of royal power and Rousseau on rule by the people. If many of the wealthier colonials put loyalty to the king above all else, the majority believed that they were being unjustly oppressed and that tyranny must be resisted as it had been in the days of Charles I or of James II. Indeed the Revolution was in some senses a civil war in both America and in Britain. In every colony there was an important minority, often including many of the leading citizens who fought for, worked for, or at least hoped for the success of the British army. More than seventy thousand "loyalists" left the colonies during the course of the war or at its close. Many more than that at length made their peace with their fellow-citizens. In Britain, in the Parliament and outside it, there were, during the whole period, many who wished for the success of the colonists, sometimes because they thought the American cause was just, often because they wanted the King to be defeated in his attempt to increase the authority of the crown. Many British officers gave up their commissions rather than fight against the Americans with whom they had marched against the French. Jeffrey Amherst, the captor of Louisburg and Montreal, refused to take command of the British troops in New England.

Practically, after Lexington and Concord, and intellectually, after the ringing sen-

Thomas Paine. After a painting by George Romney (d. 1802).

Courtesy Bettmann Archive

tences of Thomas Paine's pamphlet *Common Sense* (January 1776), there was no possibility of turning back for the Americans. But the definitive breaking point was the Declaration of Independence written by Thomas Jefferson and adopted by the Second Continental Congress on July 4, 1776. Its eloquent phrases are a summary of the best political thought of the preceding centuries and a bright beacon in the intellectual history of the Western world:

We hold these truths to be self-evident, that all men are created equal, that they are endowed by their Creator with certain unalienable Rights, that among these are Life, Liberty and the pursuit of Happiness. That to secure these rights, Governments are instituted among Men, deriving their just powers from the consent of the governed. That whenever any Form of Government becomes destructive of these ends, it is the Right of the People to alter or to abolish it, and to institute new Government, laying its foundation on such principles and organizing its powers in such form, as to them shall seem most likely to effect their Safety and Happiness.

From the start the thirteen former colonies had a major problem in securing a minimum of coöperation among themselves. The Articles of Confederation adopted by the Congress in 1777 were not ratified by the requisite number of states until 1781. Even then, lack of a federal executive or judiciary and the absence of power in Congress to deal with taxation and trade made this first attempt at federal union too weak to be effective. But gradually the neccessities of war taught the new sovereign states some lessons about working together.

Despite this increasing though very imperfect unity among the states, despite the steadfast and adroit leadership of George Washington, and despite the great difficulties that the Atlantic Ocean and the large size of the area to be reconquered imposed upon the British, it is hard to see how the Americans could have won a definite victory in the war without foreign aid. For example, from the autumn of 1776 to the very end of the war the British held the central and strategic port of New York. Or again, the Congress financed the war with larger and larger issues of paper money which rapidly depreciated in value and might have become worthless without the help of funds from abroad.

But France, still smarting from defeat in the Seven Years' War, had from the start viewed the American cause with sympathy and perceived in it an opportunity for revenge against England by helping to disrupt her empire. Influenced by the adroit propaganda of Benjamin Franklin, American emissary to Versailles, and impressed by the crushing defeat of Burgoyne at Saratoga (October 17, 1777), France in 1778 formed an alliance with the United States and declared war on Britain. The French aided the Americans with money and supplies, and also with troops and naval support. It was the momentary superiority of the French navy that enabled the Franco-American forces to compel the surrender of Lord Cornwallis at Yorktown in Virginia in 1781, an event which virtually decided the struggle in America, since all the reserve strength of Great Britain was required in the West Indies, Europe, and Asia.

In addition, French diplomacy secured the adherence of Spain to the anti-British alliance (1779). Holland, indignant at the English pressure against Dutch commerce,

likewise declared war on Britain (1780). Indeed, the arrogant maritime policy of the British and their practice of stopping, searching, and seizing neutral vessels led Catherine the Great of Russia to protest vigorously. In 1780, Russia with Sweden and Denmark formed an "armed neutrality of the North" to uphold neutral rights against the British. Prussia, Portugal, the Two Sicilies, and the Holy Roman Empire subsequently confronted Great Britain with an almost unanimously hostile Europe by adhering to this "armed neutrality."

In the Mediterranean, the French and Spanish took Minorca from the British, but failed in an attempt to capture Gibraltar. In India, the French and their allies were defeated by the British. The French Admiral Suffren, however, gained such victories at sea as to threaten English maritime control in the east. It looked for a while as if the French navy, rebuilt and reconstituted since 1763, might successfully challenge British sea-power. But such hopes were dashed in April 1782, when the English Admiral Rodney overwhelmed the French fleet under De Grasse at the battle near the islands called "the Saints" in the West Indies.

Despite this naval victory, Britain, unsuccessful in America, inglorious in India, expelled from Minorca, faced with revolt in Ireland, and weary of war, was very ready for peace. But still secure behind the Channel, victorious at sea, unshaken in India, Britain was by no means humbled. Defeat, but not humiliation, was the keynote of the treaties which Great Britain concluded in 1783 with the United States at Paris and with France and Spain at Versailles.

By the treaty of Paris, the former thirteen colonies were recognized as the sovereign and independent United States of America. By the treaty of Versailles, France acquired Tobago in the West Indies and Senegal in Africa, which she had lost in 1763. Spain recovered the island of Minorca and the American territory of Florida. The Netherlands, concluding a separate peace in 1784, fared less well. It was forced to yield commercial stations in India and a share in the trade of the East Indian islands to the British.

The significance of the War of American

Independence went far beyond anything to be found in the terms of the peace treaties. It was in fact manifold:

(1) Britain lost the most populous of her colonies, and a new independent nation of European origin, destined for greatness, appeared across the Atlantic.

(2) Since the American Revolution was in good part a rising against mercantilist restrictions, it reënforced the *laissez-faire* theories of Adam Smith and cast grave doubts on the ultimate wisdom of such policies. Perhaps when other colonies became strong and wealthy they would likewise drop off the mother tree like ripe pears, and become independent. The doubts about the value of commercial restraints were accentuated by a fact which soon became evident. Before long, Britain was doing a more thriving trade with the independent United States than she had ever done with the colonies.

(3) France secured a partial revenge for her defeat in the Seven Years' War. But she did so at considerable cost. Her finances, already shaky, were cast into utter confusion by the expenses incurred. What had been a difficult financial problem now became insoluble.

(4) In Britain the ill-success of George III and his favorite ministers in the war discredited them in a very large degree and spelled the failure of the King's attempts to increase the royal power. In a very real way, the success of American (and French) arms helped to preserve limited monarchy and political liberty in Britain.

(5) The American Revolution produced a series of political innovations which were to be of the utmost importance in the coming years.

(6) The ideas and experiences of the American Revolution were ultimately to affect many lands. Almost immediately they were to have a most significant influence on France.

These last two points are of such importance that they will be treated more at length in the next two sections.

C. American Political Innovations

From the American Revolution and its attendant international war emerged the United States as an independent country basing its right to existence on popular sovereignty and successful revolution. Its very origin made this new nation a horrible example for absolute monarchs and a source of inspiration for oppressed peoples. Besides, in the course of its revolution and afterwards, the United States came to exemplify a series of very important political ideas. They can be summarized in four words: republicanism, democracy, federalism, and constitutionalism.

There had, to be sure, been republics in ancient Greece and Rome, among the Italian city states (like Venice), and in Switzerland. But the United States was far larger than the previous examples, so large that it had to invent a complicated system of representative government. It was, moreover, quite self-conscious about its republicanism. Thomas Paine's anti-monarchical slogans and their own objections to George III had convinced most Americans that the day of kings was over. There were those who had their doubts. Some would have made George Washington king. A few even thought it might legitimize the new government to have a descendant of the Stuart kings to lead it. But when the new constitution came to be written it was starkly republican and required each state to have a "republican form of government."

At first the state legislatures which supplanted the colonial assemblies were not very democratic. The franchise was limited to males and usually to landowners and the more well-to-do classes. Often, too, there were religious qualifications tending to exclude Catholics or even some kinds of Protestants. But there was no hereditary aristocracy and in a growing and developing country new people acquired wealth. If, at first, office holding was restricted to men of substance, and indirect elections were used to limit the power of the masses, still it was not long before men of the people began to rise to power. Gradually, and indeed rather rapidly, religious disabilities and property qualifications for voting or office were done away with in one state after another.

As with republics, there had also been federations before. In fact, the British empire in 1774 was a sort of a federation, since there were legislatures with some power in many of the colonies. But the United States was the first extensive, carefully and consciously thought out example of federalism. It was a working contradiction, a sovereign nation composed of "sovereign states." It pointed out a way of reconciling local and national interests and of keeping some powers close to home. It showed that diverse peoples with divergent interests could still come together under a single government for common purposes. The American example of federalism has had weighty influence on the formation of many nations, from Latin American republics (like Brazil or Colombia) to other former British colonies (Canada, Australia, India) and even to the Union of the Soviet Socialist Republics.

When a convention met in the State House at Philadelphia in May of 1787, under the presidency of George Washington, to do something about the inter-state disputes that had arisen under the old Articles of Confederation, and possibly to devise a stronger form of central government, its members were well aware of the idea of a constitution. The "Instrument of Government" in the England of Cromwell, the unwritten traditions of British government, the colonial charters, the new state constitutions, the Articles of Confederation themselves were all in one way or another examples. Yet the Federal Constitution was the first to be devised and adopted by elected representatives for a whole nation. It, so to speak, focussed and brought together all thinking on a written constitution, the experiments of the various states in forming their own governments, the experience with the (to the colonists) unfortunate flexibility of the unwritten British constitution, the writings of a hundred authors from Hobbes to Jefferson.

The Constitution, which went into effect in 1789, enshrined many important political ideas—republicanism, limited government, the separation of powers, checks and balances, representative legislatures—but it was in itself an idea of the utmost importance. Since that time, almost every new nation, whether formed by revolution or otherwise, has sought to devise a constitution and then to secure its ratification by some form of popular approval. Very shortly after 1789 another American innovation

was included in the Constitution, for the first ten amendments were declared in force in December 1791. Taken together they constitute a "Bill of Rights," designed to protect the individual citizen from the government. They guarantee the rule of law, the separation of church and state, and the freedom of speech, press, petition, and assembly.

The example of America was heightened in importance by the fact that the new ideas worked, and the government was from the start conducted with effectiveness and success. Indeed the first presidents (Washington, John Adams, Jefferson, and Madison) and their cabinet officers were men of such unusual ability and distinction that they were able rather rapidly to fill in, by setting precedents, any gaps in the constitutional framework. And from the start it was apparent that the bold American experiment had extraordinary vitality.

D. Impact of the American Revolution on France

Even before the peace treaty with the United States, George III had been forced to dismiss Lord North and his cabinet and to bring in more liberal ministers. Several reforms were soon effected. The Irish parliament was granted an almost independent position (1782) and Catholic Irishmen were given the right to vote (1793). In 1800, the Irish parliament was fused with that at Westminster,[1] and thereafter, for more than a century, the British Isles were known as the United Kingdom of Great Britain and Ireland. But even more important were the steps begun much later (1839–1849) by which former colonies were gradually transformed into self-governing dominions.

More immediate and more dramatic were the effects of the American Revolution on France. The ringing phrases of the Declaration of Independence on liberty, equality, and the rights of man woke echoes in France. The anti-monarchical writings of the Americans and their British sympathizers could be applied to Louis XVI as well as to George III. For the French such propa-

---

[1] From this, however, Catholics were excluded until 1829.

ganda was greatly reënforced by the fact that many of their navy and army officers, such as the Marquis de Lafayette, had been to America, mingled with Americans, and seen republican institutions at work. Benjamin Franklin with his great reputation as a scientist, his deliberate homespun simplicity, and his shrewd tongue had been an eloquent exponent of the new principles. French Freemasons were in contact with their American brothers.

When the American states and eventually the United States drew up constitutions, they were eagerly read and discussed in intellectual circles in France. Here was republicanism in practice. Here were the rights of men guaranteed. Here was human equality being written into law. It is not too much to say that the American Revolution was a decisive blow at both divine-right monarchy and aristocratic privilege in France. The lessons it taught were sharpened by the fact that, in good part as a result of its participation in the American war, the French monarchy was slipping into a kind of financial chaos that hampered its efforts at efficiency and reform, showed up its every weakness, and gave its opponents manifold opportunities. To understand why France was so vulnerable to new ideas and to demands for change the state of that nation in 1789 must be examined.

One factor in the situation was the fact that the seeds brought to France from America fell on ground already well plowed. The thinkers of the "enlightenment" were not merely propounding abstract notions. Much of what they said was a direct or indirect attack on the social and political order in which they lived. The existing authorities, natural upholders of traditional law, government, and religion, realized the subversive nature of the attacks; and many of the French *philosophes* spent some time in exile or in prison, while their writings were censored or banned. Yet the same authorities were fascinated by the new ideas. If condemned by church or state government, if in trouble with police or the courts, a *philosophe* could usually find a highly placed protector at home or abroad who would grant him help and refuge till the storm blew over. A book supressed in France

Benjamin Franklin. Painting by Charles Willson Peale (d. 1827).

Courtesy Bettmann Archive

could be published in Amsterdam. Sometimes it was printed in Paris with "Amsterdam" on the title page to deceive the censors.

It is true that the *philosophes* were constructing a positive system of thought which was to be the main basis of nineteenth-century liberalism. They stood in general for toleration (or indifference) in religion, for individual rights and limited government in politics, for greater equality between classes in society, for *laissez-faire* in economics, and for rationalism and materialism in philosophy. But inevitably, as they advocated these ideas, they found themselves attacking almost every aspect of of the existing society which was founded and organized on quite different principles. Because they wrote well and vigorously, because, despite their many quarrels and squabbles, they formed a sort of united intellectual front, because their ideas seemed modern, novel, and exciting, the *philosophes* exercised a tremendous influence in most intellectual or would-be intellectual circles. Even wealthy nobles and highly placed churchmen, who profited most from the existing order, took up the "enlightened" theories and discussed them with interest and even enthusiasm.

Rousseau well illustrates these generalizations. He was a very difficult person to get along with. He never kept a friend for long. He usually attacked his benefactors and quarreled with his supporters. But he never lacked patrons. Counts, dukes, high-born ladies took him in and gave him shelter. Louis XV would have given him a pension had he come to court when invited to do so. Society ladies wept over his *Nouvelle Héloïse,* and the salons eagerly argued about his *Social Contract.* Yet the ideas that Rousseau propounded were definitely revolutionary. He attacked the very basis and the whole fabric of the existing order.

For example, in his *Social Contract* he maintained that governments had been formed by men for their own benefit, and should have been instruments of social well-being. Instead, they had grown rigid and tyrannical. With their repressive laws and oppressive taxes, with their police and armies and officials, they destroyed liberty and enslaved men. Everywhere man was perverted from his natural goodness by bad government. The solution was to establish new and better governments representative of, and responsible to, the "popular will."

Criticism of the existing order was just as clear, if less radical, in the works of thinkers other than Rousseau. Thus it was that the late eighteenth century presented a curious picture. Intellectual leaders did not believe in the society in which they lived. In France, where the *philosophes* were most numerous, most active, and most able, the very defenders of the existing order were half convinced that what they defended was outworn and unjust. And in fact there were many things in France that were difficult to defend on any rational basis. France, it is true, was better organized and better managed than most of the other continental countries. But it was more conscious of its shortcomings.

France, in the second half of the eighteenth century, was the most advanced of all the continental countries. Its peasants were more prosperous, its financiers more wealthy, its upper classes more cultured than those in other European lands. But France under the "old regime" was a peculiar composite. Though in many basic ways it still resembled a country of the later middle age or of the sixteenth century, it had been changed by the ideas and institutions of absolutist, centralized government developed in the seventeenth century.

E. France of the "Old Regime"

The French monarchy was still based on the idea of absolutism and divine right, despite the notions of popular control that were gaining currency and despite the limitations on monarchy established in England. The king of France still treated his realm as a collection of personal and family possessions. In spite, too, of the growth of religious skepticism and the beginnings of religious toleration, the Catholic Church still held in France a privileged and exclusive position. Education and charity were almost entirely in its hands. Noble and peasant alike attended its services. If on the one hand the king selected the bishops, on the other he usually heeded their advice and supported their views. If the church lent some financial support to the government through "gratuitous gifts," it also possessed broad landholdings and collected compulsory taxes or tithes.

In a period when more and more people were talking about the equality and the "natural rights" of all men, the class structure in France showed glaring inequality and a wide variation in rights. The privileged orders, or the first two "estates of the realm," were the clergy and the nobles. The first estate, or clergy, was itself characterized by inequality. The high churchmen—archbishops, bishops, and abbots—often enjoyed great wealth drawn from church landholdings and from tithes. The Cardinal de Rohan, with an income of 2,500,000 livres a year, could astound the court with his magnificence and his gambling. Churchmen like him lived with the pomp and ceremony of princes, and were prone to neglect their ecclesiastical duties and to play the role of courtiers at Versailles. Often a noble family took care of a younger son by securing him a high position in the church, while an unmarried daughter was likely to be made an abbess. Some of the aristocratic churchmen were pious and hard-working. But others were dissipated, arrogant, and worldly.

In sharp contrast, were the lower ranks of the clergy. Many a shabby but devout country curate, with an uncertain income of less than $150 a year, was doing his best to make both ends meet, with a little to spare for charity. If among the lower clergy there was some lack of education, some sloth, and some merely routine formalism, there was also a vast deal of humble service and quiet toil in behalf of the common people. In the rural villages the priest was often the guide, philosopher, and friend of his flock. He defended them against the officials, taught their children to read, gave them the news of the day, and comforted them in their troubles.

Marquis de Lafayette. From a French print of 1781.

There was a similar contrast in the second order or "estate"—the nobility. There were thousands of lesser nobles who lived on their estates, patched up their crumbling châteaux, and showed pride in their coats of arms, their horses, and their dogs. If they could ever afford to come to Paris or Versailles, they were treated like country bumpkins. Their clothes were old fashioned, and it was held that they smelled faintly of the barnyard. Some of the country nobles were fairly well-to-do. Many of them were on friendly terms with their peasants and tenants. But their influence was largely local. They had no real function in the state as a whole.

Much more conspicuous were the great nobles, the courtiers. Some of them still were of use as officers in the army. But to a large degree they had become merely decorative. They formed a background for the king. The real work of government was done by lawyers and other middle-class folk. The nobles at court sought eagerly for royal attention, since that might mean pensions, gifts, and salaried (if honorary) posts. At Versailles, many of them rarely did anything more worth while than to invent a delicate compliment, or to patronize an art, or to pose as "enlightened." Their morals were not of the best—it was almost fashionable to be vicious. But their manners were perfect. Meanwhile, the landed estates of these absentee lords were in charge of salaried agents whose duty was to squeeze money out of the peasants.

Whether rich or poor, at court or in the country, the noble enjoyed special privileges. He was thought of as finer and better than common men. He was addressed in terms of respect—"my lord"—"your grace"—or the like. For him the best places were reserved in the church or in the theatre. Ordinary people drew aside to let him pass and bowed or doffed their hats. His noble birth, if it prevented him from marrying "below his class," admitted him to polite society and allowed him to seek preference in the army, in the church, or at court.

More substantial were the actual possessions of the noble. Each noble usually bequeathed to his eldest son a mansion or château, together with more or less territory from which rents and dues could be collected. High churchmen, on taking office, came into similar properties belonging to the church. Though nobility and clergy together held a large portion of the fairest lands of France, substantial pensions from the crown, and many well salaried offices, they paid far less than their share of the taxes. They were exempt from the burdensome *taille*, or land tax. While they were supposed to pay certain direct taxes like the *vingtième* and the *capitation*, their influence was such that they could usually scale down their contributions to a minimum. Even taxes like the *aides* on wine they could escape by maintaining their own vineyards. Thus the chief burden of taxation fell, not on those who were richest and best able to pay, but chiefly on the lower classes and especially on the peasantry.

The third estate which did pay taxes, consisted of all those who were not clergymen or nobles. Here, too, there were wide differences, for the wealthy merchant was in a position quite distinct from that of the humble peasant. The most powerful element of the third estate was the bourgeoisie—the merchants, bankers, businessmen, manufacturers, and professional men who lived in towns or cities. Industry, commerce, and finance had all been growing rapidly in France, as in the rest of Europe, since the late middle age, and with them the bourgeois had grown in wealth and power. By the late eighteenth century, the richest group in France were financiers. They made most of their money by collecting the taxes farmed out on contract by the government and by loaning money to it. If the government got hard up, that merely meant fatter profits for the tax-farmers, because they could then secure better terms on their contracts and higher interest on the loans.

There were many wealthy merchants. France, even after the Seven Years' War, enjoyed a most lucrative trade in sugar from the West Indies, in eastern textiles and other goods from India, and in products from the Near East. Trade was also extensive with the Baltic, with Germany and the Low Countries, and with southern Europe. There were several kinds of industrialists, some of whom were very well-to-do. There were manufacturers of the old medieval type, who belonged to guilds and made goods in their shops with the aid of journeymen and apprentices under the protection of the monopoly established by their guilds and confirmed by the government. There were "putting-out" capitalists, or merchant-employers, who bought the raw materials, sent them out to be worked up by laborers in their homes, and then sold the finished products. There was also a growing number of manufacturers who possessed large shops much like factories, where they employed dozens or even hundreds of people.

Associated in one way or another with these important groups of bourgeois, were others of varying significance. There were great numbers of shopkeepers, large and small, wholesalers, brokers, commission merchants, and bankers. To handle legal matters there were numerous lawyers, some of whom grew wealthy, while others eked out a precarious livelihood. Most of the government and municipal officials were drawn from the bourgeoisie. Indeed, many a lawyer found his career in government service rather than in private practice. If the officials were dependent on, and for the most part loyal to, the government, they were none the less bound by close family ties to the business classes.

Since the sixteenth century, the bourgeosie had grown in numbers and wealth and also in education. Most of the French *philosophes* were of bourgeois origin, and from that class came most of the persons who read the latest books on science or philosophy or government, who responded sympathetically to the current pleas for rationalism or to the criticisms of the existing order, and who eagerly discussed questions of political theory or economic policy. There was growing among these bourgeois a sense that they did not have social esteem, political influence, or economic privileges corresponding to their numbers, their wealth, or their education. They felt themselves to be the backbone of the country and the basis of its prosperity. It irked them to see a foppish noble or an idle churchman take precedence over them in society or at court, and even escape payment of most of the taxes. To the bourgeois it seemed that the privileged classes who contributed little to national well-being were getting far more than a fair share of the good things of life. The situation seemed clearly out of line with the teachings of Rousseau, or Adam Smith, or Voltaire.

Yet if there was cause for discontent, the peasantry had more reason to be restive than the bourgeoisie. France was still a predominantly agricultural country, and it was on the backs of the peasantry that the other classes were borne. It was the peasantry who raised the food and produced the raw materials. It was the peasantry who paid the bulk of the taxes, tithes, and dues. But they enjoyed no political power whatever. If they failed to pay the taxes, which they had no voice in levying, they lost their land or their equipment.

Though there were relatively few serfs left save in the most backward areas of France, conditions for the peasantry had not changed much from those of the middle ages. Peasant villages still were organized for the most part on the old "open field" system. The peasant cultivated scattered strips and followed the traditional agricultural procedures of the village. Some peasants now owned their land. Many were tenants paying money rents or a share of the crop.

But whatever his status, the peasant was subject to a number of vexatious burdens. If he owed no labor, he paid a "quit rent." If he sold his farm, part of the price usually went to the lord. If he took his goods to market, he often had to pay market fees or dues. Under a system of *banalités*, his grain must be ground, his grapes or olives pressed, and his bread baked at the lord's mill, press, or oven, and a fee paid for the privilege. Only the lord could hunt, and he could and sometimes did run his horses and dogs over the peasant's crops. To the church the peasant paid a tithe (often a twelfth or a fifteenth) of his crop.

The royal taxes were still more burdensome. The *taille* was sometimes a land tax, sometimes one on the peasant's whole re-

sources. It varied from year to year, and the village had to choose collectors who went to jail if the expected sums were not forthcoming. To the *taille* were added the *capitation* and the *vingtième*, which had originally been intended as a kind of income tax but which in practice were collected more or less like the *taille*. Often the peasant would let his house go to pieces so that he would be thought poor and might thus be taxed less. In many parts of France, there was a heavy salt tax, or *gabelle*, and in some sections the peasant was required to buy a given amount of salt each year. Beer, wine, and other beverages bore heavy taxes called *aides*. Roadmaking was a duty of the peasant, and by the *corvée* he was forced to discharge it for the crown without pay.

All these burdens left the average peasant little for himself. There were districts where the peasants were prosperous and lived in comfortable cottages. But more often they were wretched, miserable, and sometimes even hungry. They ate black bread and thought a bit of meat a luxury. They lived in thatched huts and wore rough woolens frequently patched. Their tools were few and crude. They were ignorant, superstitious, and mainly illiterate.

Yet when all has been said, the French peasants were probably better off than those anywhere else on the continent of Europe except perhaps in the Low Countries. In France serfdom was disappearing, while it was still common in Germany, the Habsburg lands, and Russia. For all his wretchedness, the average French peasant was better fed, clothed, and housed than his fellows to the east.

As with the peasantry, so with the other classes. France, for all its outworn and traditional organization, was the most advanced country on the continent. The bourgeoisie were more numerous, better educated, and more ambitious than elsewhere. The intellectuals were abler, more critical, and more vociferous than those in other lands. The nobles and high clergy were not only more polished than in other countries, they were also a little less certain about the justice of a system which gave

Jean-Jacques Rousseau (d. 1778).

Courtesy Bettmann Archive

them so many privileges. If called on to defend their "rights," some of them would do so half-heartedly or not at all. Such was the France which heard the news from America of republicanism, liberty, equality, and constitutions which ensured the freedom of all men. Such was the France which was facing the worst financial crisis of the old regime.

Marie-Antoinette and her children. Painting by Mme. Vigée-Le Brun (d. 1842).

Courtesy Bettmann Archive

CHAPTER 41

The French Revolution

A. The Financial Crisis of the French Monarchy, 1783–1789

There had been those in France who had opposed war on Great Britain in 1778, for fear of the financial costs. Four years earlier Louis XV had been succeeded by his grandson, Louis XVI. The new monarch was virtuous but dull-witted, well-meaning but lacking in decision. He was too awkward and shy to preside with dignity over the court or the royal councils. He liked to shoot deer or to play at lock-making. He had many amiable virtues, but not those which could make him a forceful or an enlightened ruler.

When Louis XVI came to the throne, hopes had at first run high, for Turgot, friend of Voltaire and other encyclopedists, was named minister of finance, and reform was in the air. But Turgot's attempts to remove the old restraints on commerce and industry, to aid agriculture, to revise the financial system, to reduce the burdens on the peasants and to tax the nobles and clergy, ran into the stubborn opposition of the privileged, and seemed to threaten the traditional rights of guilds, towns, provinces, nobles, and churchmen.

Having accomplished but little, Turgot was dismissed in 1776, and amidst general relief his reforms were abandoned. Turgot, the theorist, was succeeded by a hard-headed Swiss banker, Jacques Necker. During his five years in office (1776–1781) Necker sought to apply business methods to government finances. He borrowed 400,000,000 *livres* from his banker friends and tried to reduce expenses and improve tax collections. In 1781 he pretended to inform the public about the condition of the royal treasury by issuing a report, or "Account Rendered." The report, though favorably received, was something less than a full and honest one, for Necker was eager to secure further loans; and expenditures on the American war were rapidly mounting.

At court, Necker had a powerful enemy in the Queen, Marie Antoinette, daughter of Maria Theresa of Austria. Gay and frivolous, she was disliked by many people as a foreigner and as a symbol of the alliance with Austria which had proved so disastrous in the Seven Years' War. The young Queen had little serious interest in politics and less understanding of them, but when her friends came to her with complaints about Necker's miserly economy she begged the King to dismiss him. Well-intentioned Louis XVI could not bear to deprive his irresponsible wife and her charming friends, the courtiers, of their pleasures. He appointed as the new finance minister the suave and obsequious Calonne, who found more money for the court, but only by floating new loans at high rates of interest.

By the end of the American war (1783), the financial problem was desperate. It was indeed insoluble without the reforms which would have upset the old order in France. The country could easily have borne heavier taxes, but only if the upper classes were made to bear their fair share of the burden. To a bishop or a noble it seemed ridiculous to expect a high-born person to pay taxes like a merchant or a peasant. The privileged classes were so intrenched in the courts, the church, and the government, and so well defended by law, tradition, and precedent, that they were able to block any attempt to alter the existing system.

In 1786 the interest payments on the public debt totaled more than 160,000,000 *livres* and, since the regular income fell far short of meeting the regular expenses, the government was running deeper into debt every month. In addition, it was becoming increasingly difficult to float new loans even at very high interest rates. Something had to be done. In desperation the King convened (1787) an Assembly of Notables—145 of the chief nobles, bishops, and officials—in the vain hope that they would consent to the taxation of the privileged classes. They contented themselves, however, with recommending some minor reforms, urging that Calonne be dismissed, and declaring that the question of taxation should be referred to the Estates General. But in all their suggestions there was no real help for the treasury.

The new minister of finance, Archbishop Loménie de Brienne, politely thanked the notables and sent them home. He made so many fine promises that he was able to float a new loan. But the *parlement*, or high court, of Paris soon saw that there was nothing substantial behind his promises and refused to register new loans or taxes. Encouraged by popular approval of its stand, the *parlement* went on to draw up a declaration of rights and to assert that new taxes should only be granted by the nation's representatives—the Estates General. This sounded almost subversive, and the *parlements* were closed. At once, there was popular protest. Soldiers refused to arrest the judges. Excited crowds gathered in Paris and in provincial cities and clamored for the summoning of the Estates General. Menaced with revolt, Louis XVI finally gave way to the popular demand. In 1788, he summoned the Estates General to meet at Versailles, in May, 1789.

The Estates General was no novel institution. To be sure, it had not met for 175 years. But prior to 1614, kings had not infrequently summoned representatives of the clergy, the nobles, and the rest of the people (the "third estate") to advise them. Since each estate had met separately and had voted as a unit, the clergy and the nobles (the privileged classes) could outvote the third estate two to one. Moreover, the powers of the Estates General had been advisory, and if worse came to worse its advice could perhaps be ignored and it could be dismissed. No, the summoning of the Estates General might after all be useful and it did not seem too dangerous to the monarchy. The fact that this reasoning was to prove false arose from conditions that neither Louis XVI nor his ministers could be expected fully to grasp.

The general economic situation in France was in some ways as ominous as the strictly financial. The economic difficulties were very real, despite the fact that France was basically sound and was progressing in industry, commerce, and agriculture. A recent problem had been created by the Eden treaty negotiated between France and Great Britain in 1786. In line with the ideas of freer trade upheld by Adam Smith and other economists of the time, this treaty had reduced the import duties levied against each other's goods by the two countries. The British had agreed to receive French wines at the rates charged on the favored Portuguese wines, but had quickly nullified any advantage the French might thus have gained by lowering still further the rates on the Portuguese product. Though Britain had refused to lower the duties on French silks, France had cut the rates on English cotton goods, and just at this time the British were producing more and better cotton stuffs at costs decreased by the application of new inventions in spinning. As a result of the treaty, commerce between France and Britain had notably increased and the age-old profession of smuggling across the Channel had been hard hit. But France had been quickly flooded with English cottons and other goods. For this reason and probably for others as well, French business had entered upon a period of depression. By 1788, unemployment had become serious and business men were protesting.

To add to these problems there was a basic long-run trend which has only recently been explored and understood. From about 1735 prices of goods had been rising, while wages had risen much less rapidly. This development benefited the big landowners (who did not pay their share of the taxes), since they got more for their products and paid relatively less in wages. For this reason, land rents had been rising significantly. But it was very hard on the working classes since they got relatively less money for their labor and had to pay higher prices for their food and clothes. It has been estimated that a worker in France could, in the period 1785–1789, buy about 25 per cent less goods with his wages than a similar worker in the period 1726–1741. Nor were the peasants wholly unaffected since large numbers of them pieced out their livelihood by working part time for wages.

Before the nineteenth century, business depressions were normally associated with bad harvests and high grain prices. Such was the case in 1788–1789. The harvest of 1788 was a poor one. Soon the price of grain was going up. During the early months of 1789 it rose rapidly to a peak in the month of July, at which time the price of grain was

Mirabeau. Bust in the Louvre Museum by Jean Antoine Houdon (d. 1828).

higher than it had been since 1709, a year of great famine and suffering. When it is remembered that the French lower classes spent something like two-thirds of their total income for food and that their ability to buy food had already been seriously impaired by the current trend of prices and wages, some notion may be derived of how serious was the situation.

In considering the events of 1789, it is well to bear in mind that many members of the lower classes were hungry, fearful, and discontented. The mobs that appeared suddenly like actors on the stage came together in part at least because the people were so wretched and miserable that they felt something must be done, and the government in its financial weakness was unable to start public works or give relief or distribute cheap grain as had been done in crises in the past.

B. The National Assembly, 1789

France in the winter of 1788–1789 was undergoing a serious crisis, but that this would develop rapidly into a revolution which would overthrow divine-right monarchy and the old regime, and affect all subsequent history, was anticipated by no one. France had met and surmounted crises before. Its monarchy and social system had been so long established and had achieved such impressive success in the past that they seemed indestructible.

Elections to the Estates General were held amidst much discussion and a frantic search for precedents of two centuries earlier. In accordance with old custom and at the King's request, the groups of electors drafted reports on local conditions and made recommendations as to reforms they felt desirable. These reports and recommendations were called *cahiers*, and they were numerous. Almost every group of voters of each of the three estates prepared one. Though the *cahiers* almost uniformly expressed loyalty to the monarchy, most of them breathed a spirit of reform. In line with the "enlightened" thought of the day, they urged the removal of social inequalities and of economic, financial, and political abuses. Even the privileged orders—clergy and nobility—quite generally recognized some need for reform.

The Third Estate was naturally most insistent. Two thirds of its elected representatives were lawyers and judges, most of whom admired limited monarchy of the British sort and were well acquainted with the writings of the *philosophes*. The Third Estate had grown to be much more important than it had been in 1614, and Louis XVI had recognized this change by providing that the number of representatives of that estate should equal the number of representatives of the other two combined. The commoners naturally enough concluded that they would be the most influential group when the Estates General met.

Among the men elected by the Third Estate were two spokesmen, Mirabeau and Sieyès, both of whom belonged to the privileged classes but gladly accepted election by the unprivileged. Mirabeau was the son of a marquis who had written books on the economic principles of the physiocrats. The son had proved so wild and unruly that the father had repeatedly had him put in prison to keep him out of mischief. In 1789 he found opportunity to employ his almost superhuman energy in working for the constitutional government in which he believed. Not so forceful was the priest Sieyès, who was much less a devout Catholic than a devotee of the critical philosophy of the day. In a pamphlet issued on the eve of the meeting of the Estates General, Sieyès asked, "What is the Third Estate?" "It is everything," he replied. "What has it been hitherto in the political order? Nothing! What does it desire? To be something!"

When the Estates General finally met at Versailles in May 1789, neither the King nor his ministers had worked out a program for it. The King welcomed its members, and apparently expected them to devote themselves to financial problems. He did direct them to vote by order, that is, as three separate bodies, so that the nobles and clergy together would be able to outvote the Third Estate. If the nobles and most of the higher clergy approved this adherence to tradition, the Third Estate did not. They wished all the delegates to meet together and to vote "by head" or as individuals, so that their extra numbers would give them real power,

and so that the assemblage would represent the French nation as a whole and not the separate classes of the country.

In support of its views, the Third Estate was firm, while the King shilly-shallied, to offend no one. At length, on June 17, 1789, the Third Estate proclaimed itself a "National Assembly" and invited the other orders to sit with it and to work together for the reformation of France. Three days later, finding that the King had locked them out of their assembly hall, the Third Estate took a truly revolutionary step. Led by Sieyès and Mirabeau, they proceeded to a large nearby building used normally as a riding-hall or tennis court; they listened to a number of fiery speeches; and amid intense excitement and with upraised hands, they took an oath, as members of the "National Assembly," that they would not separate till they had drawn up a written constitution for France.

This "Tennis Court Oath" was the actual beginning of the French Revolution, for in it the representatives of the Third Estate were going against the orders of the King and far beyond the purposes for which they had been summoned. Unexpectedly, the indecisive King took no forceful action against the revolutionary commoners. Soon these were joined by a number of the lower clergy and a few liberal nobles. "We are here by the will of the people," they declared in the words of Mirabeau, "and we shall not leave our places except at the point of a bayonet." The King gave way. Just a week after the scene at the tennis court he reversed his position and directed the three estates to sit together and vote "by head" as members of a National Constituent Assembly.

The stage was now set for the new National Assembly to proceed with the work of drawing up a constitution for France. But it was not to proceed calmly, for France, in the throes of depression and near famine, was deeply stirred by the events at Versailles, and in the ensuing months a number of events occurred which gravely affected the attitude and work of the Assembly.

Early in July rumor spread that the King was concentrating troops on Versailles. Although this move may have been intended

The Tennis Court Oath. Painting by Jacques Louis David (d. 1825).

to protect rather than to overawe the Assembly, there resulted three day of wild disorder in Paris. Shops were looted and royal officers expelled, while angry crowds rioted. On the third day—July 14, 1789—a mob attacked the royal prison-fortress of the Bastille. It contained few prisoners and they were unimportant, yet it was somehow a grim symbol of Bourbon despotism. The mob took the Bastille and slaughtered the scanty garrison who sought to defend it.

The fall of the Bastille was both the first serious act of violence in the Revolution and a sign that the Parisian populace were behind the Assembly. Matters now proceeded apace, for during the disorder prominent citizens of Paris set up a new city government, or "commune," and organized a militia called the National Guard. In an attempt to allay the excitement, Louis XVI recognized the new government of Paris and confirmed the appointment of Lafayette, of American fame, as commander of the National Guard. The King did more. He visited Paris in person, praised what he could not prevent, and wore a new tricolor cockade combining the red and blue of Paris with the white of the Bourbons. The French still celebrate July 14 as the anniversary of the birth of their popular freedom.

During the summer of 1789, revolutionary violence spread to the provinces. In many regions, peasants rose, and, attacking the châteaux of nobles, burned the rolls which recorded the dues and fees they owed. Some monasteries were pillaged, some landowners were murdered. Amid the confusion, intendants and other officials left their posts and courts ceased to function. The old regime was in fact crumbling. Much affected by reports of these events, the Assembly was debating on August 4 what should be done about them, when one of the nobles—a relative of Lafayette—declared that the peasants were attacking injustices and that the remedy was not to repress the peasants but to remove the injustices. It was immediately moved and carried that the Assembly should proclaim equality of taxation for all classes, and the suppression of feudal dues. Then followed a scene of wild excite-

ment; nobles vied with clergymen in re-
nouncing the vested rights of the old regime.
Game laws were repealed, manorial courts
suppressed, serfdom abolished, tithes can-
celed, and all special privileges of classes,
cities, and provinces swept away. Within a
week the various measures had been put
together into an impressive decree "abolishing feudalism." To be sure, the peasants
were already abolishing it, and presently the
Assembly in calmer mood was voting money
compensation for surrendered privileges.
Still the "August Days" wrote into law the
dissolution of the traditional class society
and the substitution of an individualist
society.

While peasants burned châteaux and the
Assembly voted decrees, many nobles were
leaving France in fear or in protest, and the
Queen and the King's two brothers (the
Count of Provence and the Count of Artois)
were urging Louis XVI to use the army
against the revolution. It is doubtful whether
the well-intentioned King would have done
so, but news of an officers' banquet at
Versailles reached Paris and once again a
mob took action. On October 5, 1789,
numbers of the poorest women of the city
and some men dressed as women, all armed

with clubs and screaming "Bread, bread!",
straggled along the highway from Paris to
Versailles. Lafayette with his National
Guard followed them.

At the royal palace, Lafayette undertook
to guard the royal family, but the night was
a wild one and rioters actually broke into
the palace and killed some of the Queen's
bodyguard. In the morning, the King took
a fateful step. He agreed to move with his
family to Paris. In a lumbering coach, attended by Lafayette and surrounded by the
mob, Louis XVI, Marie Antoinette, and
their children took their way to Paris on
October 6, while the mob shouted, "We
have the baker and the baker's wife and the
little cook-boy—now we shall have bread!"
The National Assembly soon followed the
King to Paris, and thenceforth both Louis
XVI and the Assembly were no longer at
Versailles full of memories of Louis XIV,
but in Paris ever subject to the influence and
threats of the populace.

C. New Order in State, Church, and Society, 1789–1791

The National Assembly, both at Versailles and at Paris, was accomplishing an

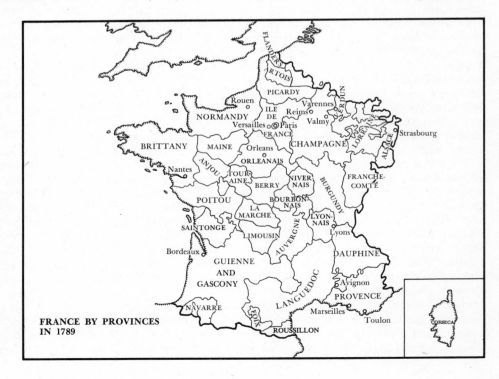

FRANCE BY PROVINCES
IN 1789

important work—tearing down the old regime and building a new order. Much of what it did would become a lasting part of French political life. Its slogans and its principles would provide the basis for French liberalism.

The first major accomplishment of the National Assembly had been the destruction of the old order in the "August Days." Its second was the assertion on October 2, 1789, of the principles on which the new order was to be built—the "Declaration of the Rights of Man." This declaration reflected the influence of *philosophes* like Rousseau and borrowed ideas and phrases from the English Bill of Rights and the American Declaration of Independence. It affirmed the principles of religious toleration, freedom of speech, and freedom of the press. It proclaimed that "private property is an inviolable and sacred right," and upheld the basic tenets of democracy by declaring that "Law is the expression of the general will. Every citizen has the right to participate personally or through his representative in its formation. It must be the same for all." It announced that "Men are born and remain free and equal in rights," and it defined these rights as "liberty, property, security, and resistance to oppression." "No person," it said, "shall be accused, arrested, or imprisoned, except in the cases and according to the forms prescribed by law."

A third and more practical achievement of the National Assembly was its reorganization of the country's administration. It swept away the old overlapping subdivisions, and abolished special privileges of guilds, towns, and provinces, the traditional local variations of justice and taxation, and even the provincial names of Burgundy, Normandy, Brittany, etc., that had endured for centuries. To replace what it was demolishing, the National Assembly set up a new and uniform system. The whole country was divided into eighty-three "*départements*," named after rivers or mountains, and each *département* was subdivided into cantons, and the cantons into communes or municipal units. Local officials were not to be appointed by the king, but elected by the people, and a new system of courts with elected judges was established. To this day

France has retained the system of local divisions devised by the National Assembly.

In its reforms the National Assembly emphasized the national unity of France. Indeed the fostering of nationalism was one of the most impressive features of the French Revolution. The Estates General had renamed itself the *National* Assembly. The new citizen militia was called the *National* Guard. The Declaration of the Rights of Man insisted that "all sovereignty resides essentially in the Nation." While the Assembly discussed plans for national military service and national education, patriotic rites to celebrate the new spirit of national unity were devised. On July 14, 1790, there was a spectacular patriotic festival at Paris, and in the provinces "altars to the fatherland" were erected and before them patriotic ceremonies were conducted. But the National Assembly went even further and preached the rights of people outside of France to national self-determination. It encouraged the people of Avignon, a city on the Rhône long owned by the papacy, to vote by plebiscite in 1791 to join France, despite protests of the Pope. Already nationalism was complicating international relations.

The Assembly could not ignore the financial difficulties which had been the occasion for its meeting. These had grown more acute, since, amid revolutiionary conditions, people simply ceased to pay taxes. Moved by a sense of national need and by anticlerical ideas which the *philosophes* had preached, the National Assembly tried to

FRANCE BY DÉPARTEMENTS
IN 1791

solve the financial problem at the expense of the Catholic Church in France. It decreed in November 1789 the confiscation of the landed estates held by the church, and against this property as security it issued paper money (called *assignats*). Since the paper money could be used to buy the confiscated land, it served as a mechanism by which the middle class and the peasants acquired the properties the state had seized. As often happens, however, too much paper money was issued; the *assignats* fell in value and a serious inflation of prices occurred.

As a partial indemnity for the confiscation of church property, the state undertook to pay the salaries of the clergy, who were thus made dependent on the state. But the National Assembly soon went further and undertook to reorganize the whole ecclesiastical system in France. In February 1790, the monasteries and other religious communities were suppressed. In July, a "Civil Constitution of the Clergy" was enacted. By this new law, the bishops and priests were reduced in number; they were to be elected by the people, paid by the state, and only nominally associated with the "foreign" pope.

Naturally enough, the Pope, Pius VI, protested vigorously against the new legislation in France. He condemned the "Civil Constitution of the Clergy" and forbade French clerics to take the required oath of loyalty to it. The issue was squarely joined. Those who took the oath—"the juring clergy"—were excommunicated by the Pope. Those who refused to take it—"the non-juring clergy"—lost their posts and salaries and were threatened with imprisonment. Many of the lower clergy who had sympathized with the course of the Revolution were now forced by their consciences to oppose the Assembly and its acts. Some priests and churchmen stayed in France and incited the devout to work against the revolutionary trend. Others left the country and swelled the numbers of the *émigrés*. A minority acquiesced in the revolution. In general, from this period dates a deep split in France between anti-clerical and devout.

Meanwhile the National Constituent Assembly was drafting the written constitution which would establish in France a limited monarchy. It was completed in 1791 and reluctantly signed by the King. Like the slightly earlier American Constitution, it provided for a "separation of powers" among executive, legislative, and judicial branches of government. But chief power was actually centered in a one-house "Legislative Assembly." The middle-class men who framed the constitution showed their distrust of the masses by arranging a complicated system of indirect election for members of the legislature, and by limiting the right to vote to "active citizens" who paid taxes, and the right to hold office, to property owners. The king's powers were reduced to a shadow and he was given only "a suspensive veto" over legislation. He could delay but not prevent the passage of laws of which he disapproved. By a decision which has been much criticized, but which was intended to show their lack of self-interest, the members of the National Constituent Assembly made themselves ineligible to sit in the new Legislative Assembly which met on October 1, 1791, amid public rejoicing, to inaugurate the era of constitutional limited monarchy in France.

Before that meeting took place, certain developments occurred which boded ill for the success of the new government. Opposition to the religious and political changes was rising within France. The number of *émigrés* was increasing and they were urging foreign rulers to intervene in France. Mirabeau, who, with his personal prestige, was a major support of limited monarchy, died prematurely in April, 1791. Worst of all, the King showed that he was out of sympathy with what was happening. In June 1791, accompanied by Marie Antoinette and the royal children, he fled from Paris in an effort to escape from the country. Detected and stopped by chance at Varennes near the border, the royal fugitives were ignominiously brought back to Paris. Louis subsequently swore to uphold the constitution. But how much faith could be placed in a monarch who had sought to leave the country and join the enemies of the new regime, and whose brothers had already fled? The King's personal popularity waned rapidly, while distrust and hatred of his wife, "The Austrian woman," grew apace.

D. Limited Monarchy and Start of Revolutionary War, 1791–1792

When the Legislative Assembly met on October 1, 1791, it faced enormous difficulties. Its members were new and untried, and the whole country was divided into contending factions. While many Frenchmen were willing to accept the new constitutional monarchy and hoped for its success, there were large groups of conservatives who thought things had gone too far, and of radicals who thought they had not gone far enough.

Many of the reactionary nobles had become *émigrés* by fleeing the country. Numbers of them gathered just over the northern and eastern frontiers, especially at Coblentz, and agitated against the new regime. Within France it was believed (correctly) that the King's closest advisers were in sympathy and in touch with the *émigrés*. Conservative clubs, moreover, had been formed in Paris and other cities by members of the upper classes. In certain sections of western France, especially in Brittany, Poitou (La Vendée), and Anjou, the peasants, devoted to Catholicism and influenced by the nonjuring clergy, had become outspokenly hostile to the revolutionary changes that were going forward.

More dangerous to the orderly working of the new government were the radicals. Elated by progress already made and eager to put into practice the theories of the extreme *philosophes,* many middle-class people wished to eliminate the king altogether, to set up a republic, to establish manhood suffrage, to root out all surviving traces of privilege, and to reduce still further the role of the clergy and the church. Such radicals could usually count on the support of urban working people to whom the Revolution thus far had not given bread or jobs or (since they did not pay direct taxes) the right to vote.

The power and influence of the radicals was greatly enhanced by the fact that they were beginning to be well organized. Back in the early days of the National Assembly, eating clubs had been formed by like-minded delegates, and informal groups had gathered at cafés for political discussion.

From such a beginning a number of political clubs had grown up, of which two were especially important. Known popularly by the names of confiscated monasteries in which they met, one was called the Cordelier, the other the Jacobin, Club. The former had been organized as a "society of the friends of the rights of man and of the citizen," and from the start it was radical. The Jacobin Club had originated as a "society of friends of the constitution," with such moderates as Mirabeau, Sieyès, and Lafayette. Subsequently under the leadership of Robespierre, it had become quite as radical as the Cordelier. It exercised nation-wide influence through its policy of organizing branch clubs of middle-class radicals all over France and showering them with propaganda—pamphlets, newspapers, letters.

Among the radical leaders, three may be mentioned—Marat, Danton, and Robespierre. Marat had been a skillful and learned physician. He had traveled in England and noted the aristocratic nature of its government. The meeting of the Estates General turned his attention to politics, and in vigorous pamphlets he had opposed the idea that the new French government should be modeled on Britain's. As demagogic editor of a newspaper, *Ami du peuple* (Friend of the People), he contended that reform must benefit all the people and could be secured by direct popular action. By 1791 he had a hold on the people of Paris, many of whom regarded him as their champion and prophet.

Less extreme and more statesmanlike was Danton. A lawyer by profession, he was a shrewd debater, and possessed a mighty voice and powerful physique. Remaining calm while he worked his hearers into a frenzy of enthusiasm, Danton was an immensely effective orator. He had become influential among the people of Paris and a leading member of the commune, or city government. With Marat he had founded the Cordelier Club, and there in 1791 and 1792 he spoke and worked against the King and for a republic.

A lawyer, too, was Maximilien Robespierre. A devout follower of Rousseau, he had taken his place among the extreme radicals of the National Assembly in the early days when they were few in number. When he failed to gain much influence in that body he turned to the people of Paris for support, and in 1791 became leader of the Jacobin Club. In a chilly way, Robespierre was a fanatic. He was ready to go to any lengths for his ideas and plans.

When the Legislative Assembly met, it became apparent that about half of its 750 members voted more or less independently on various issues before it, while the other half was divided into two camps—the Feuillants (so called because they met in a former convent of that name), and the Girondists (several of whose leaders came from the department of the Gironde). The Feuillants were relatively conservative in that they wished to uphold the new constitution and were even willing to strengthen the royal power. The Girondists were radical in that they favored a republic. They were intensely patriotic, and fond of "classical" references to the ancient republics of Greece and Rome. Among the Girondists were Brissot, an organizer; Vergniaud, an orator; Condorcet, a philosopher; Dumouriez, a general. At the home of the wealthy Madame Roland, they had a salon where they met for political discussion.

In internal affairs, the Legislative Assembly accomplished little, since from the start foreign problems loomed large. The foreign powers had at first welcomed the disturbances in France, since they seemed likely to weaken French influence in Europe. But the upper classes throughout Europe, including Great Britain, were soon horrified by the trends in France toward social equality and mob violence. This reaction was enshrined in Edmund Burke's eloquent *Reflections on the Revolution in France* (1790), which was widely welcomed as a telling defense of the old order of things. In August 1791, Frederick William II of Prussia joined with the Emperor Leopold II in the Declaration of Pillnitz, which announced that the restoration of order and monarchy in France was an object of "common interest to all the sovereigns of Europe." Such verbal interference in their affairs enraged patriotic Frenchmen and weakened the position of Louis XVI.

War might not have resulted if the chief political factions in France had not desired it. The moderate Feuillants, under such leaders as Lafayette, thought it would consolidate the French people in loyalty to the new constitutional regime. The radical Girondists believed it would discredit the monarchy and result in the establishment of a French republic and the general triumph of revolutionary ideas all over Europe. Only such extreme radicals as Marat and Robespierre, outside the Assembly, opposed war for fear it might lead to reaction or a military dictatorship.

Obtaining control of the government, the Girondists demanded that the Emperor Leopold II withdraw his troops from the French frontier and expel the *émigrés* from his territories. When he did not comply, the Girondist ministers prevailed upon Louis XVI to declare war, April 20, 1792. Leopold had just died, but his successor, Francis II, joined with King Frederick William II, of Prussia to gather an army of 80,000 men at Coblentz for the invasion of France. Among the French, patriotic enthusiasm rose to fever heat. Troops coming up from Marseilles sang a stirring new hymn, known as the *Marseillaise* (though it was written at Strasbourg). But, for all their enthusiasm, the French were ill-equipped and ill-organized for war, and the conflict opened with a series of French reverses.

As the military danger grew, many Frenchmen became convinced that they were being betrayed by the royal family. On June 20, 1792, a Paris mob jostled into the palace of the Tuileries and threatened the King, though it did him no violence. A month later, the French were further aroused by a manifesto from the Duke of Brunswick, commander-in-chief of the Austro-Prussian armies, which announced the intention of the Allies to restore absolute monarchy in France, and to punish the revolutionaries, while threatening dire penalties if meanwhile any harm was done to the royal family. The reply of Paris to the Duke of Brunswick was a bloody insurrection on August 9–10, 1792. A mob, led by extreme radicals of the middle class, rose against the constitutional monarchy. They replaced the city government with a new revolutionary commune in which Danton was the leading figure. They invaded the royal palace, massacred the Swiss Guards, and forced the royal family to take refuge with the Legislative Assembly. On August 10, the terror-stricken deputies voted to suspend the King from office and to authorize the immediate election by universal manhood suffrage of a National Convention to draw up a new constitution for France.

For the next six weeks, France was in a state of practical anarchy. The royal family was imprisoned. Lafayette, in protest, resigned his command of the French army and surrendered himself to the enemy. And the allied forces kept advancing.

Danton, now virtually dictator, decided that "the way to stop the enemy" was "to terrify the royalists," while Marat posted fierce placards calling for the blood of "aristocrats." When news reached Paris on September 2 that the fortress of Verdun was invested, a wholesale massacre of royalists began. Men, women, and children, priests, bishops, magistrates, and nobles to the number of two thousand, were hauled out of prisons and murdered.

Meanwhile Dumouriez had replaced Lafayette, and at Valmy on September 20 he checked the allied advance. On the same day, the newly elected National Convention met at Paris.

E. The National Convention and Revolutionary Republic, 1792–1795

The news of Valmy reached Paris on September 22, and simultaneously the National Convention decreed "that royalty is abolished in France." It proceeded to adopt a new calendar with September 22, 1792, as the first day of Year I of the Republic. During the next three years the Convention performed the twofold work of consolidating the Revolution within France and of waging successful foreign war. But it accomplished these tasks by terror, bloodshed, and dictatorship.

In composition the Convention was quite different from the Legislative Assembly. On the right sat nearly two hundred Girondists who were now the conservatives, since, though they desired a democratic republic, they represented the well-to-do middle class and believed in moderation. On the high seats at the left sat a group of about a hundred extreme radicals called the "Mountain" (from their position in the hall) or "Jacobins" (because of the affiliation of many of their leaders with that club). In the center sat a large group—the real majority—called the Plain. It had no settled convictions and no outstanding leaders. At first it tended to vote with the Girondists, but later the course of events and the clamor of Paris mobs inclined it toward the Mountain.

Louis XVI was brought to trial before the Convention on a charge of treason, found guilty by a vote of 387 to 334, and condemned to death. On January 21, 1793, he was beheaded in the Place de la Révolution (now Place de la Concorde). The dignity with which he met his death was the most kingly behavior of his reign.

Meanwhile the tide of Austrian and Prussian invasion was being rolled back from France. After Valmy, Dumouriez drove the foreign armies across the Rhine, invaded the Austrian Netherlands, and seized Brussels. Whereupon the Convention proposed to propagate "liberty" throughout Europe. By a decree of December 1792, it announced its opposition to all princes and privileged classes and its eagerness to help every people found "free and democratic governments."

Thus republican France definitely challenged monarchical Europe. Though the challenge was welcomed by some middle-class intellectuals in foreign lands, the masses of people outside France still gave unquestioning loyalty to their respective rulers. Even in France, a royalist reaction led to civil war in the Vendée, and the able Dumouriez, disgusted by increasing radicalism at Paris, deserted to the Austrians.

The foreign powers accepted the challenge of the French revolutionaries. The outraged monarchs of Austria, Prussia, Great Britain, Holland, Spain, and Sardinia formed a coalition against France. The allied armies reoccupied Belgium and the Rhineland and again invaded France. Against the threat, the National Convention acted with energy and dispatch. All young men were made subject to military conscription, and a new "national" army was organized under the competent direction of Lazare Carnot. Munitions and supplies for it were multiplied. Trusty young officers were trained and commissioned. By the end of 1793, Carnot had some 500,000 men under arms and most of them were fanatically devoted to France and the Revolution.

Not only did the new revolutionary principle of "the nation in arms" provide a large army, but Carnot, unhampered by tradition, was able to make important military innovations. He created the "division" as a military unit, improved the service of supply, and sent members of the government as "deputies on mission" to watch the generals and send home for execution any who faltered or showed themselves incompetent. Moreover, in the revolutionary army, men, regardless of their birth, could reach high rank. Gradually a new group of impetuous republican generals came to the fore and skillfully employed new tactics which took advantage of the numbers and ardor of their troops. Soon the French army was a powerful military force with a dash and vigor which made its opponents, with their tactics of the time of Frederick the Great, seem old-fashioned.

In this way, France met a coalition which would have staggered Louis XIV and won victories which would have dazzled him. The country was cleared of foreign foes. The war was pressed in the Netherlands, along the Rhine, into Savoy, and across the Pyrenees. So successful were the French that Carnot, at first called the "organizer of defense," earned the title of "organizer of victory."

Before the National Convention adjourned in 1795 the anti-French coalition was disrupted. Charles IV of Spain was compelled to make peace and to contract a close alliance with the Republic that had put his Bourbon cousin to death. Frederick William II of Prussia by treaty (1795) gave France a free hand on the left bank of the Rhine and turned his attention to a third partition of Poland.[1] William V, Stadholder of Holland, was deposed, and his country transformed into a "Batavian Republic" in alliance with France. French troops held the

Austrian (Belgian) Netherlands. Though Austria, Great Britain, and Sardinia still remained in arms, they seemed powerless to check the triumphant advance of the French.

But the victories of the Republic were won at a terrible cost. Pride in military triumph gradually overshadowed republican enthusiasm and democratic faith. Economic life in field and shop was increasingly directed to the maintenance of the army. The very victories of the French heightened alarm in other countries, and the plundering of conquered lands made many of the "liberated" dubious about the advantages of the new freedom. At home, the new military power had been mercilessly used to stamp out domestic protests and insurrections, whether of Catholic and royalist peasants of La Vendée, or of other provincials who opposed the radicalism of Paris.

Success abroad and at home arose not only from the new militarism but also from the strong central government established by the National Convention and by the policy of terrorism which that government pursued. In the spring of 1793, under the threat of foreign invasion, the National Convention entrusted supreme executive authority to a Committee of Public Safety composed of nine (later of twelve) members. Though the Girondists sought to control it, and though Danton was at first its leading figure, power in it gradually came into the hands of a group of Jacobins headed by Robespierre, St. Just, and Carnot. Through the local Jacobin societies and through a ruthless exercise of power, the Committee enforced its will on all France.

The policy of the Committee in suppressing dissent in the provinces and rival factions in Paris was terrorism, and the period of its chief work is called the Reign of Terror. So sensational were the methods used and so numerous were the victims who went to the guillotine (an efficient beheading device) that many writers treat the Terror as the central episode of the Revolution. In reality it was but an awful incident in a great political and social movement, an incident induced by the need for united action in crushing enemies at home and abroad, and perhaps, too, by bitter personal rivalry accentuated by fear.

---

[1] See above, p. 443, and map on p. 444.

The chief agencies used by the Committee of Public Safety in its terrorism were the Revolutionary Tribunal and the Law of Suspects. By the former, arrested persons were arbitrarily tried and condemned to death, while by the latter anyone could be arbitrarily arrested who was an "aristocrat" or was "suspected" of disloyalty to the Republic. It is estimated that at Paris some 5,000 persons were thus executed by the guillotine. The Terror spread also to the provinces. Local tribunals arrested suspects, and local guillotines beheaded them. At Lyons, hundreds were put to death. At Nantes, a brutal Jacobin, Carrier by name, loaded victims suspected of connection with the insurrection in the Vendée onto old hulks which were towed out into the Loire and sunk.

But royalists and "aristocrats" were not the only ones to be executed. At Paris, there was a constant flux, as factions strove for power. Those who lost in the struggle went to the guillotine. The Girondists were discredited by their moderation and by the treason of Dumouriez. At the end of May 1793, the Convention, incited by Marat and a Parisian mob, expelled its leading Girondist members, many of whom were afterwards guillotined. In revenge, a Girondist young woman stabbed Marat to death, and then she too was executed.

In March 1794, followers of Danton combined with followers of Robespierre against a group of extremists, led by a certain Hébert, who were intent upon destroying all Christian churches and establishing Atheism. These were outmaneuvered, condemned, and executed. Whereupon Robespierre turned against Danton, who was counseling moderation, and in April succeeded in sending him, with his closest followers, to the guillotine.

For a hundred days, Robespierre was virtual dictator of France, trying to establish a Rousseau-like "republic of virtue" and a Deistic religion. But in the Convention, members who feared that they would be victims of the next purge conspired against him. On July 27, 1794 (ninth Thermidor, Year II, in the new revolutionary calendar), Robespierre was seized and hurried to the guillotine. The death of Robespierre ended the Reign of Terror. The "Thermidorian Reaction," as this event is called, marked

also a turning away of the bourgeoisie from revolutionary radicalism. The Committee of Public Safety had exercised an economic as well as a political dictatorship. It had fixed prices, requisitioned goods, and threatened to confiscate property. Businessmen, lawyers, and "solid" citizens generally were anxious for a regime that would respect property and permit normal business and profits. And throughout the country there was widespread desire to end the "Terror" and to return to more normal conditions.

Despite foreign war and civil strife, the National Convention accomplished some long-range reforms. It devised a plan for national education, began the task of compiling a national code of laws, abolished slavery in the colonies, protected women's property rights, forbade primogeniture (inheritance of property by the eldest son alone), and established the simple and convenient metric system of weights and measures which eventually won acceptance in all save English-speaking and backward countries. With less enduring results, the Convention devised a calendar in which the months had new names (Brumaire, Thermidor, etc.) and the weeks had ten days. It authorized a "religion of reason" in the stormy days of '93, but two years later, while maintaining the ban on non-juring clergy, it promised religious toleration and restored many church buildings to Christian worship.

In republican enthusiasm, the Convention decreed that all persons be addressed as "citizen." Knee breeches (*culottes*) of the old regime went out of fashion, and were replaced by the long trousers of workingmen (*sans-culottes*). But after Thermidor, republican radicalism waned, and France edged away from revolutionary excesses. The last rioting of a Paris mob was suppressed in October 1795 by a "whiff of grape-shot" discharged at the command of a young and then obscure artillery captain named Napoleon Bonaparte.

In 1793 the Convention had drafted a radically democratic constitution based on universal manhood suffrage. But it had never gone into effect, and after Robespierre's death a new and more conservative document was worked out under the guidance of Sieyès. This, which went into effect in 1795,

THE FIRST FRENCH REPUBLIC AND
ITS SATELLITES, 1795-1799

French Republic 1799

Dependent Republics 1799

German Church States to be absorbed by
other German States under French auspices

200 Miles

is called the Constitution of the Year III, and the republican government which it established is known as the Directory. It provided for a two-chamber legislature elected by indirect and somewhat restricted suffrage and for an executive of five Directors chosen by the legislature. It was hoped that the new government would give stability to the French Republic. But in fact it lasted little more than four years.

F. The Republic under the Directory, and Advent of Napoleon Bonaparte

That the Republican Directory did not long survive was owing to a combination of factors. It was harried by pressures from radicals on one side and conservatives on the other. To have consolidated the country after six years of revolutionary upheaval would have required hard and honest labor on the part of men of distinct genius. Yet almost without exception the Directors were men of mediocre talents, and some of them were flagrantly dishonest.

In marked contrast with the mediocrity

of the Directors was the genius of the soldier whom they promoted to command a major French army and entrusted with the task of pressing the foreign war against Austria and Sardinia. This was Napoleon Bonaparte. In 1796, with lightning rapidity, infectious enthusiasm, and brilliant tactics, he crossed the Alps, humbled the Sardinians, and within a few months disposed of five Austrian armies. Soon all northern Italy was in his hands. Sardinia surrendered, and ceded Nice and Savoy to France. When Bonaparte's army approached Vienna, even Austria stooped to make peace with this amazing republican general. By the treaty of Campo Formio (1797), France obtained the Austrian (Belgian) Netherlands, and Austria, while permitted to annex the Venetian Republic, had to promise not to interfere elsewhere in Italy. Only Great Britain was left at war with France.

So great was Bonaparte's prestige as a result of his Italian campaign that the Directors were relieved when they found a way of getting rid of him temporarily. At his own suggestion, a French expedition was sent in 1798 to Egypt, with himself in command, in order to sever communications between England and India. There Bonaparte won some battles, sent home glowing reports, and encouraged scientists he had brought with him to study Egyptian monuments. But as the British Admiral Lord Nelson won a great naval victory off the mouth of the Nile, the French army in Egypt was cut off and isolated. Bonaparte himself, eluding the British warships, returned to France, where he was received as a kind of savior. For while he had been away, matters had been going very badly for France. There had been increased domestic unrest; and the foreign policy which, since the peace of Campo Formio, the Directory had pursued of installing puppet republican governments in Holland, Switzerland, and Italy, had led to the formation of a Second Coalition (Russia and Austria with Great Britain) against France.

Thanks to money subsidies supplied by the British prime minister, the younger William Pitt (1759–1806),[1] the new Allies were enabled to put large armies in the field and in 1799 they won repeated victories. The French were driven from Italy, and most of the puppet republics collapsed. Thus when Bonaparte returned from Egypt in October 1799, he found France defeated, and the public eager for a change that would remedy the situation.

Within a month the young general was able to overthrow the Directory. Adroitly intriguing with Sieyès, one of the Directors, he surrounded the Legislature with a cordon of troops, and on November 9, 1799 (eighteenth Brumaire), secured by a show of force the overthrow of the government. This *coup d'état* (blow at the state) was promptly followed by a new constitution which made Bonaparte First Consul of the French Republic. Those who had plotted with him had hoped to use him as a tool. But it quickly became clear that Bonaparte was master.

Thus, only ten and a half years after the Estates General had met in Versailles, parliamentary government fell by the sword. As Marat and Robespierre had feared, foreign war brought a military dictator to power.

The way to real liberty and democracy, never fully cleared by the French Revolutionaries, was now blocked by a reactionary dictatorship.

Yet in a sense the advent of Bonaparte did not end the French Revolution. The revolutionaries had advanced certain principles which they summed up in the words "Liberty, Equality, Fraternity." These words had been carried into foreign lands by the French armies. They brought fear to monarchs and nobles; they connoted evil to a host of devout Christians; and to many an ignorant peasant they might seem strange and dangerous. But to many of the middle class, heirs of the eighteenth-century "enlightenment," to many a dreamer or altruistic intellectual, to many a workingman in the cities, the words appeared full of hope and of the promise of better days to come when justice should reign and all men be brothers. Bonaparte did not erase "Liberty, Equality, Fraternity" from the monuments. Far from denouncing them, he applauded them. He called himself "the son of the Revolution" and declared he would complete its work. True, he twisted the principles to his own use. If he maintained equality, he sacrificed liberty.

William Pitt, the Younger. After a portrait by John Hoppner (d. 1810).

---

[1] Son of the William Pitt who became Earl of Chatham. See above, pp. 465, 471.

Yet to our own day, the principles of the French Revolution have had great and enduring significance. "Liberty" has implied certain political ideals. Government should be exercised, not autocratically by divine right, but constitutionally by the sovereign will of the governed. The individual should not be subject to the arbitrary rule of a king, but should be guaranteed possession of personal liberties which no state might abridge. Such were liberties of conscience, worship, speech, and publication. The liberty of owning private property was proclaimed by the French Revolution to be an inherent right of man.

"Equality" has signified the social principles of the Revolution. It meant the abolition of privilege, the end of serfdom, the destruction of the feudal system. It assumed that all men were equal before the law. It carried the hope that every man might have an equal chance with every other man in the pursuit of life and happiness.

"Fraternity" was the symbol of the idealistic brotherhood of those who sought to make the world better, happier, and more just. At the same time, it was the watchword of the new French nationalism. For the sake of humanity the French nation should be exalted. Schools, armies, even religion should be nationalized. No longer should mercenaries fight at the behest of despots for dynastic aims. Henceforth a nation in arms should be prepared to do battle under the banner of "fraternity" in defense of whatever it believed to be the nation's interests.

Political liberty, social equality, national patriotism—these three have remained the ideals of all who have looked for inspiration to the French Revolution.

CHAPTER 42

Career of Napoleon, 1799–1815

A. The French Republic under Bonaparte's Consulate, 1799–1804

From 1799 to 1814 the history of France and of all Europe was so closely tied to the career of Napoleon Bonaparte that these years have been called "the era of Napoleon." During this period France experienced a molding of previous revolutionary achievements into permanent institutions and yet at the same time was subjected to a military dictatorship. French militarism triumphed briefly, and French armies helped to spread revolutionary ideas all over Europe, arousing nationalism in other countries. During the first five years of the period France remained nominally a republic, with Bonaparte as First Consul. From 1804 to 1814, he ruled as Emperor Napoleon I over a French Empire.

In 1799 General Bonaparte was thirty years of age. Short, stocky, quiet, with cold grey eyes, he had already an imperious and commanding manner. Born in Corsica, he had received a military education in France and had become a junior artillery officer in the royal army. Restless and ambitious, he threw in his lot with the Jacobins after the Revolution broke out and achieved some distinction in the recapture of Toulon (1793) and the defense of the Convention (1795). But it was his First Italian Campaign of 1796 that made him famous. Bonaparte was selfish and ruthless, but he had qualities which convinced his associates that he was "a man of destiny." He was a military genius, knowing how to use the new tactics evolved for the mass armies that had been created by the Revolution. He had an amazing memory and a sense of the dramatic. He was an exceptionally able organizer and administrator. He understood politics and diplomacy, and, being unrestrained by religion, morality, or sentiment, he was prepared to use any means to gain his ends.

When Bonaparte seized power in 1799 he appreciated that the French people were weary of weak government and disorder. He set himself a constructive program which he carried into effect within a few years. First, he devised a new government for France (Constitution of the Year VIII), under which a semblance of democracy was retained by a three-house legislature, but in which real authority was centered in Bonaparte as First Consul and in his appointed Council of State. Submitted to the people in a plebiscite, the new constitution won an overwhelming majority. The vote was really one of confidence in Bonaparte and of disapproval of the Directory.

Within France, the First Consul's firm hand soon reduced the country to order. He repressed royalists on one hand, and Jacobins on the other. The press was subjected to rigid censorship; and under Fouché, an ex-Jacobin, a pervasive secret police and spy system was developed to keep watch over the citizenry.

Bonaparte effected a permanent reorganization of local government in France. In 1800 he abolished the elective officials in the *arrondissements* and *départements* and vested their functions in prefects and sub-prefects appointed by, and responsible to, the First Consul. Elective councils were retained but with very limited powers. While village mayors were to be appointed by the prefects, mayors and police officials of cities would be named directly by the chief of state. Thus Bonaparte completed the work of centralization begun by Richelieu. The system was hardly democratic but it was efficient.

Bonaparte also effected an ecclesiastical settlement in France. In 1799 the country was still divided into two camps—that of devout Catholics who were hostile to the revolutionary restriction and persecution of the church, and that of liberals and radicals who wished to maintain a separate French church or to do away with Christianity altogether. In 1801 Bonaparte negotiated a concordat (or treaty) with Pope Pius VII. By it, the Pope accepted the confiscation of church property and the suppression of monasteries in France. In return, the Republic undertook to pay the salaries of the clergy. The First Consul would nominate the bishops, the Pope would invest them with their office. Priests would be appointed by the bishops. Thus was the Catholic

Church officially restored in France, but it was tied to the state even more closely than in the days of Louis XIV. So advantageous did this concordat appear that it continued in force for over a century and under a dozen different governments. Bonaparte made similar arrangements with the Protestant churches and Jewish synagogues in France.

The First Consul put French finances in order. By rigid economy, exacting collection of taxes, and contributions levied on conquered lands, Bonaparte balanced the French budget. He completed the work of the Directory in establishing sound currency, and he set up the Bank of France (1800) as a central credit and note-issuing institution.

Surrounding himself with expert legal advisers, Bonaparte pushed through the wholesale reformation of French law which had been begun in the revolutionary period. The resulting civil code (1804)—the Code Napoléon—was followed by a code of civil and criminal procedure, a penal code, and a commercial code. Into the new legal structure were written many of the major achievements of the Revolution—equality before the law, religious toleration, abolition of

Napoleon's Crowning of Josephine (1804). Painting by Jacques Louis David (d. 1825).

Courtesy Bettmann Archive

serfdom, of feudalism, and of privilege, and equality of inheritance. If harsh punishments and the legal subjection of women were maintained, still the codes were so clear and otherwise so enlightened that they were later adopted or imitated in many other lands. Bonaparte was rightly hailed as a second Justinian.

Public works of various sorts also distinguished Bonaparte's rule. Highways were built, bridges constructed, canals and harbors improved. Paris and other cities were beautified by public buildings and monuments in the classical style, and many of them commemorated the triumphs of Napoleon Bonaparte.

In one matter, however, Bonaparte failed signally. He hoped to reëstablish the old French colonial empire. To Haiti he dispatched his brother-in-law, General Leclerc, with an expeditionary force to subdue the slaves who had revolted and killed or expelled their French masters. Spain was forced by Bonaparte to give back to France the territory of Louisiana (west of the Mississippi) which France had ceded in 1763. But Leclerc's efforts failed miserably, and anticipation of war with Great Britain determined Bonaparte to sell Louisiana to the United States in 1803.

One task which he had set himself in 1799—defeat of the Second Coalition of Britain, Austria, and Russia—Bonaparte was eminently fitted to perform. He inspirited the French army, perfected the system of supply, and appointed able officers to commands. By flattery and diplomacy, he induced the half-insane Tsar Paul (1796–1801) of Russia to withdraw from war against France and even to revive (with Prussia, Sweden, and Denmark) an armed neutrality of the North against Great Britain. Then in 1800, with lightning swiftness, Bonaparte led his armies through the Alps, and at Marengo in Italy overwhelmed the Austrian forces. Another French army crushed the Austrians at Hohenlinden in Germany. In 1801 Austria signed the treaty of Lunéville which reaffirmed the peace of Campo Formio.[1] and reëstablished French dominance in Italy. Though the British were still masters of the sea, though Nelson broke up the armed neutrality of the North

---

[1] See above, p. 542.

in 1801 by bombarding Copenhagen (without a declaration of war), and though the remnants of the French Egyptian expedition were compelled to surrender, still France seemed clearly unconquerable on the continent. Under these circumstances Great Britain and France signed, at Amiens in 1802, a treaty which was designed to inaugurate a peace, but which proved to be only a truce.

In a few short years, Bonaparte as First Consul had brought France order, prosperity, victory, and peace. If his rule was a thinly disguised dictatorship, yet he had maintained many of the social and legal gains of the Revolution. The future of France promised to be golden. Secure and firmly governed, there seemed nothing to prevent her from consolidating her position and her internal well-being. But instead, the story of the ensuing years is one of military glory culminating in disaster.

B. Creation of the Napoleonic Empire and Its Triumphant Expansion

After the peace of Amiens was signed, Bonaparte felt strong enough in France to take another step toward absolute power. A new constitution (Constitution of the Year X) was devised in 1802, submitted to the people, and approved by an overwhelming majority. It was very similar to the previous one, with the exception that Bonaparte was now made First Consul for life, and that his powers, as against those of the hand-picked legislative bodies, were strengthened. There remained only one more step for the ambitious general to take. Two years later, by still another constitution and still another plebiscite, Bonaparte assumed the title of Napoleon I, Emperor of the French. On December 2, 1804, amid imposing ceremonies in the cathedral of Notre Dame at Paris and in the presence of Pope Pius VII, Bonaparte placed a crown upon his own head. The peculiar nature of the new government was symbolized by the inscription on French coins of the time, "French Republic, Napoleon Emperor." Nor was the heritage of the recent revolutionary past eliminated by the Empire. The social gains were still intact. The tricolor was still the country's flag. The words, "Liberty, Equality, Fraternity," still appeared on public buildings.

There were changes, however. As a form of address, "monsieur" replaced "citizen." The republican calendar fell into disuse. Old titles of nobility were restored, and new ones created. The revolutionary generals who accepted the new regime became "Marshals of the Empire." Distinguished service to the Emperor was rewarded by membership in a newly created Legion of Honor. Some of the noble *émigrés* came back to add social graces to the imperial court, where they rubbed elbows with men of lowly origin who had won fame on far-flung battlefields.

If the Consulate had brought peace and reform, the Empire involved almost continuous war. Even before the Empire was established, war had broken out again (May, 1803) with Napoleon's inveterate enemy, Great Britain. Though the Revolution was in a real sense over in France, many Englishmen felt they were fighting its personification by opposing Napoleon. Moreover, in the expansion of French control there was an economic or strategic threat to Britain, especially in the Low Countries and in the Mediterranean. During the next decade, whatever else happened on the continent, Britain warred against France by every means at its disposal.

In part, the Franco-British conflict was naval. Here the British won an early and decisive victory. On October 21, 1805, their fleet under Lord Nelson crushed combined French and Spanish fleets off Cape Trafalgar (near the Strait of Gibraltar). Nelson lost his life in the battle, but Britain won unquestionable supremacy on the seas. So effective was Napoleon's censorship, however, that no French newspaper mentioned the naval disaster till after the fall of the Empire.

Before Trafalgar, Napoleon had planned to invade England and had even gathered troops along the Channel coast (1803–1804) for the purpose. He was diverted, however, by events in Austria; and after Trafalgar, British sea power rendered any such plan too hazardous. Napoleon was reduced to attacking Great Britain by indirect means. In true mercantilist fashion, he sought to bring Britain to its knees by closing its markets and thus reducing its exports. By a series of decrees, he prohibited the importation of British goods, not only into France, but into all the other parts of Europe which he controlled. This method of trying to ruin Britain was known as the "Continental System," and much of Napoleon's effort was spent in attempting to enforce it, and to persuade other Continental countries such as Russia to adhere to it.

Britain replied to the Continental System by a series of royal "Orders in Council" designed to keep neutral ships from going to French-held ports and to oblige them to come to England. Thus a neutral ship could go almost nowhere in Europe without breaking either the French or the British regulations. In enforcing their orders, the British had the advantage of sea power, and so ruthlessly did they use it in violation of neutral rights that the youthful United States at length (1812) felt impelled to declare war on Great Britain.

In the long run, Napoleon's Continental System failed of its purpose. Many British goods were in great popular demand on the Continent, and even Napoleon found himself obliged to license the importation of certain ones. There was much smuggling, and countries which were subject to Napoleon, or allied with him, sought to alleviate their shortages by buying British products and overseas goods supplied by the British, whether legally or illegally. Moreover, British sea power secured the markets of the whole world, except Europe, for British merchants, who rapidly expanded their trade in distant areas such as Spanish America.

Though the commercial war went against Napoleon and slowly sapped French strength, land victories for a while seemed to offer ample compensation. In vain Great Britain organized and subsidized a Third Coalition, with Austria, Russia, and Sweden against France. Abandoning his projected invasion of England, Napoleon rapidly marched his armies into Germany and defeated the Austrians at Ulm (October 20, 1805). Moving on, he occupied Vienna, then turned northward, and crushed an Austro-Russian army at Austerlitz in Mora-

Battle of Trafalgar. By Clarkson Stanfield (d. 1867).

Courtesy Bettmann Archive

via on December 2, his "lucky day." Austria was thus forced out of the coalition, and by the treaty of Pressburg the Austrian Emperor Francis I ceded Venetia to Napoleon and the Tyrol to Bavaria.

Prussia had not originally joined the Third Coalition, but now its King Frederick William III, relying (unwisely) on a military reputation inherited from Frederick the Great, and fearing a complete French triumph, entered the war and sent an army under the aged Duke of Brunswick against Napoleon. The French and Prussian armies met at Jena (October 14, 1806), and the

Prussians were defeated in disastrous and most humiliating fashion. At a stroke, the Prussian military prestige evaporated. Napoleon entered Berlin and occupied most of Prussia. Prussian Poland was torn away and erected into a Grand Duchy of Warsaw under Napoleon's ally, the Elector of Saxony, and Prussia was compelled to reduce her army to 42,000 men.

Russia remained to be dealt with. In a bloody winter battle at Eylau in East Prussia, Napoleon won a partial victory; and then at Friedland, he was completely successful. At Tilsit, on a raft in the middle of the Niemen River, Napoleon and the young Tsar Alexander I (1801–1825) met to discuss peace terms. Alexander was dazzled by Napoleon's personality and by his generosity, for the victor exacted hardly an inch of Russian soil and asked only that Russia join in excluding British trade from Europe. On the other hand, Alexander was given to understand that he might deal as he would with Finland and the Ottoman Empire. "What is Europe?" exclaimed the emotional Tsar, "where is it, if it is not you and I?"

Thus was the Third Coalition liquidated, with Sweden paying a heavy price for having adhered to it. In 1808 Russia seized Finland, which had long been Swedish. In 1809, Sweden recognized the Russian conquest, and agreed to exclude British goods. The Swedish King Gustavus IV was compelled to abdicate in favor of his aged and childless uncle, Charles XIII, who soon named as his heir one of Napoleon's generals, Marshal Bernadotte.

By 1808, Napoleon's French Empire was at its height. Northern Italy had been made into a kingdom with Napoleon as King and his stepson Eugene Beauharnais as Viceroy. The kingdom of Naples was ruled by his brother Joseph, as was Holland by his brother Louis. The Pope, the King of Spain, and the King of Denmark were his allies. The Russian Tsar called him friend and brother. Sweden was being brought into line. The Grand Duchy of Warsaw was a recruiting ground for his army. All Germany was under his influence. Prussia and Austria had become second-rate powers.

Germany was being entirely made over by the impact of Napoleonic France. The left bank of the Rhine had been incorporated into France, and in subsequent rearrangements scores of petty independent states east of the Rhine had been wiped out. Altogether, the number of German states was reduced from more than three hundred to less than one hundred. Bavaria, Württemberg, and Baden in the south had been enlarged to reward them for aiding Napoleon, and the rulers of Bavaria and Württemberg, and also of Saxony, had been further compensated with the title of king.

Besides, in 1806 the South German states and a number of others virtually seceded from the Holy Roman Empire and formed a Confederation of the Rhine under Napoleon's protection. Napoleon announced that he no longer recognized the Holy Roman Empire, and on August 6 the Habsburg Emperor Francis II resigned the imperial crown which had been worn by his ancestors for centuries. The work of a long line of French kings and statesmen was completed by Napoleon, and the Holy Roman Empire had come to an inglorious end. Its last Emperor contented himself with assuming the new title of Francis I, Hereditary Emperor of Austria.

By 1808, all Germany was at the mercy of Napoleon. Prussia was shorn of half her lands, the Confederation of the Rhine enlarged, and a kingdom of Westphalia carved out of northern and western Germany for Napoleon's brother Jerome. Most significant of all, wherever French rule extended, there followed the abolition of feudalism and serfdom, the recognition of the equality of all citizens before the law, and the enlightened principles of the Code Napoléon.

The humiliations of Austria were not at an end. Far from accepting French dominance, Francis I, with the aid of two patriotic assistants—the Archduke Charles and Count Stadion—busied himself with reforming the army, mustering the national resources, and stimulating national spirit. In 1809, when Napoleon was involved in difficulties in Spain, an opportunity seemed to have come for Austria to strike. Francis I declared war, and the Archduke Charles led an army into Bavaria. But with his usual rapidity Napoleon rushed from Spain, forced the Austrians back upon Vienna, and seized their capital once more. In May, the Austrian commanders inflicted a reverse upon Napoleon at Aspern but failed to follow it up, and then at Wagram in July Napoleon won a victory which induced the Austrians once again to make peace. This time, they had to yield Austrian Poland to Russia and to the Grand Duchy of Warsaw, and the Illyrian provinces on the Adriatic to France. As an additional pledge, Napoleon shortly afterwards married Maria Louisa, daughter of Francis I. The French Emperor had long desired an heir to his throne, and he made the new marriage possible by securing an annulment of his previous marriage with Josephine Beauharnais. Fate still seemed to smile on the Corsican, for in 1811 Maria Louisa bore him a son who was given the title of King of Rome.

Yet all was not well with the Napoleonic fortunes. The troubles in Spain alluded to above were beginning to be a bleeding wound in the side of the French Empire. In 1807 Napoleon had poured troops into Spain and Portugal. He had seized Lisbon and announced that Portugal, long Britain's ally and commercial vassal, was now part of the Continental System. In the next year Napoleon had lured to France the aging Spanish King Charles IV, together with the heir to the throne, Prince Ferdinand, and the flashy chief minister of Spain, Godoy. Then he had forced both King and Prince to resign all claims to the Spanish throne. Napoleon's brother Joseph was thereupon promoted from the kingship of Naples to that of Spain, while a brother-in-law, Joachim Murat, was given the vacant Neapolitan throne.

In July 1808, Joseph was crowned at Madrid. But in August he was driven out by an angry uprising of Spaniards. At last the triumphant advance of the French, inspired by their new nationalism, had run into the aroused patriotism of another people, and they were to find this much more difficult to deal with than divine-right monarchs and professional armies. Spanish priests and nobles made common cause with bourgeois and peasants. When they could not put an army in the field they employed guerilla tactics, which cut French communications and bewildered the best French generals. Moreover, the British sent an army under Sir Arthur Wellesley (later Duke of Wellington) to Portugal in August 1808, and quickly, with the aid of Spaniards and Portuguese, he expelled the French from that country. Thus began the Peninsular War, which lasted until 1813 and brought eventual disaster to the French. Napoleon might put Joseph back on the throne at Madrid. He might seize cities and win battles. But he could not subdue the Spanish people nor could he oust the stubborn British.

C. Decline and Fall of the Empire

From 1808 to 1814 Napoleon's power was on the wane, though for some time the decline was concealed by victories like that at Wagram. Certain limitations of Napoleon's genius and of his dictatorship were becoming apparent. He was growing older and less energetic, while his ambition and lust for conquest kept on increasing. He was becoming more averse to taking advice. Moreover, the armies, on which his power really rested, were changing in character. They had once been composed almost wholly of patriotic Frenchmen fighting with enthusiasm for the fatherland and the Revolution. Now, more and more, they included Poles, Germans, Italians, Dutch, and Danes recruited more or less forcibly and held together mainly by discipline and faith in the Emperor. Nor were the French officers the dashing young patriots of the earlier days. They were more cautious, more self-seeking. Some of the best had died in battle.

In the conquered and allied lands, there had been many who originally viewed the coming of the French apathetically, or else hailed with enthusiasm the introduction of the revolutionary principles and reforms. But liberty and equality somehow proved to be mirages. For the subject countries, French rule was harsh. There were taxes and requisitions, there were confiscation (or even looting) and conscription, and there was always another war to drain off resources in men, goods, and money. Gradually other European peoples came to look upon the French as conquerors who were more oppressive than the old divine-right rulers. Conquered countries became nationalistic.

Everywhere, too, the Continental System came to be hated. It led to shortages, high prices, and stagnant trade. Smuggling grew apace and the loopholes that were opened up were too numerous for the French to plug. Despite constant pressure from Napoleon, the continental states simply could not be kept in line. They bought British goods when and how and where they could. When Pope Pius VII objected to both the Continental System and Napoleon's treatment of church matters, the Emperor made

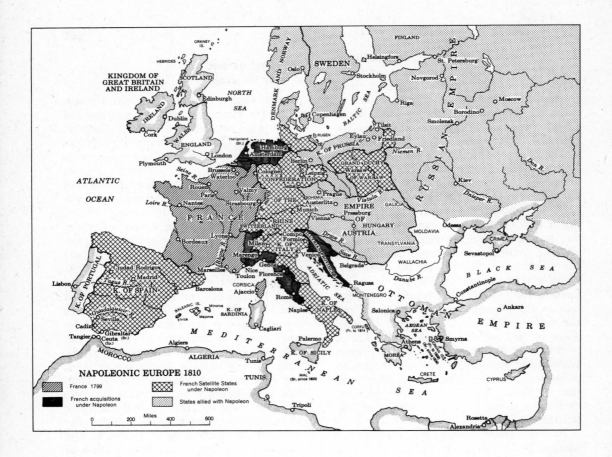

him prisoner and seized the Papal State (1809). The next year he deposed his brother, Louis, for admitting English goods into Dutch territory, and incorporated Holland into France. And all the while French generals and their armies were trying vainly to subdue Spain and Portugal and expel British forces from the peninsula.

After Wagram (1809), it seemed for a time as if Napoleon need expect no more trouble in central Europe. But the very magnitude of the French victories was raising a new kind of opposition. In Prussia, King Frederick William III turned to new advisers who, between 1807 and 1813, wrought a veritable regeneration in that kingdom. The chief of these were Baron vom Stein and Chancellor Hardenberg, who felt that only by renovating the state and removing abuses could Prussia be made strong again. Under their leadership, serfdom was abolished (1807) and the peasants were made absolute owners of part of their holdings; the administration of the government

was simplified and improved; and modernized agencies of local government were set up. At the same time two military reformers, Scharnhorst and Gneisenau, were remaking the Prussian army, despite limitations put on it by Napoleon.

To check these developments in Prussia, Napoleon forced the dismissal of Stein, who proceeded to turn to Austria and Russia, preaching hatred of the French as he went. Stirred by reforms, humiliated by defeats and aroused by French arrogance, the Prussian people, and other Germans as well, felt the stirrings of a new national patriotism. Through the work of societies like the *Tugendbund* (League of Virtue) and the writings of authors like Fichte and Arndt, a new loyalty to the fatherland was rapidly created. No longer did the French have a monopoly of national patriotism. As for liberty, to a Prussian in 1810 it seemed that it could be secured only by ousting the French conquerors.

In Austria the ill-timed campaign of 1809

was but a stage, not an end, of national effort. The army was rebuilt; diplomatic channels to Napoleon's other victims were kept open; Austria was biding her time. Meanwhile the Spanish war continued. In 1812, Wellington, with British and Spanish troops, won a resounding victory at Salamanca, captured Madrid, and drove out the French. In the same year, groups of liberal Spaniards, who had learned revolutionary doctrines from both French and British, gathered at Cadiz and drafted a new constitution for Spain. This document long served as a model for liberal constitutions throughout southern Europe. Under it, sovereignty was vested in the "nation," legislative power in a single-house legislature (or *cortes*), and executive power in the king and his ministers. But the king was to have only a suspensive veto over acts of the *cortes*. The constitution proclaimed individual liberty and legal equality. While it recognized Catholicism as "the religion of the Spanish nation," it abolished the Inquisition and limited church property.

Though the four fateful defects in the Napoleonic Empire—Napoleon's own character, the changing nature of his army, the impracticability of the Continental System, and the rise of nationalism among the peoples of Europe—were now painfully evident, it was a break between Napoleon and the Tsar Alexander that ushered in the final disasters. Alexander had been irritated by the enlargement of the Grand Duchy of Warsaw after Austria's defeat in 1809. He had been impeded, rather than aided, in his designs on the Ottoman Empire. He had been annoyed when Napoleon dethroned one of the Tsar's relatives in German Oldenburg and annexed that duchy. But most of all, he was alienated by Napoleon's efforts to enforce the Continental System on Russia. Russia needed to import manufactured goods from England and to export grain thither. Gradually Alexander permitted the resumption of trade with Britain. Napoleon had either to fight for his system—his sole weapon against Great Britain—or see the system collapse in northern Europe. Napoleon chose to fight.

Early in 1812, Napoleon was busy preparing for war against his recent ally. He forced Prussia and Austria to promise aid, and he gathered an army of 430,000 men. Less than half were French veterans; the rest were Germans, Poles, Italians, Dutch, Swiss, Danes, Yugoslavs. Nor was Alexander inactive. He made peace with the Ottoman Empire, reached understandings with Great Britain and Sweden, negotiated secretly with Austria and Prussia, and mobilized an army. Napoleon declared war on June 22, 1812, crossed the Niemen river two days later, and proceeded into Russia. Refusing to engage in open battle, the Russians retreated slowly, merely harassing the French advance. Unable to defeat or capture his foe, Napoleon penetrated ever deeper into Russia. Only once, at Borodino on September 7, did one of the Russian generals, Kutusov, fight a real battle. Both sides lost heavily, but the French were able to move on and to take Moscow a week later.

On the very night of Napoleon's triumphal entry, Moscow was set on fire. Supplies were burned up; the inhabitants fled. Already, the Russians in their long retreat had adopted a "scorched earth" policy of destroying provisions that might aid the French. Now, lack of food made it impossible for Napoleon to winter his army in Moscow. To advance was futile. He could only retreat. On October 22, he evacuated Moscow and began to retrace his steps toward Germany. The Russian forces followed, still risking no major engagements but ever attacking the French rear and cutting off stragglers.

Napoleon's retreat from Moscow is one of the most famous and horrible episodes in history. Downpours of rain changed to sleet and snow. Swollen streams checked the march. Food was short. The French forces abandoned their baggage. They ran out of ammunition. They froze to death in snow drifts. They fell from exhaustion. The retreat became a rout, the rout a disaster. It was only a pitiable and starving remnant of the *Grande Armée* which on December 13 recrossed the Niemen into Germany. Fully half a million lives had been sacrificed upon the fields of Russia to Napoleon's ambition. Yet he sought to reassure the afflicted French people by announcing, "the Emperor has never been in better health."

For a moment Alexander hesitated, for

Russia was now free. But urged on by Baron vom Stein and his own desire to play the role of deliverer of Europe, he decided to attempt the final overthrow of his rival. On January 13, 1813, Alexander led his troops across the Niemen and proclaimed the liberty of the European peoples. It was the beginning of the War of Liberation.

Russia was promptly joined by Prussia, together with all northern and central Germany. On the other side, Napoleon speedily gathered a new army of 200,000 men from France, southern Germany, and Italy. On May 2, he defeated the Prussians and Russians at Lützen, but lack of cavalry prevented him from following up his victory.

At this point, Metternich, chief minister of Austria, arranged an armistice and proposed a general peace which would have left France many of its conquests. But Napoleon only wanted time to gather more forces for a decisive victory. By the utmost effort, he got together an army of 120,000 men; and then he rejected the peace proposals. Whereupon Austria joined the coalition of Russia, Prussia, Sweden, and Great Britain.

Though at Dresden, in August, Napoleon won another victory against the Austrians, his forces were gradually hemmed in by the converging Allies. At Leipzig, in October he fought a three-day "Battle of the Nations." Outnumbered, deserted in the midst of battle by his Saxon troops, he went down to defeat. A fortnight later, Napoleon led a remnant of his army back across the Rhine. Germany was freed.

After the "Battle of the Nations" the French allies and puppets were either overwhelmed or deserted to the other side. Only the King of Saxony, on whom Napoleon had conferred the additional title of Grand Duke of Warsaw, remained loyal. Yet in the face of these events Napoleon rejected still another peace offer from Austria that would have left him a France bounded by the Alps, the Rhine, and the Pyrenees. Needlessly he prolonged the war on French soil, with the remains of his defeated army and with hastily gathered recruits.

Early in 1814 three large foreign armies moved in on France from the north and east, while Wellington, having cleared Spain of French troops, led still another army into southern France. At the end of March, despite a brilliant and desperate defense on the part of the Emperor, Paris surrendered to the Allies. Thirteen days later, by a personal treaty of Fontainebleau, Napoleon abdicated his throne, renounced all rights to France for himself and his family, and in return was granted sovereignty of the little island of Elba (off the northwest coast of Italy), an annual pension of two and a half million francs, and the Italian duchy of Parma for his wife, Maria Louisa. After an affecting farewell to his Old Guard, Napoleon departed for Elba, where he dwelt for ten months.

In 1793 European monarchs had banded together to restore divine-right monarchy and the old social order in France and to stamp out revolutionary ideas. But in 1814, while they restored a Bourbon to the throne, and gave him a France with the boundaries of 1792, they did so with the understanding that he would recognize and confirm the chief social and political reforms of the Revolution. The Restoration was engineered, in the name of "legitimacy," by the unscrupulous Talleyrand, ex-bishop, ex-revolutionist, ex-Napoleonic minister, who now courted the Tsar Alexander.

The "legitimate" heir of Louis XVI was his brother, the Count of Provence, a stout and cynical old gentleman, who had been living quietly in England these many years and who now made a solemn entry into Paris. The new king kept what forms of the old regime he could. He assumed the title of Louis XVIII, "King of France by the Grace of God." He reckoned his reign from the death (1795) of his nephew, the dauphin ("Louis XVII"). He replaced the tricolor with the lilied white flag of his family. At the same time, however, he granted a constitutional "charter," making France a limited monarchy. He confirmed the liberty and equality won by the Revolution. He left the church lands in private hands. Simultaneously there were restorations elsewhere in Europe. Ferdinand VII came back to Spain; Pope Pius VII returned to Rome; Victor Emmanuel I mounted the throne of Sardinia.

But the last had not been heard of Napoleon. He found Elba irksome and longed to get back to the Continent. By February 1815, circumstances seemed favorable. His enemies were divided, Austria and Great Britain being at odds with Prussia and Russia over the fate of Saxony and Poland. In France the return of the *émigrés* with their old airs and the tactless treatment of Napoleonic veterans were arousing ill-feeling, while the concessions of Louis XVIII did not render the majority of Frenchmen enthusiastic about the return of a Bourbon monarchy.

With a small bodyguard Napoleon escaped from Elba, eluded British warships, and landed at Cannes on March 1, 1815. Troops sent out to arrest him could not resist the familiar uniform; and without firing a shot Napoleon entered Paris on March 20. Louis XVIII was already jogging over the Belgian frontier. By an astute manifesto, Napoleon clinched his hold on France. He promised to renounce war and conquest, to maintain liberty and equality, and to establish a constitutional government. The French either rallied to Napoleon or remained quiet.

But if Napoleon was right about France, he was wrong about the rest of Europe. The four great powers forgot their differences, renewed their alliance, and rushed troops toward France. To oppose them Napoleon raised a new army and marched into Belgium. There on June 18, at Waterloo, he fought the final great battle of his remarkable career. The defeat administered by Wellington with a British-Dutch-German army was, at the close of the day, turned into a rout by the arrival of Blücher and his Prussians. Even had Napoleon won at Waterloo, he could not have hoped to make head against the combined and determined armies of Britain, Russia, Prussia, and Austria. The return from Elba was a really hopeless venture from the start. On June 22, Napoleon abdicated again, and before long the Allies reoccupied Paris, bringing Louis XVIII back "in their baggage train."

Napoleon surrendered himself to the British, and this time no chances were taken. The former Emperor was sent to the lonely and rocky island of St. Helena in the south Atlantic. There he lived for five and a half years until his death in 1821. There he dictated his memoirs, subtly compounded of truth and falsehood, in which he sought to depict himself as the true son of the revolution, the friend of oppressed nationalities, the lover of peace, who had been driven to war and disaster by wiles of the British and of despotic European monarchs. These writings in exile were to become the basis of a "Napoleonic legend" which would contribute in time to seat another Bonaparte on the throne of a second French Empire.

D. Abiding Influence of the French Revolution and Napoleon

The events of the French Revolution and the era of Napoleon brought into Europe a new kind of government based on ideas of the eighteenth-century "enlightenment" and in harmony with a social structure in which the middle class was especially strong. The new regime consisted of a highly centralized government based on the doctrine of popular sovereignty, supported by a national army and national schools, inspired by national patriotism, and capped by a parliament representing citizens rather than classes. The new society was individualistic, and insistent on the political rights and liberties of its members. Special privileges of all sorts were banished. All religions were tolerated. This was the new system so firmly rooted in France by 1815 that no restored Bourbon could overturn it. It was in France, and in Europe, to stay.

The new regime, belief in which constituted "liberalism," was in Europe to stay because it was strong in France and had also become the goal of many revolutionary liberals outside of France. The extension of direct French rule into the Netherlands, Germany, and Italy had accustomed persons there to a centralized state, to an individualistic society, to equality before the law, and to the modern Code Napoléon. Even in areas not directly ruled from Paris, like Spain or Naples or southern and central Germany, rulers dependent on France had abolished feudalism and serfdom and instituted a more liberal form of government. The ideas of democratic rule, social equality, and religious toleration, though but briefly experienced, were not forgotten. Moreover, in countries like Prussia and Austria, humbled by Napoleon, some farsighted statesmen appreciated the value of the new institutions and perceived that the old divine-right monarchies must be reformed if they were to be strong and popular.

Of all the lessons France taught Europe between 1789 and 1815 the most impressive was nationalism, and so well and so fast did Europe learn it, that nationalism has been a major and rapidly growing force in European life down to the present day. The soldiers of Napoleon who bore the tricolor flag of France from Naples to Moscow, and from Lisbon to Berlin, were effective messengers of the new nationalist gospel—the *nation* bound together by ties of language and culture and history, the nation one and indivisible, the nation as the regenerator of human society, the nation above any class or religion, the nation as the supreme object of human devotion and sacrifice, the nation with a "mission."

Wherever they went the French aroused nationalism in two ways—positive and negative. Positively they showed the peoples of Europe what nationalism was and what a nation in arms could do. Negatively by their conquests they made themselves hated as oppressors and roused a fierce national patriotism in *opposition* to French nationalism.

In Germany and Italy, where the French, at the start, were greeted by many as deliverers who were bringing liberty from old tyrannies, their rule at length fanned a fierce patriotism that led to reforms, to nationalistic books, poems, and hymns, and to patriotic societies. In Poland, where national patriotism had developed in response to the partition of the country by Russia, Austria, and Prussia, Napoleon intensified it by his partial recreation of a Polish national state in the Grand Duchy of Warsaw. Even in the conglomerate Ottoman Empire, the Napoleonic era had its repercussions. Napo-

leon's invasion of Egypt brought western ideas to Ottoman territory. Among the Yugoslavs (Serbs, Croats, Slovenes) revolutionary and nationalist ideas were introduced by Napoleon's occupation of the Dalmatian coast.

Russia, too, experienced a new surge of patriotism and a new sense of national unity. The victorious war against Napoleon was a "fatherland war," and in the hatred roused by invaders the Russians found a deeper love for their own country. The Napoleonic wars also stimulated opposition and patriotism among the Austrian peoples. But the disparate nature of these prevented the rise of a single national patriotism for the whole Austrian Empire. If there was an increase of devotion to the Habsburg Emperor, there was at the same time an increased nationalist sentiment among the several peoples—German, Hungarian, Italian, Yugoslav, and Czech—which boded ill for the Empire's future unity. Great Britain, alone among the major powers, witnessed no fighting on its own soil in the long wars. But Britain was the very heart and center of the resistance to Napoleon. Her money, her ships, and in the end her soldiers were chief instruments in breaking the power of the Corsican. Britain's role in the long struggle and her final success led to a tremendous increase in British national patriotism.

Thus, in all Europe, while monarchs were restored and many of the trappings of the old regime were brought back by 1815, and while conservatism seemed triumphant everywhere, still there were forces at work that could not permanently be held down or ignored. These forces were the new ones brought to life in revolutionary France—liberalism and nationalism—and the greater of these proved in the long run to be nationalism.

CHAPTER 43

Conservative Restoration and Liberal Rebellions, 1815–1840

A. The Congress of Vienna and Peace Settlement of 1815

At Vienna in the autumn of 1814 assembled leading statesmen of Europe to conclude the long series of revolutionary and Napoleonic wars with what they hoped would be a permanent peace settlement. Among them were the Tsar Alexander of Russia, Talleyrand as agent for Louis XVIII of France, the Duke of Wellington and Lord Castlereagh representing Great Britain, and Stein and Hardenberg, the former of these serving as adviser to the Tsar rather than to the Prussian King. Foremost in the assemblage was Prince Clemens Metternich, chief minister of Austria.

Metternich came of a distinguished Rhenish family, and his wife was a daughter of Count Kaunitz, the Austrian diplomat of the eighteenth century.[1] He had entered the Austrian diplomatic service and had rapidly advanced in it until in 1809 he became chief minister, a position he was to hold for thirty-nine years. He helped Austria recover from its defeat at Wagram. He arranged the marriage of Maria Louisa with Napoleon and at the same time schemed against the French Emperor. So well did he plan that Austrian intervention was the decisive factor in the campaign of 1813 and Austria thus became the foremost power among the victorious allies—a fact which was recognized by the choice of Vienna as the place for the peace conference.

The so-called Congress of Vienna was

_____
[1] See above, p. 469.

hardly a congress in the usual sense. Delegates of all the participating countries met together only to sign a general treaty, the terms of which had been largely determined beforehand by the "Big Four"—Austria, Prussia, Russia, and Great Britain. True, Talleyrand so skillfully took advantage of disputes among the four, and so persuasively composed their differences, that gradually he was admitted to their inner councils. Thereby defeated France had a voice in some of the most important decisions.

The chief cleavage among the "Big Four," which gave Talleyrand his opportunity, was over the fate of Poland and Saxony. Before 1813, the Tsar Alexander had promised Austria and Prussia to give them back the Polish territories they had held in 1795. But subsequently he aspired to reconstitute the old Polish kingdom with himself as King, and he accordingly proposed that Prussia, instead of receiving its former large part of Poland, should annex Saxony (whose king had stood by Napoleon to the end). Prussia accepted the proposal, but Great Britain and Austria opposed it, and the deadlock was so serious that for a while war seemed imminent among the victors. Finally, through efforts of Castlereagh and Talleyrand, a compromise was effected. Prussia got part but not all of Saxony, and the Tsar got the greater part of Poland (henceforth called Congress Poland). Of Polish territories, Austria retained Galicia, and Prussia kept Posen and the "corridor" separating East Prussia from the rest of the Prussian kingdom.

557

Congress of Vienna with Metternich presiding. After a painting by Jean-Baptiste Isabey (d. 1855).

One principle underlying the whole settlement of Vienna was the restoration, so far as practicable, of the boundaries and reigning families of Europe as they had been before 1789. It was much the same as the "legitimacy" which Talleyrand was urging in order to preserve France and to enable her, though defeated, to play a major role in the councils of Europe. In line with this principle, the Bourbons were reinstated in Spain and in the Two Sicilies, the house of Orange in Holland, the house of Savoy in Sardinia, the pope in the Papal State, and a number of German princes in their former possessions. In the name of legitimacy, likewise, Austria recovered the Tyrol and most of the other lands she had lost, and the Swiss confederation was restored under a guarantee of neutrality.

A second principle, and one at variance with the first, involved "compensations," in order to reward those who had played major roles in defeating Napoleon or to build strong states around the borders of France as a check against future French aggression. Great Britain was rewarded with the French islands of St. Lucia, Tobago, and Mauritius, with the important Dutch Colonies of Ceylon and South Africa, and, in addition, with Malta, Heligoland, the Ionian islands, and part of Dutch Guiana. To "compensate" the Dutch for their colonial losses, as well as to create a stronger country on the border of France, the southern (Austrian) Netherlands were transferred to Holland. To "compensate" Austria for this change, she was given a commanding position in Italy. To Austria went the historic Venetian Republic and the duchy of Milan, while members of the Austrian Habsburg family were seated on the ducal thrones of Tuscany, Parma, and Modena.

Russia was "compensated" with Finland and additional Polish territory, while Sweden was "compensated" for the loss of Finland, and Denmark punished for its loyalty to Napoleon, by taking Norway from the latter and giving it to the former. Prussia made notable gains to reward her contribution to the victory and to strengthen her against France. She received Swedish Pomerania, all of Westphalia, most of the Rhineland, and two fifths of Saxony, though the rest of Saxony was restored to its legitimate ruler despite his long fidelity to Napoleon. The additions to Prussia gave her mineral resources which were to be of the utmost importance in the next century, and in the long run tended to transform her from an agricultural into the leading industrial state of Germany. The kingdom of Sardinia made advances too, for not only were its former lands restored but to them was added the port of Genoa with its surrounding territory. It was hoped that an enlarged Sardinia, together with a strengthened Prussia and Holland, would keep France in check.

In reconstituting Germany, few people wanted to push legitimacy so far as to restore the hundreds of petty states of 1789, and there was no serious effort to reëstablish the Holy Roman Empire. Stein would have like to unite Germany into a single national state under the Prussian king. But Austria and the south German rulers opposed any such plan. Since states-rights' ideas were still strong in Germany, the result was the creation of a loose German Confederation of the thirty-eight remaining states, with a Diet consisting of delegates of the various rulers. Austria presided over the Diet and dominated the Confederation.

There was little concession in the peace settlement of 1815 to the forces of liberalism or nationalism, and no sympathy indicated for new ideas about individual rights, political liberties, and constitutional government. Some humanitarianism was exhibited by adoption of a declaration sponsored by Britain, to the effect that the slave trade should be abolished, though the several countries were left free to fix their own dates for its abolition. And some significant contributions were made at Vienna to existing international law, not only concerning precedence among ambassadors and ministers, but also provision for free navigation of certain international rivers, notably the Danube and the Scheldt.

Metternich was especially anxious to prevent the recurrence of revolutionary violence and international war. For this purpose he (and other leading members of the Vienna Congress) relied, not on any world league or super-state, but on joint action of a continuing Quadruple Alliance of Austria, Prussia, Russia, and Great Britain. Later in 1815, after the adjournment of the Congress of Vienna, the Tsar Alexander proposed the formation among European sovereigns of a "Holy Alliance," in which they would promise in both domestic and foreign affairs to take as "their sole guide" the precepts of Christianity, "the precepts of justice, Christian charity, and peace." Out of deference to the Tsar, this curious "alliance" with him was signed by Frederick William III of Prussia and the Emperor Francis I of Austria, although the latter confessed he did not know what it meant. Eventually all the rulers of Europe subscribed to it, except the Pope, the Sultan of Turkey, and the Prince-Regent of Great Britain.

In the minds of later liberals, the Holy Alliance became the symbol of a conspiracy of reactionary monarchs to stamp out nationalism, liberalism, and social justice. But this was unfair. The Holy Alliance never really functioned. It was the *Quadruple Alliance* of the "Big Four" which, under Metternich's guidance, provided a temporary bulwark against forces of disorder and change.

B. Metternich and the Concert of Europe

The period from 1815 to 1848 has usually been called the "Era of Metternich," for during those years the Austrian statesman was the central figure in Europe. His policies were frankly conservative. He wanted to conserve peace between states and to conserve the old regime within each country. Believing that nationalism and liberalism and other revolutionary principles were responsible for the devastating wars which had afflicted Europe from 1792 to 1815, he did his utmost to discourage and repress any reassertion of those principles in the Habsburg territories and wherever else he could bring his influence to bear. For some fifteen years, Metternich's efforts were largely successful, though afterwards he found himself obliged to accept compromises with liberalism in several parts of Europe outside of Austria, and finally in 1848 even Austria rebelled against him and his conservative system.

During the early part of this period

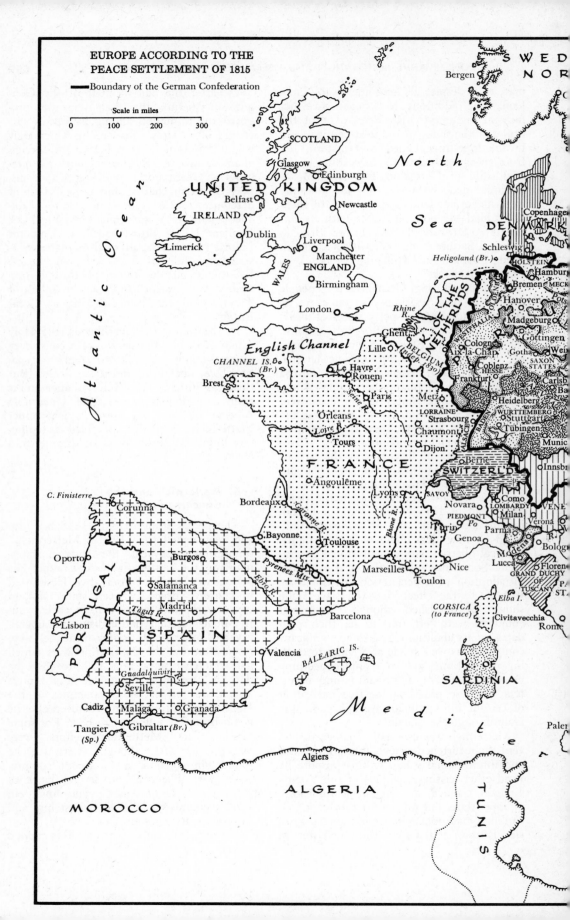

EUROPE ACCORDING TO THE
PEACE SETTLEMENT OF 1815

━━ Boundary of the German Confederation

Scale in miles

0   100   200   300

Atlantic Ocean

SCOTLAND

Glasgow
Edinburgh

UNITED KINGDOM

Belfast
IRELAND
Newcastle

Dublin
Liverpool
Manchester
ENGLAND

Limerick

WALES

Birmingham

London

English Channel

CHANNEL IS.
(Br.)

Brest

North

Sea

Bergen

SWED
NOR

Copenhagen
DENMARK

Schleswig
HOLSTEIN
Heligoland (Br.)
Hamburg
Bremen MECK

Hanover

WESTPHALIA
Madgeburg
Göttingen
Cologne
Aix-la-Chap.
Coblenz
Frankfurt
SAXON
STATES
Carlsb
Ba

Le Havre
Rouen

Paris

Orléans

Loire R.

Tours

FRANCE

Seine R.

Metz

LORRAINE
Strasbourg
Chaumont

Dijon

HESSE

Heidelberg
WÜRTTEMBERG
Stuttgart
Tübingen
Munic

Rhine R.

K. OF THE
NETHERLDS

Ghent
Lille

BELGIUM
(indep.
1830)

Berne
SWITZERL'D
Innsbr

Angoulême

Lyons
SAVOY
Novara
PIEDMONT
Turin
Po
Genoa

Como
LOMBARDY
Milan
VENE
Verona
Parma

Bordeaux

Garonne R.

Bayonne
Toulouse

Marseilles
Toulon

Nice

Rhone R.

C. Finisterre

Corunna

Oporto

PORTUGAL

Lisbon

Burgos

Salamanca

Madrid

Tagus R.

SPAIN

Guadalquivir

Seville

Cadiz
Malaga
Granada

Tangier
(Sp.)
Gibraltar (Br.)

Ebro R.

Pyrenees Mts.

Barcelona

Valencia

BALEARIC IS.

Lucca
Modena
GRAND DUCHY
OF
TUSCANY
Florence
PA
ST.

Elba I.

CORSICA
(to France)

Civitavecchia
Rome

Mediter

K. OF
SARDINIA

Paler

Algiers

ALGERIA

MOROCCO

TUNIS

FINLAND

Helsingfors

Cronstadt

St. Petersburg

G. of Finland

Stockholm

Reval

Novgorod

Volga R.

Nishni Novgorod

Baltic Sea

Riga

Moscow

Smolensk

Danzig

Königsberg

Niemen

LITHUANIA

R U S S I A

P R U S S I A

Posen

Vistula R.

K. OF Warsaw

POLAND

Oder R.

Breslau

Rep. of Cracow (to Austria 1846)

Kiev

UKRAINE

Ekaterinoslav

Don R.

Troppau

Lemberg

Carpathian

AUSTRIAN EMPIRE

Dniester R.

BESSARABIA

Pruth R.

Kherson

Dnieper R.

Sea of Azov

Vienna

Pressburg

Jassy

MOLDAVIA

Odessa

Crimea

Kerch

Budapest

HUNGARY

Sevastopol

Drava R.

Temesvar

Sava R.

WALLACHIA

Bucharest

DOBRUJA (1856)

Black Sea

BOSNIA

Belgrade

SERBIA

Danube R.

O T T O M A N

Plevna

Varna

MONTE-NEGRO

Scutari

BULGARIA

Sofia

Adrianople

Constantinople

Unkiar Skelessi

Scutari

Kiuprili

Durazzo

Salonica

Gallipoli

E M P I R E

A N A T O L I A

Adriatic Sea

Brindisi

Pindus

Janina

Larissa

Mitylene

Chios

Smyrna

Konieh

Alexandretta

Naples

KINGDOM OF THE TWO SICILIES

CORFU (Fr. 1807)

IONIAN IS.

Cephalonia (Br. 1815)

Zante

Missolonghi

Patras

Athens

Samos

Aegean Sea

Taurus

Messina

Reggio

Catania

GREECE (Indep. Kindom 1830)

Navarino

RHODES

CYPRUS

Beirut

MALTA (Brit.)

CRETE (Candia)

Sea

Acre

Jerusalem

Jaffa

Aboukir B.

Damietta

Alexandria

Metternich counted on support of the so-called "Concert of Europe." This was really the Quadruple Alliance of Austria, Prussia, Russia, and Great Britain, which in 1818, by the inclusion of France, was expanded into a Quintuple Alliance. The "Concert," under Metternich's guidance, dealt with threats to peace by a series of conferences— at Aix-la-Chapelle in 1818, at Troppau in 1820, at Laibach in 1821, at Verona in 1822. These conferences became the means of concerting measures not only for the prevention of international conflict, but also for the suppression of liberal and nationalist movements within the various countries. At Troppau in 1820, Russia and Prussia formally agreed with Austria to act jointly against revolutionary distrubances anywhere in Europe. From this decision Great Britain dissented, and henceforth the "Concert" was practically a Continental affair.

With only minor exceptions the period from 1815 to 1830 was one of triumphant conservatism. In Austria, Metternich set an example of repression of nationalists and liberals. He maintained a strong army, established a rigorous censorship of publications and theatrical performances, created an efficient police system, and put conservative ecclesiastics in charge of education. The reforms that Joseph II had attempted in Austria before the French Revolution were ignored and more or less forgotten.

So far as he could, Metternich saw to it that the same sort of policies were applied throughout Germany and Italy. Austrian influence was able to block most of the attempts to give the other German states the constitutions which their princes had quite generally promised during the patriotic War of Liberation. The Duke of Saxe-Weimar was an exception, for he conceded a constitutional government. But he brought down on himself a joint protest of the reactionary powers when in 1817 some students at the Wartburg, celebrating the tercentenary of Luther's theses against indulgences, burned various symbols of the old regime. Two years later a conservative spy named Kotzebue, in the pay of Russia, was assassinated by a liberal student. This event gave Metternich an opportunity for action. He summoned a meeting of German states-

men at Carlsbad and secured the promulgation of the resulting "Carlsbad decrees" by the Diet of the German Confederation. The decrees provided for close supervision of university professors and students, for muzzling the press, and for the establishment of a committee to investigate revolutionary plots. They likewise forbade the granting of any constitution "inconsistent with the monarchical principle."

No less complete was Metternich's influence in Italy. Austria ruled in the north, Habsburg princes and the pope in the center, and the Bourbon Ferdinand I in the south. All joined in reëstablishing the old regime. Police, troops, and spies held down all liberal agitation, and the fact that in much of Italy the repressive hand was a foreign one made it especially irksome to Italian liberals and nationalists. Only in the kingdom of Sardinia was there a ruler with exclusively Italian interests. Even here, Victor Emmanuel I, at the behest of Metternich, disavowed any idea of introducing liberal reforms. Officially all Italy was conservative and reactionary.

In France, Louis XVIII, who was restored a second time to the throne of his fathers in 1815, sought to follow a policy of compromise. He retained many Napoleonic institutions like the Legion of Honor, the Bank of France, the concordat with the pope, and the system of state education; and he recognized the Napoleonic nobility. The charter he granted, while by no means democratic, since the suffrage was limited to the very wealthy, did guarantee personal liberties as well as giving France a constitutional government and providing a legislature where public matters could be discussed. The first legislature so elected proved more royalist and reactionary than the King, who dissolved it in 1816. The second was more moderate and during the next years finances were improved, the electoral law simplified, and the censorship of the press relaxed. But in 1820, the King's nephew, the Duke of Berry, was assassinated by a fanatical liberal. Once more reaction set in. Strict censorship was reëstablished. Control of the Catholic clergy over education was strengthened. The electoral law was again modified in a conservative direction. The police and spy systems were made more effective, and the army was used to overawe any opposition.

These conservative tendencies in France were accentuated in 1824 when Louis XVIII died and was succeeded by his brother, Charles X, who had long been the leader of the ultra-royalists. He was crowned with old-fashioned pomp. He surrounded himself with conservative and reactionary advisers. He promised an indemnity of a billion francs to *émigré* nobles who had lost their lands during the Revolution.

In Great Britain, it was the conservative Tory faction which had won the long war against Napoleon, and, under the leadership of Castlereagh and Wellington, it maintained its control in the post-war period. Aging George III had become hopelessly insane in 1811. His son acted as prince-regent till 1820 and then on the death of his father ascended the throne as George IV. In both capacities he showed himself a thoroughgoing conservative in public affairs and an immoral fop in private life. Under such guidance Britain did not at first vary much from Metternich's idea of sound government. The repressive measures of the war period were renewed and strengthened. The press was censored and suspensions of the right of *habeas corpus* made arbitrary arrests possible.

Mass meetings of protest were held, and one of them at Manchester was broken up by troops who killed six persons. Parliament then (1819) passed still more repressive laws—the so-called Six Acts, which re-

stricted seditious writings and public meetings, provided for the searching of private houses for arms and the speedy trial and punishment of offenders, and levied a heavy stamp tax on newspapers to keep them from the hands of the masses. When violent radicals responded in 1820 by plotting to assassinate the Tory cabinet, this "Cato Street Conspiracy" was ferreted out and five of its participants were hanged. Even in Britain liberalism seemed to be ebbing.

C. Spanish American, and Greek Revolutions

Under the muffling blanket of Metternich's conservative system, liberalism and nationalism were concealed but not eliminated. They became underground forces ready to flare into activity when opportunity offered. In Germany, university students formed secret societies (*Tugendbund, Burschenschaft*, etc.) in behalf of national unity and liberal reform. Occasionally, they organized demonstrations noisy enough to cause uneasiness in Vienna and Berlin.

In southern Italy, the secret society of the *Carbonari*, with its oaths and passwords, was more active. It inspired in 1820 a rebellion in Naples against the tyrannical Ferdinand I (1815–1825). The King, terrified when he found that his army would not support him, accepted a liberal constitution

Royal Restoration of Law and Order in Naples. Honoré Daumier (d. 1879).

modeled after the one drawn up in Spain in 1812. But the next year, at the international conference at Laibach, he "invited" an Austrian army to Naples "to restore order." To Metternich's satisfaction, Ferdinand, supported by Austrian bayonets, annulled the constitution and began a savage campaign of reprisals, which helped to give the Two Sicilies the reputation among liberals of being the worst governed state in Christendom.

Crushed in southern Italy, liberals had a brief day in the north. In 1821, soldiers in Piedmont mutinied and seized Turin, the capital. King Victor Emmanuel I abdicated in favor of his brother, Charles Felix, while the liberal Prince Charles Albert, next in line for the throne, was made Regent. Charles Albert at once proclaimed a liberal constitution. Here again, Metternich intervened with Austrian troops. The Regent was expelled, and absolutism was restored under Charles Felix.

Even in Russia, least liberal of the great powers, there was some trouble. When Alexander I died suddenly in December 1825, revolutionary societies, led by young officers and a group of intellectuals imbued with ideas which they had learned from the French and from Freemasonry, attempted to alter the succession to the throne. Alexander had designated his second brother Nicholas as his successor, passing over his liberal but erratic first brother Constantine. The revolutionaries, with "Constantine and Constitution" as their slogan, organized a mutiny of troops at St. Petersburg. But Constantine would not aid the movement, and Nicholas quickly suppressed it. The leaders of this December revolt, who were later known as Decembrists, were severely punished. But they had shown that even Russia was not wholly unaffected by liberal undercurrents.

In Spain there was active liberal opposition to King Ferdinand VII, who, on his restoration in 1814, had abolished the constitution of 1812 and brought back the old absolutism, exempted the clergy and nobles from taxation, and reëstablished the Inquisition. The opposition centered in secret societies like the Carbonari and Freemasons, and permeated the army which the King assembled at Cadiz in 1819 for shipment to America to suppress revolts that had broken out in the colonies during the Napoleonic period. A mutiny occurred in the army, and presently rioting broke out in various parts of Spain. In March 1820, Ferdinand, quaking with fear, gave his royal oath to restore and support the constitution of 1812. In a subsequent declaration, he said, "Let us advance frankly, myself leading the way, along the constitutional path." The insurgents took him at his word and laid down their arms.

The hypocritical Ferdinand had no intention of keeping his word. While pretending to be a constitutional monarch, he was scheming to restore absolutism. The Spanish liberals themselves, mainly middle class in origin, fell to quarreling; nobles and clergy objected to reforms that were attempted; the peasants were for the most part apathetic. Meanwhile the Concert of Europe under Metternich was much disturbed by the events in Spain. The Tsar Alexander wanted to lead a Russian army thither to crush the revolution. But the French were not eager to have foreign troops march across their soil. Finally, at the Congress of Verona in 1822, it was agreed that France should send an army to Ferdinand's aid.

Early in 1823, after the Spanish liberals had rejected a joint demand from France, Russia, Austria, and Prussia to abolish the constitution of 1812, the Duke of Angoulême, nephew of Louis XVIII, led a French army across the Pyrenees. The invaders this time met no such national opposition as Napoleon had encountered, for the Spanish people were sorely divided and the conservative majority generally welcomed the French. In May, the French captured Madrid and the Spanish liberal ministers fled to Cadiz, taking Ferdinand along as a hostage. On October 1, they released the King on the understanding that he would grant a general pardon and set up a moderate government. Cadiz thereupon surrendered. But once safe in the French lines, the King annulled his promises and pronounced the death sentence on all constitutionalists. In vain Angoulême advised moderation. Hundreds were executed and other hundreds were jailed or exiled.

Events in Spain, and the threats of the

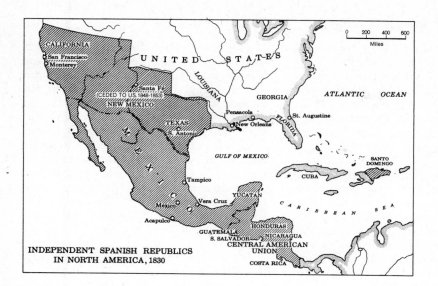

INDEPENDENT SPANISH REPUBLICS
IN NORTH AMERICA, 1830

SPANISH AND PORTUGUESE
SOUTH AMERICA, 1830

Independent Spanish republics

Independent Portuguese Empire of Brazil

great powers, likewise helped to put an end to a simultaneous liberal revolt in Portugal and to install a reactionary government in Lisbon. But in this · confused period Brazil declared its independence (1822) and became a separate Empire under a member of the Portuguese royal house.

The backing of King Ferdinand VII of Spain by most of the Concert of Europe might have enabled him to carry out his project of subduing the rebellious Spanish colonies in America except for two facts. First, the British since 1789 had developed a thriving trade with Spanish America, and they had no wish to see reëstablished a colonial system which would once more shut out their goods. Second, the United States was thoroughly sympathetic with the movement in the Spanish colonies to free themselves from Spain. Encouraged by the British, the American President James Monroe announced in 1823 a policy since known as the "Monroe Doctrine." Thereby, the United States made clear its intention of refraining from any intervention in European affairs, but at the same time insisted that any intervention by European powers in the Americas would be regarded as an unfriendly act. With the British and American navies prepared to back up the Monroe Doctrine, no foreign aid was forthcoming for Ferdinand overseas, and within a brief period all Spanish American colonies, except Cuba and Puerto Rico, were independent republics.

Meanwhile, in eastern Europe, in the confines of the Ottoman Empire, there were developing other cracks in the conservative attempt to maintain the *status quo*. In 1817, a Serbian peasant named Miloš Obrenović, who had first followed the earlier Serb leader Karageorge and had later had him murdered and who had since led a popular uprising against the Turks, won from the Sultan grudging recognition as "supreme prince" of Serbia. In 1821, a Greek prince named Ypsilanti rebelled in Moldavia in expectation of Russian help, which Metternich persuaded the Tsar to withhold. The revolt was crushed and Ypsilanti ended in an Austrian prison.

But soon afterwards occurred a general Greek revolt, to which the Turks replied with severe reprisals, including a massacre of Christians. To Metternich, the Greeks were rebels against a "legitimate" sovereign, and he would do nothing for them. But Russia, bound by ties of religion to the Greeks, was sympathetic, and western Europe was deeply stirred. Liberals saw in the Greek revolt a popular uprising for liberty. Romantics saw in it an attempt to revive the ancient glory that was Greece. Even conservative Christians could approve it as a crusade against the infidel. Money, volunteers, and arms flowed to the Greeks. The English poet Lord Byron died in Greece where he had gone to fight for Greek independence.

For a while the Greeks held their own. Then the Sultan called in the aid of fierce troops from Egypt under Ibrahim Pasha, who swept up and down the Greek peninsula with fire and sword and sold thousands of Christians into slavery. Indignation in Europe rose. When the Sultan in 1827 rejected the request of Great Britain, France, and Russia for an armistice, the fleets of these countries destroyed the Turco-Egyptian naval squadron at Navarino. The next year the Tsar Nicholas I declared war on the Ottoman Empire, and, with some help from the Serbs, the Russians fought their way almost to Constantinople and compelled the Sultan to sign the treaty of Adrianople. The treaty was a milestone in the dismemberment of the Ottoman Empire, for by it the Sultan virtually recognized the independence of Greece, and granted autonomy, not only to Serbia under Miloš Obrenović, but also to the Rumanian principalities of Moldavia and Wallachia. Despite Metternich, the status quo was being seriously altered. Nationalism was making significant gains.

On the other side of Europe also, conservatism was waning, for in Great Britain, though the Tory party still held power, new leaders were coming to the fore who favored reform. George Canning as foreign minister had encouraged the United States to oppose the Concert of Europe in the Monroe Doctrine. William Huskisson, much interested in new industries, secured reductions in the tariff and removal of the most constrictive features of the old Navigation Acts. It was a Tory parliament, too, that freed Protestant Dissenters (those not belonging to the Anglican Church) from political disabilities (1828), and admitted Catholics to parliament and public affairs (1829). But such steps seemed paltry to the growing body of liberal sentiment in England. The rising industrial towns were demanding representation in parliament. Radicals were urging that the suffrage be extended even to workingmen. Conservatism in England was weakening.

D. Liberal Revolts and Reforms of the 1830's

If Metternich's system was jarred in the 1820's, it was cracked (though not destroyed) in 1830. In France, middle-class liberals and urban workingmen had been growing restive under the increasingly reactionary regime of King Charles X. In 1829, in defiance of the legislature, he appointed as prime minister a former émigré, Prince Polignac. After repeated votes adverse to the premier, the King dissolved the lower house and called for new elections. But the chamber which was returned was even more hostile to Polignac

than the one which it replaced. Then the King decided on what amounted to a destruction of the constitutional charter. On July 26, 1830, he published four arbitrary ordinances which tightened restrictions on newspapers, dissolved the newly elected chamber, changed the electoral law so as to eliminate most of the middle-class voters, and called for new elections. With incredible lack of foresight the King did not concentrate any extra troops in the capital.

Paris responded immediately with armed insurrection, and after three days of sporadic street-fighting, Charles X abdicated in favor of his young grandson, the Count of Chambord, and left hastily for England. Thus with but little bloodshed the "July Days" of 1830 ended divine-right monarchy in France. The victors, however, were by no means in agreement on what the ensuing government should be. Some were republicans, others liberal monarchists, and there were even a few Bonapartists. The liberal monarchists, headed by a journalist, Adolphe Thiers, and a wealthy banker, Jacques Laffitte, proposed, as a new king, Louis Philippe, Duke of Orléans, heir of the

GREECE AND THE BALKANS IN 1832

younger line of the Bourbons, and son of a Philippe "Egalité" who had voted for the death of Louis XVI in 1793. The republicans (radical intellectuals and Parisian workers mainly) were won over to this proposal by the aging Lafayette. Louis Philippe had fought in the revolutionary army in 1792, and after that, whether in exile or in France, had lived a life of bourgeois respectability.

The accession of Louis Philippe to the throne was peculiar. It was not based on inheritance, nor on plebiscite, nor on constitutional processes. It was the result of the decision of the leaders of a brief but successful Paris revolution, later endorsed by the national legislature. From the start Louis Philippe tried to win middle-class support and to conciliate republican sentiment. He restored the tricolor flag, called himself "King of the French" (not "King of France"), and accepted his role as a constitutional monarch under the somewhat liberalized Charter. The establishment of the "July Monarchy" was so clearly a triumph of the middle class that it is often called the "Bourgeois Monarchy."

It was a saying of the time that when France caught cold all Europe sneezed. Such was the case in 1830. The suddenness and the success of the July Revolution at Paris alarmed conservatives and heartened liberals everywhere. In the Belgian Netherlands, forces of liberalism and nationalism were let loose by the events at Paris. The Belgians had been for fifteen years unhappy and restive under the Dutch rule imposed on them by the peace of Vienna, for not only were the two parts of the Netherlands divided by more than two centuries of history, tradition, and conflict, but the Belgians were industrial and Catholic, while the Dutch were agricultural or commercial and largely Calvinist. The Dutch King William I had, moreover, irritated his Belgian subjects by favoring Dutch law, language, religion, and officials. In 1830, the news of the revolution at Paris started riots in Brussels. The riots developed into a revolt; and when William refused to concede to them a separate legislature, the Belgians declared their independence (October 1830).

The international situation favored the Belgians. Metternich and the Tsar Nicholas had other matters on their minds, and the British and the new French government approved of a separate Belgian state. In 1831 an international conference at London reached an agreement by which Belgium would become an independent state with a German prince, Leopold of Saxe-Coburg, as its constitutional King. But the Dutch King William I was stubborn. It took pressure from the British navy and the French army and the lapse of eight years before he finally recognized the separation of Belgium from Holland and signed a treaty of peace and friendship. At this time (1839) all the great powers—Britain, France, Russia, Prussia, and Austria— guaranteed the independence and neutrality of Belgium, a guarantee that was to be respected for seventy-five years. In Belgium, liberalism and nationalism had scored a notable victory, marked by the definitive secession of Britain and France from Metternich's Concert of Europe.

What occupied Metternich and Tsar Nicholas in 1830, so that they could spare little thought for Belgium, was revolutionary disturbance in central, southern, and eastern Europe. In Germany, riots and demonstrations by liberals scared some of the rulers into granting constitutions. In the Papal State, liberals raised a new tricolor flag (red, white, and green) of Italian nationalism and democracy and repudiated the temporal rule of the new Pope Gregory XVI, while outbreaks in Parma and Modena forced their Habsburg rulers to flee to Vienna. But Metternich rushed into Italy Austrian troops, which soon restored "order" and the "legitimate" sovereigns.

It was Poland which gave trouble to Tsar Nicholas. He might favor nationalism in Greece, but Poland was another matter. Late in 1830, Poles, eager to reëstablish an independent nation and hopeful of aid from revolutionary France, rose in Warsaw against Russian rule. It took the armies of the Tsar nearly all of 1831 to crush the gallant Poles, who obtained words of sympathy but no practical assistance from France and Great Britain.

With the liquidation of the Polish and

Liberty Leading the People (1830). Ferdinand Delacroix (d. 1863).

Italian revolts, Metternich's conservative system seemed firmly entrenched once more in most of Europe. True, France and Belgium had now been added to Greece, Serbia, and Spanish America as areas where Metternich's beloved *status quo* had been drastically altered. It must be noted, however, that the alteration was not so violent as it seemed. Before many years Louis Philippe, despite his liberal gestures, showed himself so conservative at heart that he became quite friendly with Metternich.

Great Britain experienced no revolution in 1830. Yet the forces of liberalism were at work there, too, and they were strengthened by the growing importance of industry and the growing strength of the middle class. Britain already had national unity, a limited monarchy, and a good deal of individual liberty. It did not, however, have anything approaching democracy. The hereditary House of Lords wielded much

influence, and the House of Commons was unrepresentative of the masses of people. Thriving industrial cities like Manchester, Birmingham, Sheffield, and Leeds had no representatives in Parliament, while, under the centuries-old system of apportionment, certain towns that had disappeared were still represented by two men in the House of Commons. In addition to these "rotten boroughs," there were also "pocket boroughs" where wealthy landlords controlled elections because the voters were few. Thus it was that great landlords, titled or otherwise, dominated the House of Commons as they did the House of Lords. And it was for this reason that the growing middle class of the cities, who wanted a government responsive to the needs of business, added their clamor to the outcries of liberals and radicals.

In 1830, demand for liberal reform of the House of Commons led to the resignation of the Tory ministry. The new Whig government under Earl Grey put a parliamentary reform bill through the lower House in 1831, but it was defeated by the House of Lords. New elections gave Grey a Whig majority in the Commons. But the Lords turned down a second reform bill. Then in 1832 noisy demonstrations in the cities, coupled with the inability of the Tory Duke of Wellington to form a government and with the King's reluctant pledge to create enough Whig peers to pass the bill in the House of Lords, had their effect. Enough Tory peers stayed away from the crucial vote to enable a third reform bill to pass and become law.

The reform of 1832 was a very moderate affair. It took 143 seats away from small towns and "rotten boroughs" and gave them to the new towns and cities and the most populous counties. It provided new and uniform qualifications for voters which in effect increased their number somewhat and gave the ballot to prosperous members of the urban middle class. Thus political power was henceforth shared between the landed and the business classes, and the latter were growing while the former declined in strength. Those who now had control regarded this solution as a happy and permanent one, a concession to democracy which did not endanger order or stability and would not lead to "mob rule." This arrangement, later to be called the "Victorian Compromise," carried Britain still further away from conservatism.

The reform of 1832 hastened certain changes that were already under way in Great Britain. It strengthened the Whigs who won the first elections under the new system, and who, in gratitude for the support of the industrial middle class, sponsored certain liberal reforms and indeed began to call themselves Liberals. Thus the Whig party was transformed into the Liberal party which was now composed of a right wing of tolerant aristocrats (the old Whigs), a center of ambitious business men (the real Liberals), and a small left wing of intellectuals and reformers (the Radicals). At the same time, the Tory party underwent changes. Its mildly "liberal" element was reënforced by the defeat in 1832 of the die-hards like Wellington. It accepted a

new leader in Sir Robert Peel, himself a factory owner. It began to call itself the Conservative party, and, if its right wing was still devoted to the landed interests, the Anglican Church, and intense nationalism, its left wing was not unsympathetic to business and not unwilling to coöperate on occasion with the Liberals.

The work of the reformed parliament moved England still further in a liberal direction. In 1833 Negro slavery was abolished throughout the British Empire, though the slave owners received financial compensation. In the same year, there was introduced a system of subsidizing private (church) schools from public funds so as to make education available to more people, and three years later the University of London was created by Parliament to compete with conservative Oxford and Cambridge. Other acts pushed forward the reform of the penal law, created a governmental bureau of public health, and prescribed more merciful treatment for debtors.

The reform of the "corn laws," advocated by liberal economists, was not so easy. England, which had exported grain till the mid-eighteenth century, had become, as the population grew, dependent in years of bad harvest on imports of grain ("corn") from abroad. To keep up the price of grain for the benefit of the landlords, a system of protective import duties had been developed. The lower the price of grain in England, the higher went the import duties on a "sliding scale." To the landlords who made the enclosures and adopted improved agricultural methods, these corn laws seemed like the keystone of national prosperity and the assurance of reasonable profits from their lands. Without them, they argued, England would become dependent on foreigners for food. But to the middle class and the new industrialists, the corn laws seemed like a way of raising the price of food (and thus of wages) so as to subsidize the conservative landlords.

Backed by such interested manufacturers as Richard Cobden and John Bright, there was formed in 1838 an Anti-Corn-Law League which launched a strenuous campaign of propaganda by speeches and pamphlets. The urban middle class was easily convinced. The workers thought the reform would give them cheaper food. Nature assisted the free-traders. In 1845, the English wheat crop was ruined by rain, and the blight of the potato crop in Ireland ushered in a period of starvation and emigration for that island. In Parliament the Conservatives had a majority. But in this crisis their own leader, Sir Robert Peel, deserted them. Aided by the Liberals he put through the repeal of the corn laws in 1846 and established free trade in grain.

It was the central group of the Liberal party, satisfied with the reform of 1832, which had the most influence in succeeding decades. But there were a few Radicals in Parliament and a good many outside it, who were urging further changes in a democratic direction. By 1838 groups of workers and some middle-class reformers agreed on a "People's Charter" of six points which would have made Great Britain a real democracy. The six points were: (1) universal manhood suffrage; (2) annual election of parliament; (3) equal electoral districts; (4) vote by secret ballot; (5) removal of property qualifications for members of parliament; (6) salaries for members of parliament so that poor men could afford to sit in it. For a time the "Chartists," by widespread agitation and propaganda, seemed to be gaining ground. But in Parliament the Liberals joined the Conservatives in rejecting their proposals; the government showed itself ready to put down any violence by force; and the Chartist leaders fell to quarreling among themselves. After 1842 the Chartist movement declined in numbers if not in noise. Enough of it remained, however, to cause a near-crisis in 1848.

France, despite the liberal July Revolution of 1830, did not move in a democratic direction under Louis Philippe. The right to vote was restricted by property qualifications to a quarter million owners of landed or industrial properties, and legislation was chiefly for the benefit of business men. The construction of railways was subsidized. A protective tariff was maintained. Workers' organizations remained illegal.

In one respect, Louis Philippe rather hesitantly pushed a policy inaugurated by Charles X. In 1830, to avenge an insult to a French consul by the ruler of Algiers, and in the hope of winning some glory for his regime, Charles X had sent a military expedition to that country. After much wavering, Louis Philippe and his government decided to occupy, not only the city of Algiers, but the interior as well. Soon they found themselves with a full-fledged war on their hands, for a native leader, Abd-el-Kader, rallied the tribesmen against the French. Not until 1847, after long fighting, was Algeria subdued. But by then it was a French possession, with some 40,000 Frenchmen settled in it.

Within France, while the bourgeois monarchy of Louis Philippe pleased some of the wealthy middle class, it commanded little popular support. Gradually, at least six large groups crystalized in opposition to it: (1) *Legitimists*—nobles, clergy, and some peasants—who looked upon the Count of Chambord, grandson of Charles X, as the rightful King; (2) *Catholics*, both legitimist and liberal, who objected to existing restrictions on church schools and other anti-clerical legislation; (3) *Patriots*, who thought Louis Philippe's foreign policy of peace-at-any-price inglorious, and, inspired by the "Napoleonic Legend," looked back with longing to the glories of the Empire; (4) *Reformers*—middle class liberals—who wanted an evolution of the monarchy in a democratic direction; (5) *Republicans*, radical workers, artisans, and intellectuals who looked back with sympathy to 1793 and desired a popular democracy; and (6) *Socialists*, who were disturbed by social problems and the growth of an impoverished urban working class. Some of these last sought to establish Utopian coöperative communities. Others, like Louis Blanc, wanted to end unemployment by setting up coöperative factories called "national workshops." Still others followed Proudhon, who wished to abolish private property and authoritarian government and to create a new order based on anarchistic, voluntary coöperation. With such widespread dissent, the bourgeois monarchy was shaky.

Throughout continental Europe, except in France and Belgium, the conservative regime sponsored by Metternich and maintained in the face of the troubles of the 1820's and of 1830, still seemed solid in the early 1840's.

SELECT SUPPLEMENTARY READINGS FOR PART VIII

General. C. J. H. Hayes, *Political and Cultural History of Modern Europe*, 2 vols (1932–1939); S. B. Clough and C. W. Cole, *Economic History of Europe* (1952); *Cambridge Modern History*, Vols. VI–X (1904–10).

Chapter 39. Godfrey Davies, *Early Stuarts, 1603–1660* (1937); I. D. Jones, *The English Revolution* (1931); William Haller, *The Rise of Puritanism* (1938); C. V. Wedgwood, *The King's Peace, 1637–1641* (1955); John Buchan, *Cromwell* (1934); M. P. Ashley, *Financial and Commercial Policy under the Cromwellian Protectorate* (1934); G. P. Gooch, *English Democratic Ideas in the Seventeenth Century*, 2nd ed. (1927); G. N. Clark, *The Later Stuarts, 1660–1714* (1934); Arthur Bryant, *King Charles II* (1931); D. Ogg, *England in the Reign of Charles II*, 2 vols. (1934); and *England in the Reigns of James II and William III* (1955); Sir George Clark, *Three Aspects of Stuart England* (1960); G. M. Trevelyan, *English Revolution, 1688–1689* (1939), and *England under Queen Anne*, 3 vols. (1930–1934); Winston Churchill, *Marlborough, his Life and Times*, 6 vols. (1933–1938); A. F. Pollard, *Evolution of Parliament* (1920); Andrew Lang, *History of Scotland*, vol. iii (1905); Richard Bagwell, *Ireland under the Stuarts and during the Interregnum*, 2 vols. (1909).

Chapter 40. Additional to books listed for chapter 38: Leo Gershoy, *From Despotism to Revolution, 1763–1789* (1946); Henri Sée, *Economic and Social Conditions in France during the Eighteenth Century*, Eng. trans. (1926); J. B. Perkins, *France in the American Revolution* (1911); L. H. Gipson, *The British Empire before the American Revolution*, 10 vols. (1936–   ); J. Steven Watson, *The Reign of George III, 1760–1815* (1960); C. L. Rossiter, *Seedtime of the Republic* (1953); S. F. Bemis, *The Diplomacy of the American Revolution* (1935); R. Coupland, *American Revolution and the British Empire* (1930); J. F. Jameson, *The American Revolution considered as a Social Movement* (1926); C. L. Becker, *Declaration of Independence, a Study in the History of Political Ideas* (1922); R. L. Schuyler, *Constitution of the United States, an Historical Survey of Its Formation* (1923); R. R. Palmer, *The Age of the Democratic Revolution: A Political History of Europe and America, 1760–1800* (1959). See also, the new American Nation series edited by R. B. Morris and H. S. Commager especially the volumes by L. H. Gipson, L. B. Wright and J. R. Alden.

Chapter 41. Crane Brinton, *A Decade of Revolution, 1789–1799* (1934); G. Lefebvre, *The Coming of the French Revolution* (1947); P. H. Beik, *The French Revolution seen from the Right* (1956); Leo Gershoy, *French Revolution* (1935); Albert Mathiez, *French Revolution*, Eng. trans. (1928), and *After Robespierre the Thermidorean Reaction*, Eng. trans. (1931); Louis Madelin, *French Revolution*, Eng. trans. (1916); F. V. A. Aulard, *French Revolution, a Political History*, Eng. trans., 4 vols. (1910); Crane Brinton, *The Jacobins* (1930), and *The Lives of Talleyrand* (1936); G. G. Van Deusen, *Sieyès* (1933); Louis Barthou, *Mirabeau*, Eng. trans. (1913); J. S. Schapiro, *Condorcet* (1934); Louis Gottschalk, *Marat* (1927); Louis Madelin, *Danton*, Eng. trans. (1914); J. M. Eagan, *Maximilien Robespierre* (1938); Geoffrey Brunn, *Saint-Just* (1932); R. R. Palmer, *Twelve Who Ruled* (1941); W. T. Laprade, *England and the French Revolution* (1909); G. P. Gooch, *Germany and the French Revolution* (1920); C. J. H. Hayes, *Nationalism* (1960), and *Historical Evolution of Modern Nationalism* (1931); S. B. Clough, *France, a History of National Economics, 1789–1939* (1939).

Chapter 42. Geoffrey Bruun, *Europe and the French Imperium, 1799–1814* (1938); F. M. Kircheisen, *Napoleon*, Eng. trans. (1931); J. H. Rose, *Life of Napoleon*, 11th ed. (1934); August Fournier, *Napoleon*, Eng. trans., 2 vols. (1911); J. M. Thompson, *Napoleon Bonaparte, his Rise and Fall* (1952); F. M. H. Markham, *Napoleon and the Awakening of Europe* (1954); Sir Charles Oman, *Studies in Napoleonic Wars* (1929), and *History of the Peninsula War*, 7 vols. (1902–1930); R. G. Burton, *Napoleon's Campaigns in Italy* (1912); K. von Clausewitz, *Campaign of 1812 in Russia*, Eng. trans. (1843); R. B. Mowat, *Diplomacy of Napoleon* (1924); E. F. Heckscher, *The Continental System* (1922); H. A. L. Fisher, *Studies in Napoleonic Statesmanship: Germany* (1903); G. S. Ford, *Stein and the Era of Reform in Prussia* (1922); R. M. Johnston, *The Napoleonic Empire in Southern Italy and the Rise of the Secret Societies*, 2 vols. (1904); A. T. Mahan, *Influence of Sea Power upon the French Revolution and Empire, 1793–1812*, 10th ed. (1898), and *Life of Nelson* (1899); J. H. Rose, *William Pitt the Younger*, 2 vols. (1911); Philip Guedalla, *The Duke of Wellington* (1931); Lord Rosebery, *Napoleon, the Last Phase* (1901).

Chapter 43. Sir Charles Webster, *Congress of Vienna, 1814–1815* (1920), and *Foreign Policy of Castlereagh* (1925); Harold Nicolson, *The Congress of Vienna, a Study in Allied Unity, 1812–1822* (1946); Algernon Cecil, *Metternich* (1933); Arthur May, *The Age of Metternich, 1814–1848* (1933); F. B. Artz, *Reaction and Revolution, 1814–1832* (1934); W. A. Phillips, *The Confederation of Europe* (1914); F. B. Artz, *France under the Bourbon Restoration, 1814–1830* (1931); J. M. S. Allison, *Thiers and the French Monarchy* (1926); Elie Halévy, *History of the English People, 1815–1841*, 3 vols. (1924–1928); H. B. Clarke, *Modern Spain, 1815–1898* (1906); W. R. Thayer, *Dawn of Italian Independence*, 2 vols. (1892); C. M. Woodhouse, *The War of Greek Independence* (1952); William Miller, *A History of the Greek People, 1821–1921* (1922); H. W. V. Temperley, *History of Serbia* (1917); W. W. Kaufmann, *British Policy and the Independence of Latin America, 1804–1828* (1951); G. Masur, *Simon Bolivar* (1948).

From Mazzini
to Napoleon III

PART IX
ROMANTIC AND

Westminster Houses of Parliament, rebuilt in Gothic style. By Sir Charles Barry (d. 1860).

LIBERAL EUROPE, 1848–1871

THE PERIOD from 1848 to 1871 opens with revolutions which upset the conservative system of Metternich but do not lead at once to a triumph of either liberalism or nationalism. The ensuing years are, however, ones in which nationalism makes great progress. It gradually becomes an inspiring goal for conservatives as well as liberals. Through a series of brief wars considerable progress is made in redrawing the map of central Europe along national lines. A united Italy, a united Rumania, and a very strong and united Germany emerge.

At the same time, liberalism does progress too. Not in a leap, but by a series of changes, all western and central Europe moves toward liberal democracy. France, for example, at the end of the period substitutes for the quasi-liberal dictatorship of Napoleon III a democratic republic. Only in eastern Europe, in the Russian, Austrian, and Ottoman Empires, do barriers remain against nationalism and popular government, and even here there are signs of weakness in the barriers.

The age is one of romanticism in the arts not unrelated to the nationalism in political life. Artists, writers, and composers throw off the bonds of classic restraint and exuberantly seek for color, emotion, and vitality.

There is an increasingly rapid progress in science, and the results of scientific research begin to be applied to technology. Great Britain is transformed from a predominantly agricultural and commercial society to one which is preponderantly industrial. And industry begins to grow apace in Belgium, France, Germany, and across the Atlantic in the United States.

All this change is not accomplished without protest. On the one hand, some conservatives bemoan and resist the new developments. And on the other, radical protests begin to be heard from industrial workers and those who seek to speak for them.

By the end of the period, an age of optimism is dawning. It seems to many as if science and industry are actually bringing the kind of progress that which was foreseen in the Enlightenment of the eighteenth century and that the cure for surviving ills is more democracy, more liberalism, more nationalism, more science, more industry.

CHAPTER 44

Romanticism and Scientific Progress

A. Romantic Movement in Literature and Art

For more than four centuries, from the fourteenth through the eighteenth, Europe had chiefly sought its models of taste and excellence in art, literature, architecture, philosophy, and politics by looking backward to ancient Greece and Rome. At the height of the "Enlightenment" in the eighteenth century, most dramatic writing followed classical rules; poetry dealt with classical themes and assumed classical forms; architecture was inspired by classical remains; education was in the classics. Portraits of statesmen frequently depicted them as clad in Roman togas. Revolutionaries like the French Girondists thought of themselves as playing roles of a Brutus or of the Gracchi.

In the latter half of the eighteenth century there were signs of reaction against classicism. The reaction gained ground in the early years of the nineteenth century. Between 1815 and 1848 it became the dominant note in the artistic and intellectual life of Europe. It is called romanticism.

Romanticism defies definition. Basically it was a revolt against the conventions and restraints of classicism. But the revolt took many different forms, and among its exemplars were revolutionaries and reactionaries, poets and business men, agnostics and devout Christians. The most important characteristics of romanticism were: (1) its emphasis on sentiment and nature as against reason and artificiality; (2) its glorification of the individual as against society as a whole; (3) its insistence on diversity and change as against uniformity.

With some romantics, the central theme was the veneration of nature, not as an abstract force imbued with laws and mathematics, but as something sweet and lovely, compounded of hills and fields, lakes and waterfalls, stormy seas and trackless forests. With others, romanticism meant an intense interest in history, not of Greece and Rome, but of the middle ages and the European peoples, not for the sake of the "lessons of the past" but for the sake of color, adventure, and pageantry. Still other romantics turned their attention to distant lands and peoples, to imaginary Utopias in the future, or to the exotic and the unusual. They looked before and after, and pined for what was not. Many of them were revolutionaries. Many found solace in mysticism and religious experience.

The sources of the romantic movement were manifold. In part, it arose from a disillusionment with the eighteenth century, with the "enlightenment" and its faith in reason and natural law, which had apparently led only to bloody wars and revolutions. In part, it sprang from a reaction against the growing drabness of urban life. In part, too, it was a recognition of great achievements of immediately preceding centuries, achievements which made those of classical antiquity appear pallid.

It was in English poetry that romanticism took earliest and strongest hold. In 1798,

Wordsworth and Coleridge published their joint volume of *Lyrical Ballads,* which found its inspiration in a mystical approach to life and the beauty of· the commonplace in nature. Coleridge later added other strangely magical poems like *Kubla Khan* and *Christabel* to *The Ancient Mariner,* while Wordsworth described his emotional response to nature and to life in *The Prelude* and *The Excursion.* Soon Sir Walter Scott was composing historical ballads like the *Lady of the Lake* on Scottish love and valor. But the startling success of a new poet, Lord Byron, turned Scott to the long series of the romantic Waverley novels. Byron's stirring poems proclaimed his rebellion against society and the world, although they had, perhaps, less real poetic feeling than the word pictures of Keats, or the lyrics of the revolutionary Shelley.

Literature on the continent underwent a similar change as the nineteenth century advanced. Goethe, who had heralded romanticism in the eighteenth century, and then won fame as a classicist, completed his romantic masterpiece, *Faust,* just before his death in 1832. Schiller in his historical dramas had become thoroughly romantic by the time he wrote *William Tell* (1804). Heinrich Heine, a rebellious exile in Paris, was composing sentimental German lyrics in the 1820's. But it was French lyric poetry that under romantic influence reached new heights with Alfred de Musset, Alfred de Vigny, and Victor Hugo. Hugo won even greater fame with his dramas like *Hernani,* which at its production in 1830 started a riotous demonstration among the classicist critics, and with his historical novels such as *Notre Dame de Paris* and *Ninety-Three.*

Nor was romanticism in literature confined to western Europe. In Russia, Pushkin wrote romantic poems in the manner of Byron and historical dramas in imitation of Shakespeare, infusing both with Russian spirit and his own genius. Gogol gained distinction with romantic tales of country life, and with his masterpiece *Dead Souls,* a series of humorous and unflattering sketches of provincial society. In Poland, Mickiewicz glorified the Polish countryside in his historical poems. In Italy, Manzoni turned from classicism to romantic poetry and wrote the greatest Italian novel of the century, *I Promessi Sposi.* Elsewhere—in Spain, Portugal, Austria, Scandinavia— romantic writers broke loose from the classical tradition in poetry, drama, and the novel.

·Pictorial art was less rapidly affected by romanticism than literature. Though they showed signs of the new tendencies, artists such as David or Ingres continued to paint in the classical tradition, while sculptors like Canova or Thorwaldsen sought to make their statues even more severely classical than those of the Renaissance. But the English painters Constable and Turner and the Frenchman Delacroix brought romanticism into painting by emphasis on vivid color, nature, history, and, in the case of the last, violent action. When François Rude was set to work on the sculptures for Napoleon's Arch of Triumph at Paris he put into them an intensity of emotion and dramatic action that was typically romantic.

At first in the nineteenth century, architecture tended to adhere to a severe classicism—the so-call "pure Greek." But before long the new vogue of the middle ages, exemplified by the success of Scott's novels, produced a tremendous interest in, and revival of, medieval gothic architecture. All sorts of buildings from churches to private homes were constructed in some approximation to the gothic style. When, after a

Immanuel Kant. After a painting done in 1791.

Courtesy Bettmann Archive

fire, the British houses of parliament were rebuilt in the 1840's, the new edifice was gothic.

Music went romantic earlier than pictorial or monumental art. Though the towering genius of Beethoven defies classification, his later work contains distinctly romantic as well as classical elements. Clearly romantic in their colorful melodies and their escape from restraining rules were such German composers as von Weber, Schubert, and Mendelssohn. Italian opera also became quite romantic, both in manner and subject, with the work of Rossini, Bellini, and Donizetti. The last based one of his most popular operas, *Lucia de Lammermoor*, on an historical novel by Sir Walter Scott.

B. Philosophy and Religion

In some ways Immanuel Kant (1724–1804) represented the culmination of the rationalist philosophy of the seventeenth and eighteenth centuries. Seeking to approach God and religious truth by reason, Kant decided that some features of the universe and of human experience can not be discovered or understood by rational processes. He concluded that God, the freedom of the human will, and the immortality of the soul are known by man, not through reason, but through a sort of inner moral instinct. This doctrine, that certain vital truths transcend human reason, is described, in some forms, as transcendentalism, and in others as "idealism." Kant's emphasis on the moral duties of man and his concepts of "spirit" and "will" paved the way for such a disciple as Fichte, who stood for a kind of transcendental pantheism and applied his philosophical "idealism" to the practical task of arousing German patriotism against Napoleon.

In the chair of philosophy at the university of Berlin, Fichte was succeeded by Hegel, who was at once an "idealist" and a mystic. Hegel's eloquent use of semi-scientific, semi-poetic phrases, his personification of abstract forces, his constant reference to "spirit"—world spirit, time spirit, national spirit, and so on—stirred romantic if somewhat misty thoughts in his hearers and readers. His emphasis on free-dom gave hope to many liberals, while his survey of world history with its conclusion that the peak of the progress of the human spirit had been reached in the contemporary Prussian monarchy, where "man as man is free," reassured conservatives. Hegel thought that progress took place by a process which he called dialectic: a situation (thesis) gives rise to its negation (antithesis), and the two fuse to create a new situation (synthesis).

While philosophy was moving toward romantic "idealism," trends in religion were also distinctly away from the rationalism of the eighteenth century. Indeed, the period of romanticism witnessed a remarkable religious revival, a renewed faith in the supernatural and in Christianity, and a special emphasis on mystical religious experience. This was helped undoubtedly by current disillusionment about rationalism and also by romantic interest in the middle ages.

In the era of Napoleon, when Pope Pius VII was a prisoner of the Emperor and revolutionary ideas were in the ascendant, it had seemed to many persons as if Catholic Christianity were decaying and before long might disappear. But the years after 1815 produced a remarkable restoration of Catholic influence and prestige. The quiet dignity with which the Pope resisted Napoleon's persecution won general respect. When he returned to Rome in 1814, he formally reconstituted the Society of Jesus which had been suppressed forty-one years earlier. With France he continued the Napoleonic concordat, and with other Catholic states he concluded similar agreements. With Protestant Prussia, he negotiated a friendly agreement for the regulation of Catholic affairs in that country.

Under Pius VII a number of intellectuals of other faiths or of no faith were converted to Catholicism, and defenders of it wrote books which met with an enthusiastic response. In 1817 appeared *Du Pape* by a French scholar, Count Joseph de Maistre, which upheld the ancient claims of the papacy, insisted that the pope was infallible in matters of faith and morals, and argued that the way to care for the ills of the world was to recognize the pope as the supreme and inspired head of all Christian nations.

Even more influential was Chateaubriand's *Le Génie du Christianisme*, published in 1801, which, with glowing figures of speech, upheld Catholicism as the historic religion that had produced the best in European civilization. Inspired by such works, many Catholics in France and other lands ceased to feel that they were on the defensive against rationalist attacks. In most Catholic countries, moreover, the authorities, in their efforts to suppress liberalism, gave support to the church and strengthened the control of the clergy over education.

England was deeply affected by the religious revival in a number of ways. At the death of John Wesley in 1791 there had been, in Great Britain, about 77,000 Methodist church members. So rapidly did the movement grow in ensuing years that by 1837 they numbered over 300,000. The rise of the Methodists wrought changes in the Anglican Church, which began to show a new interest in popular preaching and evangelical religion. Alongside the Methodists, other evangelical sects, like the Baptists, grew in numbers and activity.

But a counter tendency soon manifested itself in the "Oxford movement." At the University of Oxford a group of young clergymen headed by John Henry Newman and Edward Pusey, who were disturbed by rationalism, liberalism, and the effects of evangelical Protestantism, began to stress the historic, traditional, and Catholic elements in the Anglican Church. In a series of famous tracts during the 1830's they stressed the authority of the Church as against the individual or the Bible and upheld the view that the Anglican Church was a branch of the "undivided Catholic Church." In 1845, Newman's search for religious authority convinced him that ultimately it was to be found only in the voice of the pope, and he joined the Catholic Church. A considerable number followed him, with consequent strengthening of the Catholic Church in English-speaking countries. At the same time, other leaders of the Oxford Movement, including Pusey, remained in the Anglican Church, and strove to make it more Catholic in its beliefs and ceremonies. Thus there arose, within the Anglican Church, an Anglo-Catholic "high church" party which combated both the severely Protestant "low church" and the looser "broad church" groups

In Germany the earlier "pietism" waned, and the Lutheran churches remained closely bound to, and supervised by, the governments of the various states. Doctrinal differences had so far lost their meaning, however, that the civil authorities were able forcibly to unite the Calvinist and Lutheran churches in Prussia and several other German states. On the whole it was in the new "idealist" philosophy, rather than within established Protestant churches, that religious impulses of the romantic period found chief expression in Germany.

C. Contribution of Romanticism to Nationalism and Liberalism

So closely related were nationalism and romanticism in the era of Metternich that it is difficult to separate them. Nationalism was romantic, and most romanticism was nationalist. Everywhere, devotees of romanticism displayed patriotic emotions and sentiments. Usually they extolled the common people of their respective nationalities. Frequently they ransacked historical records to find evidence of their nation's glorious deeds in the past. As heirs to the fervor engendered in the Revolutionary and Napoleonic eras, the patriotic romantics glorified the nation, its language, its culture, its folk songs, its past, with an ardent and often poetic emotionalism. In those countries which were already national states, romantic nationalism strengthened patriotic devotion to the fatherland. Not infrequently, political and religious conservatives were just as patriotic and romantically nationalistic as the liberals or the radicals. In lands still divided into various states, like Italy and Germany, or subject to foreign rule, like Poland and Czechoslovakia, romantic nationalism led to intense and often revolutionary movements for unification and liberation.

Nationalists and romantics could join with enthusiasm in exalting folk culture— the myths, ballads, proverbs, dances, customs, and costumes of the several European peoples. The more scholarly could investigate the peculiarities of local laws and

John Henry, Cardinal Newman. From a photograph (1887).

Courtesy Bettmann Archive

institutions or devote themselves to the study of the national language in its varieties and dialects. In this connection the fashion was more or less set by Jacob Grimm, who was the author of an elaborate *German Grammar*, a detailed *History of the German Language*, and an imposing *German Dictionary*. In addition, Grimm collected fairy tales that he found current among the people and wrote a history of the pre-Christian myths and religion of the Germans. The same sort of work was done with great diligence and more or less success for France, England, Hungary, Czechoslovakia, Poland, Russia, Finland, Bulgaria, and almost every other European nation.

Romanticism and nationalism shared an enthusiasm for history. National pride prompted historical research, and romantic interest in the past built up national pride. Stein, the German patriot, sponsored a project for publishing all the source materials for the ancient and medieval history of Germany, and the first volume of the great resulting collection, *Monumenta Germaniae Historica*, appeared in 1826. Soon Great Britain and France had commissions of scholars at work on the publication of their medieval documents. It was indeed an age of history. In Germany, Niebuhr and Ranke; in Britain, Carlyle and Macaulay; in France, Michelet and Guizot: these were busy preparing monumental historical works. If some like Niebuhr turned to ancient history, or, like Carlyle, wrote mainly of foreign countries, still in most histories the patriotic note was seldom absent and it was often dominant. Indeed, histories were frequently the means by which the patriotism of "oppressed," or subject, peoples was aroused. Thus, Francis Palacky stirred the Czechs with his five-volume *History of the Bohemian People*, which began to appear in 1836.

In France or Great Britain, conservatives could join with liberals in nationalist manifestations. But in Italy or Germany or Poland, liberals were the outstanding nationalists, for national unification or liberation could be attained only by upsetting the conservative *status quo* which Metternich was so vigorously maintaining. It seemed clear that national unity in Germany and Italy, or national liberation in Poland or Czechoslovakia, could be gained only by revolution. There were moderate liberals and nationalists who hoped to obtain their goals by the slow process of education and reform. But in the divided and subjected countries most nationalists and liberals were perforce revolutionaries.

Revolutionary activity had to be carried on underground. Frequently its leaders were in exile. There was often a romantic note in their work. There were oaths taken by the dim light of candles and signed in blood. There were secret passwords and handclasps. There were meetings in the woods or in caverns. There were symbols like skulls and naked daggers. But in spite of all such trappings, the work was deadly serious.

As a conspicuous example of the romantic nationalist revolutionary, we may mention Joseph Mazzini (1805–1872). A native of Genoa and the son of a university professor, he early became both a liberal and a nationalist. As a young man he joined the secret revolutionary society of the *Carbonari*, and took part in its activities, and was betrayed to the authorities while initiating a new member. Jailed for six months without trial, he was finally released, but under so many restrictions that he went into exile in France. In 1831 he projected a new non-secret organization, "Young Italy." It was composed of intellectuals under forty years of age, who would conduct an incessant campaign among all Italians for the purpose of instilling in them the desire to liberate their country from foreign and domestic tyrants and to unify it into a democratic "Roman Republic." In 1833 Mazzini was sentenced to death *in absentia*, for his part in an abortive revolutionary movement in the Sardinian army. By word and pen, Mazzini worked for his cause. He was not a good organizer, and the groups of collaborators he gathered shifted and changed. But he did inspire large numbers of Italians and fire them with the flame of his purpose. The flood of pamphlets, newspapers, letters,

and instructions which he poured into Italy from his exile in France and England slowly bore fruit—but fruit that was one day to be bitter in his mouth, for nationalism was to prove stronger than liberalism, while to Mazzini the two were inseparable.

There was an engaging quality in the teachings of Mazzini. The banner he designed for "Young Italy" bore on one side the words "Unity" and "Independence," and on the other, "Liberty, Equality, and Humanity." Even his nationalism had a broadly international aspect. Though, as he once said, he "loved Italy above all earthly things," he dreamed of a Europe that would be a peaceful brotherhood of free nations. In 1834 he organized "Young Europe," an association "of men believing in a future of liberty, equality, and fraternity for all mankind, and desirous of consecrating their thoughts and actions to the realization of that future."

D. Scientific Progress

While romantic, liberal nationalists sought to alter the existing political order,

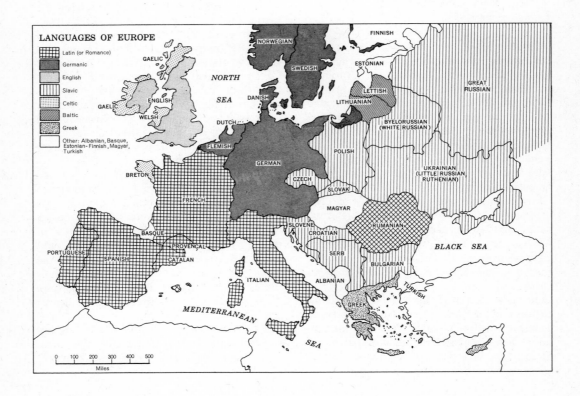

scientists in their laboratories and observatories were extending the boundaries of knowledge. The scientific work of the seventeenth and eighteenth centuries was carried ahead, and a peculiar phenomenon of modern times became evident—that of accelerating tempo. One scientific discovery led to others, and each of these to still others, so that as the nineteenth century progressed science made ever more rapid advance.

When the century opened, two famous French professors, Lagrange and Laplace, were systematizing and developing the work of preceding mathematicians and scientists since the time of Newton. Lagrange, who in 1793 had devised the metric system of weights and measures for the French government, perfected a series of mathematical innovations, some of them very useful for astronomical calculations. His friend Laplace devoted his chief attention to astronomy and published between 1799 and 1825 his five-volume *Celestial Mechanics*. In it he gave convincing mathematical proof of Newton's principle of gravitation and worked out many of the implications of Newton's theories. In another work he put forward his celebrated "nebular hypothesis," an ingenious supposition as to the way in which the whole solar system developed from a vast, whirling, gaseous cloud.

In the footsteps of these French scientists followed Leverrier, director of the observatory at Paris. By mathematical calculations he showed in 1845 that there must be another unseen planet in the solar system out beyond Uranus and he predicted its orbit. The next year occurred one of the great triumphs of modern astronomy when the new planet, which was given the name of Neptune, was actually observed close to the spot which Leverrier had foretold.

In physics, the early nineteenth century witnessed a rapid development of thermodynamics, optics, magnetism, and electricity. Thermodynamics, the study of the mechanical action of heat, became a subject of much interest as the use of the steam engine developed. Earlier physicists had thought of heat as a subtle fluid which they called "caloric." But that it was a form of motion, rather than a substance, was demonstrated by an American, Benjamin Thompson, who in 1798 presented to the Royal Society in London a paper entitled *Enquiry concerning the source of heat which is excited by friction*. A loyalist at the time of the American Revolution, Thompson had gone to England and later to Bavaria, where he gained the title of Count Rumford. His work was carried on by Sir Humphrey Davy in England, and in France by Carnot, son of the Jacobin statesman. In 1843, James Joule upheld the view that, whenever mechanical force is expended, an exact equivalent of heat always results. He had already been able to show that electrical energy, like mechanical, had its equivalent in heat. His name has been given to a scientific unit of energy—the joule.

From the work of these men, scientists were able to formulate two great principles of physics. The "first law of thermodynamics," that of the "conservation of energy," was largely a discovery of Helmholtz, who read a paper on the subject in 1847. It held that the quantity of energy which can be brought into action in the whole of nature is unchangeable and can neither be increased nor diminished. Four years later William Thomson, better known by his later title of Lord Kelvin, stated the "second law of thermodynamics," that of the "dissipation of energy," that, while the sum total of energy in the universe is unchangeable, the amount of energy available is constantly diminishing by a continual degeneration into non-available energy such as "dissipated" heat.

But what were perhaps the most exciting developments of the time in physics were in the field of electricity. In the eighteenth century Franklin had shown that lightning was an electric phenomenon; Galvani had experimented with the action of electricity on the muscles of frogs; Volta had in 1799 devised the voltaic pile, a sort of dry cell; and there had been much experimenting with the static electricity of "Leyden jars." But in the nineteenth century, electricity rapidly ceased to be a laboratory curiosity and became an important new force. In 1820 Ampère suggested the use of electricity for sending messages, and in the 1830's practical systems of telegraphy were developed by Wheatstone in England, and Morse in America. Already, Sir Humphrey Davy and others had been producing electric cur-

Samuel F. B. Morse (1791–1872). Self portrait.

rents from improved voltaic piles, and it was quickly shown that such currents could decompose chemical compounds and also be used for electroplating one metal with another. In 1808 Davy produced an electric arc light between two carbon poles.

In 1819 a Dane, Oersted by name, showed that, since an electric current affected a compass needle, electricity and magnetism were related. This connection was investigated by Michael Faraday, who in a series of brilliant experiments produced magnetism by electric currents and discovered the principle of the electric motor and the dynamo (1831). With the development of the dynamo, electric current could be generated in larger quantities and more easily than by the voltaic pile. Experiments of all sorts with electricity and even its industrial use became much more practicable.

Through the work of chemists and physicists, an old idea dating back to the ancient Greeks was definitely established in the nineteenth century. Philosophers and scientists had often speculated as to whether the matter of the universe might not be made up of minute particles or "atoms." About 1803, John Dalton, arguing from facts of chemistry, persuasively presented the idea that all matter consists of atoms, that the atoms of various chemicals are distinguished from each other by different relative weights, and that atoms combine in definite relationships to form compounds. At almost the same time, an Italian nobleman, Count Avogadro, at the University of Turin, demonstrated that gases consist of minute particles which he called "molecules" and proposed the hypothesis that "equal volumes of gases, under the same conditions of temperature and pressure, contain the same number of smallest particles or molecules." For a time there was confusion in terminology between Dalton's "atoms" and Avogadro's "molecules." But gradually "atom" came to be accepted as the name of the smallest unit of simple elements, while "molecule" was used for a unit composed of two or more atoms in a gas or in a compound.

Organic chemistry was actually born in 1828, when Friedrich Wöhler showed that urea, a substance hitherto thought of as purely animal, could be artificially synthesized from chemicals in the laboratory. The old distinction between living creatures and inorganic substances was thus broken down. Apparently, everything was made of chemical elements and compounds. Wöhler likewise helped to establish another connection between chemistry and living matter, for he did some work with Justus von Liebig, whose experiments at the universities of Giessen and Munich showed that vegetables require certain chemicals in order to grow well. Liebig's efforts paved the way for the development of chemical fertilizers, which eventually revolutionized modern agriculture.

Meanwhile biologists and botanists were making strides in knowledge of animals and plants. Lamarck, in his *Natural History of Invertebrate Animals*, not only gave a wealth of detailed information about various forms of life, but proposed a general theory, which, though not entirely new, was to undergo significant development in ensuing years. This was the idea of evolution—that one species of animals is derived from another, and that "higher" forms develop out of "lower" forms. The idea was significant, but Lamarck's suggestions as to how evolution took place proved mistaken. He held that need felt in an animal body tends to produce a new organ, which use develops, and that such changes can be passed on to succeeding generations. In short, he erroneously believed that "acquired characteristics" are inherited.

In geology, the outstanding scientist was Sir Charles Lyell. In 1830 he published his classic *Principles of Geology, an attempt to explain the former changes of the Earth's surface by reference to causes now in operation*. His basic idea was not new, for James Hutton in a book published forty-five years earlier had held similar views. But Lyell reenforced Hutton's argument by a wealth of scientific observations and presented it in a lively and entertaining style. It was Lyell's contention that the present surface of the earth was the product, not of past floods and catastrophes or of special acts of the Creator, but rather the result of observable forces that were still in operation—winds, frost, rain, streams, ice, volcanoes, earthquakes. Coal came from buried vegetation, fossils from buried plants and animals, and they had been buried not by a catastrophe but by natural agents. Mountains had been lifted by the slow folding of the earth's crust; valleys had been formed by the erosion of rivers. It had all been a slow, continuous, evolutionary process.

Another scientific landmark, this one in the field of embryology, is attributable to a physician, Dr. von Baer, who worked in East Prussia and Russia. His *Letter on the Egg of Mammals* (1827) pointed out that human beings, in common with all other mammals, and with birds, fishes, and reptiles, are reproduced by the fertilization of eggs. Baer's later work and that of other scientists were improved in accuracy and range by the development in the 1830's of the compound microscope. And it was the improved microscope that enabled Theodor Schwann to discover in 1837 that yeast is made up of living organisms. Two years later he formulated the highly significant "cell theory," that all living things originate and grow tiny structural units, or "cells."

Basically, the newer developments in science militated against the emotional and mystical impulses of the era of romanticism. As some of the mysteries of nature were cleared up and some of its marvels better understood, there was a renewed tendency on the part of many intellectuals to become indifferent, if not actively hostile, to current conceptions of religion and the supernat-

ural. Over against the romantically inspired religious revival of the era, a new generation of skeptics, absorbed in science, turned from those things which they felt man could not know positively to fields like chemistry or physics which, they thought, contained the factual and the certain. In a sense this trend was a continuation of the influence of Newtonian physics on the eighteenth century, which had seen thinkers move from Christian faith to Deism and even to Atheism. But science was now scoring so many triumphs that its prestige was affecting a larger number of persons. When combined with the development of industry, which will be discussed in the next chapter, the influence of science in the nineteenth century was toward materialism—a paramount interest and faith in those things which man can detect with his senses and examine in the laboratory.

Disciples of Nature. Caricature of romantic painters by Honoré Daumier (d. 1879).

CHAPTER 45

Advance of Machine Industry

A. Early Stages

The term "industrial revolution" is so well established in historical usage that it cannot be readily abandoned, although there is some reason for doing so. The process of improving manufacturing techniques, developing the factory system, and increasing industrial output has been long and slow, whether in England or in the world at large. In England it can be traced back at least to the mid-sixteenth century and is still continuing. What is spread over four centuries is hardly a "revolution."

The "industrial revolution" used to be assigned to eighteenth-century England. Sometimes such dates as 1740–1800 or 1760–1820 were specified, with emphasis on certain inventions in the cotton and metal industries, on the building of roads and canals, and on the Watt steam engine. But it was gradually realized that, while cotton and iron manufacture did grow rapidly in the eighteenth century, the period of real mechanization and mass production came after 1800 or even after 1820. In 1800 the power loom was not yet in practical use, the processes of steel manufacture were still costly and slow, and only a few score low-power Watt steam engines were in operation. The building of roads and canals in eighteenth-century England only repeated what had been done in France in the seventeenth century. The real revolution in transportation came after 1830 with the introduction of the railway and the steamship.

If the term "industrial revolution" is to be used, it should be applied to the period in which a country is fairly rapidly changed over from predominantly agricultural and commercial pursuits to those of mechanized industry. In England this change occurred, roughly speaking, between 1830 and 1870. Before 1830 most Englishmen were still engaged in farming or in trade. By 1870, most Englishmen were connected in one way or another with mechanized industries. That the change—the "industrial revolution"— took place originally in England, is attributable to the fact that certain prerequisites for it had been more completely fulfilled there than in any other country. These prerequisites, which must be briefly examined, may be listed under six heads: capital, labor, techniques, resources, transportation, and markets.

1. Capital. For intensive industrialization, capital in large quantities is necessary to build factories and machines, to hire workers, and to buy raw materials. This was available in England as profit from the successful British commerce of the seventeenth and eighteenth centuries and from the capitalist type of agriculture which grew up especially after 1740 in connection with the enclosure movement. In England, moreover, the use of capital was expedited by the Bank of England, by efficient handling of governmental finances, and by the rise of a London money market where bills could be discounted and shares bought and sold. The British coinage and paper money were on a sound basis from the early eighteenth cen-

James Watt. Sir Francis Legatt Chantry (d. 1842).

tury onwards, save for a brief period during and after the Napoleonic wars. Just when the need for financing industry was becoming great, joint stock banks other than the Bank of England were legalized (1826). In the ensuing decades the formation of joint stock corporations for industry, commerce, and finance was made simple and easy. It must be noted, however, that much of England's industrial capital was self-generated. That is, a manufacturer, starting with a small capital, enlarged his plant by plowing back his profits into the business.

2. *Labor.* Workers for the new English industries of the nineteenth century came from a number of sources. The British population was growing rapidly. It almost doubled in the eighteenth century, and doubled again in the first half of the nineteenth, despite considerable emigration. There was some immigration into England of Continental European labor in the eighteenth, and of Irish in the nineteenth, century. Perhaps most important of all, labor was made available for factory-production through the gradual destruction of the old peasant farming as a result of the enclosure movement and capitalist agriculture.

3. *Techniques.* England, in the late eighteenth and early nineteenth centuries developed techniques, processes, and machines necessary for large-scale industry. France was probably ahead of England in technology as late as 1750. Afterwards England rapidly outstripped all rivals. The story of the cotton textile inventions is familiar, though it has probably been unduly conventionalized, and the work of a number of inventors has been attached to a single name. In any case, the flying shuttle (John Kay, 1733), the spinning jenny (James Hargreaves, about 1767), the water frame (Richard Arkwright, 1769), the spinning "mule" (Samuel Crompton, 1779), the power loom (Edmund Cartwright, 1785), the cotton gin (Eli Whitney, 1792, in the United States), the cylindrical calico printing machine (Thomas Bell, 1785), and chemical bleaching and chemical dyes—all these had been developed before the end of the eighteenth century. They had been successfully grouped in factories operated by water or even steam power, and cheap large-scale production in factories had put out of business the small-shop and the home production of cotton thread. In the early nineteenth century, the factory cotton industry grew by leaps and bounds. By 1835 there were nearly 106,000 power looms in the British Isles.

The story of the metal industries is almost as familiar. Shortage of wood to make charcoal for the smelting of iron ore, impelled experimentation with coal, which had been mined in ever-increasing quantities in England since the sixteenth century. The Darbys at Coalbrookdale, in the first half of the eighteenth century, attained success in this endeavor by transforming coal into coke and then using a strong blast of air in the smelting process. English iron production had been declining for lack of charcoal; it was rejuvenated after the mid-eighteenth century by the use of the Darby's coke-blast process and by a series of other inventions and improvements: John Smeaton's air pump (1760), the reverberatory furnace, "puddling," and the rolling mill (all developed by Henry Cort and Peter Onions about 1783), James Watt's steam hammer, Huntsman's steel process (about 1740), the hot blast (Nielson, 1828). By the early nineteenth century, iron was being produced in rapidly increasing quantities. From it were made the new machines. Enthusiasts were urging the use of iron for bridges, for ships, and even for coffins.

In the eighteenth century the power most generally used was, as in the past, that of man, mules, wind, or water. A steam (or atmospheric) engine—the Newcomen—had been invented in the early 1700's, but its use was restricted to pumping water out of mines. It was vastly improved upon by James Watt's engine, patented in 1769 and first put to industrial use in 1776. By the first decade of the nineteenth century, steam was becoming a major motive force. No longer did a mill have to be located beside a running stream. Steam engines were being put on boats (Robert Fulton's *Clermont*, 1807), and the first moderately successful locomotive was made by George Stephenson in 1814. Watt had encountered difficulty in making his early engines for lack of proper machine tools. But gradually this was surmounted by the development and use of drills, lathes, the slide rest, and stamping presses.

4. *Resources*. England was well endowed with just the resources needed for industrialization. Its climate was damp enough to be highly suitable for mechanical spinning and weaving. Its water power was ample. More important, England was abundantly endowed with iron and coal.

5. *Transportation*. With its many ports and extensive shipping, Great Britain was well equipped, by the eighteenth century, for sea-borne transport. Then, during the latter half of the century, Britain modernized its medieval inland transportation by the construction of a network of roads and canals. Since no part of England is much more than sixty or seventy miles from salt water, these roads and canals soon put many inland towns in a position to share in the growing British trade.

6. *Markets*. England and Scotland, since the Act of Union of 1707, had constituted a consolidated open market, free of tariffs. To them, Ireland was united in 1800, giving English industry a still more extensive home market. English merchants had opened up channels of trade to all Europe, to North America, to Africa, and to the Far East before the mid-eighteenth century. Afterwards, British markets continued to expand. The United States kept on buying British goods, even after the American Revolution. India bought more and more British wares, especially the new, cheap cottons. The Spanish colonies were opened to British commerce in the period of the French Revolution and Napoleon, and Britain increased its trade with them when they became independent countries in the 1820's. All over the world, from Canton to Buenos Aires, and from Capetown to North Cape, British commerce, from the beginning of the nineteenth century, had no serious competitor.

Thus by 1815 or 1839, England had all the prerequisites for the rapid growth of large-scale factory production. She had them more fully than any rival. She had already undergone a certain degree of industrialization in cotton textiles and the metal trades. In the ensuing decades she was to become indeed the workshop of the world. She was to undergo her "industrial revolution" a generation ahead of any other major country. When this revolution was under way in England (and later in other countries) it proved to be self-generating, self-perpetuating, self-reinforcing. Once industry really got going, there was a sort of take-off into more rapid, more extensive industrialization. The point of take-off seems to be that at which the new industry begins to produce at such a rate that it can provide large quantities of capital for further industrial expansion. That point came in England about 1830.

B. Industrial Revolution in England

The industries already developed in England expanded with amazing rapidity after 1830. For example, English exports of cotton goods rose in value from 19 million pounds sterling in 1830 to 56 million in 1870. In 1821, England bought 93,500,000 pounds of raw cotton from America, her principal source of supply. By 1859–1860 such purchases ran well over a billion pounds. In 1871, moreover, 88 per cent of all workers in the cotton industry were employed in factories.

Iron progressed almost as fast. British production of pig iron rose from 750,000 tons in 1830 to six million in 1870. Coal production similarly increased from 26 million tons in 1830 to 110 million forty years later. In the metal industries, the biggest advance was the improvement of methods for large-scale conversion of iron into steel. The Bessemer process, introduced in 1856, was rapid and inexpensive. It made steel available for machinery, rails, and ships, and steel was stronger and more durable than iron. Then to the Bessemer process was added the Siemens-Martin "open hearth" process in the 1860's, while in the 1870's the Thomas-Gilchrist developments made it possible to use iron ores with a high phosphorous content. Between 1856 and 1870, the price of steel was cut in half in England.

In the same period, factory organization and machine production were applied to such old and formerly small-scale industries as shoe-making, brewing, flour-milling, and furniture-making. Production of arms and munitions was likewise revolutionized both by mechanization and by new inventions such as the percussion cap (as against the flintlock), the rifle (as against the musket), and breech-loading (as against muzzle-loading). In 1862 an American, Richard Gatling, invented a machine gun which would fire 350 shots a minute. With the "Gatling gun," the "industrial revolution" was carried into warfare.

New industries came into existence alongside the older ones. In the 1840's growing urban demand, increasing scientific knowledge, and better methods of producing glass jars and tin receptacles permitted the introduction of canned foods. By the 1860's fresh fruits, fish, and vegetables were being canned in considerable quantities, and "extract of beef," just invented by the German scientist Liebig, was enjoying a popularity quite out of line with its nutritional value. Gail Borden in America had just patented "condensed milk," and dried milk was first made in England in 1855.

From the making of coke for iron smelting, there developed a new industry, for, in producing coke, coal gas is released. A gas-lighting company was incorporated in London in 1812. Gas was first used for cooking in 1832. By the mid-century many streets and many homes were being lighted by it, and "gas works" and gas tanks disfigured most of the larger cities.

But scientific progress in the field of electricity was already preparing a rival to gas. The invention of the carbon arc light and improved dynamos made electrical lighting practicable by 1870, and the invention of the incandescent lamp in 1878 put it in widespread use. Meanwhile, electricity was being widely employed for the electroplating of metals as early as the 1850's, and in the previous decade the telegraph had spread a network of wires over the face of Europe. Together with a submarine cable to America, successfully laid in 1866, the telegraph made it possible to get news transmitted with unheard-of rapidity and gave a stimulus to newspapers, which were likewise aided by mechanical steam presses and cheaper paper.

A new industry that arose between 1830 and 1870 was photography. Though the first crude photograph had been made in 1822, it was a Frenchman, Daguerre, who rendered the process practicable. By 1839 he could "take pictures" in thirty minutes; and "daguerreotype" was long a synonym for photograph. In 1841 Fox Talbot, an Englishman, developed a faster process; and a decade later, almost instantaneous photography was realized. Henceforth the new art developed swiftly as a great commercial industry.

The invention, by the American Charles Goodyear in 1839, of a process of vulcanizing rubber in order to make it stronger and more elastic laid the foundation of another new industry. By the 1860's there was a marked growth of factories for the production of rubber articles, but the great days of rubber still lay ahead. Similar was the story of petroleum products. In the 1850's a Scottish industrial chemist, James Young, discovered how to make naphtha, lubricating oils, paraffine, and kerosene by distilling crude oil. Gradually these new products found a market, and kerosene or "coal oil" was especially popular for use in lamps. World production of petroleum, a mere two thousand barrels in 1857, rose to five and a half million in 1870. Only ten years later it would be thirty million.

The mechanization of industries, old and

Locomotives of 1831 and 1893 as displayed at the Chicago World's Fair, 1893.

Courtesy Bettmann Archive

new, produced what amounted to another profession—that of engineer. Originally, engineers had been men who designed and constructed fortifications and engines of war. But as industrial invention proceeded and became more complicated, it gave rise to "civil engineers" trained to plan and build roads, docks, canals, aqueducts, drainage systems, lighthouses, etc. In 1828 the civil engineers of London formed a society. But rather rapidly the engineers became more specialized. Some, dealing with steam engines, machine tools, mill work, and moving machinery in general, became "mechanical engineers." Others, busying themselves with the technical problems of mines, became "mining engineers." By 1870 there were "marine engineers," "sanitary engineers," "chemical engineers," and "electrical engineers." In a way the engineers were a link between industry and science. Many of them were competent scientists and some of them made significant contributions. Gradually science and industry became closely interlocked.

Probably even more "revolutionary" than the rapid progress of industry, between 1830 and 1870, were the startling improvements in transportation. In 1830 men still went afoot, or rode on horseback or in carriages. In 1870 they and their goods could be whisked about at previously unheard-of speeds over shining roads of rails. The first steam railway was that between Stockton and Darlington in England, opened in 1825, with stationary engines to draw the cars over the hills and locomotives to pull them on level stretches. In 1830, the Liverpool-

Manchester line was inaugurated, and on it Robert Stephenson's improved locomotive, the *Rocket*, covered the forty-mile distance in an hour and a half. The success of this venture ushered in a period of extensive railway building. There were forty-nine miles of steam railways in 1830 in England. In 1870 there were 15,300 miles. Small lines were consolidated into larger systems, and London was linked with all the major English and Scottish cities. Locomotives were vastly improved, railway building techniques developed, and speed and safety increased.

The revolution in ocean transportation was slightly slower. In 1838 two ships crossed the Atlantic under steam power, the *Sirius* in eighteen days, and the *Great Western* in fifteen days. Two years later Samuel Cunard inaugurated the first regular trans-Atlantic steamship service. In the 1850's, the screw-propeller was widely adopted in place of the earlier paddle wheels, and iron began to replace wood as the building material for the larger ships. In 1858, when an iron liner, the *Great Eastern*, was constructed with a gross tonnage of 18,337, a horsepower of 11,000, and a speed of thirteen knots, it was regarded as a triumph of marine engineering. The number of British steamships increased from 298 in 1830 to 3,178 in 1870, and their net tonnage rose in the period from 30,339 to 1,112,934. But it was not until the 1880's that the tonnage of Britain's steamships surpassed that of her sailing vessels.

Not only was there a shift from sail to steam. There was a remarkable growth of the merchant marine as a whole. The tonnage of British ships more than doubled between 1830 and 1870, and just at the end of the period the opening of the Suez canal in 1869 gave another impetus to sea-borne transport. The swift decrease of the costs of shipping goods by water made it possible for England to sell its wares, even bulky ones of iron, all over the world, and also made it easier and less expensive to import both raw materials like cotton and wool, and food like wheat.

The impact of industry, science, and cheap transportation on English agriculture worked first in one direction, then in the other. By the enclosure movement and the new techniques of the eighteenth century,

British farming had been changed over into a large-scale, profit-making enterprise. High prices in the Napoleonic era had brought wealth to the landowners, but in the twenty-five years after 1815, prices were relatively low, workers were drawn off into the growing factories, and competition of cheap food from the continent was increasing. For a while, agricultural profits were low.

But from 1840 to 1874, British farming became very profitable once more, despite the repeal of the corn laws in 1846. Machinery, applied to agriculture, drastically cut labor costs. In 1853 the "Crosskill reaper" was perfected in England, and at about the same time the "McCormick reaper" began to be imported from America. Moreover, Liebig's work on fertilizers had practical effect. Manufacture of superphosphate of lime was begun in England (1846), use of nitrate of soda grew, and guano from Peru was imported in swiftly increasing amounts. As the age of chemical and mechanical agriculture advanced, the crops of the English landlords rose while their labor costs dropped. They did very well till about 1874, when a combination of diseases among their animals and the impact of cheap food imported on steamships from Russia, Argentina, United States, Canada, and Australia brought depression.

If the big landlords were seeking and making profits in the period from 1830 to 1870, they were merely reflecting the fact that England had become by this time a thoroughly capitalist country. To older capitalists who had made money by commerce and banking, had been added new industrial capitalists. The factory and the machine gradually supplanted the old craftsman and the artisan, for these could not afford to buy the new machines nor could they compete with them. Work in homes and small shops declined, nor could the putting-out system face the competition of the factory. The changes thus wrought were far-reaching. No longer was ownership of tools and shops spread among thousands of workers. The factories and machines were owned by a relatively small number of industrial capitalists, men who brought together labor, raw materials, and machines in a single spot and organized the production and sale of goods.

The early industrialists had often been poor men, like Arkwright or Watt, who, starting in a small way, by intelligence and persistence and (sometimes) ruthlessness, built up a factory. Rapidly, however, the "self-made" men were joined by those who already had wealth from land or trade or inheritance and who now "invested" in factories and shared the profits. As joint stock companies grew in number and popularity in the mid-nineteenth century, it became easy for the man with money to "invest" in industry and reap the profits, while the technical work of production and management was carried on by hired employees of the corporation. There were, of course, risks. Many enterprises failed. To the capitalists, it seemed that the risks they ran justified the rewards they got. In any event, industrialization greatly increased the amount of capital in England. One estimate is that it rose from 1,500 million pounds sterling in 1750 to 2,500 million in 1833, and 6,000 million in 1865.

C. Spread of Machine Industry to the Continent

England was so closely bound to the Continent by commercial ties that industrialization of the former was certain to affect the latter. Machines, such as water frames of the Arkwright type, were introduced sporadically into France and the Belgian Netherlands in the latter part of the eighteenth century. As early as 1781 an English iron master founded the famous metal and munitions works at Creusot north of Lyons and installed a steam engine there. Coke smelting was employed at Creusot in 1810, and though the enterprise declined when munitions orders fell off at the close of the Napoleonic wars, it was later revivified by the Schneider family and became one of the most famous metal works in Europe.

Another Englishman, William Cockerill, mechanic and inventor, constructed in Belgium (at Verviers) in 1799 the first wool-carding and wool-spinning machines on the continent. In 1807 he established a large machine shop at Liége and made a handsome fortune from it. After the peace settlement of 1815, machine production was quickened and extended.

Though the process of industrialization was begun in Belgium well before 1830, it was the ensuing decades that witnessed its triumph. By 1870, Belgium, aided by British investments and engineers, was a nation of foundries, factories, and mines. It was the most densely populated country in Europe. The majority of its inhabitants lived in cities and got their livelihood from industry or trade. As early as 1834, the Belgian parliament adopted a plan drawn up by George Stephenson for the construction of a national system of railways radiating from Liége and Brussels. Through loans floated in England, the plan was speedily carried into effect.

France was more slowly and less completely industrialized. Her traditions of hand-work and luxury manufacture had become solidly entrenched before the political revolution of 1789. Her system of small-scale agriculture had been reënforced by that Revolution. She had lost both colonies and markets during the long wars. She lacked adequate supplies of coking coal, and much of her iron ore had too much phosphorus in it to be useful before the development of the Thomas-Gilchrist process in 1878. Yet the "industrial revolution" gradually penetrated into France. First it affected mining and metallurgy. The output of coal rose from 800,000 tons in 1815 (about the same as in 1770) to 1,800,000 tons in 1830, and of pig iron from 100,000 to 300,000 tons, while the number of steam engines (still used mainly for pumping water out of mines) increased from 16 to 625.

After 1830, with the aid of the business-minded government of Louis Philippe and later subsidies and assistance from Napoleon III, French industries developed behind a wall of tariffs which were maintained at high levels till 1860. Especially vitalizing for industry was the construction of railways, which was begun in 1842 with a line from Paris to Rouen and thence to Le Havre (built by an English company, with English capital, and English engineers and workmen). By 1870 a network of main lines radiated north, south, east, and west from Paris.

From 1830 to 1870 the output of French coal increased from 1,800,000 to 16,000,000 tons, and of pig iron from 300,000 to 1,400,000 tons, while the horsepower of steam engines, other than locomotives, rose from 20,000 to 336,000. After 1840, power-driven machinery began to compete with hand work in the French textile industries. Most of the new factories were concentrated in the north of the country, in Alsace and Lorraine or near Lille, Rouen, and Paris. By 1870, many an urban Frenchman was a machine-tender in a factory, although small shops and the putting-out system still flourished and the bulk of the population was still definitely agricultural.

Germany, despite vast resources of coal and iron, was originally more backward than France. Although some machinery was brought in from England and a few factories were built prior to 1830, there was scarcely a beginning of industrialization till after that date. The formation of a customs union (*Zollverein*), including by 1833 most German states (except Austria), removed many trade barriers. It had been designed primarily to help landowners by enlarging markets for agricultural goods, but it also served to stimulate commerce and to create a desire for improved means of communication. In 1839, with aid from British capital, the first important German railway was built from Dresden to Leipzig, and by the time of the political revolutions of 1848, there were some 4,000 miles of railway connecting Berlin with Hamburg, the Rhine, Prague, and Vienna. In Germany, in contrast to England, Belgium, and France, railway building preceded real beginnings of industrialization, but just as railways speeded up the foundries and factories of those countries, it served to create them in Germany.

German coal output, less than that of France in 1850, rose to 16 million tons in 1860 and to more than 37 million in 1870. Production of pig iron jumped to half a million tons in 1860 and soared to almost two million tons ten years later. Meanwhile, steam-driven machinery was being applied to cotton spinning, and textile factories were springing up in Saxony, Silesia, Westphalia, and the Rhineland. Cotton weaving and the manufacture of other textiles was, however, as late as 1870, still predominantly a hand industry, and 64 per cent of the population of Germany was still classed as rural and agricultural. Germany was clearly beginning to experience her "industrial revolution." But its sweeping consequences were to become obvious only after 1870.

Elsewhere on the continent, large-scale manufacturing, with the factory system and industrial capitalism, appeared only spottily before 1870. There were a few instances in Holland, Sweden, and Spain. There were considerably more in Russian Poland, particularly near Warsaw. Bohemia (especially Prague) and German Austria (especially Vienna) participated somewhat in the new mechanized industry. In the 1850's a few steam engines were brought into northern Italy (Piedmont), and Count Cavour acquired wealth and his first fame as a promoter of industrialization. But, by and large, Europe, with the exception of England, Belgium, France, and Germany, was before 1870 almost as solidly agricultural as it had been a century or two earlier.

D. Accompaniments of Industrialization, and Temporary Triumph of Economic Liberalism

For centuries up to the eighteenth, the population of Europe had been static or only slowly rising. In 1700, it did not number more than 125 million. By 1800, it totaled about 187 million; by 1850, 226 million; and by 1900, 400 million. In a general way, with exceptions as to eastern Europe, this tremendous growth of population occurred in areas where industrialization was taking place. It was probably caused more by a decline in the death rate than by an increase in the birth rate, and seems to have been connected with improved diet and sanitation.

Most of the population growth was centered in cities, which were heavily augmented by influx from rural areas. In Great Britain, London expanded into an urban colossus far overshadowing all other English cities. Old cities like Bristol or Glasgow grew; while new ones, which had been mere villages in the early eighteenth century, came to be great, busy, densely populated centers, as in the case of Liverpool, or Leeds or Sheffield, or Manchester, or Birmingham. Similar changes occurred on the Continent with sensational growth of such cities as Brussels, Paris, Lille, or Berlin. In addition, hundreds of towns grew into cities, and villages grew into towns.

With the rise of the cities came significant changes in the structure of classes. The familiar division of landowner and peasant, merchant and artisan, persisted. But to it was added another division of industrial capitalists (with dependent managers, foremen, engineers, lawyers, etc.) and wage-earning proletarians. By 1870 in England the most numerous type was the "factory hand," the proletarian who owned no property and made his living by a daily labor at some kind of a machine.

Under the new industrialization, the lot of the wage-laborer was hardly a happy one. While the peasant or rural artisan of the eighteenth century had most likely worked long hours and been ill-housed and ill-clad, he had been, to a considerable degree, his own master. He often owned some land, some tools, and a cottage. He had some security. He was part of a friendly community that felt some responsibility for him. The worker in the factories, forges, and mines of the 1840's had few such advantages. He labored twelve or fourteen hours a day at a machine in dismal, unsanitary, and unsafe factories. If he was a miner he worked underground and scarcely saw the light of day. He went to work at the sound of a whistle. He was fined for absence or lateness. He was clad in rags or shoddy cloth. He ate unwholesome food. He lived in a rented room in some sort of human rabbit-warren with much dirt and little or no sanitation. His work was intensely monotonous and he had few amusements. He was often unemployed because the factory owner found it cheaper to hire his wife and children. Even six-year-olds were found useful because of their nimble fingers. The bad living and working conditions of industrial laborers, with the grimy industrial cities, appeared first in Great Britain, but they were duplicated on the continent wherever industrialization occurred.

In earlier rural life, there had always been work to do. But in newer industrialized life there were usually some jobless men—the unemployed. And every few years, there recurred a business "crisis" or "depression" that produced widespread mass unemployment with intense suffering for the hapless urban proletarians. Such depressions occurred in 1818–1819, 1825–1830, 1837, 1847–1848, 1857–1858, 1866–1867, 1873–1878.

On the other hand, the new industrialism was attended by many advantages. Increased production meant increased wealth. The new inventions brought such comforts and improvements as better food, better clothes, running water, gas and electric light. With the growth of science, medical knowledge was advanced. Man could travel speedily. News could be sent almost instantaneously. Machinery was doing some of the back-breaking toil formerly done by man. But at least in the first or second generation of industrialization, these advantages accrued more to the wealthy than to the wage workers.

The way in which the economic life of Europe was developing was explained and defended by British economists of the time, variously known as "economic liberals," the "classical school," or, after the cotton manufacturers who had fought for the repeal of the English corn laws, "the Manchester school." All were deeply influenced by the laissez-faire doctrines of Adam Smith's *Wealth of Nations*,[1] though they made distinctive additions. Malthus promulgated a "law of population," that the number of persons tends to grow faster than the food supply and that over-population can be prevented only by "positive checks" of famine, war, and disease, or by "preventive checks" of continence and abstention from marriage. The poor, said Malthus, were "the authors of their own poverty"—they had too many children. Ricardo argued that "rent" is determined by population growth, forcing use of ever more sterile land for the production of food. He also enunciated an "iron law of wages," that wages tend to fall toward the level of bare subsistence. Nassau Senior demonstrated to his own satisfaction that daily hours of factory labor should not be reduced from fifteen to fourteen, because it was the fifteenth hour which gave the capitalist his needed profit. McCulloch advanced a "wage fund" theory, that there was just so much money to pay the laborers

---

[1] See above, p. 491.

of a country; if one group of workers succeeded in raising their wages, they were merely reducing the pay of some of their fellow laborers. Meanwhile Jeremy Bentham, philosopher of "utilitarianism," maintained that the application of *laissez-faire* and the ideas of economic liberalism would result in the greatest good for the greatest number of people.

As developed by such British writers, economic liberalism became by the 1830's a well-organized body of doctrine. Like political liberalism, with which it was closely associated, it stressed the individual. It made individual self-interest the motive force of economic life. Again like political liberalism, it stressed freedom—freedom of trade (no tariffs or subsidies), freedom of contract between individuals (no labor unions), freedom from government interference or regulation (*laissez-faire*), freedom of competition (no monopolies, especially none chartered by governments). The economic liberals were the heirs of eighteenth-century thought in that they believed that economic life was guided by supposedly "natural laws," such as "laws" of rent and wages and population. Man could not prevent, though he might impede, the operation of such "laws." The best thing to do was to remove all man-made restrictions and let the "laws" work automatically.

Despite a growing pessimism of classical economics from the time of Malthus and Ricardo (which earned for it the title of "the dismal science"), its doctrine of economic liberalism won many followers. Industrial capitalists found in it justification for the system under which they were growing wealthy, and many statesmen were quite convinced of its validity. Economic liberalism gained firmest foothold and most victories in Great Britain. Between 1800 and 1860, almost all the longstanding British restrictions on private industry and trade were repealed by parliamentary action. Thus disappeared the statute of apprentices, laws regulating woolens, leather, and linens, the assize of bread, navigation acts, tariffs, usury laws, monopolies of East India Company and Hudson's Bay Company, and the Elizabethan poor law. By the time he last of the English import duties (except a few retained for revenue) were removed by the Cobden treaty with France in 1860, England had adopted free trade and *laissez-faire* as thoroughly as any nation has ever done.

In France and Germany, economic liberalism won some converts. Yet it never triumphed completely and many industrialists pleaded for tariff protection against cheap British imports. France kept her high tariffs till Napoleon III reduced them to a moderate level by agreeing to the Cobden treaty in 1860. The German Zollverein tariff of 1834 was a low one—Germany did not yet have many industries to protect. Writers on the continent who espoused economic liberalism usually did so because it seemed consonant with the political liberalism they favored. On the whole, continental countries never adopted economic liberalism with the wholehearted thoroughness evinced by Britain.

E. Protests Against Economic Liberalism

Meanwhile the "dismal science" of liberal economists and the more dismal conditions created by industrialization did not go unchallenged. Among groups in England who reacted against the shocking conditions to which workers were subjected, the following may be mentioned: (1) Political radicals and extreme democrats, like William Cobbett, contended for the rights and the dignity of the common man. (2) Certain clergymen, like Denison Maurice and the novelist Charles Kingsley, thought the squalor and degradation of the working classes unchristian, and urged a "Christian Socialism" of coöperation and profit-sharing. (3) An humanitarian factory owner, like Robert Owen, first improved conditions in his own mills, then tried and failed to secure effective legislation from parliament, then turned to "Utopian Socialism" and endeavored to establish in Britain and America coöperative, agricultural-industrial colonies. (4) Some Tory aristocrats, like Michael Sadler and Lord Ashley, reacting against the growing dominance of middle-class industrialists, wrote books and pamphlets exposing current social ills, and worked for legislation to remedy them. (5) A Tory politician like Benjamin Disraeli felt that the old landed classes must win the support of the lower classes and together limit the excesses of the middle class and strengthen the country by improving social and economic conditions. (6) Miscellaneous persons opposed existing conditions from some special interest in popular education or in public health (7) Persons from among the laboring classes sought to better their lot by political agitation (as with the Chartists), by formation of mutual benefit or coöperative societies (like the coöperative grocery store founded at Rochdale in 1844), and by labor unions (which were partially legalized in England in 1824–1825).

No one of the British groups just listed would have been strong enough to make headway in Parliament, or in the country at large, against economic liberalism, but through joint action advantage could be taken of political circumstances to win some of the measures sought. Thus Great Britain witnessed, even in the period of the triumph of *laissez-faire,* some legislation that went against doctrines of economic liberalism and sought to protect workers or to improve their condition by means of government action.

As early as 1802 a "factory act" limited the hours of labor and regulated the working conditions of pauper-apprentice children who were rented out by the parish authorities to factory owners. Other factory acts in 1819, 1831, and 1833 limited night work and the hours of labor of all children and the employment of children under nine years of age. The act of 1833 was the first important one, for it provided mechanisms of inspection and enforcement. In 1842 an act forbade the employment of women and girls, and of boys under ten, in mines, while subsequent "mines acts" required certain minimum working conditions and precautions against accidents. A supplementary factory act of 1844 limited still further the hours of employment for women and children, and a maximum work-week of sixty hours was provided for them by an Act of 1847. Despite the outcries of economists, this last act, together with later additions, gradually forced a ten-hour day in British industry. Meanwhile a Public Health Act of 1848 sought to improve sanitation, and in the next five years almost two hundred local boards of health were set up. In the

1860's a series of acts was passed to prevent adulteration of food and drink.

Thus before *laissez-faire* completely triumphed in Great Britain by wiping out all the old restrictions that had come down from mercantilist days, new considerations based on the results of industrialism, and new pressures from those who opposed economic liberalism, were already leading to legislation by which the government was newly regulating business and interfering with its functioning. Very gradually the condition of urban workingmen was improved.

On the continent, criticism of industrialism and its attendant economic liberalism was more radical than in England, but for a considerable time it was less productive of protective legislation for workingmen. Of the distinctive critical movements which originated on the continent, the following may here be mentioned:

1. "Utopian Socialism" was advocated by a number of persons, including the Frenchman Charles Fourier, who pleaded for a new social organization based on coöperative communities raising their own food and making their own goods.

2. A variety of "radical" opponents of economic liberalism offered various criticisms or alternatives. A Swiss, Sismondi, insisted that the equitable distribution of goods was just as needful as their increased production. A German, Friedrich List, questioned the "laws" of the classical economists, especially their doctrine of free trade, and urged that economic regulation, including tariff protection, should be utilized to promote nationalist development. The Frenchman, Louis Blanc, who was particularly shocked by unemployment, preached the "right to work" and proposed coöperative factories to be guaranteed by the state. He was a kind of "state socialist." Another Frenchman, Proudhon, was the father of "anarchism." He wanted to abolish all compulsion by state or church, and, with it, all private ownership (though not private use) of property, and to make credit available to everyone without interest charges.

3. "Social Catholicism," led by such persons as Ozanam in France and Bishop Ketteler in Germany, combated on moral and religious grounds the individualism and

selfishness of industrialists and urged state intervention and a revival of guilds in order to safeguard the working classes. The liberalism which Gregory XVI condemned in the 1830's included economic liberalism.

4. "Marxian Socialism" or "Communism" was derived from the middle-class German writers Karl Marx and Friedrich Engels, who lived and worked in exile, chiefly in England. Their views were first set forth clearly in the *Communist Manifesto* (1848), and later elaborated in *Capital*, the first volume of which appeared in 1867. Marx and Engels believed that history was the story of the struggle between economic classes. The bourgeois capitalists, they claimed, had defeated the old feudal classes in the French Revolution, but immediately had to face a new struggle with the industrial proletariat. The proletarians were exploited by the capitalists, the fruits of their labor were taken from them, and they were ravaged by unemployment. But they were growing in number and discipline and would shortly seize power from the bourgeoisie, probably by violent social revolution.

None of the foregoing movements accomplished very much in the early period of industrialization on the Continent, but the last three laid foundations for influential popular action after 1870.

CHAPTER 46

Liberal and Nationalist Revolutions of 1848-1849

A. The February Revolution at Paris and Creation of the Second French Republic

By 1847 the groups in France which opposed King Louis Philippe were becoming stronger and more vocal. Prevented by press censorship from expressing its views in print, the opposition voiced its demand for electoral reform at a series of political banquets held at Paris and in the provinces. In alarm the government forbade a "monster banquet" at Paris scheduled for February 22, 1848. This prohibition precipitated another Paris revolution—the "February Revolution" of 1848.

On February 22 angry workers, reckless students, and earnest liberals crowded the streets shouting for reform. The next day as the tumult continued, Guizot, the prime minister, ordered the National Guard to restore order. But soon the guardsmen were joining the crowds in the popular cry, "Down with Guizot." Guizot resigned. The rioting might then have subsided, had not some soldiers guarding Guizot's residence fired into a crowd of boisterous demonstrators, killing twenty-three and wounding thirty others. For a moment the crowd was stunned. Then in a rage it bore off the corpses for all Paris to behold.

Dawn of February 24 found the streets of Paris ominously barricaded by workmen and placarded with such signs as, "Louis Philippe massacres us as did Charles X; let him go join Charles X." Prudent as always, Louis Philippe tarried only long enough to

abdicate in favor of his ten-year-old grandson, the Count of Paris, and then, as "Mr. Smith," he drove off in a closed carriage to follow Charles X to England.

The Count of Paris was ignored, and a "provisional government" installed itself at the city hall in Paris. It was an odd mixture, for it included the Catholic liberal poet Lamartine, the Jacobin republican Ledru-Rollin, the socialist Louis Blanc, and a workingman, Albert. So unpopular had Louis Philippe become that even extremists, legitimists on the right and anarchists like Proudhon on the left, rallied temporarily to the new government. Since two monarchies had failed in thirty-three years, a republic seemed the only practicable solution. So the provisional government proclaimed France a republic—the second republic in French history. But what kind of a republic would it be?

At the outset the Second French Republic was impelled by the Paris proletariat in a radical and socialist direction. It is to be noted that this revolution was the first in Europe to have a definitely socialist tinge, though, oddly enough, because Louis Philippe had alienated Catholics, it was almost the only European revolution of the period which was not marked by a good deal of anti-clericalism.

The provisional government ordered the election of a National Assembly by universal manhood suffrage. The National Guard, hitherto reserved to the middle classes, was opened to all citizens. "National workshops," in response to demands of Louis

Guizot. By Honoré Daumier 1879).

Blanc and his followers, were promised to guarantee work for everyone. A commission was set up to develop a program of social reform. From February to May there was the utmost enthusiasm among socialists, radicals, and workmen in Paris and in some of the other towns and cities. Liberty trees were planted. Red flags of revolution were flown. Proudhon and his followers openly attacked the system of private property.

But all was not well with the revolution. Blanc had urged workshops which would be coöperative and productive factories. Instead, the "national workshops" of 1848 were really work projects such as digging trenches, improving parks, and the like. They had little utility, and were only an excuse for paying the unemployed a dole of two francs a day. Moreover, the elections for the National Assembly in May showed that the rest of France was much less revolutionary than Paris. The peasants and property owners of the provinces elected men who were on the whole republican, but conservative as to social and economic matters. They looked with much fear on "red" Paris. They were prepared to defend private property. They had no desire to spend public funds in doles for the workers of Paris. One of the first things that the Assembly

did when it met at Paris in June 1848 was to abolish the so-called "national workshops."

The withdrawal of the wages of two francs a day meant starvation for many of the Parisian workmen, who were well aware of the conservative intentions of the National Assembly. Once again, rebellion flared up and barricades were built in the streets. The Assembly, in alarm, entrusted dictatorial powers to General Cavaignac, who called out regular troops and bourgeois national guardsmen to put down the rioting. In a futile effort to prevent bloodshed, the archbishop of Paris lost his life. For three days, the terrible "June days" (June 24–26, 1848), there was fierce and stubborn fighting in the streets of Paris. In the end, the forces of "order" triumphed. Some of the rebels were shot, and 4,000 were transported to penal colonies overseas. Louis Blanc fled to England. Proudhon was jailed. The socialist side of the February Revolution was liquidated.

With the "red menace" of socialism thus eliminated, the National Assembly proceeded during the summer and autumn of 1848 to lay the foundations of the Second French Republic in line with the ideas of moderate, bourgeois liberals. Much emphasis was put on "the family, rights of property, and public order." At the same time, concessions were made to the workers by establishing a "commission of thirty" to study social reforms; to Catholics, by promising more religious teaching in the schools; to humanitarian liberals, by abolishing slavery in the colonies, freeing the press from censorship, and doing away with capital punishment; to Jacobin democrats, by adopting a democratic republican constitution.

This constitution of 1848 provided for a president with a term of four years, and for a one-house legislature, both to be elected by universal manhood suffrage. The president would choose his own cabinet (as in the United States), but he might not veto an act of the legislature and he would not be eligible for reëlection. The National Assembly arranged for elections to take place in December 1848.

B. Revolutionary Wave Throughout Central Europe

There had been signs in the years just before 1848 that central Europe was restive under the bonds of Metternich's conservative system. When news of the February Revolution in Paris spread quickly over Europe along the railways and telegraph lines that had recently been built, the latent restiveness became widespread revolt.

Revolt occurred throughout the Austrian domains. On March 3, 1848, Louis Kossuth, an Hungarian patriot and advanced liberal, called upon Metternich to grant to Hungary a free parliament and self-government. Eight days later a group of Czech liberals in Prague made like demands in respect of Bohemia. On March 13 a turbulent mob of students and workers clashed with police in the streets of Vienna.

Metternich called out the civic guard. But it refused to disperse the crowds that gathered around the imperial palace; while a deputation urged the Emperor Ferdinand I to dismiss Metternich at once. Assured that his hour had at last arrived, the white-haired old minister presented his resignation. His residence was already sacked and burning. On March 14, 1848, he hurriedly departed from Vienna for London. Metternich, the veteran foe of revolution, was fleeing for his life before a revolution.

By the time Metternich reached safety in London a little more than a month later, the revolutionary storm was racking, not only the chief cities of the Habsburg Empire, but all central Europe as well. At Vienna, promptly after the flight of Metternich, Ferdinand I named a liberal ministry, freed the press, authorized a national guard, and promised a constitution. In April he promulgated a constitution. But the Viennese liberals, now in control of the capital city and backed by the new national guard, were unwilling to accept a constitution which was granted by the Emperor and might later be revoked by him. They forced him to convene a Constituent Assembly, so that the new constitutional government would be based on the people's, not the monarch's, will. Ferdinand, practically powerless, retired to Innsbruck, and in July 1848 the Assembly met in Vienna. It had been elected nominally by universal manhood suffrage, but in fact largely by bourgeois voters. It represented all the Habsburg Empire save only Hungary and Lombardy-Venetia, where other plans were afoot.

In Hungary, in March and April of 1848, the liberals organized their own revolution. It was arranged that the Hungarian Diet would meet annually and include representatives of middle-class taxpayers as well as the hitherto dominant landowners. It would make laws for Hungary, and to it an Hungarian ministry, separate from the Austrian, would be responsible. Ferdinand, yielding to pressure and panic, was persuaded to appoint the first such Hungarian ministry, and it included leading Hungarian liberals like Kossuth and Francis Deák. Revolutionary legislation was rapidly enacted. The press was freed; a national guard was organized; serfdom, feudal privileges, and the exemption of nobles from taxation were abolished. Though no step was taken to depose the Emperor Ferdinand as King of Hungary, the liberal government at Budapest adopted a national flag and otherwise acted as a free national state. Backed by the liberals at Vienna, the Hungarians felt it safe to ignore the hostility of the King at Innsbruck.

In Prague, too, liberals—both Czech and German—seized the opportunity offered

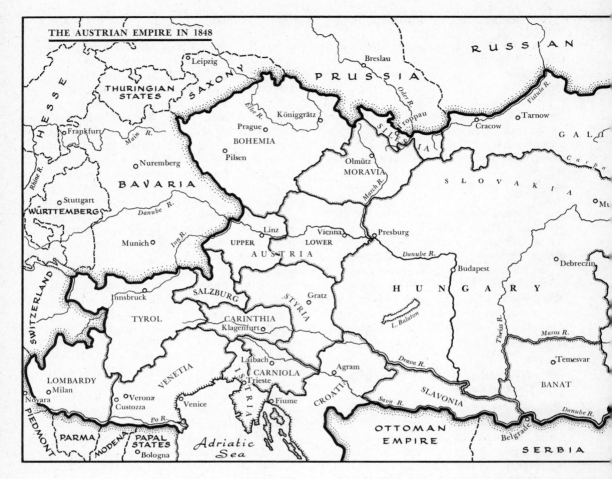

them to set up a separate ministry for Bohemia, to transform the local Diet into a national parliament, and to create a national guard. In April, the Emperor felt compelled to agree in general terms to this autonomous, liberal regime for Bohemia. But the German liberals at Vienna and the Hungarian liberals at Budapest were not eager to see the Czechs or other Slavs obtain real self-government. The Czech liberals and nationalists accordingly convoked at Prague, in June 1848, a Pan-Slavic Congress consisting of Czech, Slovak, Polish, Yugoslav, and Russian delegates to devise measures which might assure liberty and autonomy to the Slavic peoples, especially those within the Habsburg Empire.

In Italy, a revolt had broken out within the kingdom of the Two Sicilies even before the February Revolution at Paris, and in January 1848 King Ferdinand II was forced to accept a liberal constitution. Influenced by events in France, the King of Sardinia-Piedmont, Charles Albert, promulgated a liberal constitution, called the *Statuto*, on March 4, 1848. Then with the collapse of Metternich's power at Vienna and the ensuing confusion, the tide of liberal and national revolution rolled all over Italy.

At Milan, the populace, after five days of street fighting (March 18–22), expelled General Radetzky and his Austrian garrison, and cheered for the transfer of Lombardy from Austria to Sardinia. At Venice, under the leadership of Daniel Manin, a patriotic liberal, the townspeople drove out the Austrian officials and proclaimed the restoration of the Venetian republic. But if the Austrians had been expelled from some of the larger cities, they still had in Lombardy a large army, which might be used to reestablish Austrian rule. To get rid of this threat and drive the Austrians from Italy, Charles Albert of Sardinia declared war on Austria,

MPIRE

erg

Dniester R.

Pruth R.

Czernowitz

BUKOVINA

MOLDAVIA

NSYLVANIA

Hermannstadt

ALLACHIA

But when crowds flocked to the palace square to applaud him, they were received with musket-shots from his royal guard. Again the barricades went up and street-fighting broke out, in which two hundred citizens lost their lives. On March 19 the King showed a change of heart. He called off his troops, appointed a liberal ministry, and convoked a Constituent Assembly. The Assembly was elected by universal manhood suffrage and met in Berlin in May 1848. It was overwhelmingly liberal.

In the smaller German states, simultaneous revolutionary movements met with similar success. In Bavaria, the liberals compelled King Louis I to abdicate in favor of his son, Maximilian II, who swore to uphold and liberalize the constitution which had been granted thirty years earlier. In Baden, Württemberg, Hesse, Hanover, Saxony, Nassau, Brunswick, and the petty Thuringian States, the rulers were frightened into appointing liberal ministries, promising constitutional government, and granting freedom of the press. In Bremen, Hamburg, and Lübeck riots led to a liberalizing of the governments of these "free cities," which had long been ruled by wealthy oligarchies.

On the borders of Germany, both Denmark and Holland were affected by the liberal upheaval. The Danish King Frederick VII promised liberal rioters (March 21, 1848) to summon a constitutional convention. It met in October, and drafted a constitution which was put into effect in June 1849. The Dutch King William II put himself at the head of the liberal movement and sanctioned in October 1848 a constitution, which transformed the old States-General into a national parliament.

Even England did not wholly escape the effects of the general commotion of 1848. The Chartists, reawakened by liberal successes on the continent, prepared a petition for a democratic reform of parliament and planned to present it with a tremendous demonstration. The ministry and upper classes were alarmed. The aged Duke of Wellington was called upon to defend the government with regular troops and 170,000 special middle-class constables. But rain dampened the ardor of the Chartists and the demonstration fizzled out.

March 23, 1848. To his army of 60,000 men, were soon added detachments from the Two Sicilies, the Papal State, Tuscany, and Lombardy. Charles Albert captured the fortified town of Peschiera from Radetzky at the end of May. It looked as if Italy was well on the way to securing both liberal government and national independence.

Meanwhile, Metternich's fall was the signal for rejoicing and for liberal (and national) revolution throughout Germany. The most sensational upheaval was in Prussia. King Frederick William IV of Prussia was a romantic and somewhat dramatic prince, who, though arbitrary and paternalistic by nature, had indulged in some mildly liberal gestures. He was much surprised when his "beloved" Berliners took to rioting and erecting barricades (March 15–17, 1848). To quiet the excitement he promised to convene a Prussian Parliament and to work for a national union of Germany.

The revolts which swept the continent of Europe were not only liberal, but nationalist. In Italy, many patriots rallied behind Charles Albert to win national freedom and unity under the banner of the house of Savoy. In Germany, popular demands grew urgent that something be done to unify the separate states into a single nation. In response, the new liberal governments of the several states instructed their delegates in the Diet of the loose German Confederation at Frankfurt to authorize the democratic election of a National Assembly to devise a new federal government for the whole of Germany. Elections were duly held in Austria, Prussia, and other German states, and, since many conservatives refrained from voting, the liberals won a large majority. In May 1848, the representatives came together at Frankfurt, and the body is known in history as the Frankfurt Assembly.

The Diet of the German Confederation ceased to function. The new Frankfurt Assembly proceeded to proclaim a German National Empire and to select a temporary administrative head for it in the person of a liberal Habsburg prince, the Archduke John of Austria. It then set to work to draw up a constitution. From the start, most of the members assumed that the new Germany, like the old Confederation and the older Holy Roman Empire, would include Austria—not the whole Austrian Empire, but the German part of Austria centering in Vienna—that it would be a federation something like the United States, and that the central government would be monarchical but parliamentary and liberal. The task of writing such a constitution was both difficult and delicate, and there was much difference of opinion as to whether the emperor of Austria or the king of Prussia should be the new German emperor.

On the new constitution and the negotiations connected with it, the Frankfurt Assembly labored for a year. Meanwhile, in December 1848, it reached agreement on a document called the "Fundamental Rights of the German Nation." This statement was similar, in a general way, to the French "Declaration of the Rights of Man and of the Citizen" of 1789, though it was more detailed, more frankly nationalist, and at the same time less dogmatically democratic. It was in fact the classic expression of the middle-class, liberal nationalism of the mid-nineteenth century. It summed up the hopes and dreams of 1848. With it as a guide, the new nation which the Assembly was striving to create would have been both constitutional and liberal.

C. Nationalist Conflicts and Conservative Reaction

During the first half of 1848, liberalism made startling advances all over Europe. Then it began to suffer setbacks which wiped out most of the liberal gains. The explanation, both of the rapid liberal victories and of the subsequent defeats, lies in the very nature of the revolutions of 1848. They were primarily urban, middle-class affairs. The cities spoke first and loudly in favor of a new liberal regime. Then in due course the countryside of conservative landowners and peasants spoke less noisily but with greater weight.

The rural areas were rooted deep in traditional ways and usages. The great majority of the inhabitants of Germany, the Austrian Empire, and Italy belonged to agricultural classes. They distrusted townsfolks. They respected the clergy. They had a lingering regard for their landlords. Most of the clergy and landowners were hostile to revolutionary change, and in the course of time they rallied to the support of the bureaucrats and army officers, who, though pushed aside in the first stages of the upheaval, were likewise opposed to revolution. Moreover, even the cities were divided by cleavages between bourgeois and workers, and between radicals and moderates. As the revolutions made rapid progress, many middle-class moderates drew back in alarm. Then, too, while the liberals could appeal to national sentiment, so could the conservatives. Before long the masses of people, rural and urban, were being urged to prop up their tottering governments for the sake of national strength and prestige.

The first serious setback to the liberal revolutionary movement in central Europe occurred in Bohemia. Here in June 1848 the Austrian governor and army commander, Prince Windischgrätz, enraged by

ITALIAN STATES IN 1848-1849

a renewal of rioting in Prague in which his wife had been killed, acted decisively to "restore order." His troops, backed by German elements in the province who had become alarmed by the increasing power of the Slavic Czechs, subdued Prague, dispersed the Pan-Slavic Congress, and overthrew the revolutionary liberal government. Liberal reforms were revoked, and Bohemia placed under martial law.

The next important setback was in Italy. Here the army of Charles Albert of Sardinia was weakened by the withdrawal of contingents from central and southern Italy. Both Pope Pius IX and King Ferdinand II of the Two Sicilies were frightened by "excesses" of the revolutionaries and continuance of domestic "disorder," and Ferdinand wanted all his troops to restore absolutism in his kingdom. In July 1848 a reënforced Austrian army under Radetzky decisively defeated the Italian army of Charles Albert at Custozza. Charles Albert agreed to an armistice and Radetzky reoccupied Milan and all Lombardy.

This serious reverse to the cause of Italian liberty and unity aroused Italian extremists to frantic endeavors. At Rome, the liberal papal minister, Rossi, was assassinated in November 1848. Pope Pius IX, disillusioned with liberalism and in fear of his life, fled from the city. In February 1849 a republic was proclaimed at Rome, and Mazzini assumed the leadership. Radical republicans likewise seized control of Florence and Naples and temporarily transformed them into republics. Charles Albert, driven on by the threat of a similar republican outbreak in his kingdom of Sardinia, renewed the war with Austria. But in March 1849, at Novara, he suffered a second and quite overwhelming defeat at the hands of Radetzky. Forced to conclude a humiliating peace with Austria, Charles Albert abdicated in favor of his son, Victor Emmanual II, but did not revoke the Piedmontese constitution (*Statuto*). The victorious Austrian army could now be utilized to suppress the revolutionary republics.

In May 1849 the King of the Two Sicilies and the Grand Duke of Tuscany were restored to their thrones by force of arms. Venice, blockaded by land and sea, surrendered to the Austrians. As for Rome, French troops, sent under circumstances which we shall presently note, overthrew Mazzini's republic at the end of June and reinstated Pope Pius IX in his temporal domains. By the summer of 1849 all Italy was once again under traditional control. Republicanism was stamped out, and, except under Victor Emmanuel in Sardinia, liberalism was suppressed.

The Austrian restoration in Italy was rendered easier by the triumph of conservative reaction in Austria itself. The successes of Windischgrätz and Radetzky in June and July 1848 had heartened the Emperor Ferdinand at Innsbruck and his conservative supporters, for it was clear that loyal troops could be used successfully to repress revolution. Events in Hungary likewise played into the conservatives' hands. The revolutionary government under Kossuth at Budapest was characterized not only by liberalism, but also by an intense Hungarian nationalism. It outraged Austrians by its separatist tendencies, and it aroused violent opposition of the Croats, Serbs, Slovaks, and Rumanians under Hungarian rule, for it showed no

Joseph Mazzini. From a photograph.

Courtesy Bettmann Archive

Louis Kossuth. From a daguerreotype.

Courtesy Bettmann Archive

tendency to make any concessions to their national sentiments and demands. These anti-Hungarian nationalists found an able champion in Joseph Jellačić, a Croatian soldier and patriot, who pointed out to the Emperor that the Croats and other Slavs would make common cause with Austria against the Hungarian pretensions. In September 1848, Jellačić was made governor of Croatia and authorized to attack Hungary with a Slavic Austrian army which would be aided by German Austrian troops from Vienna.

The liberals of Vienna sought to prevent the despatch of troops against the Hungarian liberals. A mob hanged the minister of war to a lamp post and seized the imperial armory. But on Vienna were already converging the army of Windischgrätz from Bohemia and that of Jellačić from Croatia. To assist the Viennese "rebels," marched a Hungarian army. But it was defeated and turned back by Jellačić. On the last day of October 1848, Windischgrätz beat down the resistance at Vienna and occupied the city by force. A score or so of radical leaders were executed and the liberal government was supplanted by a reactionary ministry headed by Prince Felix Schwarzenberg, brother-in-law of Windischgrätz and disciple of Metternich.

Schwarzenberg's first important act, once "order was restored," was to persuade Emperor Ferdinand to abdicate in favor of his eighteen-year-old nephew, Francis Joseph, and then to have the new Emperor annul the liberal concessions which the old one had made. He allowed the Austrian constitutional convention to continue its debates a while longer. But he ignored the document it prepared, and proclaimed a conservative constitution by his own authority. Eventually he withdrew even this concession to liberalism.

Schwarzenberg likewise began a vigorous offensive against the Hungarians, and sent Windischgrätz and his army to support Jellačić who was already invading Hungary. Kossuth replied by proclaiming Hungary an independent republic (April 1849) and by stirring the people to patriotic armed resistance. For a time the invading armies were held at bay. But Schwarzenberg asked and obtained the assistance of an additional army from the Russian Tsar Nicholas I, who was eager to suppress all revolution in central Europe lest a new revolt should occur in Poland. By August 1849 the three invading armies had overcome resistance in Hungary. Kossuth fled into exile. The liberal constitution was abolished. Once again Hungary was ruled as an Austrian province.

The success of the conservative forces in Italy and throughout the Habsburg Empire had a profound influence in restoring confidence to the conservatives in Germany. By the late summer of 1848, King Frederick William IV of Prussia yielded to two pressures to defy the liberals. One was pressure from Great Britain, France, and Russia to end the war on Denmark which at the request of the Frankfurt Assembly he had been waging to free the "German" duchies of Schleswig and Holstein from Danish rule. The other was pressure from conservative classes at home—landowners, Protestant clergy, army officers, civil servants—to check the liberal Prussian Constituent Assembly, which was voting to abolish the nobility, to make the King a mere figurehead, and to send a Prussian army to help the liberals in Vienna. In the autumn of 1848 Frederick William IV felt strong enough to act. He ousted the liberal ministry and installed a conservative one under the reactionary Count Brandenburg. He withdrew his troops from Denmark and used them to overawe the Constituent Assembly and the people of Berlin. When these acts caused no serious tumult, the King dissolved the Constituent Assembly and drafted a constitution which left real power in his hands and those of the ministers he chose. It did provide for a legislature which would be consulted on some matters, but by a peculiar "three-class system" two thirds of that body represented those who paid two thirds of the taxes—the upper class and the wealthiest part of the middle class.

The triumph of reaction in Prussia and Austria left the liberal majority of the Frankfurt Assembly in a most awkward position. In a desperate attempt to save the situation, the Assembly offered the crown of the projected new German Empire to the Prussian King, hoping that his romantic attachment to nationalism and his desire for personal glory would outweigh his growing aversion to liberalism. Frederick William IV hesitated. But he received ominous warnings from the Austrian Prime Minister Schwarzenberg and from the Russian Tsar Nicholas. In April 1849 the Prussian King denounced the constitution that had been drawn up by the Frankfurt Assembly and refused, as he said, "to pick up a crown out of the gutter."

In a despairing protest against the now obvious failure of the Frankfurt Assembly, liberal extremists tried in May 1849 to install republics in the Rhineland, Silesia, Saxony, and Baden, but these were quickly suppressed by Prussian troops. Many of the liberal leaders who escaped jail or execution fled into exile. Not a few found refuge in the United States.

Though now a foe of all liberalism, Frederick William IV was still haunted by the dream of uniting Germany under Prussian leadership. Accordingly, he proposed a plan for a close union of all the German states, except Austria, with himself as president. Some of the states accepted and sent delegates to a meeting of the parliament of the new "German Union" at Erfurt in 1850. But Austria, with conservatism triumphant at home, was in a position to reassert her old leadership in Germany. Schwarzenberg would not permit the union of Germany under Prussia and a Hohenzollern emperor.

For a time in 1850, it looked as if war would break out between Austria and Prussia. Schwarzenberg had the support of the south German states and of others like Saxony, which feared Prussia. It seemed likely, too, that Russia would support Austria. In the face of such powerful opposition, the Prussian King backed down. In November 1850 Frederick William IV signed the treaty of Olmütz with Austria. By its terms, the "German Union" under the presidency of Prussia was dissolved, and the previous "German Confederation" under the presidency of Austria was restored. There was no provision for a popular parliament. Instead, the Diet of delegates of the princes was reconstituted, and, acting under instructions from the now conservative governments of Austria and Prussia, it formally repealed the "Fundamental Rights of the German Nation" and set up a special commission to purge any state constitution of "revolutionary novelties."

D. Transformation of the Second French Republic into Another Napoleonic Empire, and General Restoration of "Law and Order," 1850–1852

The revolutionary upheaval of 1848 was over by 1850, and the regime of Metternich to a large degree reëstablished. Even in France, the revolutionary gains of 1848 did not endure. The elections held in December of 1848 for the presidency of the new Republic produced a curious result. General Cavaignac got one and a half million votes; Ledru-Rollin received 370,000. But five and a half million ballots were cast for Louis Napoleon Bonaparte, nephew of the Emperor Napoleon. Louis Napoleon, after a youth spent in exile and some adventures as a member of the Carbonari in Italy, had set himself seriously to the work of being the heir of the Napoleonic tradition. He had dabbled in military matters. He had written a book on poverty and social reform. He had steadily cultivated the Napoleonic legend, compounded of fact and fiction, of liberalism and dictatorship. Twice—at Strasbourg in 1836, and at Boulogne in 1840—he had tried to organize armed risings against the government of Louis Philippe.

Both attempts had been ludicrous fiascos. After the second, Louis Napoleon had been imprisoned for six years, and had escaped to England in the disguise of a stone-mason.

In 1848 came his opportunity. He had not been in France during the June days, and so had not alienated the workers by siding against them. Yet he was known to be a friend of law and order. If the Emperor Napoleon had stood for anything, it had been firm rule. Perhaps his nephew would bring peace at home and respect abroad. What especially helped Louis Napoleon was fear of the "red menace," the "ugly threat of socialism," on the part of the middle-class, the landowners, and most Catholics. Some of the radical republicans laughed at Louis Napoleon's candidacy for the presidency. His amazing success at the polls turned their amusement to dismay.

Once installed as President, Louis Napoleon set himself to increase his popularity and simultaneously to control police and army. To strengthen Catholic support, he sent to Rome the French military expedition which in June 1849 ousted Mazzini's republic and reinstated Pope Pius IX. Similarly he approved the Falloux Law of 1850, which removed the restrictions imposed by Guizot under Louis Philippe on Catholic schools. At the same time, to ensure support of urban workers, Louis Napoleon sponsored legislation which limited the hours of work (to twelve a day), restricted child labor, and improved the distribution of poor relief. To satisfy the bourgeoisie, he showed himself a friend of property, order, and business interests.

So conservative, on the whole, was Louis Napoleon's attitude that he might have lost the sympathy of workers and of liberals, had he not adroitly utilized a dispute with the national legislature, in which conservatives had a majority. In 1850 the legislature passed a law restricting the suffrage to taxpayers who had lived for three years in the same district, thus disenfranchising a third of the voters—mostly urban workers. The President gave willing ear to protests against this law and promptly declared that he could not permit the legislature to deprive millions of Frenchmen of the right to vote. In November 1851 he demanded that the legislature reëstablish universal suffrage.

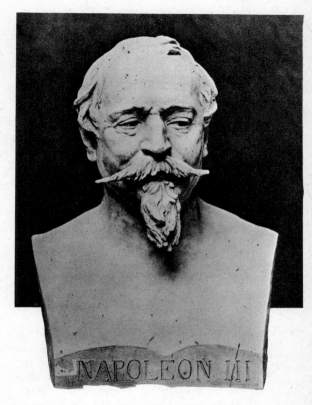

Napoleon III. By Jean Baptiste Carpeaux (d. 1875).

When it refused to do so, he executed, on December 2, a *coup d'état.*

This seizure of power was skillfully managed. Police and troops overawed all opposition. A manifesto proclaimed a temporary dictatorship, the dissolution of the Assembly, and the restoration of universal suffrage. Censorship prevented counter agitation. The most notorious critics of the President, such as Adolphe Thiers and Victor Hugo, were hustled out of the country. On December 21 the French people in a plebiscite voted, by 7,500,000 to 640,000, to empower President Louis Napoleon to prepare a new constitution for the Second Republic. He had won conservatives by standing firm for internal order, and liberals and radicals, by sponsoring universal suffrage.

The new constitution, modeled closely on Napoleonic precedent, gave the President a term of ten years and put so much power in his hands and in those of the Council of State appointed by him that he became virtually a dictator. The next year, Louis Napoleon devoted to propaganda. He appealed to national pride. He spoke honeyed words to peasants, to artisans, to capitalists, to rich and poor, to reactionaries and radicals, to believers and agnostics. He organized demonstrations at which he was greeted with cries of "Vive l'empereur." His reward was speedy and complete. On December 2, 1852, he became, through a new national plebiscite, Napoleon III, Emperor of the French.

The Second Republic was thus changed to the Second Empire, a dictatorship only partially concealed by the national plebiscites and the continued existence of a national legislature which had no real power. The February Revolution had, in a little over four years, resulted in a regime even less democratic than that of the monarchy which it had replaced.

Yet the revolutionary upheaval of 1848 left some liberal gains in Europe. In the Austrian Empire, the conservatives did not reëstablish serfdom, which had been abolished by the liberal governments. Henceforth the peasants were free to buy and sell land and to move from place to place. From the revolutions, moreover, there survived some form of constitutional government, if not in the Austrian Empire, at least in Sardinia-Piedmont, Switzerland, Holland, Denmark, and Prussia.

The enduring gains of liberalism were but scanty. By its manifold failures in 1848 and 1849, liberalism was discredited and driven underground again in France as well as in Central Europe. Yet behind the scenes it was by no means dead; if the liberals of the 1860's were less vocal than those of 1848, they became slowly more influential.

One of the factors that thwarted a liberal triumph in 1848 was clearly nationalism. Though liberals and nationalists had joined hands to start and carry on many of the revolutions, occasions had quickly arisen where national interests ran counter to liberal aims. "Liberal" Prussia had in 1848 fought "Liberal" Denmark in the name of German nationalism. "Liberal" Hungary, identified with Magyar nationalism, had aroused the nationalist opposition of liberal Croatians and other Slavs. German liberals in Bohemia, alarmed by the rapid rise of Czech nationalism, had thrown in their lot with the conservatives of German Austria. Worst of all, the struggle of Austria with Prussia for leadership in the unification of Germany had confused all the issues and resulted in thwarting liberalism, as well as nationalism.

Had the Frankfurt Assembly succeeded in its liberal national work, the subsequent history of Germany, and of Europe too, might have been very different. Had Germany been united under liberal auspices, then the whole weight of nationalism and patriotism would have been behind the new liberal state, and Germany might have remained liberal as well as nationalist.

After 1848, liberalism and nationalism displayed some tendency to split apart and take separate roads. Nationalists showed themselves ready to sacrifice liberalism to attain national ends; and during ensuing decades some of them tended to invoke "blood and iron," rather than "liberty, equality, and fraternity."

CHAPTER 47

Liberal Nationalist
Regime of Napoleon III

AND CREATION OF NATIONAL STATES OF ITALY
AND RUMANIA

A. Napoleon III's Domestic
Policies

We have already seen how the "Napoleonic legend," the fear of the "red menace," the blunders of the republican legislature, and his own crafty maneuvers combined to enable Prince Louis Napoleon Bonaparte to overthrow the Second French Republic and to make himself in 1852 the Emperor Napoleon III. His regime was essentially a dictatorship. He organized an effective secret police; he controlled the press; he manipulated elections by the use of "official candidates"; he dominated the legislature and the whole government down to the provincial prefects and mayors; and he jailed or exiled his most outspoken critics. He made much of the army and of old Napoleonic soldiers.

Napoleon III tried to make his dictatorship acceptable to both radicals and conservatives. On the one hand, he preserved at least the illusion of universal manhood suffrage and called the Second Empire "the final flower of the French Revolution." On the other hand, he resolutely defended "order"; and his marriage in 1853 with the beautiful Eugénie, a Spanish countess, gave him an Empress whose charm helped to make the French court once more the center of European styles and fashions.

The Emperor was favorably impressed by the contemporary vogue of economic liberalism. In politics, he was hardly a liberal, but in economics he was even more liberal

than Louis Philippe or Guizot. Legislation designed to aid business was the order of the day. Railway lines were multiplied and consolidated. The formation of stock companies was made easier. The Bourse, or stock exchange, became ever more active as the capital market boomed (and occasionally crashed). Government regulation of business was reduced. A system of savings banks was established. Even the tradition of high tariffs was broken, when Napoleon III cut the French import duties to a maximum of 30 per cent (after five years, to 25 per cent) in the Cobden treaty with Great Britain (1860). Despite plaintive outcries of some manufacturers, the Emperor proceeded in the 1860's to conclude low-tariff treaties with the German Zollverein, and with Belgium, Italy, Switzerland, Austria, Sweden, Spain, and Portugal. His initiative seemed to be ushering in an era of freer trade for all Europe.

Napoleon III also sponsored a remarkable series of public works to stimulate industry and commerce and to provide employment for labor. Harbors were improved, swamps drained, roads repaired, and the network of railways completed. In Paris, vast sums of money were spent on constructing broad boulevards and magnificent public buildings under the supervision of the Emperor's devoted friend, Baron Haussmann. The French capital thus became the most beautiful and attractive city in the world, a mecca for tourists and pleasure seekers. The imposing new opera house,

The Paris Opera House.
Courtesy Bettmann Archive

with its ornate architecture and glaring gas lights, was a symbol of the Second Empire.

Napoleon III, unlike Louis Philippe, did not forget the workers. He chatted familiarly with them and drank toasts to them. He subsidized their organizations. It was for the working class, he affirmed, that his government of cheap bread, public works, and national holidays existed. With all this talk, there was some actual labor legislation, just enough to encourage the proletariat and not enough to alienate the bourgeois liberals. One law permitted workers to form coöperative societies for buying and selling. Another partially legalized trade unions and recognized for the first time (though under severe limitations) the right to strike. A third extended workmen's voluntary insurance, with state guaranties, against death and industrial accidents.

Napoleon III took special care to reassure the peasants who still constituted a majority of the French population. He repeatedly affirmed his devotion to the principle of private property and his interest in the vineyards and wheatfields of the peasants. He encouraged railway construction, he said, the better to get their goods to market. He lowered tariffs, the better to sell their products in England. The Emperor likewise took pains to favor the Catholic Church. He strengthened the hold of the clergy on the universities and public schools in France, maintained French troops at Rome for the protection of the pope, and in general posed as the champion of Catholic Christianity.

For the first time since the advent of Napoleon I, it seemed as though France had a government that could secure internal peace and order, rise superior to factional quarrels, and reconcile divergent political, economic, and social interests. To most Frenchmen and most Europeans, the rule of Napoleon III seemed eminently successful, and France was widely regarded as the strongest country on the continent of Europe. But to some degree these appearances were deceptive. The Second Empire bears a superficial resemblance both to the Empire of the first Napoleon and to regimes of twentieth-century dictators. In techniques and methods, it forms a sort of link between them. It was characterized by a suppression of political liberty through censorship, secret police, and a sham constitution. It paid homage to democracy by plebiscites but thwarted all real democracy in both local and national governments. To make up for the loss of liberty, it emphasized material well-being and sought by propaganda, often inconsistent and in many cases not backed by action, to keep the support of all groups and classes however divergent their interests. Yet there was much more liberalism in the regime of Napoleon III than in the later dictatorships of Communists and Fascists. There was comparatively little dictation in economic matters, and less interference with personal liberties. Moreover, through the whole period of the Second Empire there were strong currents of opposition to it at home as well as abroad.

Doubtless Napoleon III was sincerely pacific at heart, and he aspired to be the champion of nationalities. He lacked the martial zeal of the born soldier, and he had an un-Napoleonic aversion to the sight of battlefields and the smell of gunpowder. Yet circumstances and his own ambition and heritage involved him in a series of wars. And it was war which eventually engulfed him and ended the Second French Empire.

B. The Crimean War, National Emergence of Rumania, and Napoleon III's Colonial Ventures

From the beginning of his rule, Napoleon III made friendship with Great Britain a keystone to his diplomacy. At the same time, his relations with the Tsar Nicholas I of Russia were distinctly unfriendly. The Tsar had been reluctant to recognize the Second Empire; his tariffs irked French business men; his religious intolerance irritated French Catholics; his stern measures with the Poles outraged French liberals. But it was a quarrel between Roman Catholic and Eastern Orthodox monks in Palestine which ignited the latent hostility between Russia and France. The Tsar had long been interested in carving up the Ottoman Empire, whose Sultan he described as the "sick man of the East." When Russia denounced the Sultan's inability to keep peace in the Holy Land and demanded that Russia be allowed to "protect" the Christians in the Ottoman Empire. Napoleon III encouraged the Sultan to resist.

The dispute presented a seemingly golden opportunity to the French Emperor. A war with autocratic, intolerant Russia—the power which had defeated Napoleon I, created the Holy Alliance, and crushed the Poles—would be popular at home and in western Europe with both liberals and Catholics. Moreover, he could count on British support, for if English liberals were pacific, they were also anti-Russian. It was becoming a major point of British policy to bolster up the decaying Ottoman rule so as to prevent aggressive Russia from becoming too strong in the eastern Mediterranean and threatening the British route to India. Consequently, Great Britain backed French insistence on the preservation of the integrity of the Ottoman Empire. For reasons of its own, which we shall note later, Sardinia espoused the Franco-British cause, while Austria, torn between gratitude for Russian help in 1849 and fear of Russian advance in the Balkans, preserved a troubled neutrality. Prussia was friendly to Russia but inactive.

War began between the Ottoman and Russian Empires in 1853. France and Great Britain joined the Turkish side in 1854, and Sardinia in 1855. It was easy to declare war but a little difficult to find a place to fight. At length the French and British sent a joint expedition into the Black Sea and attacked the Crimea. Since military operations were confined mainly to this peninsula, the conflict is known as the Crimean War. It is notable as the first significant struggle between major European powers after 1815. It was marked by gross military inefficiency on both sides. Sickness caused more deaths in the armies than bullets. At length, the Allies captured Sevastopol, and in 1856 Russia sued for peace. The Crimean War cost half a million lives and two billion dollars.

Napoleon III had the satisfaction of holding the peace conference at Paris. In the settlement arrived at, Russia agreed to respect the integrity of the Ottoman Empire, to renounce any claim to protect its Christian inhabitants, to restore to it a small slice of territory in Bessarabia, and not to keep any warships in the Black Sea. An international commission was created to supervise the free navigation of the Danube. Thus the Ottoman Empire was preserved, and Russia was checked. Napoleon III was cheered by returning veterans. In the midst of the popular applause, a son—the Prince Imperial—was born to the Emperor and Empress. Fortune smiled upon the Emperor of the French and lured a pacifist on to further wars.

Emperor Maximilian of Mexico. From a photograph.

Courtesy Bettmann Archive

One by-product of the Crimean War won Napoleon III considerable prestige with liberals and nationalists, even if it eventually weakened the Ottoman Empire, for which the war had supposedly been fought. This was the formation and unification of Rumania. The Rumanians were a people speaking a Latin language and inhabiting the Ottoman principalities of Moldavia and Wallachia and the Russian province of Bessarabia. Affected by the doctrines of nationalism, the Rumanians were eager to establish a free and united Rumania. At the peace conference, Napoleon III insisted on adding part of Bessarabia to Moldavia and securing for the Rumanian principalities a large measure of autonomy within the Ottoman Empire. In 1858 he secured from the Sultan and the great powers a general recognition of the right of each of the Rumanian principalities to elect its own parliament and choose its own prince, though it was expressly provided that Moldavia and

Wallachia should not be united. The Rumanian leaders neatly got around this provision by having the two principalities choose one and the same prince, Alexander Cuza. In 1861–1862, Napoleon III again showed his benevolent interest in the Rumanians by persuading the powers to recognize not only the one prince, but also the fusion of the two parliaments into a united Rumanian parliament. The Second French Empire thus helped to create the modern national state of Rumania.

Meanwhile, Napoleon III was showing his interest in colonial affairs. He completed the pacification of Algeria in 1857, and the next year established a permanent civil government there under Marshal MacMahon. He dispatched naval expeditions to occupy various islands in the Pacific, notably New Caledonia (1853). He joined with the British in a military demonstration against China, which extorted from the Chinese government the treaties of Tientsin (1860), opening several ports to European trade and promising security to Christian missionaries in the interior. South of China, the Emperor laid the foundations of a large French colonial domain, for in 1858 he sent an expedition into Annam and Cochin-China to avenge the murder of some French missionaries, and five years later he established a French protectorate over Cambodia.

One colonial undertaking, in the long run, failed miserably, though at the start it appeared a brilliant project. It was a plan to take over the republic of Mexico, which was torn by internal strife. The time seemed opportune, for the United States was too involved in its Civil War (1861–1865) to interfere. In 1861, Benito Juarez, an Indian in blood and a radical in policy, had won his way to power in Mexico. He inaugurated a series of anti-clerical "reforms," such as suppression of religious communities, confiscation of church lands, and institution of civil marriage. In addition, Juarez repudiated the foreign loans contracted by the preceding conservative regime.

Napoleon III joined with Great Britain and Spain to seize the Mexican customs houses by force, so as to compel Juarez to recognize the debts Mexico owed abroad. Within four months, a compromise satisfactory to Spain and Great Britain was reached and these powers withdrew their forces. But the French troops stayed on, since Napoleon III had more elaborate plans afoot. He did not intend to make Mexico an outright French colony, for a step so drastic might well have aroused violent opposition from other countries, but rather to install a puppet regime subservient to France. By so doing, he was confident that he would please French Catholics, who felt that their church would thereby be relieved of persecution in Mexico and also French business men, who would find continuing opportunities for lucrative investment in Mexican mines, railways, and agriculture. Accordingly, in the autumn of 1862, the French Emperor sent to Mexico a force of 30,000 French veterans. Though they required constant reënforcements, the French army captured Mexico City in June 1863 and drove Juarez into the mountain fastnesses of the north. Casting around for a ruler for Mexico, Napoleon III hit upon the Archduke Maxmilian, brother of the Austrian Emperor Francis Joseph.

But the "great idea of his reign," as Napoleon III termed it, proved disastrous. From the outset, Maximilian, who became "Emperor of Mexico" in 1864, was in a precarious position. His regime was unpopular even among Mexicans who disliked Juarez. The French troops, hampered by rough country and lack of communications, encountered difficult guerilla warfare. Most important of all, the end of the American Civil War (1865) enabled the United States to reassert the principle of the Monroe Doctrine and to back up its protests with very real threats. Whereupon, Napoleon III faced about and gradually recalled his expeditionary forces. The last of them left Mexico in February 1867. Maximilian, who was gallant or foolhardy enough to remain behind, was soon captured and shot, and Juarez was reinstated as president.

The Mexican venture of the French was not only disastrous in itself. It was a veritable boomerang against Napoleon III. The restoration of Juaraz brought in Mexico a renewal of anti-Catholic legislation and repudiation of the franchises recently acquired by French financiers. In France, there was dismay at the blood and money that had been uselessly expended, while ardent Cath-

olics and bourgeois liberals alike grew increasingly critical of the Emperor.

C. Unification and National Independence of Italy

The failures of Charles Albert of Sardinia and of revolutionary liberals like Mazzini in 1848–1849,[1] did not destroy the movement for the unification of the Italian peninsula into a single nation. In fact, the ensuing period witnessed such an intensification of nationalist agitation that it has been called the *risorgimento* (resurrection).

There had been serious disagreement among Italian patriots about methods of achieving national unity. Mazzini from exile continued to urge the formation of a liberal democratic republic. One of his most vigorous followers was Joseph Garibaldi, a native of Nice, who had fought in South America, against Austria in north Italy in 1848, and against the pope in central Italy in 1849. For a time Garibaldi was a refugee in New York, but in 1854 he returned to Italy to await a new opportunity to strike for national freedom.

Another method had been advocated by a Piedmontese priest named Gioberti, who sought to reconcile nationalism and liberalism with traditional religion, and proposed a federation of existing Italian states under the presidency of the pope. This had appealed to many persons among the clergy and upper classes, but any popular support for it was lost after 1849 by the ultra-conservatism of Pope Pius IX.

A third group of nationalists had urged the creation for all Italy of a liberal, constitutional monarchy under the king of Piedmont-Sardinia, and after 1849 this group gained strength at the expense of the others. Republicanism waned as a natural reaction to its excesses and failures in 1848–1849. Federalism practically collapsed in the face of Pius IX's hostility. On the other hand, despite the failure of King Charles Albert of Sardinia to make headway against Austria and his abdication in 1849, his successor, Victor Emmanuel II, attracted an ever increasing number of supporters by reason of his retention of liberal constitu-

---

[1] See above, p. 606.

Cavour.

Alinari Photograph

tional government and of his personal reputation for bluff honesty.

In Count Camillo di Cavour, King Victor Emmanuel had a first-rate assistant. From his youth an admirer of French culture and British political and economic liberalism, Cavour was first known as an improving landlord, as a promoter of factories and railway building, and as editor of *Il Risorgimento*, a famous journal which urged liberal and constitutional reform in Piedmont-Sardinia to prepare it for leadership in all Italy. With the establishment of constitutional government in the kingdom, Cavour came rapidly to the fore in politics. He entered the cabinet in 1850, and in 1852 became prime minister and minister of foreign affairs. At these posts, he remained, with one brief interruption, till his death nine years later.

As premier, Cavour strove to promote the material welfare of the country in current British fashion. Tariffs were lowered, industry and transportation improved, and public finances reformed. At the same time, he sought to reduce the influence of the church by restricting its privileges, expelling the Jesuits, and suppressing some of the monas-

tic establishments. His ideal, he said, was "a free church in a free state."

Despite formidable obstacles that stood in his way, but aided greatly by the National Society which had largely superseded Mazzini's Young Italy, Cavour worked steadily for the cause of Italian unity. Since he was convinced that Italy could be united only by the defeat of Austria, for which defeat foreign aid would be necessary, he turned his attention to the diplomatic field. In 1855 he took Sardinia into the Crimean War as an ally of France and Great Britain, hoping that Austria would join the Russian side. Austria disappointed him by remaining neutral, but at least Cavour won a hearing for Italian problems at the peace table, where he explained at length and in angry tones the injustice of Austrian rule in Italy.

Aided by the popularity of Piedmont-Sardinia among liberals in France, Cavour then set to work to gain the help of Napoleon III against Austria. Though the French Emperor had been an Italian Carbonaro in his youth, though he had Italian blood in his veins, though his cousin ("Napoleon II") had as a baby been entitled "King of Rome," he hesitated until a fanatical Italian nationalist, named Orsini, threw a bomb at him in January 1858. Napoleon III quickly made up his mind to risk offending the pope and French Catholics by aiding Italian liberals and nationalists.

A secret meeting between Cavour and the Emperor took place at Plombières in July 1858. Napoleon III agreed to assist Sardinia in driving Austria out of Lombardy and Venetia and to sanction the creation of a single north Italian state. Cavour agreed to arrange it so that Austria would seem the aggressor in the war, and then to cede to France the Alpine duchy of Savoy and the Mediterranean port of Nice. Forthwith, Cavour set about irritating Austria by ostentatious military preparations and a haughty diplomatic tone.

In April 1859 Austria sent Sardinia an ultimatum demanding immediate demobilization. Cavour rejected the ultimatum, and war began with Austria on one side and Sardinia and France on the other. It lasted from April to July and constituted the first major step on the road to Italian liberation and union. Hailed with enthusiasm by the Italians, Napoleon III and Marshal Mac-Mahon led a French army into Piedmont, where they united with a Sardinian army under Victor Emmanuel II and General La Marmora. In June the Austrians, defeated at Magenta and Solferino, abandoned Milan and fell back upon the strong fortresses of Venetia.

Napoleon III had promised to "free Italy from the Alps to the Adriatic." But the defeats of the Austrians had inflamed Italian nationalism, and patriots in central Italy were demanding that Modena, Parma, Tuscany, and the Papal State be incorporated into a union under Victor Emmanuel II, as well as Lombardy and Venetia.

French Catholics were alarmed at this threat to the Pope's temporal power, and one French bishop, from the pulpit, branded Napoleon III as "the modern Judas Iscariot." The French Emperor, himself, was much upset by the carnage he had witnessed in the battles already fought, and by indications that Prussia might join Austria against him. Moreover, he apparently envisaged some sort of federal, rather than a united, Italy. For these reasons, he decided to call a halt to the war, and, in July 1859, he concluded with the Emperor Francis Joseph at Villafranca an armistice, whereby it was agreed that Lombardy should be ceded to Sardinia, Austria should retain Venetia, the rulers of central Italy would be reinstated in their duchies, and the

UNIFICATION OF ITALY, 1859-1870

Pope would become president of an Italian federation.

Thus Napoleon III fulfilled only half his bargain with Cavour. It was the turn of Italian patriots and French liberals to denounce the French Emperor. Cavour in disgust resigned his offices. But Victor Emmanuel had no alternative. He acceded to the terms of the truce, which was ratified in November by the treaty of Zurich.

Napoleon III and Francis Joseph, however, had not reckoned with the resolution of Italian patriots, nor with the skill with which Cavour, who returned to office, conspired with the liberal and radical leaders of central Italy. The inhabitants of the duchies and of part of the Papal State drove out their rulers and governors, established revolutionary governments, held plebiscites, and voted to join the kingdom of Sardinia. Cavour, in the name of his King, sent commissioners to take charge of these regions.

At first, Napoleon III refused emphatically to recognize such an exercise of the "right of national self-determination." But Cavour drove a shrewd bargain. With deep regret, he offered the French Emperor Nice and Savoy (just as if Napoleon III had carried out the original agreement to free Venetia as well as Lombardy), if France would recognize the annexation to Sardinia of Tuscany, Parma, Modena, and the papal province of Romagna. In the treaty of Turin (March 1860), Napoleon III accepted this deal. Still another plebiscite was held in Savoy and Nice, and they were "restored to France," to which they had belonged briefly in the time of the French Revolution and Napoleon I. Thus Napoleon III made a tangible territorial gain for France. But the costs were rather high. French liberals and French Catholics now distrusted him more than ever. Italian patriots, who, like Garibaldi, a native of Nice, thought Napoleon had reaped a shameful reward for a half-completed bargain, denounced him. Even Victor Emmanuel II was deeply pained at parting with Savoy, the ancestral home of his family. And affairs in Italy had gotten almost completely out of French control.

Close on the heels of the unifying movement in northern Italy came a similar development in the south, led this time by Garibaldi rather than Cavour. In the Two Sicilies, Francis II had succeeded Ferdinand II in 1859, but had made no change in the tyrannical system of government. Garibaldi, with the connivance of Cavour, assembled at Genoa a volunteer army of about a thousand "redshirts." In May 1860 they sailed to Sicily where they were welcomed by enthusiastic revolutionaries. In a remarkable campaign, in which his forces grew steadily, while those of Francis II were weakened by desertion, Garibaldi made himself master of the island. Then he crossed over to the mainland and in September took possession of Naples. Francis II retired to the fortress of Gaeta.

Garibaldi's swift victories and romantic personality made him such a popular idol that he could easily have become republican dictator of all south Italy. To avoid such an eventuality, Cavour despatched a Sardinian army southward. When the army crossed into papal territory, all the European powers, except Great Britain and Sweden, withdrew their diplomatic representatives from Turin. But Cavour announced the annexation of the entire Papal State except the city of Rome and its immediately surrounding territory. The Sardinian forces went on into southern Italy and, on November 7, Garibaldi and Victor Emmanuel II rode side by side through the streets of Naples. Despite his radical advisers, nationalism was now stronger with Garibaldi than republicanism. He resigned his authority into the hands of Victor Emmanuel II, and, refusing all titles and honors, retired to his home.

Though Napoleon III made the gesture of sending a fleet to Gaeta, he could not stem the tide. The British persuaded the French Emperor to withdraw his ships, the blockade of the fortress was completed, and fell at last in February 1861. Already a plebiscite had ratified the annexation of the Two Sicilies to Sardinia; a parliament representing all Italy, save Rome and Venetia, had met in Turin; and Victor Emmanuel II had been proclaimed King of the new Italian nation.

For three months Napoleon III did not

Garibaldi. From an engraving.

Courtesy Bettmann Archive

recognize the new kingdom of Italy, and he continued to maintain a French garrison at Rome to defend the Pope. The French Emperor, once the hero of liberals and nationalists, had now been forced into a conservative position by preventing the Italians from making Rome their capital.

Cavour did not live to see the final triumph of his policies, for he died in June 1861. The completion of Italian unity fell to other hands. Venetia was won in 1866, when Italy joined Prussia in a war on Austria. Through an agreement with the Italian government, Napoleon III withdrew the French troops from Rome in 1866, but he sent a military force back the next year to defeat an armed incursion led by Garibaldi. This second French garrison was withdrawn only in 1870 when Napoleon III

was himself engaged in a desperate war. Over the protests of Pope Pius IX and a show of armed resistance ordered by him, Italian troops took Rome in September 1870, and in 1871 it became the capital of the united kingdom of Italy.

Thus Napoleon III, the chief instrument in the early stages of the unification of Italy, appeared to be its chief obstacle in its later phases. His venture into Italian politics gained him relatively little. Not only had he helped to create on the borders of France a single centralized state where formerly there had been several weak ones, but he had alienated Catholic opinion by his action in 1859, and liberal opinion by his wavering but conservative policies thereafter. He did have the territorial gains of Nice and Savoy.

D. Decline and Fall of the Second French Empire

Mexico and Italy were not the only explanations of the decline of Napoleon III's popularity at home and his prestige abroad. In the 1860's he was aging rapidly, and disaffection was growing within France. Conservatives were talking about the desirability of bringing back either a "legitimate" Bourbon king (grandson of Charles X) or a "liberal" Orleanist king (grandson of Louis Philippe). Many Liberals, including professional men and journalists, were leaning toward republicanism and lending support to the party which hitherto had comprised only doctrinaire radicals and ill-organized workingmen. In other words, the national combination which had backed the Emperor was falling to pieces, and there were reëmerging the factions of royalists and republicans which had existed before his advent.

The rising tide of opposition and its danger to the Second Empire were disclosed by the parliamentary elections of 1869. Despite governmental manipulation, fifty royalists and forty republicans were returned, and the opposition vote rose everywhere (but especially in the cities) to unheard-of proportions. Being an opportunist, Napoleon III responded by deciding to "liberalize" his government, and he at once made a number of concessions. He eased the press censorship. He promised to abandon the practice of paying election expenses of "official" candidates for the legislature. He agreed that his ministers should be responsible to the legislature rather than to himself. And he appointed a prime minister, Émile Ollivier, who formerly, as a liberal royalist, had bitterly criticized the imperial regime, but who now seconded the plan of Napoleon III to establish a "Liberal Empire."

Through the collaboration of Ollivier and the Emperor, a new "liberal" constitution for the Second Empire was drawn up. It embodied the concessions already made and assigned much of the power formerly exercised by Napoleon and his Council of State to the legislature. Such reforms might conciliate the liberal royalists, but they satisfied neither the legitimist royalists nor the republicans. The latter, in fact, redoubled their subversive agitation, openly attacking the Emperor in newspapers, speeches, and demonstrations.

The new constitution was submitted to a plebiscite in May 1870. Though the opposition vote declined from the high point of the previous year, it still reached ominous proportions. Seven million votes were cast in favor of the constitution, one and a half million against it. Nearly two million qualified voters stayed away from the polls.

Whether the "Liberal Empire" would have been a success, no one can tell, for other events intervened. But those very events were affected by internal conditions in France. There was one point on which Frenchmen were approaching agreement— opposition to the political unification of Germany under Prussian auspices. French liberals detested Prussia as a reactionary state. French Catholics disliked Prussia for its intolerant Protestantism. French patriots feared the rise of a powerful nation across the Rhine, for since Richelieu's day a weak Germany had been considered an advantage and safeguard for France. French imperialists (including the Empress) thought a successful patriotic war would ensure the popularity and continuance of the Empire.

Napoleon III had no stomach for war with Prussia. He was broken in health, and troubled by recollections of his previous wars. He knew, moreover, that France had no friend in Europe on whom she could count for sure support in a crisis. Yet he was aware, too, that if the gamble of a war with Prussia succeeded, it might bring glory to the Empire and assure the succession of his son, the Prince Imperial.

The Prussian prime minister at the time was the astute Bismarck, who believed that the unification of Germany could be completed only by a successful war with France, and he found a pretext for it in a complication arising in Spain. Spanish liberals had organized a revolution in 1868 and ousted the arbitrary and dissolute Queen Isabella II. They were seeking a new sovereign who would be liberal and constitutional. After receiving refusals from several European princes, the Spanish liberals offered the crown to Prince Leopold of Hohenzollern-Sigmaringen, a Catholic cousin of William I, the King of Prussia. Prince Leopold, not too eager for Spanish adventures, declined the offer. But Bismarck, scenting the possibilities of the situation, procured a renewal of the invitation and its acceptance by the prince (July 2, 1870).

Pressed by his wife, his ministers, and popular sentiment, Napoleon III took a strong stand and professed to see in the acceptance a projected union of Germany and Spain reminiscent of the empire of Charles V and menacing to France. He sent strong protests to the Prussian and Spanish governments, and on July 12 it was announced that Prince Leopold had withdrawn his acceptance. If the French Emperor had let well enough alone, he would have emerged the victor in a minor diplomatic skirmish. But he was urged by his advisers to push the matter further and to administer to Prussia a stinging diplomatic defeat. The French ambassador to Prussia was instructed to obtain from William I an official public promise that he would never permit a Hohenzollern to become a candidate for the Spanish throne.

The ensuing interview between the Prussian King and the French ambassador at the summer resort of Ems was indecisive. When the persistent ambassador requested another interview, the King merely stated that he was leaving Ems and could not receive him. The news of this rebuff was sent to Bismarck in a telegram by one of the King's aides. Bismarck, who was consulting the Prussian military chiefs at the time, was at first in despair, for the matter seemed ended. Then he saw a possible plan to bring on war. He secured the assurances of the military leaders that all was in readiness for the conflict. Then he gave the telegram to the press, not in its original form, but so edited by omissions as to seem very abrupt, an insult to the French ambassador. The amended telegram was nicely calculated to have the effect, in Bismarck's own cynical words, "of a red rag on the Gallic bull."

The report of the Ems despatch, published in Paris on July 14, the French national holiday, threw France into an angry frenzy. That night Napoleon acceded to popular clamor and to the counsel of his ministry, and decided on war. The next day the French legislature, with only a few dissenting votes, authorized a formal declaration of war against Prussia. The third—and last—of the European wars of the Second Empire was beginning.

The Empire entered the Franco-Prussian war (1870–1871) with much enthusiasm, but with little else. Austria and Italy, like Russia and Great Britain, remained aloof. French mobilization went badly. The attempt to use the railways led to traffic jams. Supplies were piled up in one place, while troops were shifted to another. Early in August 1870 Marshal MacMahon suffered such a reverse at the hands of the invading Germans that he was obliged to withdraw his army from the greater part of Alsace and fall back on Châlons. On August 18 another French army under Marshal Bazaine was defeated by the Germans under Moltke in a bloody battle at Gravelotte in Lorraine, and shut up in the fortress of Metz. In this crisis MacMahon advised Napoleon III to pull back the French armies to Paris and reorganize them there for a decisive battle. But when the Emperor wired the plan to the Empress Eugénie, whom he had left as regent at the capital, she replied that a general retreat would mean the overthrow of the Empire and

that he should go forward to relieve Metz.

Napoleon and MacMahon, with heavy hearts, moved their inferior forces down the Meuse river seeking to find a place where they might cross and drive back the Germans. At Sedan, almost down to the Belgian border, they made a despairing attempt, September 1–2, 1870. Outnumbered, outgeneraled, and finally encircled, the Emperor at length stopped the slaughter by surrendering with 81,000 men. The battle of Sedan ended the first phase of the Franco-Prussian war, which had so far lasted barely six weeks.

The battle of Sedan also ended the Second Empire. On September 4, when it became generally known in Paris that the main French army had been captured and that the Emperor himself was a prisoner, a self-appointed group of republicans, among whom Léon Gambetta was conspicuous, proclaimed at the city hall the deposition of the Emperor and the establishment of a republic—the Third French Republic. The Empress Eugénie hastily fled, with the aid of an American dentist, to England. A government of national defense was constituted to rule France until peace could be restored and the nation consulted on the making of a permanent constitution for the country.

The adventure of the Second Empire was over. Its promises of peace and stability had been belied. Whatever it had done for the internal development of France had been compromised by its wars and the disaster of 1870. The experiment of peaceably turning a dictatorship into a constitutional, liberal empire was a failure.

Napoleon III himself was released by the Germans at the close of the war. He went to die in England (1873), and his ill fortune pursued his son, for the Prince Imperial ("Napoleon IV") was killed fighting for the British against the Zulus in South Africa in 1879. The Empress Eugénie lived till 1920, long enough to see republican France revenge her husband by conquering imperial Germany. But for the Bonapartes, there was no renewal of the extraordinary circumstances which had enabled the nephew of Napoleon I to dominate France from 1848 to 1870.

William I, flanked by Moltke and Bismarck. Reinhold Begas (d. 1911).

CHAPTER 48

Creation of the Hohenzollern German Empire

AND THE HABSBURG DUAL MONARCHY OF AUSTRIA-HUNGARY

A. German Nationalism and the Prussian Bismarck

In Germany, as in Italy, the events of 1848–1849 [1] did not mean the end of agitation for national unification. As with Italy, the big obstacle to a unified German state was Austria, though here the Austrian role was somewhat different. In Italy, Austria was a foreign power occupying part of the peninsula and dominating much of the rest. In Germany, Austria proper was German in language and for centuries had been part of the Holy Roman Empire, and latterly of the German Confederation. Now Austria faced a dilemma. She wanted to retain her traditional leadership in Germany. Yet she could not bring into a German nation her millions of non-German subjects (Hungarian, Czech, Slovak, Polish, Croatian). German national sentiment which had been aroused against Napoleon in the triumphant War of Liberation, never died down, and during the ensuing age of romanticism it continued to inspire patriotic songs and societies. Scholars joined poets in glorifying the German nationality, its language and customs, its history and mission.

Important to at least the middle class were developments which indicated that national unity would be profitable as well as romantically desirable. In 1818, Prussia had substituted for her previous multiplicity of provincial tariffs a single one. This was low on manufactured goods and lower still

[1] See above, pp. 607–608.

on raw materials, but it taxed goods passing in transit through Prussian territory and hence provided Prussia's neighbors with a special inducement to join her economically. Between 1819 and 1826, a number of minor German states which had territories enclaved (completely surrounded) by Prussia accepted her tariffs and formed a customs union (*Zollverein*) with her. Then between 1829 and 1833, a number of the central states adhered to the union, and in the latter year even the southern states of Bavaria and Württemberg entered it.

Thus was inaugurated an enlarged *Zollverein* in which most of Germany was included, with a single set of customs duties on its exterior frontiers. In the next twenty years all the remaining states were incorporated save only Austria and Hamburg. Though not originally designed as such, the *Zollverein* proved to be a powerful instrument in uniting Germany and in increasing the influence of Prussia. The same end was also served by the construction of railways, which by 1860 bound all the German states closely together.

There were, however, forces other than Austrian influence which worked against German unity. One was fear and dislike of Prussia on the part of many Germans. Another was religious difference and conflict between Catholics and Protestants. A third was "particularism," the loyalty of the citizens of each of the separate states to it and to its ruler, their pride in local history, their preference for their own dialects and customs. Particularism was especially strong in the Catholic states of the south, of which Bavaria was the chief. Such was the general situation in Germany in the 1850's and 1860's. Liberal revolution in 1848 had failed to bring unity. It remained for the strong-arm tactics of a cynical conservative to succeed where liberals had failed. This was Bismarck.

Otto von Bismarck belonged to the class of land-owning north-German squires (or Junkers) who had long served the Prussian monarch in army, Lutheran church, and civil administration. Though deeply attached to Prussia and its king, Bismarck had led an unruly life as a young man and had even been dismissed from the civil service for "deficiency in regularity and discipline." His marriage in 1847 to the pious daughter of another landlord had steadied him and confirmed his devotion to the Lutheran state church and to ultra-conservative principles. During the upheavals of 1848–1849, he vigorously opposed the liberals. He offered to bring his peasants to Berlin to

defend King Frederick William IV and was one of two in the Prussian legislature who refused to vote thanks to the King when he promised to grant a constitution.

Bismarck scoffed at the Frankfort Assembly; and, while reluctantly accepting the Prussian constitution of 1850, he aided in forming a Conservative party to resist liberalism and to defend the royal power, the agricultural interests, the army, and the Lutheran Church. From 1851 to 1862, he was active and eminently successful in the Prussian diplomatic service. As Prussian delegate in the German Diet at Frankfurt, and as Prussian ambassador to St. Petersburg and Paris, he gained a deep knowledge of German and of European affairs.

Bismarck's great opportunity came as the result of a conflict between the Prussian King William I (Prince-Regent 1858–1861, King, 1861–1888) and the Prussian legislature. William I was far from brilliant, but he was hard-working and pertinacious; and above all he was a soldier with an absorbing

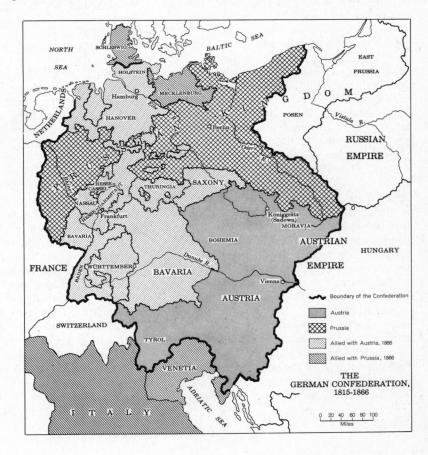

THE GERMAN CONFEDERATION, 1815-1866

Bismarck. Franz von Lenbach (d. 1904).

Courtesy Bettmann Archive

Roon's advice, summoned Bismarck to be his chief minister. Bismarck's policy was summed up, a bit ominously, in his famous sentence, "Not by speeches and majority resolutions are the great questions of the time decided—that was the mistake of 1848 and 1849—but by blood and iron." Unable to get favorable action from the Progressive majority, he proceeded, with the King's consent, to govern Prussia without a legal budget and without a parliament. As a virtual dictator and in flat violation of the constitution, he levied and collected taxes and put through the whole program of military reform. The Progressives grumbled, and liberals in other German states heaped abuse on Bismarck. But Bismarck was confident that the liberals at home and abroad were more vocal than dangerous. He worked on the dubious principle that the end justifies the means. He would overcome his opponents by his very success. In the new army he had a powerful instrument for effecting German national unification under conservative Prussian leadership.

B. The Danish War of 1864, and the German Civil War of 1866 Between Prussia and Austria

As a first step in his plan, Bismarck precipitated a war between Denmark on the one hand and Austria and Prussia on the other. The excuse for the war lay in the complicated question of the duchies of Schleswig and Holstein. These duchies, which contained a large German population, had already occasioned a brief war in 1848. That conflict had been settled when the Great Powers forced through a compromise highly favorable to Denmark, for the Danish king remained sovereign of the duchies while promising not to incorporate them into the rest of his kingdom. In 1863, King Frederick VII of Denmark died, and his successor, Christian IX, under the pressure of nationalist demands from his Danish subjects, broke the compromise agreement by accepting a new constitution which unified the political institutions of Denmark and the two duchies.

The response in Germany was a wave of patriotic agitation against Denmark. In it, Prussia and Austria competed for

passion for all matters military. As soon as he came to power, William I set about reforming and expanding the Prussian army with the aid of a gifted chief of staff, General Helmuth von Moltke, and a very able minister of war, Albrecht von Roon. To finance the army reforms, the King asked the legislature in 1861 for more money. This the legislature, under the influence of liberals, refused. Whereupon the King dissolved the legislature. The ensuing elections returned 100 conservatives, 25 moderate liberals, and 235 progressives—the last a new political party consciously modeled after the British Liberal party, and resolved to force liberal principles and real parliamentary government on the King. Thus an impasse was reached. William I, Moltke, and Roon were determined to push through the army reforms. The party with an overwhelming majority in the legislature was determined to prevent them from doing so.

To break the deadlock, William I, on

leadership, and in 1864, they both went to war with Denmark. The Danes fought heroically. But this time they got no foreign help, and, overborne by sheer numbers, they had to submit to the terms of the treaty of Vienna, imposed on them in October 1864. The treaty gave Schleswig and Holstein to Austria and Prussia. As Bismarck anticipated, the two victors were soon at odds over the division of the spoils, for while Austria, backed by the German Confederation, wanted to make a separate state out of the duchies, Prussia refused to do so. The dispute was only temporarily patched up by the Convention of Gastein in 1865, according to which Holstein would be administered by Austria, and Schleswig by Prussia.

Bismarck was determined to bring about a war between Prussia and Austria. But before doing so he wanted to make sure that Prussia would get foreign help and Austria would not. He was fairly certain that Great Britain and Russia would remain neutral. France was more doubtful.

In October 1865, at Biarritz, Bismarck made vague hints of "compensations" to Napoleon III, so as to forestall French interference in the early stages of the war. Bismarck counted on such a quick victory by the reformed Prussian army that there would be no later stages and thus no opportunity for France to intervene successfully. From Italy, Bismarck obtained more than mere neutrality. He secured an alliance against Austria. So sure was Bismarck of his ability to start the war when he wished, that the alliance ran for only three months beginning in April 1866. If within that time war broke out between Prussia and Austria, Italy promised to join the former. As a reward she would get Venetia from Austria.

Bismarck proceeded to stir up trouble for the Austrians in Holstein. When Austria responded by appealing to the German Confederation, Bismarck declared that such an appeal violated the Convention of Gastein, and he sent Prussian troops to occupy Holstein and oust the Austrians.

PRUSSIA IN THE NORTH GERMAN CONFEDERATION, 1867-1871

At the same time he proposed a reform of the German Confederation and the exclusion of Austria from it. Austria called on the Confederation to reject the reform and to mobilize against Prussia. Most of the states sided with Austria, because of the particularist fears of Prussian dominance. Liberals opposed conservative Prussia, and Catholics sympathized with Catholic Austria.

Bismarck then announced that Prussia was seceding from the Confederation, and would fight a "defensive" war against Austria and her German allies. Italy, of course, was soon found on the Prussian side. Despite the ruthless cynicism with which Bismarck precipitated the war, he managed so skillfully and concealed his moves so well that public opinion in most foreign countries favored Prussia.

The actual war, between Prussia and Italy on the one hand and Austria, Bavaria, Hanover, Saxony, Baden, Württemberg, and some lesser German states on the other, was of such surprisingly short duration (June 15 to July 26, 1866) that it is usually called the "Seven Weeks' War." Austria, though less well prepared for war than Prussia, defeated the Italians on land and sea. But in the main campaign in Bohemia, the Austrians were overwhelmed in the battle of Sadowa (or Königgrätz) on July 3, 1866. This battle was so decisive that it led to the end of the war, to drastic rearrangements in Italy, Austria, and Germany, and to a tremendous increase in the military reputation of Prussia.

By the final treaty of Prague (August 1866), Austria was obliged to cede Venetia to Italy and Holstein to Prussia, to pay a small indemnity, and to consent to the dissolution of the German Confederation. The German states north of the Main were to enter a "closer union" with Prussia. Those south of the Main were to form a union of their own. From both groups Austria was to be excluded. But Bismarck did not wish to make a mortal enemy out of Austria. He had gained his end by getting her shut out of German affairs despite her thousand years of participation in them. His territorial demands were therefore moderate, and he vetoed the idea of a triumphal Prussian parade through Vienna.

Bismarck made separate treaties with the south German states of Bavaria, Baden, Württemberg, and Hesse-Darmstadt, by which they lost virtually nothing, for he wanted to win their friendship.

The north German states which had sided with Austria came off much worse. Prussia annexed outright, not only Schleswig-Holstein, but also Hesse-Cassel, Nassau, the free city of Frankfurt, and the kingdom of Hanover (since 1837 separated from the crown of England and under its own ruler). These additions of five million subjects and 27,000 square miles of territory made Prussia for the first time a compact and continuous state stretching from Russia and Denmark to France and the Main River. Henceforth, with Austria excluded, two-fifths of the area and two-thirds of the population of Germany belonged to Prussia.

The lesser German states north of the Main which were not annexed by Prussia—twenty in number—were formed by Bismarck, in 1867, into a new and closely knit North German Confederation. Each state retained a measure of local autonomy but all were subordinated to a federal government with the King of Prussia as hereditary "President" and with a two-house legislature, Prussia clearly dominated the new organization.

C. The Franco-Prussian War of 1870–1871, and Creation of the German Empire

Amid the enthusiasm occasioned by victory over Austria, Bismarck made his peace with the Prussian legislature. Dazzled by the success of his policies, the Progressive party abandoned its opposition and voted a bill of indemnity which gave Bismarck legal forgiveness for his unconstitutional behavior in the past. Indeed, many Progressives now discovered that they were more nationalist than liberal. When the federal parliament of the North German Confederation was formed, a new party became very active in it and collaborated closely with Bismarck. It was called the National Liberal Party. Many of its members were former Progressives.

In the states south of the Main, there was still much distrust and dislike of Bis-

Parisians patronizing a butcher shop selling cat and dog flesh during the siege, 1870–1871. From a contemporary drawing.

Courtesy Bettmann Archive

marck and of Prussia among liberals, Catholics, and particularists. A step toward closer cöoperation between the northern confederation and the southern states was taken in 1867, when a joint customs parliament was created to discuss common tariff problems. But it limited itself strictly to such matters, for the southern states were jealously guarding their political independence. To Bismarck, it seemed clear that only a big patriotic enterprise such as a victorious war against a common foreign foe could bring Bavaria, Württemberg, Hesse-Darmstadt, and Baden into union with Prussia. As preparation for just such a war, certain bungling attempts of Napoleon III to obtain "compensation" in 1867 so alarmed the south German states that Bismarck was enabled to conclude secret defensive alliances with them.

We have already mentioned Bismarck's role in precipitating the Franco-Prussian War in 1870 over the question of the Hohenzollern candidacy for the Spanish throne.[1] When France declared war, the south German states honored their treaties of alliance and joined with Prussia against France. Their troops shared with the Prussians in the victories which ensued.

After the surrender of Napoleon III at Sedan, the German armies moved rapidly on to Paris, which was soon encircled and

[1] See above, pp. 620–621.

besieged. Peace might have been quickly negotiated had not Bismarck let it be known that Germany must be "safeguarded" in the future by "recovering" Alsace-Lorraine from France. The French government, unwilling to blight the new republic at the start by such a cession of territory, fought on under the inspiring leadership of Léon Gambetta. Escaping from Paris in a balloon, Gambetta raised fresh troops, who, to the surprise of the Germans, won some successes, although they were unable to relieve Paris. Strasbourg had already surrendered in September, and Metz was yielded up in October through the cowardice (if not treachery) of Marshal Bazaine.

Paris held out until January 27, 1871, and then surrendered only because its people were freezing and starving. Four days afterwards, an armistice was arranged, in order to permit the election of a French National Assembly which would have authority to conclude peace. The preliminary peace terms, agreed to at Versailles by Bismarck and Adolphe Thiers, head of the French provisional government, were reluctantly ratified by the new Assembly in March. The final peace treaty was signed at Frankfurt in May 1871.

By the treaty of Frankfurt, France ceded to Germany all of eastern Lorraine, including the fortress of Metz, and all of Alsace except Belfort, a fortress which had heroically withstood a German siege. To retain Belfort and its environs for France, Thiers had to permit a triumphal parade of the German conquerors through Paris. In addition, France agreed to pay a war indemnity of five billion francs. German troops remained in occupation of northern France till this sum was paid in full (1873). In the course of the war the Germans had lost 28,000 dead and 101,000 other casualties. The French losses were 156,000 dead, 143,000 wounded or disabled, and 720,000 surrendered or interned.

Of the numerous and far reaching results of the Franco-Prussian War, the most striking was the fulfillment of Bismarck's plan for the establishment of a German Empire under Prussian and Hohenzollern leadership. Just as Bismarck had foreseen, the triumphantly successful war in which South Germans fought shoulder to shoulder with Prussians aroused throughout the country a wave of popular patriotic ardor strong enough to overcome particularist sentiments, princely jealousies, liberal suspicions, and Catholic misgivings. By November 1870, while the war was still in progress,

Bismarck negotiated treaties of union between the North German Confederation and the southern states of Bavaria, Württemberg, Baden, and Hesse-Darmstadt. These treaties, duly ratified by the respective sovereigns and parliaments, simply extended the North German Confederation so as to include the southern states, and changed its name to the "German Empire" (*Deutsches Reich*). The King of Prussia, instead of being "President of the Confederation," was henceforth to be "German Emperor."

By a curious coincidence the solemn ceremony of inaugurating the German Empire was held on January 18, 1871, exactly 170 years after the Prussian Hohenzollerns had assumed the title of king.[1] And by the irony of fate, since the Germans were still besieging Paris, it was held in the Hall of Mirrors in the palace of Louis XIV at Versailles, "in the ancient center," the official German report explained, "of a hostile power which for centuries had striven to divide and humiliate Germany." There, surrounded by

---

[1] See above, p. 447.

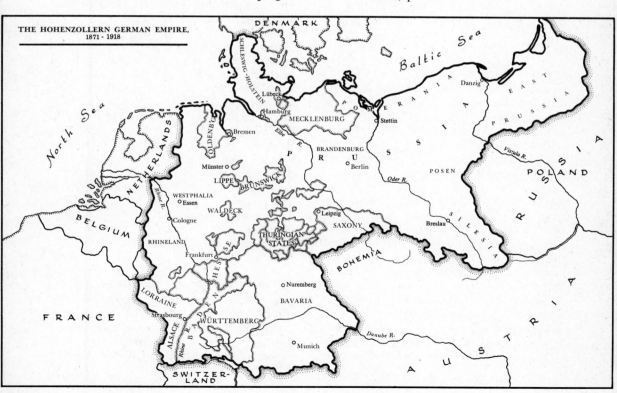

THE HOHENZOLLERN GERMAN EMPIRE,
1871 - 1918

Emperor Francis Joseph of Austria-Hungary.

Courtesy Bettmann Archive

German princes and generals, Bismarck read the imperial decrees which set the seal of success on the first part of his life work.

The Franco-Prussian War had other results than the unification of Germany and the formation of the German Empire. In taking Alsace-Lorraine from France, Bismarck over-reached himself, though he would no doubt have taken western Lorraine as well had he known how valuable the Thomas-Gilchrist process would soon make its abundant iron ore. But moved by the advice of his military counselors, Bismarck was willing to risk permanent French hostility in order to give Germany a more defensible frontier across the Rhine. He got the frontier, and he also got the hostility.

The Franco-Prussian War ushered in a new era. It broke the long peace (1815–1870) among the major powers of western Europe. It created a new and very potent nation, the German Empire. It emphasized once more the value of large, well-trained, and well-equipped armies. It aroused a fiercer nationalism not only in victorious Germany and defeated France but also in the rest of Europe. In short it sowed many of the seeds which were bitterly reaped in the twentieth century.

D. Creation of the Dual Monarchy of Austria-Hungary

In the Austrian Empire, the Seven Weeks' War resulted in drastic changes. The Hungarians, defeated in their bid for independence under Kossuth in 1849, had been restive under Austrian rule. There had been some fear at Vienna that they would prove rebellious in the crisis of 1866. But under the leadership of Francis Deák, they fought loyally in the disastrous war. It was Deák's belief that Hungary would best serve its interests by a partnership with Austria rather than by revolt against her. Indeed, the Magyars (Hungarians) had at least one major interest in common with the German Austrians, for they were both eager to hold down the subject Slavic peoples.

Deák's gamble in getting Hungary to support Austria in 1866 was successful. The military catastrophe of that year followed so closely the defeat of 1859 in Italy, that a reorganization of the Habsburg Empire was obviously necessary. In accomplishing this, it seemed less drastic to transform the Empire into a dual monarchy by granting autonomy to the Magyars, than to form a five-part federation by recognizing the claims of Poles, Czechs, and Yugoslavs as well. Accordingly, after due negotiations, a new political arrangement for the Austrian Empire was worked out by the *Ausgleich* (Compromise) of 1867. The Habsburg dominions were divided into two parts: (1) the "Empire of Austria," embracing Austria proper, Bohemia, Galicia, Carniola, and the Tyrol; (2) the "Kingdom of Hungary," including Hungary proper with its crown lands of Croatia, the Banat, and Transylvania. Each part would have a constitution and parliament of its own, and each would be independent of the other in

EUROPE IN 1871

500 Miles

most respects. Yet the two would be united by a common ruler—to be known under the dual title of "Emperor of Austria and King of Hungary"—and by a common army, common foreign relations, and certain common ministers.

Thus was the Austrian Habsburg Empire transformed into the Dual Monarchy of Austria-Hungary. The Seven Weeks' War had proved advantageous to Hungarian as well as German nationalism. The Dual Monarchy, though it was to endure for fifty-one years, contained a fatal defect. It did not recognize the national aspirations of the Slavic peoples who were left under what they regarded as the alien (and in the case of Hungary, tyrannical) rule of Germans and Magyars.

The Slavs who came off best in the new scheme of things under the Habsburg Emperor-King were the Poles and the Croats. The Poles of Galicia were given some political and economic liberty in 1868 by the Austrians and, indeed, were so favored that they coöperated with Vienna in holding down the Czechs and Slovenes. The Croats were the most western and advanced of the southern Slavs, and therefore the most likely to agitate politically and make trouble for the Magyar rulers at Budapest. They were predominantly Roman Catholic rather than Orthodox in religion, and, unlike their fellow Serbs, they used the Roman rather than the Greek alphabet. Hungary appeased them to a degree by granting Croatia some local autonomy in 1868. As for the Czechs in Bohemia and their kinsmen the Slovaks in Hungary, they were treated more or less like inferior and subject peoples within the Dual Monarchy. They responded by agitations at home and by intrigues with Slavic Russia abroad.

SELECT SUPPLEMENTARY READINGS FOR PART IX

Chapter 44. On romanticism: H. N. Fairchild, *The Romantic Quest* (1931); Oliver Elton, *Survey of English Literature, 1780–1830,* 2 vols (1920); and appropriate chapters in Kuno Francke, *History of German Literature,* 4th ed. (1901); C. H. C. Wright, *History of French Literature,* new ed. (1925); J. Pijoan, *History of Art,* vol. iii (1928); J. Barzun, *Romanticism and the Modern Ego* (1943); A. Einstein, *Music in the Romantic Era* (1941); H. R. Hitchcock, *Architecture: Nineteenth and Twentieth Centuries* (1958). On science: H. S. Williams, *Story of Nineteenth-Century Science* (1900); J. D. Dampier-Whetham, *History of Science and Its Relations with Philosophy,* 2nd ed. (1932); R. H. Shryock, *The Development of Modern Medicine* (1936); E. Nordenskiold, *History of Biology* (1928); S. P. Thompson, *Faraday* (1898); J. T. Merz, *A History of European Thought in the Nineteenth Century,* 2nd ed., 4 vols. (1912–1928).

Chapter 45. G. N. Clark, *The Idea of the Industrial Revolution* (1953); W. O. Henderson, *Britain and Industrial Europe, 1750–1870* (1954); C. Singer, E. J. Holmyard, A. R. Hall, T. I. Williams (eds.), *A History of Technology,* 5 vols. (1955–1958); Vol. IV, *The Industrial Revolution* c. 1750 to c. 1850; F. C. Dietz, *The Industrial Revolution, 1750–1927* (1927); J. L. and B. Hammond, *Rise of Modern Industry* (1926); C. S. Abbot, *Great Inventions* (1932); W. Bowden, *Industrial Society in England toward the End of the Eighteenth Century* (1925); L. C. A. Knowles, *Industrial and Commercial Revolutions in Great Britain during the Nineteenth Century* (1921), and *Economic Development in France, Germany, Russia, and the United States* (1932); H. D. Fong, *Triumph of the Factory System in England* (1930); J. H. Clapham, *Economic History of Modern Britain,* vol. ii, *Free Trade and Steel* (1932), and *Economic Development of France and Germany, 1815–1914,* 3rd ed. (1928); F. A. Nussbaum, *History of the Economic Institutions of Modern Europe* (1933); Sir Leslie Stephen, *English Utilitarians,* 3 vols (1902); C. R. Fay, *The Corn Laws and Social England* (1932); William Cunningham, *Rise and Decline of the Free Trade Movement* (1912); B. L. Hutchins and A. Harrison, *History of Factory Legislation,* 3rd ed. (1926); John Morley, *Life of Richard Cobden* (1903); J. L. and B. Hammond, *Lord Shaftesbury* (1924); Sidney and Beatrice Webb, *History of Trade Unionism,* rev. ed. (1920); W. S. Sanders, *Trade Unionism in Germany* (1916); A. F. Weber, *The Growth of Cities in the Nineteenth Century* (1899).

Chapter 46. P. S. Robertson, *Revolutions of 1848* (1952); A. Whitridge, *Men in Crisis: the Revolutions of 1848* (1949); J. A. R. Marriott, *The French Revolution of 1848 in Its Economic Aspects*, 2 vols (1913); D. C. McKay, *The National Workshops, a Study in the French Revolution of 1848* (1933); F. A. Simpson, *Rise of Louis Napoleon* (1925); H. von Treitschke, *History of Germany in the Nineteenth Century, 1815–1848*, Eng. trans. 7 vols. (1915–1919); K. R. Greenfield, *Economics and Liberalism in the Risorgimento, a Study of Nationalism in Italy, 1814–1848*, (1934); G. Salvemini, *Mazzini* (1920); H. A. L. Fisher, *The Republican Tradition in Europe* (1911); J. L. and B. Hammond, *The Age of the Chartists, 1832–1854* (1930); A. Briggs (ed.), *Chartist Studies* (1959).

Chapter 47. R. C. Binkley, *Realism and Nationalism* (1935); *New Cambridge Modern History*, vol. X (1960); G. P. Gooch, *The Second Empire* (1960); A. L. Guerard, *Napoleon III* (1942); Philip Guedalla, *The Second Empire* (1928); F. A. Simpson, *Louis Napoleon and the Recovery of France, 1848–1856* (1923); J. M. Thompson, *Louis Napoleon and the Second Empire* (1954); F. C. Palm, *England and Napoleon III* (1948); H. B. Parkes, *A History of Mexico* (1950); W. R. Thayer, *The Life and Times of Cavour*, 2 vols (1911); D. Mack Smith, *Cavour and Garibaldi, 1860* (1954); and *Garibaldi* (1956); Bolton King, *History of Italian Unity, being a Political History of Italy from 1814 to 1871* (1899); G. M. Trevelyan, *Garibaldi and the Thousand* (1909), and *Garibaldi and the Making of Italy* (1911); T. W. Riker, *The Making of Roumania* (1931); H. C. F. Bell, *Life of Palmerston* (1941).

Chapter 48. H. Friedjung, *The Struggle for Supremacy in Germany*, Eng. trans. (1935); W. O. Henderson, *The Zollverein* (1939); W. H. Dawson, *The German Empire, 1867–1914*, 2 vols (1919); R. H. Lord, *The Origins of the War of 1870* (1924); F. Darmstaedter, *Bismarck and the Creation of the Second Reich* (1948); W. O. Henderson, *The Zollverein* (1960).

PART X
PROGRESSIVE AND

From Bismarck
to Lloyd George

IMPERIALIST EUROPE, 1871–1914

THE LAST PART of the nineteenth century was an era of optimism. After 1871, it began to seem as if the age of major wars was over. In one country after another democracy made visible progress. At the same time, the spread of industrialization and the resultant increase in the output of goods seemed to usher in a period when poverty would be reduced and human well-being forwarded. Cheap food from North America and Australia, if it raised some problems for the landowners of England, improved the diet of the workers in the cities.

Meanwhile, science was making such spectacular advances that it seemed to many as if the day was not far off when the whole of the universe could be explained in the materialistic terms of matter and motion. With science, medicine and public health progressed significantly and, as the death rate dropped, population grew even more rapidly than it had in the past. A portion of the increasing numbers emigrated to America; an even larger proportion moved into the expanding cities.

But as the vision of a peaceful, prosperous, expanding world, guided by science and supplied by machine industry, developed in men's minds, there were some dark spots which people strove to forget. Conditions in the city slums were in many countries so sordid that there were attempts to improve the lot of the worker through "social legislation." It seemed, moreover, as if progress were focussed in western Europe, for in the east, particularly in the empires of the Romanovs and the Ottoman sultans, there was no democracy, relatively little industry, and scant attention to the needs or desires of the lower classes.

There was a renewal of the European imperialism of the seventeenth and eighteenth centuries. It had seemed, about 1860, as if the day of building colonial empires might be over, as if there were a general agreement that colonies did not pay and were not worthwhile. But partly because of the rapidly rising nationalism after the unification of Italy and of Germany, and partly because of the tremendous growth of industry and commerce, there was, in the last three decades of the century, a new struggle for colonies in which Africa was partitioned and much of Asia and Oceania brought under European sway.

During the whole period, Great Britain enjoyed a very special preëminence. A leader in democracy and liberalism, she had made her advances since the seventeenth century without revolution. Her industry was the best developed in the world. Her commerce, guarded by the largest of all navies, traversed the seven seas almost without rival. London was the world center for banking, finance, and insurance. People of all lands turned to England as the outstanding example of a modern nation.

CHAPTER 49

Democracy in Western Europe

A. The Shining Example of Britain

Throughout the last half of the nineteenth century, Great Britain was the model which most other countries sought to copy. They looked with envy upon her far-flung empire, her mighty navy, her incomparable industry and commerce, her foreign investments, her growing population. Somehow her success in these many lines seemed to be connected with her parliamentary government, which showed itself able to move toward liberal democracy without revolution, and with her cabinet system, which seemed flexible enough to meet every expanding need.

To be sure, Britain preserved more of the class structure of the eighteenth century than countries like Belgium or Holland or even France. She was very slow in creating a system of free public education. In social legislation she lagged behind Germany. But these were merely illustrations of the gradualness of development which seemed part of the secret of British success.

The Victorian compromise, initiated by the reform of 1832,[1] did not last to the midpoint of Queen Victoria's reign (1837–1901). By 1867 the pressure from the laboring classes for the extension of the suffrage was getting too strong to be resisted. In the previous year, the Liberals and their rising leader Gladstone, who had proposed a slight parliamentary reform, had been driven from office on that issue. But popular demonstra-

tions increased to the point of violence, and in 1867 the Conservative prime minister, Lord Derby, authorized his chief lieutenant, Disraeli, to introduce a new and still moderate reform bill. To embarrass the Conservatives, Gladstone, aided by Radical Liberals, proposed a number of amendments to broaden the bill. Rather than allow the Liberals to get credit for a popular reform, Disraeli accepted the amendments and secured the passage of the bill, which was by now a good deal more radical than Gladstone's original proposal. Thus was the reform of 1867 enacted through competition between the two parties. Democratic in trend, it almost doubled the electorate by giving the franchise to most urban workingmen.

Five years later, under Gladstone's auspices, the secret ballot was introduced. Then in 1884, the Liberals put through the third great parliamentary reform of the nineteenth century by extending the vote to rural workers and bringing Great Britain fairly close to universal manhood suffrage. In 1885 the Conservatives sponsored a supplementary reform, providing that members of the House of Commons would be chosen by approximately equal districts of about 50,000 people each. Thus Britain achieved a very considerable degree of the political democracy for which the Chartists had pleaded forty years earlier.[2]

If the lower classes got the vote, the upper and wealthier classes still retained

---

[1] See above, p. 572.

[2] See above, p. 571.

ical predominance. They completely
trolled the House of Lords. They occu-
d most seats in the House of Commons.
ley held nearly all cabinet offices. Yet in
ne party competition of upper-class leaders, there was a growing tendency to seek
lower-class votes by making campaign
promises, and sometimes the promises were
kept. Gradually, therefore, Britain achieved
a measure of social reform, and, contrary
to the principles of economic liberalism, the
government increased its intervention in
economic matters for the benefit of workers.

The outstanding political leaders in the
period after the reform of 1867 were William E. Gladstone and Benjamin Disraeli.
Gladstone was prime minister from 1868
to 1874, from 1880 to 1885, in 1886, and
from 1892 to 1894, while Disraeli was prime
minister in 1868 and from 1874 to 1880.
Gladstone professed devotion to the liberal
principles of peace, *laissez-faire*, and humanitarianism; he disapproved of imperialism
and was most happy when arguing for "re-
trenchment" (economy) in the home government. Disraeli, on the other hand,
believed that the upper and lower classes
should coöperate to restrain the triumphant
middle class and to preserve the traditional
English institutions of monarchy, Anglican
Church, and landed aristocracy; and in the
1870's he started Britain off on a new stage
of imperialist expansion and stressed the
importance of India in the British Empire
by adding "Empress of India" to Queen
Victoria's other titles.

The issues which separated Gladstone
and Disraeli were not really as deep as they
appeared to the Liberals and Conservatives
of the time. Both parties were committed
to maintenance of things as they were. Both
parties were willing to accept changes of
necessity or for political advantage. The
most burning disputes were over Ireland,
which was poverty-stricken, depopulated
since the potato famine of 1845–1846, and
economically exploited by absentee landlords and Anglican churchmen. When the
Irish became sufficiently violent, or sufficiently organized, something had to be
done for them, though concessions were
usually accompanied by "coercion acts." In
1869 Gladstone prevailed on parliament to
disestablish the Anglican Church in Ireland,

Queen Victoria.

so that Catholic Irishmen were no longer
required to pay for the support of Protestant
churches and ministers. A Land Act of 1870
forbade arbitrary evictions of Irish tenants,
arbitrary raising of rents, or failure to reim-
burse the tenant for improvements he had
made. Another Land Act of 1881 granted
Irish peasants the "three F's" for which they
were then agitating—fair rent, fixity of tenure, and free sale.

But it was a political situation which gave
weight to Irish demands. In the general
election of 1885, an Irish Nationalist party,
which had been organized and was led by
Charles Stewart Parnell, obtained a balance
of power between the evenly matched Liberal and Conservative parties. Whereupon
Gladstone, anxious for Irish support of himself and the Liberal party, acceded to Parnell's demand for "home rule" for Ireland,
and in 1886 introduced such a bill in Parliament. By doing so, however, Gladstone split
the Liberal Party, as Peel had earlier split
the Conservative Party.

A group of liberals led by Joseph Chamberlain and calling themselves Liberal
Unionists, joined the Conservatives in voting down home rule. For the next twenty
years the Conservatives, supported by the
Liberal Unionists, were in office continuously, except for 1892–1895, when Gladstone again introduced a home rule bill and
got it through the Commons only to have

it defeated by the Lords. But while the Conservatives stood firm against home rule, they made some concessions to Ireland. Thus they sponsored a series of land purchase acts which wrought a veritable social revolution in Ireland by advancing government funds (on easy terms) to Irish tenants and thus enabling them to buy out their landlords and become peasant proprietors.

There were other British reforms. An Education Act of 1870 gave increased support to the old religious schools and inaugurated a system of state schools (called "board schools"). Full legal recognition was granted to labor unions by an act of 1871, and before the end of the century unionism had spread from the skilled crafts to semiskilled factory workers, and to unskilled laborers as well. Slowly the pressure of lower class voters, of trade unions, and of social reformers made itself felt. Before he devoted himself to the Irish question and an unsuccessful attempt to reëstablish English tariffs, Joseph Chamberlain made a reputation for "municipal socialism" by reforms he instituted as mayor of Birmingham. In the Conservative party, Lord Randolph Churchill led a group of "Tory Democrats" who worked for social legislation.

Disraeli.

The period from 1873 to 1896, ma~~r~~ by these democratic, social, and educati~~o~~ reforms, was a difficult one in some w~~ay~~ for Great Britain. World prices were lo~~w~~ Profits in trade and commerce dwindle~~d~~ British agriculture, in the face of overseas competition of cheap wheat and frozen meat, ceased to be profitable. Germany and the United States were becoming serious competitors in manufacturing. But all this was relative, and after 1896, as prices rose again, Britain made handsome profits once more from industry and commerce if not from farming.

B. The Third French Republic

The Third Republic in France was proclaimed amidst the gloom attending the defeat at Sedan in 1870. It was organized by a National Assembly elected to ratify an humiliating peace with Germany, and comprising an anti-republican majority. And in its first days, it was torn by civil as well as foreign war. Yet, though no other French regime since 1789 lasted more than eighteen years, the Third Republic endured for seventy.

When the National Assembly was elected in 1871, the royalists were eager to make peace, while the republicans, unwilling to saddle the new republic with the shame of defeat, wished to continue the war. Since the country was sick of war, it voted heavily for the peace party and, out of 650 deputies elected, some 400 were royalists. This majority naturally refused to sanction the republic. It made the peace and appointed Adolphe Thiers as "head of the executive power" to keep the throne warm for a king, who, it was expected, would soon occupy it. But meanwhile the masses of Paris, distrustful of the royalist Assembly, ravaged by economic distress, and injured by the Assembly's decision not to pay wages to national guardsmen any more and to enforce the payment of debts and rent which had been suspended, rallied to the support of the city Commune (city government) in armed revolt against the National Assembly. In April and May 1871, the city, which had so recently been besieged by Germans, underwent a second siege. The attacking French

...y sent by Thiers fought fiercely, and the ...ommunards" resisted furiously. In des-...ration, Parisian extremists slew the hos-...ages they held, including the archbishop of Paris, and burned a number of public buildings, including the palace of the Tui-leries. But at last they were overwhelmed. The Commune was crushed and its sur-viving leaders were killed or exiled.

Having crushed the Parisian radicals, the National Assembly turned to the business of establishing a permanent government. It soon found itself facing a nearly insoluble problem, for, though its majority was royal-ist, this was divided into two almost equal camps. "Legitimists" wanted the Count of Chambord (grandson of Charles X) as king, while "Orleanists" wanted the Count of Paris (grandson of Louis Philippe). For months the two factions wrangled, until in 1873 they were temporarily shocked into joint action by Thiers's announced conver-sion from royalism to republicanism. Out-raged, they ousted Thiers and elected in his stead the staunchly royalist Marshal Mac-Mahon. Soon afterward they agreed upon a compromise: the childless Count of Chambord would become King, and the Count of Paris would be his heir. But this was upset by the rock-ribbed conservatism of the prospective king, who declared that the flag of France under his rule would be the white banner of the Bourbons, symbol of the old regime. Such a seemingly insig-nificant point proved a major stumbling block, for it meant that the Count of Chambord, as "Henry V," would try to take France back to the days before 1789, and the majority of Frenchmen, including French royalists, had moved too far along the road of liberal democracy for any such retreat.

With the failure of the royalist plan, the National Assembly set about organizing a French republic. But the royalist majority still hoped to fashion the republic so that it could easily be transformed into a mon-archy after the death of the aging Count of Chambord. In November 1873 the Assembly made MacMahon "President of the Republic." In January 1875, by the nar-row margin of one vote, it provided for the election of future presidents. Three more "constitutional laws" in 1875 completed the framework of government. Filled in by precedent, interpretation, and amendment, they were all the constitution which the Third Republic ever had. The laws provided for a two-house legislature (Senate and Chamber of Deputies), a ministry respon-sible to the legislature, and a president elected for a seven-year term by the two houses meeting jointly. On paper, the presi-dent seemed to enjoy considerable powers. In practice, authority rested with the par-liament.

In the first elections under the new sys-tem, France showed its true sentiments by electing a majority of republican deputies, among whom Gambetta was foremost. But MacMahon was unwilling to accept this verdict, and on May 16, 1877, he appointed a royalist ministry, dissolved the Chamber of Deputies, and ordered new elections. Both MacMahon and Gambetta toured the country in a spectacular campaign. The republicans won a decisive victory, and MacMahon had to appoint a republican ministry. Two years later, after the republi-cans gained control of the Senate, they were able to force MacMahon out of the presi-dency and to put in a colorless politician named Grévy. One result of the "sixteenth of May" was that no future president dared to used his power to dissolve the Chamber. Another was a tendency to elect undistin-guished and "safe" men as presidents.

Thus by 1879 republicans finally con-trolled the Third Republic. During the en-suing decade they consolidated the new regime. They made the tricolor the national flag, the Marseillaise the national anthem, July 14 the national holiday, and Paris (instead of Versailles) the national capital. They made the Senate wholly elective in-stead of partly appointed. They passed laws guarantying freedom of speech, assembly, and the press. At the same time they assailed Catholic "clericalism" as an enemy of re-publicanism. Under the leadership of Jules Ferry, they passed a series of educational laws designed to restrict church schools and to erect a system of national non-religious lay education. They banned many of the religious orders. They made civil marriage compulsory.

From 1879 the Third French Republic showed two interesting peculiarities. The

General Boulanger.

taxes for the land taxes, then by subsid
and aid to peasant coöperative and crec
associations, and finally by protective tariffs
The Méline tariff of 1892 represented a
major decision. By placing heavy duties on
such products as wheat, meat, and sugar, it
indicated that the French (unlike the British) were determined to preserve the peasantry and to keep agriculture prosperous
even if it meant expensive food for the rest
of the population.

There was a good deal of opposition to
the Republic, even after 1879, and within
the next twenty years this assumed serious
proportions on two occasions. One was the
Boulanger Affair, and the other the Dreyfus
Affair.

General Boulanger, a radical republican
at the start and war minister in 1886–1887,
became popular with patriots by champion-
ing a "war of revenge" against Germany,
and before long he was intriguing with conservative elements to make himself a dictator, presumably in Napoleonic fashion. In
1889 he was elected to the Chamber from
Paris by a huge majority, and might then
have successfully executed a *coup d'état*.
But he lacked courage, and when the government ordered his arrest he fled the country. In 1891 the "brave general" committed
suicide in Brussels.

More serious was the Dreyfus Affair. In
1894 a secret court-martial of the French
army convicted a certain Captain Alfred
Dreyfus (a French Jew) and sentenced him
to life imprisonment on Devil's Island (near
French Guiana). A little later, when question was raised about evidence used at the
trial, the general public divided sharply between "Dreyfusards" and "Anti-Dreyfus-
ards." The former, contending that Dreyfus
was innocent, included the majority of
republicans; the latter, holding that he was
guilty, embraced foes and critics of the
republic—a noisy group of anti-Semites,
most royalists, many Catholics, and officers
intent upon upholding the "honor of the
army." As proofs eventually accumulated in
favor of Dreyfus's innocence, he was
brought back to France and retried in 1899,
but so intense was the feeling against him
in the army that he was again found guilty,
though "with extenuating circumstances."
Whereupon he was pardoned by the

first was an apparent instability arising from
the large number of political parties, or
"groups." Few of the ministries lasted more
than a year. Many endured only a few
weeks or months. But policy was actually
stable, because a new ministry usually contained a number of ministers from the preceding one and represented merely a slight
reshuffling of cabinet posts. The second
peculiarity was a tendency to move toward
the left (radicalism). The major republican
group of the 1880's, led by men like Gambetta and Ferry, was called "Opportunist,"
since it had no fixed programs other than
republicanism and anti-clericalism. To the
left of the Opportunists were the "Radicals," including Georges Clemenceau. By
the 1890's these were growing in strength,
and to their left, socialist groups were
emerging.

In the first twenty years after 1879 the
Opportunists guided the destinies of the
republic. They led it into new imperialist
adventures, which we shall note later. They
favored business by raising tariffs on industrial products, subsidizing shipping, and
constructing public works. They helped agriculture, first by substituting a host of indirect

sident of the Republic, and in 1906 was completely exonerated and restored to military rank.

The Dreyfus Affair had several important consequences. (1) The republic was strengthened. (2) Royalists were discredited, and weeded out of the army. (3) Opportunists who had shilly-shallied in the case were supplanted by Radicals who, with some Socialist support, became the leading political group. (4) Anti-clericalism was greatly intensified, so much so, that in the ensuing years the triumphant Radicals expelled almost all religious orders from France (1901), made provision (1904) to prevent clergymen from teaching even in church schools, and, by abrogating the Concordat of 1801, separated church from state (1905).

C. Other Successes of Liberal Democracy

In the latter part of the nineteenth century, while liberal democracy was the rule in Great Britain and France and partially recognized in Germany, it made notable progress elsewhere in western Europe. In Italy, there were special difficulties. There was cleavage between the progressive industrial north and the backward agricultural south, and there was papal hostility to the new Italian kingdom. Pope Pius IX refused to recognize Italy's forceful seizure of Rome in 1870 and became "the prisoner of the Vatican." The Italian government attempted to meet the impasse by a "law of papal guaranties," which promised sovereign independence to the Pope within the Vatican and granted him an annual subsidy in return for the territory he had lost. Pius IX promptly rejected the law, refused the subsidy, and forbade Catholics to participate in Italy's political life. Though the Pope's attitude strengthened his international position by making it clear that he was not subservient to the Italian government, it created grave difficulties for Italy. It was not until 1929 that an amicable settlement was reached between Italy and the Vatican.

Despite these difficulties, parliamentary government made considerable progress in Italy. There were a number of parties, which in general fell into two groups: the Right, whose strength lay in the industrial north; and the Left, led by middle-class intellectuals and lawyers from the south. The Right was perhaps a shade more aristocratic and less anti-clerical than the Left. But both were very much like the liberal republicans of France. The Right was in power from 1870 to 1876, and the Left for most of the next twenty years. One of the Left prime ministers, Crispi, led Italy into an ill-fated imperialist attempt to seize Ethiopia. The Ethiopians crushed the Italian expeditionary force at Adowa (1896), and the discredited Left was out of power for the next seven years.

Both Right and Left sought to better Italian economic life by constructing railways, subsidizing shipping, and granting tariff protection to industry. Despite Italy's lack of coal and iron, some progress was made, slowly before 1896, and rapidly thereafter. Yet lack of opportunity at home led millions of Italians, especially from the south, to emigrate to Argentina, Brazil, and the United States. In 1900, about 350,000 left the country; and in 1910 the figure rose to 530,000.

In both Spain and Portugal, liberalism made some advance. Spanish liberals ousted Queen Isabella II in 1868. But attempts to establish a constitutional monarchy under another dynasty were succeeded by still more disastrous attempts to found a republic. After much disorder and fighting, the Bourbon monarchy was restored in 1875 in the person of Isabella's son, Alphonso XII. For the next thirty-five years, Spain was nominally a liberal constitutional monarchy. Actually it was ruled by a group of military and political chieftains whose power rested on the indifference of the masses and the support of the army. Some were called Liberal, others Conservative, and they cheerfully shared the spoils of office with each other. Republicans continued their propaganda and helped to force the adoption of universal manhood suffrage in 1890. To counterbalance the votes of city workers, who were becoming more revolutionary (whether they wanted a republic, socialism, or provincial autonomy), the Conservatives made the suffrage compulsory in 1907 so as to oblige the more conservative peasants to vote. An unsuccessful war of 1898 against the United States lost Spain most of her remaining colonies, and proved a blow to her national pride and to the monarchy.

Conditions in Portugal were much like those in Spain after 1875. In general the ministers were less efficient and more corrupt. In addition, King Charles I was personally licentious and extravagant. In 1907 he tried to quell factional strife by giving dictatorial powers to the prime minister, but in the next year both Charles and his eldest son were assassinated in the streets of Lisbon. The monarchy staggered along till 1910, when it was overthrown by a revolt which made Portugal a republic.

By the late nineteenth century, both Belgium and Holland had become liberal, constitutional monarchies much like Britain. In Belgium the Liberal party was in power most of the time from 1847 to 1884, but its anti-clerical tendencies gave rise to a strong Catholic party which controlled the government for the next thirty years. In Holland, though the suffrage was gradually broadened, the sovereign could still initiate and veto legislation. More thoroughly democratic was Switzerland, which adopted the referendum (1874), permitting the people as a whole to vote on laws, and also the initiative (1891), enabling a specified number of citizens to force the submission of a measure to such a vote.

In Denmark, King Christian IX (1863–1906) waged a long contest with the lower house of the national legislature. Till 1901 he succeeded in ruling in a more or less autocratic manner, but in that year he was compelled to appoint a ministry representing the majority of the lower house. It was not until 1914–1915 that the age for voting was cut from thirty to twenty-five and the upper house of the legislature made wholly elective. Norway and Sweden were ruled by the same king, but with separate ministries and legislatures from 1815 to 1905. In this arrangement, the Swedes had the better of the bargain, for they held chief positions in the joint army and diplomatic services. Growing Norwegian nationalism finally led to a separation of the two countries. In 1905, the Norwegians proclaimed their independence and chose the second son of the Danish king as their ruler. Sweden reluctantly consented. Universal manhood suffrage was established in Norway in 18 and in Sweden in 1907.

By 1914 all the countries of western Europe seemed committed to political democracy. Almost all of them had something approaching universal manhood suffrage. All of them had constitutions, even though Britain's was unwritten. Most of them had governments responsible to the national legislatures, though this was not true of Germany and did not mean much in Spain or Portugal. All of them recognized personal liberties of speech, press, religion, and assembly.

D. Controlled Democracy in Germany under Bismarck

The new German Empire represented a nice compromise between nationalism and federalism, and between divine-right monarchy and popular government. In the Empire were twenty-five states besides the "imperial territory" of Alsace-Lorraine. Each state retained its respective duke, grandduke, or king, and its control over such local matters as direct taxation, education, public health, police, and landholding. Certain special privileges were conceded to some of the states. Thus Bavaria retained control of its own post offices, railways, and army (in peace time), and in Saxony the supreme court of the Empire was located. The federal, imperial government had authority over foreign affairs, military matters, foreign and domestic commerce, and criminal and civil law. For the Empire as a whole, laws were to be made by a two-house legislature: a *Bundesrat* (Federal Council), composed of agents of the various state governments; and a *Reichstag* (Imperial Parliament), elected democratically by all males over twenty-five years of age.

While democracy was recognized in the manner of electing the Reichstag, it was restricted by limiting the power of that body, for the imperial ministry, headed by a chancellor, was responsible not to it but to the Emperor. Moreover, Prussia, still under the undemocratic constitution of 1850, was given a major role in the Empire. Not only was the Prussian king, as emperor, empowered to appoint and dismiss the chancellor of the Empire at will, but usually the

...perial chancellor and the prime-minister of Prussia were one and the same person. The agent of the king of Prussia in the Bundesrat was given enough votes to enable him to veto any reduction in the army or in taxes or any amendment to the imperial constitution which the majority in the Reichstag might approve. To conduct the new imperial machinery, from the key position of the chancellorship, the Emperor William I, appropriately enough, selected Bismarck, and the statesman who had created the German Empire guided its destinies for almost twenty years afterwards.

Within a short time the governmental machinery of the new Empire was organized and perfected. The legal systems of the several states were replaced by uniform codes of law for the whole Empire. Imperial coinage supplanted the coins of the various states. An imperial bureau unified the state railroads and coördinated them with the military, postal, and telegraphic services. Control of banks was transferred from the state governments to the Bundesrat, and an Imperial Bank (Reichsbank) was set up.

To safeguard the new Germany, Bismarck turned to both diplomacy and military preparedness. In the field of foreign relations, he strove to keep France isolated so that she would have no allies if she were tempted to start a "war of revenge." At the same time, he extended the Prussian system of compulsory military service to the whole Empire, and the peace strength of the army was fixed at 400,000. Though the Chancellor would have liked to have the army appropriations made permanent, the Reichstag would grant them only for seven (later five) years at a time. But Bismarck soon learned to get the appropriation renewed each time by arranging a "war scare" at the right moment. The German military machine was always growing, never shrinking, after 1871.

In putting through his various policies, Bismarck had the support of the bourgeois National Liberal party, and of the Free Conservative party, which was composed mainly of Prussian landlords. The other major parties were the Old Conservative, made up largely of "old fashioned" Prussian squires, Lutheran clergymen, and army officers, and the Progressive party, drawn chiefly from middle-class liberals. The former was too Prussian to sympathize with Bismarck's all-German mood after 1871, and too reactionary to approve his gestures toward democracy. On the whole, however, it went along with him on most matters and backed him vigorously in his army policy. But the Progressives, who were pacifist and wanted a really democratic and liberal government, were a thorn in Bismarck's flesh. It was a relief to him that their strength was gradually waning. There were minor groups, too, who opposed Bismarck in the Reichstag. In 1875 the radical followers of Karl Marx and the more moderate followers of Ferdinand Lassalle united to form a Social Democratic party. Thereafter there were always some Socialist deputies to criticize the government and plead the cause of the workers. There were, in addition, small groups of deputies from Hanover, Schleswig, Prussian Poland, and Alsace-Lorraine, who represented people more or less unhappy under Prussian rule. Sometimes they were aided in fighting the Chancellor by deputies from the south who were eager to preserve "states' rights" or the Catholic religion from Prussian and Protestant interference.

Bismarck was particularly nettled by the Catholic, states' rights group; and his desire to repress it by striking at the Catholic Church was shared by a majority in both the Reichstag and the Prussian parliament. To many German Protestants, the Catholic Church seemed a foreign organization standing in the way of German nationalism. To many German liberals, Pope Pius IX seemed a reactionary trying to compensate for his loss of temporal power by asserting an ever greater spiritual authority. From 1872 to 1880 Bismarck waged a kind of war in Prussia and throughout Germany against the Catholic Church. On this point, the Progressives heartily approved of the Chancellor's policy, and one of them gave the conflict a high-sounding name by which it has since been known—the *Kulturkampf* (struggle for civilization).

In 1872, Bismarck began the fight by expelling the Jesuits from Germany and breaking off diplomatic relations with the pope. Then in Prussia, he put through (1873–1874) the so-called "May Laws" or "Falk

Laws," which provided that every Catholic clergymen must be a German citizen educated in German public schools and universities, and must be certified or "authorized" by the Prussian government. Ecclesiastical seminaries were put under state control, and Catholic preparatory schools for the clergy were banned. Religious instruction, even in Polish-speaking areas, was to be given in German. Backed by the pope, the German bishops condemned this legislation. Whereupon the Prussian parliament forbade "unauthorized" persons to exercise church functions and made refractory clergymen subject to loss of citizenship, imprisonment, or exile. With such severity were these measures enforced that within a single year six Catholic bishops were jailed and Catholic public worship ceased in more than 1300 parishes. In 1877, every Prussian Catholic bishop and hundreds of priests were in prison or exile, and lay Catholics were being rapidly weeded out of the civil service.

With unexpected unanimity, German Catholics fought back against Bismarck's anti-Catholic legislation. Encouraged by the pope and their "martyred" bishops, they rallied in support of "administrators" who by stealth took the place of the bishops and kept the church organization functioning. In politics they supported Catholic leaders, like Windthorst from Hanover, who were building up a distinctively Catholic party— the so-called Center Party. The new party demanded not only the repeal of the anti-Catholic laws but also a broad program of social reform. In 1874 it polled one and a half million votes and elected ninety deputies. Before long, Windthorst was skillfully lining up support from all the groups hostile to Bismarck and even from some of the Protestant Conservatives who were alarmed by the general anti-religious implications of the anti-Catholic legislation.

Finally, Bismarck decided that opposition on the religious issue was endangering his other policies. He also began to feel that Marxian Socialism was an even greater menace than Catholic Christianity. Accordingly, in 1880, he secured from the Prussian parliament authorization to use his discretion in enforcing the May Laws. Diplomatic relations with the Vatican were presently resumed, and in 1886 the most oppressive anti-Catholic measures were repealed. Bismarck thus confessed that his *Kulturkampf* had been a failure. From his standpoint it was even worse, for it raised up a new and well-organized Catholic party which was soon working with democrats and socialists to secure political and social reforms.

E. Bismarck and Socialism

Bismarck was correct in his belief that the Socialists were gaining in strength, for, as Germany became increasingly industrialized, the urban proletariat grew by leaps and bounds, and within it the Socialists obtained many converts. As we have seen, industrialism had made considerable progress in Germany before 1870. Afterwards its growth was phenomenal. It was stimulated by the French war indemnity, aided by national unity, fostered by government assistance, and forwarded by the discoveries of German scientists. German pig iron production rose from 1,400,000 metric tons in 1870 to almost eleven million in 1905, by which time it surpassed Great Britain's. German steel output by 1895 was greater than British. German coal production multiplied nine times between 1860 and 1900. By 1895 nearly seven million workers were employed in German industry and less than thirty-seven per cent of the population was making its living from agriculture.

Germany, coming late into the field, got off to a very good start in the newer industries, at the same time that she was making such rapid progress in the old. In photographic goods and optical instruments, in electrical products, and in chemicals, Germany held a commanding position by 1900. In many lines, from novelties to cutlery and from toys to textiles, the Germans won markets by making a relatively good product at a very cheap price. The government encouraged the business men to get together in associations or "cartels" to eliminate competition, fix prices, and expand sales abroad. Railway rates were cut on goods for export. Consuls with business experience were stationed in foreign cities, and schools were established to train salesmen for work abroad.

As trade and commerce grew, the German cities increased in size and number.

Between 1870 and 1900 German population rose from forty-one to fifty-six million and most of the growth was concentrated in cities. From the 1840's to the early 1880's many Germans had emigrated to foreign lands. In the peak year the number leaving the country had topped 200,000. But after 1880, economic opportunities increased so rapidly at home that emigration diminished. The German peasant seeking to better himself went no longer to North or South America, but to thriving industrial, mining, or commercial centers in his own country, such as Hamburg, Leipzig, Essen, Stuttgart, Cologne, or Berlin.

With industrialization and urban life, there came for workers new problems of unsanitary housing, long hours, insecurity, and the like. Many laborers embraced the teachings of the Socialists as a promising way out of their troubles. In 1877, the newly united Social Democratic party polled a half million votes and elected twelve deputies to the Reichstag. The doctrines which these Socialists preached—revolution, class conflict, thoroughgoing social and political democracy, abolition of private property, internationalism, and pacifism—were the very opposites of Bismarck's ideas and to him they seemed destructive to the state, the family, and civilization itself. He was outraged by the propagandist speeches of the Socialist deputies and by their opposition to every measure he sponsored. He therefore sought to suppress Socialism in two ways: to crush it by force, and to kill it by kindness.

In 1878 there were two unsuccessful attempts by madmen to assassinate the venerable Emperor William I. Bismarck made use of the resulting public excitement by claiming that the insane men were associated with the Socialists. He dissolved the Reichstag and secured the election of a new one which shared his opinion of the Social Democrats. At once, over the protests of Catholic Centrists and of Progressives, the majority of Conservatives and National Liberals passed a severe law against Socialist propaganda. Though enacted at first for only four years, it was reënacted several times and remained in effect till 1890. It forbade the circulation of Socialist books, pamphlets, and newspapers, empowered the

police to break up Socialist meetings and suppress Socialist publications, and put the trial and punishment of Socialist offenders in the hands of the police.

Yet here again Bismarck failed. The more rigorous was the enforcement of the law against the Socialists, the more effective became their propaganda and the example of their "martyrs,"—and the more solid and influential became the Social Democratic party. The party maintained its organization in Germany, waged a war of words against Bismarck from neighboring countries, and even increased its representation in the Reichstag. In 1881 it won twelve seats in that body, and by 1890 it won thirty-five.

But Bismarck did not rely on repression alone. He realized that the workers had many just grounds for complaint. As a "junker" landlord he had no great sympathy for the new industrial capitalists. As a nationalist and militarist he wanted the mass of the German people to be strong, healthy, and contented. In addition, Bismarck thought that by removing the most acute economic grievances of the laboring class, he could make it loyal to the state and immune to Socialist propaganda. Consequently, in the 1880's he sponsored an elaborate and well-considered program of social legislation—a kind of "new deal"—which was eventually imitated in most other industrial countries, in the United States, for example, some fifty years later. For this program, he secured support from the Conservatives who believed in the old Prussian tradition of benevolent paternalism and from the Catholic Center Party which was pledged to work for social reform.

In 1883 a law established insurance for workers against sickness. The next year employers were compelled to insure their employees against accidents. In 1887 the labor of women and children was drastically limited, the hours of work were restricted in various industries, Sunday was set aside as a day of rest, and an elaborate system of government regulation and supervision of factories and mines was set up. In 1889 arrangements were made to insure laborers against old age and inability to work. Thus by 1890 the German workers were better protected against exploitation and were

Dropping the Pilot. Cartoon in *Punch*, March, 1890.

more secure from the misfortunes of industrial life than their fellows in any other country. But instead of killing Socialism, this legislation, put through by the conservative Chancellor, seemed to have the opposite effect. The Socialists called the new laws half-measures and pleaded for more drastic reform.

Even before Bismarck tried to win the support of labor for the imperial government, he took another step designed in some degree to benefit the industrialists. The *Zollverein* had in general pursued a policy of low tariffs, but as German industry grew, it seemed desirable to help it to compete against older British industries by giving it an assured position in the home market. In addition, Bismarck wanted to get revenues for the imperial government without the necessity of levying assessments on the various states, which controlled local taxation. For these reasons, and against opposition of the Progressives, who believed in free trade, Bismarck in 1879 put through a much higher tariff on industrial goods.

This change did give effective protection to many German industries, but it did not help agriculture which was suffering from overseas and Russian competition. Bismarck, as a conservative and landowner, sympathized with the agricultural classes, wished to preserve a balance between agriculture and industry, and hoped, for military reasons, to keep Germany from becoming dependent on food from abroad. Accordingly in 1885 and 1887, he secured the passage of tariffs which greatly raised the import duties on agricultural products, and especially on grain. This policy served to prevent a decay of German agriculture comparable to that which occurred in England.

Austria and Italy had raised their customs duties in 1878, a year before Bismarck's first protective tariff. But it was Bismarck's action which seemed to set off a wave of higher tariffs all over Europe, and reversed the trend toward freer trade so noticeable in the 1860's. Of the major countries, only Great Britain clung to the "liberal" principles of free trade.

Against Danes, Poles, and Hanoverians who persisted in their objections to Prussian rule, Bismarck directed repressive legislation. In the Polish areas, he not only tried to force the use of the German language and to prevent hostile political activity, but also to transfer farms from Polish to German ownership. Alsace and Lorraine received some favors, but the hostility of their deputies in the Reichstag convinced Bismarck that he was right in treating them as conquered provinces and not as equals of the other German states. Toward the Jews, Bismarck was none too kindly disposed, though for political and financial reasons he refrained from public attack on them and even rebuked Adolf Stöcker, a Lutheran chaplain of William I, for his anti-Semitic activities in the 1880's. Nevertheless the bitterly anti-Jewish agitation of Stöcker and the anti-Semitic party (called National Socialist) which he founded were quite in accord with the illiberal attitude of the Chancellor toward most minority groups in Germany.

William I, whom Bismarck had made Emperor and with whom he had worked so long, died in 1888. He was succeeded by his son Frederick, but within a few months he too died, and was followed by his son, William II. The new Emperor was a young man with the same ideas on divine-right monarchy and the importance of the army as had characterized William I, but with a vanity, volubility, and impulsiveness which irritated the aging Bismarck. At the start, William II announced that he was going to continue the Chancellor in office and follow his advice. But Bismarck was set in his ways and used to running things, while William II was eager to try new ways and to be the directing force in the government. From the standpoint of the Emperor it soon became a question of "whether the Hohenzollern dynasty or the Bismarck dynasty should rule."

In March 1890 friction between the young Emperor and the old Chancellor reached a climax. They differed on Germany's policy toward Russia. They differed on the anti-Socialist policy. To check Bismarck, William II ordered that cabinet ministers should have access to him directly rather than through the Chancellor. Bismarck declined to accede to the order and William II demanded his resignation. The "Iron Chancellor" retired to his estates, where, until his death at the age of eighty-three (1898), he lived in more or less open criticism of the Emperor.

When Bismarck retired in 1890, his task was done. He had founded the Hohenzollern German Empire and put his stamp upon it. It was indeed fateful that the new Germany was created by a conservative Junker who believed in blood and iron, who distrusted democracy, and who thought that the end justified the means.

CHAPTER 50

Relative Backwardness
of Eastern Europe

A. The Russian Tsardom

While western Europe was moving toward political democracy, the Russian Empire remained autocratic. Its core was the "Great Russian" nationality, stretching out in all directions from Moscow; but by the mid-nineteenth century the expansion of the country had brought under Russian rule not only such closely related Slavic peoples as "Little Russians" (Ukrainians) and "White Russians" (Byelorussians), but many other European peoples, including Finns, Estonians, Latvians, Lithuanians, Poles, and Rumanians, besides a bewildering variety of Asiatic peoples living east of the Urals in Siberia or Turkestan. Both the Great Russians and the subject peoples were ruled autocratically by civil and military agents of the Tsar, though the Finns retained some local self-government throughout the century, and the Poles until 1831.

The Tsar Alexander I (1801–1825) had shown some sympathy with liberalism in his early years, but the reign of his sucessor, Nicholas I (1825–1855), was one of stark reaction. He stifled liberal criticism in Russia by use of secret police. He wiped out Polish liberties after the insurrection of 1831. Though he aided the Greeks in gaining their independence in 1829, he helped to prevent the Hungarians from gaining theirs in 1849. In 1850, Russia was an autocracy as despotic as that of Peter the Great.

Nicholas I died in the midst of his unsuccessful Crimean War against the Ottoman Empire, Great Britain, and France. His successor, Alexander II (1855–1881), was faced with the necessity, not only of signing a humiliating peace treaty, but of allaying criticism and discontent within Russia. Though the Russian middle class of officials, professional men, business men, and intellectuals was relatively small, it was becoming more vocal. One group with whom Nicholas I had sympathized was that of the "Slavophiles," for they believed in resisting western influences and glorifying things Russian, such as the Orthodox Church and the autocratic rule of the Tsar. Another group, the so-called "Westernizers," wished to modernize Russia by importing western science, laws, industry, and education, and to develop within the Empire some such constitutional government as existed in Great Britain or France.

To these Westernizers, Alexander II made certain significant concessions between 1861 and 1864. One of the most notable was his abolition of serfdom. Though there were areas held by free peasants and by Cossacks, nine-tenths of the land of Russia was owned in 1855 by the imperial family and some 100,000 noble families. These estates were tilled by serfs, who formed the great majority of the Russian population. Part of the produce of the fields went to the landlord. Part went to the support of the peasant village communities, or *mirs*. The serfs were bound to the soil. They paid the landlord dues in money, kind, and labor. Some two million household serfs who held no land were virtually slaves, whose services could be rented out like those of horses or oxen. The situation

649

Tsar Alexander II.
Courtesy Bettmann Archive

in this respect was worse than that of western Europe in the early middle age. Though there were exceptions, most of the Russian serfs lived in squalor, ignorance, and poverty.

First the Tsar freed the serfs on the imperial estates. Then, in the face of dogged opposition from landowners, he promulgated a decree of general emancipation in 1861. The decree abolished all legal rights of the landlords over the persons of his serfs. It gave personal freedom but no land to the household serfs. The serfs who were working on the large estates received not only freedom, but an interest in a portion of the land, which was bought from the nobles with money advanced by the government and then turned over to the village communities (*mirs*) to be parcelled out among the peasants. The whole process was very complicated and there were some in-

justices. Many peasants received too little land to afford them a living. Many landlords did not have adequate labor to work their fields. The peasants were left with a consuming hunger for more land. They were burdened by the annual payments which they had to make to the government to refund to it the purchase price of the lands. While they were freed from the authority and courts of the nobles, they were subjected to the harsh and often corrupt rule of imperial officials, judges, and tax collectors. Nevertheless, the benefits of even such emancipation as this soon showed themselves in gradually enlarged areas under cultivation, greater yield of taxes, growth of grain exports, and slowly improving conditions for the peasantry.

Another "westernizing" reform of Alexander II was the establishment of provincial assemblies. A decree of 1864 provided that each district of the thirty-four provinces, or "governments," of Russia, should have a local assembly, or *zemstvo*, composed of landed nobles and of delegates indirectly elected by townsfolk and peasants. For its district, each *zemstvo* would have authority to levy taxes, and to supervise public works, churches, schools, prisons, poor relief, and public health. Optimistic "Westernizers" thought this reform might lead to constitutional government.

Likewise the Tsar reformed the judicial system. A decree of 1862 transferred the trial of civil and criminal cases from imperial administrative officials to law courts modeled after those of western Europe. At the bottom were justices of the peace. Then came district and circuit courts. A senate acted as final court of appeal. With the decree were issued instructions for codifying the laws, establishing jury trials for criminal cases, and holding trials in public rather than in secret. But exception was made in the case of political offenders. These would still be subjected to secret, arbitrary trials by administrative officials.

Alexander II also did something to encourage elementary and technical schools, construction of railways, and development of mines. But by 1865 his reforming zeal was spent, partially as a result of a Polish revolt in 1863, which, though forcefully suppressed with comparative ease, indicated to him that western ideas were dangerous. From 1865 to 1905, the rule of Russia under Alexander II and his successors, Alexander III (1881–1894) and Nicholas II (1894–1917), was thoroughly reactionary. Critics of the government and zealous reformers were ruthlessly silenced by execution, imprisonment, or exile to Siberia. Discontent was driven underground into revolutionary secret societies, which occasionally committed acts of terrorism against the authorities. One such act occurred in 1881, when the assassination of Alexander II brought Alexander III to the throne.

Under Alexander III the policies of the Russian autocracy were both reactionary and nationalist. Centralization of administration reduced the authority of the *zemstvos* and brought even the *mirs* under government supervision. The educational system was carefully controlled from elementary school through university. The press was subjected to drastic censorship. And everywhere were agents of the secret police ready to pounce on reformers or critics of the government. In behalf of nationalism, a policy called "Russification" was pursued. It was an effort to impose the language and the Eastern Orthodox Christianity of the Great Russian people on other nationalities within the Empire. Russian sectarians who had split off from the Orthodox Church, "Uniates" (Eastern Christians reunited with the papacy), Roman Catholics (in Poland and Lithuania), and Protestant Lutherans (in the Baltic provinces) were all persecuted or harassed, in order to force them into the Orthodox fold. Similar attempts were made to enforce the use of the Great Russian language by Poles, Lithuanians, Ukrainians, and other subject peoples. One phase of Russification was persecution of Jews. They were forbidden to hold land (1882). They were ordered to live in a special district called the Jewish Pale (1890). Officials permitted or even encouraged anti-Jewish riots (*pogroms*) accompanied by the plundering and burning of Jewish property and the massacre of Jews. So intense was the persecution that in the single year 1891 some 300,000 Polish and Russian Jews emigrated from Russian territory, many of them to the United States.

In carrying out his repressive policies, Alexander III used throughout his reign, in important posts, two energetic men who were as enthusiastic as he about the bolstering of autocracy and the suppression of dissent. One was Viatscheslav Plehve (1846–1904). A lawyer of Lithuanian stock, trained at the universities of Warsaw and St. Petersburg, he organized the police throughout the Empire so well and used the ministries of justice and interior so effectively that agitation of all sorts was to a degree driven underground. Ironically enough he was, in the end, killed by the bomb of a revolutionist. The other was Constantine Pobyedonostsev (1827–1907). A teacher of civil law at Moscow, he became the tutor of Alexander III and from 1880 to 1905 was Procurator of the Holy Synod. In this position he made attempts to improve the religious education of the Orthodox clergy. But he also sought to use them and their church as instruments of propaganda for the Tsardom and for Russification. To him, as he makes clear in his *Reflections of a Russian Statesman*, western liberal and democratic innovations like jury trial and freedom of the press were dangerous if not downright immoral.

The advent of Nicholas II to the imperial throne in 1894 brought no change in policy. Centralization, repression, and Russification continued. The new Tsar was mystical and fatalistic, weak and obstinate, and much under the influence of his neurotic wife, who, though a granddaughter of the English Queen Victoria, was passionately devoted to Russian autocracy and the Orthodox Church.

Yet under Alexander III and Nicholas II events were taking place that in the long run would contribute to the downfall of the Tsarist regime in Russia. The country was undergoing industrialization, especially in textiles and metallurgy. Railways were being built. Population was growing, from 57 million in 1850, to 103 million in 1900, and to 130 million in 1914. While it continued to be largely agricultural, by 1914 one seventh of it lived in cities as against only a tenth in 1874, and one seventh of so big a population was no small number. The Empire now had as many town dwellers as France and many more factory towns than Italy.

Closely associated with the industrialization of Russia was Count Sergei Witte (1849–1915). Of Dutch extraction, he was a native of Tiflis, where his father was a government official. He began his career as a conservative journalist, but before long he became interested in railways and finance. Appointed to the imperial service by Alexander III, he continued in it for more than a decade under Nicholas II. Though an apostle of Slavophile political conservatism, Witte was an ardent advocate of western industrial and commercial development. First as head of the railway bureau, later as minister of finance, he worked for the construction of railways, and for policies of economic nationalism favorable to big business. He stabilized the currency, gave bounties to new industries, and provided protection for old ones. He sponsored some regulation

Count Sergei Witte.

of factories and some social insurance. Among his varied achievements were the construction of the Trans-Siberian railway and the introduction of the government monopoly of the sale of vodka. Despite all he did to strengthen Russia economically, he was so clearly identified with the "Westernizing" movement that, in 1906, he was forced out of office by reactionaries who had the ear of the Tsar.

In 1861, Russia had 700 miles of railway; in 1882, 15,000 miles. By 1914 the figure rose to 47,000 miles. Though it could hardly compare with Britain or Germany, Russia was already a significant producer of iron and textiles. In fact, by the early twentieth century Russia had undergone the early stages of an industrial revolution. It had developed a transportation system, a factory system, and a body of more or less skilled workers to a degree that made possible additional and more rapid industrialization. It is worth noting that the government played a larger part in this movement than in many other countries. The first railroads, for example, had been built by private capital, but usually with a guarantee by the state of a return on the money invested. In 1881, the imperial government went further and decided on outright state ownership of the railways.

As the twentieth century opened, Russia was politically an autocracy comparable with that of Louis XIV. Economically, it was a vast land of peasant agriculture, with industrialized islands bound together by a network of railways. Socially, it was primarily a peasant country with a strong landowning nobility whose main function was still service of the state, especially in the army. But it had a growing bourgeoisie, a considerable number of intellectuals dissatisfied with the political backwardness of the nation, and a rising proletariat already infected with revolutionary teachings.

B. Disruptive Nationalism in Austria-Hungary

The Dual Monarchy of Austria-Hungary showed tendencies both like those of western and like those of eastern Europe, with Austria more typical of the west and Hungary of the east. By 1867 Austria-Hungary was thrust out of both Germany and Italy. Henceforth, its attention was focussed on its own domains and on the hope of repairing its fortunes by expansion in the Balkans. But in the Balkans it encountered mounting native nationalism and growing Russian ambition, while at home it had to cope with a trend toward industrialization, liberalism, and democracy and a most ominous rising tide of nationalism among its own subject peoples.

During the period from the *Ausgleich* in 1867[1] to the World War of 1914, Austria-Hungary was ruled by the Emperor Francis Joseph (1848–1916), who sought to maintain the traditions and ceremonies appropriate to the most renowned of all the ruling houses, the Habsburgs.[2] He had had to grant constitutional government to both Austria and Hungary. But in both countries, the parliaments were long dominated by the landowning nobility and the upper middle class; and the Emperor retained the right to veto legislation and to maintain in office ministries of which the majority of the parliaments did not approve.

The legislatures of the two parts of the Dual Monarchy were supposed to settle their differences and jointly to supervise the imperial ministries of army, finance, and foreign affairs through an odd kind of joint parliament called the "Delegations," consisting of sixty representatives from the Austrian parliament and sixty from the Hungarian. They met alternately in Vienna and in Budapest. The Austrian delegates used German; the Hungarian, Magyar. Each group normally met in a separate chamber and communicated with the other in writing. In cases of failure to agree, they did meet together, but only to vote, not to debate. Such a clumsy mechanism was scarcely sufficient to cope with the increasing problems that kept arising between Austria and Hungary.

Austria, particularly in the neighborhood of the cities of Vienna and Prague, witnessed a considerable development of factory industry and of an urban proletariat, while Hungary remained more thoroughly agricultural and almost feudal in character. This difference helped to make the *Ausgleich* of 1867 an uneasy compromise. Austria wanted a protective tariff on industrial products; Hungary wished to protect farm products. The solution, which was worked out in the 1880's and which satisfied neither country, was to protect both. There were disputes, too, about the army, for the Hungarians wanted their regiments commanded exclusively by Magyars and all military orders given in the Magyar language. There was friction also about the central bank established in Vienna in 1878, about the negotiation of commercial treaties, and even about foreign policy. Yet the existence of the Dual Monarchy brought many advantages, since it maintained a large area of central Europe as an economic unit without barriers to trade. It supported a great capital at Vienna where the arts and sciences flourished amidst a conglomerate population from all parts of the Empire. And the joint strength of Austria and Hungary was sufficient to give the monarchy considerable weight among European great powers.

In the 1870's Austrian politics were much influenced by a Liberal party with anti-clerical tendencies which ran counter to the country's long Catholic tradition. But the next decade saw the rise of a Catholic party, called Christian Socialist, which was headed by a Viennese lawyer named Karl Lueger.

---

[1] See above, pp. 630–631.

[2] See picture of Francis Joseph, above, p. 630.

It won a large following among the peasantry and the lower middle class, and allies from among Catholic Poles and Czechs. Under stimulus from the Christian Socialists in the 1880's, trade unions were legalized, factories and mines regulated, working hours limited, and the labor of women and children restricted. As mayor of Vienna, Lueger made that city famous for its municipal ownership and operation of public utilities. But there was an ominous note in his leadership, for he won many followers by his passionate attacks on Jews and "Jewish capitalism." It was in the atmosphere of anti-Semitism abetted by Lueger that Adolf Hitler grew up.

In the 1880's and 1890's, the Austrian government had tried making some concessions to its subject nationalities—Czechs, Italians, Slovenes, Rumanians, Ruthenians, and Poles. It allowed relatively free use of their respective languages. It split the University of Prague into two parts, one German and one Czech. It permitted the local administrations of such cities as Cracow, Prague, and Trieste to be managed respectively by Poles, Czechs, and Italians. But all concessions only led to a demand for more and it seemed clearly impossible to give political power to the subject peoples. The Germans in Bohemia would have resented Czech rule, while the Poles would have opposed any liberties for the Ruthenians in Poland, and the Italians in Istria would have opposed rule by the Yugoslavs.

Pressure from the lower classes produced an important extension of the franchise in 1896. In 1907 universal manhood suffrage was granted and voting was made compulsory. By this time, however, Marxian Socialism was spreading among urban workers. The election of 1907 returned to the Austrian parliament 115 Christian Socialists, 62 Liberals, and 87 Socialists. These parties all found their strength in the German-speaking parts of Austria. But the rise of nationalism was ominously evidenced by an array of deputies who represented not parties, but nationalities, each eager for cultural and in some cases political autonomy. There were 82 Czech deputies, 72 Poles, 37 Slovenes, 30 Ruthenians, 15 Italians, 5 Rumanians, and 5 Jewish Zionists, a total of 246 as against 264 for the "German" parties. Yet neither the Emperor nor his advisers made any serious attempt to solve the national problem confronting Austria.

The Hungarians, too, had difficulties with subject nationalities. But they ruled with a harsher hand. They strove to impose their own Magyar language on Slovaks, Croatians, and Rumanians under their control. They abolished all local self-government in the Rumanian districts, and restricted the local autonomy that had been granted the Croatians. They kept the suffrage so limited that in 1910 there were only one million voters (chiefly Magyar) in a population of twenty million. They retained political power firmly in the hands of the Hungarian landowners and their middle class allies.

Imperial parliament building, Vienna.

Courtesy Bettmann Archive

Sultan Abdul Hamid II.

Courtesy Bettmann Archive

C. Disruptive Nationalism in the Ottoman Empire and the Balkans

While Austria-Hungary had its troubles in the late nineteenth century, the Balkan peninsula verged toward chaos as Ottoman rule gradually crumbled away. The Ottoman Sultan Abdul Hamid II began his reign in 1876 by making a pretense of adopting western institutions. He promulgated a constitution of the liberal type. But it was almost at once suspended and for thirty years it remained a dead letter. From the outset, too, the Sultan was faced with insurrections of Bulgarians and Bosnian Serbs and with Russian aggression. An ensuing Russo-Turkish war of 1877–1878 resulted in a crushing defeat for the Ottoman Empire. True, the Sultan gained interested diplomatic support of Great Britain and Austria-Hungary, who insisted, at the international congress of Berlin (1878), on softening the harsh peace conditions which Russia had demanded. But for this aid, the Sultan had to agree to British occupation of Cyprus and to Austrian administration

of the Yugoslav provinces of Bosnia, Herzegovina, and Novibazar. He also had to promise to coöperate with the great powers on a program of internal reforms, and Ottoman finances were so disrupted by the war expenditures that the country was practically mortgaged to foreigners. In 1881 control of the finances was entrusted to a commission of foreign bankers.

In addition, the treaty of Berlin of 1878 gave marked impetus to the most disruptive force at work in the Balkans—nationalism. The Sultan was compelled to recognize the complete independence of Rumania, Serbia, and Montenegro, the full autonomy of a part of Bulgaria, and a measure of autonomy for the remaining part (Eastern Rumelia). Each of the Balkan peoples at once sought, by means of propaganda, secret societies, conspiracies, and armed bands, to realize its national ambition for expansion. In vain the Sultan tried to play off the great powers against each other, especially Russia against Austria-Hungary. In vain he called in German experts to reorganize his army and his treasury. In vain did he employ terrorism, a spy system, and even massacres. The Ottoman Empire continued to crumble.

In 1882, Great Britain effected a military occupation of Egypt and established a virtual protectorate over that dependency of the Ottoman Empire. But the loss was nominal rather than real, for Egypt had been more or less independent since the early part of the century. In the Balkans, however, the decay of Ottoman rule was more meaningful. The semi-autonomous province of Eastern Rumelia revolted in 1885 and secured union with the principality of Bulgaria. Serbia, seeking "compensation" for this addition of territory by its neighbor, attacked Bulgaria and was soundly beaten. Thus Bulgaria was not only enlarged but also strengthened by a successful war, though it did not become completely independent under its own tsar till 1908.

Greece, independent since 1832, made some modest acquisitions of territory. Great Britain turned over to it, in 1864, the Ionian Islands, and, as a result of the Congress of Berlin, Greece obtained Thessaly on its northern boundaries in 1881. In 1896 the Greeks in Crete revolted, and the next

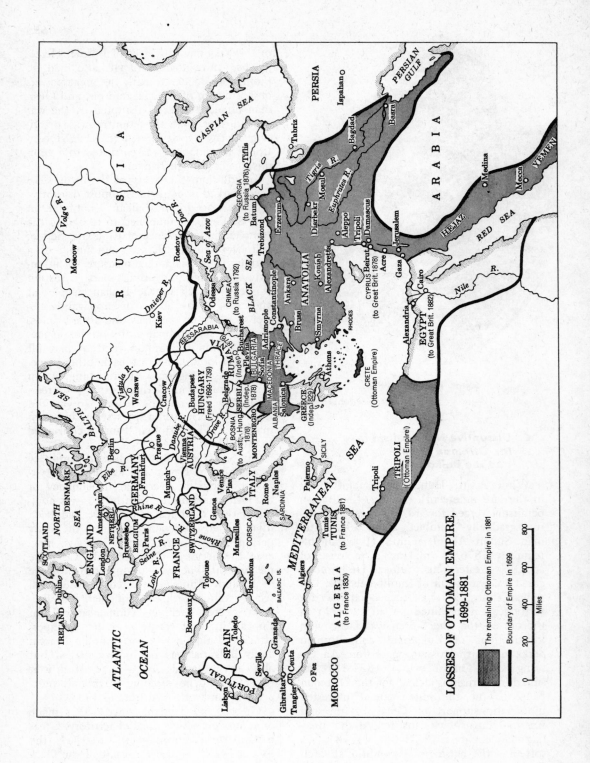

LOSSES OF OTTOMAN EMPIRE,
1699-1881

The remaining Ottoman Empire in 1881

Boundary of Empire in 1699

0   200   400   600   800
Miles

year the kingdom of Greece went to war with the Ottoman Empire on their behalf. This time the Turkish army put up a firm and successful fight. But when the Turkish army advanced on Athens, Russia, Britain, France, and Italy intervened and stopped the Graeco-Turkish War. Greece was compelled to pay an indemnity and to cede a little territory in the north. But Crete was made autonomous, put under the protection of the intervening powers, and given a son of the Greek king as its governor. In 1905 another Cretan insurrection led to an increase in Greek control of the island, for, though the fiction of the Sultan's suzerainty was maintained, Greece was permitted to appoint the Cretan governor and to drill the militia and provide officers for it. One effect of the Cretan developments was to bring to the fore an outstanding Greek patriot and statesman, Eleutherios Venizelos (1864–1936). A leader in the rising of 1896, he became the chief political figure in Crete, and so great was his popularity in Greece itself that he was summoned to Athens to be premier in 1910.

Within the Balkan countries there were many similarities of development. Each brought in a foreign prince to rule it: Greece, the Danish George I (1863–1913); Rumania, the Hohenzollern German Charles I (1866–1914); Bulgaria, the German Alexander I (1879–1886), and then another German, Ferdinand I (1887–1918). Only in Montenegro and Serbia did native dynasties rule. In the former Nicholas I (1860–1918) came from a local family of princes. In the latter the throne was fought over by two rival families whose founders had played leading roles in securing Serbian independence—the Karageorges and the Obrenovićs. The Obrenović dynasty

ruled from 1817 to 1842, and from 1859 to 1903; the Karageorge dynasty, from 1842 to 1859 and after 1903. The sway of the Obrenovićs in the second half of the nineteenth century was punctuated by occasional Karageorge insurrections, which kept the country in turmoil, and by brutal assassinations, one in 1868 and another in 1903.

Most of the Balkan countries had constitutions, parliaments, and theoretically responsible ministers. But rule was actually by factions rather than by parties. The leaders generally came from a thin upper crust of urban professional men. The influence of foreign countries played a major role in the factional politics. Despite the building of some railways and a few scattered factories, the rural life of the peasants was little changed by independence. Some schools were opened, but the great masses of the people remained illiterate.

In each Balkan country there was an intense desire to expand frontiers so as to add areas claimed for racial, linguistic, or historic reasons. One warred, openly or secretly, with another; and all cast longing eyes on territory still held by the dwindling Ottoman Empire.

Thus western Europe—industrial, democratic, and liberal—had, on its southeast border, a Balkan region which was backward, chaotic, and tumultuous. The implications of the disintegration of the Ottoman Empire were already making themselves felt. Russia and Austria were competitively seeking to gain strength by expanding their influence over the newly emerging Balkan nations. These now constituted a veritable powder magazine, highly dangerous to international peace. It would presently set all Europe in flames.

President Krueger visits his troops during Boer War.

Courtesy Bettmann Archive

CHAPTER 51

Arms, Alliances, and the New Imperialism

A. Competitive Armaments and International Alliances of the Bismarckian Era, 1866–1893

Prussia demonstrated in 1866 and 1870 what could be accomplished by a well-equipped and well-trained army based on conscription. In the ensuing decades, nearly every European state, save Britain, organized a national army based on compulsory service of all able-bodied males. In some states men had to serve one year in the military forces, in others two or three. More and more, Europe came to resemble a great armed camp with bayonets glinting along the frontiers and artillery roaring in the annual maneuvers and war games. This militarism was definitely competitive. If one country increased the size of its standing army, its neighbors felt compelled to enlarge theirs. If one nation developed an improved rifle or machine gun, all the others strove to acquire a still better one.

Britain alone continued to rely on the old-fashioned, small professional army, because her position as an island made a navy much more important to her than land forces. For many years, the British navy was unchallenged as mistress of the seas. To compete with Britain in this sphere seemed hopeless and unnecessary. But in 1898, the German Emperor William II, influenced by the writings of an American naval officer, Captain Alfred Mahan, who in a series of books was stressing the importance of sea power in warfare, and backed by aggressive German nationalism, decided

to follow the advice of his naval secretary, von Tirpitz, and to build up a great German navy. Beginning with laws enacted in 1898 and 1900, Germany created an imposing fleet of battleships, cruisers, submarines, and destroyers, second only to Britain's. In the fifteen years after 1898, Germany's annual naval expenditures rose from 30 million to 120 million dollars. Britain at once responded by increasing the number and size of her warships, so that in 1913 her naval expenditures were more than double those of Germany. Meanwhile, other nations—France, Italy, Japan, and the United States—were enlarging their navies. Naval force thus became an object of international competition like armies.

From 1871 to 1914, there were numerous war scares in Europe, but no actual wars save in the Balkans. For the first twenty years of the period, it was Bismarck (who previously had precipitated three wars) who did most to maintain peace. He now felt that it would best serve German ends. The keystone of his foreign policy was to keep France diplomatically isolated, so as to prevent her securing allies with whose aid she might wage a war of revenge on Germany. With this end in view, he developed a new kind of alliance. Before 1870, alliances had almost always been temporary affairs entered into during the actual course of a war or when an outbreak of hostilities seemed imminent. Bismarck, after the successful Franco-Prussian war, proceeded to negotiate alliances in peacetime designed to create a permanent line-up of powers which by its very strength could prevent war or, if need be, ensure victory.

In 1872 Bismarck arranged a conference in Berlin of Emperor William I of Germany, Emperor Francis Joseph of Austria, and Tsar Alexander II of Russia, to advertise to the world the cordial relations between the three powers of central and eastern Europe. The next year the members of this so-called Three Emperors' League formally agreed to work together to preserve peace and, if war should threaten, to consult together "to determine a common course of action." Despite strained relations between Russia and Austria at the time of the Russo-Turkish War of 1877–1878, the Three Emperors' League was renewed in 1881 and lasted until 1887 when it was superseded, for another three years, by a special Reinsurance Treaty between Germany and Russia.

Meanwhile in 1879 Bismarck negotiated a close defensive alliance between Germany and Austria-Hungary. This, by the inclusion of Italy in 1882, was expanded into a Triple Alliance which, repeatedly renewed, lasted until 1915. Moreover, so long as Bismarck remained at the helm in Germany, he could count, in any threatened conflict, on the neutrality of Great Britain if not on its active coöperation.

The isolation of France, so carefully secured by Bismarck, did not long survive his fall in 1890. The Tsar Alexander III of Russia was troubled by the refusal of the Emperor William II of Germany to renew the "Reinsurance Treaty." Slavophiles were urging that "Holy Russia" be purged of German cultural influence. Russian economic interests complained about the high German tariffs on wheat and rye established in 1885 and 1887. Moreover, Russia needed foreign capital to enable her to build railways and factories, to equip her armies, and to stabilize her currency. Bismarck had discouraged German loans to Russia. But what the Berlin Bourse withheld, the Paris money market supplied, and by 1890 Russia was already financially dependent on France. It must be remembered, too, that since the eighteenth century the Russian nobility had been brought up to speak French, and many spoke it in preference to Russian, while Paris and the French Riviera were favorite playgrounds for Russian grand dukes and lesser nobles.

The Tsar Alexander III disliked and distrusted the democratic politics of France. But the other forces at work gradually overcame his scruples. An informal diplomatic *entente* (understanding) between France and Russia was inaugurated in 1891. In 1893, by a military convention, Russia promised to aid France in case she were attacked by Germany, while France promised to help Russia in similar circumstances. Thus was inaugurated the Dual Alliance; and henceforth Europe was split between it and the Triple Alliance.

B. Sources of Renewed Imperialism

From 1815 to 1880, there was a slackening in colonial activities of the great powers. France lost all but the remnants of her earlier overseas empire; Spain retained only fragments of hers. Portugal's colonies, after Brazil broke away, consisted only of stagnant trading posts. To be sure, Holland still held a large domain in the East Indies, and Britain's empire encircled the globe. But the theories of *laissez-faire* were opposed to colonialism. Economic liberals pointed out that colonies were useful only for trade and this could be had without the maintenance of expensive political and military control. In addition, the example of the United States, of the Spanish American colonies, and of Brazil seemed to indicate that, once colonies had matured, they would sever their ties with the mother country and "fall away like ripe pears dropping off a tree."

Yet even in the period of waning interest in imperialism, there was some colonial activity. France, as we have seen, got complete control of Algeria in the years following 1830, and under Napoleon III acquired colonies in the Pacific and Indo-China, not to mention the ill-starred attempt to make a protectorate of Mexico.

For Great Britain, the possession of an extensive empire raised numerous problems. In Canada, conflict between royal governors and provincial assemblies led at length to a brief rebellion (1837). As a result, a commission headed by Lord Durham was sent to investigate Canadian grievances. In 1839 Durham published a lengthy report in which he advocated the union of the Canadian colonies and the grant to them of responsible government under a royal governor who should be, like the British king, a mere figurehead. Ten years later, Canadian self-government was formally recognized by the British parliament. And once this principle was sanctioned for Canada, it was soon applied elsewhere. Between 1850 and 1875, responsible self-government was granted to all the major, white-inhabited, British colonies.

But the teeming peninsula of India presented a far more difficult problem. Until past the middle of the nineteenth century the British East India Company, under general supervision of the government in London, had exercised political powers. In 1857 native unrest flamed into a revolt led by native troops (sepoys) and called therefore the Sepoy Mutiny. With some difficulty the rising was put down and the mutineers punished. The next year the British parliament deprived the Company of its political powers and vested control in a cabinet minister in London and a viceroy in India, each assisted by a small council. Though it gave no self-government to India, the Act of 1858 envisioned the possibility that some day such a grant would be made.

Even while popular interest in colonies was lessening, Britain kept acquiring new ones, for her far-flung older possessions made it easy, and sometimes defensively needful, to appropriate additional territories. Thus, for example, Britain added New Zealand (1840), Hong Kong (1842), Natal (1843), the Malay States (1874), and the Fiji Islands (1874). In addition, the older colonies received a heavy immigration from the British Isles, as Irishmen were impelled by famine to leave home, and Englishmen and Scots by bad conditions accompanying industrialization. There was heavy migration to Canada, South Africa, New Zealand, and Australia. The discovery of gold in Australia and in British Columbia, about 1850, led to a rush of gold-seekers to those areas.

During the 1870's there was a shift in the attitude toward colonies, not only in Britain under Disraeli's influence, but in other countries as well. By 1880, the new imperialism was gathering strength, and in the ensuing twenty-five years there was a scramble among the major powers to appropriate "unoccupied" or "backward" regions. In this period practically all Africa was partitioned among the rival imperialist nations, and many areas in Asia and the Pacific were seized. Though the chief competitors were Britain, France, and Germany, other nations were infected by imperialist fever. It is not easy to determine what led to this rather sudden change of attitude, for it was and is still clear that most colonies do not "pay" in the ordinary sense of bringing in more money than they cost. But some of the explanations which have usually been offered are these:

1. *Economic.* The return to high tariffs in Europe in the late 1870's and in the 1880's tended to close European markets to foreign industrial products at the very time when the growing industrialization of France, Germany, the United States, and Italy was greatly increasing the potential industrial output, and when the rise of industrial rivals was forcing the British to worry about opportunities to sell their goods. In the same period, the decline of world prices was accompanied by a prolonged depression, which, with only a few short breaks, lasted from 1873 to 1896, when the increased output of gold from South Africa tended to raise prices and stimulate business. Industrial countries eagerly turned to a search for new markets. To many, it seemed that colonies, under one's own political control, provided the safest and best kind of markets, since in them no hostile nation could put up prohibitive tariffs.

With the improvement of ocean transportation, even distant overseas colonies took on a new importance as sources of cheap food, tropical goods, and raw materials. There was growing demand not only for cotton, wool, and minerals, but for relatively new products such as palm oil, bananas, rubber, or guano, and for older ones like coffee and tea. From its own colonies, a nation might advantageously secure such goods and also ensure the dominance of its own merchants and ships in the carrying trade. The improvements in transportation (steamships) and communication (cables and telegraphs) made it much easier to acquire and govern distant overseas areas.

The same sort of explanation applies in the matter of investments. As low prices after 1873 cut profits of the new industrialists, these began to look about for new opportunities to invest their capital at more attractive rates of return. Before 1870 much money was loaned at high rates to Spanish American and other undeveloped foreign countries. But the defaults on these debts were so frequent that many capitalists welcomed the chance to invest in colonial enterprises (railways, mines, plantations) where political control seemed to give a greater assurance of safety, while need for capital kept the rate of return high.

2. *Social.* The maturing of industrial economy in Great Britain, and to a lesser degree in Germany, seemed to reduce the opportunities of quick advancement at home for ambitious young men of good education and family. Such men were the ones who traditionally could expect to find successful careers in colonial armies, governments, and business enterprises. At the other end of the scale, colonies held promise of draining off surplus population of depressed or unemployed classes, though actually there was never much emigration to tropical areas, which were the main object of the new imperialism.

3. *Political and military.* Great Britain could always find an excuse for taking a new colony in her need for coaling stations, seaports, and naval bases. Once Germany began to develop her merchant marine, and later her navy, she could advance similar reasons. With France, the fact that the country was being rapidly outstripped in population by Germany made peculiarly attractive the idea of recruiting dusky soldiers overseas. There was widespread feeling that possession of a colonial empire added to a country's influence and prestige.

4. *Nationalist.* For renewed European imperialism after 1870, there is doubtless some validity in all the reasons advanced under the three headings above. Yet there is also much of the fallacious. Colonies did not form as good markets, sources of food and raw materials, or fields for investment as did independent countries like Russia, Brazil, Argentina, or the United States. Emigration to colonial areas was relatively light after 1870. Colonies were as often political and military liabilities as they were assets.

The real driving force behind the new imperialism came from the rise of intense nationalism. The fact that Britain possessed a great empire led other countries to want one. There was a notable fascination in seeing new areas on the map colored pink or green or blue like the mother country. There was a strong feeling that an advanced and cultured nation had an obligation to spread its language and superior culture to "backward" peoples of the earth. This idea of "civilizing mission" was often mixed up with Christian missionary zeal and activity, or with the humanitarian heritage of the eighteenth-century "Enlightenment."

As the nationalism of the European nations grew more vigorous after 1870, it found outlet, not only in political speeches, military competition, and economic rivalry at home, but also in expansion overseas. National pride was swelled by raising the flag over territories whose names had the day before been unknown to the patriotic masses. National honor could be vindicated by avenging a murdered trader or missionary.

The new imperialism was all a little vague, especially as to facts and figures. But it was a rosy and compelling vision to statesmen and to newspaper readers of Europe in 1890. If liberals still raised voices against imperialist ventures, their laments were now usually drowned out by the swelling chorus of popular patriotic approval.

C. Partition of Africa

In the 1870's, except for a few coastal areas, Africa was still a dark and little known continent. Rich in resources and inhabited mainly by Negro tribes whose primitive weapons were no match for modern rifles and machine guns, it formed a most attractive sphere for the new colonial activity. Strangely enough, however, the scramble to seize and divide Africa was

Leopold II of Belgium.
Courtesy
Bettmann Archive

begun not by the great powers but by the ruler of one of the lesser countries. This was Belgium's King Leopold II (1865–1909), who was a shrewd business man as well as a rather dissolute monarch. He became interested in Africa in a curious way.

In 1840 a Scottish physician and missionary named David Livingstone had gone to Africa. In the ensuing three decades he won fame by his exploring expeditions in the south-central part of the continent and by his discovery of Lake Nyasa and of the upper courses of the Zambesi and Congo rivers. Toward the close of his life, Dr. Livingstone was reported lost in the jungle, and a New York newspaper proprietor capitalized the widespread interest in the missionary's fate by despatching an ad-

venturous Anglo-American journalist, Henry Stanley, to find him. Stanley "found" Livingstone in 1871, and then engaged in a series of important explorations of his own, which he described in thrilling fashion in his book *Through the Dark Continent*. Unable to get backing for his plans in either America or Great Britain, Stanley eventually obtained the ear of King Leopold II of Belgium and aroused his interest in the Congo River region.

Leopold, with much talk of scientific purposes, organized a private commercial company, with himself as president and chief stockholder. Through Stanley and other agents, native Congo chieftains were beguiled into turning over their lands to the company, and the work of exploiting the rubber and other products of the region

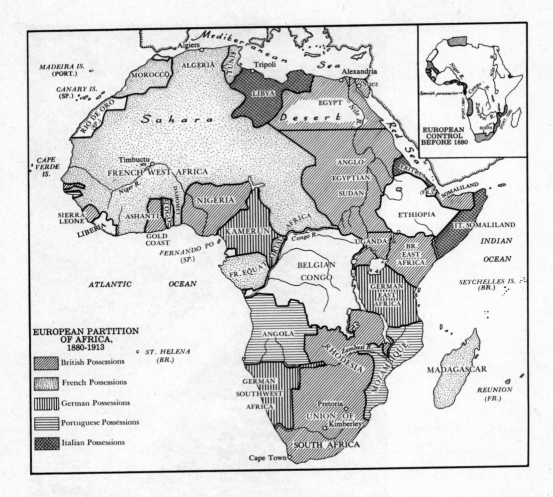

by forced labor was begun. Leopold's venture raised some questions among the other powers, and an international congress was convened at Berlin in 1885. It sanctioned the erection of Leopold's African holdings into the "Congo Free State" and laid down a few simple rules to be observed by nations acquiring African territory.

Into the Congo Free State, Leopold poured considerable capital. But he was soon reaping a rich reward. Rubber exports soared in value from $30,000 in 1886 to ten million dollars in 1908. By the latter date, however, there were numerous disclosures of outrages visited upon the natives and of the virtual enslavement of laborers who gathered the rubber. Insistent demands for sweeping reform in the Free State arose both outside and inside Belgium. Leopold yielded to public opinion, and, in return for a handsome financial compensation, transferred the Congo Free State to the Belgian

government. In what was henceforth called the Belgian Congo, Belgium thus acquired a colonial empire with an area almost eighty times her own.

But the Congo was merely a start. In the incredibly brief space of twenty-seven years, beginning in 1885 with the international congress at Berlin and ending in 1912 when Morocco passed finally under Franco-Spanish rule, the whole of Africa (save only Ethiopia and Liberia) was taken over by European countries. By 1914, of the continent's eleven and a half million square miles, the French held almost four million, the British three and three-quarters million, the Germans nine hundred thousand, the Belgians about nine hundred thousand, the Portuguese eight hundred thousand, the Italians six hundred and fifty thousand, and the Spanish a hundred thousand. Liberia remained independent because of the friendly interest in it of the United States;

Ethiopia, because of its defeat of the Italians at Adowa in 1896.

The lion's share in the partition went to Britain and to France, which had already had African holdings before 1880—Britain in the Cape Colony at the extreme south, and France in Algeria at the extreme north and in Senegal on the west coast. But Germany, after Bismarck's reluctant conversion to colonialism, got no mean extent of territory in the competition.

In tropical central Africa, the technique of acquisition was much the same. Selecting a spot, preferably one where his nation had some previous association through missionary or trading activities, the colonizer (soldier, explorer, adventurer, or official government agent) went in among the natives and persuaded their chieftain to affix his mark to a treaty turning over the territory to a European power.

In this manner, Karl Peters, by a dozen treaties secured in ten brief days, acquired for a German company 60,000 square miles in east Africa in 1884. The next year he prevailed upon Bismarck to take the company and its land under the formal protection of the German government, and within five more years, by methods similar to those of Peters, German East Africa was expanded into an imperial domain of 200,000 square miles. In much the same fashion, de Brazza of France snatched the northern part of the Congo basin from Stanley's hands, while German agents north and south of the Congo region were acquiring Kamerun and German Southwest Africa.

When the scramble in equatorial Africa was over by the 1890's, the Germans possessed, on the west side, Togoland in addition to Kamerun and German Southwest Africa; the French owned the French Congo, Dahomey, Senegal, the Ivory Coast, and French Guinea; and the British held Gambia, Sierra Leone, the Gold Coast, and Nigeria. The Portuguese had expanded their coastal trading posts into the extensive territory of Angola south of the Congo Free State, while the Spanish held Rio de Oro opposite the Canary Islands and the tiny Rio Muni in the mid-continent. On the east side of Africa, the Portuguese enlarged their old holdings on the coast to include all of Mozambique. To the north

of this was German East Africa, and still farther north was British East Africa. Thence onward to the Red Sea, Somaliland was divided among the Italians, the British, and the French, while on the Red Sea itself the Italians held the torrid coastland of Eritrea.

The conditions under which northern Africa was partitioned were somewhat different, for along the Mediterranean coast were more or less civilized Moslem countries. One of these, Algeria, had been appropriated by France long before 1870. In 1881 the French statesman Jules Ferry despatched a military expedition from Algeria into the troublesome neighboring state of Tunisia and obliged its Moslem ruler—the bey—to submit to a French protectorate. From Tunisia and Algeria, the French pushed southward, exploring along caravan routes and establishing military posts in the enormous expanse of the Sahara desert and the western Sudan, until at length they linked up their northern African colonies with their equatorial ones like French Congo and the Ivory Coast. Thus most of the great northwest shoulder of Africa came under French control.

Egypt, exploited by foreigners since the time of ancient Greeks and Romans, likewise fell prey to the new imperialism. Under its Turkish ruler, Ismail, who assumed the title of Khedive, Egypt loosened the bonds that previously tied it to the Ottoman Empire and appeared to be progressing toward full independence. But Egypt acquired new significance from the hundred-mile Suez canal which was constructed by a French company, largely financed by the Khedive through loans contracted on exorbitant terms in Europe, and opened by a gala fete in 1869. The British had originally shown slight interest in the canal, imagining it would prove impracticable. Once it was built, however, it provided a short and vital route between England and India. In 1875 Ismail, unable to meet the interest on his loans from Europeans, was desperate for money. He sought relief by selling his large holdings of shares in the Suez Canal Company, and the British government bought them.

Egyptian finances went from bad to worse, and in 1876 Ismail turned them over to a "dual control" of French and British agents. Three years later, when he tried to get rid of the foreigners, he was deposed. His successor had to submit once more to the dual control, but some of his subjects resented it, and in 1882 they revolted.

Though the French, in a momentary reaction against imperialist projects, refused to use force, the British bombarded Alexandria. A British army occupied the country, suppressed the revolt, and restored the Khedive to nominal rule, while imposing on him the duty of doing what the British told him to do. In this manner was established what amounted to a British protectorate over Egypt. The Khedive continued to "reign," but a British army remained and British "advisers" made all important decisions. Some notable reforms were instituted. Finances were put in order, the administration of justice improved, and irrigation works instituted. Moreover, a representative assembly was created in 1883, and in 1913 it was given limited legislative powers.

Up the Nile lay the Egyptian Sudan, which the British practically abandoned in 1885 after a fanatical native leader, "the Mahdi," had annihilated an Egyptian garrison, under a British general, at Khartum. But in 1898, when a French expedition under Captain Marchand proceeded overland all the way from the Congo to the upper Nile valley and at the little village of Fashoda in the Egyptian Sudan hoisted the French flag and claimed the territory for France, Great Britain insisted that the area was in its sphere of influence and sent against Captain Marchand a larger expedition with bigger guns under General Kitchener. The two commanders dealt politely with each other, while they sought instructions from home by telegraph. For a time there was a serious war scare, but eventually the French government withdrew Marchand and his men, and an Anglo-French treaty of 1899 recognized British predominance in the Egyptian Sudan.

D. British-Boer Conflict in South Africa

In South Africa, British expansion involved conflict with white people of European stock—the Boers, descendants of Dutch colonists of the seventeenth and eighteenth centuries. During the Napoleonic wars, Great Britain had taken Cape Colony from Holland. The Dutch farmers resented British rule, and when their Negro slaves were freed by the government in London in 1833, a large number of the Boers quit Cape Colony, "trekking" (emigrating) to Natal, and thence northward to the Orange and Vaal rivers. The British tried to extend their rule wherever the Boers trekked. They annexed Natal in 1843 and five years later claimed the settlements on the Orange and Vaal rivers. But the Boers in the north stubbornly withstood the extension of British rule, and in the early 1850's Britain acknowledged the independence of the Transvaal Republic and the Orange River Free State. Though in 1877 the British tried to reassert their claim to the Transvaal, the Boers defeated a small British force at Majuba Hill (1881). Gladstone, still representing anti-imperialist liberal doctrines, withdrew the British troops and recognized anew the country's virtual independence.

Elated by their success, ignorant of the full power of Britain, fanatical in their devotion to Calvinism, the Boer farmers

Cecil Rhodes. From a bust by Henry Pegram.

became more truculent and even dreamed of expelling the British from all South Africa. But the discovery of diamonds at Kimberley (about 1870) and of gold in the Rand region (1886) brought numerous foreign fortune hunters, most of them British. Among them was Cecil Rhodes, who won enormous wealth in gold and diamond mines and became the outstanding promoter, financier, and statesman of South Africa, and a leading exponent of aggressive British imperialism. In 1889 he organized the British South Africa Company which acquired title to a vast area of unsettled land and began developing this territory, later known as Rhodesia. From 1890 to 1896 Rhodes, as prime minister of Cape Colony, schemed to take over the Dutch republics of Transvaal and the Orange River Free State. He dreamed, too, of extending British sway northward and of building a Cape-to-Cairo railway. He is best remembered in the United States for the endowment he left after his death to bring young American "Rhodes Scholars" to study at Oxford where they might learn to understand Britain and to advance Anglo-American friendship.

By annexing Zululand in 1887, the British shut off the Transvaal from the sea, and in 1895 a certain Dr. Jameson, a friend of Rhodes, responding to complaints of British gold-seekers who were denied citizenship by the Boers, led an armed raid into the Transvaal with the avowed purpose of overthrowing its government. Though the Jameson raid failed of its purpose, it greatly embittered relations between the British and the Transvaal government headed by Paul Krueger, a hardy old Dutch pioneer. At last in 1899 the republics of the Transvaal and the Orange River Free State, in alliance, went to war with Great Britain. At the outset the Boers took the offensive and won some brilliant victories. But though they knew the country as only frontiersmen can and had able generals like Louis Botha and Christian de Wet, they could muster only an ill-equipped and irregularly formed army of 40,000 men or less.

The British, stirred by their defeats, raised volunteers in Britain, Canada, Australia, and New Zealand, and eventually poured an army of 350,000 men into South Africa under the command of Lord Roberts and Lord Kitchener. It was an odd, elusive, bushwacking war, with the Boers retreating into the hinterland only to sweep out on isolated British detachments, and it was long and bitterly fought. Even after Pretoria, the capital of Transvaal, fell, a sort of fierce guerilla warfare ensued for two years. Finally the weight of numbers and equipment told, and in May 1902, by the treaty of Vereeniging, the Boers laid down their arms on condition that the British respect the Dutch language and grant self-government to the former Dutch republics. The British lived up to their pledge.

Despite the lingering hostility of the Boers, a plan for confederation of South Africa won approval and was ratified by the British parliament in 1909. By it, Cape Colony, Natal, Transvaal, and the Orange River Free State were formed into the Union of South Africa, a union modeled after the Dominion of Canada. In a sense the formation of the federation was a triumph for the Boers. They elected a majority of the members of the Union Parliament and one of their number, General Louis Botha, who had fought valiantly against the British, became prime minister and remained in office till his death in 1919. He was succeeded by another Boer, General Smuts, who likewise had fought against Great Britain. Anti-British sentiment did not altogether die among the Boers, and in both the First and Second World War, there was, at the start, serious difficulty in securing South African support for Great Britain.

The Boer War had many repercussions on Britain. The physical examination of volunteers for the army showed the ravages of two generations of slum-living and factory work on the health of the British lower classes and gave a marked impetus to social legislation and town planning designed to remedy conditions. The war provided an opportunity for anti-imperialists to point out the costs, the dangers, and the wastefulness of imperial expansion.

But anti-imperialist criticisms were drowned out by the rising chorus of patriotic enthusiasm. Young newspaper correspondents like Winston Churchill sent back from the battlefields glowing accounts of British bravery, and Rudyard Kipling, who had been telling in prose and verse of the romance and color of British rule in India, turned his attention to South Africa. Newspaper readers were provided a highly flavored and much romanticized version of the glories of imperialist expansion.

E. Imperialism in Asia, the Pacific, and the Caribbean

If the last years of the nineteenth century and the first years of the twentieth witnessed intensive imperialist activity in Africa, other sections of the world were by no means neglected. Germany, Great Britain, and the United States vied with each other in economic penetration of Latin American countries by selling goods and making loans there. The United States in 1898 fought a brief war with Spain over conditions in Cuba. At the end of the conflict, Cuba was given independence qualified by certain American controls, and the United States took possession of Puerto Rico, Guam, and the Philippines. In 1898 Hawaii was likewise annexed, and in 1899–1900 the United States shared with Britain and Germany in the partition of the Samoan Islands.

By 1900 almost all the Pacific Islands had been taken over by European nations or the United States. Britain and France, first in the field, got the majority. But Holland still held the major part of the extensive and very valuable East Indies, and Germany not only secured a portion of New Guinea, and of the islands to the northward, and the two largest islands of the Samoan group, but purchased in 1899 the Caroline Islands from Spain.

On the mainland of Asia, Europeans were also extending their sway. Russia was colonizing Siberia, which had been enlarged by the forced cession from China of all territory north of the Amur river (1858). Britain moved outward from India by taking over Burma and Baluchistan in the 1880's and the Malay States north of Singapore. France added Annam and Tonkin (1884) to Cochin-China and Cambodia, thus creating an extensive Indo-Chinese domain, which was partly a colony and partly a protectorate. But the really

crucial question from the 1890's onwards was whether foreign powers would seize and partition the gigantic and decaying Chinese Empire. Here a new imperialistic competitor entered the scene. It was Japan.

Japan had closed itself off from Europeans (save for a Dutch trading post) from the seventeenth century till 1853–1854, when an American Commodore, Matthew Perry, "opened" Japan and negotiated a treaty permitting American ships to use Japanese harbors. Other nations quickly obtained similar concessions, and Japan experienced an inrush of western influences. In the ensuing decades, Japan underwent a veritable revolution. The emperor (or mikado) was restored to the authority long exercised in his name by "shoguns"; feudalism was ended; western industrialism, education, and militarism were imported and adapted to native traditions. Japanese pride in their race and their history soon found expression in something much akin to western nationalism and imperialism.

Britain had wrested Hong Kong from China in 1842, and other nations had secured special rights in the "treaty ports." But the real despoilment of China was begun by the Japanese. In 1894–1895 Japan waged war on China and by the peace treaty detached Korea from the Chinese Empire (she did not annex it outright till 1910), acquired the large island of Formosa, and obtained Chinese recognition of her rule in Liu Chiu islands, including Okinawa. Japan would likewise have taken over the Liaotung peninsula and Port Arthur, had not Russia, backed by France and Germany, intervened. At this point, European countries rushed in to acquire, by lease, control of Chinese port areas. Britain got Wei-haiwei; France, Kwangchow; Germany, Kiaochow. Russia, having prevented Japan from taking the Liaotung peninsula and Port Arthur, leased them for herself (1898).

The Chinese Empire, under the weak rule of the Manchu dynasty, was without military power to resist foreign aggression, and pleas of the United States for an "open door" in China for all foreign traders went more or less unheeded. In 1900 a Chinese patriotic anti-foreign society, called the "Boxers," committed outrages on foreigners which led to a joint British-French-German-

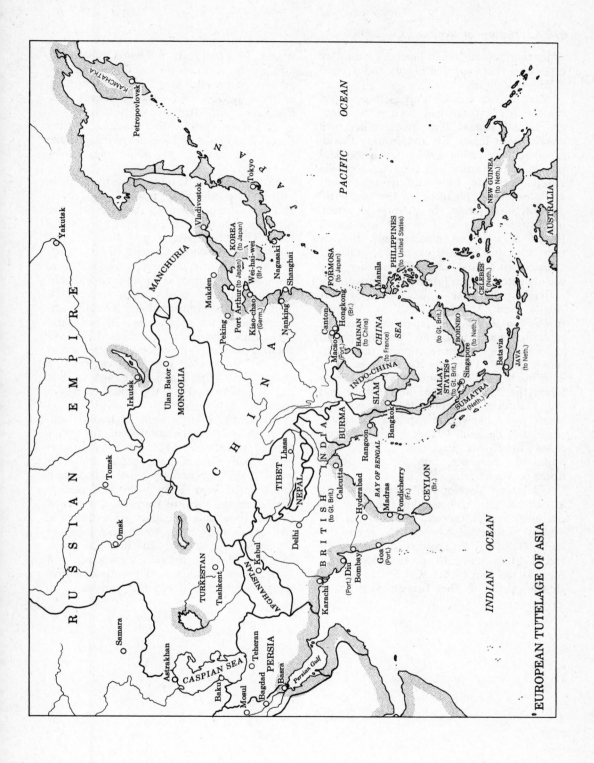

EUROPEAN TUTELAGE OF ASIA

American-Russian-Italian-Japanese military expedition that captured Peking and exacted a large indemnity.

After Russia secured Port Arthur, it became clear that she had designs on Manchuria and Korea. This brought her into conflict with Japan. For the ensuing Russo-Japanese War (1904–1905), Japan was well prepared. Her army had been doubled between 1895 and 1904 and its equipment vastly improved. Japan began the war, without any declaration, by a surprise attack on Russian ships at Port Arthur. Russia fought at a serious disadvantage, for her trans-Siberian, single-track railway was not sufficient to handle war traffic and her navy was defeated by the Japanese. The war was marked by Japanese land victories at Port Arthur and Mukden, and by internal troubles in Russia. But Japan was well-nigh exhausted when the conflict was brought to a close through the mediation of the American president, Theodore Roosevelt, in 1905. The treaty of Portsmouth (N. H.) transferred the leased areas of Port Arthur and the Liaotung peninsula from Russia to Japan. Japan likewise re-acquired the southern half of Sakhalin Island, which had been ceded to Russia back in 1875. Russia promised, moreover, not to interfere in Korea or Manchuria.

While such developments were occurring in eastern Asia, the western fringe of the continent also witnessed the clash of imperialist interests. Moving in from the south, Great Britain acquired between 1839 and 1901 a series of protectorates from Aden at the foot of the Red Sea to Kuwait at the head of the Persian Gulf, and

sought to extend its influence northward into Persia (Iran). Meanwhile Russia was pressing southward into Persia, intervening in local politics and seeking concessions. Finally in 1907 Russia and Britain agreed to divide up Persia into "spheres of influence." Russia was to have the north, Britain the south, while both could operate in the center.

Everywhere the Europeans went in their imperialistic advances into Africa, Asia, and the Pacific Islands, they carried the blessings and the curses of modern civilization. They brought in new diseases and improved medicines to cure them. They brought the Christian religion and sectarian disputes. They brought in modern industry and the exploitation of workers in factories. They brought improved agriculture and forced labor on plantations. Though the French and the Portuguese treated civilized colored peoples more or less as equals, the British, Americans, and Germans drew a sharp "color line" and were apt to live like exclusive aliens in the midst of native peoples.

But in the balance sheet of imperialism, some things must be entered on the credit side of the ledger. The imperialist powers built roads and canals, ports and railways. They "opened up" many backward and isolated areas. They introduced modern sanitation and medical knowledge. To some degree they succeeded in educating the natives, in implanting some knowledge of Christian ideals, and in instilling such Western ideas as those of democracy and nationalism, which would eventually prove dangerous to the occupying powers.

CHAPTER 52

Revolutionary Cultural Developments

A. In Science

Science had made dazzling advances in the period between the French Revolution and the middle of the nineteenth century.[1] This progress was accelerated in the years from 1850 to 1914. There were new discoveries of great importance, and every phase of life—health, food, transportation, industry, agriculture, education, philosophy, religion —were increasingly affected by the impact of science. Scientific research became firmly established in universities and as an adjunct of business enterprises. Scientific knowledge (of greater or less accuracy) was spread among the masses by schools, books, lecturers, and newspapers. The physical conditions and the intellectual climate of European life were increasingly shaped by the onward march of science.

For influence on later thought, the most significant scientific development of the period was the idea of evolution and theories as to how it took place as propounded by Alfred Russel Wallace (1823–1913) and Charles Darwin (1809–1882). For Wallace, the theory was to some degree a flash of inspiration. For Darwin, it was the result of careful observation in the South Seas (1831–1836) and suggestions drawn from Lamarck, Lyell, and Malthus's *Essay on Population*. With due credit to Wallace, who had also been reading Malthus, Darwin set forth his new ideas in his chief work, *On the Origin of Species by Means of Natural Selection, or the Preserva-*

[1] See above, pp. 582–586.

tion of Favored Races in the Struggle for Life (1859). Darwin held that the separate species of animals and plants were not the results of special acts of creation, but that they had "evolved" from earlier species by natural processes. Of these processes, "natural selection" was the most important. The argument ran like this. All individuals vary from each other. Certain of these variations will favor the individual's survival in its struggle to live and reproduce. Such favored individuals will survive longer and have more offspring. Thus the advantageous variation will tend to be fixed in the species, and as such variations accumulate a new species will be developed from the old one. The idea of "evolution" was by no means new. But here was a seemingly simple and natural way to explain how it could come about.

On the popular mind, Darwinian biology made a most profound impression. A philosopher like Herbert Spencer tried to lift all history and all thought into a Darwinian pattern. Publicists attempted to apply Darwinism to the evolution of nations and classes and to justify aggressive nations or capitalists as evidencing "survival of the fittest" in a "struggle for existence."

While all this pseudo-Darwinism was being spread about, actual Darwinian biology was undergoing important modifications. The central fact of biological evolution came to be accepted by all reputable scientists, and the discovery of skeletal remains of prehistoric human beings or near-human beings in England, France,

Germany, and far-off Java indicated that man as a physical being was descended from some earlier form of life. But it was demonstrated that "acquired characteristics" could not be inherited, as Lamarck and Darwin had imagined. And an Austrian Augustinian monk, Gregor Mendel, by a series of experiments on sweet-peas in the garden of his monastery, indicated that evolution is more likely to occur by sudden leaps or "mutations" than by gradual change. Clearer understanding was reached of the mechanism of heredity.

If biology made the most impact on the minds of people, it was probably medicine that affected their lives most directly. Before 1870, Lister and Pasteur had laid foundations for antiseptic surgery and the germ theory of disease. In the ensuing decades medical knowledge advanced by leaps and bounds, and medical practice was revolutionized. Pasteur himself developed a method of immunization against rabies. The bacilli of cholera, lockjaw, diphtheria, bubonic plague, and other diseases were isolated. The means of transmission of typhoid fever (polluted water, milk, etc.) and of malaria and yellow fever (mosquitoes) were detected. Innoculations were developed, and preventive measures taken. Along with these advances came others in

Louis Pasteur.

Photograph from Underwood and Underwood, New York

surgery, such as those which made appendectomy a relatively simple and (by the use of anaesthetics) painless operation. Such progress was soon reflected in a falling death rate in all civilized countries. For example, in Germany it dropped from 25.3 per thousand in 1881 to 11.1 in 1930.

In physics and chemistry, progress was no less notable. Hertz discovered the "ether waves" that Marconi presently utilized for wireless telegraphy (1895). Modern radio was made possible through the vacuum tube which grew out of the work of two British scientists, Thomson and Richardson, and was invented by De Forest in the United States (1907). Röntgen discovered X-rays in 1895, while Pierre Curie and his wife Marie isolated radium from pitchblende three years later. Meanwhile other scientists were beginning to open up the field of sub-atomic physics and to show that the atom itself was made up of a nucleus and of electrons. As for chemistry, it was yoked ever more closely to industry. Factories turned out chemical products cheaply and in large quantities. Organic and inorganic compounds were synthesized. One of the most significant achievements was the development, on the eve of World War I, of processes by which nitrogen in the air could be turned on a commercial scale into either munitions or fertilizers.

In the realm of psychology, Wilhelm Wundt, "the father of physiological psychology," indicated in his major book (1872) a physical basis for thought and behavior and a relationship of human minds to those of lower animals. Under his leadership, psychology turned from introspection to observation and from speculation to experiment, and became a laboratory science.

At the end of the nineteenth century, just when it seemed to many persons as if scientific progress might speedily lead to a new synthesis of human thought, which would be strictly materialistic and deterministic, any such outcome was rendered dubious by novel developments in physical science. In the very last year of the century, Max Planck advanced a new notion called the "quantum theory," according to which energy is given off by a vibrating body in little lumps or packets or units (called quanta) and not steadily or with a wavelike

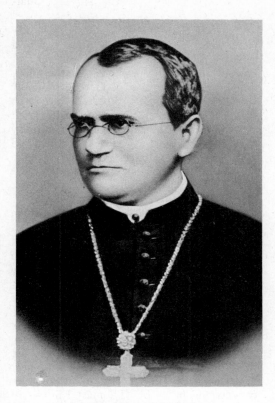

Gregor Mendel (d. 1884).

Courtesy Bettmann Archive

ebb and flow as the older physics had assumed. Planck's work soon received confirmation and extension from a wide variety of sources. Investigations of stellar spectra and of the sun bore out the new ideas and it came to be held that heat and light from the sun and other stars, never satisfactorily explained by the older physics, arose from energy given off by atoms as they changed from one state to another. Work with radium also demonstrated that the old idea of the immutability of elements was not correct. Radium itself is always breaking down into lead, and other elements like uranium undergo similar disintegration. On the eve of the first World War, the "new physics" was already unsettling the minds of scientists and casting doubts on long accepted axioms.

Another shock to nineteenth-century physics came from the Michelson-Morley experiment in 1887. Michelson and Morley, two American scientists, showed that the ether, long assumed to be the medium in which light waves (and later radio waves)

undulated, could not be detected, and therefore could not be held to exist. This conclusion eventually led Albert Einstein to propound his "Special Theory of Relativity" in 1905 and his "General Theory of Relativity" in 1915. According to Einstein, Newtonian physics had been guilty of a kind of scientific provincialism. It had treated motion in space either as relative to our own solar system, or later as relative to a great motionless ocean of ether filling all space. Now that the idea of ether had to be discarded, Einstein worked out ways of stating motion so that the statement would be equally correct for an observer on the Earth, or on Sirius or some other star. These statements involve very elaborate mathematical concepts. They use the velocity of light as an absolute (the same for all observers) and they make time a fourth dimension (in addition to length, breadth, and thickness). Einstein's "Relativity" did not change ordinary measurements on earth, but it did alter astronomical concepts.

While physicists and astronomers were plunging deeper into an un-Newtonian world of electrons, relativity, and space-time, psychology too was undergoing revision. From the time of Hobbes and Locke, man had been regarded as a thoroughly rational animal. The social sciences, like economics, had been built on the notion that man made rational choices and behaved in a logical manner. Now this was changed, partly through the work of Wundt's disciples, who stressed the animal character of man's mental behavior, and partly through the rise of psychiatry and "psychoanalysis." The latter, as practiced by Sigmund Freud, showed that a good deal of human behavior springs from unconscious or subconscious sources—repressed sexual urges, forgotten childhood experiences, suppressed fears and conflicts. Altogether, the newer psychology indicated that man is only a partly rational animal, and that much of his behavior is conditioned not by logical thought but by psychological forces of which he is partly or wholly unaware.

Influenced by these trends, sociologists contended that human groups are just as lacking in rationality as individuals. From such work, together with the development of modern advertising, were derived techniques for influencing mass behavior, which were to be tentatively tried out in World War I and used with appalling effects in the 1930's.

B. In Technology

As science progressed, it produced a continuing and increasing impact on industry. New processes were evolved; new ideas were applied; new products were developed; the total volume of production increased with startling rapidity.

Coal and iron had been the basis of the Industrial Revolution and they remained basic in the swift advance of industrialism. British production of coal grew from 110 million tons in 1870 to 265 million in 1910, and of pig iron from six to nine million tons. But in Germany, output rose in the same period even faster. That of coal increased from 37½ million tons to 222 million, and that of pig iron from two to almost fifteen million tons. By 1910, not only had Britain lost her industrial predominance, but so had Europe, for in that year the United States was producing 415 million tons of coal and more than 27 million tons of pig iron.

The application of the Bessemer and Siemens processes made it easy to produce steel from iron in large quantities and cheaply. Cheap steel made it possible to expand the railroads and to build steamships. By the 1890's, a revolution in ocean transportation had taken place; the sailing ship was being driven from the seas by the faster and more reliable steamship.

Cheap steel also made possible all sorts of machinery, and improved machine tools like the power lathe and the power press made for better and more precise machines. Britain's power looms in the cotton industry increased from 475,000 in 1870 to 700,000 in 1910. But whereas they had constituted far more than half the world total at the former date, they were only thirty per cent of it at the latter. Moreover, a new factor was appearing in the world of textiles. A French nobleman, Count Hilaire de Chardonnet had patented, in 1884, a process for making a fiber resembling silk from wood pulp. By 1910, some two and a half million pounds of "artificial silk" or "rayon" were being produced, by the Chardonnet process, and a good deal more by the British "viscose" process. And such amounts were merely an augury of the great expansion of the synthetic fiber industry that was to come. Moreover, textiles, old and new, were no longer being dyed by the old natural coloring agents like indigo, but rather by a profusion of new chemical dyes, often derived from coal tar.

Even more revolutionary was a new force which man was beginning to master. Electricity had been known since the eighteenth century, and the principle of the dynamo to generate it had been discovered by Faraday in 1831. But a whole series of developments, inventions, and adaptations were necessary before electricity could be widely used. Electric motors and dynamos were common by the 1890's. Electric lighting, which had begun with the use of the arc light in the 1870's, began rapidly to oust gas jets with the invention of the incandescent bulb by Thomas Edison in 1879. Three years earlier, Alexander Graham Bell had exhibited the first telephone, and before the end of the century telephone lines stretched for thousands of miles through Europe and America. These continents had been linked by a cable in 1866. But communications across oceans were eventually made much easier by the invention of radio or "wireless" in 1895 by Guglielmo Marconi. The uses of electricity seemed endless, for it could be applied to vacuum cleaners, sewing machines, stoves, refrigerators, trolley cars, railways, and industrial machinery. The age of electricity was even symbolized by the substitution in New York in 1888 of electrocution for hanging as the means of executing criminals.

Local transportation was much affected by improvements in the bicycle which gave it a great popularity in the years after 1890. But even more significant was the development of the automobile. After a variety of experiments in the 1880's, practicable automobiles were introduced in the 1890's. At first, France took a lead in producing them, but by 1910, the United States was making 181,000 each year, three fourths of the world output. And already some were Fords, for by that time Henry Ford was introducing the assembly line techniques of mass production that were to make cheap cars possible.

Though some of the early automobiles were powered by steam or electricity, the rapid improvement of the internal combustion gasoline engine soon made it not only the most efficient motive power for cars, but also available for other uses. Motor boats were not uncommon by 1900, and before that date the Count von Zeppelin and the Brazilian Santos-Dumont were experimenting with motor driven dirigible balloons. While "zeppelins" proved practicable, and truly successful flights were being made by 1906, the future lay with heavier-than-air craft. The first airplane flight was in 1903 by a machine constructed by the American brothers Wilbur and Orville Wright. In 1909, the French aviator Blériot flew a monoplane across the English Channel from Calais to Dover. The age of aviation was dawning.

A competitor to the gasoline engine was the internal combustion engine using heavier oil for fuel and fired by compression. It was developed by the German Rudolf Diesel in the 1890's, and was soon applied to ships, locomotives, and the generation of electricity. Another power source for dynamos was the steam turbine. Though the principle of the turbine is as old as the windmill, it remained for Sir Charles Parsons, an English engineer, to adapt it to steam in the 1880's. As turbines were improved they turned out to be much more efficient for many uses than the old Watt-type steam engine.

In other fields, too, innovation proceeded apace and one improvement led to another. For example, from wood pulp or cellulose, "celluloid" was first made in the United States in 1869. From cellulose, artificial silk was produced, as we have seen. From cellulose, too, was made in 1887, by George Eastman, the roll film which dramatically improved and speeded the processes of photography, made the simple camera possible, and permitted the development of the motion picture by Thomas Edison (1891) and others. But even more important, ways of making paper from wood pulp were developed in the 1880's that made it much cheaper than the earlier rag paper. Cheap paper meant cheaper magazines, books, and newspapers. The invention of a machine for setting type, the linotype, by Mergenthaler, a German-born American, in 1885 made it still less expensive to produce printed matter. Similarly the typewriter developed in the 1870's and 1880's made correspondence easier and created not only the new profession of typist, but opened up ever growing possibilities of employment for women.

Not all the new inventions were designed for peaceful purposes. Both the zeppelin and the airplane were capable of military use. Alfred Nobel, a Swedish chemist, intended dynamite for peaceful ends when he introduced it in 1867, but his invention ushered in a new era of high explosives. Sir Hiram Maxim, an American who became a British subject, invented the first truly automatic machine gun in 1884 and later an explosive called cordite. His brother, Hudson Maxim, developed a smokeless powder, and his son, Hiram Percy Maxim, created the Maxim silencer for making firearms noiseless. It was an American, too, John Holland, who in 1875 made the first practical submarine. By 1900, most of the great powers were adding them to their navies.

This incredible series of inventions and technological changes did not consist in a series of isolated events. They tended to be interconnected and one development led to another and the two of them to a third. Automobiles forced the improvement of highways, tremendously stimulated the rubber industry, and greatly expanded oil production and refining. But the improvement of small electric motors made the "self-starter" possible and led to a more rapid increase in automobile production. Or again, steamships made it possible for Great Britain to import much of its food, and, at the same time, shipbuilding became a major industry in Britain.

Taken as a whole, the scientific, industrial, and technological developments in western Europe and the United States from 1870 to 1914 changed the way of living of the peoples concerned much more than they had been changed in the two centuries preceding 1870. They permitted an astounding increase in population. The population of Germany, for example, grew from 40 million to 65 million in the forty years after 1870. They led to rapid enlargement of cities and a relative (and often an absolute) decline in the rural areas. In Germany there were in 1870 eight cities of over 100,000 inhabitants. In 1910 there were forty-one. Moreover, the growing cities were linked together by rapid transportation (trains, ships, automobiles) and by rapid communications (telegraph, cable, telephone, radio). In them dwelt vast masses of people, most of them industrial workers of one sort or another. These new urban masses were better educated than previous generations, for state-supported education was becoming more general and more democratic. But they were also easily influenced by the strident slogans of the new mass media like the cheap newspapers. Europe was rapidly becoming richer and more prosperous. It was also getting to be less stable as the unrooted city-dweller replaced the old-time peasant as the typical European.

C. Materialism in Philosophy and Realism in Literature and Art

Amid the sensational advances of science and industry in the latter half of the nineteenth century, there was a vogue for "materialism" in philosophy and for "realism" in literature and art. Broadly speaking, materialism meant an explanation of everything by reference only to forces detectable by human senses, and a consequent ignoring of spiritual concepts.

Evolutionary thought as applied, not only to the origin of man and animals, but to the geologic features of the earth, the formation of the solar system, and the development of human society and institutions (including law, government, the family, language, and religion), seemed to many persons to provide a satisfactory explanation of how things got to be as they are, without the help of any supernatural Creator. This was apparently reënforced by developments in anthropology, archaeology, and biblical criticism.

Archaeologists uncovered a vast mass of data about primitive and prehistoric man. Anthropologists made elaborate studies of primitive myths and religions and of primitive cultures. Critics subjected the Bible to a searching investigation as a document in the evolution of religion. Some of this "higher criticism" was done in a reverent spirit, but much of it with a feeling of antipathy to revealed religion.

The outstanding philosopher of Darwinian materialism was Herbert Spencer. In 1860 he issued the prospectus of his *Synthetic Philosophy*, an enormous work in ten volumes, upon which he was engaged for the next thirty-six years. In it he applied the principles of evolution to philosophy, psychology, sociology, and ethics. He held that everything, organic and inorganic, had evolved naturally by a progression "from the homogeneous to the heterogeneous," from the undifferentiated to the highly specialized. Behind this evolution Spencer thought there was an unknowable power or cause, but in his work he focussed his attention on knowable combinations of matter and motion. To him society was an evolving organism, religion originated in the worship of ancestral ghosts, and the industrial competition and extreme individualism of the capitalist age was an example of the "struggle for existence."

If trends of the nineteenth century led to materialism in fields of thought, they tended to produce a new "realism" in literature. To be sure, there was much surviving romanticism in all countries. Rudyard Kipling was quite romantic about British imperialism, Robert Louis Stevenson about Scottish history and the South Seas, and Edmond Rostand about French history. But the outstanding movement was toward a realistic treatment of men and society—a realism grimed with factory smoke, sordid with slum-living, and full of toil and sorrow and discouragement. The tendency had been evident in the great English novelists of the mid-century, for, though Dickens, Thackeray, and George Eliot retained romantic elements, they also tried to depict real people, occupied with contemporary problems. If Thackeray often dealt with historical subjects, if George Eliot chose romantic Italy for the setting of some of her books, and if Dickens was frequently sentimental, still Thackeray bitterly satirized the British upper classes, George Eliot put very real country people and poor people in her books, and Dickens exposed the conditions of the working classes with a humor that was sometimes grim.

After the mid-century, realism steadily gained ground. Flaubert in *Madame Bovary* gave an intensely sordid picture of French country life and human passions. Even more consciously realistic was Émile Zola, who in the years after 1871 turned out twenty somber volumes in which he traced the lives of several generations of a French family and sought to portray every phase of French life and society. Anatole France, with a glittering and facile style that won him fame and fortune, mingled witty satires and philosophical and critical works with realistic novels dealing both with contemporary life and historical scenes.

In England, George Meredith employed realism in a psychological analysis of his characters, while Thomas Hardy devoted his talents to studies of the fateful workings of the "struggle for existence" in village and peasant life in the English countryside of "Wessex." Psychological analysis of the upper classes was carried further by Henry James, who was born in America but lived in England, while social criticism reached a high point in the pungent dramas of George Bernard Shaw, published with long expository introductions, and in the fantasies and novels of H. G. Wells.

The Norwegian Ibsen carried realism on the stage to a new peak in his grim dramas. In Germany, Sudermann wrote both dramas and plays about city dwellers, while Hauptmann turned to a realistic presentation of peasant life. In Russia, a whole galaxy of novelists endowed that country with a great literature, much of it terribly realistic in its portrayals of peasants and nobles, officials and intellectuals, and gloomy with an oppressive sense of the social problems that weighed on the country. The greatest of all the Russians was Leo Tolstoy, whose *War and Peace* is an immense and incomparable panorama of Russia at the time of the Napoleonic invasions. In his later life Tolstoy turned to pacificism and a kind of revolutionary, Christian mysticism.

Against the major realistic trend in European letters was a series of reactions or counter trends of some significance. One was toward "symbolism," which sought "not a literal exactness but a suggestive use of words." It was exemplified in France by the poetry of Mallarmé and Verlaine, and in England by the prose of Walter Pater and the verse of Swinburne. Symbolism at length degenerated into "art for art's sake," a conscious decadence, an emphasis on form rather than content, in a school known as that of the *fin de siècle* (end of the century), which reached its zenith in the affectation and the wit of Oscar Wilde.

Painting may have been prevented from going realistic in the same way as literature by the invention of photography. When a camera could reproduce a scene with exactness, pictorial artists, if they were to surpass the machine, had to seek for more than accuracy. The major school of painters of the late nineteenth century was that of the French "impressionists," who sought by a skillful use of light, shade, and color to give a sense of how an object looked at a fleeting instant. Impressionism was akin to symbolism in literature. It sought to suggest the reality more vividly than could classical accuracy of line and brushwork. Among prominent "impressionists" were Édouard Manet, Claude Monet, and Auguste Renoir.

The impressionists were succeeded by "post-impressionists." Among these were Cézanne, who by thick layers of paint, slight distortions, and careful draftsmanship, tried to give greater solidity to his paintings; Gauguin, who fled from Paris to the South Seas and turned out canvases that were a luxuriant riot of tropical colors and dusky-skinned natives; and Vincent Van Gogh, a Dutch pastor's son who, half-insane, painted startling but most effective pictures with great blobs of fierce color often laid on with a palette knife rather than a brush.

The music of the age of realism remained predominantly romantic. Such were the operas of Richard Wagner, with their emphasis on medieval German folk lore; of Verdi, with their patriotic Italian sentiment; and of Saint-Saens and Massenet in France. Romantic, with an emphasis on German and Hungarian nationalism, was the music of Brahms, and likewise the compositions of those who sought inspiration in national

Count Leo Tolstoy. From a portrait painted in 1887 by I. J. Repine.
Courtesy Bettmann Archive

folk music like the Czech, Dvorak, and the Norwegian, Grieg. Romantic too was the Russian school exemplified by Tschaikovsky. There was, however, some turning away from romantic music. The outstanding innovator was Claude Debussy, who began experimenting impressionistically with unusual scales and the use of dissonances and who paved the way for the "modern" music of the twentieth century.

Of all the arts, architecture was the most confused. Gothic in the best romantic tradition vied with classical temples, Byzantine basilicas, French châteaux, Swiss chalets, and Georgian country homes. Spain, Italy, and even Egypt and Japan supplied architects with more or less unfortunate inspirations. There was a continuing tendency to use classic models (rather freely) for public buildings—banks, courts, memorials, city halls, post offices, and the like. But private homes were constructed in almost every conceivable style.

Gradually, however, new materials like steel and concrete, and the need of erecting buildings suited to some special purpose—railway stations, grain-elevators, factories—gave rise to the modern tendency toward functionalism, the adaptation of the edifice to its use.

The confusion in architecture reflected the lack of guidance in an age which was losing old faiths and not finding new ones. Science and materialism could change human life, but somehow they could not infuse it with inspiration. Realism sought to depict life as it was, rather than to lead men toward something better.

D. Marxian Socialism to the Fore

In the 1830's and 1840's there had been a series of radical protests against the growing capitalism and advancing industrialism of western Europe. There had been the Utopian socialism of Fourier and Owen, the anarchism of Proudhon, the social workshops of Louis Blanc. To a certain degree opposition to entrenched wealth and power had mingled with the liberal and romantic nationalism of revolutionaries like Mazzini. In the latter half of the nineteenth century, radical protests continued, but on the whole they tended to be swallowed up in Marxian socialism.

Karl Marx (1818–1883) was a native of Trier in Rhenish Prussia and the son of a Jewish lawyer. For revolutionary activities he was forced to leave Germany and spend most of his life in exile in Paris, in Brussels, and after 1849 in London. In 1844 in Paris, Marx met Friedrich Engels, the son of a wealthy German manufacturer. They found their ideas to be much alike and henceforth collaborated closely in writing and other activities. Of the two, Marx was undoubtedly the more intelligent, and his reputation has tended to obscure that of Engels. But it should be remembered that Engels had an incisive mind and shared in the authorship of all Marx's major works.

The first important production of the collaborators was the *Communist Manifesto*, published in the revolutionary year of 1848. It was called "Communist" to distinguish it from the writings of contemporary Utopian socialists. Later, after the Utopians faded out of the picture, Marx and Engels called themselves Socialists. The *Manifesto* was a ringing call to the European laboring class to rise in revolt. It concluded with the summons, "The proletarians have nothing to lose but their chains. They have a world to win. Workingmen of all countries, unite–" Though this document defined the basic position of Marx and Engels, their teachings were later elaborated in other writings, especially in the massive three-volume treatise *Capital*, of which the first volume was published by Marx in 1867, and the others after his death by Engels.

In the socialist movement of the last half of the nineteenth century Marx played a multiple role: 1. He was its scholar. During his long years of exile in London, Marx familiarized himself with the peculiar economic history of England, and concluded from it that as other countries became industrialized they would follow the English pattern. For his philosophic ideas and "dialectic" method, Marx drew heavily on Hegel,[1] but, whereas Hegel had seen spiritual forces as shaping material conditions, Marx believed that material conditions molded spiritual forces. Marx was also indebted for some of his ideas to the British classical economists, especially Ricardo.

2. Marx expounded a new theory of history. It has been variously called "economic determinism," "historical materialism," and the "economic interpretation of history." Marx held that economic factors determined the form and nature of all historical development, whether of law, government, art, literature, religion, or social institutions. Among economic factors, the most important were what Marx called the "relations of production," that is, who owned the means of production (land, factories, and the like), and how they were exploited. Whence resulted a struggle—or series of struggles—between economic classes. For centuries a developing bourgeoisie had struggled against the nobles and the feudal relations of production. At last in the French Revolution, they had pulled down the feudal nobility and created a capitalist society. But no sooner was the bourgeoisie in power than it was confronted with a new struggle against the rising proletariat.

3. Marx was an insistent prophet. From his historical analysis, he argued that, as time went on, big capitalists would absorb smaller ones until at last a stage of monopoly capitalism would be reached in which there would be a very few, but very powerful, bourgeois capitalists. Meanwhile the proletariat of workers would be growing in size, as peasant farmers were forced to become agricultural laborers and as small capitalists lost their shops and became wage workers. At length the proletariat, overwhelming in numbers, disciplined by factory work, and organized by socialist leaders,

---

[1] See above, p. 579.

would rise up in revolution and overthrow the few remaining monopoly capitalists. The struggle would be bitter, for the capitalists would still control government, army, police, courts, churches, schools, and newspapers. But the triumph of the proletariat would be inevitable. In most countries the revolution would be a violent one. In a few democratic nations like Britain, it might possibly be accomplished by ballots, without violence.

Marx thought 1848 might be the year of the great revolution, and, though disappointed in this, he still imagined he would live to see proletarian seizure of power. Once the laborers had overthrown the bourgeoisie, Marx expected that there would be a period of a "dictatorship of the proletariat," during which the victors would forcefully liquidate the institutions of capitalist society and stem any attempts at counter revolution. Then would be ushered in a classless, socialist state, in which all the people would own the means of production and exploit them for the benefit of all. The class struggle would be at an end, for there would be only one class.

4. Marx attempted revolutionary organization. Though he believed that a successful proletarian revolution was inevitable, he felt it could be speeded by an organized party of class-conscious socialists who accepted his interpretation of history and his prophecies. In 1848, Marx had attracted little attention. But as industrialism progressed, he won followers, impressed by his ideas and attracted by their seemingly "scientific" nature. In 1864 Marx helped to found an International Workingmen's Association, usually called the "First International." It was composed of groups from various European nations and the United States, and it held several international congresses. It stressed the international aspect of socialism and denounced religion, militarism, and nationalism as capitalist devices to delude the workers. Though it succeeded in spreading the Marxian teachings, the First International remained small and poor. It was rent by internal dissension, and weakened by national passions aroused in the Franco-Prussian War and by disillusionment with the ensuing failure of the Paris Commune. It was formally dissolved at a meeting of a few faithful assembled at Philadelphia in 1876.

Failure of the "First International" did not mean failure of Marxian socialism. In most European countries, socialist parties were formed and gradually grew. By the end of the 1880's these commanded the loyalty of many workingmen and some bourgeois intellectuals. They were supported (especially in Germany) by affiliated trade unions. They could boast parliamentary representatives, newspapers, and paid propagandists.

In 1889 delegates of socialist parties from different countries met in Paris and formed a new federation, usually termed the "Second International," which maintained a central office and held a series of congresses until the World War of 1914. But the real strength of socialism lay in the growing parties within each country. In Germany, by 1914, the Social Democrats were the largest party, with 110 members in the Reichstag representing four and a quarter million voters. To attain such popularity the Socialists sometimes compromised their principles. Many of them tended to work for reform and social legislation rather than for revolution. Some thought that socialism could best be achieved by democratic processes. Disputes over compromises and tactics led to repeated splits and controversies among the Marxians. In Germany, though the party held together, its right wing tended to follow "revisionist" or "reformist" ideas of Eduard Bernstein, who urged collaboration with bourgeois parties to put through social reforms, advocated the achievement of socialism by ballots, not violence, and even challenged such basic Marxian tenets as the tendency of capital to concentrate in fewer hands.

Though Marxian socialism after 1870 tended to swallow up all other movements of radical protest against industrial capitalism, there were some extreme left-wing trends that broke away from and even opposed Marxism. Prince Peter Kropotkin won some followers to his doctrine of anarchism. More important was the "syndicalist" or "direct-action" movement which emerged in the late 1890's in France, Italy, and Spain and was represented somewhat later by the I.W.W. (International Workers of the World) in the United States. It kept out of politics and devoted itself to the economic and "moral" preparation of the proletariat for a "general strike" which would usher in a social revolution. In Spain syndicalism fused with anarchism to form curious radical offshoots of the main Socialist movement.

Both in its regular and its irregular forms, the Socialism of the late nineteenth century was as thoroughly materialistic as any capitalist counting his profits or any philosopher seeking to explain the universe in terms of matter and motion. It insisted that the effective forces in the world were material. It denounced religion as an opiate with which the bourgeois tried to dope the proletarians. It advocated the use of material means to gain material ends. The classless state of the socialist dreams was a thoroughly materialistic paradise where the ownership of capital by all would give material goods to all.

E. Impact on Christianity

Since the seventeenth century, there had been rising religious skepticism and indifference in western Europe. They were accelerated by the "enlightened" philosophers of the eighteenth century and by the French Revolution. They were temporarily retarded by the evangelical movements (like pietism and Methodism), and by the romantically inspired religious revival after 1815. Then in the late nineteenth century they received powerful new stimuli from the material progress that came with industrialism, and from the materialist philosophy that was associated with the advance of the natural sciences.

By the 1890's large numbers of the middle classes and of intellectuals were quite indifferent in matters of religion. Some of them might still go to church out of habit, or they might stay at home and let their wives and daughters go for them. There was also a growing group distinctly hostile to religion. Some were anti-clericals, who assailed the "reactionary" influence of the clergy, or saw possible political advantage in attacking organized religion. Others, like the Marxian socialists, thought of churches as tools of the capitalists used by them to keep the workers quiet and orderly. Still others felt that religion consisted of outworn superstitions at variance with, and opposed to, the findings of modern science.

Intellectually, the churches probably lost most ground by opposition of some of their leaders to certain developments of science. The doctrine of evolution, with its insistence on the animal origin of human beings and its denial of the literal accuracy of the story of creation as told in *Genesis*, was opposed by some Catholics and even more strenuously by many Protestants. Similarly, the findings of geologists as to the age and development of the earth were denounced by many churchmen. It was frequently said that "science" and "theology" were at war with each other.

The Catholic Church was confronted in the nineteenth century by political as well as intellectual difficulties. Pope Pius IX (1846–1878), despite his early liberalism, was driven into a conservative position by his experiences with the revolutions of 1848–1849. While he strengthened the church by concordats with Catholic countries and by reëstablishing Catholic hierarchies in England and Holland, he issued a series of documents against liberalism which culminated in a famous encyclical, *Quanta Cura*, and an accompanying *Syllabus of Errors* (1864).

In the encyclical, Pius IX condemned modern liberal ideas of extreme individualism and the supremacy of the secular state over the church, and lauded the earlier ideal of the "Christian state." The *Syllabus* listed in abbreviated form "the principal errors of our time" which had latterly received papal condemnation. The "errors" included those of freethinkers and agnostics who denied or doubted the divine origin and mission of the church; those of materialists who repudiated the spiritual or subordinated it to the physical or temporal; those of anti-clericals and nationalists who sought to restrict the church and exalt the lay state; those of the liberals and the indifferent who thought one religion as good as another, held that the church should be a private, voluntary association, and imagined that the pope should reconcile himself to "modern civilization."

In 1869, while discussion of the *Syllabus* was still heated, Piux IX convened a general council of the Catholic Church, the first such council since that of Trent three centuries before. The Vatican Council, attended by nearly eight hundred prelates from all over the world, reaffirmed and deepened the traditional teaching of the church on the relationship between faith and reason. But its most striking achievement was the definition in July 1870, despite earnest preliminary opposition from a minority of its members, of the dogma of papal infallibility. It was solemnly proclaimed, as a "dogma divinely revealed," that the pope is infallible when he speaks *ex cathedra,* that is officially as the "pastor and doctor of all Christians," regarding faith or morals. The dogma was denounced by Protestants, liberals, agnostics, and nationalists, and was utilized for anti-clerical campaigns in France, Italy, and Spain, and in the *Kulturkampf* in Germany. And simultaneously the Italian government forcefully seized Rome from the Pope.

The successor of Pius IX was Leo XIII (1878–1903), who was a first-rate scholar and a sympathizer with democracy and social reform. In the intellectual sphere, while he stood firm for the historic dogmas of Catholic Christianity, he promoted the renewed study of the writings of St. Thomas Aquinas, who had taught that science and religion could not be in basic conflict since truth is one. In political matters, Leo XIII continued to condemn the "errors" denounced by Pius IX and to insist on the "right" of the church to a privileged position in the state and in education. At the same time he encouraged the formation of popular and democratic Catholic parties in Belgium, Austria, and Germany, advised French Catholics to support the Third Republic, and expressed admiration for the constitution of the United States.

In social and economic problems, Leo XIII showed keen interest. He encouraged the development of a Catholic "social" movement which sought to combat both economic liberalism and Marxian socialism and to christianize industrial society. To this movement which had been gathering headway, especially in France and Germany since the 1870's, Leo XIII in 1891 gave a guiding charter in a famous encyclical, *Rerum Novarum.* Against the Marxians, this document defended private property as a natural right and the family as the cornerstone of society. It condemned the exaltation of the state, economic determinism, and the doctrine of the class struggle. Against the economic liberals, it held that labor is not a commodity and that the state should prevent exploitation of workers, encourage collective bargaining, and enact social legislation. Specifically the encyclical urged the wider distribution of private property, the fostering of trade unions and cooperatives, the restriction of labor by women and children, and the assurance of a "living family wage."

If the Catholic Church was weakened under Leo XIII and his successor, Pius X (1903–1914), by anti-clerical legislation in traditionally Catholic lands like France, Spain, Portugal, and Latin America, and by continued strife with the Italian state, it was strengthened by the growth of Catholicism in traditionally Protestant countries like England, Holland, Canada, Australia, and the United States. Pius X was faced with a special problem in the rise of "modernism" within the church. Its advocates sought to modify Catholic teaching so as to bring it into line with what they regarded as the findings of science and of the "higher criticism" of the Bible. Though "modernism" proved troublesome, Pius X stood firm against it, excommunicated some of its outstanding leaders, and reaffirmed the traditional position of the church. It thus ceased to be a significant movement in Catholic Christianity at the very time when it was becoming influential in Protestant churches.

The first reaction of most Protestants to "Darwinism" and the "higher criticism" was, generally speaking, one of hostility. But shortly, as materialism progressed and the new science was popularized, they produced more complex reactions, so that by about 1900 three distinct movements were obvious in nearly all Protestant churches.

First, a minority of Protestants, including a relatively large proportion of intellectuals, moved toward an agnostic position. Unable to square the Bible with science, they threw over the former. Some of them sought refuge in "ethical culture," "unitarianism," or in a vague pantheism.

Second, at the opposite extreme, large

numbers of devout Protestants, relatively more numerous among the masses and in agricultural areas, were impelled to take a *fundamentalist* position. Holding the Bible to be literally inspired, they denounced any scientific explanation which contradicted or questioned their own traditional interpretation of that sacred book.

Third, a gradually growing number of Protestants became *modernist*, that is, they remained Protestant Christians in name and in actual church membership, but they tended to neglect church creeds and dogmas and the Bible itself, and to emphasize the beauty of Christianity and its ethical teachings as a guide to moral conduct. Innumerable as were the shades of modernism within the Protestant churches, they were almost all marked by an evolutionary attitude toward religion in general and Christianity in particular. Such an attitude marked a sharp reversal in the traditional Protestant habit of seeking pure religion by a return to primitive Christianity and a dependence on the authority of the Bible. It also involved a sharp reversal in the original Protestant emphasis on faith as against "good works." As the faith of Protestants in creeds and dogmas declined, they threw themselves with increasing vigor into good works of all sorts. They worked for social reform, foreign missions, popular education, public health, organized recreation, and against alcoholism, political corruption, and juvenile delinquency. Many churches became social centers of recreation and organized charity. Special Protestant organizations were developed such as Young Men's Christian Association, Salvation Army, etc.

Neither among the Protestants nor among the Catholics was there any unified reaction to the age of materialism. Religion appeared to be on the defensive, in a world that was responding more and more to nonreligious stimuli. For the first time in more than fifteen hundred years, Western European civilization seemed to be ignoring the Christian heritage to which it had been born and in which it had been nurtured.

Yet in one respect historic Christianity was not on the defensive in the decades that followed 1870. Both Catholics and Protestants engaged in a greatly expanded missionary effort that affected almost every part of the world. Using both institutions founded in earlier periods, the Congregation of the Propaganda (1622), the Society for the Propagation of the Faith (1822), the Society of Foreign Missions at Paris (1658), together with the old orders (Jesuits, Franciscans, Dominicans) and new societies like the White Fathers established in France (1868) for work in Africa, the Catholic Church developed a missionary enterprise of very considerable proportions. By 1910, some 41,000 persons were working in Catholic missions in Africa, Asia, and Oceania. Nor was this mission work without significant effects. Though except in the Philippines there had been relatively few Catholics outside of America and Europe in the middle of the century, it was estimated that in 1900 there were two and a quarter million in India, more than a million in China, two and a half million in Africa, sixty thousand in Korea, and a like number in Japan.

Before 1790 there had been relatively little Protestant missionary activity among non-European peoples. But in the next decade missionary societies were formed in England by the Baptists, by the Presbyterians and Congregationalists, and by the Anglicans. The movement spread to the United States, and before the middle of the nineteenth century there were numerous Protestant missionary groups competing with each other and with the Catholics in an effort to evangelize the people of the non-European world. The scope of this effort expanded greatly in the last decades of the century as new lands were explored and opened up. In 1910, there were some 18,000 active Protestant missionaries, and by this time some form of Protestantism was the religion of a million and a half people in India, two and a half million in Africa, a quarter of a million in China, and eighty thousand in Japan.

Both Catholics and Protestants also paid some attention to "home missions." Devoted priests and ministers tried to bring religion into the lives of the industrial workers in the city slums. They set up chapels and settlement houses and sought to give guidance and comfort to those who were crushed and oppressed by the changing society of the western world.

Lloyd George.

Photograph from Underwood & Underwood, New York

CHAPTER 53

Peace Movement
and Spasmodic Violence

AT THE TURN OF THE CENTURY

A. Progress of Democratic Social Reform, Particularly in Britain

The twentieth century opened with general optimism. Peace reigned among major European countries. The progress of industry and agriculture seemed to be ushering in a new period of abundance. Science was conquering disease. Democracy was advancing. Social reforms were being accomplished by legislation. Prophets of war and revolution seemed like pessimists left over from another and less enlightened era. Was not the eighteenth-century dream of peaceful and rapid progress at last being realized?

Great Britain still led the way in economic and political life. London was the economic heart of the world from which radiated the arteries of commerce and finance. In British politics, significant changes were taking place. Marxian socialism had never won much of a place in British life, though it had inspired the formation of a small "Social Democratic Federation" in 1881. More important were the "Fabian" Socialists, a group of intellectuals, including Shaw and Wells, who preached socialization by gradual reform. Still more important was the steady growth of the trade union movement, which before 1890 had been confined mainly to the skilled trades, but afterwards came to include a large proportion of unskilled labor as well. In 1892 there had been 1,500,000 trade-union members in Great Britain. Twenty-one years later there were over 4,000,000.

In 1893 Keir Hardie, a Scottish miner, had tried to take the trade unionists into politics by forming an "Independent Labor Party." But it made little progress before 1901, when the House of Lords, acting as the supreme court of law, decided (in the so-called Taff Vale decision) that a trade union was legally liable for damages arising from any strike conducted by its members. Almost at once, the trade unions, Independent Labor Party, the Social Democratic Federation, and the Fabian Society formed a coalition known as the Labor Party, which in 1906 elected twenty-nine members of parliament and in 1910 forty-two members. A new force thus arose in British politics, a force which pushed the older parties, especially the Liberals, into sponsoring vigorous measures for social reform.

The Conservative Party, long in power, found itself by 1906 seriously divided over imperialism and tariff protection, and compromised by the Taff Vale decision. In the elections of that year, it campaigned for the imposition of tariffs so that preferential treatment could be granted the colonies, while the Liberals fought back with their old slogan of a "free breakfast table" (no tariffs on food) and a promise to repeal the Taff Vale decision by legislation. The Liberals won a resounding victory, which brought them to power and kept them there for a decade. Between 1906 and 1914 they put through a series of significant acts.

In aid of trade unions, the Liberals reversed the Taff Vale decision by the Trade

Disputes Act of 1906, authorized payment of salaries to members of the House of Commons in 1911 so that poor unionists could afford to sit there, and in 1913 strengthened the Labor Party by allowing the use of union funds in elections. A Workmen's Compensation Act extended the principle of the employer's liability for injuries to his laborers. A Labor Exchange Act set up free, public employment bureaus. A Trade Boards Act arranged for the fixing of minimum wages in "sweated industries." In 1912 minimum wage legislation was enacted for the benefit of coal miners. Meanwhile, a series of laws was passed for the benefit of children, old people, and the health of the public. One act enabled local school boards to give free lunches to under-nourished school children. Another sought to improve many phases of the life of children by providing free medical attention, better recreational facilities, and special treatment for juvenile delinquents. An Old Age Pensions Act set up a system of relief for aged persons. A Housing and Town Planning Act aimed at eliminating slums. Capping the whole series of social enactments, a National Insurance Act (1912) provided health insurance for most workers and unemployment insurance for many.

Taken as a whole, this legislation marked an important step towards the socializing of Britain. Opposition to it grew into a fierce controversy over the "Lloyd George Budget" of 1909. Lloyd George, a gifted Welshman, had long been interested in land reform and social legislation. As Chancellor of the Exchequer in the Liberal cabinet, he decided to kill a number of birds with one stone by submitting to Parliament a frankly radical budget, proposing a steeply graduated income tax, a heavy inheritance tax, a tax on unused land designed to break up great estates, and special taxes on motor cars and other luxuries. With the revenues thus to be secured chiefly from the wealthy, Lloyd George planned to finance the Liberal program of social legislation.

By a party vote, the House of Commons passed the 1909 budget. But the Conservative majority in the House of Lords rejected it, despite the long tradition against interference by the upper house with finance bills. Each side said that the other was try-ing to overthrow the British constitution, and the ensuing elections in 1910 were hotly fought. The Liberals lost ground, but with the aid of Labor allies and the Irish (to whom they promised "home rule") they retained control of the Commons. With minor modifications, the Lloyd George budget was passed again, and this time the Lords did not venture to reject it.

But the fight over the budget led to another fight of a constitutional nature over the House of Lords. The Liberals put through the House of Commons a bill drastically limiting the powers of the upper house. It was rejected by the Lords, and new elections were held in December 1910. The results were about the same as before, with the consequence that the Lords finally gave way and consented to the enactment of the "Parliament Act." This provided: (1) that finance bills passed by the Commons would become law without the approval of the Lords; (2) that other public bills would become law even though rejected by the Lords, if they were passed by the Commons in three successive sessions with at least two years elapsing between the first and the third passage; (3) that general elections for the Commons would be held at least every five (instead of every seven) years. Thus the House of Lords was left with only a suspensive veto over most bills and no veto at all on financial measures. The democratic House of Commons was supreme.

The British reforms were more or less duplicated in other major European countries. Between 1900 and 1914 the movement toward democracy registered important victories. Universal manhood suffrage was established in Austria, Sweden, and Italy. Portugal became a republic in 1910, and even Russia, after 1905, was toying with liberal constitutional reforms.

There was also widespread pressure for social legislation on the part of both Socialist and Catholic parties and of the growing trade union movement. The growth of unionism was indeed an outstanding feature of the period. In Germany the number of union members rose from about 350,000 in 1891 to over 3,000,000 in 1913, and in France it increased from 150,000 in 1904 to 400,000 in 1912. The social legislation

Industry. By Preston Dickinson.

Courtesy Whitney Museum of Fine Arts, New York

of the period followed the pattern set in the 1880's in Germany and after 1905 in Great Britain. Almost every industrial country enacted some scheme for insuring workers against sickness, accidents, death, old age, and unemployment. Trade unions were completely legalized, their funds protected, the right to strike recognized, and collective bargaining encouraged. Education for children was made free and compulsory in most countries, and many enactments were designed to protect women and children. Public health was the aim of measures on housing, sanitation, water supply, medical service, and the purity of food and drugs.

The optimists in 1913 could point with

enthusiasm to the progress made in recent years. It seemed as if Europe was adjusting itself to the new industrialism. It was eliminating the ills of urban life and many of the hardships and uncertainties that had faced factory workers. It was spreading ever more widely the benefits derived from increased production and from modern science. It was doing all these things, moreover, through democratic means, through legislation passed by parliaments ever more responsive to the popular will.

B. General Material Progress

Between 1890 and 1910 world production of pig iron increased from 27,500,000 metric tons to 66,250,000. Of this latter figure Britain produced a little less than a sixth, Germany a good deal more than a fifth, France about a sixteenth, and the United States considerably more than a third. In coal production in 1913, though Britain still led Europe with almost 300,000,000 metric tons, its total output was less than half of that of the United States. But in merchant shipping and commerce, Britain still triumphantly led all the world. In 1914 over 44 per cent of the steamships of the world were British. Germany came second with 11 per cent. No other country had more than 4.6 per cent. World trade (in contemporary dollars) had risen from 14.8 billion in 1880 and 20.1 billion in 1900 to 40.4 billion in 1913. Of this, 17 per cent was British, 15 per cent American, 12 per cent German, and 7 per cent French.

In Britain the number of cotton spindles increased from 36,700,000 in 1870 to 53,500,000 in 1910, and the number of power looms from 475,000 to 700,000 in the same period. But whereas in 1870 Britain had dominated cotton textile production, by 1910 only about 40 per cent of the spindles and 30 per cent of the looms were hers. Most of the rest were distributed among the United States, Germany, France, Italy, Russia, Austria, Spain, India, and Japan. In 1885 British foreign investments had totaled £1,302,000,000. In 1913 they amounted to £3,763,000,000 and represented, it was estimated, a quarter of Britain's national wealth. But France had become a major lender, too, and her investments abroad in 1913 amounted to almost half as much as those of Great Britain. Germany, Switzerland, and Holland were now lenders also, although their foreign investments together were not as large as those of France.

Such figures as the foregoing indicate a number of things. (1) World production and trade were growing very rapidly. (2) Britain's share, while still most impressive, was becoming proportionately less, as Germany, France, and the United States increased their portions. (3) World industry and commerce had so developed that the whole earth was bound together by the buying, selling, and transportation of goods. National self-sufficiency was gone. Each country depended more or less on its neighbors and on distant lands, not only for food or raw materials or manufactured goods, but also for markets in which to sell its own products.

This dependence was less marked in the case of great continental powers like Russia or the United States. It was more marked in the case of Germany, and most in the case of Great Britain. Britain paid for her imports of food and raw materials by exports of manufactures, by sale of shipping, banking, and insurance services, and by income from investments abroad.

The progress of science, industry and the arts was periodically put on show in great World Fairs, or International Exhibitions. The first notable exhibition of the sort had been that in London in 1851, when crowds came to admire a "Crystal Palace" of glass and iron. But it had been surpassed by the Paris fairs of 1878 (for which the Trocadero Palace had been built) and of 1889 (at which the great spidery Eiffel Tower had been the object of much attention). Dozens of other exhibitions, including those at Philadelphia (1876), Sydney (1881), Amsterdam (1883), Chicago (1893), Bucharest (1894), and Berlin (1896), gave the various nations a chance to vie with each other in displays of manufactured goods, agricultural products, artistic handicrafts, and exotic wares from overseas, while African villages, Japanese pagodas, artificial lagoons, wild animals, and scores of other attractions were designed to lure visitors in hordes. The fairs continued into the twentieth century (Buffalo 1901, St. Louis 1904, Liége 1905, Milan 1906, Dublin 1907, London 1908, Seattle 1909, etc.), though it seemed that the Paris Exhibition of 1900 was almost unsurpassable. It occupied 549 acres, had 211 pavilions, attracted almost forty million paying visitors, and cost more than 200 million francs. At it almost every civilized nation and a great many of the colonies put on exhibits designed to sell goods or to indicate the development of the arts and sciences.

The world fairs somehow symbolized the interdependence of the nations of the earth, their willingness to coöperate, and their general spirit of optimism. There seemed indeed ample reason to look forward to the future with hope and confidence. Science was opening up new vistas; medicine was prolonging human life; industry was providing ever-increasing wealth and giving the lie to the Marxists who insisted that the lot of the workingman would ever grow worse. Education was more general; democracy and parliamentary government were coming to seem the norm; order, law, and justice were more and more characteristic of the European and Western world. It seemed reasonable for men, in 1910, to believe that those trends which had been evident since 1815 and increasingly clear since 1870 would continue indefinitely into the future. It was not only possible, but easy, to envision a world where poverty and disease had been conquered, where educated voters elected wise and just men

The Eiffel Tower. Maurice Utrillo (d. 1955).

to rule them, and where the various nations worked together peacefully for the benefit of all mankind.

C. The Peace Movement

The very interdependence of the nations of the world in industry, trade, and finance convinced many persons that there would never be another major war. This was re-enforced by movements deliberately de-signed to maintain world peace and increase world coöperation. The idea of a Concert of Europe in which the Great Powers would act together, did not die with Metternich. All the major nations were represented at the Congress of Paris (1856) which ended the Crimean War, at the Congress of Berlin (1878) which readjusted the Balkan situation, and at another Congress of Berlin (1884–1885) which laid down rules for the opening up of Africa. The great powers of Europe at a Congress in Brussels agreed in 1890 to end the traffic in arms and liquor with African natives. They acted to-gether with Japan and the United States to end the Boxer disturbances in China in 1900. Paralleling this European coöperation were periodic Pan-American conferences at which all American nations amicably dis-cussed matters of common interest.

Peaceful international coöperation was becoming the rule in many matters. In 1864, for humanitarian purposes, a con-gress at Geneva set up an international Red Cross society, which soon had branches in almost every country. Most nations joined a Telegraph Union (1875) and a Postal Union (1878), and many agreed to stand-ardized patent laws (1883) and uniform copyright laws (1887).

As early as 1816 a peace society had been founded in England, another was instituted at Geneva in 1828, and a third at Paris in 1841. Thenceforth, and especially after 1878, associations of professed pacifists multiplied throughout the Western world, until in 1914 there were some 160 of them with numerous branches and many mem-bers. International congresses of pacifists were held, and a permanent peace head-quarters maintained at Berne. To the peace movement, several great industrialists made notable contributions. For example, the Swedish Alfred Nobel willed the major part of the princely fortune he amassed from the manufacture of dynamite and other high explosives, to establish prizes for those who forwarded the cause of international peace as well as for those who promoted science and literature. Likewise, Andrew Carnegie, a Scottish-American steel mag-nate, established and heavily endowed a special peace "foundation" and built a "temple of peace" at the Hague.

In 1899 the Tsar Nicholas II, eager to cut down the military burden on his budget and to increase Russia's international pres-tige, convoked an international peace con-ference at the Hague to try to reach some agreement for a reduction of armaments. Twenty-six sovereign nations of Europe, Asia, and the Americas were represented. It proved impossible, because of mutual suspicion and jealousies, to agree on any general limitation of arms. But steps were taken to restrict the use of certain weapons in war, to codify international law with regard to war, and to establish at the Hague an international court of arbitration to which the nations might submit their quar-rels.

In 1907, prompted by the American President, Theodore Roosevelt, Nicholas II summoned a second peace conference at the Hague. This time, forty-four govern-ments were represented. Again it proved impossible to establish a general limitation of armaments, but humane amendments were added to the "laws" of land and sea warfare, an international prize court was provided for, and conventions were adopted requiring that wars be begun by formal declarations and restricting the use of force in the collection of foreign debts. It was recommended that similar conferences be held at regular intervals in the future.

D. Unsettling Domestic Violence

If, in the decade before World War I, peace and democracy seemed to be in the ascendant, there were signs of impending difficulties. Liberal democrats had held that education and democracy would raise the tone and dignity of politics, that calm de-

King Cophetua and the Beggar-Maid. A 1908 cartoon from *Punch* on Prime-Minister Asquith's lukewarm attitude toward woman suffrage.

bate would be the method of solving disputes, and that the masses, once they were literate, would respond soberly to reasonable arguments. But even in liberal Britain there were signs of stress and strain and ominous notes of violence.

There was serious trouble, for example, in Ireland. Irish nationalists had been much disappointed at Gladstone's failures to put through a home rule act. One of them, who was convinced by these failures that new tactics were necessary, was Arthur Griffith, who, in his newspaper, the *United Irishman*, established in 1899, advocated cultural, economic, and political independence for Ireland. In 1906 a new party was formed under Griffith's leadership. It took the Gaelic name of *Sinn Fein* ("we ourselves").

Meanwhile the bulk of the Irish nationalists continued to work for home rule by parliamentary means under the leadership of John Redmond. They were able to secure some local self-government for Ireland (1898) and two important land purchase acts (1896, 1903) designed to provide the Irish peasantry with farms. But more they could not get, until the Liberals, after the 1910 elections, found themselves in need of Irish votes. The Irish supported the Lloyd George budget and the Parliament Act. In return, Asquith, the Liberal prime minister, put through the House of Commons an Irish Home Rule bill in 1912. It was rejected by the House of Lords, passed again by the Commons (1913), and again turned down by the Lords. One more passage by the Commons in 1914 and it would become law, despite the upper house.

In Ireland itself, while the Sinn Fein group denounced the Home Rule Bill of 1912 as a weak compromise, Ulster Protestants, under the militant leadership of Edward Carson, swore by a "solemn covenant" to resist the Catholic majority and never to submit to an Irish parliament; and they raised a volunteer army of 100,000 men. In response, Sinn Feiners joined with other Irish nationalists to form a force of "Irish Volunteers." By 1914, violent clashes were occurring and civil war seemed near at hand—so near that Germans thought Britain was immobilized by the threat. But when foreign war actually came, Redmond and his Irish followers rallied to the British cause. The Home Rule bill was passed again and made law, but its execution was suspended for the duration of the war.

On the continent, most of the violence came from extreme radicals, from the left wing of the labor movement, and from Balkan nationalists. Between 1890 and 1914, anarchists assassinated several prominent political figures, including King Humbert of Italy (1900), the Empress Elizabeth of Austria (1898), President Carnot of France (1894), President McKinley of the United States (1901), King Charles I of Portugal (1908), and a number of Russian officials and grand-dukes. The support of anarchism waned somewhat after 1900, but syndicalists with doctrines which glorified violence, or "direct action," took their place. Under syndicalist influence, a great railway strike was organized in France (1909). It was stopped only when the premier, the former socialist Aristide Briand, mobilized part of the army and thus put many of the strikers in uniform and under military discipline.

In the name of nationalism, much violence was done. Nationalistic Russians murdered Jews and oppressed subject peoples like the Poles or the Finns. Pan-German Prussians tried to suppress Polish political activities by force. Turks massacred Armenians and other Christians. Serbs, Bulgarians, Greeks, and Rumanians resorted to strong-arm methods in Macedonia and elsewhere to further their nationalistic aims. Others who did not so often employ violence urged war or revolution. There were Frenchmen who dreamed of a "revenge" war to recover Alsace-Lorraine, Italians who hoped to fight Austria to win *Italia irredenta* ("unredeemed Italy," areas inhabited by Italians but still under Austrian rule), Serbs who cast covetous eyes on Bosnia and Herzegovina, Czechs and Poles who longed to oust their foreign rulers. Left-wing Socialists all over Europe worked for a revolution that would redden the streets with bourgeois blood.

Outwardly Europe appeared calm, peaceful, progressive. But within, to those aware of forces at work, it seemed a seething mass of class and nationalist discontent, ready to boil over into turmoil and chaos.

Émile Zola. Aubrey Beardsley (d. 1898).

SELECT SUPPLEMENTARY READINGS FOR PART X

General. C. J. H. Hayes, *Political and Cultural History of Modern Europe,* vol. ii (1939); S. B. Clough and C. W. Cole, *Economic History of Europe* (1952); R. C. Binkley, *Realism and Nationalism, 1852–1871* (1935); C. J. H. Hayes, *A Generation of Materialism, 1871–1900* (1941); *New Cambridge Modern History,* vol. xii (1960).

Chapter 49. James Bryce, *Modern Democracies*, 2 vols (1921); R. C. K. Ensor, *England, 1870–1914* (1936); Esme Wingfield-Stratford, *The Victorian Sunset* (1932); Anthony Wood, *Nineteenth Century Britain, 1815–1914* (1960); G. M. Young, *Victorian England* (1936); G. Slater, *The Growth of Modern England* (1939); J. H. Clapham, *The Economic Development of France and Germany* (1936); D. W. Brogan, *France under the Republic, 1870–1939* (1940); S. B. Clough, *France, a History of National Economics, 1789–1939* (1939); R. H. Soltau, *French Parties and Politics, 1871–1921* (1922); Benedetto Croce, *A History of Italy, 1871–1914* (1929); R. Albrecht-Carrié, *Italy from Napoleon to Mussolini* (1950); W. H. Dawson, *The German Empire, 1867–1914*, 2 vols. (1919); E. Eyck, *Bismarck and the German Empire* (1950).

Chapter 50. M. Karpovich, *Imperial Russia, 1801–1907* (1932); J. D. Clarkson, *A History of Russia* (1961); G. T. Robinson, *Rural Russia under the Old Regime* (1932); G. Fischer, *Russian Liberalism* (1958); H. Seton-Watson, *The Decline of Imperial Russia, 1855–1914* (1952); R. A. Pierce, *Russian Central Asia, 1867–1917: A Study in Colonial Rule* (1960); H. W. Steed, *Hapsburg Monarchy* (1919); J. Redlich, *Emperor Francis Joseph of Austria* (1929); Oscar Jaszi, *Dissolution of the Hapsburg Monarchy* (1929); R. Kann, *The Multinational Empire: Nationalism and National Reform in the Habsburg Monarchy, 1848–1918*, 2 vols (1950); A. J. May, *The Habsburg Monarchy, 1867–1914* (1951); Ferdinand Schevill, *History of the Balkan Peninsula*, rev. ed. (1933); D. C. Blaisdell, *European Financial Control in the Ottoman Empire* (1929); E. E. Ramsaur, Jr., *The Young Turks* (1947).

Chapter 51. W. L. Langer, *European Alliances and Alignments, 1871–1890* (1931); R. J. Sontag, *European Diplomatic History, 1871–1932* (1933); P. T. Moon, *Imperialism and World Politics* (1926); R. G. Trotter, *The British Empire-Commonwealth* (1932); Mary E. Townsend, *Rise and Fall of Germany's Colonial Empire, 1884–1918* (1930); H. I. Priestley, *France Overseas, a Study of Modern Imperialism* (1938); T. F. Power, *Jules Ferry and the Renaissance of French Imperialism* (1945); F. H. Skrine, *The Expansion of Russia, 1815–1900*, 3rd ed. (1915); R. J. S. Hoffman, *Great Britain and the German Trade Rivalry, 1875–1914* (1933); Herbert Feis, *Europe, the World's Banker, 1870–1914* (1930); E. M. Winslow, *The Pattern of Imperialism* (1948); J. Schumpeter, *Imperialism and Social Classes* (1955); W. L. Langer, *The Diplomacy of Imperialism* (1951); J. T. Pratt, *The Expansion of Europe in the Far East* (1947); R. A. Oliver, *Sir Harry Johnston and the Scramble for Africa* (1957); S. G. Millin, *Rhodes* (1952); L. M. Thompson, *The Unification of South Africa, 1902–1910* (1960); Eric Walker, *A History of Southern Africa* (1957).

Chapter 52. On Science, in addition to works cited for chapter 44, see F. A. Lange, *History of Materialism and Criticism of its Present Importance,* 3rd ed. (1925); E. Boring, *History of Experimental Psychology* (1929); A. N. Whitehead, *Science and the Modern World* (1926); Jacques Barzun, *Darwin, Marx, Wagner, the Fatal Legacy of "Progress"* (1941), and *Race, a Study in Modern Superstition* (1937); C. Singer, E. J. Holmyard, A. R. Hull, T. I. Williams (eds.), *A History of Technology,* 5 vols. (1955–1958), Vol. V, *The Late Nineteenth Century,* c. 1850 to c. 1900; E. Diesel, G. Goldbeck, and F. Schildberger, *From Engines to Autos* (1960). On Marxism, see Isaiah Berlin, *Life of Marx* (1939); G. D. H. Cole, *What Marx Really Meant* (1934); Karl Federn, *The Materialistic Conception of History* (1939); G. M. Stekloff, *History of the First International* (1928); W. H. Dawson, *German Socialism and Ferdinand Lassalle* (1888). On Anarchism: E. H. Carr, *Michael Bakunin* (1937). On the churches and religion: K. S. Latourette, *History of the Expansion of Christianity,* vol. iv (1941); Adrian Fortescue, *The Orthodox Eastern Church,* 2nd ed. (1908); S. W. Baron, *Social and Religious History of the Jews,* vol. ii (1937); and articles in the *Catholic Encyclopedia.*

Chapter 53. J. W. Swain, *Beginning the Twentieth Century, a History of the Generation that Made the War* (1933); E. P. Cheyney, *Modern English Reform, from Individualism to Socialism* (1931); C. R. Fay, *Coöperation at Home and Abroad,* 4th ed. (1939); A. P. Higgins, *The Hague Peace Conferences* (1909); D. C. Somervell, *Modern Britain, 1870–1939* (1941); E. C. Wingfield-Stratford, *The Victorian Aftermath, 1901–1914* (1933); Francis Hackett, *Ireland, a Study in Nationalism* (1918); G. Dangerfield, *The Strange Death of Liberal England* (1935).

From William II
to Hitler

The German "War Lords."

Photo by Underwood & Underwood, New York

v. Mackensen	v. Moltke	Kronprinz Wilhelm	v. François		v. Falkenhayn	v. Beseler	v. Bethmann-Hollweg
		v. Preussen		Ludendorff	v. Einem		
v. Bülow	Kronprinz Rupprecht	Herzog Albrecht	v. Kluck	v. Emmich	v. Haeseler	v. Hindenburg	v. Heeringen
	v. Bayern	v. Württemberg	Kaiser Wilhelm II.				v. Tirpitz

PART XI

WORLD WAR I

Hitler addressing a youth parade at Nuremberg, 1936.

Courtesy Wide World Photos

AND ITS AFTERMATH

THE LATEST AGE—the twentieth century—marks, in some respects, the greatest advance and the highest achievement of European, or Western, civilization. This is doubtless so in science and technology, and likewise in popular aspiration for fuller, freer, and richer life. In other respects, however, the age suggests comparison with the early middle age (the "Dark Age") or with the ancient age of Eastern Mediterranean empires. Its violences are even more deadly and destructive, its instability as manifest, and its dictatorships as despotic.

The age opens with optimism inherited from the previous century concerning material progress and democratic politics. It also opens with portents, similarly inherited and now multiplying, of international conflict. While seeming progress is made in extending liberalism and nationalism into eastern Europe, the fate of the old border-empire of Austria becomes a very real issue between Germany and Russia, and hence between their respective allies in the game of power politics.

For over four years, from 1914 to 1918, is waged a war involving every great power of Europe, together with Japan and the United States, and most lesser nations of the world. It is called the First World War. Strictly speaking, it was not the first war fought globally, but it was quite unprecedented in its magnitude and destructiveness.

There follows a decade of renewed hope and optimism. Old empires are broken up, their subject nationalities liberated, and the European state-system put squarely on a national basis. Within the new nations, as within older ones, democracy is well-nigh universally professed and individual liberty pledged. And to preserve peace and prevent recurrence of war, a league of nations is fashioned. Democracy and peace, it is imagined, will stimulate the art as well as the technology of a dawning new era.

Already, however, Western democracy has failed to take root in Russia, and, instead, a novel type of dictatorship is forcefully fastened upon it—Marxian, "popular," and "totalitarian." Presently, amid deteriorating economic conditions in central Europe, dictatorships, ostensibly anti-Marxian but equally totalitarian and fiercely nationalist, are installed in Italy and Germany and are imitated, in greater or lesser degree, in many smaller countries. All such dictatorships represent a repudiation of traditional Western liberty, and the major ones are antagonistic to the Judaeo-Christian spiritual heritage. Without scruples, they exalt militarism, make propaganda a fine art, and readily employ force and violence alike in domestic and in international affairs.

The example of the dictatorships of eastern and central Europe tends to widen the gulf in western Europe between "Left" and "Right," to impair the operation of remaining democratic government, and to break down the League of Nations. Only when the democratic Western powers are exasperated beyond endurance by aggression of the totalitarian dictatorships, particularly by Nazi Germany, do they abandon compromise and go to war.

CHAPTER 54

Toward World War I

A. Russo-Japanese War and Revolt in the Russian Empire

As we have seen, Russian expansion in Asia had, in 1904, brought the empire of the Tsars into armed conflict with the rising power of the vigorous and intensely nationalistic Japanese; and this led to an internal upheaval in European Russia. We have already noticed that the Russian peasants were left unsatisfied by the land settlement which accompanied their emancipation in 1861.[1] Then, too, by the end of the nineteenth century a Social Democratic party was winning urban workers to Marxian Socialism. Peasant dissatisfaction was exploited by a Social Revolutionary party, which, adapting Marxian teachings to the traditions of Russian agricultural life, proposed that the land be given to those who actually worked it. Simultaneously, a Constitutional Democratic ("Cadet") party had appeared among middle-class "Westernizers," and the policy of "Russification" pursued by Alexander III and Nicholas II had aroused bitter resentment among "subject peoples" in the Empire—Poles, Finns, Letts, Lithuanians, Jews, Georgians, Armenians, etc.

All the latent opposition to the autocratic Tsardom became active as soon as it was borne in upon the Russian people that they were suffering one reverse after another in the war with Japan. Naturally enough the Tsar's government was blamed. Middle-class liberals held political banquets and

[1] See above, p. 650.

made provocative speeches. Workers staged political strikes at Moscow, Vilna, and other industrial centers. At St. Petersburg a procession of strikers, led by an Orthodox priest named Gapon, was fired on by troops while on its way to present a petition to the Tsar. The resulting bloodshed earned for that day (January 22, 1905) the title of "Red Sunday." The Tsar's uncle, the Grand Duke Sergei, was assassinated in Moscow in February 1905, and other political murders ensued. Armed outbreaks occurred in Poland and the Caucasus. The state railways could be operated only under martial law. The universities were closed. Most significant of all, in rural districts bands of peasants, under Social Revolutionary leaders, wandered about pillaging and burning the mansions of noble landlords and country gentlemen.

Faced with growing disorder, the Tsar made concessions. Hoping to appease the subject peoples, he promised religious toleration, permitted the use of Polish in private schools, and relaxed the enforcement of anti-Jewish legislation. Hoping to quiet the peasants, he cancelled the arrears they owed on the payments to the state for the land they had received. Hoping to win over the liberals, he consented to respect legal formalities in the trial of political offenders and promised to work out a plan for constitutional government. After further hesitation and delay and further rioting and disorder, the Tsar announced in August 1905 that he would establish a parliament, or Imperial Duma.

In October 1905, Nicholas II issued a kind of constitution in the form of a "manifesto," guaranteeing personal liberties of conscience, speech, and association, establishing moderately popular franchise for the election of the Duma, and clearly stating that henceforth no law would be valid without the Duma's consent. In December the Tsar was prevailed upon to grant practically universal manhood suffrage for Duma elections, and (in March 1906) he provided a two-house parliament by designating the Duma as the lower chamber and the old Council of State as the upper chamber. Of the latter, now to be called the Council of the Empire, half the members would be appointed, and half elected indirectly by certain privileged classes. Meanwhile a general strike in Finland led the Tsar to reëstablish the Finnish Estates General suppressed in 1899; and, when it proceeded to draft a modern, liberal constitution, the Tsar ratified it.

In Russia, however, the revolutionary upheaval soon spent its force. The conclusion of peace with Japan in the autumn of 1905 ended the series of defeats, reduced the pressure on the government, and released troops for the "restoration of order" at home. Many Russians were tired of foreign war and domestic rioting. The revolutionary elements fell to quarreling among themselves. Extreme (Bolshevik) Social Democrats clashed with moderate (Menshevik) Social Democrats, and both were in conflict with the Social Revolutionaries, while all the radicals were distrusted by the liberals. The liberals themselves disputed about the Duma and the policies it should pursue. The Constitutional Democrats thought the Tsar's decrees were merely a first step in the right direction, and hoped that the Duma would draw up a constitution that would make the Russian government like the British. A rival group, called "Octobrists," were content to accept the Tsar's "October Manifesto" as definitive, even though it made the Duma only a mild check on the autocracy.

As the revolutionary elements fell to quarreling, reactionary elements in Russia plucked up courage, closed their ranks, and prepared to fight for the preservation of the autocracy, the great landed estates, and the

traditional regime as a whole. Landlords, officials, courtiers, army officers, Slavophile patriots, and numerous Orthodox clergymen organized a "Union of the Russian People," which early in 1906 began a counter-revolutionary movement. "Black bands" or "black hundreds," as certain agents of the Union were popularly called, terrorized radicals and incited mob violence against Jews. Leaders of the Union put pressure on the Tsar to withdraw the concessions he had made, and Nicholas II showed himself more amenable to conservative than he had

Peasant Bargemen of the Volga. I. J. Repine (d. 1930).

been to liberal influence. In the decree of March 1906 establishing the Council of the Empire, he forbade the new parliament to discuss constitutional laws, asserted his own autocratic control of military and foreign affairs, and authorized imperial ministers to promulgate laws when the Duma was not in session, and to proceed on the basis of the old budget if in any year a new budget was not approved. Then Nicholas II installed as premier an energetic conservative, Peter Stolypin.

Stolypin repressed revolutionary agitation and treated quite cavalierly the Duma which had been elected and had assembled at St. Petersburg in May 1906. When the Cadet and Social Revolutionary majority in the Duma proposed parliamentary control of the imperial ministers and a program of land reform to break up large estates, Stolypin rejected their proposals, dissolved the Duma, and ordered new elections. Thereupon, two hundred Cadet members of the Duma, in imitation of the Tennis Court meeting of the French deputies in 1789, assembled at Viborg in Finland and drew

Nicholas II. Valentine Syerov (d. 1911).

up a manifesto calling on the Russian people to refuse taxes and military service till the Tsar's government should respect the Duma. The Viborg manifesto produced only a feeble response. Its authors were disfranchised; the Cadet clubs were suppressed; the few attempts at insurrection were put down; some revolutionaries were executed and many others banished.

Despite governmental interference, the opponents of autocracy obtained a majority in the second Duma, which met in March 1907. Again there was a collision between the ministers and the legislature. Again the government dissolved the Duma. This time, however, Nicholas II issued a new "constitutional law" obviously intended to assure the election of future Dumas which would not oppose the government. The suffrage was elaborately restricted. Electoral districts were redrawn so that conservative rural voters could swamp the radically inclined cities.

The new system worked as Nicholas II and Stolypin intended. The third Duma, chosen in October 1907, contained an overwhelming majority of Conservatives and Octobrists, who were quite willing to have the Duma restricted to a consultative role. Outside the Duma, revolutionary opposition continued from radicals and members of the subject nationalities, but it no longer terrified the government. The revolutionary upheaval of 1905 had subsided and left behind only the democratic reforms in Finland and a slightly altered form of imperial government which the official almanac of 1907 appropriately described as "a constitutional monarchy under an autocratic Tsar."

B. Diplomatic Crises Over Morocco and the Balkans

We have seen in an earlier chapter how the Triple Alliance of Germany, Austria, and Italy was balanced in the 1890's by the Dual Alliance of France and Russia.[1] For a time, Great Britain tended to coöperate with the former, but as naval rivalry developed with Germany, it veered toward the Dual Alliance. In 1904, negotiations between Britain and France, by settling colonial disputes between them, linked them in

[1] See above, p. 660.

an *Entente Cordiale* (friendly understanding). It was not an alliance, but it rapidly developed into something closely approaching one, for the two countries supported each other in one diplomatic crisis after another, and, under Sir Edward Grey, the British Foreign Minister, military and naval "conversations" were initiated which by 1912 resulted in "understandings" as to how the two countries would support each other in case of war. Britain agreed to protect the French Channel and North Sea coast by her navy in the event of war between France and Germany, so as to enable the French to concentrate their fleet in the Mediterranean.

The *Entente* was soon extended by the inclusion of France's ally, Russia. The defeat of Russia by Japan in 1905 eased British fear of Russian advances in Asia. With French encouragement, Britain and Russia settled in 1907 their pending conflicts in Asia. Henceforth, the Triple Alliance of Germany, Austria, and Italy was confronted by the Triple Entente of France, Russia and Great Britain, with Japan as a close associate of the latter. Moreover, Italy was not wholly loyal to the Triple Alliance, for in 1902 she secretly joined France in a mutual pledge of neutrality if either should be attacked. Though the line-up of the European great powers was reasonably clear by 1908, it must be remembered that the exact terms of most of the treaties and understandings were secret. This secrecy tended to increase mutual suspicion and fear, and in ensuing crises no nation was quite sure where its enemies or even its supposed friends stood.

Between 1905 and 1913 there were recurrent diplomatic crises. Some had to do with Morocco, and others with the Balkans. All were settled by diplomatic means without bringing about a war among the major nations. But each might have caused a war; each shook the foundations of European peace; each alarmed statesmen and lent weight to the arguments of those who pleaded for bigger armies and navies.

The French had long been increasing their influence in Morocco, and by 1905 the French foreign minister, Delcassé, had plans well advanced for the establishment of a French protectorate over the greater part of that country. He secured the assent of Italy (1900), and of Britain (1904), and he reached an agreement with Spain, whereby the Spanish would be given a protectorate over the part of Morocco not appropriated by France. Morocco was a backward and brigand-ridden country, and, though its independence had been affirmed by an international congress at Madrid in 1880, its fate seemed to Delcassé to concern only France and Spain.

The German chancellor, Bülow, thought otherwise. He was eager to check France by asserting Germany's interest in Morocco and to weaken the entente between France and Great Britain. Picking a favorable moment, just three weeks after the defeat of France's ally, Russia, by the Japanese at Mukden, he arranged to have the German

Emperor William II land at Tangier and ostentatiously salute the Sultan of Morocco as an "independent" ruler in whose lands "*all* foreign nations" would enjoy equal rights.

There followed a brief moment of awful suspense. Then Delcassé resigned and France agreed to submit the whole Moroccan question to an international congress. The congress met at Algeciras in Spain in 1906 and proved a disappointment to Bülow. Britain consistently backed France, and so did Italy. The final agreement, while paying lip service to the independence of the Sultan and the "open door" for the commerce of all nations in Morocco, authorized the French and Spanish to instruct and officer a native police force and to oversee the execution of "reforms." Thus, to all

Luncheon of the Boating Party. Pierre Auguste Renoir (d. 1919).

Photo by Lewis P. Woltz; courtesy Phillips Memorial Gallery, Washington, D.C.

intents and purposes, despite Bülow's efforts, the Algeciras conference resulted in a French victory.

Another and acute Moroccan crisis was precipitated in 1911 when the French sent an army to Fez "to restore order," and Germany despatched a warship, the *Panther*, to the port of Agadir, ostensibly to safeguard German mining interests, but with a significant hint that the warship would be withdrawn only when the French left Fez. So grave was the situation that military preparations were hurried forward in France and Germany. Russia was not sufficiently recovered from the Japanese war to promise much assistance, but the British proclaimed their full support of France.

After some bickering and much tension, a Franco-German convention was concluded, whereby Germany promised not to oppose the establishment of a French protectorate in Morocco, and France agreed to maintain the "open door" there. In addition, as a sort of bribe, which represented a real reward to the Germans for their obstructive tactics, France ceded to Germany two strips of French Equatorial Africa. Though both Moroccan crises were thus resolved without war, they served to quicken hostility between Germany and France and to consolidate the friendship of France and Great Britain. Germany by her strong-arm methods assumed, in the eyes of the outside world, something of the role of a bully.

Even more disquieting than the Moroccan crises were those in the Balkans, where Austria-Hungary and Russia were the major opponents rather than France and Germany, though the two latter nations were involved through their efforts to support their respective allies. Germany had special motives for backing up Austria, since she was eager to spread her own influence in the Ottoman Empire. In 1899 the Emperor William II paid a ceremonious visit to the Sultan. From 1903 Germans were involved in plans for building a "Berlin-to-Bagdad" railway. German officers were training the Turkish army.

A major crisis in the Balkans occurred in 1908, when Austria-Hungary took advantage of a Turkish revolution to annex outright the Serb-speaking provinces of Bosnia and Herzegovina, which she had been "administering" under the provisions of the treaty of Berlin,[1] and which Serbia coveted. A storm of indignation arose in Serbia, which aroused sympathetic response in Russia. But Germany announced her firm intention of giving full military support to Austria-Hungary. Russia, still not fully recovered from the Japanese war, had to give way and Serbia was compelled to promise that she would not countenance anti-Austrian propaganda and would live on "good neighborly terms" with the Dual Monarchy. Peace was preserved. But Russia and Serbia, humiliated by the incident, drew closer together; and Serbia was swept by a fierce wave of expansionist nationalism.

By 1911, the international situation was extraordinarily perilous. Recurrent crises in Morocco and the Balkans had cost every great power some measure of prestige. Germany had been outplayed in Morocco by France and Britain. But France had been forced to cede African territory to Germany, and Britain had lost influence in the Ottoman Empire. Russia had been outplayed in the Balkans by Austria-Hungary and Germany, but was now backing Serbia and was resolved not to be outplayed again. Germany was coming to believe that, instead of exercising predominance in Europe as she had done in the days of Bismarck, she was now "encircled" by a ring of potentially hostile powers. But the more a great power was threatened with the loss of prestige, the less yielding and conciliatory it was likely to be.

C. Revolution in the Ottoman Empire, and the Italian and Balkan Wars of 1911–1913

Three years after the Russian revolutionary upheaval of 1905, the Ottoman Empire underwent a revolution. Since the 1890's there had been movements aimed at reforming and modernizing the Empire. The most vigorous in its radicalism and nationalism was that of the "Young Turks," led by Enver Bey, who formed a revolutionary "Committee of Union and Progress." In July 1908, this committee, with the

---

[1] See above, p. 655.

support of the army, executed a *coup* at Salonica, proclaimed in force the long-suspended constitution of 1876, and threatened the Sultan Abdul Hamid II with deposition if he should offer resistance. Thoroughly frightened, the Sultan endorsed the restoration of the constitution, abolished the censorship, and put a Liberal, Kiamil Pasha, at the head of the ministry.

The new regime failed to maintain internal order or to prevent foreign aggression; and in 1909 Enver and the committee executed a second *coup*, deposed the Sultan, and put in his place his mild-mannered brother, Mohammed V. The liberal cabinet of Kiamil Pasha was replaced by a Young Turk ministry, and the parliament was transformed into a National Assembly. From 1909 to 1918 the government of the Ottoman Empire was practically a military dictatorship headed by Enver Bey (who soon was promoted to be Enver Pasha). The aim of the Young Turks was a vigorous nationalism. They planned to "Turkify" the Empire by forcing all its peoples to use the Turkish language, to accept a system of national education, and to serve in a common national army. Though they had the existing army back of them, the program of the Young Turks was impracticable, for there were too many Christians and non-Turkish Moslems in the Empire who were opposed to it; and such opposition was encouraged from abroad.

In September 1911 Italy suddenly announced her intention of annexing the Ottoman north African provinces of Tripoli and Cyrenaica. The Young Turk government replied by a resolute declaration of war and sent Enver Pasha to undertake the defense of the provinces. But the war resulted in a double loss for the Turks. Enough Turkish troops could not be sent to Africa to prevent Italy from making good her conquest there. But enough were sent to encourage the Balkan nations to attempt to seize lands of the Ottoman Empire in Europe. Before the Turco-Italian war was ended in October 1912 by the treaty of Lausanne, which gave Italy Cyrenaica and Tripoli and permitted her to administer the Dodecanese Islands in the Aegean, the Balkan War of 1912–1913 had begun. The Ottoman Empire was in its death throes.

Shrewdly sizing up the growing weakness of the Empire, King Ferdinand of Bulgaria organized a Balkan League of Bulgaria, Serbia, Greece, and Montenegro. After feverish military preparations, it attacked the Ottoman Empire in October 1912. The Turks brought back Kiamil Pasha as prime minister, won some diplomatic support from the Great Powers, terminated the war with Italy, and threw all their military strength into the defense of their European territories. But in spite of these efforts, the Balkan allies, to everyone's surprise, overwhelmed the Turkish resistance, captured Salonica and Monastir, overran Macedonia, and by March 1913 the Bulgarians were in possession of Adrianople, while the Serbs took Scutari in April. Finally in May 1913 Enver Pasha had to accept the peace terms of the Balkan League as amended by the great powers, even though the Ottoman Empire thus lost all its European territory save Constantinople and a narrow strip along the Bosporus and Dardanelles.

It was one thing to despoil the Turks and quite another to divide the booty, for not only were Balkan allies very jealous of each other, but Austria-Hungary was determined to prevent the enlargement of a pro-Russian Serbia. In this determination, Austria was backed by Germany and Italy and opposed by Russia and France. For a time it seemed as if the major powers would go to war over the Balkan problem. But at last a compromise was reached. Serbia was allowed to expand southward but was barred from the Adriatic by the erection of an independent state of Albania under a German prince.

If a world war was thus staved off, another Balkan war was let loose. Serbia, deprived of the portion of Albania she had expected, demanded a part of Macedonia which had been tentatively assigned to Bulgaria, and Greece was at odds with Bulgaria over the division of Thrace. By June 1913 Serbia and Greece were fighting Bulgaria and they were soon joined by Rumania, which, though hitherto passive, was fearful of an enlarged Bulgaria. The Turks, hopeful of regaining some of their losses, likewise threw their troops against Bulgaria. In July 1913 the Turks recaptured Adrianople,

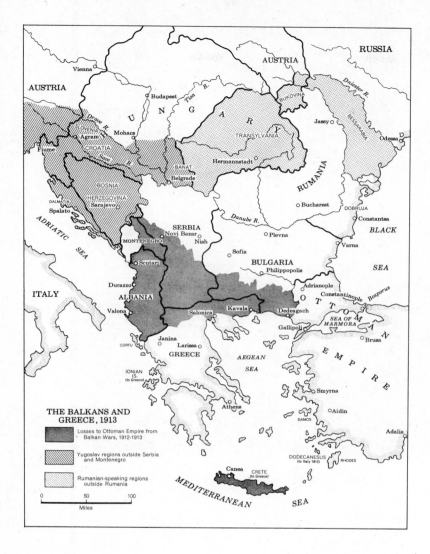

THE BALKANS AND
GREECE, 1913

Losses to Ottoman Empire from
Balkan Wars, 1912-1913

Yugoslav regions outside Serbia
and Montenegro

Rumanian-speaking regions
outside Rumania

while the Greeks, Serbs, and Rumanians were closing in on the Bulgarian capital of Sofia. Unable to secure aid from the great powers, King Ferdinand of Bulgaria had to make peace. The treaty of Bucharest in August 1913 reassigned the spoils of the previous war. Serbia got a large chunk of Macedonia. Greece secured Crete, southern Epirus, southern Macedonia (including Salonica), and part of western Thrace. Bulgaria retained a bit of Macedonia and the region of central Thrace. But to Rumania, Bulgaria had to cede her northeastern territory of Dobruja and subsequently she had to give back Adrianople to the Turks.

By the two wars of 1912–1913, all the Balkan states were enlarged at the expense of the Ottoman Empire, and a new nation, Albania, was created. But Bulgaria was left feeling cheated and revengeful. The nationalism, the jealousies, and the rivalries of the Balkan countries were greatly intensified. And the great powers eyed each other with ever greater suspicion and hostility. The Balkan Wars proved a prelude to much vaster conflict.

D. Multiple Origins of World War I

The First World War scarcely deserves the title, for the War of the Spanish Succession, the Seven Years' War, and the

Memorial to Peter I, King of Serbia 1903–1918 and of Yugoslavia 1918–1921. Ivan Mestrovic (d. 1962).

Napoleonic conflicts had all been struggles waged on the high seas and on several continents. But because of its magnitude, the number of participants, the costs in men and money, and the ending of a long period of comparative peace, this war seemed to contemporaries to be of a completely new order. Its origins were multiple, and their general nature may be indicated as follows:

1. *Diplomatic.* We have seen how, between 1891 and 1914, the great powers of Europe had become aligned in two camps, each bound by secret engagements, and each jealous and suspicious of the other. We have seen likewise how a series of crises, especially those connected with Morocco and the Balkans, heightened the tension between Triple Entente and Triple Alliance. By 1914, each group of powers felt cheated or thwarted, and unwilling to make the kind of concessions necessary to surmount the next crisis by compromise. Diplomacy certainly did not cause the World War, but it helped to create a situation in which it could take place.

2. *Political and Nationalist.* Behind most of the occurrences which led toward the war lay political rivalries and nationalistic aspirations. It was the excesses of modern nationalism which induced democratic and not-so-democratic statesmen to squabble over their nations' interests in Africa, Asia, and the Balkans. It was nationalism which made the French long to recover Alsace-Lorraine, and the Russians to extend their control southward. It was nationalism which embittered the rivalries of states like Great

Britain and Germany and encouraged them to military and naval competition. Most important of all, nationalism was an explosive force which had already disrupted the Ottoman Empire and now seriously threatened the integrity of other conglomerate Empires—most notably the Austrian, but even, perhaps, the Russian. Nationalistic Serbia, fresh from helping to break up the Ottoman Empire, was aflame with zeal to expand at the expense of the Austrian Empire; and the statesmen of the latter made frantic efforts to safeguard it against any nationalist dissolution.

3. *Economic*. Deeply ensnarled with other factors were those of an economic nature. Germany and Great Britain were engaged in industrial and commercial competition. Germany by great efforts was gaining ground. Britain was in danger of losing her preëminent position. Such economic contention led to friction and suspicion between the two nations and prepared the people of one to look upon people of the other as rivals. In lesser degree there were similar economic rivalries between Russia and Germany, between France and Germany, and so on. Excited by nationalistic propaganda, economic rivalry became just as real as the bonds of economic solidarity that held nations together.

4. *Military*. From the rising nationalist sentiments and the anarchical state of international relations arose military and naval rivalries that themselves led toward war by making Europe an armed camp and putting in the hands of each country a military machine ready for use. More than anything else perhaps, naval rivalry embittered Anglo-German relations, while the competitive race in land armies and armaments increased fear and hostility among all the continental countries. Advice of general staffs was usually asked in each diplomatic crisis, and sometimes, as in the case of Austria or Russia, the military experts found reasons for urging steps more warlike than those advocated by diplomats or politicians. Indeed, the balance of military power on the continent was close enough to make each nation fearful lest another obtain the advantage by a head-start in mobilization.

5. *Social*. There was a wide variety of social factors. They ranged from a belief in "social Darwinism"—that the fittest nation (in a military sense) would survive and grow, or that war was a healthy part of the "struggle for existence"—to a belief in the superiority of the French or German or Russian or some other "culture." They included unfortunate effects of mass journalism in an age of literacy, and of patriotic oratory in a period of democracy. Basically, the decline of Christian faith among many people helped to create a mood in which war was less shocking to the ethical sense of mankind. In a materialist world, what was wrong with the use of material force to gain material ends?

Unsuspected by masses of Europeans still basking in the declining sun of "peace and prosperity," war clouds were gathering in 1914 on every horizon.

Archduke Francis Ferdinand of Austria and his wife.

Photo by Underwood & Underwood, New York

CHAPTER 55

World War I, 1914–1918

A. Outbreak of the War: Central Powers versus Allied and Associated Powers

On June 28, 1914, the Archduke Francis Ferdinand, nephew of the Emperor Francis Joseph and heir to the thrones of Austria and Hungary, was assassinated, together with his wife, in the Bosnian town of Sarajevo, by a band of nationalist Serbs. The assassination evoked a storm of indignation in Austria-Hungary and invited the Austrian foreign minister, Count Berchtold, to have a reckoning with Serbia. It is now known that the assassins, though natives of Bosnia and thus subjects of the Habsburg Empire, were members of a Serbian secret society, the "Black Hand," that they had been armed and trained in Serbia, and that they had been assisted by high officers in the Serbian army. It is also fairly certain that important Serbian officials, including the prime minister, had foreknowledge of the conspiracy and yet gave the Austrian government no adequate warning.

At the time, despite his suspicions, Count Berchtold could get no proof of the complicity of the Serb government. But determined to crush Serbia, he proceeded as if he had the necessary evidence. With some difficulty, he won over the Hungarian premier and the Emperor Francis Joseph to his plans. On July 5–6, an emissary of his secured from the German Emperor William II a pledge of un-

qualified support for Austria in any action she might take against Serbia. This "blank check" with which Germany underwrote Berchtold's schemes was a serious mistake, since William II, though eager to back up his Austrian ally and to avenge the Archduke, does not appear to have wanted a major war at this juncture.

Having gained the support of Germany, Berchtold presented Serbia, on July 23, with an ultimatum, acceptance of which he demanded in forty-eight hours. In it he called upon Serbia to suppress anti-Austrian propaganda, to dismiss anti-Austrian officials, and to accept the aid of agents of the Austro-Hungarian government in repressing the revolutionary movement which sought to gain for Serbia lands of the Dual Monarchy. On July 25 the Serbian government replied, accepting all demands that would not impair its "independence and sovereignty" and offering to refer disputed points to the Hague Court or to an international conference. At the same time, the Serbs ordered the mobilization of their army. Whereupon the Austro-Hungarian government pronounced the Serbian reply evasive, broke off diplomatic relations with Serbia, and likewise ordered mobilization. War was clearly impending between Austria and Serbia.

But a vaster war was also impending. The Russian government felt that if it stood aside and let Austria crush Serbia, Russian prestige in the Balkans would be shattered. From the French President

Raymond Poincaré, who was paying a state visit to St. Petersburg, Russia received assurance of French support. France had no eagerness for war, but feared lest she lose her ally or the alliance lose prestige. On July 26 the British Foreign Minister, Sir Edward Grey, urged that a conference of diplomats try to find a peaceful solution to the crisis. France and Italy responded in a favorable manner. But Germany, afraid that at such a conference she would be outplayed as at Algeciras in 1906,[1] replied that the dispute concerned only Austria and Serbia and hence that the other powers should strive merely to "localize" the dispute, that is, to keep the war a small one. With this evidence of Germany's support, Austria declared war on Serbia on July 28.

Events then marched fast. Amidst frantic diplomatic efforts to preserve peace, military preparations were pushed ahead with feverish haste. On July 29, when news of the Austrian declaration of war reached St. Petersburg, the Tsar Nicholas II was prevailed upon to order a general mobilization of the Russian army. That evening, von Moltke, German chief of staff and nephew of the Prussian commander in 1870, argued in a council at Potsdam that war was inevitable and that Germany should mobilize at once.

That night, William II, alarmed at the prospect of war, tried to persuade Austria to negotiate with Russia and begged the Tsar to take no military measures which "would precipitate a calamity we both wish to avoid." But it was too late to swerve Berchtold from his course, and, when the Tsar tried to change the general mobilization to a partial one, the Russian foreign minister, urged on by the Russian military men who had no plans for a partial mobilization, soon persuaded him (July 30) to renew the orders for general mobilization. Russian mobilization transformed the Austro-Serbian war into a general conflict. Von Moltke now had no difficulty in convincing William II that Germany could not delay her own mobilization without risking disaster. On July 31 Germany

presented Russia with a twelve-hour ultimatum demanding immediate demobilization. Russia did not reply. Germany declared war.

Germany knew that war with Russia was almost certain to involve France. Accordingly on July 31, Germany presented an eighteen-hour ultimatum to France, demanding that she should declare her neutrality. Had France agreed, Germany would then have demanded the right to occupy the French fortresses of Toul and Verdun till peace was restored. But France did not agree. Instead, she merely stated on August 1 that she "would consult her interests" and at once began mobilization. On August 3, 1914, Germany declared war on France.

The British on the whole were sympathetic to France, and Sir Edward Grey on August 2 told the Germans that Britain would not tolerate naval attacks on the French coasts or shipping. But there was strong pacifist sentiment both among the people and in the cabinet. Germany, however, soon solidified British opinion against her, for on August 2 she occupied the neutral Grand Duchy of Luxembourg, and presented a twelve-hour ultimatum to Belgium requiring free passage of German troops across Belgian territory. The Belgian government refused and appealed to Britain, which, with Prussia and the other great powers, had guaranteed Belgian neutrality in 1839. Aroused by this violation of international law, and by the threat to the Low Countries whose independence Great Britain had always sought to maintain, the British government declared war on Germany at midnight on August 4. In his disappointment, the German Chancellor, Bethmann-Hollweg, berated the British ambassador for Britain's going to war "just for a scrap of paper."

The major contestants were now at war with each other. But gradually other nations were drawn into the conflict. On August 7, tiny Montenegro joined her fellow Yugoslav state of Serbia against Austria-Hungary. Japan, perceiving a chance to advance her interests, declared war on Germany on August 23. The Ottoman Empire, hoping to regain its recently lost territories, signed

---

[1] See above, p. 704.

A Dawn in 1914. After an etching by the British artist C. R. W. Nevinson.

on August 1 a secret treaty of alliance with Germany, and on October 29 bombarded Russian Black Sea ports, thus forcing the Entente powers to declare war. At the outbreak of the conflict, Italy and Rumania, though nominal allies of the Central Powers, remained neutral on the ground that the war was not defensive on the part of Germany and Austria-Hungary. Thus Italy lived up to a secret agreement of 1902 with France. Soon, both sides were bidding for the support of these neutrals and in the game of promising bribes the Entente Allies had the advantage, for they

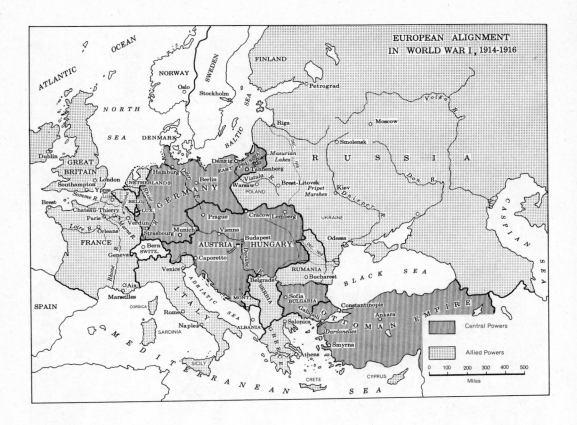

could agree to give to Italy long-coveted blocks of Austrian territory, and to Rumania large slices of Hungarian lands.

In April 1915, Italy signed a secret treaty with the Allies at London, whereby she was promised financial aid and territory in Africa as well as in Austria and the Ottoman Empire, if she would come into the war. On May 23, despite the fact that the armies of the Allies were suffering reverses, Italy declared war on Austria. Italy's entrance was balanced to some degree by the fact that Bulgaria, still smarting from her losses in 1913 and encouraged by German victories, allied herself with the Central Powers in September 1915, in return for promises of territorial gains, and on October 14 declared war on Serbia. Rumania held off until 1916, by which time the pro-German King Ferdinand had been succeeded by his pro-Ally nephew Carol and the Allies had won some encouraging victories. In return for promises of territorial extensions, Rumania declared war on Austria on August 27, 1916. By this time Portugal, long an ally of Britain,

had declared war on Germany (March 9, 1916). Thus all Europe, save Scandinavia, Holland, Switzerland, and Spain, was engaged in the struggle, for the Allies were using Greek territory for operations as early as 1915, though they did not force that country formally into the war till July 1917.

At the outbreak of the war the American President, Woodrow Wilson, had proclaimed the neutrality of the United States and had urged its people to be "neutral in fact as well as in name." As the war progressed, however, such neutrality proved difficult to maintain. Britain halted and searched American ships and seized contraband cargoes. But such violations of American rights could be paid for, later, in cash. More serious were the sinkings of American ships by the submarines with which Germany fought the British blockade. Against such sinkings, Wilson protested sternly, and likewise against the sinking of British vessels with American cargoes and passengers aboard. On May 7, 1915, the British liner "Lusitania" was sunk with the loss of about a hundred

American lives. Backed by the growing pro-Allied sympathy at home, Wilson took a strong stand and forced Germany to promise to refrain from sinking merchant vessels without providing for the safety of the passengers.

Thus the action of the United States put a stop to the one effective German weapon against the British blockade. But early in 1917 Germany announced her intention of resuming unrestricted submarine warfare. The German leaders felt sure that Britain could be starved into submission before American aid could be effective. The United States at once broke off diplomatic relations with Germany, and, when the Germans carried out their threat of sinking merchantmen regardless of the flag they flew or the passengers they carried, the United States declared war on Germany, on April 6, 1917. In the following months a number of Latin American countries, together with Siam, Liberia, and China, followed the lead of the United States. The whole world seemed to be arraying itself on the side of the Allies.

B. First Stage (1914–1916), from German Success to Deadlock

The war came as a terrific shock to Europe. In an instant, dreams of peaceful progress evaporated. Yet everywhere, stirred by patriotic sentiments, people rallied to the support of their respective governments. Pacifism evaporated, and neither the Christian churches nor the Socialist parties were able to maintain any international solidarity. It was quickly apparent that nationalism was the strongest sentiment in Europe.

At the start, it was generally expected that the war would be a brief one, and for a time German successes were such that it seemed as if the conflict might be ended in a few months. The German military plan was to strike first and with superior strength in the west against France, and then when France was crushed, to turn eastward and overwhelm Russia. In pursuit of this plan, huge German armies advanced rapidly through Belgium, overcoming all resistance there, and driving French armies and a

British "expeditionary force" backward toward Paris. Only a few days after the outbreak of hostilities, the German commander-in-chief, von Moltke, wired the Emperor William II, "In six weeks the whole story will be concluded."

But the Germans were overconfident. They made tactical blunders. They allowed a gap to open up between two of their advancing armies. On September 6, almost in sight of Paris, they were halted by the French and the British and in the next three days, in a series of actions known as the Battle of the Marne, they were forced to retreat. By September 14 the Germans were on the defensive.

The "miracle of the Marne," as the French called it, prevented a speedy German victory and produced a stalemate. Both sides rapidly extended their lines and dug themselves in, until a series of entrenched armies opposed each other from the North Sea coast of Belgium to the Swiss border. A war of movement and maneuver had been expected. Instead, it was now trench warfare, in which the machine gun was king, and advance obtainable only by appalling casualties. As the war progressed, attempts were made to break up the trench warfare by heavy artillery barrages, by the use of poison gases (Germans), and by tanks (British). But until 1918 none of these attempts achieved more than partial and momentary success. The western front was deadlocked.

It was otherwise in the east. At the start of the war, the Russians, with surprising speed, invaded Austrian Galicia and German East Prussia. In Galicia, they met with success, but in East Prussia their early advance was turned into a crushing disaster involving the loss of 300,000 men and vast amounts of material, when the Germans under Generals Hindenburg and Ludendorff routed one Russian army and broke up another in the battles of Tannenberg (August 26–31, 1914) and the Masurian Lakes (September 5–15, 1914).

The Austrians not only were defeated in Galicia, but their invasion of Serbia was checked and then pushed back. The Germans, even though it meant weakening the west front, had to come to their aid. In a great offensive at Gorlice (May 1915)

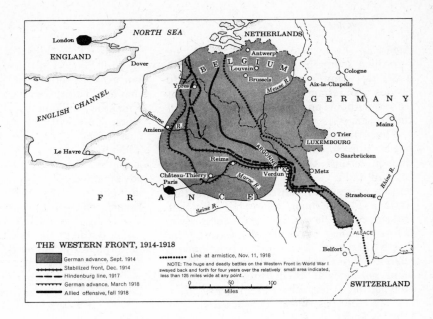

THE WESTERN FRONT, 1914-1918

- ▨ German advance, Sept. 1914
- ━━━━ Stabilized front, Dec. 1914
- ┅┿┅┿┅ Hindenburg line, 1917
- ━┰━┰━ German advance, March 1918
- ━━━━ Allied offensive, fall 1918
- •••••••• Line at armistice, Nov. 11, 1918

NOTE: The huge and deadly battles on the Western Front in World War I swayed back and forth for four years over the relatively small area indicated, less than 125 miles wide at any point.

0   50   100
Miles

the Germans and Austrians under General Falkenhayn pushed back the Russians and exploited this success so well that by September 1915 all Poland and most of Lithuania were in the hands of the Central Powers. Though Italy declared war on Austria, the Austrians for almost a year easily held their mountainous frontier against the Italians.

Fresh from his eastern victories, Falkenhayn hurried west in September 1915 with reserve troops and checked a French offensive in Champagne. Then joined by Bulgaria, Germany and Austria turned on the stubborn Serbs. By the end of the year they had overrun all Serbia and Montenegro and occupied Albania as well. Linked up by land with the Ottoman Empire, the Central Powers now were dominant from the Persian Gulf to the North Sea, and their improved position was emphasized by a British failure. Early in 1915, in a plan inspired by Winston Churchill, a Franco-British fleet attempted to force the Dardanelles in order to open a short supply route to Russia, which was already desperately short of munitions. The attempt failed, and a costly landing on the Gallipoli peninsula was held in check by the Turks under German leadership. In December 1915 the whole venture was abandoned.

In February 1916, the Germans opened up a tremendous offensive on the western front, designed to take the French fortress of Verdun and to "bleed France white" in the process. A gigantic battle dragged on from February to July, but in face of heroic French defense, the Germans failed to take Verdun. On both sides, the losses in men were staggering. In May the Austrians weakened their Russian front for a drive on Italy. But though the Italians retreated at first, they soon held, and the Austrians had to shift troops back to the Russian front to try to stem a Russian offensive under General Brusilov that won back most of Galicia. The victories of Brusilov, and of an Italian counteroffensive that gained the key city of Gorizia, helped to persuade Rumania to come into the war (August 1916). But the Rumanians had waited too long. An Austro-German army under Falkenhayn quickly overran Rumania, so that, by the end of 1916, its resources of oil and wheat were at the disposal of the Central Powers.

By this time, such resources were becoming of crucial importance. At the beginning, all the participants, even Germany, were ill-prepared for a long war. But once it was realized that the struggle would be long and very costly, every belligerent undertook an economic mobilization. Never before had governments been so active nor their influence so pervasive. If at first they hesitated and fumbled, gradually their efforts became more effective. Germany was first, and most perfectly, organized. In Austria-Hungary more than 80 "centrals" were set up to handle various phases of production and distribution. France established a whole series of committees, commissions, and "offices." Britain had "control boards" and committees composed of representatives of capital, labor, and the state. Even corrupt and backward Russia tried to organize its economic effort through a "central war industries committee" instituted in May 1915.

Among the Central Powers, Germany was clearly the leading partner, though she sometimes had difficulty in keeping Austria in line. Among the Allies there was a difficult task of coördination which was handled with only partial success. The Allied military command was not unified till the last months of the war. In the economic field there was earlier and better coöperation. Britain and France established commissions to make common purchases, and a joint agency for control of ships and shipping which served not only to speed supplies to France or Britain, but also to discipline neutral powers by cutting off their imports and exports.

In the economic warfare between the Allies and the Central Powers, the most effective weapons were, respectively, the British blockade and the German submarines. By its control of the sea, Britain captured or sank or drove into hiding practically all German ships. Gradually, by a system of control and inspection, she throttled even the imports Germany could get via neutral countries like Holland or Sweden. Within the bonds of the British blockade, Germany writhed to no avail. She was short of food (desperately so by 1918), short of copper, oil, and rubber; and *ersatz* (substitute) products by no means filled the gap. On only one occasion did Germany challenge the British fleet, the basis of the blockade. That was off Jutland at the end of May 1916. In a great naval battle, a German fleet which had ventured out into the North Sea encountered a

British armada. The British lost more ships and lives. But the German warships retreated to their home harbors and did not again emerge.

If Germany was strangled by the blockade, Britain was vulnerable as an island. By commerce raiders, floating mines, and especially by submarines, the Germans sought to destroy the shipping by which England drew on the outer world for food and supplies. In April 1917 submarine warfare reached a peak, and one ship out of four that left the British Isles was torpedoed. If the Germans could have redoubled their efforts, Britain might have been put out of the war. But the British (and now the Americans as well) met the threat by a gigantic shipbuilding campaign, by anti-submarine weapons (depth bombs, wire nets, listening devices), and by sending vessels in convoys guarded by warships. The crisis was past and before the war was over 200 German submarines were destroyed. But the shipping losses of the Allies (especially of Britain) were staggering. Before the end of the war they amounted to about 6,000 vessels totaling almost fifteen million tons, or some three-fifths of the shipping with which the Allies had begun the war.

C. The Russian Revolutions of 1917

By 1917 the Allies were generally victorious outside the European Continent. The Japanese had seized the German treaty ports in China and the German islands in the Pacific. British, French, and Belgians had captured all the German colonies in Africa, except German East Africa, and this could not hold out much longer. In the Near East, the British, after a series of failures in 1915, had captured Bagdad and most of Mesopotamia (Iraq); and in 1917, under General Allenby, and with Arab support, they conquered Palestine.

Within Europe the Allies were less successful. True, the Central Powers had experienced discouragement in 1916 by the failure of the Verdun campaign, by heavy losses from a British offensive on the Somme, and by the entrance of Rumania into the war. Falkenhayn had been dismissed from chief command (August 1916), and Hindenburg (with Ludendorff) had been made virtually a military dictator. Under Hindenburg's guidance, the Germans on the western front early in 1917 retreated to the heavily fortified "Hindenburg Line." Thereby they gave up about a thousand square miles of territory, but straightened their lines and conserved their waning man-power. Some of the German Socialists and Centrists commenced to clamor for peace, while the new Emperor of Austria, Charles I (1916–1918), began secret but fruitless peace negotiations with the Allies.

Nevertheless the Central Powers were clearly dominant throughout the Balkans. They had pressed the Russians far back and were easily holding the Italians in check. Germany was in a strong defensive position in the west, and its leaders hoped that unrestricted submarine warfare would bring success in 1917. Such was the general situation when a series of events in Russia proved as encouraging to the Central Powers as it was discouraging to the Allies.

Since 1915 things had been going from bad to worse in Russia. Brusilov's victories in 1916 had been more than offset by the incompetence and corruption of the Tsarist regime. The Russian armies were desperately short of munitions and supplies. In vain, the Cadets and Octobrists in the Duma urged the establishment of constitutional government and a responsible ministry. The Duma was dissolved and its members sent home or jailed. In vain, a convention of *zemstvos* endorsed the Duma's recommendations. It too was dissolved. In vain, Russian patriots of all classes pleaded for reforms. The Tsar and his government went on with their incompetent blundering.

During the winter of 1916–1917 popular disaffection overspread Russia. The subject nationalities grew restless. The middle classes grumbled. There were riots of peasants and strikes of workers. Revolution was precipitated by the decrees of the autocratic government on March 11, 1917, that the Petrograd strikers should go to work and that the recently reassembled Duma should again go home. The strikers refused to obey and won over to their side the soldiers upon whom the government relied to suppress them. They formed a revolutionary "soviet" (or council) of soldiers and workingmen. The Duma likewise refused to obey, and, by agreement between it and the Petrograd Soviet, a provisional government was set up on March 14 under the chairmanship of Prince George Lvov, a liberal landlord. The next day a deputation waited on the Tsar at Pskov and obtained his abdication.

The provisional government at once proclaimed freedom of speech, press, association, and religion. It released political prisoners, permitted the return of political exiles, restored full autonomy to Finland, and promised it to Poland. It announced that a National Constituent Assembly would shortly be elected by universal manhood suffrage to draw up a constitution for Russia. At the same time, it strove to infuse new energy into Russia's prosecution of the war.

There was momentary rejoicing among the Allies, for they imagined that a democratic Russia would fight more vigorously than an autocratic one. In this, they were grievously disappointed. For three years Russia had suffered heavier losses than any other country. The masses were sick of war and soldiers wanted to get home. The provisional government could not agree on a program of reform or resist the pressures of the "soviets of soldiers, workers, and peasants" that were everywhere being formed. In May the discouraged Prince Lvov resigned and was succeeded by Kerensky, a member of the Social Revolutionary party.

Kerensky brought several moderate (Menshevik) Socialists into the ministry, but he failed to halt the subversive activities of the most radical group of Socialists, the "Bolsheviks" or "Communists." These were skillfully led by Nikolai Lenin (revolutionary name of Vladimir Ulyanov), who had returned from exile in Switzerland under a safe conduct from the Germans who were eager to foment further troubles in Russia, and by Leon Trotsky (revolutionary name of Lev Bronstein), who came back from exile in America. The Bolsheviks were a tiny minority of the population, and even of the proletarian and middle-class

Nikolai Lenin.
*Courtesy
Bettmann Archive*

radicals. But they had a philosophy, a program, and a technique of revolutionary organization. They got their members into key positions within the soviets at Petrograd, Moscow, and elsewhere. They urged a dictatorship of the workers and no compromise with capitalism. They proposed the nationalization of all factories and landed estates. For the war-weary population they promised a cessation of hostilities. For the hungry workers they promised food. Lenin's slogan, "Peace! Land! Bread!" struck deep chords among the Russian people and evoked favorable response from multitudes who were quite hazy about the principles of Marxian Socialism.

Kerensky vainly begged the Allies to consent to a general peace "without annexations or indemnities." He vainly tried to combat both Bolshevik and German propaganda and to restore discipline in the faltering Russian armies. He vainly launched a desperate offensive in July 1917. The Russian troops mutinied. The Austrians recovered all of Galicia. The Germans captured Riga and penetrated into Estonia.

In November 1917 a second revolution occurred in Russia. Kerensky's provisional government was overthrown, and Lenin, at the head of the Bolsheviks and working through the local soviets, took charge of affairs. One of the first acts of the new Communist regime was to agree to a truce with Germany and Austria-Hungary; and in March 1918, after protracted wrangling, a peace treaty was signed at Brest-Litovsk by Russia on one side and Germany and her allies on the other.

The peace thus dictated by Hindenburg and Ludendorff was harsh in the extreme and showed what the Allies might expect if they were defeated. It involved what amounted to a partition of the Russian Empire. Poland, Lithuania, and the Latvian province of Courland were ceded outright to Germany and Austria. Bessarabia was turned over to the Central Powers for transfer to Rumania. Armenian districts south of the Caucasus were surrendered to Turkey. Finland, Estonia, the Latvian province Livonia, and the huge area of the Ukraine were detached from Russia and recognized as independent states under German protection.

Rumania, completely isolated by the defection of Russia and largely in the hands of the Central Powers, felt obliged to sue for peace and to agree to a treaty which was imposed upon her at Bucharest in March 1918. Thereby Rumania yielded Dobruja to Bulgaria and certain mountain passes to Austria-Hungary. But in return for pledges of close coöperation with Germany and Austria, Rumania was promised Bessarabia.

Thus in 1917–1918 the Allied eastern front completely collapsed. Germany was free to devote her attention to the western front, and Austria-Hungary, though torn by a rising tide of nationalism among her subject peoples, had only to stand firm against Italy.

D. Last Stage (1917–1918): Defeat and Collapse of the Central Powers

The withdrawal of Russia from the war was a blow to the Allies. Yet before the treaty of Brest-Litvosk was signed, other events were turning the balance against the Central Powers. The Allies were receiving increasingly effective aid from the United States, first in ships, food, and munitions, but by 1918 in men as well. Disaffection was spreading rapidly among Poles, Czechs, and other subject peoples of Austria-Hungary. The German submarine campaign was not achieving its object,[1] but the British blockade was depriving Germany of direfully needed food and materials. The Allied war-aims set forth by

---

[1] The toll of Allied shipping taken by German submarines declined from four million tons in the first half of 1917 to two and a quarter million in the second half of 1917, and to a scant two million in the first half of 1918.

President Woodrow Wilson of the United States in his "fourteen points" of January 1918, strengthened morale of Allied peoples and correspondingly weakened that of peoples within the Central Powers. These points may be summarized thus:

1. "Open covenants of peace, openly arrived at," and no secret diplomacy in the future;
2. Freedom of the seas in peace and war;
3. Removal of economic barriers to the interests of subject peoples;
4. Reduction of armaments;
5. Impartial adjustments of colonial claims with due regard to the interests of subjected peoples;
6. Evacuation of Russian territory with full opportunity for Russia to determine her own future development;
7. Evacuation and restoration of Belgium;
8. Evacuation and restoration of French territory, and the return of Alsace-Lorraine to France;
9. Readjustment of Italian frontiers along clearly recognizable lines of nationality;
10. Autonomous development for the peoples of Austria-Hungary;
11. Evacuation and restoration of Serbia, Montenegro, and Rumania, an outlet to the sea for Serbia, interrelations of the Balkan states according to historical lines of allegiance and nationality;
12. Secure sovereignty for the Turkish parts of the Ottoman Empire, autonomy for the other portions, freedom of shipping through the Straits;
13. Establishment of an independent Poland with all territories inhabited by indisputably Polish population and with access to the sea;
14. Formation of a general association of nations to guarantee "political independence and territorial integrity to great and small states alike."

As their submarine campaign weakened and their man-power lessened, the Germans

under Hindenburg and Ludendorff made a supreme effort to smash the Allied armies in France before the full weight of American man-power became effective. In March 1918 they smote the British trenches in the valley of the Somme with a terrific assault and plowed through to Amiens. In April, they hit the British west of Lille and gained some fifteen miles. In May, with the last of their reserve troops and with boys called to military service ahead of time, they struck the French along the Aisne and fought their way forward to Château-Thierry on the Marne only forty-odd miles from Paris. Here, Marshal Ferdinand Foch, who had been named commander-in-chief of all the Allied armies, checked the Germans with the help of fresh American troops.

The furious drives and sledge-hammer blows of the Germans in the spring of 1918 netted them considerable territory, as well as prisoners and guns, and served to restore the western front almost to what it had been in 1914 on the eve of the first battle of the Marne. But they were supremely expensive, for they were accompanied by a frightful loss of life not only of French and British but of Germans as well, and German man-power was running low. In June the Germans could still push forward near Noyon another six miles. But a similar effort in July, aimed at Reims, encountered unyielding resistance and was quickly succeeded by a great Allied counter-offensive. Meanwhile, in June, an Austrian offensive against the Italians along the Piave River had been stopped and turned back. The day of military successes for the Central Powers was over, and the final triumph of the Allies began.

In 1918 the war governments of the Allies were in strong hands. Wilson directed the American effort. Lloyd George headed the ministry in Great Britain. Italy had a vigorous prime minister in Orlando. In France, the aged Clemenceau was virtual war dictator, with a fierce will to victory. The Allies now had satisfactory coördination in both military and economic matters, and their troops were at last well supplied with munitions of all sorts. Thanks to conscription in the United States, there were

a million American soldiers in France by July 1918, and in the next four months that number was doubled.

Having checked the Germans in the second battle of the Marne (July 1918), the Allies, flushed with victory and guided by the master hand of Foch, hammered at the German lines everywhere in France. While Franco-British armies recaptured Cambrai and Lille, Franco-American armies forced the Germans from St. Mihiel and cleared them out of the Argonne. By the end of October, the Germans had been driven almost completely out of France, and compelled to evacuate most of Belgium. Along the whole western front they were retreating so rapidly as to resemble a rout.

Meanwhile in the Near East, the British were pressing Turkey hard. With Arab aid they overran all Palestine and advanced into Syria. In October 1918, they captured both Damascus and Aleppo. From Salonica an Allied army, under a French general, Franchet d'Espérey, struck north, in September 1918, against the Bulgarians. Within two weeks Macedonia was cleared and Bulgaria itself was tottering.

Almost simultaneously, Austria-Hungary collapsed. Encouraged by Allied victories in the west and in the Balkans, the Czech and Yugoslav deputies in the Austrian parliament on October 1, 1918, proclaimed the right of their peoples to self-determination. On October 18, a declaration of independence was issued by the provisional government of the "Czechoslovak Republic" headed by Thomas Masaryk, an outstanding Czech scholar and patriot. Eleven days later the Croatian Diet voted to break its ties with Hungary and to join Serbia in creating a union of all Yugoslavs. The Rumanians reëntered the war and invaded Hungary. The Italians advanced into the Austrian provinces of Istria and the Tyrol.

The confederacy of the Central Powers, which had stood like a granite fortress for four years, was finally crumbling. Its armies were defeated and demoralized. Its generals were discredited. Its monarchs and statesmen were panic-stricken. Its peoples were clamoring for peace. Bulgaria, the last to join the confederacy, was the first to quit it. She surrendered unconditionally to the Allies on September 30, 1918. A month later, the Ottoman Empire and Austria-Hungary followed suit. Germany was left to end the First World War as best she could.

Already, in August 1918, General Ludendorff had told William II that the war was lost, and at the end of September, prostrated by the news of Bulgaria's surrender, he had besought the Emperor to make peace at once. William II responded by appointing a liberal chancellor, Prince Maximillian of Baden, and instructing him to negotiate with the Allies. After a month's interchange of notes between Prince Maximillian and President Wilson, the Allies agreed to make peace on the basis of the "fourteen points," subject to reservations on the fate of Austria-Hungary and on an explicit pledge of German reparation "for all damage done to the civilian population of the Allies." On this basis an armistice between Germany and the Allies was signed on November 11, 1918, in a railway car on a siding in the forest of Compiègne in northern France. But by this time revolutionary movements and naval and military mutinies in Germany had brought about the downfall of the imperial German government and the succession of a republican and socialist government. It was consequently the latter which signed the armistice. William II had already taken refuge in Holland.

In accordance with the armistice, the Allies occupied the left bank of the Rhine. To the Allies, moreover, Germany surrendered all her war material, though most of the German naval ships were sunk by their officers at Scapa Flow (June 1919). The confederacy of the Central Powers, broken and disarmed, lay prostrate at the feet of the triumphant Allies.

The First World War lasted four years and fifteen weeks. It was waged by thirty nations, including all the great powers. Sixty-five million men bore arms in it. Eight and a half million were killed, twenty-nine million were wounded, captured, or missing. The direct costs of the war have been estimated at something like 200 billion dollars. Its indirect costs in property and lives are incalculable.

With the First World War, an era ended, an era of optimism and "progress." The new age that was dawning began with high hopes at the peace conference, but those hopes soon gave way to disillusionment. For the next two decades Europe was in an unstable equilibrium, which, when it finally broke down, plunged the world into a second and even greater disaster.

CHAPTER 56

Peace Settlement of 1919–1920

A. Paris Peace Conference and Treaties

Paris and its environs were naturally chosen as the setting for the peace conference following the First World War. It was decided in advance by the victorious Allies that they would first reach agreement among themselves on peace terms and afterwards summon the vanquished Central Powers, beginning with Germany, to accept the terms. Accordingly, the conference was formally inaugurated by an assemblage of eminent Allied representatives on January 18, 1919, in the Hall of Mirrors at Versailles, where, forty-eight years earlier to the day, Bismarck had proclaimed the German Empire. Altogether, the participating "allied and associated nations" numbered thirty-two. But in all ensuing negotiations, the crucial decisions were made by the "Big Three"—Wilson for the United States, Clemenceau for France, and Lloyd George for Great Britain.

After four months of incessant labor and spasmodic disputing, the draft of a peace treaty with Germany, 80,000 words in length, was submitted to, and endorsed by, the conference in a formal plenary session on May 6, 1919. The next day German delegates were admitted and presented with the draft. They protested that it was intolerably severe and that it violated the "fourteen points." The Allies made only minor concessions, and at length on June 23 a German Constituent Assembly at Weimar

voted to accept it unconditionally. Five days later the treaty was signed in a solemn ceremony in the Hall of Mirrors at Versailles.

With the completion of this "treaty of Versailles" with Germany, the major work of the conference was done and its leading figures went home. But others stayed on and labored over the settlements with the remaining defeated states. Peace was formally concluded with Austria in September 1919 (treaty of St. Germain); with Bulgaria in November 1919 (treaty of Neuilly); with Hungary in June 1920 (treaty of the Trianon); and with Turkey in August 1920 (treaty of Sèvres). The last never really went into effect. The others, including that with Germany, endured for two decades. Since they were all signed in the vicinity of Paris, they may be called collectively the Peace of Paris. Into each was written a "covenant" providing for the establishment of a League of Nations and a Permanent Court of International Justice, which we shall discuss later.

By the treaty of Versailles, Germany ceded Alsace-Lorraine to France, the towns of Eupen and Malmédy to Belgium, the province of Posen and a strip running to the sea through West Prussia (the Polish corridor) to Poland. The town of Memel was ceded to the Allies, and was appropriated by Lithuania in 1923, as partial compensation for Polish seizure of Vilna. Further, Germany agreed to the holding of plebiscites to determine the fate of East

Prussia, Upper Silesia, and Schleswig. East Prussia voted to remain German; the northern third of Schleswig joined Denmark; Upper Silesia, after much disorder, was arbitrarily divided between Germany and Poland. Danzig became an international "free city," and the coal region of the Saar was placed for fifteen years under the administration of the League of Nations and the economic control of France.

In addition, Germany yielded all her overseas empire. Her lease of Kiaochow and privileges in Shantung were transferred to Japan, and also her Pacific islands north of the equator. The German portion of Samoa went to New Zealand, and the other German possessions south of the equator in the Pacific were transferred to Australia. German Southwest Africa was assigned to the Union of South Africa; German East Africa to Great Britain (save for the northwest corner which went to Belgium); Kamerun and Togoland were divided between Britain and France. In most cases the powers receiving German colonies did so, not as absolute sovereigns, but as "mandatories"

of the League of Nations, to which they promised to give periodic accounts of their stewardship.

Germany recognized, moreover, the independence of Poland, Czechoslovakia, and German Austria, denounced the treaties of Brest-Litovsk and Bucharest, and gave the Allies a free hand to settle affairs in eastern Europe. Militarily Germany promised to abolish conscription, reduce her army to 100,000 men, raze all fortifications for thirty miles east of the Rhine, reduce her navy to six battleships, six light cruisers, and twelve torpedo boats with no submarines, to abandon military and naval aviation, demolish the fortifications of Heligoland, open the Kiel canal to all nations, build no forts on the Baltic, and surrender her transoceanic cables. Though Germany expressly consented to the trial of the former Kaiser and other "war criminals," Holland refused to surrender William II, and attempts by the Allies to prosecute other offenders were soon abandoned.

By a special section (the "war guilt clause"), Germany was compelled to

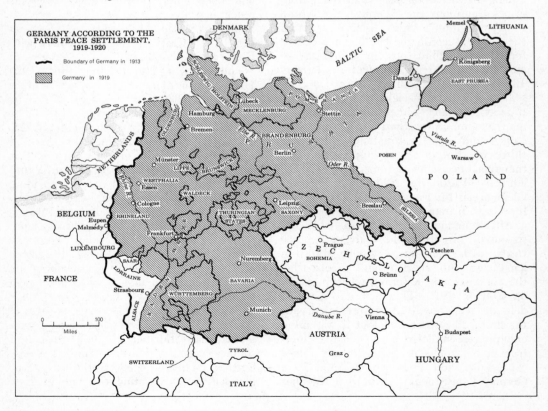

GERMANY ACCORDING TO THE PARIS PEACE SETTLEMENT, 1919-1920

The "Big Four" at the Peace Conference 1919. Left to right, Premiers Lloyd George, Orlando, and Clemenceau, and President Wilson.

Photo by Underwood & Underwood, New York

acknowledge responsibility for bringing on the First World War and to promise "reparations" for the damage done to Allied civilians and their property. On this account she was to make an immediate payment of five billion dollars and such further payments as the Allied Reparations Commission should direct. In the meantime she was to make payments in goods of all sorts —ships, railway equipment, cattle, coal, books, etc.—as compensation for the destruction she had wrought. The total amount of reparations was left unsettled. It was to be the most that Germany could pay. Until the treaty was executed in full and the reparations paid, the Allies might occupy the left bank of the Rhine and bridgeheads on the right bank, although, if Germany were fulfilling her obligations, partial evacuation would take place within fifteen years.

The treaties with other defeated powers followed in a general way the pattern of the treaty of Versailles with Germany, and involved a drastic rearrangement of the map of Europe. By the treaty of St. Germain, Austria recognized the independence of Hungary, Czechoslovakia, Poland, and Yugoslavia, and ceded to them and to Rumania and Italy the bulk of the old territories of the Dual Monarchy. Austria was left as a small, independent, German-

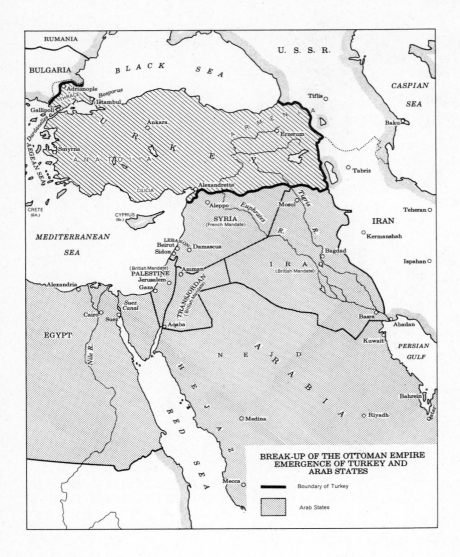

**BREAK-UP OF THE OTTOMAN EMPIRE
EMERGENCE OF TURKEY AND
ARAB STATES**

━━━━━ Boundary of Turkey

▨ Arab States

speaking state with an area and a population about the same as Portugal's. She was deprived of seaports, and her army was restricted to 30,000 men. Her formerly great capital city of Vienna now resembled a head without a body.

From Bulgaria were taken, by the treaty of Neuilly, most of the lands she had won in the Balkan War of 1912–1913 and all her World War conquests. Dobruja went to Rumania, most of Macedonia to Yugoslavia, the Thracian coast to Greece.

By the treaty of the Trianon, Hungary was stripped of almost all her non-Magyar subjects and many who were Magyars. The Slovak provinces went to Czechoslovakia. Transylvania was ceded to Rumania.

Croatia was yielded to Yugoslavia. Hungary shrank from an imperial domain of 125,000 square miles to a little land-locked state of 36,000 square miles, and from a population of twenty-two million to one of eight million.

Determination of the fate of the Ottoman Empire was delayed by acute quarrels between France and Britain and between Italy and Greece, as well as by the existence of two rival Turkish governments, the Sultan's at Constantinople and that of Mustafa Kemal, an army officer and ardent nationalist who established a revolutionary republican regime at Ankara in Asia Minor. At length in August 1920 the Allies signed a treaty at Sèvres with the Sultan, by which the Arab state of Hejaz, east of the Red Sea, and Armenia, in Asia Minor, would be independent. Palestine, Mesopotamia, Trans-Jordania, and Syria would become mandates, the first three of Britain, the last of France. Cilicia would be a sphere of influence for France, and southern Anatolia for Italy. Smyrna, Thrace, Adrianople, Gallipoli and the Aegean islands would be ceded to Greece. The Straits would be demilitarized and internationalized. Of all the conquered countries, Turkey alone, under the vigorous Mustafa Kemal, was able to resist the execution of the peace terms imposed on it. Armenia did not become independent. Adrianople and Smyrna remained Turkish. The spheres of influence did not materialize. The Straits were not demilitarized or internationalized.

The reason why Mustafa Kemal was able to oppose the peace settlement lay in the fact that the Allies had demobilized their forces, while he had an army still in being. He wiped out the Armenian Republic, compelled the Italian troops to leave southern Anatolia, and obliged the French to end their occupation of Cilicia. The French, Italians, and Russians all began to treat directly with Mustafa Kemal, but the British encouraged the Greeks to attempt, in 1921, to enforce the terms of the treaty of Sèvres by armed might. The Turks in a vigorous campaign drove the Greeks out of Asia Minor, and in November 1922 occupied Constantinople and deposed the Sultan Mohammed VI. The success of Mustafa Kemal and his Turkish Nationalists led to new and difficult negotiations. Eventually in July 1923 at Lausanne in Switzerland another treaty was signed. It ended the Turkish Empire, and made Turkey a more or less consolidated national state. Turkey resigned all claims to Hejaz, Palestine, Trans-Jordan, Mesopotamia, and Syria, but kept the whole of Anatolia and also Cilicia, Adalia, Smyrna, Constantinople, Gallipoli, Adrianople, and eastern Thrace— a total area of about 300,000 square miles with a population of some thirteen million.

The peace settlement of Paris and the later treaty of Lausanne did not resolve all questions, but they did establish a political framework and a territorial settlement for Europe. Unlike the settlement at Vienna,

a hundred years earlier, they made some attempt to redraw the map of Europe along lines of nationality. This proved very difficult; and the new nations that sprang from the Peace of Paris were required to sign "minority treaties" guaranteeing civil equality and cultural opportunities to national minorities within their borders.

B. The New Nations

Several nations gained independence in 1919–1920 as a result of the partial breakup of the Russian Empire. Finland, long used to some degree of autonomy under the tsars, established a successfully functioning political democracy, and, like the neighboring Scandinavian states, achieved a quiet prosperity based in part on co-operative enterprises. Latvia and Estonia became democratic republics, and so did Lithuania. In the last named country there was much political turbulence, aggravated by the Polish seizure (1920) of Vilna, the city claimed by the Lithuanians as their capital.

To reconstitute an independent Poland had seemed impossible in 1913, for it required the dissolution of the three Empires of Russia, Germany, and Austria. Yet this actually occurred in the course of the First World War. For some time afterwards there was fighting between the Poles and the Russians, but at length, by a treaty signed at Riga in March 1921, Communist Russia recognized the independence of Poland and accepted a compromise frontier well to the east of that (the Curzon line) tentatively suggested earlier by the Allies.

With an area of about 150,000 square miles and a population of about thirty million, Poland was the largest of the new states of central Europe. But it had been grievously devastated by war, and its electorate and parliament were split into an extraordinary number of political factions whose chronic rivalries made successful constitutional government difficult. From 1926 until his death in 1935, Marshal Josef Pilsudski, Polish hero of the First World War, exercised a kind of veiled military dictatorship, and during these years considerable progress was made in breaking up large landed estates and in promoting popular education.

In the new nation of Czechoslovakia, which emerged from the disruption of Austria-Hungary, democratic practices were steadily adhered to, despite difficulties with neighboring countries and with a large minority of "Sudeten" Germans in Bohemia, and despite differences between Catholics and Socialists and between Czechs and Slovaks. The personal prestige of Thomas Masaryk, who was in a very real sense the "father of his country" and its president until 1935, combined with the parliamentary skill of other leading statesmen to preserve democratic government. Political stability was enhanced by a modest but solid prosperity based in part on reforms which gave land to the peasants and on industrial development, especially the large-scale production of munitions and shoes.

Both post-war Austria and post-war Hungary, now stripped of their subject peoples, were essentially new states. Austria was harried by adverse economic conditions, centering in depressed Vienna, whose fac-

tories were cut off from their former markets and sources of supply and whose people for the most part joined the Social Democratic party. Rural and provincial Austria remained Catholic and tended to vote for the Christian Socialist party. Immediately after the war the Social Democrats were the largest party and governed the country in a coalition with the Catholics. But from 1922 to 1930, the Christian Socialists in coalition with the smaller Nationalist Party were in charge of affairs. Aided by loans from abroad, Austria struggled along until 1931, when, caught in the backwash of the world depression, her economic difficulties led her into political troubles which were soon gravely complicated by pressures from abroad.

Hungary after a brief experience of Communist dictatorship fell into the hands of reactionary aristocrats led by Admiral Horthy and Count Stephen Bethlen. From 1920, Hungary was technically a "constitutional monarchy," without a king and with Horthy as "regent." There was little real democracy, for power rested with the great landowners and wealthy bourgeois. There

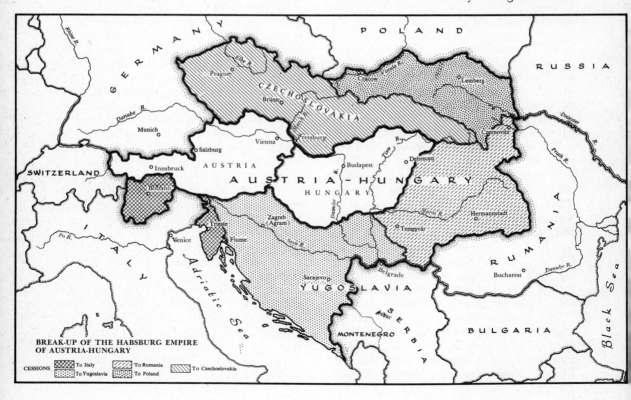

BREAK-UP OF THE HABSBURG EMPIRE
OF AUSTRIA-HUNGARY

CESSIONS   To Italy   To Rumania   To Czechoslovakia
        To Yugoslavia   To Poland

was much bitter nationalism summed up in the slogan "No! No! Never!," which referred to the loss of territory imposed on Hungary at the end of the war.

Yugoslavia, which was Serbia enlarged by territories transferred from Austria-Hungary, was deeply troubled by differences in religion, culture, and politics among its constituent peoples—Serbs, Croats, and Slovenes. The Serbs were Orthodox in religion and "backward" in economics and culture. The Croats and Slovenes were Catholic in religion and more progressive. In addition, there were more than a million Moslems, mainly in the province of Bosnia. The Croatians urged a federal state and home rule for Croatia. The more numerous Serbs insisted on a centralized administration. This difference, intensified by religious, educational, and economic disputes, led to bitter quarrels and even fights among the deputies in the Chamber at Belgrade. Violence reached a peak in 1928, when Stefan Radić, the Croatian leader, and several of his lieutenants were killed. Whereupon, early in 1929, King Alexander, supported by the army, dissolved the parliament, suppressed the constitution, proclaimed himself dictator, and repressed all criticism and dissent.

Rumania, with her area and population doubled as a result of the First World War, was almost a new state. Vexed by minorities which constituted two-ninths of her population, the government sought to win the support of the peasantry by a drastic policy of breaking up large estates. But in so doing it roused the ire of former landlords. Though nominally democratic, Rumania was actually ruled by cliques of professional politicians, some of them notoriously corrupt. Moreover, there was trouble with the crown, for after the death of Ferdinand I (1927), he was succeeded, not by his son Carol who had been legally debarred from the succession because of his infatuation with a woman of doubtful reputation, but by Carol's son, Michael. In 1930, however, Carol, with the support of army officers, seized the throne, and the government became more arbitrary and irresponsible.

One of the most vigorous of the smaller countries in the post war period was Turkey.

Cut down to a population overwhelmingly Turkish, intensely nationalist, infused with patriotic pride by the victory over the Greeks in 1921–1922, and possessed of a beloved leader in Mustafa Kemal, Turkey made rapid progress. Nominally Turkey was a constitutional, democratic republic, but actually it was a nationalistic dictatorship under Mustafa Kemal, who proceeded rather rapidly to westernize the country. The sultans had been religious leaders (caliphs) as well as political rulers. Mustafa Kemal abolished the caliphate (1924), reduced the role of the Moslem religion, substituted western law for that based on the Koran, abolished the wearing of the fez and the veil, changed from the Arabic to the Roman alphabet, prohibited polygamy, emancipated women, adopted the western calendar, developed public education, introduced the metric system of weights and measures, and in 1932 brought Turkey into the League of Nations. Few countries have been transformed so fast or so successfully. Turkey began to look toward the future not the past. It built railways, dams, electric plants, and irrigation projects. It organized a compulsory exchange of minority populations with Greece, by which a million Greeks, resident in Turkey, were sent to a homeland they had never known, and 400,000 Turks, resident in Greece, were brought to Turkey. It put down by force revolts of the stubbornly Moslem Kurds. It developed a lively and relatively free press. When Kemal died in 1938, he left a strong country and one that moved, though fitfully, toward a more democratic government.

Of the national states which were newly constituted or newly enlarged in 1919–1920, only Czechoslovakia and Finland made a real success of democratic republican government. In the rest, for a variety of reasons, including internal conflict and fear of foreign nations, the trend was toward some sort of arbitrary or dictatorial rule. It seemed as if democracy was something that could not be attained suddenly, but rather must grow by a slow evolution nurtured by experience. It is possible that greater prosperity in the new nations might have led to a longer maintenance of popular government. But despite moments of economic well-being in the 1920's, a serious depression harrassed Europe most of the time in the two decades after 1919. Even the older democracies had their troubles in the post-war world.

C. France and Great Britain

Though victorious in the war and re-possessed of Alsace-Lorraine, France faced a multitude of grave problems after 1919. At the start, the most pressing seemed to be the rehabilitation of her devastated areas in the north, the cost of which she expected Germany to bear. In 1920, after much haggling, the Allies agreed that France should get 52 per cent of German reparations, and the next year the total of these was fixed at thirty-two billion gold dollars. But it was one thing to determine the debt and another to collect it. There were serious obstacles to accepting payments in kind, for free importation of such commodities as coal, steel, or machines from Germany threatened to ruin corresponding English and French industries. Money payments proved no less difficult, for Germany could not make them unless she had a large favorable balance of trade, and this could be secured only by letting her win back all her pre-war markets and many new ones. Against any such outcome, France, as well as the United States and many other countries, quickly erected high tariff walls. In 1922 Germany declared her inability to make further payments. Whereupon French troops occupied the German industrial district of the Ruhr. But the Germans met this step with well-organized "passive resistance," and the French found it as difficult to secure payments by force as by negotiation.

In 1924, an international commission of experts headed by an American banker, Charles Dawes, devised a plan whereby German payments would be spread over a long period of years. France withdrew her troops from the Ruhr, and for a while the "Dawes Plan" seemed to work fairly well. But the Germans were irked by the economic controls it imposed, and the transfer of payments was still difficult. In 1929, a second commission of experts headed by

another American, Owen Young, recommended that the reparation payments be reduced to eight billion dollars spread over the next fifty-eight years. This proposal, together with provision for the Allied evacuation of the occupied areas of the Rhineland, was embodied in an international agreement signed at the Hague in 1930.

But in the very next year, in the face of world-wide depression, Germany declared herself unable to meet even the Young Plan payments. At the suggestion of the American President Herbert Hoover, Germany's creditors granted her a temporary moratorium, and in 1932 they agreed to scale the remaining reparations payments down to 700 million dollars, if at the same time the United States would forgive the war debts (totalling over ten billion dollars) owed by the various Allied nations to it. This the United States refused to do. Whereupon the Allied countries (except Finland) stopped payments to the United States as Germany had stopped payments to them. Practically, though not legally, both reparations and interallied war debts, which had so long weighed down the economy of the world, were thus wiped off the slate.

The total of reparation payments actually made by Germany was about six and a half billion gold dollars, of which over a third represented American loans to Germany that were not repaid. Meanwhile, French reconstruction was financed less by receipts from Germany than by domestic taxes, loans, and issuance of paper money, which brought on an inflation that reduced the value of the franc by four-fifths and bore hard on the salaried classes and on all those who lived on savings or fixed incomes.

Meanwhile, in the international sphere, France sought to bolster her position and ward off any German "war of revenge" by a system of alliances. She contracted a formal military alliance with Belgium in 1920, with Poland in 1921, and with Czechoslovakia in 1924. The last-named country had already formed, in 1920–1921, a "Little Entente" with Rumania and Yugoslavia for the purpose of safeguarding the territories they had each acquired from Hungary. This arrangement helped France

A Figure. Henri Matisse
(d. 1954).

to enlarge her circle of alliances by drawing into it Rumania in 1926 and Yugoslavia in 1927. But in the event, the alliances proved slender reeds to lean on, for not only did France have to continue to strengthen her allies by costly loans, but the countries of eastern Europe (except Czechoslovakia) were drawn in the 1930's by economic motives towards Germany, which promised them a better market for their goods than France.

In internal politics, France oscillated between the Right and the Left, with the Left tending to gain strength. The Right parties, or "National Bloc," controlled the government from 1919 to 1924. But the failure of Poincaré's strong policy toward Germany brought in the "Cartel of the Left" in the elections of 1924. It proceeded to adopt a conciliatory attitude toward Germany, and in 1925 it agreed to the "Locarno Pact," whereby Germany entered the League of Nations, while Germany, France, and Belgium promised to respect their mutual frontiers, and Italy and Britain guaranteed the arrangement. In the crisis of financial inflation, however, the Left failed to command popular support, Poincaré was recalled to the premiership, and parties of the Right won the elections of 1928. The Left again triumphed in 1932, and once more in 1936.

In Great Britain, the political scene was marked by the almost complete disintegration of the Liberal party. Its old faith in free trade seemed no longer tenable, for in the post-war world Great Britain was in a precarious economic position. Her veins of iron and coal were running thin. She had lost markets to the United States and Japan. The new countries were trying to build up their own industries behind protective tariffs. Unemployment hung like an ominous cloud over the British Isles. In 1921, two million workers were idle in a country of only forty-two million people. Even in 1928, a boom year in most lands, the number of British unemployed hovered close to the million mark.

The Lloyd George coalition government, which had triumphed in the "khaki election" of 1918, made the peace. It reluctantly recognized the Irish Free State as a separate dominion (1921). It extended social insurance for labor and greatly increased the government subsidies ("doles") for unemployment payments to workers. But in 1922, the coalition broke up and in the ensuing election the Liberals won only 118 seats in the Commons against 347 for the Conservatives and 142 for the Labor party.

Britain had already adopted some emergency tariffs. Now the Conservatives under Stanley Baldwin came out for thorough-going protection as a cure for Britain's ills, and an election was fought on the issue in 1923. The Conservatives lost some 90 seats, while the Laborites gained fifty, with the result that early in 1924 Britain's first Labor cabinet was formed under Ramsay MacDonald. But this was short-lived, for it was dependent on Liberal support, and when MacDonald decided to recognize the Bolshevik government of Russia the Liberals deserted him.

New elections in 1924 gave a thumping majority to the Conservatives, and a second Baldwin government lasted until 1929. It fought and beat a "general strike" of the workers arising from unemployment in the coal mines. It extended the suffrage (1928)

League of Nations Buildings at Geneva.
Courtesy Wide World Photos

to all women on the same basis as men. In foreign affairs, it pursued a cautious policy, hostile to Russia, friendly to Germany, and not too coöperative with France. In domestic matters it tried to improve economic conditions by gingerly experimenting with housing and the "rationalization" of industry and by "sound" financial policies.

In the regular general election of 1929, Labor won a plurality and Ramsay MacDonald formed a second ministry. But his government almost at once ran into an acute economic crisis resulting from the worldwide depression which began in 1929. MacDonald tried no radical reforms and his careful policies met with little success. When, in 1931, he proposed drastic economies in governmental expeditures including the "dole" to the unemployed, he split the Labor party. Only a minority under the name of National Laborites stuck with the prime minister. But instead of resigning, MacDonald invited Conservatives and Liberals to join with him in forming a "national government" to meet the economic crisis, and in the ensuing election his coalition won a sweeping victory. But the chief beneficiaries were the Conservatives, who almost doubled their representation.

A protective tariff was now enacted, and in 1931 the so-called Statute of Westminster recognized the self-governing dominions of the British Empire (Canada, Australia, New Zealand, South Africa, and Ireland) as "nations" groups in a "Commonwealth," and bound together only by ties of sentiment, by allegiance to a common king, and by occasional conferences. In 1935, Stanley Baldwin replaced MacDonald as prime minister, and the Conservatives won the election of that year.

D. The League of Nations

The First World War created a widespread demand for some sort of association of nations to preserve world peace. Various plans were proposed by statesmen and publicists. But it was Woodrow Wilson who was most insistent on providing for a definite League of Nations by a solemn international "Covenant" incorporated in the Paris peace settlement of 1919–1920.

The Covenant provided for an international body of two houses—an Assembly in which every nation had one vote, and a Council in which the great powers had permanent seats and a few lesser powers held temporary elective seats. In addition, there were a Secretariat staffed by officials with headquarters at Geneva; a Court of International Justice at the Hague for the settlement of disputes; and an International Labor Office designed to further interests of labor all over the world. Though in some ways the League resembled an international government, it was in reality much more like a continuous conference of diplomatic agents of the various states. Its main purpose was to prevent war, but it also had special duties imposed on it by the treaties of 1919–1920, and was expected to promote general international coöperation.

The Covenant obligated the member nations "to respect and preserve as against external aggression" each other's "territorial integrity and political independence." It required the submission of disputes to arbitration, and, if arbitration failed, to the Council. Members were forbidden to wage war in contravention of a unanimous decision by the Council, and provision was made for economic and military measures ("sanctions") against recalcitrant states, whether members or non-members. All treaties contrary to the League were to be abrogated and all treaties old and new were to be registered with the League Secretariat. The League was to push forward the reduction of armaments, to administer Danzig and the Saar, and to supervise mandated colonies.

In January 1920, at the call of President Wilson, the League of Nations was formally inaugurated at Paris with an initial meeting of the Council, and the first Assembly convened at Geneva in the following November. By this time all the Allies in the First World War, except the United States and Russia, had joined the League; and the invited neutrals brought the number of members to forty-two. It was ironical that the United States, whose President had taken the leading part in launching the League, should have held aloof from it.

The reason for this was that unfortunately the League became an issue of American partisan politics, and in the presidential election of 1920 "isolationist" foes of the League triumphed.

Other states were admitted to the League from time to time, for example, Germany in 1926 and Russia in 1934. By 1935, there were sixty-two members: twenty-eight in Europe, twenty-one in America, eight in Asia, three in Africa, and two in Australasia. But there were also significant secessions. Above all, the continuous abstention of the United States was calamitous for the League.

Despite its weaknesses, the League accomplished a great deal. The Secretariat gathered and published much useful data about world conditions. The League supervised the repatriation of 400,000 prisoners of war belonging to twenty-six nationalities. It aided in caring for refugees. It helped in the financial rebuilding of Austria and Hungary. It conducted plebiscites with impartiality and successfully administered Danzig and the Saar. Through its agencies, it did much to check the spread of typhus and the international traffic in opium. Through its commission on intellectual coöperation, it brought together scientists and scholars from all parts of the world and facilitated the exchange of scientific, artistic, and literary information and the movement of students and teachers from one country to another. Through its associated Labor Office, it promoted international collaboration in collecting facts and in dealing with problems of industrial labor. Through the Court of International Justice, a considerable number of controversial matters were successfully arbitrated, and through special committees a start was made toward a codification of international law.

Thus the League proved a valuable and indeed indispensable instrument of international coöperation. But its record in its primary function of settling disputes which might lead to war was not so shining and by the mid-1930's was beclouded. A few minor disputes it settled: between Finland and Sweden over the Aland Islands (1920); between Poland and Germany over their boundary in Upper Silesia (1921); between Greece and Bulgaria over border incidents (1925); between Peru and Colombia over a border province (1933). In dealing with disputes affecting major powers, the League was far less effective. It ended a dispute between Great Britain and Iraq over the Mosul oil fields, but it did so only by a pro-British decision. In 1923, when Poland, backed by France, was in conflict with Lithuania over Vilna, League mediation was pushed aside and Poland's seizure of the city was upheld by an independent agreement among France, Britain, and Italy. In the same year, in a violent quarrel between Greece and Italy, the Italians seized the Greek island of Corfu, and ignored the League. Only through the mediation of France and Britain was Italy persuaded to evacuate Corfu, and then on terms necessitating Greek acceptance of Italy's major demands. In the 1930's the League was flouted with impunity by Japan, Germany, and Italy.

In respect of disarmament, the failure of the League was well-nigh complete. Outside its framework, a conference of naval powers at Washington in 1921–1922 agreed to a limitation of battleship tonnages to a ratio of 5 for Great Britain, 5 for the United States, 3 for Japan, 1.67 for France, and 1.67 for Italy, but no agreement was reached about limitation of light cruisers (advocated by the United States) or prohibition of submarines (urged by Britain). At a second naval conference at Geneva in 1927, the United States and Britain still could not agree about cruisers. They finally reached an agreement at a third conference at London in 1930, but Japan now acquiesced most reluctantly, while France and Italy refused altogether. Consequently the London commitments bound only three of the five naval powers and were further weakened by an "escalator clause" which permitted a nation to exceed the specified tonnage totals if it thought its "national security" was "materially affected" by the naval building of another country.

In the matter of land armies, even less progress had been made. In 1925 the League created a special commission to study the problem, which proved to be

Self Portrait. Vincent Van Gogh (d. 1890).

extraordinarily complicated and difficult, especially in view of the fears of some nations like France and the ambitions of others like Germany and Italy. After five years of labor, the Commission brought forth a draft treaty providing for limitations "in principle" of number of men under arms and of expenditures for armaments. But it included also an "escape clause" pro-

posed by the United States and permitting any country to "suspend temporarily" any restriction imposed on it by the treaty. The long awaited Conference on Disarmament met in Geneva in February 1932 to discuss and improve the draft treaty. All League members were represented, and also the United States and Russia.

The Conference was protracted. In vain

the American President Hoover proposed a cut of one third in the armies of all countries. In vain the British prime minister, MacDonald, urged a standard army of 200,000 men for each of the major powers. Each proposal aroused fears or suspicions. In October 1933, Germany, now dominated by Adolf Hitler, impatiently quit the Conference and announced her purpose of re-arming without regard to restrictions of the Versailles treaty. In the summer of 1934, Britain acknowledged the failure of the Conference. It then faded away, and in 1935 Germany independently reëstablished the kind of army which she had in 1914.

E. Economics and Culture After World War I

Despite its devastation, World War I increased the productive capacity of major nations and in some lines stimulated scientific advance. Internal difficulties removed Russia from world trade, and most of the countries of Europe were upset by currency inflation, violent in defeated lands like Germany and Austria, partial among victors like France and Italy. Inflation enabled Germany to slough off its internal debt, but most other countries, especially Britain, staggered along under a tremendous burden of indebtedness. Reparations and war debts complicated international finance. Agricultural reforms in central and eastern Europe produced a more equitable distribution of land, but often decreased productiveness since the new peasant proprietors lacked capital.

By 1926, despite difficulties, general European production, including even Russia's, approximated pre-war levels, and for the next three years comparative prosperity reigned; political tensions eased somewhat; international relations improved; people became optimistic. Then in the autumn of 1929, the American stock market crashed; business slackened, unemployment rose, and the United States experienced a prolonged depression. As American loans to Europe ceased, as American purchases of European goods fell off, and as American tourists to Europe thinned out, the depression rapidly overspread Europe. Internal

and international friction increased, and in gloom and mutual suspicion Europe moved down the slope toward catastrophe.

Unsettled economic and political conditions after the First World War were reflected by a notable unsettling in art and literature. In painting there were numerous conflicting tendencies. "Cubism," inaugurated by a Spaniard in Paris, Pablo Picasso, utilized planes, straight lines, and geometrical forms. "Futurism," developed mainly in Italy, criticized the "static" quality of past painting and tried to show objects in motion, frequently by duplicating them in slightly altered positions. "Surrealism" attempted to depict a Freudian character of the human mind by showing incongruous objects associated in a wildly dreamlike manner. Less extreme artists, Henri Matisse for example, followed lines laid down before the war by post-impressionists like Cézanne and Van Gogh.

Architecture, though much of it was still traditional, developed a "modernist" school which achieved some striking results. "Modernism" in architecture was born of attempts to realize the potentialities of new materials like steel and concrete. It was fathered by designers of skyscrapers, office buildings, garages, and factories, with an eye upon the uses to which such edifices were put. It was consolidated into a "school" and achieved its greatest popularity in Germany. By 1930, many of the new buildings all over Europe were "modern" and "functional," with great sweeping planes, geometrical forms, and many windows.

In popular music, American jazz swept Europe, and syncopated rhythms were common not only along the Mississippi but on the Danube, the Seine, and the Thames. Serious composers like the Austrian Arnold Schönberg moved toward "modernism" in music, using dissonance, abandoning old harmonic relationships, employing novel sound effects, and trusting often to "natural inspiration."

The literature of the era was chaotic. Spread of literacy had greatly increased the size of the reading public, and if many were satisfied with daily newspapers and trashy magazines or novels, others created a demand for almost every conceivable type of book. There was a vogue for non-fiction works on travel, history, economics, politics, and especially biography. One trend, represented by Lytton Strachey's *Eminent Victorians*, was toward "debunking" great figures of the past by stressing their oddities and shortcomings. There were also many realistic but nostalgic works, such as those of the French Marcel Proust or the German Thomas Mann.

Most striking of all, though not very popular, were a number of authors who experimented with words, figures of speech, punctuation, capitalization, and all the old rules of writing. Some of them like Gertrude Stein and James Joyce carried their experiments so far that many of their works became partly or wholly incomprehensible to the average reader. Likewise, there was a notable vogue of the introspective novel, exploring and emphasizing the vagaries, rational and non-rational, of the human mind.

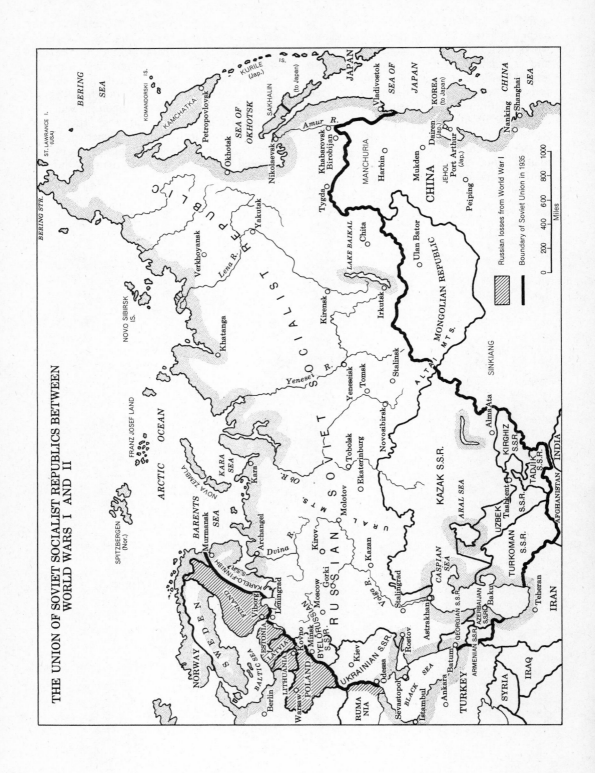

THE UNION OF SOVIET SOCIALIST REPUBLICS BETWEEN
WORLD WARS I AND II

Russian losses from World War I

Boundary of Soviet Union in 1935

Miles

0 200 400 600 800 1000

CHAPTER 57

Rise of Communist, Fascist, and Nazi Dictatorships

A. Communist Russia and the Soviet Union

At the close of the First World War, liberal democracy was the rule in every country of Europe except Russia. Here, it had been promised by the popular revolution of March 1917 which overthrew the autocratic tsardom, but the promise was nullified by the *coup d'état* and revolution of November 1917 which inaugurated a forceful dictatorship. This was called a "dictatorship of the proletariat." It was really a dictatorship of the Bolshevik Communist leader, Lenin, actively supported by a small but fanatical following, and employing methods of the utmost ruthlessness. It was more despotic than any recent European regime. It proved to be the forerunner of other dictatorships, which, whatever their professed principles might be, would copy its practices, and not only repudiate liberal democracy at home but oppose it abroad.

Just prior to Lenin's seizure of power, a Constituent Assembly had been freely and democratically elected. As it contained relatively few Bolsheviks, it was dissolved when it tried to meet in January 1918. Meanwhile the country at large was being terrorized. Nobles, landowners, army officers, and priests who would not accept the new regime were driven into exile or put to death. The ex-Tsar, his wife, and children were slaughtered. All dissident groups, including Cadets, Social Revolutionaries, or Menshevik Socialists, were mercilessly crushed.

Lenin's withdrawal of Russia from the First World War and his making peace with the Germans in March 1918, coupled with his repudiation of debts and his strident preaching of world revolution, angered the Allies and prompted them to give financial and military aid to "white" opponents of the "red" dictatorship. For the next two or three years Russia was prey to spasmodic civil war and foreign intervention, and also to a famine which in 1921–1922 carried off some five million people.

Yet the dictatorship triumphed. The Allies were too sick of war and too divergent in purpose to sustain any effective intervention in Russia. On the other hand, Lenin had in Leon Trotsky an exceptionally able war minister who successfully organized, equipped, and inspirited a remarkable "red army." And masses of Russian peasants and workers rallied to the support of the dictatorship lest its overthrow involve a reversal of its decrees for the break-up of large landed estates and the confiscation of privately owned factories. By 1921 domestic opposition was overcome and foreign interference ceased. In 1924 the Russian Communist regime was formally recognized by Great Britain, France, and Italy, and ten years later by the United States.

A kind of constitution for the Communist regime was promulgated in 1923. It provided for several "Soviet Socialist Republics," joined together in a "Union," and each guaranteed some measure of cultural nationalism. At first there were

Stalin at the 16th Congress of the Russian Communist Party. Painting by A. Gerasimov.

four of these, but by 1936 they numbered eleven.[1] Nominally the form of government for both the Union and the several constituent states was democratic. Persons over eighteen years of age who were engaged in "productive work" or enlisted in the army could vote for members of local "soviets." Local soviets chose delegates to regional soviets, and these elected deputies to a congress of soviets in each state and to an All-Union Congress of Soviets for the whole federation.

In practice, however, there was little more of democracy than of personal liberty under the Communist dictatorship. Many classes of persons were definitely debarred from voting: former tsarist officials, clergymen, employers of labor, private traders, well-to-

do peasants (*kulaks*). And all who could vote found themselves obliged to vote for nominees of the small minority belonging to the Communist party.

No other party was allowed to exist, and no person might belong to the Communist Party unless he avowed unquestioning faith in the principles of Marx and Lenin, promised the strictest obedience to party discipline, and proved his zeal during a probationary period. All members had to be continuously "active" and "above reproach." Their organization paralleled the governmental structure of the Union. Local party "cells" in factories, offices, or villages sent delegates to regional committees, which in turn were represented in an All-Union Party Congress. This Congress elected a Central Committee with a supreme "political bureau" of nine members. Here rested the center of authority for the entire Soviet Union, for the "political bureau" proposed major policies for the country and utilized the party machinery, along with elaborate espionage and censorship, with secret police

---

[1] (1) Russia, with its capital at Moscow, and embracing ninety per cent of the area and nearly seventy per cent of the population of the entire Union; (2) Ukraine, with capital at Kiev; (3) White Russia, with capital at Minsk; (4) Georgia; (5) Azerbaijan; (6) Armenia; (7) Turkoman; (8) Uzbek; (9) Tajikistan; (10) Kirghiz; (11) Kazakstan.

and arbitrary arrests and executions, to secure unquestioning adoption of such policies at any point from the local soviets up to the All-Union Congress. Though in theory they were separate, the party and the government were so intertwined as to be practically indistinguishable. He who controlled the party, controlled the country as a supreme dictator.

First the dictator was Lenin, who was both prime minister of the government and president of the party's political bureau, but by 1922 he was suffering from overwork and was partially paralyzed. There ensued a bitter rivalry for the succession between Trotsky, the war minister, and Stalin (Joseph Dzugashvili), scion of a Georgian peasant family and secretary of the Central Committee of the party. When Lenin died in 1924, Stalin's control of the party machinery and his popularity with the party members enabled him to become the acknowledged dictator. Trotsky was expelled from the government in 1924 and from the party in 1927. In 1929 he fled into exile and was murdered in Mexico eleven years later. By a series of "purges," his followers and other dissidents were rooted out of the government and the party.

During the first years of Soviet rule in Russia an attempt was made to apply the principles of Marxian socialism in thoroughgoing fashion. Private property was confiscated; debts repudiated; land, mines, and factories nationalized. But peasants disregarded the nationalization of the land, and took it for themselves. Workers' committees who strove to run the factories often lacked technical competence. The country as a whole was racked by civil war, foreign intervention, disease, and famine. The grain harvest of 1921 was only two-fifths that of 1913, and the transportation system was in a state of almost complete breakdown.

In the circumstances, Lenin proclaimed in 1921 a "new economic policy" (NEP). This, while preserving a communistic basis in public ownership of the major means of production, promised liberal rewards for Russian and foreign technicians, permitted small scale private production and trade, and allowed the peasants to rent land, hire labor, and sell their crops to private traders. The NEP stimulated production, both agricultural and industrial, and helped Russia to recover from the worst effects of war.

But to Stalin and other leaders, the NEP was only a temporary makeshift. To realize their ambition of making Russia a great industrial country and of socializing agriculture as well as industry, they worked out a series of "Five Year Plans." Under these, Russia did become a great industrial nation. Between 1928 and 1938 its production multiplied almost five times. By the latter date Russia was the fourth nation in the world in industrial output, being surpassed only by the United States, Germany, and Great Britain. In iron, steel, and certain other commodities, Russia was ahead of Britain.

Socialization of agriculture encountered special difficulties. Before the end of the first "Five Year Plan," it was decided to liquidate the kulaks (well-to-do peasants who had prospered under the NEP) and ruthlessly to push forward the creation of collective farms. Hundreds of thousands of kulaks were dispossessed and sent into exile or to concentration camps. Many peasants slaughtered and ate the livestock that was about to be confiscated and collectivized. As a result, there was more famine, especially during 1932–1933 in the Ukraine, where large numbers starved to death. But socialization was achieved, whatever the costs. By 1936, over 98 per cent of all tilled land was in state or collective farms, and agricultural production was again increasing.

The Communist dictatorship of the Soviet Union persistently endeavored to suppress all varieties of historic Christianity. It closed most of the churches, persecuted priests, forbade missionary enterprise, and denied advancement to practicing Christians. At the same time, it sponsored a "Society of the Godless" and the stream of propaganda by which this organization helped to de-Christianize the youth of the Soviet Union.

The dictatorship zealously promoted popular literacy. Thousands of schools— primary, secondary, and technical—were established. Scientific institutes were organized, and research conducted, especially along practical lines. Radio stations, newspapers, and books multiplied. Schooling was free at all levels, but, like all publicity and intellectual activity in the Soviet Union, it was subject to official censorship and propaganda and dominated by the Marxian ideas and approved policies of the Communist party.

In 1936 the Soviet Union adopted a new constitution, broadening the franchise and containing a declaration of individual liberties. It was largely "window dressing," however. Actually the dictatorship of Stalin and his Communist party continued as before.

There was some alteration of internal policy at about this time. National patriotism, which previously had been scorned, was now inculcated. Differentials in compensation for various sorts of labor were widened, until the bureaucracy of officials and managers was so well-paid that "socialist millionaires" became possible. Piecework wages, and what would be called in capitalist lands the "speed up," were introduced. Russia under Stalin was moving away from Lenin's principles of 1917, and the trend was now toward some form of state capitalism and an intensification of nationalism.

The Communist dictatorship in Russia had significant influence outside. Its example and propaganda served to split off from foreign Socialist parties, which were normally democratic, new Communist parties that were pro-Russian and anti-democratic. These were federated in 1919 in a "Third International" (Komintern), with headquarters at Moscow, in competition with the "Second International" of the more moderate Socialists. Through the Komintern, the Russian dictatorship directed the policies and activities of sizeable Communist parties in Germany, France, Italy, and most other countries on the European continent. Thereby it rendered the operation of liberal democracy more difficult in those countries, not only directly, but also indirectly by stimulating counter activity on the part of anti-democratic conservatives and reactionaries.

B. Fascist Italy

Among countries fatefully affected by the rise of totalitarian dictatorship, Italy was one of the most conspicuous. The Italian government which waged the First World War was liberal and democratic, and the first general election after the close of that struggle seemed to indicate that Italy, like Britain and France, would continue to adhere to liberal democracy. In addition to a slender majority of old-line Liberals in the newly elected Chamber of Deputies, there were increased numbers of Social Democrats and also a large representation of a new Catholic Popular party, led by Don Sturzo and committed to democracy.

Conditions in Italy were not conducive to orderly progress. Many patriots blamed the existing regime for Italy's relative military weakness in the war and for her failure in the ensuing peace negotiations to get as much territorial extension in Africa and the Near East as they thought she should have. The majority of Italian Socialists, influenced by example and propaganda of Lenin's Bolshevik dictatorship in Russia, turned Communist and abandoned democratic methods in favor of "direct action." They instigated a series of strikes, accompanied by much violence, and in many instances they dispossessed owners of factories and assumed control.

Against such extremes of "Right" and "Left," the Liberal ministers from 1919 to 1922 were unable or unwilling to take any effective action. They disputed among themselves, while the domestic situation grew rapidly worse. The budget was unbalanced, the public debt large, the currency inflated. The balance of trade was highly unfavorable; and rising tariff walls abroad, together with America's refusal to receive any more immigrants (who might have sent remittances home) and Italy's need for foreign raw materials, rendered improvement well-nigh impossible.

The circumstances provided opportunity for an ambitious man, Benito Mussolini. Son of a blacksmith and himself an elementary school-teacher in his early years, he was, before the war, a left-wing Socialist, vehemently anti-Catholic and anti-imperialist. He served a jail-sentence for pacifism, lived for a time in exile, and at length became editor of the official publication of the Italian Socialists. During the war he became an ultra-patriot, broke with the pacifist majority of his party, served in the trenches as an ordinary soldier, and founded a newspaper through which he exerted ever widening influence. He now urged the employment, in behalf of an intensive nationalism, of essentially the same tactics as the Communists used; and for such a program he gained support of restless demobilized soldiers, dissatisfied white-collar workers, youthful intellectuals, and groups of frightened business men. His movement was called "Fascism."

Mussolini greeting crowds at the 15th anniversary of the founding of the Fascist party.

Courtesy Bettmann Archive

The word Fascism was derived from the *Fascio* (or "club") which Mussolini organized at Milan in 1919 and which gave rise, during the next two years, to a network of similar *fasci* all over Italy. In November 1921 these were consolidated into a political party, with Mussolini at its head and with a wealth of symbolism and ceremonial. Fascists wore black shirts in imitation of Garibaldi's red shirts, and revived the ancient Roman usages of saluting with outstretched arm and carrying as their emblem the *fasces* of the Roman lictors.

With mounting enthusiasm and violence and with perfected organization, Fascism gathered momentum during 1921–1922, while its opponents—Liberal, Socialist, and Catholic—remained divided and irresolute. In October 1922 the Fascists held a great congress at Naples, paraded the streets, and listened to a grandiloquent speech by Mussolini, who declared, "Either the goverment will be given to us or we shall march on Rome." Then as the Liberal prime minister resigned, Fascist crowds moved on Rome by train and auto. The regular army stood aside, and King Victor Emmanuel III asked Mussolini to form a ministry. Whereupon the Fascist leader extorted from the terrified parliament a grant of dictatorial powers.

Fascists were speedily put into key positions throughout the country, and given a monopoly on propaganda. Socialists were suppressed and their strikes stopped. For a brief time, following the murder of the Socialist leader Matteoti, the opponents of Fascism threatened to coalesce in dangerous unity. But by strict censorship and forceful police measures, Mussolini weathered the storm and followed it up with a veritable reign of terror. Opponents were imprisoned or exiled. Critics were silenced.

By a series of enactments from 1925 to 1928 Mussolini consolidated his dictatorship. Political parties other than the Fascist were banned. Censorship was tightened. "Seditious" persons were subjected to summary "justice." Mussolini as prime minister of the state and "leader" (*Duce*) of the Fascist party was authorized to initiate legislation and appoint local officials. Elections for parliament were transformed to a

744

mere "yes" and "no" vote on a list of Fascist candidates.

Formally, Italy continued to be a "constitutional" monarchy. The king was still nominal sovereign. A parliament still existed. But actually the whole government was dominated by the Fascist party, which, like the Communist party in Russia, consisted of a small minority, and which was similarly organized, with local groups, provincial federations, and Grand Council. As chairman of the Grand Council and prime minister of the country, Mussolini centered all power in his hands. To enforce his will he had not only the governmental agencies but a special Fascist militia. To win the loyalty of the youth and to train future members of the party, quasi-military organizations were set up for boys and young men.

Mussolini and his Fascist dictatorship sought to gain the support of workingmen by undertaking social changes and substituting a "corporate" state for the previous liberal state. Non-Fascist trade unions and all strikes were banned in 1926, but at the same time were organized thirteen "syndicates" (six of employers, six of employees, and one of professional men), under whose auspices tribunals were established to settle labor disputes.

Mussolini sought also to win the approval of Italian Catholics by negotiating with Pope Pius XI the Lateran treaty of 1929, which recognized the sovereign independence of the papal state of "Vatican City," and likewise a concordat, which regulated relations between state and church within Italy and promised the latter important functions in education. It was not long, however, until the church and the Fascist party were at odds over the schools and the youth organizations. Catholicism and totalitarian dictatorship were fundamentally incompatible.

Nationalism was continually emphasized by Mussolini and the Fascists. Italians were ceaselessly reminded of their past greatness and future destiny as a nation. For patriotic reasons as well as to give work to the unemployed, the government fostered a great variety of public works. Pride in the past was stimulated by repairing and unearthing ancient Roman monuments and erecting grandiose memorials. Faith in the future

Pope Pius XI.
Courtesy Bettmann Archive

was aroused by a host of "modern improvements." Railways were refurbished, palatial steamships built, marshes drained, electric power plants constructed. As far as might be, Mussolini aimed at economic self-sufficiency for Italy.

Closely associated with nationalism, was an ostentatious militarism. The army was increased and its equipment improved. Military reviews were staged. Special youth organizations trained small boys in the manual of arms. In speeches, Mussolini ranted about war and the warlike virtues and tried to fill Italians with an unaccustomed martial ardor. And related to this militarism was an aggressive imperialism.

C. Republican Germany and Its Difficulties

German defeat in the First World War brought about, in November 1918, the overthrow of the Hohenzollern Empire which Bismarck had created in 1871, and the substitution of a provisional republican government headed by Friedrich Ebert, a prominent Socialist. Not all Germans took kindly to the change. There was opposition from a monarchist "Right," which comprised former Conservatives (now renamed "Nationalists") and former National Liberals (reorganized by a wealthy industrialist, Gustav Stresemann, as a "People's" party).

There was also opposition from an extreme "Left," composed of Socialists who sympathized with Bolshevik Russia and wanted to effect a thoroughgoing social revolution in Germany by means of a similar dictatorship. At first, it was this Communistic opposition which made chief trouble for the provisional government by inciting workers to riot and revolt. It was promptly and sternly suppressed, however, by Ebert with the support of a majority of Socialists, who were resolved to maintain the tradition of their party as Social Democratic.

Meanwhile the provisional government sponsored the election, by universal suffrage, of a National Constituent Assembly. Coöperating with Ebert and the Social Democrats in support of democracy and republicanism were the Catholic Centrists and the Progressives (now known simply as "Democrats"); and this coalition obtained an overwhelming majority of the popular electorate and hence dominated the Assembly, which met at Weimar in February 1919, ratified the treaty of Versailles in June, and completed a constitution in July.

The Weimar constitution of the new German Republic was thoroughly democratic. While it retained the federal organization of the previous Empire it lessened the powers of the several states and broadened those of the central government. In the latter, it entrusted legislative power to a two-house legislature composed of a Reichstag, representing the people, and a Reichsrat, representing the states. The executive authority was vested in a president, elected by the people for seven years, and in a chancellor and ministry responsible to the Reichstag. The suffrage was granted to all adult citizens of both sexes. The constitution included a detailed and liberal bill of rights, and provisions for the initiative, referendum, and recall, for proportional representation of all parties, and for a National Economic Council, representative of labor and capital, to advise on social and economic legislation. Similar changes at the same time in the state constitutions of Prussia, Bavaria, Saxony, and all others, seemed to guarantee the democratic character of the whole German Republic.

Grave difficulties confronted the German Republic. Internally, there was continuing embittered opposition of a monarchist and nationalist "Right" and of a communist, pro-Russian "Left." In foreign affairs, Germany was penalized and fettered by the terms of what seemed to most of its people a harsh and unjust peace treaty. To make matters worse, the country's economic position was extremely precarious.

There was currency inflation, which reached a climax in 1923, when a basketful of notes would not buy a dozen eggs, and a cow or a chair could be procured only for billions or even trillions of marks. While public indebtedness (war bonds, etc.) was wiped out, so too were savings accounts, life insurance, and investments of the middle class. Though the currency was stabilized on a new basis by 1924, Germany never recovered from the effects of the inflation. The German bourgeoisie had lost so much of its money and property that it remained a middle class only in its psychology. It was restive and eager to regain its lost status.

For a time the Republic appeared to gather strength. As "Leftist" insurrection had been suppressed in 1919, so a "Rightist" attempt at a *coup d'état* (the "Kapp Putsch") was thwarted in 1920 by a general strike of Socialist workers. Then, from 1924 to 1929, when the inflation and the Ruhr occupation were over and the Dawes Plan and Locarno agreements in effect, matters perceptibly improved. Despite frequent changes of ministry, the governing coalition of Centrists, Democrats, and Socialists retained a comfortable majority. At the general elections of 1924 the coalition polled 18 million votes out of 29 million cast. Four years later it polled almost 23 million out of 31 million. Besides, the People's party was now coöperating, and its leader, Stresemann, was chancellor in 1923 and then foreign minister until his death in 1929. At the same time, economic conditions improved somewhat. Germany gradually regained a considerable part of her foreign markets despite high tariffs in many countries. American loans enabled her to meet her reparations payments. And the towns, states, and national government were able to borrow heavily for public works.

Then came the financial crash of 1929, ending American loans and creating a most fateful economic depression in Germany. Unemployment, which even in 1928 had amounted to 1,350,000, rose to 3,150,000 in 1930, and to 5,600,000 in 1932. Such depression served to bring out inherent weaknesses of the Weimar Republic. The coalition which so far had triumphantly maintained it, now weakened and tended to disintegrate. Some of the Democrats, as well as most of the People's party, turned toward the "Right" and helped to swell the opposition from that quarter, while a growing number of Social Democrats heeded propaganda from Moscow and, under the leadership of Ernst Thälmann, a Hamburg mechanic, definitely joined the Communist opposition on the "Left." These organized local "cells" and regional "soviets." In 1930 they polled 4½ million votes, and in 1932 nearly 6 million. They took orders from Moscow, preached internal revolution and external coöperation with Russia, and stubbornly refused to work with the democratic Socialists or support the republic.

While the subversive activities and propaganda of the Communists were dangerous, so too, increasingly, was the opposition of the Nationalist Right. Here the original core of hostility to the republic consisted of Junkers (landed Prussian aristocrats), long identified with the monarchy, the army, and the civil service. They were scandalized by the defeat of German arms, and the overthrow of the Hohenzollern Empire. They chafed at the military and other restrictions of the Versailles treaty, and they eagerly put forward the myth that the German armies had never been defeated but had been "stabbed in the back" on the home front by traitorous Socialists and internationally minded Jews and Catholics.

It was the Junkers who provided the leadership of the Nationalist Party. At first, the following of this party was not impressive. In 1920, though it polled some 4 million votes in the general election, it was discredited by the failure of the Kapp Putsch. Another *coup* was attempted at Munich in 1923 by an odd team of nationalist fanatics, the renowned and elderly General Ludendorff and the youthful and hitherto unknown Adolf Hitler. Both were arrested, and Hitler was imprisoned.

Early in 1925, by clever maneuvering, the Nationalists obtained an ominous success. They put forward as their candidate for President of the Republic, to succeed the Socialist Ebert, who had just died, the aged war-hero, Field-Marshal Hindenburg, who; thanks to his personal popularity, won the election. Hindenburg's basic loyalties were those of a Junker—to empire, army, landed aristocracy, and Lutheran Church. Yet during the seven years of his first presidential term he observed his oath to uphold the republic and loyally coöperated with the republican majority in the Reichstag.

In 1932 Hindenburg was reëlected as the candidate of the republican coalition against candidates that stood for dictatorship rather than for democracy. One of these was the Communist Thälmann and the other the "Nationalist Socialst" (or Nazi) Hitler. A year later the democratic German Republic was practically ended by Hindenburg's delivering it to Hitler.

D. Nazi Germany

Adolf Hitler was born in Austria in 1889 of a lower middle-class family. He grew up with only ordinary schooling, and as a young man eked out a meager livelihood in an architect's office in Vienna and as a free-lance illustrator in Munich, solacing himself with devotion to Wagner's operas and Nietzsche's philosophy of the superman. He became an ardent German nationalist, adoring "Aryan" Germany, despising the polyglot Austrian Empire, and detesting Jews, Socialists, liberals, and pacifists. He served in the German army throughout the First World War. He was wounded and gassed, and for his valor he was awarded the Iron Cross. But he was not promoted beyond the rank of corporal.

At the close of the war, Hitler joined with a handful of youthful army acquaintances to form the "National Socialist" (or "Nazi") party, whose "unalterable program," adopted in 1920, was a mixture of radicalism and nationalism. It denounced the Versailles treaty, demanded the union of all who spoke German in a Greater Germany, and insisted on the return of Germany's lost colonies and the full rearmament of Germany. It assailed German Jews as aliens who should be denied citizenship. It condemned liberalism and parliamentary democracy. It proposed economic reforms designed to appeal to both the workers and the lower middle classes: abolition of unearned income, of department stores, and of land speculation.

Hitler speedily assumed leadership of the group and discovered that he had oratorical ability. By "letting himself go" in frenzied recital of the woes of Germany and in fierce denunciation of Jews and foreigners, he could attract and stir large audiences and exercise over them an almost hypnotic influence. The attempted Nazi *coup*, with General Ludendorff, at Munich in 1923 (the "Beer Hall Putsch") fizzled miserably, but it gained notoriety for Hitler and his ideas. A kind of bible for Nazism, under the title of *Mein Kampf* (My Battle), was written by Hitler while in jail.

Hitler and his lieutenants built the Nazi party along lines already adopted and tested by the Communists in Russia and the Fascists in Italy, with local cells, youth organizations, party guards (the *Schutzstaffeln*, or S. S.), and "storm troops" (the *Sturmabteilung*, or S. A.). They adopted a brown-shirt uniform and the emblem of a black swastika on a red field. They indulged in most strident propaganda and violent tactics, terrorizing their opponents and dis-

regarding law and personal rights. The party attracted many jobless youths, discontented war veterans, and impoverished bourgeois, but prior to 1929 it had relatively slight electoral success and was deemed less dangerous to German democracy than its Communist rival.

Nazi opportunity came with the economic depression of 1929. Hitler won most of the lower middle class, and new allies among aristocrats of the conservative Nationalist party, who thought they could use him for their own ends. Even industrial and commercial magnates began to support him as a barrier against the rising tide of Communism.

In the elections of 1930, while the Center Party more than held its own, the vote of the People's and Democratic parties fell off by 1¼ million, that of the Socialists by a half million, and that of the conservative Nationalists by two million. But the Communists gained a million votes, and the Nazis almost six million. The radical "left" and the radical "right" were winning mass support at the expense of the democratic coalition. From 1930 to 1932 the republican government, under Chancellor Heinrich Brüning, was dependent on wavering coöperation of the Social Democrats and support of the ultra-conservative President Hindenburg.

Brüning and other republicans worked manfully for Hindenburg's reëlection to the presidency in 1932. Thälmann, the Communist candidate, polled 3,700,000 votes, and Hitler, 13,400,000. But Hindenburg won with 20,000,000 votes. Once reëlected, Hindenburg, out of growing senility or deep-seated prejudices, began to give heed to Junker aristocrats who surrounded him. He dismissed Brüning and appointed as Chancellor Franz von Papen, who had allied himself with the conservative Nationalists and who now, with the aid of General Kurt von Schleicher, executed a military *coup* against the Socialist premier and police officials of Prussia. The Socialists, receiving no aid from the Communists, meekly surrendered their posts. But from ensuing general elections, neither Papen nor Schleicher (who succeeded him in the chancellorship) could obtain anything like a majority of Conservative supporters in the Reichstag.

Eventually, conservative Nationalists convinced Hindenburg that their cause could best be served, and any Communist dictatorship most surely prevented, through collaboration with Hitler's Nazi party, which, with the conservative Nationalists, now commanded a parliamentary majority. Accordingly, on January 30, 1933, the senile President dismissed Schleicher and appointed Hitler chancellor.

It had taken Lenin and Mussolini several years to crush opposition and establish their respective dictatorships. Hitler did likewise within a few months. From the start, he regarded his Nationalist allies in the ministry and the Reichstag as merely a convenient link with Hindenburg and legality. The important thing was that he now commanded the public police as well as his own storm troops; and these were ruthlessly employed to terrorize opponents and assure to the Nazis a majority in elections scheduled for March 1933. Just prior to this election the Reichstag building was burned, undoubtedly by Nazis, although at the time Hitler made political capital out of it by blaming it on the Communists. Out of 39 million votes, the Nazis polled 17 million, and their Nationalist allies some 3 million. It was by no means an overwhelming electoral victory for Hitler, but it sufficed.

A week later, Hindenburg decreed that the Republican flag (black, red, gold) be hauled down and replaced by two flags, that of the old German Empire (black, white, red), and the swastika of the Nazis. On April 1, 1933, the Reichstag voted to delegate its powers for four years to the Hitler government. Thus began what the Nazis called the Third Empire, counting as its predecessors only the old Holy Roman Empire and that of Bismarck and William I.

The revolution which inaugurated the "Third Empire" was attended by intense popular excitement skillfully worked up and exploited by the new regime. Press, radio, cinema, and public meetings were all used for intensive propaganda. One of Hitler's chief lieutenants, Joseph Goebbels, exhibited a veritable genius for showmanship, and under his guidance a whirlwind of hysteria swept the country. Deprived by censorship of all impartial news and critical opinion, many Germans, even normally sober and sensible ones, began to believe implicitly in Nazi propaganda and especially in the genius of "The Leader" (*Der Führer*), Adolf Hitler.

The hysteria of the Nazi revolution was heightened by spectacular anti-Semitism. Jews (and Christians with Jewish blood) were dismissed from all public posts. Jewish shops were looted. With sporadic intensifications, the persecution continued until thousands of Jews fled abroad, while others were immured in concentration camps and brutally tortured. This ruthless anti-Semitism was embodied at length in a code of public laws, while youths were encouraged to despise and even to destroy Jewish books, art, and music.

Meanwhile, Hitler consolidated his hold on the governmental machinery. His associate, Hermann Göring, was made premier of Prussia, and the rest of the states were subjected to other leading Nazis. The Nationalist party and the People's party were absorbed by the Nazis, while all other parties were abolished. Labor unions were dissolved and "replaced" by a "German Labor Front" completely dominated by Nazi officials. Marxian books were burned. Strikes were forbidden.

By November 1933 Hitler was ready to seek national endorsement of what he had done. He held simultaneously the election of a new Reichstag and a plebiscite on Germany's withdrawal from the League of Nations. The results as given out by the Nazis, who superintended the polls, were 40½ million "yes" and 2 million "no" on withdrawal from the League, and 39½ million ballots for the Nazi list of Reichstag candidates as against 3½ million "blank" or "spoiled."

When Hindenburg died in 1934, Hitler became president as well as chancellor of Germany, and this step was endorsed by another plebiscite. In the same year he crushed opposition within the Nazi party and conspirators outside it by a "blood purge" in which a number of leading Nazis and non-Nazis like Schleicher were murdered.

From 1934 to 1939, the story of the Nazi dictatorship was one of strengthening hold on Germany. The government was com-

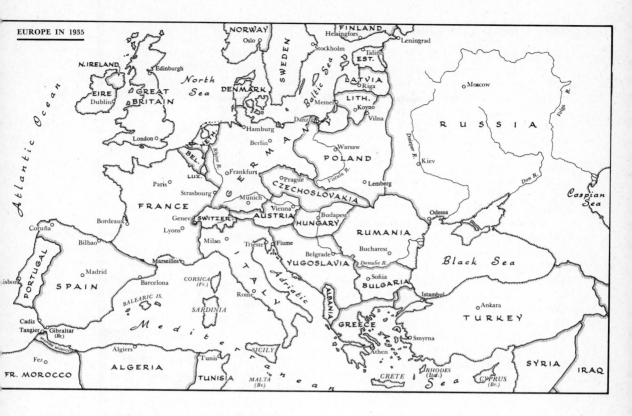

pletely centralized; the old rights of the states were eliminated; new districts were set up and put under Nazi *gauleiters* who firmly carried out Hitler's will. The new regime, like the Russian or Italian, was thoroughly totalitarian in that it denied individual rights and regulated all domestic activities, social, political, economic, cultural. Those who ventured to oppose or criticize it, including a considerable number of Catholic and Protestant clergy, were imprisoned or executed. Some fled the country and found refuge abroad.

The dictatorship ended unemployment by a program of public works, and especially of rearmament, which it began secretly in 1933 and openly not long afterwards. Fortifications were constructed, munitions factories built, a whole military aircraft industry established. Compulsory military service was reinstituted and gradually Germany moved onto a war footing. The whole economy of the country was brought under state control. Exports were pushed, especially to the Balkans, while imports were regulated so as to stockpile war material. Eventually it was foreign war,

not domestic revolt, which brought Nazi Germany to an inglorious end.

E. Wide Trend Toward Dictatorship

The trend toward dictatorship and the abandonment of democratic and constitutional forms of government was by no means confined to Russia, Italy, and Germany. It had seemed in 1920 as if the whole world were moving toward liberal democracy. But the next two decades saw a major reversal as country after country developed some type of authoritarian or dictatorial rule, usually with a definite admixture of control by the military. So strong, however, was the popular belief in democracy that the dictators almost without exception cloaked the new methods of governing in the trappings of the liberal institutions that had been evolved since 1789—constitutions, plebiscites, elections, bills of rights, legislatures chosen by a broad electorate, and the like.

In Hungary a liberal government under Count Michael Károlyi (1918) and a

Communist dictatorship under Béla Kun (1919) were quickly succeeded by monarchy without a king organized by a group of aristocrats, and approved by an election (1920). Admiral Horthy became "Regent," and in 1921 Count Stephen Bethlen was made premier. In fact, for ten years, Bethlen, supported by the well organized National Unity party, ruled in a thoroughly arbitrary fashion, as did his successor (1932), Julius Gomboes. Similarly in Poland, the large number of parties and factions made government ineffective under the very democratic constitution of 1921, and Marshal Pilsudski, a general as well as a former Socialist and revolutionary, assumed control in 1926. Sometimes as war minister, sometimes as premier, Pilsudski was in fact the dominating figure in Poland until his death in 1935. Just before he died, he secured the adoption of a new constitution which provided for the continuation of a qualified dictatorship.

In the Balkan countries, likewise, democratic procedures tended to give way to authoritarian techniques. The Rumanian constitution of 1923 had democratic features, including universal suffrage, but it gave the king the power to appoint and oust ministers without reference to the legislature. Indeed King Carol II did succeed for periods (1931–1932, 1938–1940) in ruling quite arbitrarily. There was, moreover, a strong reactionary party, the Iron Guards, which wanted to establish a thoroughly Fascist kind of government. Bulgaria in the post-war period moved from a nominally democratic government, that was often in the control of reactionaries, to authoritarian rule, whether by army officers (1934–1935) or by the King, Boris III (after 1935). It was the monarch, too, who in Yugoslavia became in effect the dictator, for in 1929, Alexander I with the support of the army dissolved the parliament, suspended the constitution, and suppressed all dissent. A new constitution two years later, though it had liberal features, in reality confirmed royal control. Albania likewise became a kind of royal dictatorship when a young Moslem and army officer, Ahmed Zogu, who had been elected president in 1925, proclaimed himself King Zog I in 1928. In Greece, on the other hand, it was a premier,

General John Metaxas, who eventually installed a dictatorship in 1936 and had himself made premier for life in 1938. Greece came to this solution only after a stormy period of confused political strife both as a monarchy (till 1924 and again after 1935) and as a republic (1924–1935). We have already noted that the Turkish post-war leader, Mustafa Kemal, was in fact a dictator, though toward the end of his life he was developing some of the elements that might make democratic government possible.

It was not only in the troubled areas of central Europe and the Balkans that democracy seemed to be weakening in the years after 1920. In the new Baltic countries, which had adopted radically democratic constitutions, the paralyzing agitation of Communists, Fascists, and dissident democrats led to the establishment of dictatorial rule in Lithuania (1926), Latvia (1934), and Estonia (1934). Even Finland, which was sturdily republican, had to adopt rather arbitrary techniques to repress dissident extremists of the right and of the left. At the other corner of Europe, in Portugal, General Antonio Carmona seized the presidency (1926), revised the constitution in a Fascist direction, and got himself continued as president with nearly complete dictatorial powers. In 1928, he brought into the government a professor of economics from the University of Coimbra, Dr. Antonio de Oliveira Salazar, who as premier was soon managing the dictatorship and continued to do so after Carmona's death in 1951. In Spain, the course of events was both more troubled and more violent. The constitutional monarchy there under King Alphonso XIII was weakened by increasingly unsuccessful military operations in Morocco, and in 1923 the King connived at the establishment of a military dictatorship under a nobleman and army officer, Primo de Rivera. But Primo's attempts to make a Fascist corporate state of Spain won little popular support, and when he resigned in 1930, the democratic constitution was restored. The next year the monarchy was abolished, the King driven out, and a republic established. It, in turn, was to endure for only eight years, and, after a bloody civil war, to give way to another dictatorship under General Francisco Franco.

The trend away from democracy was by no means confined to Europe. Iran was a more or less constitutional monarchy under its Shah Ahmed in 1921. But in that year an able general, Reza Pahlavi, took over the government. First as war minister, then as premier (1923), he organized a strong, nationalist rule, and in 1925 he arranged the deposition of Ahmed and had himself made Shah. He was in fact a military dictator. In China, a republic had been established by the democratic leader Sun Yat-sen in 1911. But for years China was in a state of near chaos with rival governments, independent "war lords," and the infiltration of Russian and Japanese agents. Finally, with the backing of Sun Yat-sen's Kuomintang party, an able general, Chiang Kai-shek, came to the fore and installed a Nationalist government at Nanking in 1927 and at Peking the next year. Peking was renamed Peiping. Nanking was made the capital, and Chiang was made President of the Republic. Conditions were, however, so unsettled, and pressure from the Russians and Japanese so continuous, that Chiang ruled as a military, nationalist dictator rather than as a democratic, constitutional leader.

Developments in Japan seemed superficially different. After World War I, the Japanese constitutional empire appeared to be stable enough and increasingly democratic. Universal manhood suffrage was, for example, granted in 1925, and for some years the government was controlled in turn by the Seiyukai (conservative) and the Menseito (liberal) party. But there was much corruption, and nationalist and militarist groups and individuals were increasingly dissatisfied with the government and its policies. In 1931, the Japanese army,

without approval from the appropriate ministries, began hostilities against the Chinese in Manchuria—an undeclared war that was eventually to merge into World War II. The next year the Menseito party leader and the Seiyukai premier were both assassinated. Thereafter, the government was in the hands of violently nationalist army and navy officers who believed in, and increasingly used, thoroughly dictatorial procedures.

Thus the trend toward authoritarian rule, in one form or another, was world-wide in the two decades after 1920. Only the old and stable countries of western Europe, Scandinavia, and North America, plus one new nation, Czechoslovakia, remained democratic during that period. Far from "making the world safe for democracy," World War I led to an era in which democracy weakened or disappeared in a number of countries where it had been at least partially established in 1914—Japan, Italy, Spain, Portugal, Greece. It seemed as if the confused conditions of the world were an invitation for strong men, army officers, and nationalist parties to seize power and to exercise it in an authoritarian fashion. Once in command, they were often able to retain control and to repress dissent by means of the improved weapons and more effective methods of communication, propaganda, and organization which modern technology had put at their disposal. Or, to state it another way, the rapid changes in society all over the world induced by war, economic development, spreading education, and technological innovation had dissolved the cement that held society together in many countries and had produced a condition of instability which opened the road to ruthless men with motives which varied from the most self-seeking to the most patriotic.

Neville Chamberlain leaving Munich, September, 1938.

CHAPTER 58

Undoing the Paris Peace Settlement

A. Intensifying Economic and Ideological Conflicts

Hopes of the early 1920's that humanity was entering upon an age of assured peace and democratic progress were pretty well dispelled by the mid-1930's. The League of Nations was obviously weakening. Promised limitation of armaments was proving vain, and in the case of the newer totalitarian dictatorships (Russia, Italy, and Germany) military establishments were being strengthened in an increasingly alarming manner.

Everywhere economic nationalism was being competitively practiced. As early as 1922 the United States, despite its being a creditor nation which could be paid only by importation of goods, adopted an intensely protective tariff, and most European countries, in imitation or retaliation, raised their tariffs. Such tariff conflict became acute and bitter following the depression of 1929. Again the United States led the way, and, against the advice of prominent economists, raised its import duties sharply in the Hawley-Smoot tariff of 1930. France inaugurated a policy of admitting only specified quotas of certain foreign goods. Great Britain adopted a protective tariff in 1932. The Netherlands and most other countries on the Continent were soon copying France, while Britain by the Ottawa agreements (1932) sought to raise a tariff barrier around the whole British Empire.

Quotas and tariffs were supplemented by currency restrictions. In the 1920's almost all European countries worked their way back to an international gold standard, but after 1929 every nation began to tinker with its money in the hope that, by cheapening it, prices could be raised at home and unemployment relieved by expanding sales abroad. Britain went off gold in 1931, the United States in 1933. With these pivots of world economy loosened, all other countries went the same way, and further competitive reductions in the value of national currencies were made. International exchange was disrupted, and most countries restricted the export of money. World economy was breaking up into national units and associated "blocs."

In coping with depression and unemployment at home, countries were driven not only to restrictions on trade and finance, but also to the assumption of increasing control over all phases of economic life. Agricultural subsidies, labor legislation, and governmental direction of industry grew rapidly in importance and scope.

Complicating the economic depression and conflict of the 1930's was an intensifying ideological conflict. Instead of the liberal and democratic Europe which had been expected at the close of the First World War, there was now a Europe in which liberal democracy was retreating before a rapid advance of dictatorship. The newer dictatorship was of two main types: (1) Marxian or Communist, as in Russia; and (2) Fascist or Nazi, as in Italy and

Germany. Each of these was to its followers a veritable religion, inspiring them with fanatical devotion, and each claimed to be absolutely opposed to the other. Yet, while one represented an extreme "left" and the other an extreme "right," they both employed essentially the same organization and methods and both were thoroughly hostile to liberal democracy.

Though neither type of dictatorship permitted any domestic dissent or criticism, both fostered the spread of their respective ideologies abroad, and this the democracies could not prevent without violating their distinctive liberalism. Thus, while no democratic parties existed in Russia, Italy, or Germany, nearly all democratic countries had Communist and Fascist parties, denouncing each other but both working to subvert the democratic regimes that harbored them. In the United States and most democratic countries of western Europe along the Atlantic seaboard, the subversive parties were vocal but not immediately menacing. Elsewhere, however, they tended to paralyze the orderly operation of democratic government and to provoke forceful action against them leading to at least partial dictatorship. This actually occurred in Poland, Lithuania, Latvia, Estonia, Rumania, Yugoslavia, Austria, Hungary, Bulgaria, Greece, Turkey, and Portugal.

In Spain, King Alphonso XIII had connived at the establishment of a dictatorship by General Primo de Rivera which lasted from 1923 to 1930. In 1931 a revolution ousted the King and established a republic. Though this endured for six years, it was torn by bitter conflict between "left" and "right." A "leftist" revolt was suppressed with bloodshed in 1934. A "rightist" revolt in 1936 led to three years of civil war.

B. Weakness of the League of Nations, and Japanese Seizure of Manchuria

The Paris peace-settlement of 1919–1920, with the Covenant of the League of Nations, was supplemented in the 1920's by the so-called "Nine-Power" treaties (1922) designed to maintain the integrity of China and the *status quo* in eastern Asia, and also by the "Kellogg-Briand" pact (1928) by which all countries pledged themselves to "renounce the use of war as an instrument of national policy." By 1935, however, Germany was repudiating the peace settlement which she had promised to observe, while Japan and Italy were waging wars against fellow members of the League of Nations. Thenceforth, matters went from bad to worse, and violence or the threat of violence increasingly dominated world affairs.

The sequence of these sorry events was initiated by Japan in 1931. Though she had signed the Nine-Power treaties, joined the League, and adhered to the Kellogg-Briand pact, she was ambitious to control China. She already had important investments in Manchuria and a hold on its strategic railways, but it appeared difficult for her to gain more, because of her international commitments, and because the Chinese Nationalist government of Chiang Kai-shek was consolidating its hold on China and insisting on the maintenance of Chinese sovereignty over Manchuria. In Japan the more or less liberal leaders who had signed the peace pacts were being harassed by extreme nationalists, who resorted to assassination and terrorism, and who succeeded in establishing in the spring of 1932 what amounted to a military dictatorship.

Already hostilities had been opened in Manchuria. In September 1931, to "protect" Japanese property, to "repress banditry," and to "restore order," Japanese troops attacked Chinese forces, and, expanding their hold rapidly from the railway zones, soon overran the entire territory and drove out the Chinese governor and his forces. China appealed to the League of Nations, and a League commission, after six months' investigation, recommended that Japan be censured and Manchuria be given an autonomous government under Chinese sovereignty. Japan ignored the recommendations, resigned from the League, and proceeded with the plans of her militarists in Manchuria.

The League, unable to agree on any joint action or "sanctions" against Japan, contented itself with expressing regret. Unavailing, too, were China's pleas to the United States under the Nine-Power

Generalissimo Chiang Kai-shek reviewing his staff officers, 1940.

Courtesy Wide World Photos

treaties and the Kellogg-Briand pact, though the American government did announce the "Stimson doctrine," to the effect that it would not recognize any territorial changes resulting from aggression in violation of treaties. The simple fact of the matter was that only force applied by a great power could have checked Japan. The United States, Great Britain, and France were too busy with the problems of depression and those created by the rise of dictatorships in Europe to be willing to use force in defense of China. Thus the basic principles of the League and of international peace were sacrificed, and Japan pursued her aggressive way unhindered.

In 1932 Japan set up a puppet government in Manchuria under the ex-Emperor of China, Henry Pu-yi, renamed the country Manchukuo, and recognized it as "independent." In response, the Chinese organized a patriotic boycott of all Japanese goods. But this action only inspired Japan's

military clique, now firmly in the saddle at Tokyo, to further aggression. A Japanese expeditionary force landed at Shanghai, and Japanese armies occupied the Chinese province of Jehol south of Manchuria. At length in 1933 the Chinese government of Chiang Kai-shek, powerless to resist and without aid from abroad, consented to a truce which left Jehol and Manchuria in Japanese hands. The United States and the League of Nations merely withheld recognition of the new Japanese-dominated state of Manchukuo.

Sure now that she could proceed without interference from the great powers, Japan in 1934 denounced the Washington and London naval agreements and started strengthening her navy. The next year, Japanese troops pushed across the Great Wall into the Chinese provinces of Chakar and Hopei and compelled the Chinese government to replace its officials in these provinces and in Peiping and Tientsin with persons acceptable to Japan. Under this pressure from Japan, Chinese patriotic feeling was aroused, and there were signs that the Chinese might achieve political unity and be able to resist further Japanese advances. In 1936 Chiang Kai-shek ended the civil war in Kwantung and the next year reached an agreement with the Communist forces in northwest China for a "united front" against Japan. Whereupon, fighting between Chinese and Japanese troops near Peiping in July 1937 was the signal for the delivery of a Japanese ultimatum to China. When China rejected it, Japan launched an actual, if undeclared, war against China, which continued until it was merged (in 1941) with the greater struggle of the Second World War.

C. Italian Conquest of Ethiopia, and Civil War in Spain

While Japan waged a war of aggression in eastern Asia, Mussolini and Hitler were directing aggressive policies for Italy and Germany in Africa and Europe. Mussolini cherished dreams of expanding Italy's colonial empire. In particular, he cast envious eyes on the independent African kingdom of Ethiopia (Abyssinia), and longed to avenge the defeat it had inflicted on Italy at Adowa in 1896.[1]

In pursuit of his policy, Mussolini negotiated an agreement with Great Britain in 1925, whereby Italy might seek "concessions" in Ethiopia. But Ethiopia, a member

[1] See above, p. 665.

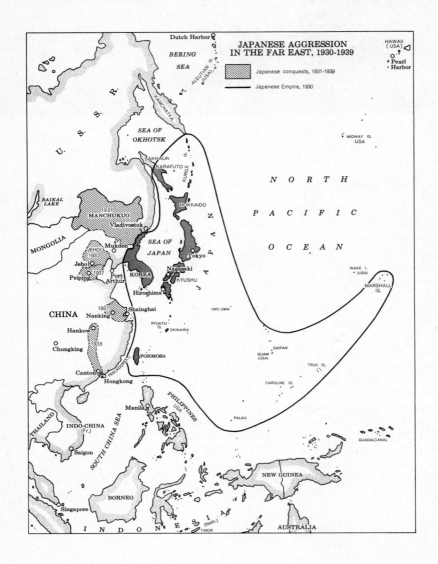

Generalissimo Francisco Franco being greeted by Dr. Antonio de Oliveira Salazar.

Courtesy Wide World Photos

of the League of Nations since 1923, promptly protested to that organization, and Italy, posing as a special friend of Ethiopia, signed with it in 1928 a treaty of "perpetual friendship" and arbitration. But still the Ethiopian King, Haile Selassie, doggedly refused all Italian requests for special favors or concessions, and Mussolini gradually reached the conclusion that Italy could gain her ends in Ethiopia only by the use of force.

Such use of force would violate existing treaties and the principles of the League of Nations. But Japan had shown that this could be done with impunity. In January 1935 Mussolini secured from France, which was eager to keep Italian friendship as a check against Hitler's ambitions, an agreement that Italy should have a free hand in Ethiopia. Then alleging the necessity of repressing disorder along the ill-defined border between Ethiopia and the Italian colonies of Eritrea and Somaliland, he despatched an Italian army to east Africa.

Ethiopia appealed to the League and won popular and presently governmental support in Great Britain, which now perceived in Italy's aggressive attitude a threat to its own imperial interests in Egypt, as well as to the cause of collective security. Britain sent a fleet to the Mediterranean and besought the League to take a strong stand. In vain France tried to effect a compromise which would give Italy part of Ethiopia. Mussolini went ahead with his preparations and in October 1935, in flagrant violation of the League Covenant, the Kellogg Pact, and the Italian-Ethiopian treaty, Italian troops invaded Ethiopia, captured Adowa, and pushed on into the interior. Though the natives fought bravely, they had no arms to match the tanks, planes, and artillery of the Italians. By May 1936 Haile Selassie had fled abroad, his capital of Addis Ababa was occupied, and the whole country was formally annexed to Italy. King Victor Emmanuel III assumed the title of Emperor of Ethiopia.

Meanwhile, in October 1935, the League of Nations had pronounced Italy an aggressor. Britain backed the action of the League, and France reluctantly supported Britain. In November, the League voted to apply economic sanctions against Italy, including a ban on the shipment of oil to her. The sanctions caused some distress in Italy, but they failed of their purpose, for they solidified the Italian people in support of Mussolini, while Italy obtained needful war materials from Germany. With scrupulous regard for treaties and international law, Britain made no attempt to shut off the flow of Italian troops and supplies through the Suez Canal.

In Italy's conquest of Ethiopia, as in Japan's war against China, there was ruthless use of force, violation of treaties, and disregard of the League of Nations. Italy responded to her condemnation by the League by merely withdrawing from it in May 1936, and in July the League acknowledged its impotence by rescinding the sanctions against Italy. Aggression scored a notable victory.

No sooner was the Italian conquest of Ethiopia completed than the outbreak of civil war in Spain afforded opportunity for

forceful interference on the part of all three
of the major European dictatorships—Italy,
Germany, and Russia. Ever since the establishment of the Spanish republic in 1931,
it had been sorely troubled by conflict between "Right" and "Left," and in 1934
a revolt of the Left had been suppressed
with no little bloodshed. Elections early
in 1936 gave a majority of seats in parliament (though not quite a popular majority)
to a "popular-front" coalition of Leftist
groups—Radical Republicans, Socialists,
Syndicalists, and Communists—which
promised to break up large landed estates,
to enforce measures against the church,
and to make drastic reductions in the army.
Considerable mob violence ensued, and in
July 1936 a group of high army officers
(who later chose General Francisco Franco
as their chief, or *caudillo*) attempted a *coup
d'état* against the popular-front government. The *coup* failed of its immediate
purpose, but it precipitated an extraordinarily destructive civil war lasting for almost
three years (1936–1939).

The Spanish Civil War was primarily a
Spanish affair. It was a struggle between
the Leftist groups which comprised the
"popular front" and were known as "Loyalists," and Rightist groups of Monarchists,
Carlists, and Conservative Republicans,
which, with a newly created fascist group
called the Falange, were known as "Nationalists." Loyalists were stronger in northern
and eastern Spain; Nationalists, in western
and southern Spain. The former had allies
in nationalistic Basques and Catalans; the
latter, in the majority of clergy and army
officers.

But the Spanish Civil War also had ominous international aspects. Almost from the
start, General Franco received aid in men,
money, planes, and material from Fascist
Italy and Nazi Germany, and gradually his
Nationalist movement became popularly
identified with the cause of fascist dictatorship. On the other hand, the popular-front
government received similar aid from Communist Russia and fell increasingly under
its influence, with the result that the Loyalist cause was represented by its adversaries
and critics as essentially the cause of
Marxian dictatorship. Under Communist

auspices, "international brigades" were recruited and sent into Spain to battle anti-
Communist "volunteers" and expeditionary
Italian and German forces. There was constant danger that the Spanish Civil War
might develop into a huge international war
involving not only the two contrasting
types of dictatorship but also the remaining democratic great powers.

Anxious to avoid entanglement in any
such war, and, if possible, to stave it off
altogether, the United States strengthened
its neutrality legislation, while Great Britain adhered to a similar policy of non-
intervention in Spain and sought to persuade other European powers to do likewise. With perfect cynicism the several
dictatorships assured Britain they were not
intervening or would at once cease to intervene, and then kept on giving aid to one
side or the other in Spain. France was less
cynical, but its "popular-front" ministry of
the time, under Léon Blum, was sympathetic with the Spanish Loyalists and inclined to wink at private violations of public
neutrality.

Meanwhile the civil war dragged on in
Spain, with fortune slowly favoring the
Nationalists. In 1937 Franco accomplished
the piecemeal conquest of the Basque provinces in the north, and in March 1938 his
armies drove eastward to the Mediterranean
and cut off the Loyalist forces in Catalonia
from those in the Madrid-Valencia zone.
This marked the beginning of the end.
During the next year Franco conquered all
of Catalonia; and finally, after a twenty-
nine-months' siege, Madrid capitulated to
him in March 1939. Thousands of Loyalists fled abroad, principally to France,
Mexico, and South America. Spain itself
was subjected to a military dictatorship of
a fascist type.

The outcome of the protracted violence
in Spain was as heartening to Mussolini and
Hitler as it was uncomfortable for Stalin
and ominous for the democracies. Even in
Western Europe, on the Atlantic seaboard,
dictatorship was now triumphant over liberal democracy; and for any final reckoning
with France and Britain (or with Russia),
Italy and Germany had gained prestige and
valuable military experience.

D. Hitler's Repudiation of the Versailles Treaty

Before he came to power Hitler had won popularity in Germany by denouncing the victors of the First World War and preaching the most intense kind of German nationalism. Once his dictatorship was established, he used the field of foreign relations for a double purpose—to increase his personal prestige with the Germans, and to gain territory and prestige for Germany. His objective was piecemeal destruction of the Paris peace-settlement, and his tactics were unusually simple. He focussed attention on some particular German demand and insisted that when this was granted Germany would live like a good neighbor with the rest of Europe. When it was granted, he proceeded to make a new demand. He was satisfied to obtain his ends by threats and bluster. But he rapidly pushed forward German military preparations in case war should result from his tactics.

Early in his dictatorship, Hitler turned his attention to Austria, his native land, which he was resolved to bring into an *Anschluss* (union) with Germany, contrary to express provision in the treaty of Versailles. He actively encouraged Nazi propaganda within Austria, and connived at an attempted *coup d'état* there in July, 1934, attended by the murder of the Austrian chancellor, Dollfuss. The *coup* failed, partly because the Nazis had insufficient popular support within Austria, and partly because Italy, seconded by Czechoslovakia and France, took a strong stand and threatened war if Germany should take over Austria. Consequently, on this occasion, Hitler backed down; he denied that he had had anything to do with the trouble in Austria or had any intention of annexing that country.

Common opposition to Hitler drew France and Italy temporarily together, and in January 1935 they signed a pact at Rome designed to maintain Austrian independence, give Italy a free hand in Ethopia, and uphold the treaty of Versailles. At the same period, Hitler scored a victory. In the plebiscite held according to the Versailles treaty to determine the fate of the Saar, ninety

per cent of the votes were for reunion with Germany, and accordingly, on March 1, 1935, amid much Nazi rejoicing, the Saar was formally turned over to Hitler's Third Empire. Elated by this success (legitimate for once), Hitler intensified Nazi propaganda among German-speaking people outside Germany—in Austria, Danzig, Memel, and the Sudentenland (western fringe) of Czechoslovakia. He made no secret of his hope of absorbing such areas, and even the Russian Ukraine, into his greater Germany.

As if to give speedy effect to this ambitious program, Hitler dramatically announced, on March 16, 1935, Germany's repudiation of all treaty limitations on her armaments, the reëstablishment of universal military service, and the creation of an air force equal to the British or the French. Applauded with patriotic enthusiasm in Germany, Hitler's violation of the Versailles treaty naturally aroused alarm elsewhere. In a conference at Stresa, in April 1935, Mussolini joined the premiers of France and Britain in proclaiming that the three countries would work together to support the League of Nations and the Versailles treaty. In May, France concluded a defensive military alliance with Russia, and Russia made a similar alliance with Czechoslovakia. It seemed as if Nazi Germany might be restrained by joint action of the other dictatorships with the democracies.

In the autumn of 1935, however, Fascist Italy, as we have seen, began her Ethiopian adventure. Mussolini had reason to believe that the French government and possibly the British would regard it with benevolent eyes. But popular feeling in Britain and France opposed the compromises suggested, and regard for the League of Nations and the principle of "collective security" led both countries to participate in the sanctions against Italy. Germany, on the other hand, openly sympathized with the Italians and supplied them with war material. Moreover, Hitler seized the moment when cleavage was widening between Italy on one hand and France and Britain on the other to deliver a major blow at the European treaty structure. In March 1936, German troops marched into the demilitarized zones of the Rhineland in flat violation of both the Versailles treaty and the Locarno pact.

The German general staff had been very reluctant to take this step, fearing that France would fight and defeat the new German armies, which were not yet ready for a major war. Hitler had insisted on the gamble, and fortune favored him. Though the Council of the League of Nations adopted a resolution condemning Germany for violation of treaties, France and Belgium were the only nations at all minded to take any real action, and they were deterred by pacifism at home and indifference abroad. Russia refused to collaborate with France. Italy was now hostile to France. Great Britain was more concerned with Italian aggression than with German. In the circumstances, Germany remilitarized her western frontiers with impunity, while Belgium broke off her military alliance (of 1920) with France and resumed her neutrality. French prestige and the cause of peace suffered a most serious setback.

By October 1936 the course of events brought Germany and Italy into an open accord, the so-called "Rome-Berlin axis." It was the logical result of their close relations during the Ethiopian War, their common disdain for the League of Nations, their opposition to France and Great Britain, their similarity in government and ideology, and their ambitions for expansion.

In November 1936, Germany concluded with Japan an "Anti-Comintern" pact, ostensibly directed against the spread of Russian Communism, but clearly intended to serve Japanese purposes in eastern Asia and German ambitions in Europe; and a year later, Italy adhered to this pact. Thus emerged a new balance of power, with Germany, Italy, and Japan on one hand, and France, Great Britain, and Russia on the other. It was a most precarious balance, however, for continued and effective collaboration of Communist Russia with the western democracies proved well-nigh impossible.

Meanwhile Nazi Germany continued her violations of the treaty of Versailles. In November 1936 she repudiated its provisions for international control of her water-

NAZI GERMANY AND ITS AGGRESSIONS, 1933-1939

Remilitarized, 1936
Appropriated, 1935-1939
Allied 1936, 1939
Threatened, 1939
Boundary, 1933

ways. In January 1937 she denounced its clauses charging her with war-guilt. Then early in 1938 she violated its guarantee of Austrian independence. The Austrian Chancellor Schuschnigg had been contending desperately against a rising tide of Nazi inhltration and propaganda in his country. At length in March 1938, when direct overtures to Hitler proved vain, Schuschnigg suddenly called for a plebiscite, in which he hoped to show that most Austrians were opposed to union with Germany, despite the noisy claims of the Austrian and German Nazis. To prevent the holding of the plebiscite, Hitler swiftly occupied helpless Austria with German troops and proclaimed its incorporation in the Nazi German Empire.

Other powers might protest, but Italy, which in 1934 had threatened war to prevent Germany's seizure of Austria, was now so absorbed in Ethopian and Spanish adventures and so closely allied with Germany that Mussolini pretended to approve the extension of the German Empire to the borders of his own country. With Italy acquiescent, the protests of other nations were merely verbal.

Thus Germany by the spring of 1938 had destroyed the restrictive clauses of the treaty of Versailles, helped to discredit the League of Nations, and made considerable territorial gains. Hitler's bloodless successes convinced the German people of his genius, and many of those who did not like his policies of dictatorship and terrorism at home were dazzled and won over by his successes abroad.

E. "Appeasement," Partition of Czechoslovakia, Russo-German Pact, and Outbreak of World War II

From 1935 to 1938, Anthony Eden as British foreign secretary had tended, though somewhat hesitantly, to work with France, the League of Nations, and even Russia in an attempt to check Italy and Germany. But his efforts seemed fruitless, for Italy and Germany drew closer together and won a series of successes in Ethiopia, Spain, and Austria. Neville Chamberlain, who succeeded Stanley Baldwin as British prime

minister in 1937, dismissed Eden in the spring of 1938 and tried a new tack. While retaining ties with France, he would strive to reach an understanding with Germany and Italy. With Italy he at once negotiated a set of treaties (signed April 1938), by which Italy promised to get out of Spain as soon as possible and to stop anti-British propaganda in Palestine and Egypt. In return, Britain promised to work for general recognition of Italy's conquest of Ethopia. Amidst recriminations and the despairing protests of the native ex-ruler, Haile Selassie, Great Britain obtained from the League of Nations authorization for individual members to recognize the King of Italy as Emperor of Ethopia, and herself granted such recognition.

But no sooner was Italy "appeased" than Germany demanded "appeasement." Hitler was following up his success in Austria with virulent propaganda against Czechoslovakia and ostentatious preparation for giving forceful aid to its "oppressed" German-speaking minority—the Sudetens. These were being stimulated by Nazi agents to demand not mere autonomy but outright annexation to Germany. The Czechs mobilized in defense and called on France, Russia, and the Little Entente for their promised assistance. On the other side, Italy and Hungary backed Germany's truculent attitude. For a few days the crisis was acute, war seemed at hand, and popular emotion was intense. Dramatically Chamberlain flew back and forth between England and Germany begging Hitler not to precipitate war, while Daladier, the French premier, flew back and forth between Paris and London. No united stand could be made against Hitler. The position of Russia was uncertain. The Little Entente dared not break with Germany unless France did. France felt horror at the prospect of war, and was determined to stick to Great Britain. Britain imagined that by permitting Germany to annex German-speaking districts of Czechoslovakia, Hitler would be "appeased" and there would be no war.

So the crisis was suddenly ended by an accord signed at Munich in September 1938 by Chamberlain, Daladier, Mussolini, and Hitler, by which peace was maintained but democratic Czechoslovakia was sacrificed. Hitler got a free hand to annex the Sudetenland, which he promptly did. Simultaneously, Poland seized the Teschen district of Czechoslovakia, and Hungary occupied a strip of Slovakia. Altogether, Czechoslovakia lost a third of her territory and no longer had a strategically defensible western frontier. All she received in return was a joint guarantee attached by the four great powers to the Munich pact. Hitler, triumphant, announced he had no further territorial ambitions. Chamberlain, flying back from Munich, declared he had given Europe "peace in our time." Almost everywhere (outside of Czechoslovakia) people hailed the Munich pact with relief. It seemed to remove the threat of war and to indicate that there could be pacific collaboration among the major European powers whether dictatorial or democratic.

How far Hitler could be trusted to observe his pledges was soon apparent. In March 1939, only six months after the Munich pact and without even consulting its other signatories, he completed the partition of Czechoslovakia. With German encouragement, a separatist Slovak cabinet had been set up, and when the Czech prime minister tried to depose its head, Hitler not only forced the Czech government to accede to the Slovak demands but to place itself under his direction. German troops poured into Prague. Bohemia and Moravia were made dependencies of the Third Reich. Slovakia was transformed into a German protectorate. Simultaneously, Hungary seized the Ruthenian province of Carpatho-Ukraine.

These events of March 1939 convinced Neville Chamberlain that Nazi Germany could neither be trusted nor "appeased" by concessions. With dismay he saw Hitler bully Lithuania into surrendering Memel to the Third Reich, while Mussolini, eager to share in spoils of forceful expansion, occupied Albania and added it to Italy. Almost immediately Hitler launched a vituperative campaign against Poland, charging that it was committing "atrocities" against its German minority, and demanding that it agree to German annexation of Danzig and a "rectification" of the Polish Corridor.

This was too much for Chamberlain. In April 1939 he suddenly and radically recast British foreign policy. Great Britain entered into a formal alliance with France and Poland to guarantee one another's independence and territorial integrity, by war if necessary, against any aggression. At the same time Britain announced its readiness to give like guarantees to Rumania, Greece, and Turkey. At long last, a serious attempt would be made to compel Nazi Germany to desist from further treaty violations and aggressions against its neighbors.

It was a belated attempt. The totalitarian dictatorships would hardly have ventured upon their aggressions, if, at the first threat of such aggressions, the democratic great powers had acted in concert and with the superior forces which they then commanded. Combined and resolute action by Great Britain, France, and the United States would almost certainly have prevented the Japanese seizure of Manchuria in 1931, the Italian conquest of Ethopia in 1935, and German rearmament in 1936. As late as the Munich crisis in the autumn of 1938, there was still a good chance that a strong united stand by the democratic powers might have enlisted Russian coöperation and resulted, without war, in halting Hitler and sparing Czechoslovakia.

Why the democratic powers neglected their earlier and more favorable opportunities to stop totalitarian aggression, and why, instead, they followed so long a policy of "appeasement," is explicable primarily by the deep-seated pacifism of their peoples. Democratic peoples were as reluctant to face the threat of war as the dictators were eager to commit aggression. While the latter concentrated upon preparedness for war, the former pressed their governments to cut expenditures for army and navy and to avoid any step which might lead to war. The United States, throughout the 1920's and 1930's, was popularly pacifist and isolationist to an extreme degree. Its criticism of the totalitarian dictatorships and their aggressions was purely verbal; it held aloof from the League of Nations, even from the World Court; it would not consider any joint action with France or Great Britain; it adopted legislation aimed at maintaining a strict neutrality in the event of any foreign war. And the pacifism and practical isolationism of Britain and France were scarcely less pronounced.

Only an accumulation of German aggressions finally brought the British and French governments to the alliance of April 1939 with Poland. The alliance was none too strong. Neither the French nor the British people displayed any enthusiasm about it, and the United States clung to neutrality. On the other hand, Germany had at least potential allies in her Axis associates—Italy and Japan—and perhaps in Spain. She was now once again better armed and equipped for war than the opposing alliance. Under Hitler she had a unity of purpose, command, and enforced public opinion, which the Allies lacked; and her recent annexations had given her a manpower superior to theirs. Moreover, she had a will to war which in Britain and France was still gravely qualified by continuing pacifism and, in France, by bitter partisan strife.

Hitler might yet have hesitated to attack Poland and thus defy France and Great Britain, had it not been for the decisive stand of Communist Russia. During the critical summer of 1939, Stalin and his Foreign Minister Molotov spurned the overtures made to them for Russian coöperation with Britain and France. Already, in the spring of 1939, they had secretly indicated to the Nazi Foreign Office a willingness to arrange, for a price, an entente with Germany. Stalin doubtless believed that, by favoring Germany, he could share in a partition of Poland and have a free hand to recover what the Russian Empire had lost in the First World War along the Baltic and Black Seas. And by maintaining a nominal neutrality while the Nazi dictatorship was locked in what he imagined might be a gigantic and exhausting struggle with the western democracies, he would be able at the close of the struggle to dominate all Europe in the interest of the Soviet Union, communism, and his own dictatorship.

At first, Hitler hesitated to negotiate with a Russian regime which he heartily disliked and which in the past he had stridently denounced. But as the crisis developed, he perceived advantages in a deal with Russia and pushed the negotiations for it. Consequently, late in August, a "non-aggression pact" was concluded at Moscow between Russia and Germany, and proclaimed to the world. Accompanying it were secret articles which provided for a partition of Poland, allowed Russia a free hand in the Baltic states, and promised Germany a copious supply of foodstuffs, petroleum, and other needful war supplies from Russia.

This Russo-German pact was a signal to Stalin that he might proceed with forceful aggressions of his own. It was also the final signal for Germany's attack on Poland and the outbreak of war. Hitler was now assured that he would have collaboration, not opposition, in the east, and that in the west, especially in France, military effort against him woud be impeded by an extreme Fascist "Right" sympathetic with Nazi Germany and still more by an extreme "Left" of pro-Russian Communists who would follow directions from Moscow and obediently acclaim the new German-Russian pact.

On September 1, 1939, scarcely more than a week after the German-Russian pact, and without any formal declaration of war, German armies invaded Poland. Two days later, Great Britain and France, honoring their treaty obligations, declared war on Germany. It was the beginning of what is termed the Second World War.

SELECT SUPPLEMENTARY READINGS FOR PART XI

General. C. J. H. Hayes, *Contemporary Europe since 1870* (1958); S. B. Clough and C. W. Cole, *Economic History of Europe* (1952); *The Columbia Encyclopedia; New Cambridge Modern History*, vol. xii (1960).

Chapter 54. B. Romanov, *Russia in Manchuria, 1892–1906* (1952); M. T. Florinsky, *Russia, a History and an Interpretation*, vol ii (1953); Hugh Seton-Watson, *Decline of Imperial Russia, 1865–1914* (1953); W. L. Langer, *The Diplomacy of Imperialism, 1890–1902*, 2 vols. (1935); B. E. Schmitt, *Triple Alliance and Triple Entente* (1934), and *The Annexation of Bosnia* (1937); E. C. Helmreich, *The Diplomacy of the Balkan Wars, 1912–1913* (1938); George Young, *Nationalism and War in the Near East* (1915); R. J. Sontag, *European Diplomatic History, 1871–1932* (1933); W. C. Buthman, *Rise of Integral Nationalism in France* (1939); R. Albrecht-Carrié, *Italy from Napoleon to Mussolini* (1950); R. A. Kann, *The Multinational Empire, Nationalism and National Reform in the Habsburg Monarchy*, 2 vols. (1950); K. S. Pinson, *Modern Germany* (1954); L. L. Snyder, *From Bismarck to Hitler, the Background of Modern German Nationalism* (1935); R. W. Tims, *Germanizing Prussian Poland, 1894–1919* (1941).

Chapter 55. C. R. M. F. Crutwell, *A History of the Great War* (1936); B. H. Liddell Hart, *History of the World War* (1935); C. J. H. Hayes, *Brief History of the Great War* (1920); S. B. Fay, *Origins of the World War*, 2 vols. (1930); B. E. Schmitt, *The Coming of the War, 1914*, 2 vols. (1930); T. G. Frothingham, *Naval History of the World War*, 3 vols. (1924–6), and *The American Reinforcements in the World War* (1927); R. Gibson and M. Prendergast, *German Submarine War, 1914–1918* (1931); N. N. Golovine, *The Russian Army in the World War* (1931); F. P. Chambers, *The War behind the War, a History of the Political and Civilian Fronts* (1939); Charles Seymour, *American Diplomacy during the World War* (1934); W. H. Chamberlin, *The Russian Revolution, 1917–1921*, 2 vols. (1935); E. H. Carr, *A History of Soviet Russia*, vol. I, *The Bolshevik Revolution, 1917–1923* (1951); R. H. Lutz, *Fall of the German Empire* (1932); W. S. Churchill, *The World Crisis, the Eastern Front* (1931); B. Pares, *The Fall of the Russian Monarchy* (1939); G. F. Kennan, *Soviet-American Relations, 1917–1920* (1956–58); E. H. Carr, *A History of Soviet Russia*, 6 vols. (1950–60).

Chapter 56. H. W. V. Temperley, *A History of the Peace Conference of Paris*, 6 vols. (1920–4); E. M. House and Charles Seymour, *What Really Happened at Paris, the Story of the Peace Conference, 1918–1919* (1921); Harold Nicolson, *Peacemaking, 1919* (1939); F. P. Walters, *A History of the League of Nations*, 2 vols. (1952); H. C. F. Bell, *Woodrow Wilson* (1945); R. S. Baker, *Woodrow Wilson, Life and Letters*, 8 vols. (1935–9); C. K. Webster and S. Herbert, *League of Nations in Theory and Practice* (1933); M. O. Hudson, *Permanent Court of International Justice* (1934); F. G. Wilson, *Labor in the League System* (1934); H. L. McBain and L. Rogers, *New Constitutions of Europe* (1922); B. C. Shafer, *Nationalism, Myth and Reality* (1953); C. J. H. Hayes, *Historical Evolution of Modern Nationalism* (1929); C. A. Macartney, *National States and National*

Semi-abstract "modern" sculpture by Amadeo
Modigliani (d. 1920).

Minorities (1934); Arthur Rosenberg, *Birth of the German Republic* (1931); R. J. Kerner (ed.), *Yugoslavia* (1949); and *Czechoslovakia* (1940); G. L. Lewis, *Turkey* (1955); William Miller, *The Ottoman Empire and its Successors*, 3rd ed. (1934); C. L. Mowat, *Britain between the Wars, 1918–1940* (1955); Arnold Wolfers, *Britain and France between Two Wars* (1940); J. M. Keynes, *Economic Consequences of the Peace* (1920); J. C. Stamp, *Financial Aftermath of the War* (1932); D. Wecter, *The Age of the Great Depression, 1929–1941* (1948); P. Birdsall, *Versailles Twenty Years After* (1941).

Chapter 57. On Communist Russia, in addition to works by Chamberlin and Carr cited for Chapter 53: M. T. Florinsky, *World Revolution and the U.S.S.R.* (1933), and *Toward an Understanding of the U.S.S.R.*, 2nd ed. (1951); Waldemar Gurian, *Bolshevism* (1952), and ed., *The Soviet Union* (1951); Hans Kohn, *Nationalism in the Soviet Union* (1933); M. Fainsod, *How Russia is Ruled* (1953). On Fascist Italy and Nazi Germany: M. T. Florinsky, *Fascism and National Socialism* (1936); R. Albrecht-Carrié, *Italy from Napoleon to Mussolini* (1950); H. W. Schneider, *Making the Fascist State* (1928); D. A. Binchy, *Church and State in Fascist Italy* (1942); H. Finer, *Mussolini's Italy* (1935); K. S. Pinson, *Modern Germany* (1954); A. Rosenberg, *History of the German Republic* (1936); R. T. Clark, *Fall of the German Republic* (1935); Alan Bullock, *Hitler, a Study in Tyranny* (1952); Karl Heiden, *Hitler* (1936); J. W. Wheeler-Bennett, *Wooden Titan, Hindenburg in Twenty Years of German History, 1914–1934* (1936); F. L. Neumann, *Behemoth, the Structure and Practice of National Socialism* (1942); W. L. Shirer, *The Rise and Fall of the Third Reich* (1960); F. Zweig, *Poland betweeen Two Wars* (1944); E. A. Peers, *The Spanish Tragedy, 1930–1936* (1936).

Chapter 58. C. J. Haines and R. J. S. Hoffman, *Origins and Background of the Second World War* (1947); Joseph Grew, *Ten Years in Japan* (1943); Francis C. Jones, *Japan's New Order in East Asia: Its Rise and Fall, 1937–1945* (1954); H. Feis, *The Road to Pearl Harbor* (1950); Arnold Wolfers, *Britain and France between Two Wars* (1940); M. H. H. Macartney and P. Cremona, *Italy's Foreign and Colonial Policy, 1914–1937* (1938); Elizabeth Wiskemann, *The Rome-Berlin Axis* (1949); Keith Feiling, *Life of Neville Chamberlain* (1947); Kurt von Schuschnigg, *Austrian Requiem* (1946); R. Machray, *The Poland of Pilsudski, 1914–1936* (1937); R. L. Buell, *Poland, Key to Europe* (1939); R. J. Sontag and J. S. Beddie, eds., *Nazi-Soviet Relations, 1939–1941* (1948); Hugh Thomas, *The Spanish Civil War* (1961).

The meeting at Yalta. Stalin, Roosevelt, and Churchill.
Courtesy Bettmann Archive

PART XII
WORLD WAR II, 1939–1945

President Kennedy greets Chancellor Konrad Adenauer of West Germany, April 1961.

Courtesy Wide World Photos

From Stalin

to Kennedy

AND SINCE

THE SECOND World War lasts six years from 1939 to 1945 and even surpasses the First in terrifying destruction. At the outset, it is clearly a struggle between democracies and totalitarian dictatorships, with Communist Russia giving support to Nazi Germany and Fascist Italy. Later a rupture between Germany and Russia throws the latter dictatorship into an ill-assorted but eventually victorious alliance with the democracies.

The outcome of World War II raises more questions than it settles. Only two powers are the real victors—totalitarian Russia and democratic America. A new world situation thus arises with two super-powers and a series of countries, new and old, of secondary economic and military potential. The various nations tend to align themselves with one or the other super-power. All western and central Europe—the traditional seat of European and Western civilization—is sorely weakened. Part of it is held to the Russian system by force or fear of force, and other parts are not wholly unreceptive to Russian influence. And between a Communist world and a free world a "cold" war ensues.

Colonial empires overseas break up. Dozens of new nations more or less unready for self-government are created. A brave effort is made to re-suscitate an international organization under the name of United Nations. It proves increasingly effective in some spheres and makes progress despite the fact that the world is divided into two alignments. But there remains the question as to whether through it or outside it the nations of the earth can find ways of living together in peace, security, and stability.

Meanwhile, there is rapid progress in science and technology bringing changes more significant and of greater effect on the lives of men than in any previous period of similar duration. Improved communications spread knowledge of the productivity of modern industry and of the standard of living in the advanced countries. The less developed countries undergo a "revolution of expectations" and strive to win for themselves the fruits of the new kinds of production and national independence.

The period is one of change, of hope, of fear. No one can predict the ultimate outcome. Nor is it clear that the highest spiritual values of historic Western civilization can be preserved as its outward forms, its nationalism, its science are spread throughout the world.

CHAPTER 59

World War II, 1939–1945

A. Initial German Successes and Russian Coöperation (1939–1940)

The Second World War began on September 1, 1939, with a slashing German attack on Poland. It proved a very one-sided affair. The invading German armies outnumbered the defending Polish armies almost three to one, and gave brilliant and terrifying demonstration of the new military technique of *Blitzkrieg* ("lightning war"). This involved heavy bombing, by superior air force, of fortifications, roads, railways, industrial plants, power stations, etc., and, amid resulting confusion and destruction, a quick infantry advance spearheaded by a superior and mobile force of armored tanks. Even the weather favored the Germans, for the clear bright days of that September were ideal for air operations, and kept the Polish plains dry and firm for tank maneuvers.

The Poles fought bravely and furiously, and at Warsaw they held out until their capital city was a shambles. It was all in vain. Within a very few days after the initial German attack, the outcome was a foregone conclusion. And in little more than two weeks, Soviet Russian armies were collaborating with the Germans and occupying the eastern part of Poland. Within five weeks all Polish resistance was crushed, the government was in exile, the country partitioned between the dictatorships of Nazi Germany and Communist Russia, and the surviving population subjected to merciless exploitation.

Meanwhile, Poland's allies, France and Great Britain, were powerless to help. Both were astounded by the swiftness and terror of the Blitzkrieg in the East, and quite unprepared to cope with it. They possessed no such numbers of planes and tanks as Germany. Britain, while enjoying naval superiority, had a relatively small and ill-equipped army, the transport of which to the Continent took time. France had a larger army, but it was subordinated to a great system of fortifications (the "Maginot Line") which had been constructed for defensive purposes along the Franco-German frontier after the First World War, and which was paralleled, since the remilitarization of the Rhineland in 1936, by an even stronger German system of fortifications (the "Siegfried Line"). Thus the forces of the Western Allies, if seemingly sheltered from German attack, were practically prevented from invading Germany, and hence from affording any relief to Poland.

This curious situation in the west continued throughout the winter of 1939–1940, with some patrol activity and with occasional dropping of propaganda pamphlets, but without serious fighting. The Allies optimistically hoped that while their armies sat safe behind the fortified frontier, their superior economic and commercial resources would gradually weigh against Germany and bring it to terms. Consequently they tended to overlook the lessons of the German Blitzkrieg in Poland and to neglect taking special precautions against its repetition in the West. They were not sufficiently heedful of their loss of prestige from Poland's subjugation and partition, or of the defeatism spreading within France, or of the ominous activities of the three chief European dictatorships during that winter of 1939–1940.

Nazi Germany was free to transfer its major forces from the east to the west and to increase its already superior number of planes and tanks, preparatory to a supreme effort to overwhelm France. Simultaneously, Mussolini busied himself with denouncing France and laying claims for Fascist Italy to Corsica and Tunis and Savoy and Nice. And the Communist Russian dictatorship of Stalin, in continuing collaboration with Nazi Germany, and with no effective opposition from the Allies, proceeded to tear up treaties and to commit a series of aggressions against all its European neighbors.

Following its seizure and incorporation of eastern Poland, Russia made demands on the three Baltic republics of Lithuania, Latvia, and Estonia which they were in no position to resist and which led to their transformation into Russian "protectorates" with Russian garrisons at strategic points. By agreement with Hitler, the German-speaking minorities in these lands were sent "home" to Germany, and finally, in July 1940, all three countries were incorporated in the Soviet Union.

But this was not all. Russian troops invaded and occupied the Rumanian provinces of Bessarabia and Bukovina; and Rumania, mindful of the fate of Poland, surrendered them to the Soviet Union. Russia likewise made demands on Finland for military and naval bases and for certain outright cessions of territory. Here, however, resistance was encountered, and at the end of November 1939 Russia began a war with Finland by bombing its capital city of Helsinki. In an amazing display of courage and military skill, and with surreptitious aid from the Scandinavian countries, especially Sweden, the Finns withstood for several months Russian invasions from the south, north, and east. But by March 1940, sheer weight of numbers and material bore down the Finns and broke their "Mannerheim Line." Finland surrendered, and on March 12 signed peace terms which yielded to

Winston Churchill.

Courtesy Bettmann Archive

Russia the Karelian peninsula in the south, the Petsamo region in the north, and a naval base close to Helsinki. Communist Russia was now dominant in nearly all the territories it had lost at the close of the First World War; and wherever it newly established itself, it drove existing governments into exile and terrorized the populations.

Shortly after the conclusion of the Russian conquests in eastern and northern Europe, the Germans were ready to strike with overwhelming force in the west. On April 9, 1940, they seized Denmark and launched an air and naval invasion of Norway. At some points, they encountered resistance, but it was confused, and was interfered with by traitors within the country. One of these, a certain Major Vidkun Quisling, was later to enrich modern languages with a new word, for "quisling" came to stand for the "fifth-column" traitor who betrayed his homeland to a foreign country.

For a brief space, it seemed that Great Britain might be able to come to the rescue of Norway. But German air power drove British ships out of the straits between Denmark and Norway, and soon compelled them to quit Norwegian ports. King Haakon VII of Norway fled, and set up a "government in exile" in England, and the greater part of the Norwegian merchant marine continued to carry goods for the Allies.

On May 10, 1940, as a result of the British fiasco in Norway, Winston Churchill succeeded Neville Chamberlain as prime minister of Great Britain. In Churchill the British found a great war leader, capable of uniting the country in the face of disaster and eventually of leading it to victory. Son of an American mother and a father who was descended from the Duke of Marlborough, Churchill had had a long experience in public affairs. He had consistently warned his country of the rising menace of Nazi Germany and had severely criticized Chamberlain's pre-war policy of "appeasement." He now took the helm in Britain's gravest crisis.

B. Fall of France and Isolation of Britain (1940–1941)

On May 10, 1940, the very day on which Winston Churchill became prime minister of Great Britain, the Germans launched an offensive against France. It was not a frontal attack on the heavily fortified "Maginot Line," which would have been much too costly, but rather an outflanking of the Line by a surprise attack through the neutral countries of Holland and Belgium. War was declared by both, but their armed resistance was not great, and it was quickly mowed down by the same sort of Blitzkrieg which the Germans had employed against Poland—a skillful use of air power, lightning movements of armored columns, spearheaded by tanks, some "fifth column" work, the employment of parachute troops, and relentless. pressure against a disorganized foe.

In Holland, German parachutists, wearing Dutch uniforms, hurtled down from the air, while German ground forces, in rubber boots, swarmed across canals and flooded fields. The Rotterdam airfield was captured on the first day, and the city itself was turned to rubble by a murderous and unopposed bombing. Armored columns raced across the country, cutting the Dutch army into bits. Within a week all resistance was. crushed, and Queen Wilhelmina and her government took refuge in England.

Belgian resistance lasted not much longer. At the very start, the Germans captured bridges over the Meuse River and the Albert Canal. British and French troops were pushed forward to help the Belgians hold a second line from Antwerp to Louvain and Namur. But the German armored columns swept through the Ardennes, which the French had thought almost impassable for them, and crossed the Meuse near Sedan. This was a crucial breakthrough. It obliged the armies in Belgium to fall back and it brought the Germans into France beyond the west end of the Maginot Line.

The Germans exploited their breakthrough, not by swinging to the left, toward Paris, as in 1914, but to the right, toward the sea. German spearheads reached Abbeville on May 20 and turned north to Boulogne on the coast. Quickly the million Allied soldiers in Belgium (including the entire British army on the Continent) were cut off from the main French armies, and against them the Germans drove fast and furiously from all directions. On May 27 King Leopold III of Belgium surrendered and became a prisoner of war; and during the next week the British worked manfully with all sorts of water craft to evacuate their army from the port of Dunkirk. The latter had to abandon guns, munitions, and supplies, but, despite almost continuous air attack and shell fire from land, the boats managed to get to England some 225,000 British troops and about 110,000 others (mostly French).

Meanwhile, the same tactics which the Germans used to cut off Belgium and the British were being employed to demoralize, cut through, isolate, and overwhelm the several French armies within France itself.

In vain the French high command was transferred from General Gamelin to General Weygand. The French armies were without adequate planes and tanks, and they employed those they did have ineffectively; they were confused and blocked not only by the Germans, but by enormous numbers of civilian refugees and, in some instances, by internal Communist and "fifth column" activity. And, to cap the climax, Fascist Italy seized the opportunity to join Germany in the attack on France, just as Russia had seized a like opportunity to assist in the destruction of Poland. Italy declared war on France and Great Britain on June 11. Three days later the Germans occupied Paris. French armed resistance was already nearing an end, and the French government moved to Tours and thence to Bordeaux.

France had promised Britain not to make a separate peace, and Churchill flew to Tours with a proposal that France and Great Britain be merged into one country, with one government, and fight on together. There was some discussion of the possibility of removing remnants of French troops and equipment to French North Africa, or of concentrating forces for a final stand in the peninsula of Brittany. To a majority of the French cabinet, such possibilities appeared impractical, and by a vote of 13 to 11 it decided to quit the struggle. Reynaud, the premier who had succeeded Daladier, resigned and was replaced by the aged Marshal Pétain, who had won fame as the defender of Verdun in the First World War. On June 17 the new cabinet asked Hitler for an armistice, and for its conclusion the Germans brought out of a museum the railway car used for signing the armistice of November 11, 1918, which had registered Germany's defeat in the First World War. At the same spot, in the forest of Compiègne, on June 21, 1940, the French delegates signed an armistice that registered the disastrous defeat of their country. A camera at the scene caught Hitler dancing a little jig.

By the terms of the armistice, France north of the Loire River and the entire Alantic coast would be occupied and administered by the Germans; the remainder would have a measure of autonomy; the country would have to pay heavy "costs of occupation." To the Germans the price of this sensational victory was comparatively small. They had lost about 25,000 killed and 70,000 wounded. They had captured, killed, or wounded more than two million French soldiers.

The fall of France had several immediate effects. (1) It practically ended the Third French Republic. Marshal Pétain obtained from the Parliament a grant of dictatorial power, which he used to set up at Vichy an essentially fascist regime for the part of France left him by the armistice. For a time, most Frenchmen regarded Pétain as a patriot who only awaited a favorable chance to strike back at the Germans. Gradually, however, as certain high officials of his regime, especially Pierre Laval, urged "collaboration" with the Germans, there developed in France an "underground" resistance, some of which was brought into clandestine contact with a "Free France" group that the British government collected and sponsored in London under the leadership of General DeGaulle.

(2) Italy formally entered the war on the side of her Axis partner, and undertook to dominate the Mediterranean. Expeditionary forces were despatched to Italian North Africa to oppose the British in Egypt and, if possible, to deprive them of the Suez Canal, while diplomatic pressure was exerted on Spain to get it to enter the war, seize Gibraltar, and thus close the western end of the Mediterranean to the British.

(3) Throughout the European continent Germany and collaborating Russia were now all-powerful, less than a year after the outbreak of war. They had partitioned Poland between them; and while Russia had appropriated Lithuania, Latvia, and Estonia, and despoiled Finland and Rumania, Germany had conquered Norway and Denmark, Holland and Belgium, and now France; and Italy was her active ally. And for self-preservation, other and lesser powers now felt constrained to hold aloof from Great Britain and to be friendly with the Axis. Hitler acted as a kind of arbiter among the nations of central and east-central Europe. For example, he directed a veritable partition of Rumania, agreeing to Russian seizure of Bessarabia and to

Bomb destruction in London. St. Paul's Cathedral is in the background.

Hungary's annexation of part of Transylvania. In vain the Rumanian government expressed dissatisfaction. German "tourists" filtered into the country and in September 1940 abetted a *coup d'état* which sent King Carol into exile and eventually established a pro-Nazi dictatorship.

(4) Great Britain was left without allies and was separated from Germany's triumphant forces only by the narrow waters of the British Channel. The whole Atlantic coastline of Europe from Norway to southernmost France was in German hands, and all the resources, factories, and labor of western and central Europe were at Germany's disposal. Britain had suffered the loss of the best part of its war-equipment (except planes) during the rout in Belgium and the evacuation from Dunkirk, and considerable time would be required to replace it.

There is little doubt that Germany might have overwhelmed its one remaining foe if it had concentrated its attention, for a year after June 1940, on preparations for an actual large-scale invasion of England—building and marshalling transports along the Continental coast and providing them with adequate airplane coverage and submarine protection for the crossing. That Germany did not do this, is mainly attributable to a naive belief of Hitler and some of his chief advisers that a devastating air attack on Britain would suffice to bring it to terms.

The Germans opened their air attack on British coastal towns on August 8, 1940, and early in September extended it, with some 1,500 planes, to London. Then until the late spring of 1941 British cities were under more or less continuous air attack. Some 50,000 high explosive bombs (not counting incendiaries) fell on London.

Coventry was almost obliterated. Ports and manufacturing cities, such as Cardiff, Portsmouth, Swansea, Glasgow, Liverpool, Manchester, and Sheffield were badly battered. Some 40,000 persons were killed and twice as many wounded.

Yet the air attack of Germany on Britain failed. First, it failed because the British still had a sizeable defensive air force, which, during 1940–1941, knocked down three thousand German planes at a loss of less than a thousand to themselves. As Winston Churchill said, in tribute to British flyers, "Never in the field of human conflict was so much owed by so many to so few."

Second, British civilian, as well as airforce, morale proved tough and firmly resistant. When Britain stood alone against a victorious enemy, its people showed their finest qualities.

Third, the British had important resources and manufacturing skill, which enabled them to replace their losses and to add to their airforce and other defenses. Moreover, they still were dominant on the seas and, despite heavy losses inflicted on their shipping by German submarines and planes, they continued to receive invaluable assistance in men and supplies from overseas, especially from the British Dominions of Canada, Australia, and New Zealand.

Fourth, and most significant of all, the British had an increasingly important source of supply in the United States. At the outbreak of the war, most of the American people were isolationist and anxious to keep out of it. But as the Germans scored one triumph after another, alarm grew in the United States, and its sentiment became increasingly pro-British. Under the leadership of President Franklin Roosevelt, it began to give the British "all aid short of war." In September 1940 it turned over to Britain fifty naval destroyers in return for leases on naval bases in Newfoundland and the West Indies. In November it shared its own rapidly rising production of war material on a fifty-fifty basis with Great Britain, on condition that the latter pay for and transport its share on a "cash and carry" basis. This arrangement was later eased for Britain by a "Lend-Lease Act" passed by the American Congress in March 1941.

Fifth, and last, Germany was diverted in 1940–1941 from concentrating against Great Britain by a number of extraneous developments. Hitler, imagining that he could get full French coöperation from Marshal Pétain which would enable him to shut the British out of the Mediterranean, neglected to force Spain into the war and to secure Gibraltar. Then, too, he found that his Italian ally was so weak and dispirited as to require constant bolstering.

In September 1940, an Italian army under Marshal Graziani, advancing from the North African province of Libya, crossed the Egyptian border and reached Sidi Barrani, while other Italian forces from Ethopia edged their way into Kenya and the Sudan. Then in October, another Italian army, based on Albania, launched an attack on Greece, partially for conquest and partially as additional aid against the British in the eastern Mediterranean. Both Italian efforts failed dismally. In December 1940 the British in Egypt, under General Wavell, counter-attacked, rolled Graziani's army far back into Libya, and took 130,000 prisoners and much material. Then, between January and May 1941, South African and other British Dominion troops overwhelmed the Italian garrisons in Somaliland, Eritrea, and Ethiopia, and restored Haile Selassie to the throne from which he had been driven five years previously.[1] Meanwhile, by January 1941 the Greeks had decisively beaten the Italians and driven them back into Albania.

In these circumstances, Germany had to pull Italy's chestnuts out of the fire. In February 1941 Hitler sent into North Africa several highly trained and armored German divisions under General Rommel, who replaced the Italian commander and pushed the British back through Libya and far inside the Egyptian frontier. In March 1941 Hitler moved to end the Graeco-Italian conflict by establishing German control in southeastern Europe. He demanded of Bulgaria and Yugoslavia that they grant passage of German troops. King Boris III of Bulgaria readily acceded, and the Regent Paul of Yugoslavia more reluctantly on March 25. In the latter country, however, a popular and army revolt deposed Paul

---

[1] See above, p. 757.

and led to a brief German-Yugoslav war. Within two weeks the Germans, with their Blitzkrieg, overran Yugoslavia and ended its formal resistance. But in the mountainous wilds of the country, a prolonged guerrilla war continued.

Then into Greece the German war machine proceeded. In vain the British sent an expeditionary force from Egypt to help the Greeks. By the end of April, Greece was overrun and the British saved 44,000 of their force only by another Dunkirk-like evacuation. For a little longer the Greeks, with British aid, clung to Crete, but this too they had to abandon in the face of overwhelming attacks of German airplanes and parachutists.

Yet the very reverses which Great Britain suffered in the spring of 1941 in Greece and Crete were evidence that Germany was far afield from a knock-out blow against England itself. And any such blow was now indefinitely postponed by a break between Germany and Russia.

C. Break between Germany and Russia, and Participation of the United States (1941)

From the summer of 1939 to the spring of 1941 there had been apparently friendly coöperation between Nazi Germany and Communist Russia, with consequences advantageous to themselves and disastrous to the rest of Europe. Then suddenly, on June 22, 1941, the anniversary of Napoleon's break with Russia in 1812, Hitler broke with Stalin and launched a gigantic German invasion of Russia. This marked a radical change in the setting and course of the Second World War.

Stalin and his Communist associates had undoubtedly feigned greater friendship with Hitler and Nazi Germany than they felt, and they were certainly piqued in the spring of 1941 by German military intervention in Bulgaria and Yugoslavia which they thought of as being within Russia's sphere of influence. Fundamentally, of course, they sought to serve Russian and Communist ends, not

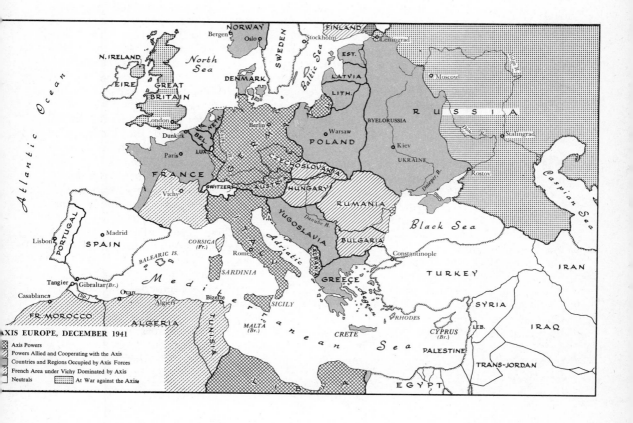

AXIS EUROPE, DECEMBER 1941

Axis Powers
Powers Allied and Cooperating with the Axis
Countries and Regions Occupied by Axis Forces
French Area under Vichy Dominated by Axis
Neutrals   At War against the Axis

Hitler's; and if at any time fortune should cease to smile on Hitler, they would be pretty sure to be his enemies instead of his friends. Yet, whatever may have been their ultimate intentions, they were hardly minded to break with Hitler in June 1941. The break was on the other side.

Hitler had long been obsessed with anti-Slavic, as well as anti-Communist, feeling, and his pact of 1939 with Communist Russia was only a needful temporary expedient. He was convinced that sooner or later Germany must fight Russia for the hegemony of Eastern Europe, and particularly for the rich agricultural region of the Ukraine; and the moment now seemed propitious. Germany had quickly overwhelmed every nation with which her army grappled, including the reputedly great military nation of France, while Russia had experienced much difficulty in subduing petty Finland. Hence, a German war against Russia should be brief and highly successful. It could be represented as a "crusade against the red menace," and as such would enlist sympathy throughout western Europe. Hitler felt sure that once he had crushed Russia he could make some sort of reasonable peace with Great Britain. If the British proved unduly stubborn he would have the resources and the security to bring about Britain's defeat at his own leisure.

The sudden break of Hitler with Stalin in June 1941 had numerous repercussions. Churchill, speaking for Great Britain, declared: "Any man or state who fights against Nazidom will have our aid. Any man or state who marches with Hitler is our foe. . . . We shall give whatever help we can to Russia and to the Russian people." In France, the Communists quickly changed their earlier pacifist and pro-German stand into an active resistance to the Germans. American Communists, who until June 1941 had been denouncing the war as an imperialist conflict from which America should remain isolated, now called loudly for all-out aid to Russia and Britain. On the other hand, countries which had been despoiled by Russia between 1939 and 1941, such as Finland and Rumania, actively supported Germany in warring on Russia, as also did Hungary and Bulgaria.

Germany gave promise in 1941 of repeating in Russia what had been done in Poland in 1939 and in France in 1940. Its armies, using the tactics of the Blitzkrieg, with planes and tanks, rapidly pierced the protective belt of East Poland and the former Baltic republics and pushed deep into Russian territory. In less than four weeks, German armies hammered into Smolensk. Then, as their central thrust slowed down a hundred miles from Moscow, they launched a drive to the south which engulfed Kharkov and reached Rostov at the mouth of the Don. They occupied all of the rich agricultural and industrial Ukraine. Simultaneously, other German armies in the north swept forward to the very gates of Leningrad.

In early October the Germans resumed their direct drive on Moscow, and by the end of the month they had it partially encircled. By late November it seemed as though they must shortly capture it and oblige Stalin to sue for peace. The moment was opportune for an associate of the Axis—faraway Japan—to merge its protracted war with China into a general drive for supremacy in Asia and the Pacific.

Already in July 1941, Japan had taken advantage of the fall of France to obtain military and naval bases in French Indo-China; and shortly afterwards, in pursuit of what it euphemistically termed the establishment of a "co-prosperity sphere" throughout eastern Asia, it adopted an aggressive attitude toward the Dutch East Indies. The United States and Great Britain were alarmed, and both countries imposed a partial embargo on shipments to Japan. The Japanese response was the installing, in October, of a new and bellicose premier in the person of General Tojo and his despatching, in November, of a pretended "peace mission" to the United States. This was merely a cover. The Japanese government decided to strike while Russia was being overborne by Germany, while Britain was isolated and seemingly powerless, and while the United States was unprepared. On December 7, without any declaration of war, Japanese planes made a surprise attack on the American fleet at Pearl Harbor in Hawaii, destroyed a considerable part of it, and won temporary naval supremacy in the Pacific.

On December 8 the United States and Great Britain declared war on Japan. Three days later Germany and Italy declared war on the United States. The Second World War was now indeed global. Every major power was engaged in it.

As Germany won notable initial successes in Russia, so Japan won similar successes in the Pacific. By the end of December 1941 the Japanese were in Siam and were threatening Burma. They captured Guam and Wake Island from the Americans and Hong Kong from the British. In another month they had overrun most of the Philippine Islands, and by the middle of February 1942 they had reduced the great British fortress and naval base of Singapore.

D. Passing of Axis Powers from Offensive to Defensive (1942–1944)

The Axis powers of Germany, Italy, and Japan maintained offensives throughout the greater part of 1942. Though they were now opposed by an alliance of Great Britain, Russia, and the United States, the latter continued to suffer reverses.

The Japanese, between January and March, conquered Burma, thereby cutting the main supply-route over the Burma Road to China, and at the same time threatening India. They defeated a combined Dutch, American, British, and Australian naval force in the strait of Macassar, in the Dutch East Indies, and on March 1 effected a landing on Java. Within the next few weeks they overwhelmed the Dutch, took possession of nearly all the extensive Malay archipelago, and menaced Australia. In May they forced the surrender of Bataan and Corregidor, the last American footholds in the Philippines.

In Europe, the Germans had met with more stubborn resistance in Russia than they anticipated, and although their armies in 1941 had conquered the Ukraine and gotten to the gates of Leningrad and Moscow, they not only received no peace plea from Stalin, but were actually pushed back a bit during the ensuing winter by a Rus-

President Franklin D. Roosevelt signing the declaration of war against Japan.

Courtesy Bettmann Archive

sian counter-offensive. By the spring of 1942, however, they had recovered and were making new advances. They still failed to take either Leningrad or Moscow, but they overran the Crimea and captured Sevastopol. Then, in the summer, they made two extensive drives. One was southward, netting them Rostov and carrying them hundreds of miles into the Caucasus with its rich oil fields. The other was eastward between the Donetz and the upper Don, and on to Stalingrad on the Volga.

In North Africa, there had been fluctuations in the desert fighting between the British, based on Egypt, and the Italians and Germans, based on Tripoli. In January 1942 the latter were driven back from the Egyptian frontier, but in the summer, under command of the German General Rommel, they returned, recrossed the frontier, and advanced to El Alamein, only sixty miles from Alexandria. Axis conquest of Egypt and the Suez Canal seemed imminent.

In the latter part of 1942 each of several offensives of the Axis powers was halted and changed into a defensive operation; and the Allies began important offensives of their own. The main reason for this change was that, whereas the Axis at the start had been better prepared for war, possessing superiority in planes, tanks, guns, and munitions, and having more technically trained men, it was now being equalled and surpassed in all these respects by its foes. Russia not only had an extraordinarily large pool of man-power, but it removed many of its vital industrial plants out of reach of the invader and mightily expanded them. It also received enormous quantities of war material from Great Britain and especially from the United States.

The United States performed industrial prodigies. Once it was tooled up for war production on a mass basis, it turned out, from 1942 to 1945, a gradually overwhelming avalanche of weapons—over 400,000 planes, 70,000 naval craft of all types, 80,000 landing craft, 8,000 cargo ships, nearly 2 million heavy machine guns, over 2 million sub-machine guns, 12 million rifles and carbines, nearly 6 million bombs to be dropped by aircraft, half a million depth charges for use against submarines, 110 million grenades, 86,000 tanks, nearly 2½ million trucks. By 1945, much more than half the war-production of the world was in America.

Nor was it merely a matter of quantity. Coming into the war late, the United States was able to focus its production on the latest models. The Germans improved their tanks more rapidly than the Americans. But in planes, the bombers and fighters of the United States surpassed those of their opponents. On both sides scientists were mobilized and developed new weapons of offense and new mechanisms of defense. But in the long run the achievements of the British and Americans overshadowed even the most spectacular German inventions, such as the jet-propelled flying bomb and the rocket bomb.

The farthest extension of Japanese conquests was reached in June 1942. In that month American fleet-based planes, in the crucial naval battle of Midway, stopped a major Japanese thrust at Hawaii. In August, American marines landed at Guadalcanal in the Solomon Islands, and held it against repeated counter-attacks in the autumn.

Germany's second-year offensive against Russia was halted by fierce, protracted, and eventually successful Russian resistance at Stalingrad. In November the Russians struck back against the Germans with a well-prepared counter-offensive, which encircled a German army of some 300,000 men and compelled its surrender at the end of January 1943. The defense of Stalingrad, and the succeeding Russian counter-attack, marked the turning point of the war on the eastern front, if not of the whole war.

In Egypt, the invading Germans and Italians were finally driven back by the British from El Alamein in a spectacular battle of tanks. It began in October 1942 and resulted in heavy losses for General Rommel and his retirement to fortified positions four hundred miles west of Egypt. Stalin, to relieve his hard-pressed Russians, had been urging Britain and America to assume an offensive in Europe and to open a "second front" in France. In 1942, however, Roosevelt and Churchill were agreed that sufficient men, ships, planes, and materiel for such a difficult operation were not yet available. Instead, they decided to seize French North Africa, preparatory to an attack on what Churchill called the "soft under-belly" of the Axis through Sicily and Italy. The British drive westward from Egypt was deemed a part of this plan.

On November 8, 1942, an Anglo-American expedition, carried by hundreds of craft and protected by heavy naval escort, effected landings near Casablanca on the Atlantic coast and at Oran and Algiers on the Mediterranean. It had been feared that Spain, under General Franco, might seriously interfere with the operation. This did not occur, however, and what difficulty the landing forces had was not with Spaniards but with French units loyal to Marshal Pétain. Even this difficulty was soon surmounted through special agreement between Admiral Darlan, representing at the moment the Vichy regime in North Africa, and General Dwight Eisenhower, who was commander-in-chief of the Anglo-American forces. Subsequently, Darlan was assassinated, and in time a "Free French" government was established at Algiers under General de Gaulle.

Meanwhile, the Allied seizure of French North Africa had repercussions within France. The Germans swiftly reacted by seizing the part of France which, in accordance with the armistice, had remained under French (Vichy) administration. They completely discredited the Vichy regime, rendered Marshal Pétain virtually a prisoner, and gave a big impetus to the French resistance movement and its eager coöperation with the Allies.

For a time, Rommel's army of Germans and Italians put up a stubborn fight in Tunisia against the British advancing westward from Egypt and Libya, and the Americans pressing eastward from Algeria. At length the Allies effected a juncture, and on May 6, 1943, they won a decisive victory. The city of Tunis and the naval base of Bizerte fell to them, and within a week German resistance in Africa ceased.

With North Africa entirely in their hands, the Anglo-American forces prepared for the next operation. On July 9, 1943, after prolonged air bombing, they landed in Sicily and quickly overcame the Italian defense. But German forces, which had been evacuated from North Africa, fought fierce rearguard actions across Sicily and safely reached the mainland. Sicily itself, within forty days, was an Allied conquest.

The defeats in Africa and Sicily produced important results among the Italians, who, as a people, had not been enthusiastic about Mussolini's getting them into the war. There were mutterings even inside the Fascist party. On July 24, 1943, at a meeting of the Fascist Grand Council, a motion was passed asking King Victor Emmanuel to assume real leadership. Mussolini was arrested; the King placed the government in the hands of Marshal Badoglio; and Fascism was outlawed.

Badoglio then opened secret negotiations with the Allies. The Germans still had large forces in Italy, and the Allies demanded "unconditional surrender," as Roosevelt and Churchill had agreed to do in a meeting the previous winter at Casablanca. The negotiations were kept secret until the Allies actually landed in Italy on September 9, 1943, when it was announced that Badoglio and the King had agreed to an armistice, amounting to unconditional surrender. The Germans, however, were not caught napping. They had already taken over the defense of southern Italy and they moved quickly to seize control of the entire peninsula. Thus Italy was in an odd position. It had signed an armistice, but it was largely in German hands. Mussolini escaped to the north to conduct a sort of phantom puppet government for the Germans.

The Anglo-American army put ashore on the beaches of Salerno on September 9, met fierce German opposition. It was supported by planes from Sicily and by heavy fire from naval vessels, but its position was difficult until it was joined by a British army which had taken the southern ports of Taranto, Brindisi, and Bari, and moved rapidly northward. By October 1 the Allied forces captured Naples, but not before the Germans had destroyed the port facilities and wrecked much of the city.

The mountainous nature of the Italian peninsula and the skillful defense of the Germans made Allied advance northward extremely difficult. In January 1944 the Allies tried to hasten matters by a landing behind the German lines at Anzio. But the Germans reacted so quickly as to imperil the landed troops, and the Anzio expedition was not safe until May when it was joined by the main Allied army which had been painfully pushing forward. This had been delayed by a heavily fortified German "Gustav Line" which ran through Cassino. It was not until May 11 that the Gustav Line was breached. Then Cassino was finally taken and the Anzio beachhead relieved; and on June 4, 1944, the Allied forces entered Rome. But the German General von Kesselring dexterously extricated his troops and prepared new defense lines still farther north.

One of the factors which made von Kesselring's retreat inevitable, despite his military skill and the advantages of the terrain he defended, was an increasing difficulty in securing supplies from Germany. This difficulty in turn arose from the rising tempo with which Allied bombers were striking at production centers and transportation lines in Italy and more especially in Germany. As early as May and June of 1942 the British staged three raids of a thousand bombers each on Cologne, Essen, and Bremen. Afterwards, improved airplane design and increased production, plus the participation of the American air force, rendered such heavy bombing more frequent and more destructive. British bombers specialized in night raids; American, in daytime operations. By early 1943 Germany was subjected on successive days to "round the clock" bombing, and the bomb-carrying capacity of the planes was gradually increased.

The main targets of the Allied air forces were submarine pens and other German installations on the Channel Coast, German industries with special emphasis on refineries and synthetic fuel plants, and railways and other means of communication. Germany was not "knocked out" from the air, but the bombing did produce shortages and a creeping paralysis of communications which seriously hampered the German armies.

Growing Allied air power paid another dividend. Air patrols from Newfoundland, Iceland, North Ireland, and later from the Azores (with Portugal's permission), together with the use of "baby flattop" carriers, checked the submarine menace. In May 1943 the Germans for the first time lost more submarines than they put into operation. Thenceforth the threat to Allied shipping decreased, though it was held in check only by constant vigilance.

While the western Allies were clearing the Mediterranean, concluding an armistice with Italy, and bombing Germany, Russia was likewise scoring notable successes. At the beginning of 1943, while one German army was being crushed at Stalingrad, another was being driven out of the Caucasus. The siege of Leningrad was broken on January 18, and in early March the threat to Moscow was practically ended.

Throughout the spring and summer of 1943 there was heavy fighting in southern Russia, with certain towns and areas changing hands several times. Finally, in the autumn, energetic Russian offensives captured Kharkov, the strategic railway junc-tion of Bryansk, and the city of Smolensk, which had been the German eastern headquarters in 1941–1942, and pushed the Germans out of the Donetz basin. In November 1943 they won the Ukranian capital of Kiev.

By June 1944 the Russians had cleared the Nazis out of most of the territory held by the Soviet Union in 1938. In the south they had advanced into pre-war Rumanian and Polish territory. In the center they had liberated much of White Russia. In the north they had come nearly to the old Estonian border. They had inflicted tremendous losses on the Germans which the Nazis could in no wise repair. These successes they had achieved by remarkable strategy, by hard fighting, and by an ability to maintain supply lines with few railways. This last ability was greatly enhanced by American motor trucks shipped to them by the tens of thousands under the Lend-Lease arrangement and brought in from Arctic Ocean ports and by an overland route which had been opened up through Persia.

Though President Roosevelt had made the crucial decision of devoting the bulk of American resources to the prosecution of the war in Europe and to such enterprises as the landings in North Africa and the invasion of Italy, the year 1943 and the first half of 1944 were not without gains in the Pacific against the Japanese, made possible by a growing control of the air and of the sea. During the summer and fall of 1943, American forces extended their hold in the Solomons by taking New Georgia and the air base at Munda, together with adjacent islands. In November, American marines captured airfields on Bougainville. Already a most effective naval and military strategy was being worked out. Instead of painfully digging out the Japanese garrisons on every island, General MacArthur, the American commander in the Pacific, was content to seize key airfields and ports, isolating other Japanese contingents, cutting their supply lines, and leaving them to wither away. Thus Rabaul, the principal Japanese base on New Britain, was rendered ineffective in December.

Early in 1944 the Americans struck into territory that had been Japanese before Pearl Harbor by capturing the atoll of

General Dwight D. Eisenhower.

Courtesy Bettmann Archive

Kwajalein in the Marshall Islands. Thereby they secured a base for bombing the Japanese at Truk in the Carolines and for a further push which took them to Saipan in the Marianas by the summer of 1944. Despite isolated Japanese garrisons in the southwest Pacific, the war there was now essentially over. The American forces were in a position to strike for the recovery of the Philippines, and they had covered the longest and hardest part of the sea-and-air road leading to Tokyo.

E. Allied Victory (1944–1945)

On June 6, 1944, the very day on which the Germans evacuated Rome, American and British (including Canadian) forces landed in France. This was the greatest water-borne invasion of history. It began with air and naval bombardment of fifty miles of Normandy beaches and the dropping of paratroopers behind the coast line; and presently, despite stout German resistance, it secured a strong Allied foothold in the Cherbourg peninsula. Thence was launched an offensive with planes and tanks which beat the Germans at their own Blitzkrieg, threw them into disorder, and obliged them during the next two months to quit Paris and the greater part of France.

By mid-September it was obvious that the Allies were closing in upon Germany and that its defeat was only a matter of months. In France, the Anglo-American invasion from the west was linked up with another which came from a recent landing in the south on the Mediterranean coast near Toulon. Together the invaders numbered over two million, and already they had practically liberated France, pushed into Belgium and Luxembourg, freed Brussels and Antwerp, and entered Holland and even Germany itself.

At the same time, the Allied forces in Italy had pressed the Germans northward from Rome through very difficult mountainous terrain and had come in sight of the Po valley. The Russians, too, were driving successfully, and in overwhelming force, from eastern Europe. In August 1944, Russian armies broke through to the Baltic west of Riga, pushed into East Prussia, overran eastern Poland, and reached the Vistula River both above and below Warsaw. Simultaneously another Russian army entered Rumania and occupied Bucharest. In September, Finland surrendered anew on Russia's terms, while Russian troops penetrated into Bulgaria, Yugoslavia, Hungary, and Czechoslovakia.

In the autumn and early winter of 1944, Nazi Germany made a supreme effort to hold off the victoriously advancing Allies. Russian advance in the east was almost everywhere slackened and halted. Allied advance from the south was stopped by the German "Gothic" line in north Italy. Allied advance from the west was arrested and actually turned back in the so-called "Battle of the Bulge," which was fought in December and which temporarily brought the Germans back into Belgium. Germany, however, could not maintain for long a counter-offensive or even a defense on so many fronts. Its war material, its manpower, and its morale were now vastly inferior to the Allies'.

Early in 1945 Allied offensives were resumed and went on unrelentingly to the end. The Russians captured Warsaw in January, Budapest in February, Danzig in March, Vienna in April. In April the Allies in Italy took Bologna, crossed the Po, and reached Milan. Meanwhile, Allied forces in the west, now including substantial French contingents, wiped out the "Bulge," reached Cologne in March, gained control of the Rhineland and the Ruhr in April, and on

April 25 made first contact with the Russians near Leipzig.

On May 2, the German army in Italy surrendered. Already a group of Italian Communists had seized Mussolini fleeing toward the Swiss border, and had slain him and hung up his body for public execration in Milan.

On May 2, Berlin fell. The western Allies might have taken it, but by previous agreement they left it to the Russians, who mowed down the final furious resistance of frenzied Nazis. Hitler perished miserably amid the ruins. On May 7, German military and naval commanders met Allied commanders at Reims and agreed formally to unconditional surrender. Allied victory was complete in Europe.

Victory in the Pacific over Japan was yet to be achieved, but by May 1945 it was in clear prospect. The United States now possessed super-abundant naval and air strength. It had reconquered almost all of the Philippines since October 1944. It had obtained bases for effective bombing and eventual invasion of Japan by conquering Iwo Jima in February 1945 and Okinawa in April. In May the British recovered most of Burma; and the Chinese, aided by American supplies, were cutting the Japanese off from Indo-China and regaining some of their own coastal territory.

A large-scale invasion of Japan was planned for the autumn of 1945, but it proved unnecessary. By midsummer, the incessant bombing of the country convinced many responsible Japanese, including the Emperor Hirohito, that further fighting was futile and that they should sue for peace. On August 8 the hopelessness of the odds against them was emphasized by Russia's formally declaring war against Japan and ordering an advance into Manchuria and Korea. The final determinant was the atomic bomb, the outcome of several years' secret labor by American, British, and Canadian scientists and engineers. Two such bombs were dropped on Japan, with the most terrifying results: one on August 6, destroying the city of Hiroshima and killing some 66,000 civilians; the other on August 9, laying Nagasaki in ruins and killing 40,000.

An underwater atomic blast in Bikini Lagoon, July 25, 1946.

Courtesy Wide World Photos

The next day, Japan offered to surrender, on the one condition that its Emperor was not molested. The surrender was agreed to by the Allies on August 14, 1945, and shortly afterwards American troops, under General MacArthur, occupied Japan. This marked the end of World War II.

The costs of the war can never be accurately determined. To the American people alone, the immediate and direct cost of the war was over a million casualties, including nearly 400,000 deaths, and a financial expenditure of something like 350 billion dollars. The direct expenditure of other countries has been estimated at a trillion (1,000 billion) dollars, while loss of property must run to another trillion, and of human lives into the millions.

Three major contributions to final Allied victory may be discerned: first, the stubborn courage of the British during the year in which they stood alone against the triumphant Axis; second, the vast man-power, relentless defense, and strategically skillful attacks of the Soviet Union which wore down the Germans; third, the vast productive capacity of the United States which provided the materials for victory.

President Harry Truman addressing first session of the United Nations at San Francisco, 1945.

Courtesy Wide World Photos

CHAPTER 60

Immediate Outcome of World War II

A. Peace Plans and the United Nations

During the course of the war, shortly after Germany's attack on Russia, but while the situation of England still seemed dark indeed, President Franklin Roosevelt and Prime Minister Winston Churchill had met at sea in August 1941. One of their purposes was to formulate a statement of the objectives of the anti-Nazi powers, which would, at the same time, influence neutral opinion and form a general basis for the post-war settlement. It was to some extent modeled after Wilson's famous and influential "Fourteen Points," but it was much less specific.

The "Atlantic Charter," as it was called, declared that the United States and Great Britain sought no additional territory, and that if any territorial changes were made at the end of the war they should be in accord with the freely expressed wishes of the peoples concerned. It went on to reaffirm the right of all peoples to choose their own form of government, to promise the restoration of freedom to countries that had been conquered, and to assert that all nations, victors or vanquished, should have access to raw materials. It proclaimed that all nations must be secure within their own boundaries, and must be afforded the means of freeing their citizens from fear and want; that the seas must be free; and that ultimately the use of force must be abandoned among nations, though, pending the establishment of general security, na-

tions threatening aggression must be disarmed.

The hopes for democracy, security, and peace, thus enshrined in the Charter, fitted well the mood of the Allied governments in exile. At a conference in London, in September 1941, Belgium, Poland, Czechoslovakia, Yugoslavia, Greece, and others accepted the principles of the Charter as a basis for the post-war settlement. After the entrance of the United States into the war, there was a gradual drawing together of the powers arrayed against Germany, Italy, and Japan. Poland and Russia had already signed a declaration of friendship. In May 1942, Great Britain and Russia signed a twenty-year treaty of alliance. At the same time, "full understanding" was reached between the United States and Russia. Important conferences were held by Roosevelt and Churchill in 1943 at Casablanca, at Washington, and at Cairo; and Stalin joined them at Teheran in late November 1943 and at Yalta early in 1945. Though for the most part these consultations had to do with immediate war needs and strategy, some agreements were made looking to eventual arrangements for peace.

In November 1943, the foreign secretaries of Great Britain, the United States, Russia, and China met at Moscow and asserted the need of establishing as soon as practicable a permanent "international organization" of "all peace loving states." At the Teheran Conference, the next month, Roosevelt, Churchill, and Stalin called for "a world family of democratic nations." The implementation of these ideas was pushed forward at the Dumbarton Oaks Conference in Washington (August–November 1944), where representatives of the Big Three and China drafted a Charter for the United Nations—a name supplied by President Roosevelt. The draft, with only minor amendments, was adopted by a conference at San Francisco (April–June 1945) of fifty-one nations arrayed against Germany, Italy, or Japan, and it went into effect on October 24, 1945.

The initial members were the fifty-one represented at San Francisco.[1] But it was provided that others, including enemy states, might subsequently become eligible for membership. One of the anomalies in the original membership was the inclusion, at Stalin's insistence, of the Ukraine and Byelorussia, though these were integral parts of the Soviet Union. For a full decade afterwards, as a result of friction between the Soviet Union and the Western powers, only nine additional nations were admitted: Afghanistan, Iceland, Sweden, Thailand, Pakistan, Yemen, Burma, Israel, and Indonesia.

Not until the end of 1955 was a compromise reached whereby sixteen other nations were admitted: Albania, Austria, Bulgaria, Cambodia, Ceylon, Eire, Finland, Hungary, Italy, Jordan, Laos, Libya, Nepal, Portugal, Rumania, and Spain. Other admissions gradually followed, chiefly of newly independent states in Asia and Africa, until by 1962 the United Nations had a total and truly worldwide membership of 104. Still excluded were Communist China and the divided countries of Germany, Korea, and Vietnam.[2]

---

[1] Argentina, Australia, Belgium, Bolivia, Brazil, Byelorussia, Canada, Chile, China (Nationalist), Colombia, Costa Rica, Cuba, Czechoslovakia, Denmark, Dominican Republic, Ecuador, Egypt, El Salvador, Ethiopia, France, Great Britain, Greece, Guatemala, Haiti, Honduras, India, Iran, Iraq, Lebanon, Liberia, Luxembourg, Mexico, Netherlands, New Zealand, Nicaragua, Norway, Panama, Paraguay, Peru, Philippines, Poland, Saudi Arabia, South Africa, Syria, Turkey, Ukraine, Uruguay, U.S.A., U.S.S.R., Venezuela, Yugoslavia.

[2] The members, as of mid-1962, are listed in the rear end papers of this volume.

In a general way, the United Nations bears a close resemblance to the League of Nations. It has a General Assembly in which each nation has one vote, and a Security Council of eleven, including five permanent members (Great Britain, China, France, Russia, and the United States) and six members elected for two-year terms by the Assembly. By a most important provision, any permanent member may veto any action by the Security Council save only in the case of a merely "procedural" matter. A Secretariat under a Secretary General performs administrative and technical tasks.

In practice, the successive Secretaries General, Trygve Lie of Norway, Dag Hammarskjöld of Sweden, and U Thant of Burma, have been important not only as administrators but also as representatives and spokesmen of the whole organization. An Economic and Social Council of eighteen members elected by the Assembly seeks to improve world health, economic, social, and educational conditions. Related to the U.N. are a dozen special agencies, among them: a United Nations Educational, Scientific and Cultural Organization (UNESCO); a Food and Agricultural Organization; an International Labor Organization; an International Civil Aviation Organization; an International Monetary Fund; and a World Health Organization.

Directly responsible to the Assembly, is a Trusteeship Council designed to safeguard the interests of colonial peoples, previously supervised by the League of Nations, or taken from former holders as a result of the Second World War. The Assembly likewise chooses an International Court of Justice of fifteen members who are empowered to decide international disputes of a justiciable nature and to render advisory opinions. Under the Security Council are an Atomic Energy Commission to deal with the development and use of atomic power, and a Military Staff Committee composed of representatives of the major powers and charged with planning and directing military action against aggressor nations. Provision is also made for international armed forces to be used at the discretion of the Security Council; and these have been drafted and employed in Korea and the Congo.

The United Nations has intervened more or less effectively to prevent or limit strife or aggression in Iran, Greece, Palestine, Indonesia, and India-Pakistan, and, as we have just indicated, in Korea and the Congo. It successfully administered Libya and transformed it in January 1952 into an independent nation. But its major importance has not been in settling disputes or preventing conflicts. Rather, it has been significant as a world forum and through the work of its agencies. As a meeting place for the nations in times of tension, it has permitted small countries to be heard. It has focussed on some problems what amounts to a world opinion, whose weight even the great powers feel. It has compelled the powers great and small to make known their position—to stand up and be counted —on a host of issues.

Even more important has been the quietly effective work of many of the United Nations' agencies. The Relief and Rehabilitation Administration (UNRRA) distributed in 1945–1946 one and a quarter billion dollars' worth of aid to war-ravaged countries. The International Monetary Fund has slowly furthered the cause of monetary stability. The International Bank has provided loans totaling a billion and a half dollars for the rehabilitation and development of more than a score of countries. The International Children's Emergency Fund has benefited some sixty million children.

The World Health Organization (WHO) has provided information, supplies, and technical skills to fight a dozen endemic diseases such as malaria and yaws. UNESCO has assisted libraries, reduced illiteracy, provided for the translation of important works, and greatly accelerated the interchange of scholarly knowledge. All the while, other organs like the International Civil Aviation Organization, the Universal Postal Union, the World Meteorological Organization, the Commission on Narcotic Drugs, and the International Telecommunication Union have been carrying forward in unspectacular but vital areas the whole idea of international coöperation.

With its headquarters in New York in an impressive glass-walled building, with its pale blue flag emblazoned with a polar map of the world between two olive branches, with its postage stamps designed to symbolize international coöperation, the United Nations had taken on by 1955 many of the attributes of an enduring institution. In June of that year its tenth anniversary was marked by a special meeting in San Francisco, its birthplace. The gathering was dignified by the presence of the most important leaders of nations great and small. The speeches, which were numerous and eloquent, could almost be summarized as follows: the United Nations has not fulfilled all the hopes of 1945; the world situation has thwarted it in its major role as a peace-maker; but it has accomplished much; we may be hopeful for the future; and in any case this organization is a continuing symbol of man's aspirations for a world at peace.

B. Weakened Europe and Shift in the Balance of Power

It was a war-ravaged and weakened Europe that played a part in the founding of the United Nations. Destruction wrought by war, especially by air bombardment, was tremendous. Nor was the devastation confined, as in the First World War, to limited areas; rather, it was widespread over most of Europe—in Britain, the Low Countries, Norway, France, Italy, all Central Europe, Greece, the Balkans, and the greater part of European Russia. Many major cities were totally or in large part destroyed.

And, since the Second World War was more truly global than the First, much destruction had also taken place on a large scale in Japan, China, and the Philippines. Economic and social conditions were terrifying. Food, fuel, and fibers were wanting or in short supply in all the war-torn countries. Devastated nations, faced by a gigantic task of rehabilitation, were without many of the requisites for it. Farmers lacked tools, machinery, livestock, fertilizer, and seed. Undamaged factories lacked raw materials and coal. Many people, undernourished, ill-housed and ill-clad, lacked vitality. The transportation systems were in chaos. Inflation in greater or lesser degree was universal, and the prices of available goods soared in black markets, despite rationing and price controls.

Aggravating the chaotic conditions was the problem not only of returning millions of demobilized soldiers and prisoners of war to peaceful pursuits, but also of caring for many millions of "displaced persons"— Jews and others ejected by the Nazis; Poles expelled from the part of their country appropriated by Russia; Germans ousted from East Prussia, Silesia, and the Sudetenland; Arabs ejected from Palestine; and many a political refugee. A decade after the end of the war it was estimated that there were still two million homeless persons.

The defeated powers were not merely weakened and ravaged; they were prostrate. Germany, Austria, Italy, and Japan were occupied by military forces of the victor nations—Austria and Germany by France, Britain, Russia, and the United States; Italy by Britain and the United States; Japan by the United States; and Poland, Rumania, Bulgaria, and Hungary by Russia. There were some attempts to punish the defeated. Russia in particular removed a good deal of machinery and other capital goods from Germany. In the vanquished countries, all weapons of war were removed or destroyed, armed forces were disbanded, and war-factories were dismantled. At Nuremberg, beginning in November 1945, leading German Nazis were tried by the victors as "war criminals." Eleven were sentenced to death. Similar trials were conducted by the United States in Japan and by local or national courts in several countries. Continuing attempts were made to de-Nazify Germany by removing all Hitler's devoted followers from positions of importance. But vengeance was quickly overshadowed by the practical problems of reorganizing governments, local and national, reëstablishing transportation, providing some sort of housing, and feeding the people.

If the defeated nations were prostrate, some of the victors were in little better state. The end of the war saw neither Great Britain nor France in a position to play effectively the role of a great power. Britain had political stability, but was unable to feed itself or to produce enough exports to secure the needed food. Loans from the United States and Canada in 1945–1947, totaling some five billion dollars, were all that enabled the British to purchase needed food, raw materials, and other goods. The task of rebuilding its cities and rehabilitating its industries strained every resource of the country and it had little to spare for military or diplomatic purposes. At the same time, as we shall see, a large part of the British Empire was cutting itself loose from the homeland. France was an even worse case, for it had most of the problems faced by the British and, in addition, it could not achieve a strong, stable, and effective government.

In terms of sheer strength, either military or economic, Great Britain and France were no longer great powers. Japan, Italy, and Germany were even weaker and were in the control of their conquerors. China was lapsing into civil strife more debilitating than foreign war. Whereas in 1939 it had been possible to count seven great powers (or eight if China were included), by 1946 there were only two left—Russia and the United States. Russia had suffered much in the war. It had had untold millions of military and civilian casualties. Many of its great cities had been devastated and its factories destroyed. But it had built up new industrial potential behind the Urals. It had created and maintained a massive army and a mighty air force. It had untold resources within its expanding boundaries. It had a young and growing population. And it espoused the ideology of Marxist Communism, which if it was more or less identical in practice with Russian nationalism and imperialism and if it meant ruthless and bloody dictatorship at home, could still be exported to the discouraged and downtrodden in other lands as a gospel of economic and social democracy and justice. The Russian Soviet State had been born (as Lenin had predicted it might be) from the chaos produced by World War I. Stalin and his followers had no doubt that, in like fashion, opportunities would be offered by the aftermath of World War

II. Russia kept her armed forces and her war industry substantially intact in the years following 1945.

The United States emerged from the war more powerful even than Russia. It had suffered no war damage and relatively small loss of human life. It had dramatically and massively increased its industrial output. It had by far the most potent navy and air force in the world and it had by far the best equipped army. But the American people were eager for peace. They were optimistic about their ability to cooperate with the Russians in making a secure and stable world, just as they had worked with them to defeat Hitler. They wanted the soldiers, sailors, and airmen returned to civilian life as rapidly as possible. Thus it was that in 1946 and 1947 the great American military machine was taken to pieces. Tanks and planes and ships and artillery were junked. The armed forces were cut back to a small size. The nation strove to return to a peace basis as quickly as possible. By 1948, there was only one great military power—Russia. Its armed might, nevertheless, was to a considerable degree counterbalanced by the fact that the Americans still had a monopoly (and a stockpile) of the fantastic new weapon, the atom bomb. Until Russia matched the United States in atomic strength it could not venture too freely to use its military might.

In the United States itself, leadership fell to President Harry Truman, who had succeeded to the office on the death of President Franklin D. Roosevelt on April 12, 1945. Under Truman the demobilization took place with less dislocation than had been expected. Soon the factories of the country were pouring out a spate of goods—automobiles, refrigerators, textiles, tractors, radios, washing machines—to make up for the wartime deficit. Soon new types of goods like plastics and television sets were added to the flow. As the gross national product and per-capita income rose to unprecedented heights, the world, including many Americans, waited uneasily to see if the United States would not slump from fabulous prosperity into another and worse depression than that of 1929–1933. The

Russians were confident that this would happen, for Marxist theory insisted that the "contradictions of capitalism" were bound to produce ever more frequent and ever more severe economic crises. But the reforms of the prewar and war period in economic matters and the extremely varied nature of the economy had by now created a stability that stood the country in good stead. Though there were minor recessions, they were short-lived. The sheer weight of post-war production made the United States as important in the economic sphere as its atom bombs made it in the military.

C. Failure to Effect a General Peace Settlement

The Atlantic Charter of 1941 had set forth some of the general principles which, it was hoped, might be embodied in a peace settlement. Other and more specific points were agreed on at some of the wartime conferences. At Cairo in November 1943, Roosevelt and Churchill agreed for their respective countries to seek no territorial gains, and promised Chiang Kai-shek that Japan would lose all areas acquired since 1895, with Formosa going to China, and Korea becoming independent. At Teheran (1943) the same leaders, with Stalin, promised to maintain after the war "the independence, sovereignty, and territorial integrity of Iran." More important were the decisions reached by the Big Three at Yalta in February 1945.

Though the atomic bomb was then in the making, its success was by no means assured, and Roosevelt and Churchill were told by their military advisers that Russian help would shorten the war against Japan and save innumerable casualties. During the Yalta meeting, therefore, in return for a promise of Russian aid against Japan once the European war was over, the American President and the British Prime Minister promised Stalin that Russia would receive the Kurile Islands and the southern half of Sakhalin from Japan, and control, at China's expense, of Outer Mongolia, Port Arthur, Dairen, and the Manchurian railways, and that they would persuade China to accept this settlement. Stalin agreed that in the liberated countries of Europe self-government should be restored and free elections held. As to Poland, it was arranged that Russia might continue to hold eastern Polish territory up to the old "Curzon line," that Poland would be compensated by being given German areas to the west and north, and that the Poles should be allowed to choose their own government at free elections with universal suffrage and a secret ballot. Germany, it was agreed, should be divided into zones and occupied by Russia, Great Britain, the United States, and possibly France; its war factories should be dismantled, and it should be made to pay heavy reparations with half of them going to Russia.

When Germany had been defeated and another conference was necessary in August 1945, to implement the Yalta agreements, Roosevelt had died and Churchill had lost the general elections in England. At the Potsdam Conference, therefore, it was President Harry Truman and Prime Minister Clement Attlee who met with Stalin. At this meeting the zones of military occupation were delimited, with Russia holding the eastern part, Britain, France, and the United States holding the west, and Berlin (embedded in the Russian eastern zone) under joint control. Pending a final peace treaty, German frontiers were tentatively set along the Oder and Neisse rivers. Russia got the northern half of East Prussia. Poland, in compensation for its territorial losses in the east to Russia, received Danzig, Upper and Lower Silesia, eastern Brandenburg, most of Pomerania, and the southern part of East Prussia. France recovered Alsace-Lorraine; Belgium, Eupen and Malmédy; and Czechoslovakia, the Sudetenland. The much disputed Saar was put in the French zone and two years later it was detached from the rest of Germany and united economically with France, while remaining politically autonomous.

The losses to Germany in territory were much more severe than after World War I. In 1937 Germany had comprised some 182,000 square miles. What was left of it in 1945 amounted to about 137,000 square miles, with 42,000 (population about 17,-500,000) in Russian hands and 95,000

square miles (population 49,000,000) under control of the Western Allies. It is to be noted that most of German industry lay in the Allied zones in the west, but it was agreed that the remaining war plants and war potential should be dismantled and destroyed.

At the Potsdam Conference it was also arranged that Austria should be detached from Germany, but that it should be divided into four zones for occupation by the victors. The Russian zone in the east included the oil fields and some of the most important industrial and agricultural areas.

In eastern Europe and the Balkans, the matter of military occupation was settled not so much by agreement as by the situation itself. Russian armies were in effective control of Hungary, Bulgaria, and Rumania. Here they were to stay, and, as we shall see, to secure the creation of satellite governments managed from Moscow. The situation in Poland and Czechoslovakia was more complicated, but in the end came to the same result. Thus Russia from 1945 on was overwhelmingly dominant in all of eastern and much of central Europe.

At Potsdam it had been agreed to proceed at once with the drafting of peace treaties with Italy, Rumania, Bulgaria, Hungary, and Finland. The actual drafting of the treaties proved difficult and led to much dispute among the Allies. But eventually definitive treaties were agreed on and were signed at Paris in February 1947. All of them provided for reparations, most of which were to go to Russia. Italy was to pay 360 million dollars, Bulgaria 70 million, Hungary, Rumania, and Finland 300 million each. In each country, the size of any future armed forces and the amount of military material were drastically limited. A number of territorial changes were imposed. Italy lost all its colonies. Part of Venetia Giulia and some Adriatic islands went to Yugoslavia and some small frontier areas to France. Long-disputed Trieste was placed under international control. The Dodecanese Islands and Rhodes were turned over to Greece. Hungary was forced to return Transylvania to Rumania and a small region to Czechoslovakia. Rumania in turn lost Bessarabia and Bukovina to

Russia, and the southern part of Dobruja to Bulgaria. Finland had to cede to Russia the Petsamo province and a large part of Karelia and also to grant to Russia a naval base dominating the Gulf of Finland.[1] Bulgaria lost no territory and made the gain indicated above. The United States had no part in the treaty with Finland since it had never declared war on that country.

In the negotiation of these treaties there were some traces of principle, for regard was occasionally paid to history and nationality. But for the most part they recognized the actual post-war situation and took account of Russia's military predominance in eastern Europe and the military and strategic needs of the great powers. They legally established peace over much of Europe. But the terms of the treaties were in many ways less important than the developing realities of international power politics.

[1] Russia, seeking Finnish favor, agreed in 1955 to return the naval base.

D. Communist Conquest of Eastern Europe

It is a curious fact that Communism, which claims to be social and economic democracy, has always been imposed by armed force. In the post-war period, Russia, instead of liquidating its army, used it ruthlessly to create Communist regimes in countries adjoining its territories. During the war, Russia had crushed and annexed the republics of Latvia, Lithuania, and Estonia. In the years after 1945, it created dependent, "satellite," Communist regimes in Poland, Czechoslovakia, Hungary, Rumania, Bulgaria, Albania, and East Germany. There was no pretense of free and democratic elections with a secret ballot even when these had been promised (as at Yalta in the case of Poland).

The technique of establishing a Communist puppet regime in an area occupied or influenced by Russian armed forces varied somewhat from country to country, but the general pattern soon became familiar. The existing or provisional government

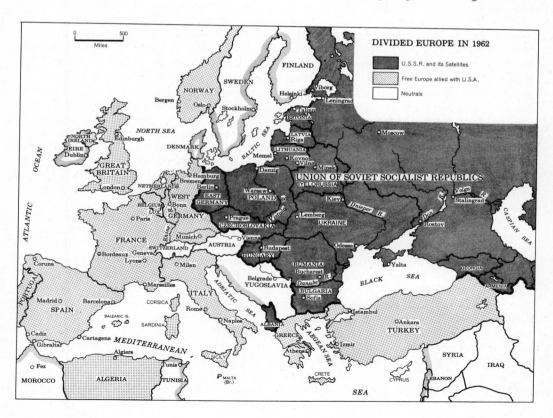

DIVIDED EUROPE IN 1962

U.S.S.R. and its Satellites

Free Europe allied with U.S.A.

Neutrals

would first be denounced as fascist and reactionary and would be superseded by a coalition "popular front" cabinet in which Communists held key positions, such as minister of interior (in charge of the police) and minister of information (in charge of propaganda). Then the Communist ministers, backed by military aid, pressure, or threats from Russia, and led by a native who had been trained in Leninist tactics in Moscow, would get rid of their non-Communist fellow ministers and establish an authoritarian government. Next a constitution like that of the Soviet Union would be drawn up and ratified by an election theoretically democratic but actually controlled. Finally the disciplined Communist party, even though a small minority, would take complete control and more or less rapidly liquidate all opposition parties and leaders. Thereafter, it was easy to control the schools, universities, newspapers, courts, and communications, to terrorize the churches, to suppress civil liberties, and to establish a thoroughgoing dictatorship, which would take orders from Moscow in both internal and external matters.

It is not hard to understand why the Western democracies did not at first oppose this new type of imperialism by which Russia extended its sway over neighboring peoples—not remote and backward tribes, but civilized folk with proud traditions of culture and independence. They trusted that the wartime coöperation with Russia could be maintained in the post-war years and that Russia would live up to the commitments it had made at Yalta and Potsdam and in endorsing the United Nations Charter. They demonstrated this trust by a speedy disarmament which left them incapable of intervening forcibly, especially in areas near to Russia. They had raised no serious objections to the outright annexation by Russia of eastern Poland, northern East Prussia, Carpatho-Ruthenia (from Czechoslovakia), and Bukovina and Bessarabia (from Rumania). They had entrusted the sole military occupation of east-central Europe to Russia and were in no position to prevent what ensued, save by the use of military force which they were no longer willing or able to apply.

Thus it was that much of what they had fought for (such as an independent Poland) was lost in the peace. The case of Poland was particularly poignant.

During the war when the Polish government-in-exile at London had objected to the idea of permanent Soviet annexation of eastern Poland, Russia had recognized a pro-Soviet "provisional government" at Lublin headed by a Polish Communist, trained in Moscow, Boleslav Beirut. At Yalta, Stalin had persuaded Roosevelt and Churchill to recognize Beirut's government, provided non-Communist members were added to it and free elections were held. In August 1945, the Beirut government ceded to Russia 70,000 square miles of Polish territory in the east.

The next year "the capitalist system" was abolished. Non-Communists were added to the government but were hemmed in and kept quite without power. Elections were held in 1947 under the dominance of police, troops, and disciplined Communist party members. The National Assembly, thus elected, adopted a constitution like that of Russia, with Beirut as president. The Communist and Socialist parties were merged (1948). Non-Communist parties were destroyed and their leaders driven into exile or put to death. Pressure was applied to the Catholic Church to prevent its interference with developments, and the Catholic primate, Cardinal Wyszynski, with several other bishops, was imprisoned. A marshal of the Russian army, Konstentin Rokossovsky was made Polish Minister of National Defense. The Poles might regret their independence and chafe under the new bonds they bore, but the Russian grip on the Polish satellite was firm.

Despite the presence of Russian troops and organized pressure from a Communist minority, Hungary strove to maintain a democratic and independent government in 1945. Elections in November of that year gave the democratic elements a large majority in the National Assembly. A liberal republican constitution was adopted, and Ferenc Nagy, a leading democrat, became premier. But a *coup d'état* in May 1947 ousted the Nagy cabinet. By the middle of 1949 Hungary had a Communist constitution, a single Communist party,

Three Musicians. Pablo Picasso, painted in 1921.

Courtesy Museum of Living Art

and close ties with Russia. All domestic dissent had been crushed. Cardinal Mindszenty, who had been a stalwart opponent of the Nazis, was condemned in February 1949 to life imprisonment and many another Hungarian patriot suffered a like or worse fate.

In Bulgaria, George Dimitrov, a Communist returning from Russia, forced his way, with the help of Soviet troops, into the government, and dominated a referendum which in September 1946 dethroned the youthful King Simeon II (who, in 1943, had succeeded his father Boris III). Controlled elections, the next month, enabled the Communists to take over the government, to found another "people's republic," and to reduce the opposition to impotence. The next year, the leader of the democratic Agrarian party was executed and a constitution of the Soviet type was adopted.

In Rumania, elections held in November 1946 put Communists in the government. Led by Peter Groza, the premier, and Ana Pauker, a fanatical disciple of Stalin, and supported by Russian troops, they forced the abdication of King Michael at the end of 1947. By 1952 all parties other than the Communist "People's Democratic Front"

had been completely eliminated and in that year a Russian-type constitution was put into effect.

The story in Albania was much the same. After the Germans had been driven out (by the end of 1944), a provisional government was established by a Russian protégé, Enver Hoxha. It was recognized by Russia, and also by the United States and Great Britain with the added proviso that free elections must be held. But the elections were not free, and American and British recognition was withdrawn. Nonetheless, with Russian support, King Zog was formally deposed (December 1945), and a "people's republic" under the dictatorship of Hoxha was set up. The 1945 constitution was modeled after that of the Soviet Union and the army was closely tied to that of Russia.

The case of Czechoslovakia is parallel. In 1945, its government-in-exile under President Beneš returned home. Under compulsion it ceded the province of Ruthenia to Russia, and established (in 1946) a six-party coalition cabinet in which the leading figure was a Russian-trained Communist, Klement Gottwald. Backed by pressure from Moscow, the Communists slowly gained control over the government and over the entire country. In February 1948, by a *coup d'état* which met with little opposition and secured the reluctant consent of Beneš, this control was made complete. In March, Jan Masaryk, liberal foreign minister, and son of the heroic founder of the Czechoslovak republic, ended his life under mysterious circumstances. He had hoped to make his country a political and cultural link between the east and the west, but the Russians wanted puppet states not links. In June Beneš felt compelled to turn the presidency over to Gottwald, who promptly promulgated a Soviet-style constitution and proceeded to eliminate all opposition.

The events in Yugoslavia form a significant variation on the theme, for in that country there were in existence, at the end of the war, native armed forces with a good deal of equipment and a strong spirit of patriotism. There had been, in Yugoslavia, during the war, rival resistance movements. One was headed by General Draja Mikhailovich, loyal to King Peter II and the government-in-exile in London; the other led by Joseph Broz, a Russian-trained Communist popularly known as Marshal Tito. In 1944, Russia persuaded Great Britain and the United States to insist on a merger of the two movements, with the result that, after the withdrawal of the German troops, King Peter was obliged to appoint Tito prime minister. Using his governmental powers and armed forces, Tito saw to it that the Communists won the elections of November 1945. The monarchy was abolished and the Federal People's Republic of Yugoslavia established. During the ensuing year, opposing factions were destroyed, General Mikhailovich was executed, and the Catholic primate, Archbishop Stepinac, was sentenced to sixteen years in prison.

So far the story is like that of the other satellites. But during 1947 and 1948 as the Russians sought to confirm their control over yet another puppet, things did not work out as expected. Tito and the Yugoslavs were at first much favored by the Russians: for example, Belgrade was made the headquarters of the Communist international organ—the Cominform. But as Russian "advisers" and secret police moved

President Eduard Beneš of Czechoslovakia, 1945.
Courtesy Wide World Photos

into the country, Tito reacted against the Russians. In June 1948, he and his government were denounced in vitriolic terms by the Cominform and many expected that he would soon be replaced by another leader more amenable to Soviet control. Instead, he was able to maintain his position and to retain the loyalty of the Yugoslav Communists and the army. The break between Russia and Yugoslavia soon appeared complete, and Tito was wooed and supported with economic aid and military supplies by the Western democracies even though his regime was a dictatorship and its principles and techniques were Communist. Not until 1955 did the Russians seek to heal the breach with Tito and it was then clear that they were willing to accept Yugoslavia as a smaller partner rather than a satellite. Tito seemed eager to continue in an independent position in which he could obtain advantages from both the Soviet Union and the Western powers. Though Tito and his ministers were convinced Communists and though they often talked as if they were the most rigid and extreme Marxists, still as time passed they allowed economic experiments that were quite unlike the Russian system. There was, indeed, some private ownership and a good deal of decentralization in industry and commerce, and peasant proprietorship of the land was widespread.

Altogether, between 1939 and 1948, Russia, in an imperialist expansion movement almost unparalleled in history, had been able to ring itself about on the west, first with a band of territory seized and absorbed (Lithuania, Latvia, Estonia, Petsamo province, part of Karelia, eastern Poland, part of East Prussia, Ruthenia, Bukovina, Bessarabia) and then to add to that ring another outer one of firmly controlled satellite puppet states (Poland, Czechoslovakia, Hungary, Rumania, Bulgaria). Albania was an exception in not being contiguous to Russian controlled territory, but this situation arose only from the fact that Yugoslavia had been able to assert its independence from Russia. In terms of Russian propaganda, this expansion was the "liberation of peoples from capitalist domination," the "establishment of peoples' democracies," the spreading of the "socialist revolution," and the safeguarding of the "Communist homeland" by interposing territorial barriers between it and the "aggressive" and "warmongering" capitalist West. To a more impartial view it seemed like the ruthless exploitation of cynical diplomacy and armed force to further the cause of Russian nationalistic imperialism. The Soviets had expanded Russian territory and control far beyond the farthest limits ever dreamed of by the most fanatical of the Russian nationalists of the days before 1914.

E. Communist Triumphs in East Asia

As things turned out, the greatest Communist successes in the post-war period were scored not so much in Europe as in Asia. It was in Asia, too, that the most acute crises arose and that the "cold war" was attended by a series of hot "shooting" wars.

At Yalta, in 1945, Stalin may have thought that the government of Chiang Kai-shek and his nationalist Kuomintang party would dominate China after the war. At any rate, Stalin pledged Russian support to Chiang Kai-shek, and Russia and the Nationalist government of China negotiated a treaty in 1945. What actually happened, therefore, may have been a surprise to the Russians, but they were certainly quick to take advantage of it.

During the war, Chiang's government had been opposed not only by the Japanese but also by Communist forces, under the Moscow-trained Mao Tse-tung, who dominated areas in the northwest of China, whither they had been driven in previous years. Weakened by the long war, by inflation and corruption, and by the dissatisfaction of some elements of the population, Chiang Kai-shek's Nationalists encountered grave difficulties in coping with the Communist army which had been extending its sway in the last years of the war, and which, in the immediate post-war period, was making still more advances.

When the Chinese Communists showed themselves stronger than had been expected, the Russians at once began to support them with arms taken from the Japanese, and with technical assistance, though at the same time Russia continued to loot Manchuria of all the machinery that could be carried away. By 1949, Mao and his Communist armies were winning victory after victory. They captured Tientsin and Peiping in January, Nanking in April, and by December were substantially in control of the whole of continental China. Chiang Kai-shek, his government, and the remnants of his armies were forced to take refuge in Formosa (Taiwan), so recently reacquired by China from Japan.

Thus China, with its extensive territories, its rich resources, and its population numbering nearly half a billion, came under Communist sway. In September 1949 a government of the Soviet type was organized, and the next February a treaty of mutual aid and friendship was signed by Russia and Communist China. In the ensuing years, Russia supported the Chinese with military equipment, goods, technical assistance, and advisers. In 1951, the Chinese felt strong enough to expand into Tibet and to set up

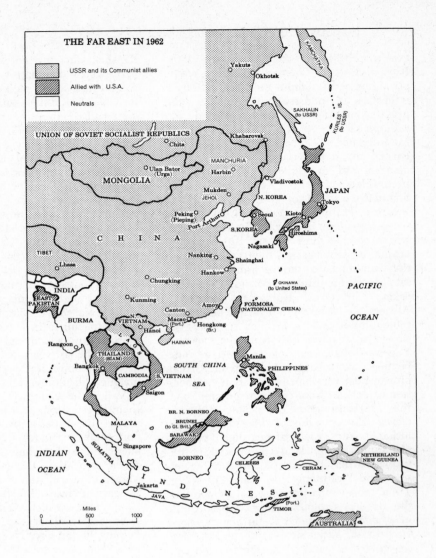

THE FAR EAST IN 1962

- USSR and its Communist allies
- Allied with U.S.A.
- Neutrals

a puppet government there. Before many years were out the Chinese were deporting Tibetans, bringing in Chinese, liquidating the "wealthy" peasants and destroying the Buddhist monasteries and other religious centers. The Tibetans rose in hopeless revolt, but without success. In 1959 the Dalai Lama, who had been both the political and religious leader of the country, fled to India, whither he was followed by thousands of refugees unwilling to submit to Communist rule.

Meanwhile in China the new regime was consolidating itself rapidly and successfully. Foreigners were driven out. Christian missionary enterprise was stopped. The merchant class and landowners were destroyed or "re-educated" in work camps. The peasants were forced into communal life on collective farms and employed on giant projects of flood control and irrigation. Industry, both of the household and factory type, was stimulated. Vast campaigns of Communist education and propaganda were undertaken. The developments were similar to those in Communist Russia, but Mao and his followers claimed to be even purer and more rigorous in their Marxism than their Russian comrades. In any case, China was already overshadowing all other Communist regimes in the world, save only the Russian.

Nor were the expansionist tendencies of Communism in Asia confined to the seizure of Tibet. Even before that move had been made, Korea had become the object of a major Communist drive. It had been arranged at the Cairo Conference in 1943 that Korea should be independent, and at the close of the war the victors proceeded on this basis. But like Germany, Korea was divided into zones of military occupation. That part of the country north of the thirty-eighth parallel (containing most of the mineral and industrial resources of the country) was entrusted to Russia, while the area south of that parallel (containing the best agricultural land) was to be held by the United States. The Russians at once set about transforming their half of the country into a puppet Communist state despite the fact that the native population, the United States, and the United Nations all wanted Korea to be a unified nation. In the South, the Republic of Korea was set up in 1948 after an elected national assembly had drawn up and adopted a democratic constitution and chosen Syngman Rhee, a veteran patriot, as its first president.

In December 1948 the Soviet Union withdrew its army of occupation from North Korea. It could afford to do so, for it had organized there not only a dependent Communist regime, but also a large native army indoctrinated in Communist ideology and well armed. The withdrawal was, moreover, useful for Russian propaganda purposes, since it could be hailed as proof of the Soviet Union's respect for the "freedom" of Asian peoples, in contrast with the "imperialism" of the Western powers and especially of the United States. Not to be outdone in championship of freedom for Asiatics, the United States followed the Russian example, and in June of 1949 with-

drew its occupation forces from South Korea. It left there, however, to defend the Republic, only a relatively small and very scantily supplied native army. It was in this same year that Mao and his Communists triumphed in China and were soon recognized not only by Russia and its satellites, but also by Great Britain (anxious over the fate of Hong Kong) and by other countries including India.

Alarmed by the Communist success in China, President Truman and his Secretary of State, Dean Acheson, adopted a policy designed to arrest Communist expansion in Asia no less than in Europe. In May 1950, the American government promised active aid to French Indo-China (Vietnam) in suppressing native rebellion and warding off aggression by Communist China. But Indo-China proved not to be the immediate object of Communist conquest.

In the early morning of June 25, 1950, without previous warning North Korean Communist armies, many thousand strong, crossed the thirty-eighth parallel and swept into South Korea. Taken by surprise and desperately short of arms and munitions, the forces of the republican government of South Korea could not withstand the attack. In four days, they lost the capital city of Seoul and were in full retreat. Communist conquest of all Korea appeared imminent and it seemed likely that Russia and Communist North Korea would be able to present the world with an accomplished fact which no one would feel called upon to alter by armed force. This would doubtless have been the result if the United States had not intervened, with results which will be discussed later.[1]

[1] See below, pp. 814–817.

General Charles de Gaulle.

Courtesy French Embassy Press and Information Division. Copyright Paris-Match

CHAPTER 61

Post-War Free Europe

A. Democratic Britain

The democracies of western Europe emerged from the war in a sorry state. Democracy itself had been weakened, for if it had fought off the Nazi-Fascist attack from the Right in a prolonged and bloody struggle, it now had to confront an invigorated Communist menace from the Left. Communism usually feeds and grows on human misery and there was misery aplenty in post-war Europe. Moreover, the military victory of Russia added to the prestige of Communism. In many countries, too, the Communists, after the German attack on Russia, had won popularity by their vigor and courage in the underground resistance movements.

Thus in most of the Western countries, while the right-wing reactionaries of the fascist type were non-existent or discredited, the Communist were, save in Britain, an important political factor. In France and Italy the Communists were especially numerous and well organized. In several countries democratic strength came from Catholic parties which had become more radical in their demands for social reform, but were firm in their defence of political democracy, religion, the family, private property, and the dignity and integrity of the individual. Another element of democratic strength was the Socialist parties, including the British Labor Party, for if some leftist elements in them flirted continuously with the Communists, the majority believed steadfastly in democratic political methods and procedures. Parties such as the Conservatives in Britain and the Radical Socialists in France seemed weaker immediately after the war, but tended to gain in strength as time passed.

In July 1945, while the war in the Pacific was still going on, British elections gave the Labor Party some 390 out of 640 seats in the House of Commons. Thus Winston Churchill, despite his contributions to victory, was pushed from power and replaced as prime minister by the Labor leader, Clement Attlee. Labor used its parliamentary success to advance its program of socializing the basic industries. One by one it nationalized the Bank of England, the coal mines, communications, the railways and long-distance trucking, the iron and steel industry, civil aviation, electricity and gas. Medicine was also nationalized or socialized, and the extension of social legislation promised the British a security "from the cradle to the grave."

But the problems of post-war Britain were not the same as those of the nineteenth century in which socialization had seemed a hopeful remedy. Britain had lost much of its overseas investment and its shipping; New York, not London, was the financial center of the world; the Empire was falling to pieces; iron-ore reserves were running out and coal had to be secured from thinner and deeper veins. In such circumstances the British problem was to create enough goods and services to sell abroad so that sufficient food and raw materials could be purchased. The socialized industries, coal for example, seemed no more productive than under private ownership. Rationing, import restrictions, and high taxes had to be used to keep consumption down, so that for some years after the war, the British continued under wartime austerity. Repeatedly, Britain had to be helped by loans and subsidies from the United States.

Amid these difficulties the British maintained their courage and their solidarity. Indeed, they accomplished much that seemed to them to be constructive. The National Insurance Act and the National Health Service Act (both of 1946), with the Family Allowance Act of 1945, raised the standard of living of the lower classes. Drastic income and inheritance taxes reduced the importance of established wealth. Subsidies kept the price of food relatively low. The Town and Country Planning Acts (1947) provided for rational procedures in rebuilding the cities and in the use of land. Agriculture was regulated and subsidized to increase productivity. Education at all levels was extended and higher education was made available to a much larger proportion of the youth. The pound was devalued to aid exports.

Slowly British productivity increased until by 1953 it was well above pre-war levels. Despite recurring crises, the balance of trade improved and less dependence on American aid was necessary. But progress was too slow and the results of the nationalization of industry were discouraging. In the elections of 1950, the Labor Party was able to retain only a minute majority in the House of Commons. The Labor Party, moreover, was divided into factions. That led by Prime Minister Attlee decided to slow the progress of socialism and to continue coöperation with the United States, while the left-wing under Aneurin Bevan espoused opposing policies. Hoping to improve his majority, Attlee called for special elections in the fall of 1951. But the results were a victory for the Conservatives who gained a slender majority of 19 in the House. Winston Churchill returned to the post of Prime Minister. Thus the famous war leader was in office when King George

VI died in February 1952 and was succeeded by his twenty-five-year-old daughter, who was crowned as Elizabeth II with traditional panoply and pomp.

The Conservatives retained all the social legislation passed by the Laborites. But they returned the iron and steel and trucking industries to private ownership, reduced food subsidies, slowly eliminated rationing, and sought to stimulate private enterprise. Prosperity increased in Britain and there was full employment, rising industrial production, and an improvement in the housing situation. It was difficult to say how much of the betterment arose from the Conservative policies and how much from world conditions. But in any case when Churchill (now a Knight of the Garter and thus Sir Winston) resigned in the spring of 1955, Sir Anthony Eden, his successor as the Conservative Prime Minister, called special elections at the end of May. Aided by the continued split in the ranks of Labor, the Conservatives tripled their majority in the House of Commons.

Despite this initial success and despite the favorable reaction of the British people to increasing prosperity and a retreat from socialism, Sir Anthony Eden was soon in trouble. In July of 1956, President Abdul Nasser of Egypt nationalized the Suez Canal and seized the assets of the Canal Company. Nasser was planning to construct a gigantic high dam on the Nile at Aswan. He had had indications of support by loans from Great Britain, the United States, and the International Bank. When those offers were withdrawn, he responded by taking over the Canal. At the same time, the continuing border troubles between Egypt and Israel grew in intensity. At the end of October, Israel invaded Egypt and was soon supported by the air and land forces of Britain and France. Both the United Nations and the United States objected so strongly that the invaders had to accept a cease-fire agreement and to withdraw their forces. A United Nations emergency force superintended the withdrawal and policed the frontier, while the Canal which had been blocked by the Egyptians was cleared under United Nations supervision.

Eden's participation in this venture had

Queen Elizabeth II.

Courtesy
British Information Services

been motivated by a sense of the importance of the Suez Canal to Britain and by the difficulties of dealing with Nasser. The adventure came to nought because the aggressive use of force to settle a dispute shocked world and American opinion and seemed too perilous in an age of atomic weapons. Though he had the approval of some elements of the Conservative Party, Eden's prestige declined so fast and so far that he was compelled to resign in January of 1957. He was succeeded by Harold Macmillan.

Under Macmillan's quiet but firm guidance, the Conservatives rather rapidly regained the support that the Suez fiasco had temporarily lost them. They were strengthened by divisions in the Labor Party on the foreign policy issues and on the question of retreating from socialism at home. They were strengthened further by the steadily increasing income of the average Briton who found himself able to buy television sets, refrigerators, and even automobiles. New elections were held in October 1959. The Conservatives won again, with a majority of some hundred members in the House of Commons. This third successive victory for one party was almost without precedent in modern times and led to renewed quarreling and questioning in the ranks of defeated Labor.

B. The Fourth and Fifth French Republics

The economic problems in post-war France were not dissimilar from those in Great Britain. But the political developments were quite different. The French elected a National Assembly in October 1945. It chose General De Gaulle as head of a provisional government and, amid growing strife among the political parties, it drafted a new constitution providing for a weak executive and an all-powerful legislature. De Gaulle protested and resigned, and a popular plebiscite, in May 1946, rejected the new constitution. A new Assembly drafted another constitution creating only a slightly stronger executive. This document, establishing the Fourth French Republic, was adopted by plebiscite in October 1946, but with little popular enthusiasm. The vote was nine and a quarter million for it, eight million against it, with eight and a half million abstaining. The new constitution replaced the former Chamber of Deputies by a National Assembly elected by universal suffrage including women, and the former Senate by a Council of the Republic, chosen by indirect election and having only advisory powers. The president was still elected as previously, for seven years, by the two houses. As in the past he could act only with the consent of the ministry, and thus the National Assembly was supreme.

In the first two assemblies and in the first legislature elected under the constitution, the three major parties were the Communist, the Socialist, and the Popular Republican Movement (M.R.P.), a liberal democratic Catholic party which included many of the former leaders of the resistance against the Germans. The Socialists, the M.R.P., and the Radical Socialists (mildly conservative democrats) united to elect a Socialist, Vincent Auriol, as the first President; he was succeeded in 1953 by René Coty. Meanwhile, in 1946, a fourth major party of conservative followers of De Gaulle emerged. It was called the *Rassemblement du Peuple Français* (R.P.F.). But it refused to participate in ministries, gradually split into factions, and lost influence.

Racked by inflation, pinched by a continuing shortage of food and raw materials, torn by dissensions left over from the war period, threatened by Communists on the left and the R.P.F. on the right, French governments had a difficult time in the post-war years. France was governed for the most part by a coalition of the Socialists, the M.R.P., and the Radical Socialists (who were slowly gaining strength). But there were differences within the coalition. The Radical Socialists disliked the social legislation and the high taxes favored by the Socialists and the M.R.P. The Socialists and Radicals opposed the M.R.P. on state aid for Catholic schools. All three feared to support deflationary legislation lest they lend strength to the Communists.

The tendency to temporize and the disputes among the ruling parties led to an instability of ministries no less notable than under the Third Republic. There were, for example, eight premiers between 1948 and 1953. Even Mendès-France, a Radical, who became premier in June 1954, and, with much popular backing, espoused a policy of liquidating French commitments in Indo-China and inaugurating needed economic reforms at home, could not retain office for even a year. Elections held in January 1956 resulted in gains for the Communists and for a new right-wing party headed by a youthful tax critic named Poujade. The National Assembly appeared much too divided to provide a stable government.

Underneath the political instability, however, improvements were taking place. The currency inflation was at length checked, though the franc was stabilized at about one-fourteenth of its pre-war value. Hydro-electric plants were built. Agricultural machinery was widely introduced. Industrial production was increased. Public health was bettered. The birthrate rose. By 1955, France was more prosperous than it had been at any time since the First World War. By 1960, the French were enjoying a standard of living unprecedented in that country. Housing projects rose in the suburbs. New broad highways were swarming with automobiles. The consumption of meat and milk was rising rapidly. Workers even had to be imported from other lands to till the fields and man the busy factories.

But despite the economic development, there was one problem so difficult, so divisive, and so acute that it led to one political crisis after another and finally to the liquidation of the Fourth Republic. This was the problem of North Africa and in particular of Algeria. In 1955 France ruled North Africa from the boundaries of Libya to the Atlantic Ocean. Tunisia and Morocco were technically protectorates, the former under a bey, the latter under a sultan. But in fact, both were dominated by France. Against the French there was growing Arab and Moslem nationalist agitation of such violence that at length the French government was compelled to yield. By a treaty of March 1956 the protectorate established in 1911 was ended and the independence of Morocco was recognized. The Sultan, Mohammed V, who had played an important role in resistance to the French, changed his title to King. At his death in 1961 he was succeeded by his son. Similarly, Tunisia became independent in 1956. But here the bey was deposed and a republic was proclaimed with Habib Bourguiba, who had been the leader of the Neo-Destour or nationalist party, as President.

Such a solution was not as practicable for Algeria. It had been invaded, "occupied," "annexed," "subdued," and "pacified" between 1830 and 1871, and its northern region had in 1947 been divided into *départements* and declared to be a part of metropolitan France, though it had also a certain degree of autonomy. Beginning in 1954, nationalist agitation in Algeria passed into a violent stage, and for the next seven years the French army was engaged in a fierce and large-scale guerrilla war against the Algerian "rebels"—a war that cost billions of dollars and thousands of lives. What complicated the problem was that more than a million of the ten million inhabitants of Algeria were European. Some French families had lived there for generations and regarded themselves as Algerian, just as did their Moslem neighbors.

The Algerian issue, moreover, divided France, with all the more conservative or reactionary elements insisting on a solution that would leave Algeria French. The army, too, at some points, seemed unwilling to support any move that might lead toward a French withdrawal from Algeria. A special crisis came in 1958, when it seemed that France was about to lapse into civil war. It was solved by the reëmergence of General De Gaulle. In May, pro-Gaullist army and civilian groups seized power in Algeria. In June De Gaulle became premier of France with the approval of the National Assembly. In September a new constitution prepared by De Gaulle was approved by an overwhelming majority of the voters, and the General himself was elected President of the Fifth Republic in December. The new constitution gave greatly increased powers to the executive branch of the government and in particular to the President. De Gaulle used them to quiet the political turmoil, to repress dissent, to order the finances, and to attempt to bring the Algerian strife to an end. In early 1961, by another overwhelming vote, the French people supported the President's Algerian policies. With this mandate, De Gaulle proceeded to negotiate with the Algerian nationalists (the F.L.N. party, or National Liberation Front) and with its "government in exile" under "premier" Ferhat Abbas. In April another threatening revolt in Algeria, led by four French generals and backed by some professional elements of the army, collapsed in a few days, and by its failure further strengthened De Gaulle.[1]

De Gaulle's constitution of 1958 provided new arrangements for the French Community—the former overseas colonies. It had been voted on in these territories as well as in France and had won approval, save in French Guinea which chose to leave the Community and became a separate republic in October 1958. The new constitution contained provisions which enabled the former African colonies to become independent nations while remaining within the French Community. By the end of 1960, twelve of them had done so and assumed a position which was technically not unlike that of the Dominions within the British Commonwealth. The twelve were the Sudanese Republic, the Republic of Senegal,

[1] See below, p. 837.

Foreign ministers Alcide de Gasperi of Italy and Robert Schuman of France, 1951.

the Republic of Dahomey, the Republic of the Niger, the Islamic Republic of Mauritania, the Republic of the Upper Volta, the Republic of the Ivory Coast, the Republic of the Congo, the Republic of Chad, the Central African Republic, the Gabon Republic, and the Malagasy (Madagascar) Republic.

C. Italy and Other Free Countries of Western Europe

Defeated Italy had many problems in common with France. Like France, for example, it had a large and disciplined Communist party eager to foment disorder and revolution and always ready to follow the dictates of Russia. In 1946 King Victor Emmanuel III, in an effort to preserve the Italian monarchy, had abdicated in favor of his son, who became King Humbert II. But a popular vote went in favor of a republic and Humbert abdicated in his turn. It seemed possible at the start that the Republic would be a Communist one, for many Italians turned to Communism, as

reaction against discredited fascism, as a quick road to economic improvement, and as a method of winning the support and friendship of victorious Russia. In the elections for the Constituent Assembly in June 1946, out of a total of 556 members the Communists under Palmiro Togliatti got 104 seats and the Socialists under Pietro Nenni, who was prepared to work with the Communists, got 115 seats. The largest party opposing them was the Christian (Catholic) Democratic Party led by Alcide de Gasperi, who succeeded in winning the support of the smaller liberal parties and some right-wing Socialists who broke with Nenni. In 1947, De Gasperi was able to form an anti-Communist coalition with a slender majority.

De Gasperi secured the reluctant ratification of the peace treaty with the Allies, the withdrawal of the Anglo-American forces of occupation, and the adoption of a new constitution (December 1947). The new government consisted of a Chamber of Deputies elected by universal suffrage, a Senate chosen partly by the people and partly by regional councils, a president elected for seven years by the parliament plus some regional representatives, and a cabinet responsible to the legislature. The ensuing elections in 1948 were critical. The United States played a role by providing for economic aid to Italy and proposing with Britain and France that the peace treaty be revised to give Trieste to Italy. In the event, De Gasperi's Christian Democrats won 306 of the 574 seats, and the Communists and Nenni Socialists only 182. As President was chosen Luigi Einaudi, a political liberal who was definitely anti-Communist. De Gasperi remained as premier till August 1953, not quite long enough to see a settlement negotiated in October 1954 by which the city of Trieste was turned over to Italy though most of the surrounding territory went to Yugoslavia. He was succeeded by other Christian Democrats, the first of whom was Giuseppe Pella at the head of an all-Christian-Democratic cabinet, and the second, Mario Scelba with a coalition cabinet. The elections of 1953 had given the Christian Democrats 261 members out of 590, while the Communists got 143 and the Nenni Socialists secured 75. In the elections of 1958, the democratic parties of the center increased their margin in the Chamber, and the Christian Democrats continued to provide the premiers. The President elected in 1955, Giovanni Gronchi, belonged to the same party.

Italy in the post-war period faced not only problems produced by the war—rebuilding factories and housing, paying reparations, fighting off the threat of internal Communism—but also others of longer standing—overpopulation, scanty resources, large estates inefficiently farmed. Every cabinet promised land reform, but progress was slow. Industrial development, sparked by aid in goods, money, and technical skills from the United States, did slowly cut down unemployment. Italian manufactured goods —textiles, shoes, typewriters, motor scooters, small automobiles—began to compete in the world markets. In 1959, for example, Italy exported more than two hundred thousand automobiles. But most of the industrial activity was in the north and the contrast between that prosperous region and the area south of Rome, where unemploy-

ment continued at a high level, became more and more painful. In the cultural field, Italy did score post-war triumphs. Italian movies were exported in large numbers, Italian novels were translated into many languages, Italian clothing styles for women began to compete with those of Paris.

The smaller democratic countries of western Europe confronted many of the same problems as the larger ones, and like them responded in a variety of ways. The Low Countries had been overrun by the Germans and fought over in the later stages of the war. Belgium rapidly stabilized its currency, checked inflation, and, supported by the prosperity of the Belgian Congo, rich in uranium and copper, made a rapid recovery. It was governed after the war by the Christian Social (Catholic) and Socialist parties. But these fell into a dispute over King Leopold III who had surrendered, perhaps precipitately, to the Germans in 1940. A crisis was averted when the King, in July 1951, abdicated in favor of his son Baudouin. But a new one threatened at the end of 1960, when, shaken by the loss of the Congo and by internal disputes between the Christian Social party and the Socialists and between the French-speaking and the Flemish-speaking citizens, the country was paralyzed by a series of prolonged strikes.

In Holland, recovery was slower, for the loss of the Dutch empire in Indonesia required painful adjustments. The government was conducted by the Catholic and Labor parties. In the 1959 elections to the Second Chamber of the States-General the Catholic party secured 49 members, the Labor party 47, and all other groups a total of only 53. In 1948 the revered Dutch Queen Wilhelmina abdicated for reasons of health and age and was replaced by her daughter, Juliana. Economic conditions in the Low Countries were improved somewhat by economic coöperation among them, particularly by the Benelux Customs Convention among Belgium, the Netherlands, and Luxembourg (effective 1948), which reduced the tariff barriers they had raised against each other.

Other small countries that had been involved in the war included Finland, Denmark, and Norway. Despite its defeat by

Football. A modernist painting by André Lhote.

Russia, its proximity to that country, and the territorial concessions that had been wrung from it, Finland steadfastly clung to its independence and to a democratic form of government. Ruled by a coalition of Socialists, Agrarians, and Liberals under a Socialist president, Juho Paasikivi (elected 1945 and again in 1950), the Finnish people by heroic efforts paid their reparations to Russia and strove to keep the peace with their mighty neighbor. This they did with such success that in 1956 the ten-year treaty of assistance and friendship signed in 1948 was extended to 1975. At the same time, the Soviet Union returned to Finland the Porkkala area which it had obtained in 1944.

In agricultural Denmark, post-war recovery was fairly rapid, but the country emerged from occupation by the Germans shorn of its most important overseas dominion, for Iceland in 1944 had voted to become an independent republic. Denmark was governed after the war by a succession of coalition cabinets under Social Democrat, Liberal, and Liberal-Conservative leaders. A modernized constitution adopted in 1953 changed the national legislature to a one chamber instead of a two-chamber body and made Greenland, which had been a colony, into a full-fledged member of the Danish Commonwealth with elected representatives in the parliament. In Norway, the Labor party secured a majority in the first post-war election and conducted the government in the ensuing years. When the King, Haakon VII, died in 1957 at the age of eighty-five, he was succeeded by his son Olav V. In both Denmark and Norway, Communists were unable to muster more than a small fraction of the voters. But in Finland they elected a substantial minority of the deputies in the Diet. The elections of 1958, for example, returned fifty Communists out of a total of two hundred.

The five countries of western Europe which had remained neutral during the war —Sweden, Switzerland, Eire (Ireland), Portugal, and Spain—were confronted after 1945 by problems rather different from those faced by the nations which had been involved in the conflict. They had no devastation to make good. But they did have to adjust to a situation in which they could no longer make high profits by exports to the warring countries. Sweden, troubled as to how to conduct its diplomacy as between Russia and the Western democracies, was governed by Social Democratic cabinets and continued to develop its democratically planned economy and welfare state. Switzerland maintained its traditional federal democracy and sought to build up its peacetime exports of clocks and watches, machinery, textiles, chemicals, and drugs. Eire secured its complete and final independence from Britain in 1948. De Valera, leader of the nationalistic Fianna Fail party, alternated with John A. Costello of the more moderate Fine Gael party as premier in the post-war years. In 1959 de Valera became President after a hard-fought election.

The Iberian neutrals, Spain and Portugal, can hardly be counted among the democratic countries, for they both retained their pre-war dictatorial regimes. The Spanish government of General Franco was long treated by the Western democracies as an outcast both because of its alleged fascist nature and because of its alleged wartime sympathy with Hitler. But the Spanish people, eager to prevent a renewal of civil war, acquiesced in the Franco regime. In 1947 a "succession law" was endorsed by popular vote. It provided that in case of the death or incapacity of the Chief of State a regency council would propose a king or regent who must be accepted by two thirds of the Cortes (or parliament, established in 1942). By 1956 negotiations between Franco and the royalist pretender to the throne had progressed far enough to make it seem likely that the Spanish monarchy would eventually be restored. By then, moreover, Spain was being wooed and supported by the United States in its efforts to build an anti-Russian coalition. And though Spain had been specifically and ostentatiously barred from membership in the United Nations in 1945 by the Western democracies as well as by the Communist Soviet Union, it was admitted without serious opposition ten years later. Funds from the United States for air bases and other military installations were, by 1961, having a significant effect on the Spanish economy. In industry, transportation, and the general standard of living definite improvement was apparent.

In Portugal, Marshal Carmona, who had seized power in 1926, was able, through his control of elections, to retain the presidency for a quarter of a century. But power was actually in the hands of his prime minister, Dr. Antonio de Oliveira Salazar, and no change in this situation was effected by the election of General Francisco Lopes as president in 1951, or that of Admiral Americo Rodrigues Tomaz in 1958. Internally, Dr. Salazar maintained his authority by his watchful police and his control of the army, though by 1962 several incidents had made it clear that there was still a liberal opposition dissatisfied with Portugal's regime. Externally, Salazar coöperated with the Western democracies, but he and his people resented Western sympathy with native unrest in the African colony of Angola and the United Nations' failure to prevent, or to condemn India's forceful seizure of Goa and other coastal enclaves which Portugal had held since the fifteenth century.

Fidel Castro explaining his plans for redistribution of the land to a group of farmers, 1959.

CHAPTER 62

Defense of the Free World

A. American Leadership and the Cold War

In 1945–1946, the United States and the other Western democracies were, on the whole, trustful of Russian intentions and promises, and hopeful that the great powers could work together in coöperation to make "one world" free from aggression and fear. Stalin and his foreign minister, Molotov, said that Russia was "democratic" and "peace-loving." They endorsed the Atlantic Charter and the United Nations. They pledged the Soviet Union to respect the right of liberated peoples to have free elections and to set up and maintain governments of their own choosing. It seemed reasonable to expect that the Western powers could work with Russia on friendly terms. Of course occasional concessions might have to be made on both sides. But not to make concessions might lead to friction, hostility, and even armed conflict. The prospect of a Third World War, with atomic weapons, was too terrifying to contemplate.

For a brief time such optimism seemed justified. It was a bit shaken as early as the autumn of 1945 by a Russian attempt to take over the important oil-producing province of Azerbaijan in northern Iran. But in this instance, the Soviet Union yielded to pressure from the United Nations. The troops were withdrawn and optimism reigned again.

Not for long, however. By the end of 1946, it was becoming quite obvious that the Soviet dictatorship attached quite different meanings to "democracy," "free elections," and "self-determination" from those usual in the United States or Western Europe. It became clear, too, that, instead of adhering to its earlier promises and honestly coöperating with the Western democracies for the realization of a free world, Russia was aggressively seeking to transform as much of the world as possible into a Communist empire dependent on Moscow. It was retaining its war-time armies. It was paralyzing the United Nations by the frequent use of its veto in the Security Council. It was fostering subversive Communist movements in other lands, especially France and Italy. It was, as we have seen, imposing puppet Communist governments on one country after another in eastern Europe. It was directing a continuous and abusive propaganda campaign against the Western nations, and particularly against the United States. These were denounced as war-mongering, capitalistic countries, seeking to obtain more markets so as to bolster up a decaying economic system and hence bent on encircling and throttling the "homeland of socialism," the Soviet Union. If Russia did join, after much haggling and delay, in making peace treaties in 1947 with Italy, Hungary, Bulgaria, Rumania, and Finland, it became evident that it would agree to no reasonable settlement of peace terms with Germany.

With Austria the situation was somewhat different. For ten long years Austria had been subjected to a four-power (British, French, American, and Russian) occupation, with joint control of Vienna by the four. The Austrians had nonetheless been able to organize a democratic republic governing the whole country and to arrange for fairly free trade and travel among the several zones. The new Austrian government had been organized by a respected socialist statesman, Dr. Karl Renner, who became its first President. It had been governed in the succeeding years by a cabinet representing a coalition of the Popular (Catholic) and the Socialist parties. In three elections (1945, 1949, 1953) the Communist party had not been able to elect more than four or five deputies out of a total of 165. Starting with United Nations' help in 1946, Austria had received much foreign aid in food and goods, and by 1955 had achieved a modest level of prosperity. The Western powers were eager to end the occupation, but in scores of meetings, held off and on through the post-war years, the Soviet representatives always interposed some frustrating obstacle that made the negotiations abortive and fruitless. Russia seemed to resent the failure of Communism to attract support from the Austrian people. It appeared anxious to maintain troops in Austria so as to have a good excuse for keeping other military detachments in Hungary and Rumania as lines of communication from Russia to Austria. It insisted on retaining control of Austrian industries and oil wells which it had seized in 1945 as belonging to Nazi Germany. Great, therefore, was the surprise in the West when, at further meetings in the spring of 1955, the Russians showed themselves conciliatory on the points they had so long, so stubbornly, and so unreasonably upheld. Greater even was the astonishment, when in May a treaty was actually signed between the four powers and Austria with provision for ending the occupation and neutralizing the country.

But if, at long last, the Soviet Union showed itself willing to reach an agreement on Austria, still in other directions it continued to evince unyielding hostility to the Western powers. Opinion in the Western countries was most affected by the man-

ner in which Czechoslovakia was taken over by the Communists. By then (1948) it was clear that the Soviet Union was implacably hostile to the democracies and was in fact engaged in what came to be termed a "cold war" (as opposed to a "hot" or shooting war) against them. Eastern Communist Europe was cut off from the West by what Winston Churchill called an "iron curtain," for the Russians, with the utmost severity, restricted travel, trade, and communication in the lands they controlled. Historic ties were broken. The continent of Europe stood divided into two parts, the one free, the other subject to the dictates of Communist Moscow.

The first significant American countermove came in 1947. Russia had recently denounced its non-aggression treaty with Turkey and was demanding from that country territorial concessions and a share in the control of the straits leading from the Black Sea into the Mediterranean. At the same time it was inciting Yugoslavia (still under Moscow's influence), Albania, and Bulgaria to give military assistance to a Communist insurrection in Greece. Great Britain had helped to free Greece from the Germans in 1944 and to reëstablish order there, but it now lacked the resources to protect Greece or Turkey from Communist aggression by Russia and its Balkan satellites. Into the breach, with British approval, stepped the United States. In March 1947, President Truman asked the American Congress for funds for troops and supplies to oppose Communism in Greece and Turkey. In May, the so-called "Truman Doctrine" (that the United States would use its economic strength to arrest the advance of Communism) was endorsed and an initial appropriation of 400 million dollars was made.

In the event, American aid was sufficient to turn the tide in both cases. It enabled Greece to suppress the internal Communist menace and the guerrillas operating in the border areas, to improve economic conditions, and to maintain an orderly democratic government. It so strengthened Turkey that Russia halted its aggressive pressures.

A second step was taken by the United States in June 1948, when Truman's Secre-

General George C. Marshall, Chief of Staff of the U.S. Army during World War II, and after it both Secretary of State and Secretary of Defense.

Courtesy Wide World Photos

tary of State, General George C. Marshall, proposed a plan for giving American aid to other European countries. Russia was invited to participate, but it denounced and rejected the "Marshall Plan" and prevented all satellites (plus Finland) from accepting American help. The plan was accepted by France, Great Britain, and fourteen other European nations. And it was implemented in the United States by the Foreign Assistance Act of 1948 under which was set up an Economic Coöperation Administration (ECA), headed by Paul Hoffman, to administer the European Recovery Program (ERP). Before the emphasis turned to military aid and ECA was replaced by the Mutual Security Agency (MSA) at the end of 1951, it spent twelve and a half billion dollars, and the money and goods which it provided were of incalculable value in rebuilding a prosperous West Europe and greatly lessening the want and misery on which Communism thrives. Nor was American aid confined to Europe. Over the years

much went to Asiatic countries such as Pakistan and Nationalist China, and under President Truman's "Point Four Program" (announced in 1949) technical assistance and financial help were extended to underdeveloped areas. In 1953, MSA and the Point Four Program were consolidated into the Foreign Operations Administration (FOA).

In April 1949, moreover, the United States entered into a twenty-year defensive alliance with a number of Western nations —Canada, Great Britain, France, Italy, Norway, Iceland, Denmark, Netherlands, Belgium, Luxembourg, and Portugal. The pact established a "North Atlantic Treaty Organization" (NATO), with an executive committee of foreign ministers, a defense council of war ministers, and a military committee of chiefs of staff. To the European members of NATO, the United States, in October 1949, granted an initial subsidy of a billion dollars to help them rearm. Supervision of the planning and coördination of the defense efforts was entrusted to the American General Dwight Eisenhower.

Greece and Turkey were later admitted to NATO, and the United States by special agreement with Spain secured air and naval bases in that country to supplement the defense of western Europe and the Mediterranean. When General Eisenhower returned home in 1952 to be elected President in succession to Harry Truman, supreme command of the NATO military forces was turned over to another American, General Matthew Ridgway.

As a supplement to NATO a Council of Europe was also organized in 1949. It represented an expansion of the alliance which had been created at Brussels the previous year by France, Great Britain, and the Benelux countries. It did not include Canada, the United States, or Portugal, but it did eventually include, in addition to the other NATO countries, Eire, Sweden, and West Germany.

Thus free Europe drew together to defend itself against Soviet pressure and the threat of Russian expansion. But the military situation was changed dramatically in September 1949, when President Truman announced that an atomic explosion, presumably that of an atom bomb, had taken place in Russia. Up to this point it had been possible to believe that Russia would be restrained in its use of force by fear of the atomic bomb stockpile in the hands of the United States. Now it became easy to envision a day when Russia, equipped with a number of the new bombs, might use them suddenly in a surprise attack, or a situation in which neither side would use such weapons for fear of retaliation. Moreover, it soon became clear that the atom bomb, producing its effects by atomic fission, had been much surpassed in power by a hydrogen fusion bomb, and there were rumors of even more deadly missiles—a cobalt bomb and an uranium fission-fusion bomb. In addition, it was no longer necessary to deliver bombs by means of airplanes, for both Russia and the United States were developing rockets capable of journeys into space with bombs as warheads. That the Russians were technically very competent in this field was demonstrated dramatically, on October 4, 1957, when they launched an artificial satellite called "Sputnik I" which circled the earth every ninety minutes for three months. The United States sent its first satellite (Explorer I) into orbit in January 1958, and in the next two years more than thirty man-made satellites were successfully launched by the two powers.

The change in the military picture led the United States to propose as early as 1950 that West Germany be rearmed, and that a German army be included in the plans for defense of the West. France, always fearful of a militarized Germany, countered by suggesting that a European army be established with only small German units scattered through it. Thereby the creation of powerful military forces under German command could be avoided. In 1952 this proposal was made part of a treaty setting up a European Defense Community (EDC), but ratification of the treaty proved difficult and France eventually rejected its own plan. Then Sir Anthony Eden, British Foreign Minister, in a surprising reversal of traditional policy, offered to keep British troops on the continent indefinitely if Western Europe could reach an understanding on an appropriate defense system which would include Germany. Finally, agreements were signed at

Paris in 1954, by which West Germany was recognized as a sovereign state, given the right to have armed forces, and admitted to NATO. The Brussels treaties of 1948 were to be expanded into a defensive alliance to be called the Western European Union with Italy as well as West Germany included. Agreement to these proposals was secured from the countries concerned during 1955. Arrangements were made to end the occupation (save in divided Berlin) by France, Britain, and the United States, though it was understood that their troops would remain there as part of the European defense system. In 1955, West Germany set about recreating an army. Conscription was introduced in 1957, and the number of soldiers was raised so that by 1961 the army had some 170,000 men in it.

All was not completely harmonious within NATO, however. After De Gaulle came to power, he pressed for a larger role for France and for less complete integration of the NATO forces in Europe. He reënforced his position by pushing forward French development of atomic devices to such a point that France was able to detonate an atomic bomb in the Sahara desert early in 1960. Shortly afterwards an agreement was reached that Great Britain, France, and the United States would each contribute a battalion to a task force that would have atomic as well as conventional weapons. Britain had already set off several atomic bombs and a hydrogen bomb as well (in 1957).

B. Divided Germany

From the very close of the war the problem of Germany intensified the tension between the Soviet Union and the Western powers. At first, the problem concerned matters of military occupation. The division into zones was awkward enough with the British occupying the northwest, the French the west and southwest, the Americans the center and south, and the Russians the northeast. But even more awkward was the fact that Berlin, under the joint control of the occupying nations, lay deep in the Russian zone, though access to it for the other powers was pledged by Russia.

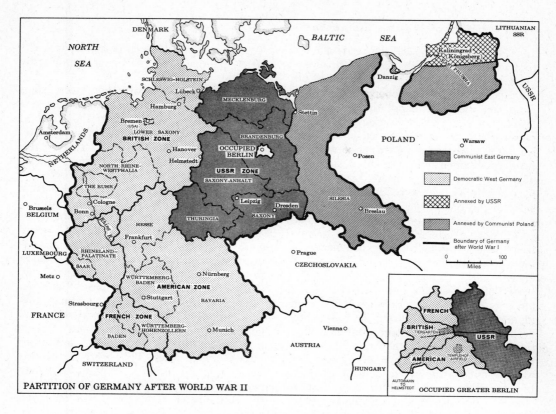

PARTITION OF GERMANY AFTER WORLD WAR II

Map legend:
- Communist East Germany
- Democratic West Germany
- Annexed by USSR
- Annexed by Communist Poland
- Boundary of Germany after World War I
- 0 — 100 Miles

OCCUPIED GREATER BERLIN

The city of Berlin was divided into two zones, the western under French-British-American control, the eastern under Russian.

At the start, the four powers coöperated in trying "war criminals" and "de-Nazifying" Germany. The Russians took all the machinery they could lay their hands on as reparations, but the Western Allies seemed not unwilling to have Germany kept weak. They agreed in 1946 on the abolition of the historic state of Prussia and the division of Germany into seventeen states—five in the eastern Russian Zone, the others in the west. The Russians in their zone set about creating a Communist regime subservient to Moscow, and the Americans busied themselves trying to democratize theirs and to break up the great industrial cartels into competing units.

But as the tone changed from one of hesitant coöperation to one of "cold war," policy toward Germany changed also. The Western powers began to see in Germany a possible counterweight to Soviet influence in central Europe. Gradually it became their policy to work for a strong and stable Germany. Inflation was checked and the currency stabilized. Relief materials and "Marshall Plan" credits were poured into the country. And the Germans responded. A decade after the close of the war West Germany was the most prosperous and productive country in western Europe. With factories rebuilt, its industrial output was far above that of pre-war years, and its exports were rising. It had even been able to absorb into useful employment a large number of the millions of German refugees who had fled from East Germany, the Baltic countries, the Sudetenland, and the German areas seized by Communist Russia and Poland.

Meanwhile, West Germany was achieving a very considerable degree of political stability. The occupying powers sponsored democratic constitutions and elections in the several states and in 1948 a democratic election for an Assembly that met at Bonn and drew up a federal republican constitution. Under this constitution, a Federal Diet was elected in 1949, consisting of 139 Christian Democrats, 131 Social Democrats, 52 Liberals, and 80 others including

14 Communists. A coalition cabinet was formed with the sturdy, seventy-three-year-old Christian Democratic leader, Dr. Konrad Adenauer, as Chancellor. In East Germany, on the other hand, the Russians allowed no free elections. They sponsored, rather, the creation of a Social Unity Party led by a Communist, Otto Grotewohl. A People's Council was appointed in 1948. The next year it was converted into a People's Chamber which promulgated a constitution of the Soviet type for the "German Democratic Republic" in the Russian zone. East Germany, which had always been largely agricultural, experienced no such economic recovery as did West Germany.

As West Germany grew stronger and more prosperous, the Russians cut it off more and more strictly from East Germany by commercial barriers and frontier restrictions. In March 1948 they virtually ended the period of coöperative occupation by walking out of the Allied Control Council. In June, they tried to drive the Western officials from Berlin and to end the joint control by shutting off all access to it from the west by highway, railroad, or water. The Western Allies, unwilling to use force, found an answer in the "airlift." For a year, American and British planes flew in all the food, fuel, and raw materials needed by West Berlin. Checkmated and realizing the propaganda value of the airlift for the Western democracies, since it was a peaceful yet dazzling display of logistical skill and of air power, the Russians eventually gave in and in 1949 again opened the roads to Berlin.

The policy of the West German government at Bonn was coöperation with the Western powers. These, more and more eager for a strong West German ally and convinced that Russia would not agree to a peace treaty, proclaimed in 1951 an end to the state of war with Germany. The growing coöperation between the Federal Republic of Germany and the Western nations was marked by a rapprochement even with France. One of the difficult problems was that of the Saar which after the war had been made semi-autonomous but united economically with France. But by an agreement reached in 1956 between France and West Germany the Saar was joined to the latter, politically in 1957 and economically in 1960.

In the post-war years there were signs that all was not well in East Germany. As the country was subjected to the standard apparatus of a Communist police state, with control in the hands of a single party (the Socialist Unity Party) and "order" maintained by a ministry of state security, a militarized "People's Police," and a large army provided with Soviet equipment, the contrast with the freedom and prosperity of West Germany became more and more glaring. There was a steady stream of refugees, numbering sometimes more than a thousand a day, who left the Russian zone to find haven in West Germany. Finally in June of 1953, when the East German government sought to increase production by decree, without increasing wages, violent riots broke out in East Berlin and other East German cities. They were suppressed but only by the use of force and in a bloody fashion. During the ensuing years, though the complicated status of Berlin remained a source both of friction and of diplomatic interchange between Russia and the Western powers, no solution satisfactory to both sides was evolved.

C. The Korean War

The most acute episode of the post-war conflict in Asia between the Communist bloc and the free world arose from the conflict over Korea which for more than three years turned the cold war into a hot one. As we have seen above,[1] on June 25, 1950, armies of Communist North Korea swept over the thirty-eighth parallel in a massive thrust into South Korea. On the morrow of the invasion, President Truman took the courageous decision of ordering armed American resistance to the aggression. Troops, planes, munitions were hurried to Korea from General MacArthur's command in Japan and were gradually added to directly from the United States. The Congress later approved the President's decision, and in July voted large increases in the armed forces of the United States.

[1] See p. 797.

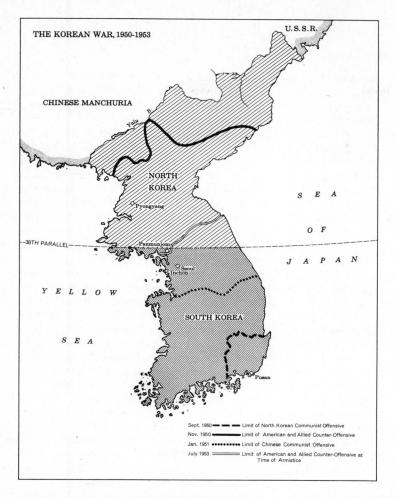

THE KOREAN WAR, 1950-1953

U.S.S.R.

CHINESE MANCHURIA

Yalu R.

NORTH KOREA

Pyongyang

SEA

OF

-38TH PARALLEL-

Panmunjom

JAPAN

Seoul
Inchon

YELLOW

SEA

SOUTH KOREA

Pusan

Sept. 1950 ▬ ▬ ▬ Limit of North Korean Communist Offensive
Nov. 1950 ▬▬▬ Limit of American and Allied Counter-Offensive
Jan. 1951 ●●●●●●● Limit of Chinese Communist Offensive
July 1953 ═══════ Limit of American and Allied Counter-Offensive at
Time of Armistice

Truman also immediately laid the problem of the Korean invasion before the Security Council of the United Nations. Through the fortuitous circumstance that the Russian delegate had walked out (in protest against the refusal to admit Communist China), there was no Soviet representative to exercise the veto. On June 27, therefore, the Security Council, with Russia absent and Yugoslavia abstaining, declared that North Korea had broken the peace, directed it to withdraw its troops from South Korea, and urged all United Nations members to help South Korea to repel the invasion. Collective action by United Nations' forces was authorized, with General MacArthur in command. In the event, sixteen members sent military forces (though most of them were merely of token size), and thirty-seven others contributed supplies, medical equipment, or the like. The brunt of the war was borne by the United States and South Korea.

During the summer of 1950, the North Korean invaders made steady progress southward. By early September they had pushed the South Korean and American forces into the southeastern corner of the country. But by this time, American reinforcements were arriving in sufficient number to turn the tide. General MacArthur launched a counter-offensive with surprise landings at Inchon, a hundred miles behind the fighting front. It recaptured Seoul, and at the end of September, in conjunction with the South Koreans, it drove the invaders back of the thirty-eighth parallel. The allies continued to advance through North Korea, and on November 21 they reached the Manchurian frontier. It seemed as if the Korean War was about to end with the complete and decisive defeat of Communist aggression.

The Communists of North Korea were indeed routed. But already Chinese Communist armies, with Russian equipment, had been massing behind the Manchurian border for a new and fiercer offensive. On November 26, a quarter of a million men, plentifully supplied with planes and tanks, crossed the frontier and threw back the American, South Korean, and United Nations forces with heavy losses. On they pressed, conquering all North Korea, capturing Seoul again and carrying the war even further southward.

The Korean War, and especially this second phase of it, had peculiar international aspects. There was no doubt that the Soviet Union inspired the aggression and supplied the weapons for it. Nor was there any doubt that the Chinese government of Mao Tse-tung was fighting the United Nations in Korea. Yet there was no declaration of war on either side and little disposition to call Russia to account. There was widespread fear that otherwise the conflict could not be "localized" in Korea and would bring on another world war. The British and other governments of western Europe were especially fearful lest American aid and interest be diverted from them to the Far East; and, besides, the Indian and other Asian governments showed an embarrassing tenderness toward both Communist China and Communist Russia. No government which had previously recognized Mao's regime in China broke off diplomatic relations with it even when its armies were fighting the United Nations forces in Korea. Some even supported the Russian contention that Communist China should supplant the Nationalist Chinese government as a member of the United Nations and of the Security Council.

All this influenced and handicapped the United States government in its conduct of the Korean War. General MacArthur was kept on the defensive and was strictly debarred from bombing Chinese bases and supply lines in Manchuria and from using the Chinese Nationalist army on Formosa. When he complained publicly about these and other restrictions, President Truman replaced him by General Matthew Ridgway.

Meanwhile, American reinforcements continued to pour in, and eventually the Chinese invasion into South Korea was halted and turned back. Once more Seoul was recaptured by the United Nations forces. By autumn of 1951 the contending armies were facing each other along a battle-scarred and bloodily contested line across Korea close to the thirty-eighth parallel, but north of it in the east and south of it in the west. In September, in an effort to halt the carnage and with the sanction of the United Nations, the United States opened truce negotiations with the army commanders of Communist China and North Korea. These, intent upon gaining time, strengthening their forces, and improving the positions they held, greatly prolonged the negotiations. As the discussions dragged on, sporadic fighting continued, and it was not until July 27, 1953, that an armistice was signed at Panmunjom.

One of the difficult questions in negotiating the armistice had been the problem of the repatriation of prisoners of war. The Communists wanted the Chinese and North Korean prisoners turned over to them, but it was clear that many of them did not want to return to their Communist-ruled countries. The United States, therefore, insisted that each prisoner be allowed to choose whether to go home or not. In the end, a United Nations repatriation commission supervised the whole matter. The Communists were shocked and the world surprised to learn that more than 21,000 Chinese and North Koreans refused to be repatriated. The armistice left the line between North and South Korea in approximately the position attained by military force.

Once hostilities were ended the United States set to work immediately to assist in the economic rehabilitation of South Korea. But the task in that war-torn country was a formidable one. An attempt to turn the armistice into a more permanent peace at a nineteen-nation conference (which included Communist China), in Geneva in 1954, broke down when the Communists refused to accept the idea of genuinely free elections throughout Korea and argued that the United Nations as an "aggressor" should be debarred from further activity there. There was much left to be settled in regard to Korea, despite the war which had lasted more than three years and cost the United States a third as many casualties as World War II.

Bolstered by American economic and military aid, South Korea made some progress under its aging President, Dr. Syngman Rhee, who had been elected in 1948 and re-elected in 1952, 1956, and 1960. But since corruption was rampant and inefficiency widespread, much of the American assistance was frittered away. The government more and more employed police methods to suppress opposition and rigged elections to stay in power. Finally in April 1960, student demonstrations and growing protest drove the President from power in a relatively peaceful revolution. The constitution was amended to place power in the hands of the cabinet rather than the president, and Dr. John M. Chang became premier. The new government attempted to rule in a more democratic fashion, but it was faced with the continuing and difficult problems of poverty and lack of education. In May 1961, a military junta, headed by General Song Yo-Chan, overthrew the government and at beginning of 1962 condemned Chang to death. The avowed objectives of the new regime were to oppose Communism and to end corruption. Its premier was General Song Yo-Chan.

D. Democratic Japan

The Korean War, and the loss of China to Communism which had preceded it, worked a dramatic change in the American attitude and policy toward Japan. After the close of World War II, the United States had been chiefly concerned with eliminating Japan as a threat to the peace of Asia and of the Pacific. The American occupation under General Douglas MacArthur had tried "war criminals," purged the government, education, and business of right-wing nationalists and militarists, reformed the land system to encourage small peasant landholdings, broken up the big business combines, outlawed the nationalist Shinto religion and the emperor-worship connected with it, and arranged for the writing, acceptance, and promulga-

tion of a new democratic constitution. So thorough was the purge of rightist elements in schools, universities, labor unions, and agricultural coöperatives, that many of these were left in the hands of Socialists. The constitution (effective in 1947) retained the emperor, but with no more power than the British sovereign. By the constitution, Japan renounced war and the use of force in international affairs, and the maintenance of armed forces was prohibited. Meanwhile, the United States supported the Japanese people by importation of food and raw materials, and sought to improve public health and economic conditions.

After 1949 American policy toward Japan underwent a drastic change. Japan began to seem like a bulwark against the advance of Communism in Asia. In 1950, the United States approved the creation of a national "police" force that much resembled an army, and pressed for the creation of armed forces (despite the constitutional prohibition) until in 1954 legislation was enacted providing for military, naval, and air "defensive" forces.

Though the occupation of Japan was under American auspices, it was supervised by an Allied Council for Japan in Tokyo and a Far Eastern Commission (composed of representatives of the United States, Australia, Canada, Nationalist China, France, Great Britain, India, the Netherlands, New Zealand, the Philippines, and Russia) meeting in Washington. Lack of agreement within the Commission long prevented the preparation of a peace treaty. But in 1950, despite Russian objections, President Truman decided to go forward with this task and appointed a mission under John Foster Dulles (later Secretary of State under President Dwight Eisenhower) to negotiate a treaty with Japan and the other interested powers.

The treaty was eventually signed in September 1951 at a conference in San Francisco by Japan and almost fifty other countries. Russia refused to sign and India to attend. China was not party to the proceedings because there was disagreement among the Allies as to which of its governments—Nationalist on Formosa or Communist on the mainland—was the legal and therefore recognizable government. By the treaty the state of war with Japan was ended and its full sovereignty reëstablished. Its losses of territory were confirmed: the Kurile Islands and the southern half of Sakhalin went to Russia; the Pacific islands "mandated" to Japan after World War I were entrusted to the United States; Formosa was assigned to Nationalist China; and Korea was to be independent. Reparations in goods and services were to be arranged for by Japan with its former enemies. At the same time the United States concluded a mutual assistance pact with Japan, by which the latter's independence and territorial integrity were guaranteed, but the United States was allowed to retain military and naval bases in Japan and to continue its occupation of Okinawa and the other Ryukyu Islands. A similar pact was made by the United States with the Philippines, and the United States resumed its support of Chiang Kai-shek and his nationalists on Formosa. At the end of 1956 Japan was admitted to the United Nations.

In the years after the end of the American occupation, Japan entered upon a period of tremendous economic growth and prosperity. In part, this development arose from the continuing flow of American funds for the bases on Japanese territory. In part, it came from the fact that Japanese debts had been liquidated by inflation and that the cost of maintaining military forces had been greatly reduced. But it was also due to the energy and skill of the Japanese people, to the fact that machinery and other equipment destroyed in the war were replaced by the most modern facilities for production, and to improvements in the quality of Japanese goods (textiles, toys, electronic devices, automobiles, optical instruments, cameras, etc.) which found them an increasing market in the United States, Europe, and Asia. There was, indeed, almost a vogue for things Japanese in America. The occupation troops had come to like the Japanese, whose stylized good manners and way of life in their homeland made a most favorable contrast to their ruthlessness in war abroad. In any case, many Americans became enthusiastic about Japanese architecture, prints, gardens, and flower arrangement.

The enthusiasm was not wholly reciprocated in Japan. If the Japanese became more and more westernized and welcomed such American innovations as television and electrical kitchen equipment, still, on the other hand, there was a considerable growth of anti-American sentiment, not unnatural after military defeat and occupation by the victors. Most of the students were, moreover, so imbued with Marxist thought that in the teeth of the contrary facts they thought of the United States as "imperialist" because it was "capitalist" and Russia as not "imperialist" because it called itself "socialist." There was even some feeling that Japan should draw closer economically to Communist China.

The post-war cabinets in Japan were in the hands of the conservative party (Liberal-Democrats) supported by the business elements in the cities and the peasant-farmers of the countryside. The opposition was largely composed of Socialists of varying hues, though there was some Communist leadership among students, teachers, and labor unions. Under such premiers as Yoshida, the government was cautiously coöperative with the United States. Anti-American feeling became a major political factor, when in the face of rising and vocal opposition the premier, Nobusuke Kishi, forced through, in early 1960, the ratification of a new mutual security treaty with the United States. It reduced the role and influence of America in Japan, but not enough to satisfy its critics. Matters came to a head when riots by students and others forced the cancellation of a proposed goodwill visit of President Eisenhower to Japan in 1960. As a result, Kishi was compelled to resign. But the ensuing elections in November confirmed the continuing control of the conservative Liberal-Democrats under a new premier, Hayato Ikeda.

E. From Stalin to Khrushchev

An event in 1953 seemed briefly to give promise of altering the character of the cold war and of changing conditions in the

Soviet Premier Nikita Khrushchev speaking in Leipzig, 1959.

Courtesy
Wide World Photos

Soviet Union and in the neighboring countries that it dominated. That event was the death of Stalin from a brain hemorrhage on March 5. Stalin had been all-powerful in the Soviet Union before World War II, but after it he had the added prestige of military victory and of imperial success— the annexation of some 260,000 square miles of territory with more than twenty million inhabitants, the creation of a ring of satellite states in the west, and the triumph of Communism in China and North Korea. Russian propaganda and folklore made Stalin into such a superman that sometimes it seemed as if he were being confused with God.

During eight years following World War II, there is little doubt that Stalin dictated the policy of Russia both internal and external. He was responsible for both its successes (the creation of the satellites) and its mistakes (miscalculations in respect to Yugoslavia and to the American reaction to the invasion of South Korea). He was responsible for the cold war and for Russia's strategy in it. It was Stalin, too, who decided to keep up Russia's military strength, maintaining a big army, enlarging the navy (especially as to submarines) and the air force, pushing forward atomic weapon research, and emphasizing heavy industry (for war material) as against light

industry (for consumer goods). As always in a dictatorship, where censorship reigns, there were inexplicable events. Writers, composers, and scientists gained favor, or lost it, at the whim of the Dictator, for failing to understand or to follow the party line as he drew it. There was a definite trend toward anti-semitism in government circles, despite the Soviet preachments about racial equality. There seemed to be at least a temporary relaxation of government drive against religion; some Orthodox churches, monasteries, and seminaries were reopened and a few shrines were restored. Most curious of all was the arrest in January 1953 of nine physicians high in official circles who were charged with plotting the death of important officials. (The doctors were released in April 1953, shortly after Stalin's death, with the explanation that the charges were mistaken.)

There was clearly some confusion in the Kremlin when Stalin died. But it was shortly announced that he would be succeeded by a five-man group, consisting of Georgi M. Malenkov as premier, and four deputy premiers—Vyacheslav Molotov as foreign minister, Marshal Nikolai Bulganin as defense minister, Laurenti Beria as minister of internal affairs and head of the secret police, and Lazar Kaganovich in charge of economic affairs. That there was a continuing, if hidden, struggle for power became evident in July when Beria was arrested, and he and his followers "purged." His fall was accompanied by the rise of Nikita Khrushchev, secretary of the Communist Party (the position through which Stalin had attained power). There was, at the same time, a significant increase in the importance of military men, indicating perhaps that the new government felt the need of special support from the army. In any case, Marshal Voroshilov was soon made president of the Presidium of the Supreme Soviet, a post much like that of president in other European republics. Malenkov was demoted from the premiership in February 1955 and replaced by Marshal Bulganin, and Marshal Georgi Zhukov took charge of the military.

At the Soviet Party Congress in Moscow in 1956, in a long, detailed, and surprising speech, Khrushchev denounced Stalin and his regime. Stalin, he said, had used cruel and ruthless procedures that were inappropriate to Communism. He had created a one-man rule based on a "cult of personality." He had by police methods interfered improperly with the lives of the people and with orderly government. This bitter attack on "Stalinism" led to hopes and stirrings both in Russia and in the satellite nations. In Poland, where the majority of the people were still devoutly Roman Catholic and intensely patriotic, there had long been restiveness under the domination of Communist leaders chosen by and subservient to Russia. In June 1956, massive riots of workmen broke out in Poznan and there were troubles in other cities. The risings were suppressed by force, but only after numbers of people had been killed, wounded, or imprisoned.

The Polish situation was sufficiently ominous to force a change in Soviet policy. Wladyslaw Gomulka, a Polish Communist leader who had been jailed because of his anti-Russian, or at least anti-Stalinist, tendencies, was allowed to become party leader in October and to take over control of the government. In the ensuing months a compromise was developed by which the Polish government under Gomulka was allowed a good deal of leeway on matters of internal policy, in return for relatively strict adherence to the Russian position on external matters. Under Gomulka the government was thoroughly Communist, but it allowed more personal freedom, including some freedom of speech and of religious worship. The attempt to collectivize the farms was more or less abandoned. Cultural relations with the Western nations were to some degree renewed. The Poles, under the shadow of Soviet armed might, remained deeply nationalistic, but thought of themselves as better off than in the days of Stalin.

A major factor in leading the Soviet government to accept the modified situation in Poland was the even more serious challenge that it had to face at the same time in Hungary. The rule of Russia's puppets in Hungary had been even tougher than in Poland. When the premier, Imre Nagy, showed some signs of relaxing economic pressures and controls in 1955, he was ousted. But during the next year there was growing unrest and opposition to the secret police and to the Communist party. Imre Nagy was allowed to resume the premiership in October 1956. But the unrest spread, workers' councils were formed, and when the police fired on a crowd there was open and armed rebellion. Everywhere the revolution seemed to be making progress and there were even reports that the Russian troops in Hungary were hesitant about firing on the people. But the revolt was quieted on October 28, when Nagy announced that Russia had promised to remove all Soviet troops from the country. By a monstrous act of treachery, however, the Soviet Union sent in new and reliable forces with tanks and artillery, surrounded Budapest, and on November 4 attacked.[1] There was heroic resistance and thousands of Hungarian patriots died in a vain effort to maintain their briefly enjoyed independence. Budapest and the other cities were subdued. Nagy was imprisoned and eventually executed (1958). Tens of thousands of Hungarians fled the country. The Russians put into power a premier they could rely on, Janos Kadar, who proceeded slowly

---

[1] See picture of Russian tanks in Budapest, below, p. 849.

but surely to liquidate the opposition to Communist rule.

One factor in the Hungarian crisis was that those who rose in revolt and, with inadequate weapons and organization, fought heroically for freedom fully expected some sort of aid, at least in arms, from the Western powers. But the United States and the other NATO countries apparently feared that any move would precipitate a general and atomic war. They were, moreover, inhibited by another crisis, that of Suez, which occurred at exactly the same time.[1] The Suez conflict not only separated the United States from France and Great Britain and occupied the attention of the United Nations, but to a degree it prevented the world from becoming fully aware of the ruthless way in which Russia put down the Hungarian revolt.

Those who expected that the Polish and Hungarian difficulties would discredit the new leadership in Russia that had seemed to pave the way for them by a relaxation of pressures were surprised to find that Khrushchev was able gradually to consolidate his position. In March 1958, the Supreme Soviet elected Khrushchev premier and it was soon apparent that he was in firm control of the Russian governmental machinery and of the Communist party in the Soviet Union. One after another possible rival to Khrushchev, such as Zhukov, Bulganin, Malenkov, and Molotov, were either liquidated or demoted. And the body of the once god-like Stalin was removed from its shrine beside Lenin's in Moscow's Red Square.

Yet the Russian people seemed quite resigned and generally loyal to the regime. They were now used to it, and thoroughly indoctrinated by it. Moreover, they benefitted from rising Russian industrial production and consequent improvement in the standard of living, and they felt patriotic satisfaction in Russian achievements in the fields of science and engineering in general and in astronaut accomplishments in particular.

---

[1] See below, p. 835.

F. Latin America in Evolution

During World War II, Latin America had been relatively quiet, relatively prosperous, and coöperative with the United States and its allies. But the post-war period was one of rapid change. Airplanes opened up quick access to many parts that had been remote. Industry began to develop significantly in countries like Brazil and Mexico. Better communication in the form of motion pictures, radio, and eventually television made many people dissatisfied with the rather low standard of living prevalent outside the wealthy sections of the large cities. There was also a general feeling that the "good neighbor" policy developed by President Franklin D. Roosevelt had been replaced by one of neglect on the part of the United States. And it was a fact that American attention was so highly focussed on Europe and later on Asia that not much economic aid flowed into Central or South America.

The problems of Latin America were manifold and varied. In Mexico, for example, there was a shortage of good land, though improved techniques were rapidly increasing agricultural output. In Colombia and Brazil, on the other hand, the question was how to proceed with the development of much unexploited territory. But, in general, there were many difficulties shared by most of the Latin American countries. One was inadequate education. Literacy was generally low, and even where it was not, secondary school, university, and technical (medical, engineering) education was deficient, and there were insufficient numbers of trained people. Another difficulty was the rapidly growing population. Introduction of improved public health techniques and the elimination of major diseases, such as yellow fever, smallpox, and malaria, had resulted in a drastic reduction of the death rate without a corresponding decrease in the birth rate. Yet industry and agriculture were not growing fast enough to take care of the increased numbers and at the same time to produce a rapid improvement in the standard of living. Mexico with a population in 1960 of some 34 million was, for example, growing at the rate of a million a year. And it was estimated that forty per cent of the Latin American population was under fifteen years of age.

There were also continuing problems of political stability. In the immediate postwar period a number of the Latin American countries were under regimes that somewhat resembled European dictatorships, though they were often based on older local traditions and customs. In 1953, for example, Argentina was ruled by Juan D. Peron, Paraguay by Fredrico Chaves, Venezuela by Marcos Perez Jimenez, Cuba by Fulgencio Batista, the Dominican Republic by Rafael Trujillo, and a number of other Latin American countries had quasi-dictatorial regimes, as in Brazil where Getulio Vargas had been in control with only a five-year interruption since 1933.

During the ensuing years there was a trend away from dictatorship, and in most instances it was replaced by a more liberal regime, as in Venezuela, Brazil, and Argentina. In Paraguay, however, one dictator was merely replaced by another (Alfredo Stroessner) after a revolt in 1954, and in the Dominican Republic Trujillo remained in power until his assassination in 1961. Often, as in Venezuela, the Catholic Church aided and supported the change to a democratic regime.

A special instance of the ousting of a dictator, and his supplanting by another, was that of Cuba. Here people grew more and more dissatisfied with the harsh and corrupt rule of General Batista. The opposition gradually drew together under the leadership of Fidel Castro who, with small forces, waged a long guerrilla warfare against government from the mountains of the Oriente Province. At first the United States preserved relatively strict neutrality, but by 1958 it was clear that the forces of young (thirty-one years old) Castro were securing aid from sympathizers and others on the American mainland. Finally, on the first day of 1959, Batista fled the country and the revolutionary forces took over. Castro himself became premier and practical dictator. It was soon apparent that his regime was under Communist influence. Opponents were executed in large numbers. A drastic land reform law was decreed (May 1959). And before long Castro was pursuing a definitely anti-United States policy. The property of American individuals and business firms was confiscated or nationalized, and the Dictator made long and bitter speeches in which he blamed the United States for all of Cuba's ills. President Eisenhower cut drastically the amount of sugar which Cuba, under a quota, had been permitted to export to the United States on favorable terms and finally, late in 1960, broke off diplomatic relations with Castro's government.

Meanwhile, the Soviet Union, Communist China, and Czechoslovakia had been making friendly gestures toward Cuba, selling it needed oil and machinery, buying its sugar, and providing it with arms and technicians. Khrushchev took repeated opportunities to display his support of Cuba and in July 1960 declared that Russia would retaliate if the United States intervened in Cuba. Castro, in turn, publicly acknowledged in 1961 that from the outset he had been a convinced Communist, and he redoubled his Communist propaganda.

If there were divisions and troubles in the Western Hemisphere, there was also some effort, outside Cuba, to improve communication and increase coöperation. There was a definite tendency for most of the Latin American nations most of the time to follow the lead of the United States in crucial votes in the United Nations, but if these states were eager for American loans and economic support they were also alert to resist any symptoms of "Yankee imperialism" or "dollar diplomacy." And there was in some of the countries an increasing, even threatening, amount of Communist infiltration and propaganda.

There were certain formal developments of note. As far back as 1890, the Pan-American Union had been created and occasional Inter-American Conferences had been held. The ninth such conference was opened at Bogotá, Colombia, in March 1948. Though it was interrupted by a local political outbreak, fostered by Communists and involving bloody riots, it transformed the Pan-American Union into the "Organization of American States" dedicated to the peaceful settlement of controversies among members, mutual support against aggression, non-intervention in each other's domestic affairs, and opposition to totalitarianism. The tenth conference took place six years later (1954) at Caracas in Venezuela, with all members represented except Costa Rica. The American Secretary of State Dulles spent most of his effort securing the passage of an anti-Communist resolution, which was eventually adopted by a vote of seventeen to one (Guatemala opposing, Mexico and Argentina abstaining).

Guatemala's vote on the Dulles resolution of 1954 reflected the growing influence of Communism on the government of that country's president, Jacobo Arbenz Guzman. In June of the same year Guatemala was "invaded" from Honduras by anti-Communist military forces, armed largely from the United States. In the event, the anti-Communist forces were triumphant within ten days. Arbenz fled and was eventually replaced in the presidency by Carlos Castillo Armas, an army officer, who outlawed Communism and promised democratic government.

In 1956, at a meeting in Panama, the heads of nineteen American states drew up and signed a declaration of principles for the Organization of American States, including mutual help and non-intervention. In 1960, the Organization of American States condemned the Dominican Republic for supporting a plot to assassinate the president of Venezuela and also took a stand against the attempt of China and Russia to inject themselves into the affairs of the Americas. Various efforts by member nations of the Organization of American States to mediate between the United States and Cuba were unsuccessful. But the whole Castro situation so focussed the attention of the United States on the Latin American nations that President Eisenhower approved a plan involving a half a billion dollar program of economic and other aid to them. In his inaugural address and early press conferences President Kennedy in 1961 indicated that he would go forward vigorously with that program, and this he did. The Cuban problem was further dramatized in April of the same year when anti-Castro refugees organized,

with help from the United States, a small-scale armed invasion of Cuba. The expected help from the people of Cuba did not materialize and the whole venture was a fiasco—and one which enhanced Castro's prestige and stimulated anti-United States feeling throughout Latin America.

Latin America was no unit in its attitude toward Cuba, and there were increasing signs of Communist strength in such important countries as Brazil and Argentina. In the latter, for example, Communists decided the provincial elections of 1962 in favor of Perón, the exiled dictator, and thereby precipitated counter-dictatorial action on the part of army officers and President Frondizi.

G. West European Coöperation

If there were signs of growing coöperation as well as troubles in the Americas, there was an even more marked drawing together of the nations of Western Europe for peaceful purposes as well as to resist the Russian threat. In addition to the various efforts, discussed above, to coördinate the military strength of the democracies—NATO, and the Western European Union [1] —several organizations were set up to exploit American aid under the Marshall Plan coöperatively and to improve economic conditions in the countries involved. The Organization for European Economic Coöperation, with headquarters in Paris, worked closely with corresponding American agencies. Its success was evident in the rapid rise of industrial, mineral, and power output, the increased agricultural production, and declining unemployment in western Europe after 1948. Similar coöperation through the European Payments Union eased the problems of international payment for goods and stimulated the flow of trade.

More significant, perhaps, was the "Schuman Plan," put forward by a French foreign minister, Robert Schuman, in 1951 and effective in 1953. [2] Under this plan,

---

[1] See above, p. 812.
[2] See his picture, above, p. 804.

embodied in a fifty-year treaty among Belgium, France, Italy, Luxembourg, Netherlands, and West Germany, there was created a "European Coal and Steel Community." Its object was to stimulate and regulate the production of coal and steel and to set up a unified market for these products in the countries involved, by eliminating tariffs, quotas, subsidies, and other restrictive practices. The Community is administered by a High Authority of nine members, chosen by the respective countries but with not more than two coming from any one country. The Authority makes decisions by a majority vote and can enforce them by fines. It is empowered to take almost any action in its sphere of influence—the production and distribution of coal and steel. Thus the nations involved gave up a considerable degree of sovereignty over a vital industrial area for the sake of integrating production, so long hampered by the national boundaries which cut across the veins of coal and iron ore.

The Council of Europe, established in 1949, had more sweeping objectives, but was able to accomplish less than the Schuman Plan. Because its membership overlapped so much with NATO, it excluded defense from its spheres of interest and left military coördination to SHAPE (Supreme Headquarters Allied Powers Europe) near Paris. It was supposed to seek greater political unity and economic and social progress. It operated through a Council of Ministers and a Consultative Assembly. From its first meeting at Strasbourg (August 1949) the Assembly seemed to many to foreshadow a parliament of the "United States of Europe" which might some day come into being, for it included representatives from almost all the countries of western Europe.

For its fifteen members (Austria, Belgium, Denmark, France, West Germany, Great Britain, Greece, Iceland, Ireland, Italy, Luxembourg, Netherlands, Norway, Sweden, Turkey) the Council of Europe serves much the same purpose as does the Organization of American States for the American republics. It maintains contacts with UNESCO and other international organizations. It established a Court of Human Rights in 1959 to uphold the Human Rights Convention to which all its members save France had adhered. Since individual citizens of the various countries can appeal directly to the Court, it is, like the Council, a supra-national entity. In addition to this convention, the Council has adopted more than thirty others dealing with matters of international concern from automobiles to university students. Though the Council has elaborated a constitution for eventual union and has promoted discussion of topics having to do with European coöperation, it has remained important chiefly as a sketchy embodiment of the dream of unity.

Much more significant has been the thrust toward greater economic coöperation. Out of the Marshall Plan and the developments it engendered grew the Organization for European Economic Coöperation (OEEC) which included all the European countries outside the Communist sphere save Finland, and with which the United States, Canada, and Yugoslavia are associated. The OEEC worked in various matters through offshoot organizations such as the European Nuclear Energy Agency, the European Productivity Agency, the European Monetary Agreement (which in 1958 superseded the European Payments Union), and the European Conference of Ministers of Transport. The OEEC was governed by a Council with a representative from each member nation. Its decisions were binding but had to be unanimous. During 1960 a treaty was negotiated which had the effect of replacing the OEEC with a new body, the Organization for Economic Coöperation and Development. But OECD differs from OEEC chiefly because the United States and Canada are included as full members rather than as associates. The treaty was ratified by the United States early in 1961.

The formation of the European Coal and Steel Community led to increases in production. Steel output rose from 42 million metric tons in 1952 to about 70 million in 1960. Investment and research increased, unprofitable coal mines in Belgium were closed down, and arrangements were made so that displaced laborers could cross international boundaries. It was the success of

From an Office Window. By C. R. W. Nevinson.

the European Coal and Steel Community that led to a further and even more important step toward the economic unity of western Europe. Under the leadership of Paul Henri Spaak of Belgium and after several conferences, the Treaty of Rome creating the Common Market was drawn up and signed in 1957 and went into effect at the start of the next year.

The Common Market (or European Economic Community) consists of six nations—France, West Germany, Italy, Belgium, the Netherlands, and Luxembourg. By the treaty they agreed to a progressive reduction of tariffs among themselves and a gradual movement toward conformity in their external tariffs and internal social and economic legislation. When the process is complete in 1970, the six countries will form a free trade area and an economic unit. The Common Market Commission administers the treaty, reports to the Council of Ministers of the EEC, and works with the Coal-Steel High Authority. Arrange-

ments were made to associate some overseas territories with the Common Market and to provide funds for their economic growth (through a Development Fund) as well as for investment in the home countries (through a European Investment Bank). A Court of Justice was created to handle disputes and enforce decisions. Thus in the economic sphere the EEC represents a truly supra-national body and a real step toward unity in western Europe. The Treaty of Rome created, moreover, for its six signatories the European Atomic Energy Community (Euratom). This organization conducts research, maintains a common market for nuclear materials, and seeks to develop atomic power.

From the start, Great Britain was torn by a desire to belong to the Common Market and a fear lest membership in it would impair its economic relationships with the overseas nations of the British Commonwealth. After much hesitation and negotiation, the British decided at first to stay out

General Carlos Romulo of the Philippines addressing the United Nations General Assembly after his election as its president, Sept. 20, 1949. At his left is Trygve Lie, U.N. Secretary-General.

Courtesy Wide World Photos

and, as a counterweight to the Common Market, they formed in 1960 the European Free Trade Area, often referred to as the "Outer Seven" in contrast to the "Inner Six." EFTA was composed of Great Britain, Denmark, Norway, Sweden, Switzerland, Austria, and Portugal. It has a looser organization than the EEC and fewer supra-national features. But it, too, aims at a gradual reduction in tariffs and the creation of a free trade area. The Seven emerged from World War II in somewhat better economic condition than the Six. The Six, however, have been developing faster since the mid-1950's than the Seven. Both groups represent a major movement away from economic nationalism and toward a collaboration that may one day approach unity.

Indeed, by 1962 the British government had changed its policy and was applying for membership in the Common Market. Apparently all thirteen countries (the Seven and the Six) were moving toward a common organization embracing substantially all of non-Communist Europe.

CHAPTER 63

REACTION AGAINST WESTERN IMPERIALISM AND

Emergence of Free Nations throughout the World

A. General Factors

The war from 1939 to 1945 was more truly a *world* war than its predecessor from 1914 to 1918 and its effects were deeper and more widespread. World War I had been primarily a European struggle with only incidental campaigning in Asia and Africa; and the chief change it had wrought outside of Europe was merely the transfer of German colonies and Turkish dependencies to the victorious powers. The break-up of the Austrian, Russian, and Ottoman empires and the recognition, in the European peace-settlement of 1919-1920, of the principle of national self-determination had indeed stimulated nationalistic movements in the Near East and the Far East, especially among Turks, Arabs, Persians, Indians, and Chinese. But until World War II, the Western powers had retained enough strength and prestige to maintain their overseas imperial sway with only minor concessions to native nationalism.

World War II was quite another story. The nationalism of peoples previously subject to Western imperial rule was immensely stimulated by the ease with which Asiatic Japan ousted the French from Indo-China, the British from Malaya and Burma, the Dutch from Indonesia, and the Americans from the Philippines, all accompanied by the slogan "Asia for the Asians" and by the establishment of native, though puppet, governments. Nor did the eventual defeat of Japan profit the former imperial powers, since the United States, which was clearly the major factor in the victory, was reacting strongly against imperialism, and since France, Britain, and the Netherlands were too weak and distracted to make a major effort to repress the persistent and militant demands of their colonial subjects for national independence.

These demands were encouraged, moreover, when the United States fulfilled its earlier promise and recognized the Philippines as an independent republic on July 4, 1946. Assisted by economic, financial, and military aid from the United States, the Philippine government, under successive presidents—Manuel Roxas, Elpidio Quirino, Ramón Magsaysay, and Carlos Garcia—made progress in the rehabilitation of the country and the suppression of the Communist-inspired guerrilla bands, the so-called "Huks." In foreign affairs, the Philippines, being culturally the most "Western" of Asiatic countries, coöperated with the Western democracies.

Other factors, too, were at work to alter the non-European world and to liquidate the overseas empires of the Western nations. One was the matter of race or color. It happened that the European imperial nations were all composed of white people, whereas their colonies and dominions in Asia and Africa were the home of colored races, black, brown, and yellow. Many countries in Latin America, too, had populations largely or partly of American Indian or Negro blood. "Color bars," by which natives were excluded from white clubs, shops, and hotels, had been common particularly in the British colonies, and the conscious superiority with which the "sahib" treated the people he ruled had galled the pride of the indigenous populations. The Japanese, moreover, had, during World War II, made much of the fact that they were ousting the whites from the areas they had long been exploiting. The French, it is true, had no "color bar" and tended to treat colonials as equals if they had learned to speak and read French and had absorbed French "civilization." It was similar with the Portuguese. But opportunities to be "assimilated" were very limited for Asians and Africans.

Working in the same direction was what has been called the "revolution of expectations." During World War II, the native populations of Africa, Asia, and Oceania were introduced to modern technology as well as modern weapons. Melanesians learned to drive jeeps and Tunisian Arabs to service airplanes. The improvements in communications and the development of mass media (picture magazines, radio, comic books, television) made Asians and Africans vividly aware of the standard of living of the peoples of the industrialized countries. And the way the European and American soldiers lived, ate, dressed, and used machines on bases throughout the world was a telling reiteration of what the mass media taught. Sensing that other ways of life were possible and that disease, hunger, and poverty were not a necessary constant accompaniment of human existence, the peoples of the underdeveloped countries became eager for rapid improvement of their lot. To almost all of them it seemed that the first step toward such improvement was national independence.

The "cold war" added difficulties to the post-war situation outside of Europe and often lent them a special urgency. Part of the Marxist doctrines of the Communists dealt with imperialism and held that it was the last stage of "monopoly capitalism" when capitalist countries, having exhausted their home markets, turned to exploit peoples overseas and to fight over the loot. The theory was demonstrably untrue, for it could

be shown that the home markets of the industrialized countries continued to grow in importance and that the colonies almost invariably cost more than they yielded. It was clear, moreover, that the new imperialists were the Communists themselves, for Russia was ringing itself with satellite states and keeping them under iron control, while China was expanding into North Korea, Tibet, and North Vietnam.

Nonetheless, the Marxist ideas constituted an easy explanation for past ills and put the blame for the backwardness of the underdeveloped countries on the Western colonial powers. The Communist propaganda spoke in appealing terms of "social justice," "economic democracy," the "overthrow of capitalism," and the "establishment of socialism." And Moscow-trained Communists were available to provide leadership to subversive movements in every new nation. In addition, the Russians had an appealing story to tell. They had been a backward and exploited people until 1917. They had made themselves into a great industrial and military power by adopting Communism. They stood ready, in the name of the brotherhood of all workers, to help the emerging countries travel the same road. Russia was, in fact, almost always seeking to strengthen itself by any available means. Russian policy was intensely nationalistic and imperialist. But the siren song of its propaganda sounded sweet to peoples emerging from colonialism. Despite the efforts of the Western nations, the economic aid they gave, and their counter-propaganda for real democracy and freedom, the Communists scored successes from Indonesia to Cuba.

Thus the world picture as it took shape in the post-war years from the East to the West Indies was in some respects clear. Western imperialism, which had begun in the sixteenth century and waned in the early nineteenth century, but which had revived with renewed vigor from 1875 to 1914, was disappearing. Subject peoples were gaining nationhood. The former imperial powers were increasingly reluctant to use force to quell native agitation or uprisings. Nationalism was triumphant in Asia and Africa. The remnants of the old colonial empires seemed definitely outdated.

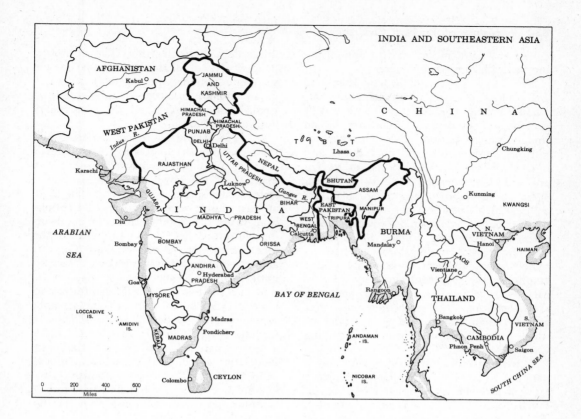

As one new country after another joined the United Nations the problems before it became increasingly those of encouraging the economic and social development of the peoples who were securing independence and nationhood.

B. India and Southeastern Asia

Winston Churchill had said, during the war, that he did not purpose to preside over the dissolution of the British Empire. But during the immediate post-war years almost all of Britain's huge Asiatic possessions obtained independence. The Labor government then in office was neither minded nor able to repress by force the native people bent on securing national freedom. For example, nationalist movements throughout India now reached such intensity as to induce the British Parliament to enact an Indian Independence Act, which became effective in August 1947. This did not provide for a united India, but, recognizing the profound religious differences and prejudices between Hindus and Moslems, it set up two states: (1) Pakistan, chiefly Moslem, consisting of two separate parts in the northeast and northwest of the peninsula, comprising together 365,000 square miles and a population of 75 million; and (2) Federal India, mainly Hindu, covering the much larger remainder, with 1,250,000 square miles and 375 million inhabitants. Both states accepted a merely nominal membership in the British Commonwealth, and Federal India loosened even this tie by adopting, in 1950, a constitution which rejected the Crown and proclaimed a Republic.

Both States had very serious domestic problems. India under the leader of its dominant Congress Party, Jawaharlal Nehru, strove to operate politically as a democracy, and to cope with grave economic and social conditions and with an extremely low standard of living and a very high degree of popular illiteracy. Pakistan, under Mohammed Ali Jinnah and his successors in leadership of the Moslem League and of the country, had to face similar difficulties and, in addition, that of administering two widely separated regions.

To add to their troubles, Pakistan and India engaged in disputes (sometimes accompanied by bloodshed on both sides) over boundaries between them, over which should gain possession of the mountainous territory of Kashmir, and over tariffs and other economic matters. While in foreign policy Pakistan leaned toward the West, India under Nehru attempted to maintain a "neutralist" position between the Communist and the democratic powers. Nehru succeeded in getting France to surrender the few coastal trading posts it had retained since the destruction of its. Indian empire in the eighteenth century.[1] Portugal, however, was less compliant, and only at the end of 1961, and then only after armed Indian attacks, did it surrender its small sixteenth-century enclaves (including Goa).

In making India into a strong and united nation, Nehru and the Congress party faced a most difficult problem because of the historic local divisions of the country. To a degree a solution was found by adopting a federal system, with many spheres of activity (such as agriculture, public order, education, and health) reserved to the fifteen states and six union territories. More difficult was the language situation. In Europe, over the centuries, language boundaries had come to coincide more or less with national boundaries and language had become an important element in national patriotism. But within India itself, the 1951 census listed 845 languages or dialects. Moreover, these languages belong to three quite different linguistic families—Indo-European (including Hindi, Bengali, Bihari, Marathi, Gujerati, and Urdu), Dravidian (including Tamil and Telegu), and Munda (with ten different dialects). Of these, Hindi, with Urdu, is spoken by about forty-five per cent of the population, and Hindi has been proclaimed the "official" language of India, though English continues to be used for all official purposes, including speeches in Parliament, and is in fact the only medium through which many Indians can com-

municate with each other. The optimistic hope of Nehru is that India can become a literate nation, through mass schooling in a common language—Hindi—and that English can be relegated to a secondary position by 1965.

In 1958, following much disputing and rioting among the linguistic groups, India's political map was redrawn so that the majority of the population in each of the states would speak, if not a single language, at least closely related dialects. Exceptions were made for Bombay and Punjab. Rioting continued in the former between the nineteen million people speaking Gujerati and the thirty million speaking Marathi, until finally in 1960 Bombay had to be split into the two states of Maharashtra and Gujerat. In Punjab demands for separate statehood grew louder from the religiously separate Sikhs. Thus in some senses India is not a national state on the European model but a federated empire of national states, held together by ties of history, religion, a common colonial past, and a common means of communication for the educated—the English language.

The basic domestic problems confronting Nehru as the Prime Minister of the second most populous nation on earth (with 438 million inhabitants in 1961) had to do with administration, industry, agriculture, education, and health. In all these fields, though the difficulties were immense, impressive progress was made. India had inherited from the British a well-organized administration and trained Indians to man it. But use was also made of British and other foreign experts hired to perform special functions. Much of the industry of the country was nationalized, though a considerable private sector existed. Under successive five-year plans (the third began in April 1961) the government sought to develop the country's productivity by controlling foreign exchange, by regulating imports and exports, and by investing heavily in new factories and mines. In this task it was aided by loans and grants from the United States, Britain, and Russia. In agriculture, too, there was considerable advance. Old crops were improved, new ones were introduced, better techniques of cultivation were employed, and large-scale irri-

---

[1] See above, p. 474.

Prime Ministers Harold Macmillan of Britain and Jawaharlal Nehru of India, 1961.

Courtesy Wide World Photos

gation projects were inaugurated. But after fifteen years of independence the per capita annual income of the Indian citizen was far less than the monthly income of an inhabitant of the British Isles. The population increase each year, moreover, tended to eat up the added foodstuffs produced and to hold down the rise of per capita income.

Internally the Congress party remained in firm control, though there was a vociferous minority of Communists on the left and some small-scale opposition from the right as well. In foreign affairs Nehru sought to maintain a "neutralist" position and to align himself with neither side in the "cold war." But, perhaps because he had been much influenced by Marxism, he in general seemed more critical of the Western powers than of the Communists down to 1956. The evidence of the ruthlessness of Russian imperialism in that year in the case of Hungary had considerable influence on the Indian leaders, and their doubts about Communism were reënforced by China's complete control of Tibet after 1959. During 1960 and 1961 India lent major support to the efforts of the United Nations to bring peace to the Congo.

In addition to the awkwardness created for Pakistan by the fact that it consisted of two distinct territorial units separated by nearly a thousand miles and united mainly by a common devotion to the Moslem religion, there were other difficulties

that arose from the scanty resources of West Pakistan and the fact that the Moslem inhabitants had been little given to commerce and industry. The death of Mohammed Ali Jinnah in 1948 left Pakistan without a leader of the stature and popularity of Nehru. Not until 1956 was it possible to adopt a constitution, and its effectiveness was short-lived. Growing economic problems, corruption in government at all levels, the failure of outside aid from the United States to raise the standard of living very much, and increasing popular unrest all led to a situation in October 1958 in which the president, Iskander Mirza, felt compelled to suspend the constitution and oust the cabinet. Within a few weeks the government was turned over to General Mohammed Ayub Khan, who ruled firmly but with the avowed intention of educating the country toward democratic, constitutional government. In 1959 a new "four level" political system was announced with a good deal of democracy in the villages and more indirect rule above. In 1960 Ayub Khan was elected President. Under him a drastic land reform was promulgated and other reforms in finance, law, education, and economic matters were promised.

Like India and Pakistan, the other former British colonies of Southeast Asia gained independence after World War II. Burma and Ceylon were freed in 1947 and organized new governments along democratic lines the next year. Burma became an independent republic, while Ceylon chose to remain within the British Commonwealth, though it gradually restricted British influence and even forced the British to give up their naval base at Trincomalee. In 1960, a woman, Mrs. Sirimavo Bandaranaike, the widow of the former premier who had been assassinated, became prime minister. Burma was harrassed by internal conflicts but for the most part managed to maintain an elective government, though it was briefly (1958–1960) ruled by a military regime.

For the Federation of Malaya, independence was somewhat more delayed, partly because of the racial divisions within its territories, and partly because of a long drawn out struggle against Communist guerrillas. But in 1957 it became a limited constitutional monarchy under its own Paramount Ruler. The federation consists of eleven states and has a population of nearly seven million divided among Malays (about half), Chinese (more than a third), and Indians. Singapore, with a population of more than a million and a half, remained a separate state and became self-governing in 1959.

In the Pacific Ocean the major British countries, Australia and New Zealand, retained their position in the Commonwealth with no thought of any other course since they had long since won complete self-government and were bound to Britain by economic ties as well as by sentiment. New Zealand, for example, continued to send more than half its exports to, and to get more than half its imports from, the mother country, which was also the leading customer and supplier of Australia. Both countries associated themselves with the United States through a defense pact called ANZUS (Australia, New Zealand, United States) and through SEATO.[1] Australia was ruled after 1949 by a Liberal-Country party coalition under Robert Gordon Menzies as prime minister. In the elections of 1958 it again won a substantial majority in the federal legislature. During the years after the war Australia made rapid progress

in industrial production, in part perhaps because it modified its immigration policy and welcomed immigrants, especially from the British empire. Between 1945 and 1959 approximately one million new settlers arrived, and the population of the Commonwealth rose to over ten million. The standard of living in Australia compared very favorably with that of the most advanced countries.

New Zealand was likewise prosperous, though it remained predominantly agricultural. Dairy production has become more important in recent years, but the major export items, meat and wool, are still derived from sheep-raising. The original Polynesian inhabitants (the Maoris) of the islands, who constitute seven per cent of the population of about two and a half million, have full citizenship. Some of them have served in Parliament and have held important official positions. Even more than Australia, New Zealand is notable for an elaborate system of social security protecting the people from problems of illness, unemployment, accident, and old age. The Labour party which had been responsible for much of the social legislation won a slender parliamentary majority in the elections of 1957, but lost it to the more conservative Nationalists in 1961.

Thailand (formerly Siam) shook off Japanese rule in 1945, signed a treaty of friendship with Britain and India the next year, and set about coping with internal difficulties. The troubles were serious and were punctuated by assassinations and *coups*. A constitution established in 1952 was suspended in 1958, and afterwards the country was under quasi-military rule.

The Far Eastern empires of the Dutch and of the French were liquidated more definitively and less smoothly than that of the British. In Indonesia, native nationalism, stimulated by the Japanese occupation, became militant in Java. In August, 1945, nationalists led by Achmed Sukarno seized power from the Japanese and proclaimed the "Republic of Indonesia" with its center in Jakarta (the former Batavia) and with a claim of sovereignty over Sumatra and Madura as well as Java. The next year another nationalist government, with its

---

capital at Macassar, was set up for East Indonesia—Celebes, the Moluccas, and the Lesser Surdas. The Dutch sought to oppose these developments with armed force, and at one point (1948) captured the Republican leaders including Sukarno. Meanwhile the United Nations had intervened, and in 1949 the Security Council induced the government of the Netherlands to recognize the independence of a new Indonesian state including all the former Dutch territories except Dutch New Guinea. In 1950, the Republic of Indonesia became the sixtieth member of the United Nations.

Lack of trained leadership made the establishment of a stable government difficult; there was continued friction with the Netherlands over New Guinea; and the Indonesians in reacting against the old style colonial imperialism were gullible about accepting Communist ideas and leadership. Under Sukarno, who was elected president at the end of 1949, there were continuing economic and political difficulties for the Indonesians who numbered nearly ninety million. There was even a serious revolt in 1952 with resistance continuing on Celebes until 1961. As president, Sukarno was, at various periods, sometimes more and sometimes less radical and sometimes more and sometimes less democratic. But he continued to work with the Communists and, after 1959, moved toward "guided democracy," which was his name for a quasi-dictatorship. He continued to stir up Indonesian nationalism by incessant demands that the Netherlands cede the western part of New Guinea which he called West Irian. This the Dutch refused to do, and in 1961 they attempted to inaugurate measures of self-government among the very backward peoples of that colony.

The French in Asia faced much the same problems as the Dutch in Indonesia. In 1946 they had reassumed control of their principal Asiatic colony, Indo-China, including the three states of Vietnam (formerly Annam), Laos, and Cambodia. But they at once confronted strong opposition in the north led by Ho Chi Minh, a Communist. Soon they were in open conflict with the Communist-led forces, called Vietminh. The French tried to cater to native nationalism by supporting the Vietnamese titular Emperor (Bao Dai) and according various degrees of autonomy to the three states. But they could not end the struggle with Ho Chi Minh, who created the "Democratic Republic of Vietminh"; and the war went on with the French making little progress and Vietminh, supported by China and Russia, gaining in strength. By 1954, defeats for the French, despite some aid from the United States, had cumulated to a point where they were willing to abandon Indo-China. This step was consummated under the leadership of the French premier Pierre Mendès-France. An accord was reached at Geneva by which Vietnam was divided into a northern part under Ho Chi Minh and Communist rule and a southern part which ousted Bao Dai, became a republic, and was to some degree dependent on economic and military help from the United States. Under Ngo Dinh Diem as premier, South Vietnam continued to be harried by Communist guerrillas, as did the small neighboring kingdom of Laos. There, despite military support from the United States, the govenment of Laos was so ineffectual that Communist rebels, supported by North Vietnam and by Red China, made considerable progress during 1960 and became a subject of international negotiation in 1961. Cambodia declared itself an independent kingdom in 1953 and was admitted to the United Nations two years later.

Thus the story of the post-war years in Southeast Asia was one of the liquidation of the Western colonial empires, the emergence of new nations imbued with an intense nationalism not always grounded in history or cultural unity, and the intrusion of the cold war as the Communist powers sought for points where expansion of their dominance was possible and as the democratic countries attempted to check and contain this new imperialist advance.

C. The Near and Middle East

In the post-war period Egypt was the most important of the Arab nations. Its intense nationalism took an anti-British form,

Emperor Haile Selassie of Ethiopia welcomed by President Nasser of Egypt at the Cairo airport, 1959.
Courtesy Wide World Photos

and from 1946 onward there were riots against the British and attempts to secure their withdrawal from the Suez Canal Zone.[1] In 1951, the government of King Farouk denounced the Anglo-Egyptian treaty of 1936, and the troubles grew more intense until much foreign property was destroyed in Cairo in January 1952. The King attempted to ease the situation, but he was ousted in July by a group of nationalist army officers under General Naguib, who seized control of the government and in 1953 made Egypt a republic. The next year Naguib was replaced as premier by another officer, Gamal Abdel Nasser, under whom an agreement was reached with Britain for the evacuation of the Suez Canal Zone. Meanwhile Britain and Egypt were disputing also over the status of the jointly ruled Sudan. In 1953 agreement was reached to establish self-government in the Sudan and after three years to let the Sudanese decide their political future. Late in 1955, following a

plebiscite, the Sudan was proclaimed independent.

Meanwhile, Nasser had become more or less a dictator as well as a vehement nationalist. Not only was he the leader of the sole political party, that of National Union, but also he was elected President of Egypt for a six-year term in 1956. Nasser preached pan-Arab nationalism and sent his emissaries throughout the Arab lands, with such effect that in 1958 Syria, though geographically separated from Egypt by Israel and Jordan, joined it to form the United Arab Republic. Both the Southern Region (Egypt) and the Northern Region (Syria) retained some separate features. There was, for example, a flag for each as well as one for the united republic. But both were ruled by Nasser, and in 1960 a joint parliament, two thirds Egyptian, one third Syrian, was elected to exercise certain restricted powers. The Union was shortlived however. In 1961 Syria seceded and restored an independent government.

In foreign affairs Nasser, with some success, sought in Egypt to play off the Com-

---

[1] See above, pp. 800–801.

munist bloc against the Western powers. He did, indeed, receive economic aid from both, without committing himself to either. Distrustful of what he was getting from the Communist powers, the United States at length withheld a large loan it had promised him toward the construction of a huge dam on the Nile at Aswan. Whereupon, in 1956, Nasser sought compensation by seizing the Suez Canal and appropriating its revenues. A brief but stormy international crisis ensued. While Israeli troops invaded the Sinai peninsula, a Franco-British naval force took possession of the Canal. Against such use of force, with attendant bloodshed, the United States protested; and so too, curiously enough, did Communist Russia, then engaged in bloody suppression of revolt in Hungary.[1] The upshot was fairly prompt withdrawal, under United Nations' auspices, of the invaders, and acquiescence in control of the Suez Canal by Egypt, which continued to deny the Canal's use to Israel.

One of the major concerns of all the

[1] See above, p.

Arab countries was the development of the Jewish state of Israel in Palestine. Great Britain, confronted by the rival nationalisms of Jews and Arabs and unable to reconcile them, surrendered its mandate over Palestine in May 1948. At once the independent Jewish republic of Israel was proclaimed at Tel Aviv. Arab natives of Palestine, supported by the bordering Arab states, strove to destroy Israel by armed force. But the Israelis fought back with much success, and finally in January 1949 a truce was arranged through the United Nations. Jordan was left in possession of an eastern strip of Palestine, including the "old city" of Jerusalem; Egypt retained a southeast coastal strip; but some 8,000 square miles went to the new state. In 1949, Israel adopted a democratic constitution and elected the veteran Zionist leader, Chaim Weizmann, as President. Peace did not reign, however, for the ensuing years were punctuated by bloody border incidents, for which responsibility seemed to lie with both Israelis and Arabs. Nor was any solution found for the problem

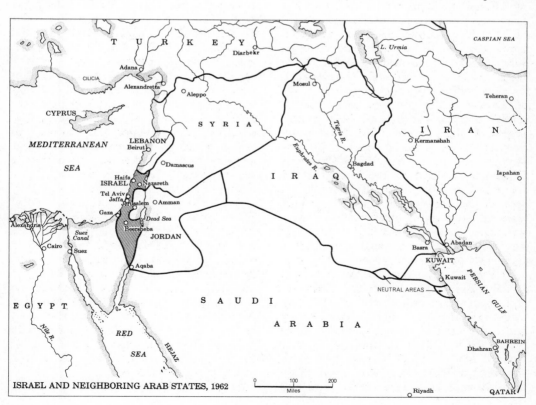

ISRAEL AND NEIGHBORING ARAB STATES, 1962

of the thousands of Arab refugees from Palestine.

Though the Arab states were so hostile that they pretended that Israel did not exist and Egypt prevented the use of the Suez Canal by Israeli shipping, yet Israel made rapid economic progress under the long premiership of David Ben-Gurion, who first took office in 1948. Irrigation, improved techniques, and pioneering communities greatly increased agricultural production. Infusions of dollars from the United States expanded such industries as textiles and building materials. The army was maintained on an efficient level because of the almost continual strife, including border incidents, with the neighboring Arab states.

One of Israel's neighbors, Iraq, underwent a violent revolution in 1958. King Faisal II was assassinated; a republic was proclaimed; and General Abdul Karim Kassim took power. Though Iraq flirted with the Soviet Union, it retained some of its connections with the West, and though there was some internal pressure for union with Egypt and Syria, it maintained its independence. Similarly, Jordan, though harried both by Communists and by a pro-Nasser party, was able to stay independent under King Hussein I, who had succeeded to the throne in 1952. Jordan did, however, end its close military ties with Britain.

Lebanon, where the government represented a precarious balance between the evenly divided Christian and Moslem influences, faced a revolt against its pro-Western regime in May 1958. President Chamoun appealed to the United States for help and President Eisenhower responded by sending in a detachment of marines. Order was gradually restored; there was little bloodshed; and a new president was chosen who was reasonably satisfactory to the various factions.

The non-Arab nations of the Near and Middle East also underwent difficulties and encountered crises. Iran in 1946 was threatened from the north when Russia failed to withdraw troops stationed there during the war. Pressure from the Security Council of the United Nations resulted in the recall of these forces. But urged on by nationalism, Iran in 1951, under a premier named Mossadegh, seized the great British-owned oil industry. Production ceased for lack of technicians. But eventually the Shah, Mohammed Riza Pahlevi, ousted Mossadegh; and an agreement was worked out with the British so that production was resumed in 1955. With some attempts at land reform by the Shah, and considerable help from the United Nations and the United States, gradual economic progress was apparent in the ensuing years.

Turkey grew in strength in the post-war years. It stood off Russian demands for territorial and other concessions in 1945–1950, supported in the latter years by military and economic aid from the United States. It developed its industry, improved its agriculture, and in 1946 permitted the appearance of a Democratic Party opposed to the dominant People's Party. In the free elections of 1950, the Democratic Party won a resounding victory and took over the reins of government, with Celâl Bayar succeeding Ismet Inönü as president and Adnan Menderes becoming premier. Under Bayar, Turkey coöperated willingly with Britain and the United States while maintaining its own intense nationalism. The Democratic Party again swept the polls in 1954 and in 1957. But its rule became gradually more restrictive and repressive and some of its grandiose economic plans fizzled out despite American aid. In May 1960, there were riots and student protests, until a group of army officers under General Cemal Gursel staged a rapid *coup* and took over the government. The new regime promised more democratic procedures, a new constitution, and early elections.

The Eastern Mediterranean island of Cyprus, which had been governed by Great Britain since 1878, became independent in 1960. In the preceding post-war years it had been racked by violence on the part of those who wanted union with Greece and by disputes between the four fifths of the population who were Greek Christians and the one fifth who were Turkish Moslems. According to the compromise eventually reached, Cyprus was to be a republic with a constitution guaranteeing certain rights to the Turkish minority, and the British would retain a naval base.

Egypt's nearest neighbor in North

Africa, Libya, was not returned to Italy after the war, but rather emerged as an independent kingdom under the leader of the Senussi tribes. After a brief period under the guidance of the United Nations, Libya became fully sovereign in 1952. Its major problems had to do with its lack of resources and scant population (less than two per square mile).

Matters did not go forward so smoothly in the rest of North Africa. As we have seen, first Tunisia, then Morocco, won independence,[1] while a struggle for it raged in Algeria. The struggle here was a long, bloody, and complicated one. The complexity and difficulty were results of a whole series of conflicting interests— French *vs.* Arab, town-dwellers *vs.* country folk, Moslem *vs.* Christian.

With dogged pertinacity, General De Gaulle strove to settle affairs by establishing an independent Algeria but one that would cooperate with France and accord equal rights to its large minority of French settlers. Eventually, in March, 1962, a "cease-fire" was agreed to and arrangements were made for the holding of plebiscites in both France and Algeria to determine the future relationship between the two countries.

Algeria was obviously on the way, after more than 130 years of French rule, to emergence as another new national state, although the way remained stormy and difficult. There was still fierce determination among French nationalists in Algeria, backed by various Rightist groups in France, to keep Algeria "French"; and a well-organized "secret army" of theirs continued to wage a terroristic guerrilla warfare.

D. New African States

The Africa which Nasser sought to lead —south as well as north of the Sahara— presented in the post-war period a confusing picture of turmoil and change, of which the most striking feature was the emergence of a whole series of new countries from colonialism to independ-

[1] See above, p. 803.

ence. The fate of the former Italian colonies had been referred to the United Nations. Libya became independent in 1952. Italian Somaliland was joined to the British Somaliland Protectorate and became independent as the Republic of Somalia in 1960. Eritrea was federated with Ethiopia in 1952 but retained a degree of autonomy.

The vast empire of France in Africa had been a concern to the French at the close of World War II. They then attempted to solve all their colonial problems by providing in the constitution of the Fourth Republic for a "French Union" composed of the mother country, overseas "départements" (Algeria, Martinique, Guadeloupe, Réunion, Guiana), "associated territories" (French West Africa, French Equatorial Africa, Madagascar, Comoro Islands, French Somaliland, New Caledonia, French Oceania), and "associated states" (Morocco, Tunisia, Vietnam, Cambodia, Laos). But the winds of nationalism were blowing strong and, as we have seen, the Indo-Chinese states, Morocco, and Tunisia had soon to be recognized as independent. It was, moreover, the bloody struggle in Algeria that brought down the Fourth Republic in France and led to the creation of the Fifth.

De Gaulle's 1958 constitution replaced the "French Union" with the "French Community," which bore a certain resemblance to the British Commonwealth of Nations. It retained the "overseas départements" of the Union and the non-African overseas territories, but the African territories were given the opportunity to choose independence and all of them did so, though all of them save Guinea decided to remain associated with the French Community. In Guinea, under Communist influence, the local leader, Sekou Touré, secured an anti-French vote and became in late 1958 the first President of his completely independent country.

The other new sovereign nations formed out of the old French colonies in 1960 are: Malagasy Republic (Madagascar), Republic of Senegal, Sudanese Republic, Islamic Republic of Mauritania, Republic of the Ivory Coast, Republic of the Niger, Republic of Dahomey, Republic of the Upper

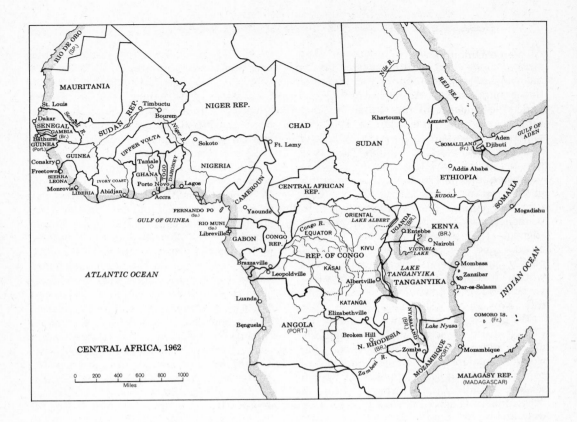

MAURITANIA
St. Louis
Dakar
SENEGAL
GAMBIA (Br.)
Bathurst
GUINEA (Port.)
Conakry
Freetown
SIERRA LEONE
Monrovia
LIBERIA
IVORY COAST
Abidjan
Accra
GHANA
Tamale
Porto Novo
Lagos
DAHOMEY
TOGO
UPPER VOLTA
Sokoto
NIGERIA
Timbuctu
Bourem
SUDAN REP.
Senegal R.
Niger R.
NIGER REP.
CHAD
Ft. Lamy
SUDAN
Khartoum
Nile R.
RED SEA
Asmara
SOMALILAND (Fr.)
Aden
GULF OF ADEN
Djibuti
Addis Ababa
ETHIOPIA
L. RUDOLF
SOMALIA
Mogadishu
CAMEROUN
Yaounde
CENTRAL AFRICAN REP.
FERNANDO PO (Sp.)
GULF OF GUINEA
RIO MUNI (Sp.)
Libreville
GABON
CONGO REP.
Congo R.
EQUATOR
ORIENTAL
LAKE ALBERT
UGANDA (BR.)
Entebbe
KENYA (BR.)
Nairobi
VICTORIA LAKE
KIVU
REP. OF CONGO
KASAI
Brazzaville
Leopoldville
Albertville
LAKE TANGANYIKA
TANGANYIKA
Mombasa
Zanzibar
Dar-es-Salaam
INDIAN OCEAN
ATLANTIC OCEAN
Luanda
KATANGA
Elizabethville
ANGOLA (PORT.)
Benguela
Broken Hill
N. RHODESIA
NYASALAND (BR.)
Zomba
Lake Nyasa
COMORO IS. (Fr.)
MOZAMBIQUE (PORT.)
Mozambique
Zambesi R.
MALAGASY REP. (MADAGASCAR)
RIO DE ORO (Sp.)

CENTRAL AFRICA, 1962

0   200   400   600   800   1000
Miles

Volta, Gabon Republic, Republic of the Congo, Republic of Chad, and Central African Republic. They ranged in population from Gabon with less than half a million people to Malagasy with more than five million and in area from Dahomey with less than fifty thousand square miles to the Republic of the Niger with almost half a million. All of them adopted constitutions, distinctive flags, and a republican form of government modeled more or less on that of France.

The two French trust territories in West Africa which had been German colonies, Cameroun and Togoland, likewise became independent in 1960. The former chose to remain in the French Community; the latter did not.

Since the boundaries of the new countries were often not meaningful geographically or on a tribal or linguistic basis, and since some of the now separate areas had been administered together by the French, there was a tendency to draw together in federations. Thus Ivory Coast, Upper Volta,

Dahomey, and the Niger Republic in 1959 formed a Council of the Entente, while the Republics of the Congo, Chad, and Central Africa created a Union of Central African Republics in 1960. On the other hand, in 1959 Senegal and the Sudanese Republic formed the Mali Federation. But Senegal withdrew the next year, fearing domination by its larger and more backward partner. Senegal, with its great sea and air port of Dakar, was, in fact, the most advanced of the new states since it had been in touch with European civilization for more than four centuries and had enjoyed a degree of self-government for many years. After the dissolution of the federation the Sudanese Republic renamed itself the Mali Republic.

Another development, occurring in 1961 and involving all but Mali of the twelve new states that remained in the loose French Community, again illustrated the trend toward federation. Meeting at Yaoundé, capital of Cameroun, the leaders of these states agreed to form an Afro-Malagasy

Economic Union. They planned a common customs pact, a common airline (*Air Afrique*), common action in foreign policy, and possibly a joint diplomatic corps. There were plans, likewise, for common defense and for association with the European Common Market. The leader in this move was President Félix Houphouet-Boigny of Ivory Coast, who had had training for many years as a representative of his country in Paris.

The formation of new African states out of former British colonies took place more gradually than in the case of the nations derived from French holdings. Ghana, the former Gold Coast, became an independent country within the British Commonwealth in 1957, and its first president, Kwame Nkrumah, strove not only to develop his own country along Communist lines but also to play a leading role in African affairs and in any pan-African movements that might arise.

Federal Nigeria, composed of Northern, Western, and Eastern Regions and with an area of nearly 400,000 square miles and a population of some thirty-five million, secured independence in 1960 but retained membership in the British Commonwealth. The Northern Region is the largest in area and population and predominantly Moslem, but it is also the most backward. Sierra Leone, tucked in between Guinea and Liberia, became independent in 1961. The British trust territory of Cameroon voted in its northern section to join Nigeria and in its southern part to unite with Cameroun.

In British eastern Africa, Tanganyika (the former German East Africa) became independent at the end of 1961 under the able guidance of its leading statesman, Julius Nyerere. And by this time it was clear that, before long, Kenya and Uganda would likewise achieve independent status. Though the movement to federate these last three countries did not make rapid progress, they did seek to work together as in the founding of a common University of East Africa in 1961. That the Federation of Rhodesia and Nyasaland, formed in 1953, would soon attain independence seemed less likely, for

President Kwame Nkrumah of Ghana with Dag Hammarskjöld, Secretary-General of the United Nations.

Courtesy Wide World Photos

there was friction among the white minority, the Indian minority, and the overwhelming Negro majority as to the political, economic, and social roles of the various races.

It was the race question, too, that took a member nation out of the British Commonwealth. In the Union of South Africa the general elections of 1948 drove from the premiership the moderate General Smuts, and replaced him by a rabid Boer nationalist, Dr. Daniel Malan. The latter, with his Afrikaaner Nationalist party, proceeded to implement anti-British, anti-Negro, and anti-United Nations policies. Against the protests of the United Nations, the mandated territory of Southwest Africa was annexed. Drastic legislation to insure racial segregation (*apartheid*) and white supremacy was passed. Native protests were ruthlessly repressed. The economy fared better than might have been expected because of the extensive uranium deposits which gave South Africa another commodity much in demand. Finally, in 1955, the Boer nationalists succeeded in packing the Senate so that they could proceed with their unconstitutional plan of taking the right to vote away from the only segment of the colored population to which the suffrage had previously been extended. Thereafter the *apartheid* policy became more and more oppressive and led to riots and demonstrations which were so ruthlessly suppressed, with much bloodshed by troops and police, that questions were asked and motions introduced in the United Nations, and the public opinion of the world was outraged. Matters came to a head in March 1961 at a meeting of the prime ministers of the British Commonwealth nations including those from Ghana and Nigeria. The Prime Minister of the Union of South Africa, Dr. Hendrik Verwoerd, a stern advocate of *apartheid*, found himself alone when he sought to defend his country's racial policies. He, therefore, announced South Africa's withdrawal from the Commonwealth. And a subsequent plebiscite ratified its adoption of the status of a totally independent republic. Yet this step was merely the culmination of a long trend, for the British flag, the British national anthem, and allegiance to the Queen had already been eliminated, and decimal currency had replaced pounds, shillings, and pence.

Far across the Atlantic there emerged another new nation which retained its ties with the British Commonwealth. It, too, had an overwhelming majority of Negroes, descendants of slaves imported from Africa. But here the racial issues had been amicably settled. The West Indies Federation was formed in 1956. It consists of ten island colonies, of which the largest are Trinidad and Jamaica, and it is moving gradually toward full independence and dominion status.

Compared to the former British and French colonies, the transition to independence of the Belgian Congo in Africa was both confused and painful. Noting the trend away from colonialism, the Belgians after World War II had developed a long-range program, with emphasis successively on primary, secondary, and university education, that would have made the colony ready for independence in the late 1970's. But the course of events moved so rapidly and the agitation for nationhood became so vociferous among native leaders that independence was granted in 1960. Elections were held and a government organized, but almost at once the country lapsed into chaos. In the first place, memories of the earlier oppressive and tyrannical rule of King Leopold II,[1] despite later reforms, still lingered and induced such violence that most of the Belgian civil servants and technicians who had planned to stay and man the machinery of government left hurriedly and went home. In the second place, tribal, regional, and personal rivalries broke out among the natives and led to intermittent struggles. In the third place, the Congo became a sort of pawn in the cold war, and at one point at least, in the autumn of 1960, the Soviet Union seemed on the point of taking control by flying in "technicians" and others, while the United States sought to check such a development. Finally, and most important of all, there were few, if any, Congolese adequately trained to run the government, the utilities, the police, the army, or the public

---
[1] See above, pp. 663–664.

Demonstration in Leopoldville in the Congo, 1960.

health services; and some of the natives seemed only too prone to evince a primitive savagery.

Into the confusion and chaos, and with American support but Russian opposition, the United Nations moved. It dispatched a multi-national armed force composed largely of Asians and Africans; it sent in experts to operate the public services; and it provided food, supplies, and funds. But the local troubles were unabated. The president, Joseph Kasavubu, was jealous of the prime minister, Patrice Lumumba, and both were opposed by Moise Tshombe, who headed Katanga, the wealthiest and best developed of the six large provinces of the country. Tshombe was determined that Katanga should secede from the Congo and constitute an independent state, and with the aid of Belgian and other interested persons he raised troops and defied the central government. In efforts to negotiate a settlement Lumumba was murdered on a trip to Katanga and Hammarskjöld, the U. N. Secretary-General,

perished in a plane crash. When, toward the end of 1961, U. N. forces fought their way into Elizabethville, the capital of Katanga, Tshombe consented to meet at Leopoldville the Congolese premier, Cyrille Adoula, the successor of Lumumba, and there he apparently repudiated secession and pledged loyalty to the Congo. Back in Katanga, however, he explained that all this was subject to approval by the provincial legislature—an approval which seemed unlikely. Further complicating the situation was the leftist and pro-Communist activity of Antoine Gizenga, chief of Oriental province, who fought both Katanga and the central government at Leopoldville.

The Congolese troubles were attended throughout by jockeying between the Communist and Western powers in the United Nations, and in the forum of African and world opinion. Possibly so far as the Congo was concerned, a compromise might eventually be found in some kind of a federation that would decrease the role of the central government and give play to regional differences and aspirations. But it seemed in 1962 as if many years would elapse before the new nation of the Congo could make much advance along the road of peaceful progress.

In any event, by 1962, most of the colonial empires in Africa had been liquidated and a score of new and independent "nations" had appeared. To be sure, some of the British colonies were not yet free, and there were unfree remnants like Gambia and the enclaves of Basutoland, Bechuanaland, and Swaziland. There were surviving Spanish colonies like the sunbaked Rio de Oro and the tiny Fernando Po and Spanish Guinea, and small Portuguese colonies like San Tome and Principe and Portuguese Guinea. But the only major exceptions were the large Portuguese holdings of Angola on the west coast and Mozambique on the east coast, plus Southwest Africa, the former German colony now held by the Union of South Africa to which it had been given under a mandate by the League of Nations. In most of these were signs of unrest as the ardor for freedom, independence, nationhood, and the ending of colonialism was communicated even across guarded borders and to natives who had been held down by repressive rule.

In the case of the Portuguese territories, the issues were complicated by the fact that they were not technically colonies but overseas provinces of the mother country. They had been founded over four centuries ago and consequently had been held longer than the African possessions of any other Western nation. Portugal was very proud of them and very reluctant to part with any of them. They meant prestige and some profit to the mother country. Political and other rights had been granted in them to all natives who had been assimilated to Portuguese culture in language and by education, although the number of such persons was small, since educational opportunities for the native population were limited. Actual native unrest and revolt did develop, especially in northern Angola, where they echoed the situation in neighboring Congo, but Portugal sought forcefully to repress them.

E. Special Problems Confronting the New Nations

In all the new nations in Africa, in the colonies approaching nationhood, and in those where a national future is not yet certain, there are problems of tribalism, language differences, and in some instances religious problems. Some units are wholly or partly Moslem; others are partly Christian and partly pagan. Some are split into cohesive tribal groups that may vary in size from a few score families to millions of people; and among these tribes there are ancient rivalries and hatreds. Most difficult of all, perhaps, is the language problem. In Ghana, with less than five million inhabitants, more than twenty vernaculars are spoken and the government radio broadcasts in six African languages. In certain parts of Nigeria it is possible to find, within a comparatively small area, half a dozen villages speaking not different dialects but quite different languages. Similar situations exist almost everywhere in Africa south of the Sahara.

On the educational and practical side, it is probable that most of the former colonies will use for some time to come a European language for education beyond the primary schools, for governmental purposes, and for communication across the linguistic barriers. The former British colonies will use English and the former French colonies French. The situation on a smaller scale resembles that in India described above.

On the political side, the tribal and language situation gives rise to three different kinds of nationalism. One is represented by such contemporary African leaders as Kwame Nkrumah in Ghana, Sékou Touré in Guinea, Tom Mboya in Kenya, Julius Nyerere in Tanganyika, and Mamadou Dea in Senegal. They and their colleagues have been educated in English or French schools. They not only aspire to liberate the former colonies and transform them into free and independent national states modeled more or less after those in Europe, but also to repress native tribalism, which they regard as an outworn survival from more primitive and barbaric times.

A second kind of nationalism is tribalism itself. Some of the tribes are large enough to have a real sense of unity and sometimes close affiliations with other tribes. Thus the Mau Maus who terrorized Kenya in the 1950's were an oath-bound unit of Kikuyu, Meru, and Embu tribes. Their nationalist movement was crushed only after much bloodshed and the jailing of 60,000 tribesmen. Again, Negro tribesmen have vigorously and persistently opposed the incorporation of Nyasaland into a federation with the white-ruled Rhodesias. In Ruanda the conflict is between two tribal groups—the tall and lordly Watusi and the shorter and less warlike Bahutu whom they had enslaved. Some of the troubles in the former Belgian Congo have arisen from the fierce hostility to each other of tribes like the Lulua and the Baluba.

The third type of nationalism is pan-African. There is a dream, which some African statesmen pursue with fervor and to which almost all give at least lip service, of a united Africa from the Mediterranean to the Cape of Good Hope, or perhaps, at the minimum, from the southern limits of the Sahara to the northern boundaries of the Union of South Africa. It is a natural hope, when the pride of the Negro has been awakened and his dignity recognized, when there is talk of an African spirit and an African "soul," when it is clear that the new African nations are for the most part too small to be truly viable economic units, and when it is to be feared that the emotions and traditions of tribalism could split Africa into hundreds of tiny and warring units. There are African leaders who believe that once colonial rule has been completely ended, the new states will more or less naturally group themselves into federations and the federations into a continental confederation. But it is likewise held by others that the political, economic, linguistic, tribal, and religious tendencies toward separatism must long prevail and entail sorry strife.

In the whole picture of disintegrating colonial empires and the disappearance of European rule, there are several interesting aspects. Colonialism had served to export to Asia and Africa a number of thoroughly West European ideas and institutions. Some of these, like liberty, equality, nationalism, have turned out to be the very notions that have brought an end to colonial rule. Others, like democracy, constitutionalism, patriotism, justice and the rule of law, even where grafted into a thoroughly alien civilization, have turned out to be integrating forces and ideals toward which some of the emerging peoples could strive. Liberal democracy has seemed to be one of the hardest to achieve; and in most of the new nations, from South Vietnam to Ghana, from Indonesia to Guinea, from Pakistan to the Sudan, there has been some version of rule by the strong leader (often a military man) in a more or less authoritarian fashion.

Another development that appeared as the colonial empires were liquidated has been the importance of education. What the new nations wanted most was to share in modern material civilization with its many benefits—health, ample food, material goods, rapid transportation, easy communication, leisure, amusements. But modern civilization clearly requires skilled administrators, professional men, and technicians. Such people are the product of a long and complicated educational process. And the new nations have had the most variant degrees of popular education. The success of the emerging countries would seem to depend, partly on whether they can retain the services of trained Europeans, but even more on how many of their own people are properly trained and educated.

Thus the difficulties in the Belgian Congo have been clearly related to the fact that there were, at independence, fewer than twenty native university graduates in the whole country, while the relative stability of Nigeria could be accounted for by the fact that it had some thousands. India or Ceylon were well provided with educated personnel compared to Indonesia or Cambodia. One of the major problems for East Africa (Kenya, Tanganyika, Uganda) was how to remedy rapidly a deficiency of adequately trained persons. In fact, for almost all the emerging nations the crucial question is whether or not an appropriate educational system can be created rapidly enough to cope with the problems of the years that lie ahead.

A related question is that of economic development. A requisite for the creation of a modern industrial country is the investment of large amounts of capital in dams, factories, mines, roads, and power plants. Such capital can be derived from saving by the people, but only if they can be persuaded or compelled to hold down their current consumption; and this is most difficult when the standard of living is low and the eagerness for more goods great. In the Communist countries consumption has been regulated by planning, discipline, and force. In non-Communist lands, while there has been a good deal of planning, efforts have been made to secure saving by persuasion. The two models have been the relative freedom of the United States and the policed state of the Soviet Union. Most of the new countries prefer freedom, but they are impressed by the success of Russia which, in less than half a century, had turned itself from a backward and poor country to a relatively modern and prosperous one, through the discipline imposed by the Communist Party.

Another source of capital for investment is a favorable balance of payments in international trade and transactions. A few countries with a highly salable export crop or product could sometimes achieve such a balance, as with Ghana when cocoa prices were high. But for most nations to secure a favorable trade balance, it would be necessary to hold down imports and thus again to restrict consumption. A third source of capital is loans or gifts from nations and investments by private firms or persons. Private investment is both difficult and risky in new countries, but on the governmental side the United States has poured large quantities of capital into the emerging nations as outright gifts, as "hard" loans to be repaid in dollars, and as "soft" loans to be repaid in the local currency and often over long periods. The motives of the United States have been partly humanitarian, partly military, partly political. Russia, in this phase of the cold war, has given economic aid on a smaller scale but with considerable propaganda effect. Great Britain invested large amounts in the former British colonies, as did France in the former French colonies.

Other sources of investment have been international. They include the International Bank for Reconstruction and Development and its affiliates established in 1960 (the International Development Association and the International Finance Corporation), and the Special Fund of the United Nations. The sums involved in economic aid have been large. By 1960 the International Bank made loans totaling more than five billion dollars. And in that year alone the various forms of assistance to other lands from the United States amounted to some four billion dollars. But the question remained as to whether even such massive infusions of capital could speed the development of the new lands rapidly enough to meet the rising expectations of their peoples.

Whatever their educational or economic status, the emerging nations have set much store by membership in the United Nations, and by 1962 the number of members passed a hundred.[1] In the Assembly, Guinea's vote counted as much as Great Britain's, and Ceylon's as much as Russia's. The United Nations meetings moreover, constituted a forum where small countries could state their views and make their complaints. On cold war issues their votes were often wooed in a pleasant fashion by the great powers. Some of the agencies of the United Nations were also in a position to be most helpful to underdeveloped countries. In this category were particularly notable FAO (Food and Agriculture Organization), UNESCO (United Nations Educational, Scientific and Cultural Organization), and WHO (World Health Organization).

When it is remembered that the charter of the United Nations was signed originally in June of 1945 by fifty-one nations, the doubling of its membership can be thought of as a symbol of much that happened in the post-war world—the breakup of the colonial empires, the emergence of new and independent countries, the needs of the underdeveloped areas. In fact, the problems posed in the seventeen years after the close of World War II were clearly going to take more than another seventeen to solve.

---

[1] See list on rear end papers.

CHAPTER 64

Aspects of Contemporary Civilization

A. Continuing Cold War

Seventeen years after the close of World War II it was clear that the Western civilization that had developed in Europe during the previous twenty-five centuries had, in one respect or another, spread into the most remote and isolated areas of the world. In New Guinea both the Australians and the Dutch were trying to introduce western-style democracy; Christian missionaries were to be found almost everywhere; jet airplanes roared into new airfields high in the Andes or the Himalayas; Congolese killed each other with Russian or American weapons; Indian parliamentary leaders debated issues in English; Chinese peasants strove to understand the writings of Karl Marx. Not only had Western ways penetrated into every clime, but also most of the backward or underdeveloped countries were striving, or at least wishing, for the benefits of modern industrialization. Former headhunters wanted to ride in jeeps; naked tribesmen hoped that their radios could be replaced by television sets.

But the world, instead of being united by common ways of doing things and common desires, was deeply divided politically and ideologically into three camps—the Communist, the Democratic, and the Neutral. Of the neutral countries, India was the largest and most important. Its neutralism was a matter of philosophy as well as

of political strategy. But many other countries, like Ghana, Egypt, Afghanistan, or Indonesia, were willing and indeed eager to accept economic help from both camps. Yugoslavia talked a vigorous brand of Communism, but maintained friendly relations with, and received help from, the Western powers. Finland was tied intellectually to the West but geographically to Russia. Switzerland was strictly neutral by tradition and Austria by recent treaty settlement. Other nations, while more or less neutral, leaned to one of the two sides. Thus Iran, Japan, and Pakistan worked closely with the democratic countries, while Cuba, Guinea, and Mali identified themselves to a degree with the Soviet Union. Most of the new African countries tried to stand aside from the struggle and to focus on their own development, while most of the Latin American countries worked with the United States, though in many of them there were parties or elements that were sympathetic to Russia and to Cuba.

Of the Communist bloc, the Soviet Union was the undoubted center and leader. But Red China, from time to time, tried to wield ideological influence and to stand for a sterner, starker Marxist line like that exemplified by Stalin. Little Albania sought to follow China's lead, and China was active in Communist propaganda in Cuba and other Latin American countries. Nonetheless, as the original Communist nation—"the homeland of socialism"—as

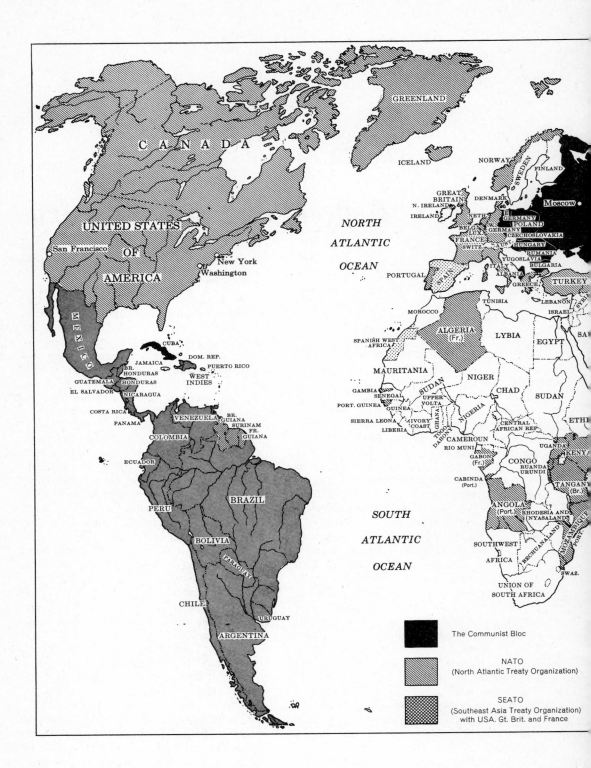

CANADA

GREENLAND

ICELAND

NORWAY

SWEDEN

FINLAND

GREAT BRITAIN

DENMARK

Moscow

N. IRELAND

IRELAND

NETH.

GERMANY

POLAND

UNITED STATES

BELG.

W. GERMANY

CZECHOSLOVAKIA

LUX.

OF

San Francisco

FRANCE

AUST.

HUNGARY

SWITZ.

RUMANIA

NORTH

New York

YUGOSLAVIA

BULGARIA

AMERICA

Washington

ATLANTIC

ITALY

SPAIN

ALBANIA

OCEAN

PORTUGAL

GREECE

TURKEY

LEBANON

SYRIA

MOROCCO

TUNISIA

ISRAEL

MEXICO

CUBA

SPANISH WEST AFRICA

ALGERIA (Fr.)

LYBIA

EGYPT

SA

DOM. REP.

JAMAICA

PUERTO RICO

MAURITANIA

NIGER

BR. HONDURAS

WEST INDIES

CHAD

SUDAN

GUATEMALA

HONDURAS

GAMBIA

SENEGAL

SUDAN

EL SALVADOR

NICARAGUA

PORT. GUINEA

GUINEA

UPPER VOLTA

COSTA RICA

SIERRA LEONA

IVORY COAST

NIGERIA

PANAMA

VENEZUELA

BR. GUIANA

LIBERIA

GHANA

TOGO

CENTRAL AFRICAN REP.

ETH

SURINAM

DAHOMEY

FR. GUIANA

CAMEROUN

COLOMBIA

RIO MUNI

UGANDA

KENY

ECUADOR

GABON

CONGO

(Fr.)

RUANDA URUNDI

TANGANY (Br.)

CABINDA (Port.)

PERU

BRAZIL

SOUTH

ANGOLA (Port.)

RHODESIA AND NYASALAND

MOZAMBIQUE (Port.)

BOLIVIA

ATLANTIC

SOUTHWEST

PARAGUAY

OCEAN

AFRICA

BECHUANALAND

SWAZ.

CHILE

UNION OF SOUTH AFRICA

ARGENTINA

URUGUAY

	The Communist Bloc
	NATO (North Atlantic Treaty Organization)
	SEATO (Southeast Asia Treaty Organization) with USA. Gt. Brit. and France

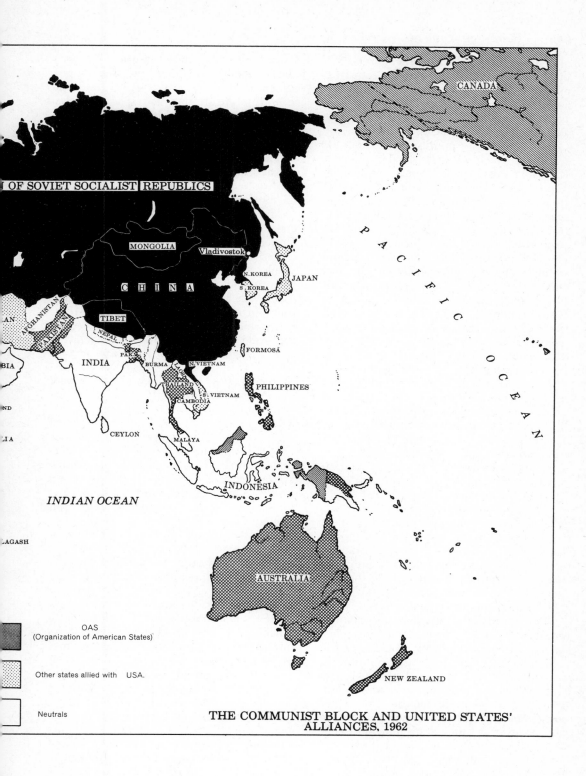

OF SOVIET SOCIALIST REPUBLICS

CANADA

MONGOLIA

Vladivostok

CHINA

N. KOREA

S. KOREA

JAPAN

PACIFIC OCEAN

AFGHANISTAN

PAKISTAN

TIBET

NEPAL

PAK.

INDIA

BURMA

N. VIETNAM

FORMOSA

THAILAND

S. VIETNAM

PHILIPPINES

CAMBODIA

CEYLON

MALAYA

INDONESIA

INDIAN OCEAN

AUSTRALIA

NEW ZEALAND

AN

BIA

ND

IA

AGASH

OAS
(Organization of American States)

Other states allied with USA.

Neutrals

THE COMMUNIST BLOCK AND UNITED STATES'
ALLIANCES, 1962

the largest geographically, the most developed industrially, and the most powerful militarily of all the Communist states, the Soviet Union was by far the most important element in determining their doctrine and deciding their policies.

Part of Russia's prestige arose from its success in World War II, its absorption of Lithuania, Latvia, and Estonia, its domination of the surrounding satellite countries from Poland to Bulgaria, its ruthless suppression of dissent in Hungary. Part came from its remarkable advances in science symbolized by its space vehicles. Part could be attributed to its obvious military strength and the effectiveness of its machinery for espionage and propaganda. But there were two other major factors in Russia's influence throughout the world. One was the Marxist-Leninist philosophy which, though it dated from the mid-nineteenth century, seemed modern in backward countries. By ignoring the unfulfilled prophecies of Marx and his outworn economics and by stressing his attacks on the exploitation of the workers and Lenin's hostility to colonialism and imperialism, the Russians were able to tell an appealing story to the underdeveloped lands. The story was, moreover, a very simple one that anyone could grasp. It "explained" the political, economic, cultural, and social situation. It attributed poverty and backwardness to exploitation by the former colonial powers, the capitalists, and the big landowners. It scoffed at religion and all non-material factors or forces. It presented itself as "scientific" and it insisted that the trend of history was inexorably with and toward Communism.

The second factor was Russia's economic progress. Starting out in 1917 not much better off than some of the underdeveloped nations, the Soviet Union had transformed itself into a great industrial power. It had done so by planning and by holding down consumption so as to increase investment in factories, dams, and mines. That it had also done so by eliminating individual freedom, sternly mobilizing the workers, and "liquidating" all who objected or dissented (*kulaks*, Ukrainians, Kazakhs, Cossacks, etc.) was less stressed by the Russians. Yet the results were clear. The Soviet Union could produce satisfactory tanks and trucks, airplanes and submarines, cameras and television sets. It led the world in missile engineering and space vehicles. Khrushchev was probably not exaggerating very much when in 1960 he claimed that the national income of the Soviet Union was increasing at the rate of eight per cent a year. And it was estimated that the rate of investment (for future production) was higher than in any other land.

The center and keystone of the democratic nations, on the other hand, was the United States. Territorially it was much less extensive than Russia. In population it was smaller than the Soviet Union and, by a wide margin, than China or India. But industrially it towered above all other countries—so much so that in some lines (e.g., automobiles) it could equal all the rest of the world combined. Its standard of living was far higher than even advanced nations like Great Britain or France. It could afford to spend some fifty billion dollars a year on defense. Its intervention had been decisive in World War II both in the east and in the west. It had, moreover, welded together a slightly uneasy military alliance (NATO) in Europe and a rather ineffectual one (SEATO) in Asia. It maintained military and air bases round the world from Spain and Libya to Okinawa and the Philippines. It had poured military and economic assistance into dozens of countries in the amount of scores of billions of dollars.

But if its industrial might lent it prestige, the wealth of the United States made it an object of envy and criticism. The standard of living of its foreign-based soldiers contrasted unpleasantly with that of the local inhabitants. The careless spending of its millions of tourists aroused mixed feelings in many lands. Moreover, some great powers of the pre-1914 period (Great Britain, France, Germany, Japan) found it a little hard to adjust to a situation in which war and circumstance had reduced them to second- or third-rate status. Its very pre-eminence, moreover, made the United States the prime target for the propaganda, the criticism, and the diplomacy of the whole Communist bloc. Red China, for example, despite the long history of friend-

Russian tanks guard the Budapest Station during the Hungarian rising, 1956.

Courtesy Wide World Photos

ship between the American and Chinese people, chose as the enemy against whom its citizens must be aroused, not the waning British Empire, which still held Hong Kong, but rather the United States.

The United States had certain advantages in the ideological struggle. It had been the first nation to throw off colonial rule, to establish modern republican government, to develop a workable democracy, to live under a constitution, to respect a bill of rights, and to fuse peoples of the most variant races, religions, and origins into a viable whole. It had been, furthermore, for almost two centuries a symbol of freedom and of opportunity for the oppressed peoples of every land. Its example had much to offer to other countries.

But it had certain disadvantages. The American people were so used to democracy that they had become a little unready to expound its virtues. Though they were making progress, they had been unable wholly to solve the problem of race relations. Despite their instinctive anti-colo-

nialism, they often found themselves in a position where it seemed important to defend an allied or friendly nation against the attacks of aspiring colonial peoples. And although they believed deeply in democracy, the exigencies of international politics, military diplomacy, and the cold war often led them to accept or even support the dictatorial rule of a strong man if he seemed likely to keep his country aligned with American interests.

Perhaps most difficult of all, the United States appeared to the rest of the world as the prime example and the chief defender of "capitalism," and most Americans were prepared to proclaim themselves supporters of "capitalism" and "free enterprise." Here a real misunderstanding of words was involved. For the African, the Asian, and for many Europeans, "capitalism" meant the kind of system that Karl Marx had seen and described in Great Britain in the mid-nineteenth century. It implied a greedy and exploiting class of capitalists who, in their search for profits, disregarded human welfare, the workers' rights, and the national interest. It implied, moreover, that labor was unorganized and helpless, that the independent farmer was so impoverished that he was being driven from the land, that urban living conditions were dismal and unhealthy, and that the government operating under the philosophy of *laissez-faire* was both unwilling and unable to do anything about the situation. To many, in addition, "capitalism," in line with the theories of the Russian Lenin, was seeking by every possible means to exploit overseas workers through political or economic imperialism because home markets, composed of underpaid workers, were exhausted. The very phrase "free enterprise" recalled to some minds Marx's comment about labor which was "free" to sell itself for low wages and to starve in slums.

To the American, on the other hand, "free enterprise" meant an economy, still competitive, in which the individual still had opportunity to organize and develop a business. To him, "capitalism" meant the system under which the United States was operating in the mid-twentieth century and which was in some respects further removed from the England of 1850 than was Soviet "Communism." In the United States of 1960, the workers were organized in powerful labor unions which were sometimes dominant and occasionally domineering. The high wages of labor had produced an enormous and continually expanding home market not only for food, clothing, and housing but also for automobiles, television sets, and outboard motor boats. The government was active in every phase of economic life. It organized some businesses and participated in others (mixed corporations). It took more than half of the profits of business through a 52% corporation tax. It subjected the rich to income taxes that rose in a steep graduation to 90% on the very affluent, and it broke up the estates of the wealthy through heavy inheritance taxes. Nor was its action predominantly negative, for an elaborate system of social security had been established which protected most people from the worst misfortunes of industrial life. The farmer, moreover, was the object of such extensive subsidies that a good many uneconomic

units were kept in existence. And banking, public utilities, stock markets, food and drug businesses, and many others were under strict regulation to protect the citizenry.

Thus when an Indonesian or an African from Ghana or a Japanese labor leader talked about American capitalism and imperialism he had one kind of a picture—largely incorrect and outdated—in mind, whereas the American, whether a member of the United States Information Service or a private individual, had quite another. If in the cold war the average Russian thought of himself as standing against capitalism, imperialism, and war and for socialism and the world-wide liberation of the laboring masses, the average American believed that his country was opposing Communism, irreligion, and war and was supporting freedom, law, justice, democracy, and respect for the individual human being. The Russian was convinced of the "aggressive" purpose of the democratic powers because of their military alliances and the American bases that ringed the Soviet homeland. The American was equally convinced that his country would never start a war and was seeking merely to check the ruthless advance of the Soviet Union which had in two decades absorbed or subjected Latvia, Lithuania, Estonia, Poland, Czechoslovakia, Rumania, Bulgaria, Albania, and Hungary, and the expansion by force of arms of world Communism which had in the same period taken over China, North Korea, North Vietnam, Tibet, and Cuba and had made threatening progress in Guinea, Mali, Nepal, Laos, Afghanistan, Indonesia, Ghana, and other lands. It seemed clear to the American, for example, that Russia had been prepared to exploit the disorder in the Congo in 1960–1961 by sending in "technical advisers," military and para-military contingents with a view to gaining control there, and had been checked only by the action of the United Nations.

B. Competition in Armaments and Production

During the decade of the 1950's the armament race between the opponents in the cold war underwent a series of changes.

Intensified by the Korean War, it had seemed to slacken after the death of Stalin and the peace in Korea (1953). Then gradually it intensified once more, as it became apparent that the Soviet Union and the Western powers were not going to be able to reach agreement or even an understanding on the status of Berlin and Germany, on disarmament, or on the cessation of atomic tests. The hopes that Khrushchev would be more conciliatory than Stalin were gradually belied as the line he followed became tougher and harder, perhaps under pressure from some elements in the Soviet government, perhaps lest the Chinese Reds, by being more aggressive, should seize the ideological leadership of the Communist world.

As the armament competition became more intense after 1955, it also changed in character. During the preceding years the Russians had focussed on land armies, tanks, artillery, and submarines as well as airplanes. The United States, while maintaining strength in other branches and putting some trust in the forces of its NATO allies, had placed its main reliance on long-range planes capable of delivering atomic bombs. But it slowly became clear that the weapon of the future was the missile, whether with an atomic or a conventional warhead. All sorts of missiles were developed by both sides—ground to air, air to air, air to ground, ground to ground—for different purposes. The whole picture changed dramatically in October 1957 when the Soviet Union put into orbit around the Earth an artificial satellite (Sputnik I). Such a feat demonstrated clearly that there was no place in the world that could not be reached by a missile from any other spot on Earth. There were, to be sure, engineering problems to be solved and ever greater accuracy to be sought, but it was evident that the day would come when the long-range bomber as an offensive weapon would be supplemented and possibly replaced by the missile. The United States immediately stepped up its program and hastened the development of missiles of various sorts, including those to be launched from deep underground pits and from submarines.

Indeed, the whole armament picture was in a state of flux. On the one hand, after the United States exploded the first thermonuclear bomb at Eniwetok in the Pacific in 1952 and the Russians developed similar devices, it became clear that the opponents in the cold war could destroy each other and perhaps through radioactive "fallout" eliminate most, or even all, life on earth. On the other hand, all attempts to reach disarmament agreements failed of success, in part at least because the United States insisted on close inspection to make sure that enforcement was adequate, while Russia would not accept more than token inspection. Even in the matter of atomic bomb tests, though Russia, Britain, and the United States temporarily stopped making them, agreement proved impossible because of differences on the question of detection and enforcement, particularly in respect to underground explosions. But the negotiations begun at Geneva in 1958 among the three nations went on and on. Meanwhile, in February 1960, France set off, in the Sahara, its first atomic bomb and thus became the fourth nation with "atomic capability." And in 1961 Russia, followed by the United States, resumed the testing of atomic bombs.

In 1960 Prime Minister Khrushchev announced that as a result of the changeover to rockets, missiles, and nuclear weapons the armed forces of the Soviet Union would be reduced from the 1959 level of 3,623,000 to 2,423,000 for the 1960–1962 period. The estimate of Russian defense expenditures for 1960 was approximately 17% of the national governmental revenue. In the United States in the same year more than half of the Federal budget was for defense. France, fighting a continuing war in Algeria, put about one third of its governmental expenditures into its armed forces, while Great Britain allocated about one fourth of its revenue to military purposes. Thus even with the changing nature of armament competition, it remained a very heavy burden on the major countries, save some of those that had been defeated in World War II, notably Japan, Italy, and West Germany. A number of the new nations, too, sought to create armies and air forces larger than necessary and too expensive for an underdeveloped economy.

International competition also existed in

more peaceful fields. Improvement in statistics and in economic analysis made it easier to get figures not only for industrial production but also for G.N.P. (gross national product—all goods and services) and for other global figures. Because the free world and the Communist world were both seeking to impress the new nations, there were frequently battles of figures on increased production, total production, G.N.P., total investment, and the like. In essence, western Europe and the United States still led by wide margins in most areas of production. But Russia had become the second most important industrial nation and was growing faster than the older industrial countries particularly in terms of percentages, since the base from which they were calculated was smaller. Indeed, in the campaign for the presidency of the United States in 1960, Senator John F. Kennedy, the successful candidate, made a major issue of the point that the recent rate of growth of the American G.N.P. (between two and three per cent) had not been large enough.

Some comparative figures will give an indication of how the production situation stood toward the end of the decade of the 1950's. The figures are for 1959 and in millions of metric tons unless otherwise indicated.

Such figures do not tell the whole story. Production, especially industrial production, was expanding more rapidly in the countries that had more recently been developing large-scale manufacturing (U.S.S.R., Japan, Mexico) than in the older industrial nations. But Italy, West Germany, and France were showing very considerable gains in industrial output as they built new, modern, and large-scale plants. In all industrial countries there was a pronounced shift

to new types of production such as electronics (television sets), plastics, and synthetics (rubber, nylon). Production of electricity seemed a fairly good index of the degree of industrialization. A little of it was being produced by atomic energy plants, but most was still thermal (coal) or hydroelectric (water power). Russia was determined to overtake the United States in production both to provide goods for its own people and to influence the new nations. But despite its larger resources in land and people, it seemed unlikely that the Soviet Union could catch up with the United States in most lines before the 1970's or even later.

In another area there was some difference of opinion as to the advantages of growth. The twentieth century witnessed a veritable explosion in population as the death rate (especially for infants) was reduced by improved medical techniques, better public health measures, and a higher standard of living. At the same time, the birth rate continued at high levels in underdeveloped countries (Latin America, India, China, Indonesia) and, surprisingly enough, rose markedly after World War II in countries like the United States and France. The estimated population of the world was about three billion in 1960. If the average growth rate of the post-war period (about 1.6 per cent) is maintained for the next four decades, the number of people on earth will exceed six billion in the year 2000 A.D. Ceylon can be taken as an illustration of the problem. Life expectancy there was 32 years in 1921. By 1954 it was 60 years. The Ceylonese death rate dropped from 19.8 per thousand in 1946 to about ten by 1960 as a result of the elimination of malaria and the establishment of better public health

	U.S.	U.S.S.R.	U.K.	W. Ger.	France	Italy	Japan
Steel	84.8	60.0	20.5	29.4	15.2	6.8	16.6
Coal	506.4	386.8	205.7	125.6	57.6	1.9	47.2
Crude Petroleum	341.0	129.6			1.4[1]	1.5[1]	.4
Aluminum	2.1	.5[1]	.1	.3	.2	.08	1.4
Cement [1]	54.8	33.3	11.8	19.3	13.6	12.6	14.9
Electricity [2]	797.4	247.6	114.4	99.5	64.6	48.9	99.0
Motor Vehicles [3]	6.7	.5	1.6	1.7	1.3	.5	.3
Wheat [1]	39.8	76.6	2.5	3.7	9.6	9.8	1.4
Meat	11.8	4.2	1.2	2.2	1.8		

[1] 1958   [2] Billions of kilowatt hours   [3] Millions of vehicles, 1958

procedures. But the birth rate remained at the high level of 35 per thousand.

In Japan, though there was a sharp drop in the death rate in the years after 1946, the birth rate also decreased sharply and thus the rate of increase in the population was moderate. India, with more than 400 million people in 1960 and a density of something like 300 persons per square mile (as compared to 220 in Europe and 50 in the United States), can expect, if the existing rate of growth continues, to have some 660 million inhabitants by 2000 A.D. It is estimated similarly that China may grow from 600 million in 1960 to 1.6 billion forty years later.

In Western countries like France or the United States many people welcomed the increasing population as a sign of national health and a source of national strength. In lands like Russia and China which adhered to the Marxist philosophy, any fears about population growth were denounced as neo-Malthusian and the view was upheld that under socialism added population is an asset. But in India, Pakistan, and other countries with an already dense population and an eagerness to raise the general standard of living, there were widespread fears that the additional population would consume most of any increases of production —that is, that the necessity of feeding, housing, and clothing the added millions of people would reduce the chances of raising the per capita income. In Mexico, where the rate of population increase of three per cent a year could raise the population from about 36 million in 1960 to 123 million by the year 2000, similar fears were expressed, as they were in South America where the population could grow from 140 million in 1960 to 394 million four decades later. On the other hand, many people held that improvements in agriculture, science, and industry would make it possible both to feed ever increasing numbers and to raise the general standard of living at the same time.

C. New Marvels of Science and Technology

Ever since the eighteenth century, science (and with it technology) had been

Albert Einstein. Emil Orlik (d. 1932).

advancing at an ever increasing rate. In the twentieth century, and especially after World War II, this acceleration of progress was evident in the most varied fields. Science became a factor in the cold war. The United States studied its science and engineering education to make sure it was not falling behind Russia's. So many men and women were engaged in scientific pursuits that it was estimated that ninety per cent of all the scientists who had ever lived were alive in 1960.

The understanding of the atom that had made possible the atomic and the thermonuclear bomb progressed rapidly both on the theoretical and the experimental fronts. The results were a little confusing. The work of Sir Ernest Rutherford, Niels Bohr, and others had led, by the 1920's, to a fairly simple concept of the atom as being composed of a positively charged proton as a nucleus with negatively charged electrons revolving around it, something like a miniature solar system. Further developments made it clear that the atom, and particularly its nucleus, was much more complex. In 1927 the German physicist Heisenberg announced his "principle of indeterminacy" which indicated that it was impossible to know at the same time where an electron was in its orbit and how fast it was going. Before long it became clear that electrons had to be treated as if they were both particles of matter and also of radiation. New atomic particles—neutrons, neutrinos, positrons, mesons, etc.—were discovered, until by 1960 there were some thirty of them with which physicists had to deal by means of newly created mathematical techniques such as quantum mechanics and new instruments like cloud chambers, betatrons, cyclotrons, and mass spectrometers. In the light of the new discoveries matter became something quite different from the hard particles governed by the laws of Newtonian physics which the nineteenth-century scientists had discussed. Rather it partook more of the nature of radiation, fields of force, and the like, and it could be shown that even the hardest substance, like steel, was almost entirely empty space.

The tremendous advances in the understanding of the nature of matter [1] made possible rapid progress in other fields. It became evident that the light and heat of the sun and other stars was the result of atomic processes, and it was possible to determine with some certainty what those processes were and how they could account for astronomical phenomena such as *novae* and the variation in star types from white dwarfs to red giants. In chemistry the work on the atom not only gave an understanding of chemical reactions, the nature of chemical bonds, and the relationship of one element to another, but also made it possible by techniques such as the bombardment with atomic particles to change one element to another, to create radioactive isotopes, and also to produce new radioactive elements. [2]

An isotope is one of two or more forms of a chemical having the same number of protons in the nucleus and thus the same atomic number, but differing in the make-

---

[1] Basic contributions to the "new physics" had been made earlier in the twentieth century by Einstein. See above, p. 673.

[2] Neptunium, 1940; plutonium, 1940; Americum, 1944; curium, 1944; Berkelium, 1950; Californium, 1950; Einsteinium, 1954; Fermium, 1954; Mendelerium, 1955; Nobelium, 1957; Lawrencium, 1961 with atomic numbers higher than that of uranium.

up of the nucleus and thus in atomic weight. It was found that there were almost three hundred stable isotopes of the various elements and some eight hundred radioactive isotopes which decayed into other forms in periods ranging from a fraction of a second to hundreds of years. The use of radioactive isotopes opened up new fields in biology, physiology, botany, and even archaeology. It became possible, for example, to introduce radioactive isotopes into a fertilizer and then trace the part of the plant in which they appeared. Or again, by studying the content of carbon 14 in a piece of wood or textile it was shown that its date could be determined with some accuracy back for several thousand years. By a similar technique the temperature of the sea water in which tiny shells were formed millions of years ago could be accurately ascertained.

The new knowledge and the new methods led to the creation of a number of previously undeveloped sciences or combinations of sciences ranging from biochemistry to astrophysics and from biophysics to paleobotany. Revolutionary advances were made in biology through the study of hormones, enzymes, and nucleic acids by biochemical and biophysical techniques. One field, genetics, profited especially from the new developments and techniques. Before World War II, T. H. Morgan and others experimenting with fruit flies had greatly advanced the understanding of heredity and the role of genes and chromosomes in determining the traits of an individual. Now, with the aid of short wave radiation, electron microscopes, radioactive isotopes, and the like, it became possible to determine much more accurately how genetic differences were actually transmitted and imprinted in the cells. Similarly, the role of viruses and how they affected healthy cells and caused diseases became clearer. The rapid increase of understanding of genetics made possible the development of disease resistant plants (blight-proof potatoes, rust-proof wheat) and more productive strains (hybrid corn), which, taken together with improvements in cultivation, irrigation, and fertilization, greatly raised agricultural output.

Hand in hand with the new knowledge

in biology and chemistry went startling advances in medicine. Physicians in the twentieth century were able to understand many diseases and pathological conditions in a thoroughly scientific manner. Part of the improvement arose from better diagnosis made possible by equipment such as the cardiograph or the X-ray camera. Part of it depended on the isolation, identification, and often the synthesis of substances which control physiological processes. Thus vitamin C was shown to prevent scurvy, and more than a dozen other vitamins were discovered and their importance determined. Adrenalin was found to affect allergic conditions, insulin (1922) to control diabetes, cortisone (1936) to alleviate rheumatic pains.

Perhaps even more significant was the development of new drugs and of antibiotics. The "sulfa drugs" were discovered and some of them were proved to be most efficacious against the bacteria that cause pneumonia, diphtheria, and other diseases. Even more marvelous were the antibiotics, of which the first was penicillin, discovered in 1929 and put to medical use during World War II. It was followed by many others such as streptomycin, aureomycin, terramycin, etc. Taken together they formed a more effective weapon against infection and disease than any that had ever before been available to physicians. Still other drugs, many of them "tranquilizers," were found to be useful in the treatment of mental disease, and drugs began to be employed with much success even against tuberculosis.

Vaccination against smallpox had been in use since the early part of the nineteenth century and the Pasteur treatment against hydrophobia since the latter part. But the twentieth century saw the development of preventive treatments based on vaccines or other immunizing injections against a wide variety of ailments ranging from diphtheria and scarlet fever to allergies, yellow fever, and eventually (1953) infantile paralysis. New chemicals were of aid in combating insect-borne diseases. DDT had been discovered in 1874 but had not been used as an insecticide until 1939. By employing it, louse-borne diseases like typhus could be controlled and mosquito-borne malaria

could be substantially eliminated. Surgery kept pace with general progress in medicine, and by the mid-twentieth century, brain, heart, and other operations of incredible delicacy were being performed in an almost routine manner. The medical advances were of great effect also in the fields of public health and sanitation. The provision of pure water, the adequate disposal of wastes, and the protection of foods all helped to save millions of lives.

As in medicine, so in technology, progress in the sciences led in the twentieth century, rather rapidly, to momentous changes. Many of them had to do with the development, improvement, and diffusion of nineteenth-century inventions. Thus the telephone (1876) became so common that it was estimated that there were almost 125 million (more than half of them in the United States) in 1959. Radio (1895) led to the development of world-wide broadcasting systems, radar (1925), television (1926), and systems for the automatic guidance of airplanes and missiles. The first clumsy airplane flown by the Wright brothers at Kitty Hawk in 1903 had, less than sixty years later, given way to jet planes capable of carrying more than a hundred passengers at six hundred miles an hour or a single pilot at more than five times that speed. The first automobile had been produced in the 1880's. In 1959, the United States alone made more than sixty-eight million motor vehicles, and had for the transportation of people and goods a highway system of roads, turnpikes, parkways, and throughways totaling more than three million miles, constructed with the aid of giant earth-moving machines which did the work of hundreds of men. The first crude phonograph of 1877 had, seventy-five years later, developed into the high-fidelity set capable of reproducing music with uncanny accuracy. Celluloid (1870) had been superseded by scores of plastics for a wide variety of purposes. Synthetic fibers such as "nylon," "dacron," and "orlon" had almost replaced natural silk by 1960 and were competing with the older fibers like wool and cotton. In 1959, in the United States alone, more than 1.4 million tons of synthetic rubber were produced.

Though much of the technological ad-

Electronically controlled line of machine tools checked by a single engineer, 1959.

Courtesy Wide World Photos

vance in the twentieth century was based on earlier developments, there were whole industries that were substantially new, including plastics, synthetics, biological chemicals, frozen foods, and electronics. The electronic industry, made possible in good part by the invention of the three-element vacuum tube (1906), was revolutionized after 1948 by the development of the simpler and smaller transistor. The use of transistors made possible the creation of relatively compact computers or "electronic brains" which could store and report information, perform routine operations, and rapidly make mathematical computations which would take a man many years to complete. The whole development of atomic ventures, ranging from engines to drive submarines and surface ships, to atomic power plants, and to the production of radioactive isotopes, arose after the explosion of the first atom bomb (1945), which had been soon superseded (1952)

by the thermo-nuclear or hydrogen bomb thousands of times more destructive.

Equally dramatic was the rapid evolution of rockets and missiles. While rockets had been known and used for military and other purposes for hundreds of years, it was the work of Robert H. Goddard (1882–1945) in Massachusetts that led to a renewed interest in them. He was, for example, the first to launch a liquid fuel rocket. Developments in World War II rapidly indicated that rockets could be used not only for long-range intercontinental missiles but also for space exploration. In this field the Russians leaped into the lead by launching on October 4, 1957, an artificial satellite, Sputnik I, which continued in orbit around the earth for three months. Before the end of 1960 the Russians had put six satellites in orbit, while the United States had sent up more than two dozen, much smaller than those of the Russians but usually heavily instrumented to send back information about radiation and other conditions in space. During the same period the Russians sent out three space probes, one of which, Lunik II, encircled the moon on September 13, 1959, while the United States launched two, again smaller in size. In April 1961, the Soviet Union put a space vehicle into orbit with a man (Yuri A. Gagarin) aboard, who successfully returned to earth after one revolution around the world. In February 1962 the United States safely put a marine officer (John Glenn) in space three times around the Earth.

All the technological and scientific advances gave rise to one momentous fact. Both agricultural and industrial output could be greatly increased without any corresponding increase in, and in fact often a decrease in, the amount of human labor required. Agricultural production per man-hour was raised rapidly not only by the use of machines for plowing, sowing, cultivating, reaping, and preliminary processing, but also by the use of better crop varieties and improved cultivation techniques. The results were startling where the new methods were applied. In the United States the number of persons employed in agriculture dropped from 12.5 million in 1930 to 7.4 million in 1959, but in the same period agricultural production increased dramatically. That of corn more than doubled. Wheat increased more than twenty-five per cent, and the number of cattle grew by about sixty per cent.

The growth of industrial output was even more startling. It arose not only from the application of new scientific knowledge, devices, and techniques, and from the use of machinery, but also from the introduction of new managerial methods. From the beginning of the twentieth century up to World War II, some of the major increases in production were achieved through new techniques of "mass production." Some of them, such as interchangeable parts, had been used in the nineteenth century. But their importance grew rapidly after 1900. The development of the "assembly line" for the manufacture of automobiles by Henry Ford in Detroit just before World War I was a striking example. After 1945 a new kind of innovation in production

became significant. This was "automation," a system whereby, for the most varied processes of manufacture, control, and inspection, machines and electronic devices replaced human beings. Through "feedback" techniques the machines could keep track of their own operation and alter it as might be necessary. In all sorts of industries —textiles, chemicals, petroleum refining, plastics—automated factories with only a few supervisory workers could steadily turn out vast quantities of goods. While automation progressed most rapidly in the United States because of the high cost of labor, it also developed to a very considerable degree by 1960 in Germany, Great Britain, France, and other countries. Automation was not so evident in Russia but mass-production methods were widely employed there.

Taken together, the new methods and techniques, the new power sources like oil, electricity, and atomic energy, the application of scientific knowledge, the development of new kinds of production (automobiles, airplanes, synthetics, plastics, electronics, etc.) constituted an industrial revolution in the twentieth century which made the changes in the nineteenth century seem puny by comparison. A few simple statistics will illustrate the magnitude of the movement. Between 1920 and 1959 in the United States the production of electricity increased eighteenfold, of aluminum more than two hundred and eighty fold, of paper more than fivefold, of electric refrigerators more than seven-hundredfold, and in the twelve years from 1947 to 1959 the index of industrial production rose by more than sixty per cent. In 1951 it took 568,000 American workers to produce 105 million tons of steel. In 1961 it required only 450,000 to produce the same amount.

What was happening in the United States was more or less duplicated in the other industrial countries. In Russia the percentage rise in output was even steeper, partly because the base was smaller. But the absolute amounts also became massive after World War II. Some illustrative figures will indicate the changes in an old industry like steel and new ones like automobile production and electricity.

American Airlines Terminal, Idlewild, New York. Architects, Kahn and Jacobs. Note abstract design in glass that dominates facade.

	Great Britain	France	Germany [1]	U.S.S.R.
Steel in millions of metric tons				
1937	13.1	7.9	20.0	17.8
1959	20.5	15.2	29.4	60.0
Automobiles and trucks in thousands				
1937	445	200	332	199
1958	1,560	1,283	1,718	496
Electricity in billions of kilowatt hours				
1927	10.9 (1928)	11.4	12.4	1.7
1938	30.7	19.3	55.2	36.4
1959	114.4	64.6	99.5	247.6

[1] West Germany after 1945.

and formulate their data and to make generalizations and predictions.

Economics did in fact become more scientific. Aided by significant improvement in the gathering of statistics and by very rapid development of refined statistical techniques, economists were able to work effectively with concepts such as the "level of prices," the "index of production," "gross national product," "national income." Economic theory likewise advanced as its practitioners, such as J. M. Keynes in Britain and J. M. Clark in the United States, improved the methods of analysis. Governments and business turned more to economists for an understanding of what was happening and what might occur as a result of changes in policy. Down to World War II, and especially in the 1930's, economists had been particularly interested in business cycles and depressions, their causes and their nature. But after 1945 the general upsurge of production and prosperity and the mildness of the economic recessions that occurred reduced the urgency of those problems, while the war-time and post-war inflations and exchange difficulties increased the attention paid to monetary and fiscal policy.

Political science and sociology made less progress in the direction of becoming scientific or developing tenable theories. But both came to use, with some effect, statistics derived from polls or otherwise to describe and analyze human behavior. Both remained predominantly descriptive and both were hard put to it to keep up with the rapid tempo of political and social change in the twentieth century. Political scientists, influenced perhaps by the rise of dictatorships after World War I, became more interested in political realities as against forms. They strove to understand the actualities of political power, where it lay, and how it was exercised.

There was great activity in the field of history, which expanded to include a vast deal of writing about the Americas, Africa, and Asia, whereas before 1900 strictly European history had seemed of overwhelming importance. Several attempts were made, with indifferent results, to describe the movement of all human history. These included Oswald Spengler's pessimistic *The*

D. Social Sciences and Philosophic Speculation

The rapid advances in science and technology in the twentieth century, taken together with the wars, the vast political changes, and the general instability, had profound effects on the non-scientific areas of human endeavor. The "social scientists" tried to become more scientific, and the phrase "behavioral sciences" came into use to express the hope that sociology, anthropology, and psychology could be more like physics or biology in their ability to control

Decline of the West, written after World War I, and Arnold Toynbee's elaborate *Study of History* (1934–1954).

Psychology seemed to move in two directions in the twentieth century. On the one hand it developed as a science based on laboratory experiments and careful observation. The Russian Ivan Pavlov had begun, before 1900, to describe human behavior in terms of observable phenomena rather than consciousness, and he originated the concept of the "conditioned reflex." This approach was carried further by a host of other workers such as the American John B. Watson whose school of psychology was called "behaviorism." Rather different were the Germans, Kurt Kaffke, Max Wertheimer, and Wolfgang Köhler, who gained insights into human actions by studying great apes and other animals and who developed "gestalt psychology" emphasizing patterns as against simple reflexes. Psychological tests were worked out and much used, especially in the United States.

On the other hand, one side of psychology developed into psychiatry which built up effective techniques for curing mental illness but was subjective and indeed almost poetic rather than scientific. The father of psychiatry was Sigmund Freud, an Austrian physician, who before 1900 was stressing the unconscious and subconscious factors (especially sexual urges) in human behavior and curing patients by "psychoanalysis." [1] His followers split into several schools, two of them led by former associates of Freud, C. G. Jung and Alfred Adler who stressed other factors more than sex. Adler, for example, invented the notions of the "inferiority complex" and the "defense mechanism" to explain the ways in which people acted. Jung recognized the importance of the human soul and of spiritual factors. Psychoanalysis, whether Freudian or post-Freudian, became very influential in many fields because of its stress on the non-rational origins of human action.

Indeed it was becoming evident, even before World War I, that there was a trend away from the rationalism and determinism of the eighteenth and nineteenth centuries. The Italian sociologist Vilfredo Pareto was stressing the non-rational bases of group behavior. Georges Sorel, a French engineer, was emphasizing the importance of myth in motivating masses of people. Modern advertising was already learning that an appeal to the emotions was more effective than a reasoned argument. The rise of nationalism, so important in leading to the two world wars of the era, and so accentuated by both of them, was clearly a non-rational phenomenon, though politicians were able to take advantage of it and to use it in a thoroughly rational and calculating fashion.

In philosophy there were, some attempts to push forward down the road of rationalism. The British Bertrand Russell, for example, who made distinguished contributions to mathematics, tried to bring the precision of that field into his philosophy of "logical atomism" and into his development of a "symbolic logic" which would not depend on words, colored as they are by emotion, by their cultural connotations, and by their history. His work was carried further by the Austrian Ludwig Wittgenstein whose "logical positivism" was so rational that it became almost anti-rational in its insistence that most communication in words is meaningless. In his later years, after World War II, Wittgenstein withdrew from some of the extreme positions he had taken, but not before he had given added impetus to the growing attempt to reach understanding of various subjects by linguistic analysis. In addition, some Christian philosophers like Jacques Maritain, who harked back to the tradition of Thomas Aquinas, appeared as the chief defenders of human reason against critics of the most varied sort. The Marxist philosophers, who were of course the only kind allowed in Communist countries, thought of themselves as materialistic and deterministic in their point of view and scientific and rational in their procedures. But as a matter of fact, Marxism was so dated by the mid-twentieth century that its methodology was antiquated, its assumptions contrary to fact, and its support based on political rather than intellectual grounds.

An important and typical twentieth-century school of philosophy was pragmatism. Though similar to the fictionalism

---

[1] See above, p. 673.

of the German scholar, Hans Vaihinger, it was principally American in origin and was developed by such thinkers as C. S. Peirce, William James, and John Dewey. The pragmatists saw truth more as a process than an end, as changing rather than as absolute. What "worked," what advanced understanding and knowledge was for them "true" until something that worked better was developed. Pragmatism was thus related to the experimental laboratory procedures of science.

But even more typical of the twentieth century were thinkers whose approach was non-rational, anti-rational, or meta-rational (beyond reason). Two philosophers, both French, may serve as illustrations, the one active before World War I, the other active after World War II. Henri Bergson (1850–1941) seized on biology as a way to escape from the rigid and rational determinism imposed by nineteenth-century physics. In his *Creative Evolution* (1907) he sought to sweep away both physics and logic. To him,

the "vital urge" (*élan vital*) of the biological organism was all important. Instinct and intuition were far more significant than reason. There might be final causes and ultimate goals but they mattered little, for immediate causes and goals were ever molded anew by creative evolution as it proceeded. Jean Paul Sartre (*b.* 1905), whose school of thought came to be known as "existentialism" and won many followers in the 1950's, especially among writers, harked back to a Danish Protestant theologian of the nineteenth century, Sören Kierkegaard, who had sharply distinguished between knowledge and faith and between thought and life. With this as a starting point, Sartre maintained that the only certainty was human existence and experience. One could be properly skeptical about knowledge, reason, ideals, and almost everything else. Indeed the only real argument against suicide was that there is inherent in human existence a kind of stoic courage and a dumb ability to endure.

Church of Notre-Dame de Royan (1958). Guillaume Gillet, architect.

Courtesy French Government Tourist Office, New York

CHAPTER 65

Religion and Art in an Age of Confusion and Change

A. Religion

The rationalistic and atheistic attacks on religion which had characterized the closing decades of the nineteenth century, and the first of the twentieth,[1] lost some of their cogency with the waning, after World War I, of faith in human reason and in the ability of natural or social science to provide ultimate answers or goals. But traditional Christianity (and Judaism also) had new foes and faced new difficulties. One was indifference. A large number of people in the Western world simply ceased to think much about religious matters and devoted themselves to other concerns, or they held that material and secular matters were so important that religion could be relegated to a minor role. Couldn't the national state do whatever worthwhile educational and charitable work the churches had been doing, and do it better?

Another and peculiarly devastating development was the repudiation of Christianty, whether Catholic, Orthodox, or Protestant, by large sections of the industrial working class. This occured chiefly in the large cities and overgrown suburbs on the European continent, though to some extent in Great Britain and in Latin America; probably the United States was least affected. It was the result in part of past neglect on the part of the churches themselves, and in part of effective propaganda of Marxian Socialism, with its emphasis on materialism, class-warfare, and eventual glorious triumph of the proletariat, and with its denunciation of supernatural religion as an "opiate," a "tool of capitalism."

The pseudo-religious nationalism which appeared after World War I in Fascist Italy and Nazi Germany was essentially anti-Christian. To be sure, Mussolini tried to conciliate the church and win its support by negotiating the Lateran treaty with the Vatican,[2] but the papacy reacted vigorously against his attempts to lessen its influence. In the case of Germany under Hitler, there was forceful suppression of Christian dissent or criticism. Here, too, in pursuit of a most un-Christian and inhuman "racialism," there was, during Hitler's dictatorship, a terrible many-sided persecution of Jews (including Christians with any Jewish ancestry), climaxed during World War II by mass extermination of an estimated five or six million in the most dreadful secret torture chambers and roasting ovens.

Communist Russia, though comparatively free of such hideous "racialism," had been, from the start in 1917, the determined and persistent foe of Christianty and has worked steadily to supplant it, among the masses, with Atheism. The Russian Communists have barely tolerated the Orthodox Church, reducing it to the status of a private, semi-secret society, preventing any propaganda or public teaching by it, and turning many of its cathedrals and other places of worship into museums,

[1] See above, pp. 681–683.

[2] See above, p. 744.

Atheistic centers, or government buildings. Within the Soviet Union, Protestantism, which used to be freely practiced in the Baltic provinces, has been even more seriously handicapped than Orthodoxy. Catholic bishops and priests have been killed or exiled and Catholic worship, once widely observed by the so-called "Uniates" in the Ukraine and Byelorussia, has been stopped althogether except in one or two small churches in Moscow that are attached to foreign embassies and are served by closely watched foreign priests.[1]

Similar policies have been followed since World War II by Communist regimes wherever they have been intruded: in the satellite states of eastern Europe, and also in China, North Korea, and North Vietnam. So far, results have varied, depending on the strength of religious loyalty in the several nations. Communist China and its satellites have rigorously persecuted all kinds of Christianity and killed, imprisoned, or expelled all foreign missionaries. In Poland, on the other hand, the Catholic Church under the leadership of Cardinal Wyszynski of Warsaw has been strong enough to obtain some concessions and a degree of freedom from Communist domination. In Czechoslovakia, there is bare toleration of Catholic and Protestant churches, and likewise of Orthodox churches in Yugoslavia, Rumania, and Bulgaria. In an attempt to smite the Catholic Church in Yugoslavia, its Primate, Archbishop Stepinac, was arrested by Tito's regime in 1946, tried on false charges of being pro-Nazi, and condemned to prison at hard labor for sixteen years; he was transferred to "house arrest" five years later, and died in 1960, a Cardinal of the Roman Church and a Christian martyr. In Hungary both Protestants and Catholics held gallantly to their faith, and for it both suffered grievously. For example, the strong-willed Catholic leader, Cardinal Mindszenty, who had been imprisoned during World War II for opposing the Nazis and Fascists was imprisoned for life in 1948 for opposing the Communists; freed amid popular acclaim by the brief revolt at Budapest in October 1956, he escaped certain death on its sup-

pression by taking asylum in the United States legation.

Despite the best efforts of Christian leaders, and the valiant stand of Christian followers, the Communist campaign against supernatural religion and in behalf of atheism cost Christianity the loss of large numbers of former adherents. In the Soviet Union the remaining Orthodox faithful consisted mostly of elderly people; and in the Communist satellites many of the younger generation were being weaned away from Christian practice. Nor was this all. De-Christianization was an obvious fact among the fairly large numbers of Communists in the West, especially in Italy, France, and Latin America.

Yet Christian losses were counterbalanced—and probably more than counterbalanced—by renewed Christian vitality and certain positive gains. The major Churches met the problems and crises of the age under notably able and devoted leadership. There were especially gifted and heroic clergymen among both Protestant and Orthodox Christians. And the Roman Catholic Popes, since Leo XIII, have been men of great intelligence and spirituality, foresighted and devout: the saintly Pius X (1903–1914), the conciliatory Benedict XV (1914–1922), the scholarly Pius XI (1922–1939), the wise Pius XII (1939–1958), and the attractive John XXIII (1958–   ).

In certain respects the intellectual climate of the period after World War II has been more favorable to Christianity than that of the era before World War I. The newer physics has undermined, among thoughtful persons, the earlier belief in the stability of matter: the older materialism now seems rather simple and naive. Natural scientists are less certain of themselves. Many phenomena, formerly regarded as fully explained, are becoming less explicable. Nor is evolution a troublesome scientific idea now to thoughtful Christians, whether Catholic or Protestant. As the eminent French scientist Lecomte du Noüy has affirmed in his *Human Destiny* (1947), evolution could not have occurred by blind chance, but only through divine guidance, and the millions of years it had taken to create man would be as a day—or nothing —to a timeless being like God. Lecomte du

---

[1] For further details about the anti-religious campaign in Russia, see above, p. 741.

Karl Barth, Swiss theologian on his 70th birthday, May 10, 1956.

Courtesy Wide World Photos

Noüy further believes that, with the appearance of *homo sapiens,* evolution ceased being physical so far as man was concerned and became spiritual, with Christ the perfect summation. Which is a far cry from the "warfare of science and religion" of seventy years earlier.

Besides, the intervening two World Wars, with their attendant political, economic, and social changes, have raised grave doubts concerning some of the optimistic teachings of earlier social scientists. Many persons, too, who had been uninterested in religion have been led by the human depravity evidenced in Hitler's concentration camps, by the ethical questions raised by the atomic bombing of the civilians of Hiroshima, or by the studied deceit and ruthlessness of the Communists, to think about ultimate human values and the traditional spiritual bases of civilization. Some came to believe that only in the tenets and ethics of Christianity could be found a cure for the destructiveness and chaos of the twentieth century.

There was corresponding intellectual vitality among religious thinkers, and renewed emphasis on theology not only in the Catholic Church but in Protestantism which had tended before the World Wars to neglect theology in promoting liberalism and social service.[1] A leading apostle of the newer tendency was Karl Barth (*b.* 1886), a German-Swiss neo-Calvinist and determined foe of Hitler. Barth insists that the time has come for the churches to return to an enlightened fundamentalism, to firm belief in divine Providence and in the Scriptures as God's word to man. But Barth's fundamentalism differs from the earlier sort in that it is set forth in the full light of recent science and philosophy. Probably his most famous follower in the United States is Reinhold Niebuhr (*b.* 1892). Among Catholics, perhaps Jacques Maritain (*b.* 1882) is the best known of a group of intellectuals seeking to adapt traditional theology to contemporary thought and needs.

Both Catholics and Protestants now strove, actively though belatedly, to evangelize the urban working classes. Pope Leo XIII's encyclical on labor, which had had slight effect when first issued (1891), was reënforced and rendered more influential by encyclicals of Pius XI (1931) and John XXIII (1961). There was a similar drive on the part of Protestant groups. And there were noteworthy results. The thriving labor movement in the United States remained respectful of religion, and so also did a considerable part of the British trade unions, while throughout western Europe a Christian trade-union movement emerged which, though having fewer members than the Socialist and Communist unions, was growing and could vie with them, and even exert some influence on them.

Missionary enterprise was pressed as never before by both Catholic and Protestant and, as far as possible, by Eastern Orthodox Christians. There was a serious setback to it—a practical stoppage—in Communist China, but missionaries who were prevented from serving there only swelled the numbers working elsewhere—in Japan, South Korea, Formosa, Indo-China, or India, for instance. Of course Christian

[1] See above, pp. 682–683.

Albert Schweitzer (b. 1875). Alsatian Protestant missionary, physician, scholar; in Equatorial Africa since 1913.

missions now have to cope throughout Asia and Africa not only with Communist propaganda and threats against them, but also with native nationalist suspicion that they are allies and agents of Western imperialism. In Africa, too, they are in competition with an advancing tide of Moslem missionary effort. Yet Christian gains have been notable. According to the 1960 Yearbook of the *Encyclopaedia Britannica*, there are now, outside of Europe and America, some 58 million Catholics, 25 million Protestants, and fourteen million Eastern Orthodox—an estimated total of close to a hundred million professed Christians.

It is an interesting and important fact that, despite losses, Christianity's stronghold has remained in the Western world of Europe and America, and that the Christian Churches—Catholic and Protestant alike—have come to accept and lend support to the cause of human liberty. As Atheism is the hallmark of the Communist world, so, it may be said, Christianity is unmistakably part and parcel of the free world. Nowadays, democratic Christian political parties flourish throughout Western Europe, and the free world's foremost statesmen are practicing Christians: Catholic Presidents of France and the United States, Chancellor of West Germany, Prime Ministers of Italy, Belgium, Eire, and Portugal; Protestant Prime Ministers of Britain and Scandinavian countries; Orthodox Prime Minister of Greece and President of Cyprus.

The United States has become not only the leading defender of the free world but the country with the largest number of professed Christians. In 1961 a Protestant source estimated the number at 62½ million Protestants, 41 million Roman Catholics, and 3 million Eastern Orthodox, comprising, together with 5½ million Jews, over two thirds of the total population. And in the world at large the nominal membership of the Roman Catholic Church was put at 527 million, of the Protestant Churches and sects at 213 million, and of the Orthodox and other Eastern Churches at 129 million—a total estimate of 869 million professing Christians, as compared with 429 million Moslems, 329 million Hindus, 150 million Buddhists, and, particularly in the Communist world, large but uncertain numbers of Atheists.

Two notable movements have characterized the Christian churches in recent times: the one, liturgical; the other ecumenical. Catholic and Orthodox have been used, from time immemorial, to "liturgies," that is, to set forms of public worship, especially in the celebration of Mass or the Eucharist. In the present century, the Catholic Church has moved steadily, particularly under Popes Pius X, Pius XII, and John XXIII, toward restoring its liturgy to earlier and simpler usage and securing greater lay participation in it. Quite as noteworthy has been the trend, under "high church" influence, to vivify and extend liturgical observance in Anglican and Lutheran Churches and to a remarkable extent in other Protestant churches. Apparently it has popular appeal. And in this connection, we should add that nowadays new church buildings, whether Catholic or Protestant, are being constructed in ultra-modernist styles and adorned with examples of the latest art.

The ecumenical movement looks toward mutual understanding and coöperation, and perhaps eventual union, among the Christian churches. It is a response to the obvious need for common defense against aggressive Communist materialism and Atheism and for common action in the missionary field. It has come conspicuously to the fore among Protestants. In 1908 some twenty-five denominations formed a "Federal Council of the Churches of Christ in North America," and in 1922 an "Ecumenical Christian Conference on Life and Work," held at Stockholm, was attended by delegates of thirty-one non-Catholic bodies. Then in 1948, after World War II, a "World Council of Churches" was created by a meeting at Amsterdam of representatives of 150 Protestant and Eastern Orthodox churches from some forty-four countries. It maintains headquarters at Geneva, and, though it has no legislative power over its member churches, it promotes coöperation in "spread of evangelism, interchurch aid and reconstruction, study of religious and social issues, and growth of ecumenical conciousness among church members."

Protestants are still much divided among themselves on matters of doctrine and organization. But the rancor that once marked their interrelations is now a matter of history, and a few actual unions have latterly been effected. Thus Anglicans have joined with Presbyterians and other Protestants to form a "United Church" in India; and in the United States the Reformed and Congregational Churches have merged into a "United Church of Christ."

As for the Catholic Church, it has an ecumenical movement of its own. It increasingly emphasizes its world-wide and supra-national nature. With its general administration now concentrated, under the papacy, in the diminutive but independent Vatican City, it yet is in close touch with the world outside through its diplomatic corps, through regular visits to Rome of its thousands of bishops and of mass pilgrimages, through the dozens of national colleges it maintains at Rome for the advanced training of priests, and through representatives on its highest counselling body—the College of Cardinals—of a widening diversity of nations. Under Pope John XXIII, the number of Cardinals, increased to eighty-six, in 1960 included 27 non-Italian Europeans, 9 North Americans, 9 South Americans, 6 Asians (Syrian, Armenian, Chinese, Japanese, Indian, and Philippine), 1 Australian, and 2 Africans (a Portuguese of Mozambique, and a Negro, Cardinal Rugambwa, bishop of Rutabo in Tanganyika). At the same time Pope John called for the assembling, in 1962, of a General or Ecumenical Council, the first since the Vatican Council of 1869–1870 [1] and the

[1] See above, pp. 681–682.

Laurian Cardinal Rugambwa, Bishop of Rutabo, Tanganyika, and Archbishop Mark Mihayo (at left) of Tabora, Tanganyika, at the first inter-territorial Episcopal Conference of the East African Catholic hierarchy.

Courtesy Religious News Service Photo

second since the Council of Trent of the sixteenth century,[1] to give special attention to the problem of church reunion. He doubtless had the Eastern Orthodox Churches chiefly in mind; he had had friendly contact with their Patriarch of Constantinople before becoming Pope, and they were nearest to Rome in doctrine and observance.

Two events of 1960 have symbolized, too, a noteworthy lessening of tension between Protestants and Catholics. One was the election, for the first time in history, of a Catholic, John F. Kennedy, to the presidency of the strongly Protestant United States. The other was the friendly call paid Pope John at the Vatican by the Archbishop of Canterbury, spiritual head of the Anglican communion. This was a courtesy call, without doctrinal discussion, but there had been no such courtesy shown on either side since the sixteenth century.

It should be borne in mind that in the current troubled age major supernatural religions other than Christianity face pressures and dangers similar to those confronting Christianity. The number of Jews in Europe has notably declined as a result of the Hitlerian massacres, of Soviet discrimination, and of emigration to the United States and to Israel. In Israel and elsewhere there is division, moreover, between religious Jews (Orthodox or Reformed) and nationalistic Zionist Jews more or less indifferent to religion. Contemporary Moslems are similarly divided by national lines, sectarian differences, and greater or lesser devotion, but, generally speaking, their common belief in God and the Prophet Mohammed renders them naturally averse to Atheistic communism and hence potential allies of the Christian free world.

In sum, the basic religious question of the later twentieth century is not one between science and theology. It is between atheism and supernaturalism. It is whether in the long run an exclusively "this-worldly" faith like Marxian Communism can and will provide the masses of mankind with a satisfying substitute for "other-worldly" faith which from earliest times to now humanity has cherished.

[1] See above, pp. 368–370.

Geoffrey Francis Fisher, Archbishop of Canterbury, 1945–1961.

Courtesy Wide World Photos.

B. Literature

Literature has responded to the violence and the rapid change of the latest age, though in a very real sense the nineteenth century continued up till 1914. English novelists like Joseph Conrad (Polish by birth), H. G. Wells, John Galsworthy, and Thomas Hardy, playwrights like George Bernard Shaw, short story writers like Rudyard Kipling, and poets like John Masefield continued in the literary veins and traditions established before 1900, as did authors like Anatole France and Romain Rolland in France and Thomas Mann in Germany. But by the time of World War I new winds were beginning to blow.

In 1913 Marcel Proust published in France the first volume of his great novel *A la Recherche du Temps Perdu*, of which the seventh and last did not appear until after his death in 1922. The work is a meticulous chronicle of the doings of people in high society, but it is notable for its delicate, searching psychological analysis of character, subtle use of symbols and metaphors, and emphasis on sex. While Proust's volumes were appearing, the Irishman William Butler Yeats was publishing books of poetry more obscure than his earlier work but fascinating and powerful in their involved use of myth and symbol. Even more significant, perhaps, was James Joyce, whose *Portrait of the Artist as a Young Man* (1916) and, more especially, *Ulysses* (1922) had a profound influence on later novel writers. The latter book is related in structure to Homer's epic, but it tells the events of a single day in Dublin and does so by attempting to reproduce the "stream of consciousness" of the individual mind with all the leaps, quirks, subconscious associations, sex preoccupations, and obscurities that occur in thought. Even earlier and with more emphasis on sex, D. H. Lawrence in his novels like *Sons and Lovers* (1913) or *Women in Love* (1921) had shown some of the same tendencies. Still more microscopic in their psychological analysis were the novels of Virginia Woolf, such as *Mrs. Dalloway* (1925) and *To the Lighthouse* (1927). Joyce in his later works experimented in such daring fashion with words and language that they are too difficult for the ordinary reader unless he has the help of an elaborate commentary.

From the 1920's onward, novels, except those written frankly for entertainment, became more and more psychological. Many authors used Freudian or other psychoanalytical ideas to probe or display human motives, and symbols rather than expositions to give insights. Some seemed more interested in turning their own psyches inside out than in communicating with the reader. But each showed his own individual variation. Roger Martin du Gard in France and Sinclair Lewis in the United States were more realistic; André Gide (France) more perverse and more interested in style; Franz Kafka (Germany) more enigmatic in his nightmarish depictions of the tragic and incomprehensible predicament of modern man; Ernest Hemingway (United States) more preoccupied with war and violence; William Faulkner (United States) more fascinated by symbols; Graham Greene (Britain) more concerned with sin and salvation; Boris Pasternak (Russia) more perturbed by the fate of the individual in an age of mass social movements; Albert Camus, Jean Paul Sartre, and André Malraux (all French) were more existentialist.

What was true of twentieth century novels was also true of dramas. Eugene O'Neill's plays, produced in the United States from 1916 on into the 1930's, were gripping but often grim portrayals of psychological conflicts, as were those of Tennessee Williams a generation later. The Italian Luigi Pirandello wrote dramas like *Right You Are if You Think You Are* (1922) which left the audience to choose one of a good many possible interpretations of the piece. Sartre and Camus wrote plays as existentialist as their novels. Jean Giraudoux modernized old myths with French wit and satire. Many of the plays, like many of the novels, were transformed into motion pictures with more or less success. Though spectacles and action dramas were most popular with the audiences, the fuller and deeper possibilities of the screen were sometimes exploited by the Germans before Hitler, the Russians before Stalin, the Italians in the early 1950's, and the "new wave" of French producers at the end of that decade.

Poets became more and more interested in myth, ambiguity, and symbol. Many of them looked back with admiration to the French Baudelaire (1821–1867) or Rimbaud (1854–1891) or were influenced by the German R. M. Rilke (1875–1926), all of whose poems had used a wealth of symbolism. Many followed Joyce in experimenting with words and language or used poems as a means of self-expression rather than communication. A seeming exception was the American Robert Frost, but his artistic simplicity was deceptive, for there were depths of metaphoric and symbolic meaning in his poems. Though Thomas Stearns Eliot, American-born Briton, was in the forefront in the new trends and in his analysis of the modern age, he differed from many in that his poems were usually infused with religious feeling, as were his poetic dramas like *Murder in the Cathedral* (1935) or *Cocktail Party* (1949). So extreme was the experimentation with words of Gertrude Stein, an American who lived most of her adult life in Paris and whose poems appeared in the 1920's and 1930's, that conservatives refused to recognize her work as poetry.

C. *Painting and Sculpture*

If experimentation was common in literature, it was even more evident in the field of painting. In the years preceding World War I the impressionist and post-impressionist painters mentioned previously [1] were still active, and Paris was still the center of art activity as it had been since the mid-nineteenth century. But there soon appeared new and more advanced schools of painting which moved further and further away from any attempt at realistic representation of scenes and objects. Inspired by Cézanne's view that everything in nature is "modeled on the lines of the sphere, the cone, and the cylinder," Pablo Picasso, a young Spanish artist working in Paris, began about 1910 trying to reduce everything he depicted to geometrical form. Other artists—Georges Braque, Juan Gris, Fernand Leger, Francis Picabia—were moving in the same direction. Their approach quickly came to be known as "cubism." Their paintings tended to minimize color and to emphasize shapes, planes, and angles to a point so abstract that the subject was no longer recognizable. A painting by Marcel Duchamp called *Nude Descending a Staircase*, which caused a great stir when exhibited in the United States in 1913, had in it no recognizable human figure nor any staircase. Though the cubists, and especially Picasso, were moving in other directions by the early 1920's their work had great influence on later developments in painting and in modern design.

A contemporary and not wholly dissimilar school was "futurism." In 1909, the Italian poet Filippo Tommaso Marinetti issued a manifesto calling for a new philosophy of art consonant with the machine age and insisting on the beauty of such things as "a racing car rattling along like a machine gun." Stimulated by his ideas, five Italian painters issued the next year their own proclamation calling for a revolt against tradition ("Burn the Museums") and urging the portrayal of machines and motions. These five—Umberto Boccioni, Carlo Carrà, Luigi Russolo, Gino Severini, Giacomo Balla—soon attracted followers who like them attempted to paint the dynamism of the machine age. As with the cubists, their subjects are often presented as abstractions, but they put so much emphasis on color, rhythm, and movement that some of their paintings convey a sense of excitement that is almost frenzied. Though the group was broken up by World War I, its influence on later artists was important.

The same period of feverish experiment spawned a half dozen other "schools" of painting, including orphism (1912), synchronism (1913), vorticism (1914), dadaism (1916), and in Russia rayonism, suprematism, and constructivism. Of all these the two most important were fauvism and expressionism. Fauvism began as a revolt against impressionism about 1906 and won its name because some critics derisively called its adherents *fauves* (wild beasts) after seeing the paintings of their first major exhibit in Paris. But a number of the *fauves*—Raoul Dufy, André Derain, Georges Rouault, Maurice de Vlaminck—went on to achieve distinctive styles and eventual fame, and Henri Matisse had great influence because of his ability to use strong and vivid color with striking effect. While most of the others tended more or less toward abstractions, Matisse,[2] though he used distortion of line, form, and perspective, usually portrayed a recognizable subject.

Expressionism was a German school which grew up after 1908 under the leadership of Oscar Kokoscha and Max Pechstein. By heightened color, distorted figures, and the abandonment of perspective, it sought to express the personal emotions of the artist, emotions which might range all the way from mystic tenderness to fierce violence. From it developed several subgroups, of which the most significant was the "Blue Riders"—Franz Marc, Wassily Kandinsky, Paul Klee, Aleksei von Jawlensky. Many of their paintings moved toward abstract exercises in color and form as with Kandinsky, though Klee and others remained somewhat more representational.

A slightly later movement was surrealism which arose after 1922. Often using a technique of almost photographic realism, the

---

[1] See above, p. 677.

[2] See above, p. 731.

The Black Circle (1924).
Watercolor by Wassily
Kandinsky.

*Courtesy Museum of
Modern Art, New York*

surrealists tried in their work to plumb the depths of the subconcious mind. Their paintings bring together incongruous objects meticulously painted so that the effect is often that of a dream or a nightmare. Among the most noted of these artists were Salvador Dali, Joan Miro, and Jean Arp. Dali's *The Persistence of Memory*, also popularly called *Wet Watches*, attracted wide public attention. Though not strictly of the school, the Russian Marc Chagall and the Italian Giorgio de Chirico were influenced by it.

After the period of ferment, artists in the ensuing decades went off in various directions, mostly those that had been indicated by experiments undertaken in the years 1908 to 1925. Picasso, for example, painted in a dozen different veins, almost always with a touch of genius. In Mexico there developed after 1920 a distinguished school of artists who painted vivid pictures (including murals and mosaics) much influenced by the pre-Columbian art of the American Indians. Diego Rivera, Jose Clemente Orozco, David Alfaro Sigueiros, and Rufino Tamayo often sought to expose the evils of capitalism and to celebrate the triumphs of the Mexican Revolution.

In the United States there had developed before World War I a group of notable artists, including Arthur B. Davies, Maurice Prendergast, and William Glackens, who were influenced by the newer tendencies and who, because they sometimes chose unromantic subjects, were called by critics "the Ashcan School." Art was much stimulated in America by the public subsidies of the depression period, but it was hard to put it into categories or schools until the abstract expressionists arose in the years between the wars. They used all the color and emotion and violence of the German expressionists but were strictly non-representational. Sometimes, as with one of their leaders, Jackson Pollock, they did not use brushes but squeezed the paint directly from tubes or swished it from cans to get sweeping and dramatic effects.

Sculpture in the twentieth century evidenced most of the same tendencies as painting. It moved away from realistic representations and toward abstractions. It frequently used distortions of various sorts and it was much influenced by an increasing acquaintance with primitive work such as the wood carvings of Africa or Polynesia. Before World War I the most influential sculptor was probably the French Auguste Rodin (1840–1917) who was both a realist and a romantic. The blurred outlines of his figures emerging from the rough stone are sometimes reminiscent of the impressionist painters. His *Man with a Broken Nose* is thoroughly realistic, while his famous *Thinker* suggests the evolution of man from the lower animals. The Croatian Ivan Meštrović, who won Rodin's praise, is notable for the powerful emotions portrayed in his work and for the strong effects he achieved by distortion. With remarkable originality his sculptures are at the same time "primitive," "archaic," and "abstract." More clearly "primitive" was Aristide Maillol whose massive women seem like the fabled earth mothers of ancient times. But the dominant trend was toward abstraction, as is shown in the work of the Italian Amadeo Modigliani who began his career as a post-impressionist painter but soon passed from cubist painting to a kind of cubist sculpture using simple geometrical forms.[1] Even more abstract were the works of Jacob Epstein, born in New York but working mainly in London. His sculptures were at first greeted with derision but won increasing appreciation, and he himself after World War I did bronze portraits in a more traditional manner.

---

[1] For an example, see below, p. 876.

Le Corbusier examining the model of an all glass apartment house designed by him, 1935.

Courtesy Wide World Photos

By the mid-century many "sculptors" were producing works in varied materials from cement to scrap iron which portrayed form or flight or the semblance of motion but which no longer bore any relationship to natural objects. Some of them moved (mobiles), others got their effect by lighting, and still others were elaborate mathematical constructs of wire and metal.

Taken as a whole, modern art has expressed the chaos, the confusion, the questing, the uncertainty, the dynamism, the change of the twentieth century. It has revolutionized design. It has proved itself capable of creating exciting decorative effects. It has served to express the artist's reaction to the world he lives in whether it be denial, frustration, antipathy, or even acceptance. Sometimes, as with the Mexican school, it can be used as a medium of propaganda. It can communicate, at least in some instances, a mood or an emotion. But it is less clear that it can set up true communication, particularly on the realm of ideas, between the painter and his audience, for in most instances the viewer is free to react or interpret in his own way with no assurance that he has fathomed the artist's intent.

D. Architecture and Music

Architecture has changed more slowly than painting, for many twentieth-century buildings have been erected in one or another of the Western traditions—classical, neo-classical, gothic, Georgian, etc. But there is also a definite "modern architecture," variant in expression but tending to exploit the new materials that have become available to the architect, such as steel, aluminum, plastics, cinder blocks, plywood, glass, reënforced or pre-stressed concrete, and so on. There has also been a strong tendency toward simplicity, an emphasis on geometric form (perhaps related to cubism), and functionalism. In fact, one of the most important new ideas has been the famous dictum "Form follows function." Many of the newer buildings have emphatic vertical lines, wide spans, the slim supports made possible by the use of steel and apparently unsupported elements cantilevered out into space. The new materials also have made possible a variety of constructions other than buildings, such as dams, highways, and bridges.

As early as 1890, the American architect Louis Henry Sullivan (1856–1924) had designed the steel-frame Wainwright Building in St. Louis in such a fashion that its functional structure was evident. His American successors like Frank Lloyd Wright carried modernism much further. Wright's buildings, from the Imperial Hotel in Tokyo (1922) to the spiraled Guggenheim Museum in New York (1959), almost invariably show imagination as well as the modern tendencies. Similarly, the Swiss architect Charles Edouard Jeanneret, who called himself LeCorbusier, always shows, from his pavilion at the Paris Exhibition of 1925 to his housing project at Marseille and the city of Chandigar he designed in India, a resourceful inventiveness in the new vein, often standing his buildings on stilts to create ground level space and vistas. Very influential also was Walter Gropius. Winning a reputation with his Fagus factory buildings in Germany (1912), he created the Bauhaus Institute of architecture first at Weimar and then (1925) at Dessau. Leaving Hitler's Germany, he came to the United States where his teachings, his opposition to all non-functional ornamentation, and his insistence on simplicity had a strong impact on the younger generation of architects—though there were those who thought his edifices too stark. By 1960, Brasilia, the half-finished new capital of Brazil, was a monument to the new architecture, while in New York the boxlike glass and steel skyscraper had become almost a cliché.

Music in the twentieth century showed conflicting tendencies. For most concerts and operatic performances the predominant fare continued to be the "classical music" of the eighteenth and nineteenth centuries. There was an increasing vogue for the works of Bach and a growing interest in the music of the centuries before 1700. On the other hand, the world was swept, beginning shortly before 1920, by a remarkable enthusiasm for American jazz—popular music with a syncopated rhythm sometimes varied by extemporization. It developed from "ragtime" and owed much to Negro musicians and thus perhaps ultimately to Africa.

Some jazz, such as *St. Louis Blues* by W. C. Handy or the more elaborate *Rhapsody in Blue* by George Gershwin, won the status of "classics" of this genre. Various subvarieties of jazz, "hot," "swing," "sweet," "boogie-woogie," "rock and roll," in their turn enjoyed popularity throughout the whole world. Jazz, indeed, poured out of phonographs, radios, and dance halls from Singapore to Helsinki and from Capetown to Tokyo. Even in Russia, where there was a tendency to regard jazz as American, capitalist, and degenerate, it had its devotees among young people. After four decades jazz seemed still so much in favor that it could be denominated *the* popular music of the century.

But there was also another kind of "modern music" which won growing acceptance as the twentieth century progressed, and was more and more presented as part of serious concerts. Moving on from the tendencies evident in earlier composers such as Claude Debussy (1862–1918), who had experimented with dissonances and unusual scales, younger men became more daring. Thus the Russian Igor Stravinsky created a sensation with his *Firebird* (1910) and his *Rite of Spring* (1913), musical ballets which startled contemporaries by their freedom in rhythm and harmony, by their impetuous violence, and by their brilliant coloring. A series of composers in the ensuing years experimented in a daring fashion with the traditional musical forms and techniques, and some even sought to introduce city noises or factory sounds or new electronic effects into their works.

Some composers, like the Russians Dimitri Shostakovich and Sergei Prokofiev, the German Paul Hindemith, or the American Walter Piston, created works that were recognizably connected with the older musical traditions though often inventive and experimental in new veins. Others, like the Hungarian Béla Bartók, were highly individualistic in their innovations. Still others, led by Arnold Schönberg, sought to find greater freedom for creativity by escaping entirely from the classical tonality in works that were subjective, emotionally violent, and even neurotic, and that were perhaps related to German expressionism in painting. In the 1920's Schönberg began employing a twelve-tone technique in which he was no longer bound by the old octave arrangement of notes. He had followers like Anton Webern and Alban Berg (who wrote a full length opera, *Lulu*, in the twelve-tone scale); and his atonalism influenced still others such as Bartók and the American Roger Sessions.

Thus as the second third of the twentieth century drew toward a close, it was clear that all the arts had changed dramatically. A critic from the 1890's would scarcely have recognized as art, much less have understood, a large portion of the painting, sculpture, poetry, or music of the 1950's and 1960's. All the arts were reflecting the confusion, the uncertainty, and the tension of their times. They were reflecting, moreover, the industrial civilization of which they were part, with its enormous cities, its mechanized transport, its mass communication media, its great factories. They were profiting greatly, too, from some of the changes that had taken place. The steady shortening of the work week in the advanced countries gave many people the time to enjoy or even practice the arts, while the new inventions brought within the reach of almost the whole population what had previously been available only to an elite. Thus, if most motion pictures and television performances were superficial and tawdry, still the best made good drama available to millions. Similarly, color reproductions of paintings by improved processes increased the accessibility of the art of all the past ages, while the phonograph, the radio, and television could bring the best as well as the most popular in music to a very wide audience. Down to the twentieth century the arts had been mainly for the delectation or amusement of the upper classes, which constituted only a small fraction of the whole population. By 1960 they were at least available to the masses.

E. "Summits" and Interaction of Historic Civilizations

After 1948 when the Communist seizure of control in Czechoslovakia convinced the Western powers that their hopes for peaceful coöperation with the Soviet Union were unlikely to be realized, international politics and indeed the whole world picture were dominated by the conflict between the East (Russia and her satellites and later China) and the West (United States and associated nations). Sometimes the struggle was muted and, as after Stalin's death, there were expectations of a change in Russian policy. Sometimes the contention was open and violent as in the Korean War. But in either case it went on and on with no end in sight.

Though the conflict was, from the Russian point of view, between capitalism and Communism, such was hardly the case, for differences in the internal economic systems are no bar to external coöperation and even friendship. Actually the East and the West were at odds because they had radically different ideologies and moralities, and because the Communists firmly believed that they must spread their system to all countries by any means from the support of internal subversion and disorder to straightforward military conquest. The Communist outward thrust was indeed the most grandiose imperialist effort in the history of mankind, for it aimed at the conquest of the whole world. And despite Communist slogans and preachments, the effort was in some senses old-fashioned, since it was shaped and colored by Russian nationalism save where it was dominated by Chinese nationalism.

Several times the world struggle came to a sharp focus in what has come to be called "summit conferences," since these have brought together the topmost authorities of the major nations. The pattern of such meetings was probably influenced by precedents from World War II when the major allied leaders had gathered to shape policies and reach agreements—Cairo 1943, Teheran 1943, Yalta 1945, Potsdam 1945. In August 1959, President Eisenhower flew to Europe for conferences with Adenauer, Macmillan, and De Gaulle. The next month Khrushchev came to America and conferred with the American President at Camp David in Maryland. The discussions led to no important understandings but seemed to generate a feeling of greater friendliness, and they paved the way for arranging, at Khrushchev's urging, a further meeting to be held at Paris in May 1960.

But when the four leaders (Eisenhower, De Gaulle, Macmillan, and Khrushchev) had actually come to Paris, the Russian priemier deliberately broke up the meeting. His excuse was that the United States had been flying observation planes over Russian territory in violation of international law and that one of them had been shot down some two weeks before. He demanded that Eisenhower halt the flights and apologize. The American President did agree to the former demand but not to the latter, and the meeting ended in bitter words. Tensions were increased when in July the Russians shot down another American plane, this time over international waters, and when Khrushchev came to a United Nations meeting in New York in September. At this gathering the Russian premier heckled his opponents, displayed violent ill temper, demonstrated his support for Castro, and denounced the attempts of the United Nations to bring order to the Congo.[1] In particular, Khrushchev attacked Dag Hammarskjold, the Secretary-General of the United Nations, and urged that he be replaced by a three-man committee composed of a representative of the East, one of the West, and one of the neutral powers. Since the suggestion was that such a committee could make decisions only unanimously, the arrangement would have given the Soviet Union a veto over all actions. Soon Russia was proposing similar committees for other international purposes, such as the policing of a ban on nuclear bomb testing—a subject which had been long and fruitlessly discussed in meetings at Geneva.

Despite the tense and unpromising atmosphere generated, another summit meeting was arranged. John F. Kennedy, the new American President elected in November 1960, wished to take stock of the Russian leader. And Khrushchev had given some indications that he thought he might be able to reach agreement more easily with Kennedy than with Eisenhower. President Kennedy, therefore, flew to Europe in May 1961 and conferred with De Gaulle in Paris, Macmillan in London, and Khrushchev in Vienna. Though the nature of the conver-

sations was not revealed, it seemed that no progress was made toward an understanding on such controversial issues as Laos, nuclear bomb testing, and the fate of West Berlin. Thus the world was left in an uneasy state of shifting balance in the struggle of the East against the West. It seemed likely that either the conflict would go on for many years, with each side trying to win the support of the uncommitted countries and the new nations, or else, before long, there might be a World War III too dreadful to contemplate.

The struggle had now far transcended the bounds of Europe and was being enacted on a world stage. Up to 1914 or even 1945, there had existed a sort of international system based on Europe, though ever since 1500 progressively affecting other continents. On the eve of World War II five of the seven nations which were accounted "great powers" were European: Great Britain, France, Germany, Italy, and Russia. At its end, four of these, and also Japan, had fallen from their high position and had become secondary to two "super powers," the American United States and the Eurasian Union of Soviet Socialist Republics. Europe no longer had a group of great powers dominating the world.

By 1961 a very important aspect of the change was obvious in the emergence of a host of newly independent nations in Asia and Africa and their admission to the United Nations. Thereby this organization has been altered from a predominantly European-American and racially "white" affair to a truly world-wide one including Afro-Asian peoples of color. The newly independent nations, generally speaking, while tending to constitute a "neutral" bloc in the United Nations, are devoted to the organization and rely upon it to safeguard them and give them help and prestige. At the same time some, in pursuit of nationalist ends, have showed themselves willing to violate United Nations' charter injunctions against using force. India, for example, has resorted to force in Goa against Portugal; Indonesia threatens to use it in Borneo against the Netherlands. It may turn out that the U. N. has been weakened, rather than strengthened, by the rapid increase of members, as well as by the

---

[1] See above, pp. 840–842.

continuing bitter conflict within it between "super powers" of democratic America and Communist Russia and their respective allies.

It should be borne in mind, however, that the present two-power balance is abnormal and not likely to be permanent. The new and extensive neutral bloc may play an increasingly significant role. Besides, Communist China, with its huge population and abundant natural resources, is a potential first-rate rival, not only of the United States but of the U.S.S.R. And the trend that now appears toward creation of a federal union of the politically mature and economically advanced countries of Western Europe may eventuate in a "super power" comparable with the United States and Russia, to say nothing of China or possibly India.

Western civilization is not a thing of the past. Its material features are now common property, or at least they represent common goals, of all peoples. Nor should its abiding spiritual aspects be overlooked. Nations in Asia and Africa of quite different background and civilization have derived from several generations, if not centuries of European tutelage and colonialism, a knowledge of European ideas and a habit of copying European manners and customs. Christianity, native of the West, has exerted greater influence on the historic religions of the East than these have exercized on Christianity. It does seem likely that the coming decades and even centuries will witness not the supersession of Western civilization, with its long past and high values, but rather the continuation and expansion of its influence in every continent as a major element in an evolving world civilization.

SELECT SUPPLEMENTARY READINGS FOR PART XII

Chapter 59. H. C. O'Neil, *A Short History of the Second World War* (1950); Winston Churchill, *Memoirs of the Second World War*, 6 vols. (1948–1953); Floyd Cave and others, *Origins and Consequences of World War II* (1948); V. Rowe, *The Great Wall of France* (1961); P. Carell, *The Foxes of the Desert* (1961); B. H. Liddell Hart, *The Revolution in Warfare* (1947); Alexander Werth, *Twilight of France* (1942); Paul Farmer, *Vichy, Political Dilemma* (1955); W. L. Langer, *Our Vichy Gamble* (1947); J. R. Deane, *The Strange Alliance* (1947); J. H. Wuorinen, *Finland and World War II* (1948); R. E. Sherwood, *Roosevelt and Hopkins* (1948); D. D. Eisenhower, *Crusade in Europe* (1948); S. E. Morison, *History of United States Naval Operations in World War II*, several vols. (1947 ff.); J. P. Baxter, 3rd, *Scientists against Time* (1946); H. R. Trevor Roper, *The Last Days of Hitler* (1947); H. Feis, *Japan Subdued* (1961); J. B. Collier, *The Defence of the United Kingdom* (1957); S. E. Morison, *American Contributions to the Strategy of World War II* (1958); R. A. Watson-Watt, *Three Steps to Victory* (1958); B. H. Liddell Hart, *The Soviet Army* (1956).

Chapter 60. J. B. Harrison, *This Age of Global Strife* (1952); W. C. Langsam, *The World since 1919* (1954); Avery Vandenbosch and Willard Hogan, *The United Nations* (1952); Eugene Chase, *The United Nations in Action* (1951); Carnegie Endowment for International Peace, *United Nations Studies*, 8 vols. (1947–1956); R. B. Russell, *A History of the United Nations Charter: the Role of the United States, 1940–1945* (1958); H. Feis, *Between Peace and War: The Potsdam Conference* (1960); B. Moore, *Soviet Politics, the Dilemma of Power* (1950); D. J. Dallin, *The New Soviet Empire* (1951); C. A. Manning, *The Forgotten Republics* (1952), Baltic states annexed by Russia; H. L. Roberts, *Rumania* (1951); D. A. Schmidt, *Anatomy of a Satellite* (1953); R. L. Wolff, *The Balkans in Our Times* (1956); J. Korbel, *The Communist Subversion of Czechoslovakia, 1938–1948* (1959); C. G. Haines, (ed.) *The Threat of Soviet Imperialism*, (1954); M. Beloff, *Soviet Policy in the Far East, 1944–1951* (1953); R. L. Walker, *China under Communism* (1955); A. D. Barnett, *Communist China and Asia* (1960); G. F. Kennan, *American Diplomacy, 1900–1950, and the Challenge of Soviet Power* (1951); J. F. Byrnes, *Speaking Frankly* (1947); Gen. W. B. Smith, *My Three Years in Moscow* (1950); A. B. Lane, *I saw Poland Betrayed* (1948); Waldemar Gurian, ed., *Soviet Imperialism* (1953); Hugh Seton-Watson, *The East European Revolution* (1950); J. P. Nettle, *The Eastern Zone and Soviet Policy in Germany, 1945–1950* (1951).

Chapter 61. M. A. Fitzsimons, *The Foreign Policy of the British Labor Government, 1945–1951* (1953); Hajo Holborn, *Political Collapse of Europe* (1951); D. C. Somervell, *British Politics since 1900* (1950); S. D. Bailey, *Parliamentary Government in the Commonwealth* (1952); E. M. Earle, ed., *Modern France, Problems of the Third and Fourth Republics* (1951); F. Goguel, *France under the Fourth Republic* (1952); M. Einaudi and F. Goguel, *Christian Democracy in*

Italy and France (1952); M. Einaudi and others, *Communism in Western Europe* (1951); A. Werth, *France 1940–1955* (1956); R. Aron, *France Steadfast and Changing: The Fourth to the Fifth Republic* (1960); P. M. Williams and M. Harrison, *De Gaulle's Republic* (1960); M. Grindrod, *The Rebuilding of Italy: Politics and Economics, 1945–1955* (1955); A. C. Jemolo, *Church and State in Italy, 1850–1950* (1960); I. Andersson, *A History of Sweden* (1956).

Chapter 62. Dexter Perkins, *American Approach to Foreign Policy* (1952); H. S. Truman, *Memoirs*, 2 vols. (1955–1956); H. A. Kissinger, *Nuclear Weapons and Foreign Policy* (1957); P. M. S. Blackett, *Atomic Weapons and East West Relations* (1956); H. L. Ismay, *NATO, the First Five Years, 1949–1954* (1954); R. Ritchie, *NATO: The Economics of an Alliance* (1956); S. E. Harris, *The European Recovery Program* (1948); G. Freund, *Germany between Two Worlds* (1961); B. L. Schwartz, *Chinese Communism and the Rise of Mao* (1950); K. S. Latourette, *The American Record in the Far East, 1945–1951* (1952); L. M. Goodrich, *Korea, Collective Measures against Aggression* (1953); E. O. Reischauer, *The United States and Japan* (1950); Sir George Sansom, *The Western World and Japan* (1950); H. M. Vinacke, *The United States and the Far East, 1945–1951* (1952); K. Kawai, *Japan's American Interlude* (1960); L. M. Goodrich, *Korea: A Study of U.S. Policy in the United Nations* (1956); D. E. Worcester and W. G. Schaeffer, *The Growth and Culture of Latin America* (1956); D. Lewis, *Five Families, Mexican Case Studies in the Culture of Poverty* (1959); T. L. Smith, *Brazil: People and Institutions* (1954); A. H. Robertson, *The Council of Europe* (1956); H. L. Mason, *The European Coal and Steel Community* (1955); W. Diebold Jr., *The Schuman Plan: A Study in Economic Coöperation, 1950–1959* (1959); Isaiah Frank, *The European Common Market* (1961); A. Zurcher, *The Struggle to United Europe, 1946–1958* (1958).

Chapter 63. C. J. H. Hayes, *The Historical Evolution of Modern Nationalism* (1955), and *Nationalism, a Religion* (1960); S. C. Easton, *The Twilight of European Colonialism: A Political Analysis* (1960); V. A. Smith, *The Oxford History of India* (1957); P. J. Griffiths, *Modern India* (1957); Khalid Bin Sayeed, *Pakistan: the Formative Phase* (1961); W. L. Holland, ed., *Asian Nationalism and the West* (1953); B. Harrison, *South-East Asia: A Short History* (1954); D. G. E. Hall, *A History of South-East Asia* (1955); D. Lancaster, *The Emancipation of French Indochina* (1961); G. M. Kahim, *Nationalism and Revolution in Indonesia* (1952); Alastair M. Taylor, *Indonesian Independence and the United Nations* (1960); G. E. Kirk, *A Short History of the Middle East* (1957); George Lenczowski, *The Middle East in World Affairs* (1952), and *Russia and the West in Iran* (1949); Majid Khadduri, *Independent Iraq, 1932–1958: A Study in Iraqi Politics* (1960); Norman Bentwich, *Israel* (1953); M. H. Bernstein, *The Politics of Israel: the First Decade of Statehood* (1957); K. Wheelock, *Nasser's New Egypt*

(1960); K. H. Karpat, *Turkey's Politics* (1959); Jane S. Nickerson, *A Short History of North Africa* (1961); D. E. Ashford, *Political Change in Morocco* (1961); T. L. Hodgkin, *Nationalism in Colonial Africa* (1956); W. M. Macmillan, *The Road to Self-Rule: a Study in Colonial Evolution* (1959); G. H. T. Kimble, *Tropical Africa*, 2 vols. (1960); Rupert Emerson, *From Empire To Nation* (1960); J. Duffy and R. A. Manners, *Africa Speaks* (1961), containing extracts from speeches by current African leaders; Mamadou Dia [Senegal leader], *The African Nations and World Solidarity* (1961); T. M. Franck, *Race and Nationalism: The Struggle for Power in Rhodesia-Nyasaland* (1960); E. J. Huxley, *Race and Politics in Kenya* (1956); D. E. Apter, *The Gold Coast in Transition* (1955); A. P. Merriam, *Congo: Background of Conflict* (1961); G. Carter, *The Politics of Inequality: South Africa Since 1948* (1958); J. Duffy, *Portuguese Africa* (1959); K. M. Pannikar, *Afro-Asian States and Their Problems* (1960); D. Lowenthal, ed., *The West Indies Federation: Perspectives on a New Nation* (1961); *Statesman's Yearbook*; *World Almanac*.

Chapter 64. See works cited for Chapters 60–63. In addition: H. A. Kissinger, *Nuclear Weapons and Foreign Policy* (1957); G. W. Elbers and P. Duncan, *Scientific Revolution: Challenge and Promise* (1959); P. Frank, *Modern Science and its Philosophy* (1962); C. T. Chase, *The Evolution of Modern Physics* (1947); F. S. Taylor, *History of Industrial Chemistry* (1957); C. J. Singer, *A History of Biology* (1950); R. H. Shryock, *A History of Modern Medicine* (1947); P. Joubert, *Rocket* (1957); M. Alperin, *et al.*, eds. *Vistas in Astronautics*, (1958 ff); A. E. Jones, *The Life and Work of Sigmund Freud*, 3 vols. (1953–1957). See also *Statesman's Year Book*, United Nations' reports and documents, and current periodicals such as the *Scientific American*.

Chapter 65. Christopher Dawson, *The Dynamics of World History*, ed. by J. J. Mulloy (1956), and *Understanding Europe* (1960); Reinhold Niebuhr, *Faith and History* (1949); A. S. Nash, ed., *Protestant Thought in the Twentieth Century* (1951); Waldemar Gurian and M. A. Fitzsimons, eds., *The Catholic Church in World Affairs* (1954); K. S. Latourette, *Christianity in a Revolutionary Age*, vols. IV–V, *Since 1914* (1962); R. Tobias, *Communist-Christian Encounter in East Europe* (1956); A. H. Barr, *Masters of Modern Art*, new ed. (1958); B. S. Myers, *Modern Art in the Making* (1959); M. Raynal, *History of Modern Painting*, 3 vols (1949–1950); O. W. Larkin, *Art and Life in America* (1949); A. C. Ritchie, *Sculpture of the Twentieth Century* (1952); C. Seymour, Jr., *Tradition and Experiment in Modern Sculpture* (1949); P. S. Hansen, *An Introduction to Twentieth Century Music* (1961); N. Slonimsky, *Music since 1900* (1949); H. R. Hitchcock, *Architecture: Nineteenth and Twentieth Centuries* (1958); J. M. Richards, *An Introduction to Modern Architecture* (1956).

APPENDIX

Partial List of European Sovereigns

I. EMPERORS

Holy Roman (German)

Ferdinand III, 1637–1657
Leopold I, 1658–1705
Joseph I, 1705–1711
Charles VI, 1711–1740
Charles VII, 1742–1745

Francis I, 1745–1765
Joseph II, 1765–1790
Leopold II, 1790–1792

Francis II, 1792–1806

Austrian

Francis I, 1804–1835
Ferdinand I, 1835–1848
Francis Joseph, 1848–1916

Charles I, 1916–1918

Ottoman (Turkish Sultans)

Ibrahim, 1640–1648
Mohammed IV, 1648–1687
Mustapha II, 1695–1703
Ahmed III, 1703–1730
Mahmud I, 1730–1754

Othman II, 1754–1757
Mustapha III, 1757–1773
Abdul Hamid I, 1773–1789
Selim III, 1789–1807

Mahmud II, 1808–1839
Abdul Medjid, 1839–1861
Abdul Aziz, 1861–1876
Abdul Hamid II, 1876–1909
Mohammed V, 1909–1918
Mohammed VI, 1918–1922

Russian (Tsars)

Alexius, 1645–1676
Theodore II, 1676–1682
Ivan V, 1682–1689
Peter I, the Great, 1682–1725
Catherine I, 1725–1727
Peter II, 1727–1730
Anna, 1730–1740
Ivan VI, 1740–1741
Elizabeth, 1741–1762
Peter III, 1762
Catherine II, the Great,
    1762–1796
Paul, 1796–1801

Alexander I, 1801–1825
Nicholas I, 1825–1855
Alexander II, 1855–1881
Alexander III, 1881–1894
Nicholas II, 1894–1917

French (Napoleonic)

Napoleon I, 1804–1814
Napoleon III, 1852–1870

German (Hohenzollern)

William I, 1871–1888
Frederick III, 1888
William II, 1888–1918

II. POPES

Alexander VII, 1655–1667
Clement IX, 1667–1670
Clement X, 1670–1676
Innocent XI, 1676–1689
Alexander VIII, 1689–1691
Innocent XII, 1691–1700
Clement XI, 1700–1721
Innocent XIII, 1721–1724
Benedict XIII, 1724–1730

Clement XII, 1730–1740
Benedict XIV, 1740–1758
Clement XIII, 1758–1769
Clement XIV, 1769–1774
Pius VI, 1775–1799
Pius VII, 1800–1823
Leo XII, 1823–1829
Pius VIII, 1829–1830

Gregory XVI, 1831–1846
Pius IX, 1846–1878
Leo XIII, 1878–1903
Pius X, 1903–1914
Benedict XV, 1914–1922
Pius XI, 1922–1939
Pius XII, 1939–1958
John XXIII, 1958–

III. OTHER SOVEREIGNS

Kings of England

James I, 1603–1625,   STUART
Charles I, 1625–1649,   "
  (*Revolution and Crom-*
  well)
Charles II, 1660–1685,   "
James II, 1685–1688,   "
Mary II, 1689–1694,   "
William III, 1689–1701,   ORANGE
Anne, 1701–1714,   STUART
George I, 1714–1727   HANOVER
George II, 1727–1760,   "
George III, 1760–1820,   "

George IV, 1820–1830,   "
William IV, 1830–1837,   "
Victoria, 1837–1901,   "
Edward VII, 1901–1910, SAXE-COBURG
George V, 1910–1936,   WINDSOR
Edward VIII, 1936,   "
George VI, 1936–1952,   "
Elizabeth II, 1952–   "

Kings of France

Henry IV, 1589–1610,   BOURBON
Louis XIII, 1610–1643,   "

Louis XIV, 1643–1715,   "

Louis XV, 1715–1774,   "

Louis XVI, 1774–1792,   "
      (*Revolution and Napoleon*)
Louis XVIII, 1814–1824,   "
Charles X, 1824–1830,   "
Louis Philippe, 1830–1848,   ORLEANS

Kings of Spain

Philip IV, 1621–1665,   HABSBURG

Charles II, 1665–1700,   "
Philip V, 1700–1746,   BOURBON
Ferdinand VI, 1746–1759,   "
Charles III, 1759–1788,   "
Charles IV, 1788–1808,   "
Joseph, 1808–1813,   BONAPARTE
Ferdinand VII, 1813–1833,   BOURBON

Isabella II, 1833–1868

Amadeo, 1870–1873,   SAVOY
(*Republic, 1873–1874*)
Alphonso XII, 1875–1885,   BOURBON
Alphonso XIII, 1886–1931,   "

Kings of Portugal

John IV, 1640–1656
Alphonso VI, 1656–1667
Peter II, 1667–1706
John V, 1706–1750
Joseph, 1750–1777
Peter III, 1777–1786
Maria I, 1786–1816

John VI, 1816–1826
Peter IV, 1826
Maria II, 1826–1853
Peter V, 1853–1861
Louis I, 1861–1889

Charles I, 1889–1908
Manuel II, 1908–1910

Kings in Scandinavia

Denmark	Norway	Sweden
Frederick III, 1648–1670		Christina, 1632–1654
		Charles X, 1654–1660
Christian V, 1670–1699		Charles XI, 1660–1697
Frederick IV, 1699–1730		Charles XII, 1697–1718
Christian VI, 1730–1746		Frederick I, 1720–1751
Frederick V, 1746–1766		Adolphus, 1751–1771
Christian VII, 1766–1808		Gustavus III, 1771–1792
		Gustavus IV, 1792–1809
Frederick VI, 1808–1839		Charles XIII, 1809–1818
Christian VIII, 1839–1848	Charles XIV, 1818–1844	
Frederick VII, 1848–1863	Oscar I, 1844–1859	
Christian IX, 1863–1906	Charles XV, 1859–1872	
	Oscar II, 1872–1907	
Frederick VIII, 1906–1912		
Christian X, 1912–1947	Haakon VII, 1905–1957	Gustavus V, 1907–1950
Frederick IX, 1947–	Olaf V, 1957–	Gustavus VI, 1950–

Kings of Poland	Kings of Prussia	Kings of Savoy and Italy
John II Casimir, 1648–1668	Frederick I, 1701–1713	Victor Amadeus II, 1675–1730
Michael Wieniowiecki, 1669–1673	Frederick William I, 1713–1740	Charles Emmanuel III, 1730–1773
John III Sobieski, 1674–1696	Frederick II, the Great, 1740–1786	Victor Amadeus III, 1773–1796
Augustus II of Saxony, 1697–1733	Frederick William II, 1786–1797	Charles Emmanuel IV, 1796–1802
Augustus III, 1733–1763	Frederick William III, 1797–1840	Victor Emmanuel I, 1802–1821
Stanislaus II, Poniatowski, 1763–1795	Frederick William IV, 1840–1861	Charles Felix, 1821–1831
	William I, 1861–1888	Charles Albert, 1831–1849
	Frederick III, 1888	Victor Emmanuel II, 1849–1878
	William II, 1888–1918	Humbert I, 1878–1900
		Victor Emmanuel III, 1900–1945
		Humbert II, 1945–1946

Kings of Netherlands
Same as Spain, 1504–1581
William I, *King,* 1813–1840
William II, 1840–1849
William III, 1849–1890
Wilhelmina, 1890–1948
Juliana, 1948–

Kings of Belgium
Leopold I, 1831–1865
Leopold II, 1865–1909
Albert I, 1909–1934
Leopold III, 1934–1951
Baudouin I, 1951–

Monarchs of Bulgaria
Alexander of Battenberg,
   Prince, 1879–1886
Ferdinand, *Prince,* 1887–
   1908; *Tsar,* 1908–1918
Boris III, 1918–1943
Simeon II, 1943–1946

**Monarchs of Serbia
(Yugoslavia)**
Karageorge, *Prince,* 1812–
   1813
Miloš Obrenovic, 1817–1839
Milan, 1839
Michael, 1839–1842
Alexander Karageorgevic,
   1842–1859
Michael Obrenovic, 1860–
   1868
Milan I, 1869–1889; *King,*
   1882–1889
Alexander, 1889–1903
Peter Karageorgevic, 1903–
   1921
Alexander I, 1921–1934
Peter II, 1934–1945

Kings of Greece
Otto I, 1832–1862
George I, 1863–1913
Constantine I, 1913–1917
Alexander I, 1917–1920
Constantine I, 1920–1922
George II, 1922–1924
(*Republic,* 1924–1935)
George II, 1935–1947
Paul I, 1947–

Monarchs of Rumania
Alexander John Cuza, *Prince*
   1859–1866
Carol I, *Prince,* 1866–1881,
   King, 1881–1914
Ferdinand, 1914–1927
Michael, 1927–1930
Carol II, 1930–1940
Michael, 1940–1947

INDEX

Index